Multimedia Computing

Preparing for the 21 Century

Sorel Reisman
California State University, Fullerton

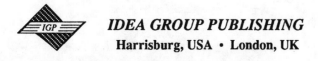

IDEA GROUP PUBLISHING
Harrisburg, USA • London, UK

Senior Editor: Mehdi Khosrowpour
Managing Editor: Jan Travers
Printed at: BookCrafters

Published in the United States of America by
        Idea Group Publishing
        Olde Liberty Square
        4811 Jonestown Road, Suite 230
        Harrisburg, PA 17109
        Tel: 717-541-9150
        Fax: 717-541-9159

and in the United Kingdom by
        Idea Group Publishing
        3 Henrietta Street
        Covent Garden
        London WC2E 8LU
        Tel: 071-240 0856
        Fax: 071-379 0609

British Cataloguing in Publication Data
A Cataloguing in Publication record for this book is available from the British Library

ISBN 1-878289-22-5

9438447

ℓ◡

Other IDEA GROUP Publishing Books

Table of Contents

Ginger L. Weilbaker, Purdue University

PREFACE

In the world of computing change sometimes seems to be the only constant. As the computer industry moves through the last decade of the 20th Century, nothing represents that change more than multimedia computing (MMC). Today, multimedia computing is on the minds and lips of almost anyone who uses computers, from chief information officers to elementary school children. In many ways this is a fascinating phenomenon since the term multimedia was largely unknown only two or three years ago. In fact, it would come as a surprise to many evangelists of MMC that multimedia computing has a history that reaches back almost 30 years, almost to when the industry of computing was just beginning. In that context it is appropriate to think of multimedia, not as a new development, but rather as the natural evolution of the computer, an evolution that by the beginning of the 21st Century will be almost one half century old. If MMC is, as it seems, a phase in the natural evolution of computing, then a study of its history may provide insight into what the future of computing might bring.

A Review of The Past
Soon after the commercialization of digital computing by Sperry Rand in the 1950's, computer scientists recognized that digital computers had far more potential than simply the processing of payrolls. As long ago as 1964, computer scientists at IBM developed the IBM 1500 System, a multimedia system for computer-assisted instruction (CAI). Later in the 1960s, the University of Illinois, funded partially by Control Data Corporation, developed the PLATO system, also for the delivery of multimedia CAI. The IBM 1500 and PLATO systems had much in common. Both used host-driven time-shared computers that controlled analog audio and video (A/V) devices that were locally attached to student workstations. Both systems delivered true multimedia applications with integrated audio, graphics, animation, and even video. Applications running on both systems were based on course authoring programming languages and tools that were models for the procedural languages that would be used to develop multimedia applications for the next 25 years. Toward the end of the 1960s and early in the 1970s, Mitre Corporation experimented with a different approach to multimedia CAI. Mitre's TICCIT system, using standard television technology, was based on a centralized host computer that controlled and distributed host-based A/V to TV-based terminals. In some ways TICCIT was a major breakthrough in multimedia computing, Mitre broke ranks from the IBM 1500 and PLATO systems which both used proprietary multimedia devices and workstations; TICCIT capital-

ized on an existing and already popular technology - television.

In the mid 1970s, IBM Canada developed a prototype multimedia CAI system that integrated television technology together with recent advances in digital computing. The system, Computerized Interactive Television (CITV), was based on a distributed processing architecture in which an IBM System/360 host communicated with an attached minicomputer (IBM System/7). The System/7 acted as a media device controller/switcher which, under control of the host, directed A/V signals to attached TV-standard terminals. Those analog signals together with host-generated digital output were electronically mixed at the terminal. Functionally, the CITV system provided integrated color, graphics, image, audio, and video in the learning environment. That the multimedia devices were mainly analog was transparent to users. For all intents and purpose, aside from the A/V function, CITV's graphics and animation were superior in quality and easier to use than similar features that three or four years later would become available on the first generation of personal computers (PC).

Probably the first, truly available multimedia computer was the Apple II+, a PC that shocked the computer industry by using off the shelf components to deliver color, graphics, animation and audio for a retail price of about $2000. The Apple II+ was not only function-rich, it also supported inexpensive and easy-to-use printers and floppy disk drives. Its local 5 1/4 floppy drives provided essential storage for the first generation of multimedia personal computing applications and data files. The Apple II+ was a watershed multimedia computer in yet another way. With its ROM-BASIC anyone could easily develop applications that used all the functions of the machine. The Apple II's ease-of-programming facilitated the training of a new generation of young and creative people, many of whom later became the multimedia application developers of the 1990s.

At about the same time as the Apple II family was breaking new price/performance boundaries for end user personal computing, companies such as Philips NV, Pioneer Electronics, Thomson CSF, RCA Corp., and Sony Corp. were experimenting with low cost mass storage technologies for audio and full motion video. From the mid 1970s through the mid 1980s these and other companies carried on relentless technology and marketing wars in an effort to produce a single A/V storage standard. Even IBM, as early as 1976 tried to develop its own solution to this problem. In 1979 IBM determined that it was more expedient to enter into a joint venture with someone who already possessed such a technology. Late in 1979 IBM, MCA, and Pioneer formed the joint venture DiscoVision Associates (DVA). From 1980 to 1982 DVA pioneered the development and marketing of the optical storage devices that became known as videodiscs, trademarked as LaserDiscs.

Although IBM itself was unable at that time to capitalize on the potential synergy of LaserDiscs and digital computers, others did. In the early 1980s many small companies developed multimedia computing systems with configurations based on the Apple II+ connected to and controlling DVA (IBM) LaserDisc players. Clever system integrators developed mixing/switching electronics that mixed the computer's digital output and the videodisc player's analog output for display on a single TV or computer screen. Functionally, these systems allowed application developers to deliver the digital outputs of an Apple II+ computer (color text, graphics, animation, and digital audio) together with the analog outputs of video and stereo audio - all integrated at a single workstation.

While it was not apparent in 1984, from a software standpoint Apple Computer's introduction of the Macintosh, and its Xerox PARC-invented graphical user interface (GUI) was a major milestone in the evolution of MMC. After almost 30 years of commercial data processing, the Mac was the first product to make computing easy and popular. Within only a few years GUIs became the only feasible interface for really personal computing on a Mac, a PC (of the IBM variety), and even on powerful workstations. The use of graphical icons to represent real-life objects and actions to simplify user/ computer interaction was the beginning of an interface philosophy that asserted that those interactions should be as natural as possible. This implied that even more natural interfaces, including the use of color, images, audio, and video could even further facilitate user/computer interaction. However, in 1984 when the Mac was first introduced, technology had still not advanced sufficiently to allow engineers to build cost-effective all-digital multimedia systems. It would be at least five years before that would become possible.

Throughout the 1980s, hardware and software companies worked with hybrid analog and digital equipment to produce applications, and develop methodologies, languages and tools that would serve as the foundation for multimedia systems that would one day be cost effective. Much of the 1980s served as a period during which a large number of small application development companies, using hybrid hardware, synthesized the application development experience and tools of the previous 20 or so years. Despite their activity, through the middle of the 1980s, multimedia computing remained an underground industry whose progress was limited by the irreconcilable technical differences between digital computers and analog videodisc storage. Yet, even in the face of these differences, many companies were beginning to discover that traditional personal computing applications could really be enhanced through the dimensions of sound and full motion video.

Recognizing this, in 1986, in an effort to promote a multimedia standard based on its own products, IBM, which had abandoned its DiscoVision LaserDisc efforts in 1982, introduced the videodisc-based InfoWindow System. The IBM InfoWindow System was IBM's version of the PC-based multimedia systems that small system integrators, using Apple II computers, had developed almost five years earlier. However, with the endorsement of IBM, MMC in the form of InfoWindow Systems became a legitimate expenditure by Corporate America. The InfoWindow System gave notice that LaserDisc-based multimedia, controlled by an IBM Personal Computer rather than by an Apple computer, could provide cost-benefits in such commercial applications as training, marketing, and corporate communications. The InfoWindow System did not offer a single technical improvement over functionally equivalent Apple II-based systems. Nonetheless, the new product established a de facto MMC standard that, despite severe shortcomings, was an important factor in the continuation of MMC hardware, software, and application development work for the next five years.

When the InfoWindow System became a supported IBM product, companies that had been developing applications for non-standard systems, began to target their work for the new standard platform. Since 1986, many companies have invested heavily in the development and marketing of LaserDisc based applications. Furthermore, companies that had been loathe to invest in non-standard MMC equipment and applications were better able to justify such expenditures because of the IBM imprimatur. The IBM InfoWindow System created a LaserDisc-based multimedia industry that, despite its reliance on increasingly obsolete hybrid analog and digital technology, could continue to exist through the end of the 1990s.

Increasingly, and in spite of the momentum of InfoWindow-like MMC systems and applications, breakthroughs in the manufacturing costs of digital components have allowed engineers to develop cost-effective methods of digitizing audio and video. Ever since the early 1960s, multimedia systems designers had been forced to integrate two intrinsically incompatible technologies to deliver both digital and A/V output at a workstation. Digital computers have, since their first introduction been high speed electronic devices. On the other hand, ever since the first IBM 1500 System, audio and video devices have been low speed, relatively unreliable electromechanical devices. The introduction of LaserDiscs essentially increased the reliability and performance of devices that could be used to deliver A/V in an MMC environment. It did not however, remove the inherent incompatibilities between digital text/graphics output and analog audio/video output. In the late 1980s even this barrier began to fall.

Throughout the 1980s, laser optical scientists and engineers improved the technologies upon which LaserDiscs were based.

Among their accomplishments was the development of devices and methodologies that made practical the use of laser optical devices for the storage and retrieval of digital data. With impetus from companies such as Sony, Philips, and Pioneer, international committees agreed upon standards that defined the physical characteristics of audio Compact Discs (CDs), small laser-readable discs that could be used as a storage medium for digitized audio. The consumer electronics industry saw CDs as an opportunity to replace easily copied tapes with an inexpensive, high quality, read-only audio medium. From the mid 1980s, as CDs virtually replaced tape as the audio medium of choice, the price of volume-manufactured CD players (i.e., disc drives) plummeted.

The same committees that established standards for audio CDs also developed logical file format standards for optical disc data files. These discs, called CD-ROMs (compact disc-read only memory) can be used to store standard computer data as well various forms of digitized audio, video, and image. With the development of these standards, and with a great deal of computer industry prodding by Microsoft Corporation, CD-ROM standards have emerged for a wide variety of platforms that include IBM PCs and Apple Macintoshes, and consumer products such as CD-I (compact disc-interactive), and PhotoCD. With the elimination of any dependency on analog technologies, CD-ROMs provide an integrated storage medium for all-digital data of text, audio, and full motion video, retrievable and manipulable by a host personal computer. Although the first versions of CD-ROM drives were prohibitively expensive, more recent versions are much more affordable, benefiting from the reduced manufacturing costs of their first cousin, the audio CD player.

A Quick Look At The Present

Today, MMC seems to be of interest to different kinds of user markets, i) industrial/commercial, and ii) consumer. Despite some apparent differences, in the context of the history of personal computing, these MMC markets have much in common. It is well-documented that Apple II+ computers found their way into Corporate America long before IBM announced and legitimized the PC. The Apple II+, running the first electronic spreadsheet, VisiCalc, was recognized by individuals in many corporate financial departments, as a salvation from the logjam of requests awaiting service by companies' overworked MIS departments.

Personnel in accounting departments, for example, had seen Apple II's in use at their children's schools, and were astounded at their simplicity, availability, and affordability. It was relatively easy for an individual department in a company to budget a few thousand dollars for new office equipment. Such expenditures easily passed unnoticed by the scrutiny of the company's MIS management. By the time IBM announced the PC, it was easy to cost-justify the purchase of personal computers, especially if the manufacturer was IBM.

So too may MMC become a pervasive influence in business environments. Today, MMC has captured the interest of the consumer market with a myriad of companies offering so-called multimedia upgrade kits for the consumer-base of home office 386 and 486-based PCs. As these kits grow in popularity (and as the price of CD-ROMs and sound boards drops), application developers are developing CD-ROM-based consumer applications that include games, education, reference, and even pornography! Even while this consumer market explodes, industrial acceptance of MMC is more conservative. After all, the cost to upgrade hundreds or even thousands of company-owned PCs is not insignificant. Furthermore, in this era of corporate reengineering, with greater emphasis being placed on decentralized decision making, integration of MMC into the corporate environment presents many technological and even legal problems. For companies to adopt MMC as enthusiastically as the consumer market appears to be doing, the MMC development community must address issues that relate to i) improvements in the technology of MMC and ii) the emergence of a discipline of MMC application development.

Technology. With an apparent solution to the long-standing problem of hybrid technologies in hand, MMC in the 1990s is facing new technological challenges. Probably one the most debated issue in the middle of the 1990s concerns the high volumes of data that need to be a stored, retrieved, and manipulated in order to work with audio and video. Until the availability of CD-ROMs, there were no special demands placed on a computer that drove and coordinated MMC applications. MMC applications were not really much different than conventional computer applications except that in addition to generating text and graphics, the computer also had to control analog A/V devices. This extra requirement required very little extra effort from the microprocessors and operating systems that are at the heart of every digital computer. The complete conversion of all data (text, graphics, image, audio, and video) to digital form now places a processing load on multimedia computers that can exceed the demands of the even largest conventional data processing task.

Today, popular CISC and RISC PC microprocessors can barely keep up with the demands to process digital audio and video. Fortunately, unlike conventional computer data, with contemporary microprocessors it is possible, with trade-offs in the quality of audio and/or video, to run reasonable multimedia applications. Such trade-offs are most apparent in the characteristics of the video that can be produced on a computer display. So called software-only methods of manipulating motion video (i.e., methods in which the

PC's microprocessor can only barely process the volumes of digital video data), fail to deliver true full motion video (i.e., full screen video at 30 frames/second). Examples of such methods are Microsoft's Indeo, and Apple's QuickTime.

Currently, the only way to deliver true full motion video is to supplement the power of the PC microprocessor with some kind of A/V coprocessor. Even with an A/V coprocessor, the processing task is only barely manageable. In order to reduce the magnitude of the task 1) the volume of data must be reduced, 2) processor/coprocessors must be more efficient, or 3) a combination of both solutions is required. Computer scientists and engineers are currently working on a variety of solutions to these challenges. Common sense might suggest that a solution to the first issue may itself be a worthy pursuit because reduced data volumes benefit any multimedia computer, whether or not it has an A/V coprocessor. However, debates rage on regarding the best methods of compressing A/V data because much of the task of decompressing the data will ultimately become an A/V coprocessor task. Ultimately, standards will emerge, benefiting the hardware manufacturers whose products will provide the sought-after solutions. Because Intel Corporation had an early start in these debates, the company's Digital Video Interactive (DVI) technology has already been endorsed and adopted as a corporate favorite. It is now clear though, that newer methods (and products) may be superior.

Another issue today concerns the best operating system for multimedia. All contending operating system companies seem to agree that GUI environments provide the best foundation from which to build multimedia extensions. However, on the desktop it does seem likely that for the foreseeable future the choices will include GUIs based on Apple's Macintosh System/7, Microsoft's Windows (with or without DOS), IBM's OS/2, or a rendition of UNIX.

Application Development. In recognition of the fact that multimedia functions are an extension of graphical applications that need to run within a GUI-based system, software developers are casting about for the best way to develop MMC applications. Although object oriented programming languages and design methodologies are becoming popular, a significant amount of excellent MMC application code is still being written with third generation, procedural programming languages. This situation too, is unlikely to change much in the foreseeable future. While languages and systems like C++, ObjectVision, SmallTalk, HyperCard, ToolBook, and VisualBasic can provide a bridge to the future of application development, these systems are really not a significant departure from the programming systems of the past. To use any of them to create a really terrific MMC application, programmers must be more than skillful, they must be creative artists

Preparing For the 21st Century

This book has been organized into four sections, each reflecting a focus of issues for readers interested in preparing for the future of multimedia computing. The first section, Technology Focus concerns technological issues that continue to be addressed by MMC technologists. The section is particularly useful for readers who would like to understand the relationship between MMC technology and the place of multimedia in emerging, decentralized enterprises.

The second section, Application/Benefits Focus, will provide guidance for reluctant corporate planners who need to justify the expense of evolving and converting a PC environment into one that capitalizes on the benefits of multimedia. The section describes a variety of business environments in which MMC applications have already proven their return-on-investment value.

The third section, Application Development Focus contains chapters related to the development of MMC applications. In addition to more traditional topics, such as development languages and environments, the section contains chapters that address matters unique to MMC. The chapters will provide readers with insight into the challenges of designing and developing MMC applications.

End User Focus, the final section, is comprised of chapters that deal with issues and considerations related to the implementation of MMC. That many of these chapters focus on training and education is no accident considering the history of MMC. I am particularly delighted to be able to conclude the book with the chapter by Ragsdale and Kassam. It seems fitting to me to be able to do that since Ron Ragsdale was the teacher, mentor, and advisor who, decades ago, set me on the path of multimedia computing when I was a graduate student at the University of Toronto.

Acknowledgments

Planning a book about multimedia computing has been a challenge, especially one with a forward looking perspective. Intellectually the challenge has been to select submissions that would stand the test of time, - submissions that really have value for readers who need to do some strategic thinking about possible roles of multimedia computing in their own endeavors, in academia, in large corporations, in small businesses, or simply as a matter of personal curiosity.

I was fortunate to be able to work with the authors of the chapters of this book, all of whom share the same vision of the place and importance of multimedia in the world of computing. I would like to thank them all for their effort, their cooperation, and their patience through the multiple revisions that were inflicted upon them.

Without logistical support, it would have been impossible to publish the excellent work of the authors of the chapters in this book. I would like to thank Grace McCormick of the Department of Management Science/Information Systems at Cal State Fullerton who kept the papers flowing from the authors, to me, back to the authors, back to me, back...

Next I would like to thank Jan Travers of Idea Group Publishing. I have no idea how Jan accomplishes everything that she does; in fact I also have no idea of all the things that she has to do, but I am certain that without her this book could never have been published.

Then I would like to thank Mehdi Khosrowpour who first asked me to edit this book. I clearly remember my very first discussion with Mehdi. I called him from a small hotel room in Carmel, California the night before I was to attend the Microsoft 1992 CD-ROM Conference (now called InterMedia) in San Francisco. At that time I really couldn't conceive of the contents of this book. But then (and many times since), Mehdi had the foresight to recognize that a serious book on multimedia computing would be possible, useful, and even valuable.

Finally, I would like to thank my wife Gail, (when the phone rings at home) "the other Dr. Reisman" who has survived with me through 25 years of my own personal involvement with multimedia computing. Over all those years I have missed dinners, teachers' meetings, children's performances, and countless other family events—now the truth can be told —playing with many of the multimedia systems and products that I described above. Without her patience I would not have accumulated the experience and perspective on multimedia computing that allowed me to work on this book.

Section 1

Technology Focus

Chapter 1

Advances in Interactive Digital Multimedia Systems*

Edward A. Fox
Virginia Polytechnic Institute
and State University

Humans communicate using a variety of senses and capabilities, especially in face-to-face situations. We should aim to emulate the bandwidth, fidelity, and effectiveness possible in those situations when we develop interactive multimedia computing systems, especially as we move from analog to digital processing environments.

That movement, a part of the evolution of information technology since the early days of computing, gained momentum with the widespread use of compact discs, which demonstrated the accurate reproduction and superb quality of digital audio. Bilevel (black-and-white) image handling, especially facsimile, has demonstrated the potential for rapid communication of documents, changing in a few years the way organizations operate.

Methods for managing computer graphics, color images, and motion video will lead to even greater changes. When fully digital multimedia computing systems are readily available, we will have powerful tools for improving human-human collaboration and human-computer symbiosis.

Televisions, CD players, telephones, and home computers will evolve and be combined, yielding systems with stereo speakers, high-resolution color displays, megabytes of RAM, fast processors for video and audio, fiber-optic network connections, hundreds of megabytes of disk capacity, CD-ROM drives, and flexible input devices, including stereo microphones, pointing devices, and text-entry units. True programming of video will be possible for personalized presentations.

High-resolution images, high-fidelity audio, nicely typeset text, and high-definition video will be available on demand, as versatile alternatives to conventional photographic, audio, newspaper, and television services. Home shopping, cottage industries, delivery of professional services, supplemental adult and child education, surrogate travel to real or artificial sites, video mail and conferencing, and diverse modes of entertainment will be supported.

Many areas of computer science and electrical engineering are aiding these developments. Fast processors, high-speed networks, large-capacity storage devices, new algorithms and data structures, graphics systems, innovative methods for human-computer interaction, real-time operating systems, object-oriented programming, information storage and retrieval, hypertext and hypermedia, languages for scripting, parallel processing methods, and complex architectures for distributed systems — all are involved.

To understand interactive digital multimedia computing systems, it is necessary to see how relevant aspects of these fields relate. The references cited in this article are a small assemblage of quality writings covering much of this broad spectrum.

First, I provide background regarding developments in interactive videodiscs, which first made images and video accessible through computer systems. Then, I deal with digital storage media, including optical, magnetic, and network options, which allow digital multimedia to be preserved, shared, and distributed. I also discuss the characteristics of audio and video and their digital representations. Because these media are so demanding of space and channel bandwidth, I review compression methods.

Technology is not all that is necessary. Vendors must follow standards — discussed in their own section — to ensure that the economics and usability of digital multimedia help this industry grow. Building on existing de facto standards and an emerging suite of international standards, digital multimedia systems (for example, from Intel, Commodore, and Philips) are already available, and the future for digital multimedia in general looks bright.

Interactive Videodiscs

Computer handling of large quantities of audio and video information became possible with the advent of the videodisc in the late 1970s. Each side of these optical discs can hold 54,000 images, or 30 minutes of motion video if the images are played in sequence at the standard rate of 30 frames per second and they run concurrently with 30 minutes of stereo sound, all recorded in an analog format. Although seek time is on the order of a second, the random-access capability allows computers to control playback in interactive videodisc systems. Videodisc output usually goes directly to a monitor; with additional boards the computer system can overlay text or graphics on the video output, or even digitize the video signal as it is received.

Preparation of videodisc applications is typically a relatively expensive process, requiring a team for design, video and audio production, graphic art, programming, project management, and content specialist duties.[1] While mastering and replication cost several thousand dollars, complete projects may cost $100,000 per disk. Recordable videodiscs are available but not common, so preparing videodiscs is essentially a publication process. When interactive videodiscs are coupled with high-quality software and a good user interface, powerful educational experiences for thousands of people can result.[2]

Videodisc applications presenting neuroanatomy and supporting surrogate or simulated travel, language study, and video research work have been developed at MIT in connection with Project Athena and the Media Lab,[3] thanks to an elaborate cable plant for analog video. Electronic books, manuals, magazines, and visual databases also have been prototyped there, showing the potential of combining interactive computer systems with videodiscs, graphics, and digitizer boards. However, similar cable systems are too expensive for widespread deployment. Instead, the shift is to digital storage and communication systems.

Digital Storage Media

In the jargon of the international standards community, "digital storage media" refers to both storage and communication capabilities. These have increased in capacity more than a thousandfold in the past decade, allowing digital multimedia to emerge as a cost-effective competitor for analog approaches. In 1985, CD-ROM (compact-disc read-only memory) with a capacity of more than 600 Mbytes but a manufactured cost under a dollar was first applied to electronic publishing.[4,5] Similarly, fiber-optic cable now makes gigabit-per-second communication channels a reality worldwide.

Storage

CD-ROMs, the most cost-effective storage medium for distributing large quantities of digital data, are related to regular compact discs — that is, CD-DA, or compact-disc digital-audio. Both support direct access to individual sectors of data that can store 1/75 second of CD-quality digital audio in CD-DA format, using 2,336 bytes, or 2,048 bytes of arbitrary digital data in CD-ROM format, with the rest of the space for error correction. Thus, CD-ROM data transfer speed is 150 Kbytes per second or 1.2 Mbits per second.

An elaborate system of optics, servos, and signal decoding circuits allows data to be accessed within a second.[6] International Organization for Standardization (ISO) 9660 (based on the High Sierra standard[7]) specifies the volume and file characteristics, allowing access through nearly any CD-ROM drive and operating system. Efforts of the Rock Ridge Group have extended the utility of ISO 9660 for Unix systems and servers.

Compact discs are part of the family of optical media.[8,9] There are prospects for further improvement, including write-once and erasable discs of varying sizes.[10] For example, announcements indicate that in 1992, write-once CD-ROM drives will cost under $3,000, and minidisk (2.5-inch, 128-Mbyte) drives will cost about the same as those for CD-ROMs, handling both formats. Further information on optical disc-publishing and access is available in the literature.[4,5]

Magnetic disks are readily available with capacities on the order of a gigabyte, but they are not low-cost, removable, or produced by mass replication. Use of caching, memory hierarchies, and minimal perfect hashing will make all storage units even more effective contributors to digital multimedia.

Networking

While fiber-optic connections are the most cost-effective scheme for rapidly transmitting large volumes of digital data, a great deal of research regarding networked multimedia is required. The Fiber Distributed Data Interface operates at 100 Mbps, and connection costs dropped below $5,000 in the early 1990s. Gigabit-per-second networks are being tested, and will form the backbone for national telecommunication. However, research regarding network protocols, local area network and workstation architectures, and operating-system support software for digital multimedia is still in its infancy. The first international workshop exclusively on these topics was held late in 1990.[11]

Asynchronous transfer mode networks support both variable and constant bit rate services at very high speeds and serve as the basis for the Broadband Integrated Services Digital Network.[12] Streams of digital multimedia, including uncompressed live video, can use the constant bit rate services. These types of fast packet switching can support real-time communication with reduced jitter. (Jitter is caused by delays of packets.) Yet many questions remain regarding synchronization of related data types, dynamic adaptation to different terminal and network services, and real-time requirements for hypermedia.[13] Research is also needed on rate structures, spectrum and channel allocation, and handling of scalable representations of video streams.[14]

Network and operating-system concerns coalesce because of the need for open systems, synchronization ("lip-sync" of audio and video), and fast transfer from network to presentation unit. High performance and reliability are also important. Research is proceeding on object-oriented models to handle the various classes of multimedia,[15] abstractions for continuous media (for example, an audio stream) I/O,[16] and connection architectures for networks and workstations.[17,18] There is a trade-off between network reliability, how closely the network approximates providing a constant rate stream, and other factors. Without buffering, the stream of data must be carefully prepared, such as by interleaving data on storage units.[19] That is especially important with CD-ROM, where seek times are one to two orders of magnitude slower than with magnetic disks. As memory prices decline, however, buffering of multimedia data will allow fast processors

Medium	Collecting	Preparing
Video	Video edit list	Digitize, enhance, compress
Image	Selection	Digitize, enhance, compress
Audio	Audio edit list	Filter, digitize, enhance, compress
Text	Text filing	Text processing, tool use
Graphics	(Composite) Object selection	Rendering, drawing, animating tool use

Publishing: ordering, correlating multiple representations, organizing (layout, order), hypermedia linking, adding interactive scripts.

Using: network distribution, optical publishing, on-line use, hypermedia enhancement by users.

Table 1: Multimedia publishing

to compensate for many performance problems in digital storage media.

Adding Audio and Video Capabilities

While issues of text and graphics processing have continuing importance in standard information systems, the current wave of development in digital multimedia deals mainly with audio and video. Luther[20] discusses many important issues, and Bottoms and Helgerson[21] and Adkins[22] cover ways to manage data-conversion projects including these media. The goal is integrated capabilities encompassing cameras, slide and filmstrip projectors, camcorders and VCRs, tape recorders, television broadcast and reception units, and postproduction studios.

Many tools are required to fully support both commercial and end-user multimedia publishing. Table 1 illustrates some key issues for important media types. First, suitable multimedia objects must be collected. These come from natural or artificial sources — for example, a captured image or a synthesized sound. While many people know how to file text documents, select a graphic object while drawing, or choose slides for a presentation, most people have had no experience editing audio or video files.

Nevertheless, tens or hundreds of hours of raw footage are often edited to produce a single hour of a video production.

After collection comes preparation. For use with computers, audio and video are digitized and then stored in the minimum amount of space suitable for subsequent use. Specialized tools for each medium are required to enhance or add new materials. Multimedia publishing then involves ordering the pool of accumulated resources and tying together the various representations of each object (for example, audio and video synchronization or sequencing of images obtained at different times). Publications must be organized both spatially and temporally, and associational links must be provided, as with hypermedia.[23] Suitable sequences of interaction must be scripted.[2] The resulting publication is shared over a network, distributed on CD-ROM, or enhanced into an even better publication as part of a hyperbase (a database of hypermedia documents).

Multimedia publications stretch the capabilities of modern computers. Enormous requirements for storage make compression necessary. Computers must provide facilities for accurate control of playback, flexible editing, and signal processing or enhancement. Combinations such as warping video onto graphic structures must be supported.

Audio

On a computer, digital sounds can supplement video, communicate when the user's other senses are engaged, or provide a suitable background or stimulus. Brewer discusses uses of audio as well as technical issues relating to CD-ROM.[24] While special VLSI chips have been developed for various digital signal processing tasks, the related matter of digital representation is a particular concern.

When sound is digitized, it is usually sampled and quantized using a scheme called *pulse code modulation.* According to sampling theory, samples should be taken at least twice for each cycle of the highest frequency component to be recovered. Because the human ear is not sensitive to sounds higher than 20 kHz, the 44.1-kHz sampling rate used for CD-DA permits fairly accurate reproduction. Each sample uses 16 bits to indicate the amplitude — that is, to quantize the sound — yielding a large dynamic range and a signal-to-noise ratio of over 95 dB. The main disadvantage of this approach is that roughly 10 Mbytes of storage are consumed by each minute of audio (171 Kbytes per second). In other words, a communication channel of about 1.4 Mbps must be allocated to handle a single stereo source.

Several approaches are commonly used to reduce the need for storage, but they reduce the quality of reproduction. Storage decreases when a system uses

- mono instead of stereo;
- fewer samples, reducing the frequency range covered; or
- fewer bits per sample, reducing the quality of waveform reconstruction.

Thus, with Compact Disc-Interactive, or CD-I, level A stereo sound requires 85 Kbytes per second, level B 42.5 Kbytes per second, and level C 21.3 Kbytes per second to give sound quality comparable to an LP record, FM radio, or AM radio, respectively. Significant further reductions are possible with *adaptive differential pulse code modulation* schemes, which use fewer bits for quantization. The differential approach involves recording the difference from the previous sample and often requires fewer bits than the actual current value. The adaptive feature involves computing parameters, so the scale for values changes as the rate of amplitude shift varies. Often, 4 bits per sample is adequate for good-quality reproduction, as in the ADPCM scheme used in the CD-ROM XA (extended architecture) standard promulgated by Philips and Sony.

Graphics, Images, and Video

Doherty and Apperson survey graphics, images, and video.[25] Many issues relate to all forms of graphics, images, and video, but there are differences in origin, storage, and presentation. Generally, graphics components of multimedia programs originate on computer systems. It is possible for natural images to lead to graphics, such as when line-tracking algorithms are applied to digitized versions of engineering diagrams, or when scanned images are converted to a "draw" representation by software that tries to fit lines and filled shapes. Sophisticated conversions to the structured representation characteristic of graphics or to higher level forms managed by artificial intelligence routines also take place in the context of computer vision.

Ultimately, images and video will be analyzed and stored in high-level and storage-efficient representations that identify and characterize objects, relationships, distances, and movement.

This will facilitate "virtual reality" investigations, support model-based compression, and allow truly scalable presentations for displays varying in size from wristwatch monitors to wall panels.[26]

Most current representations of images assume that descriptions are a two-dimensional array or raster, and that video is a sequence of such images. The "resolution" of an image is crucial as it defines the raster size. Still images that are closely examined should be stored using at least 512 X 480-pixel resolution, according to experiments we have conducted at Virginia Polytechnic Institute and State University; but, in such applications as menu selection or image database browsing, low-resolution picture icons or "picons" may suffice.

With video, the key issue is the enormous bandwidth and storage required for digital representations. NTSC television (the US standard established by the National Television System Committee) has 525 horizontal lines to define the vertical resolution or height. The theoretical width or horizontal resolution limit, based on the allowed bandwidth of 4.5 MHz, is 360 vertical lines. However, because of the scanning method and television construction constraints, the "safe" region on a television is even smaller, so 360 X 240 pixels is often the resolution achieved. This is called "normal resolution" for CD-I.[27]

Recommendation 601 of the International Radio Consultative Committee, or CCIR, specifies the international standard for digital video as 720 lines. The number of pixels per line varies depending on the television scheme used: There are 480 pixels for NTSC and 576 for PAL[28] (phase alternating line, the European standard). The International Telegraphy and Telephony Consultative Committee, or CCITT, uses the Common Intermediate Format (CIF) for video telephony, which has a resolution of 360 X 288 pixels, and Quarter-CIF (QCIF), which has a 180 X 144-pixel resolution.[29] Super VHS camcorders achieve 400 lines, and high-definition television about 1,000 lines.

Images have a third dimension, pixel depth, which refers to the number of bits used for each picture element. While monochrome uses a single bit, gray scale often uses 8 bits to get 256 levels. For color graphics, 4 or 8 bits may suffice, while for color images, 8, 9, 16, or 24 bits are standard. With 32-bit color, 24 bits are used for color and 8 bits for the "alpha channel," which indicates degree of transparency or mixing with other image planes.

Pixel depth relates to the choice of color space. Cameras or scanners will often separate the red, green, and blue (RGB) components and quantize them with a certain number of bits each. Examples are RGB 5:5:5, which is used with CD-I,[8] or 8:8:8, which produces 24-bit color. However, the human visual system is not as sensitive to color (chrominance) as it is to intensity (luminance), so color spaces other than RGB have been developed. Mappings between these color spaces can be done with linear transformations.[20] For PAL, the YUV space was chosen, and that has been adopted for use with both CD-I and Intel's Digital Video Interactive, or DVI. For analog television, 4.5 MHz can be used for luminance (Y), and 1.5 MHz each for the two chrominance channels (U and V).

Home televisions and VCRs, which are considered acceptable by many viewers, often use only 0.5 MHz for the chrominance channels. Similarly, with CCIR Recommendation 601, chrominance is subsampled, yielding a 4:2:2 scheme that provides twice as many samples for luminance. DVI's 9-bit compressed video format uses 4:1 subsampling in each dimension, yielding 1 bit of chrominance for every 8 bits of luminance.[20]

Smooth motion video requires at least 25 to 30 frames per second. PAL and Secam (Sequentiel Coleur avec Memoire, the standard used in France) use 25 frames per second; NTSC uses 30 frames per second. These are usually interlaced, so each frame is made of two fields containing alternating lines, and two fields are shown during each frame time. Eventually, noninterlaced displays like computer monitors could be refreshed with a full image 60 times per second.

To estimate bandwidth requirements, however, we can concentrate on total samples per second for various schemes. If digital video is uniformly quantized at 8 bits per sample, according to CCIR Recommendation 601, with a sampling rate of 13.5 MHz for luminance, the total bit rate is 216 Mbps. The bit rate for NTSC "network-quality" video is about 45 Mbps.[28] For CIF and QCIF the uncompressed bit rates are approximately 36 and 9 Mbps.[29] Contrast these rates with the 150-Kbps data rate of CD-ROM!

Compression Methods

Clearly, compression is essential if audio, images, and video are to be used in digital multimedia applications. A megabyte of space would be filled by roughly six seconds of CD-quality audio, a single 640 x 480-pixel color image stored using 24 bits per pixel, or a single frame — 1/30 second — of CIF video. Nevertheless, videodisc applications often have more than 20 minutes of video, perhaps 10,000 slides, and 30 minutes of stereo sound on each laser disc side. And with the tremendous volume of data that will be received each day from planned NASA missions[30] and other scientific ventures, the need for proven compression techniques is obvious.

Happily, there has been a great deal of research and many implementations using software, hardware, or both for a variety of compression methods. Research continues, with further improvements expected using wavelet and other time- and space-domain schemes. Elsewhere, I have published a brief introduction with a glossary and references.[31] Rao and Yip provide a comprehensive treatment of compression for images and video.[32] A set of useful articles appears in conference publications by NASA[33] and the IEEE Computer Society,[34] with many good references included in the bibliographies.

Compression of digital data involves computational algorithms that can be implemented in software. Some involve digital versions of signal processing methods, others involve pattern recognition, and still others use statistics or characteristics of particular data types or samples. High-speed implementations involve VLSI chips, such as for audio digital signal processing, discrete cosine transform, or vector quantization approaches. I discuss these in a later section.

Approaches

At the boundary of image processing, computer vision, and graphics is the area of model-based compression.[26] Models of faces can be analyzed, yielding facial motion parameters that can be transmitted at low bit rates and synthesized at a receiver for "talking head" video telephony. Other approaches involve feature detection at the encoder and rendering at the de-coder.

Fractals (images that can be described by a set of rules specified with a relatively small number of bits) allow compression of natural scenes where the underlying structure matches this type of model.[35] Very high compression ratios can be achieved, sometimes on the order of 1,000:1 (size of the uncompressed form versus the compressed form). However, extensive computation is required for encoding. While decoded images may be acceptable to human judgment, there is usually some quality loss. Nevertheless, several companies — for example, Barnsley Communica-

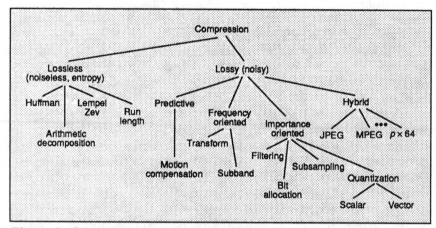

Figure 1: Selected compression approaches

tions — are marketing boards and software for fractal compression and decompression. Commodore has announced plans for software-based fractal decompression in their CDTV system.

Figure 1 shows a taxonomy of compression approaches. In *lossless* schemes, the original representation can be perfectly recovered. For text, lossless methods may achieve a 2:1 reduction. For bilevel images, 15:1 is a good figure. (A new international standard for bilevel image coding, referred to as JBIG, improves on CCITT Group 3 and 4 approaches for facsimile transmission, and in some situations achieves more than 50:1 compression.)

These approaches are also called *noiseless* — because they do not add noise to the signal — or *entropy coding* — because they eliminate redundancy through statistical or decomposition techniques. For example, Huffman coding uses fewer bits for more common message symbols, and run-length encoding replaces strings of the same symbol with a count/symbol pair. Discussions of research on lossless compression appear elsewhere.[36,37]

The other approach, *lossy* compression, involves encoding into a form that takes up a relatively small amount of space, but which can be decoded to yield a representation that humans find similar to the original.

Lossy compression

Lossy or noisy compression may add artifacts that can be perceived.[33] Careful study of the human visual system has focused attention on approaches that cause little perceived loss in quality, but achieve high compression ratios.

Prediction

Predictive approaches like ADPCM involve predicting subsequent values by observing previous ones, and transmitting only the usually small differences between actual and predicted data. An example involves motion compensation. Successive frames in a video sequence are often quite similar or have blocks of pixels shifted from one frame to the next — for example, as the camera pans or a person moves.[20] Although it is computationally expensive to analyze images and yield motion vectors, parallel computers[38] or neural networks can help with the processing.

Frequency-oriented compression

Subband coding can exploit the fact that humans have different sensitivities to various spatial and temporal frequency combinations.[39] The idea is to separate (for example, using a series of filters) the different frequency combinations, and then to code with greater fidelity the frequencies that humans pay particular attention to. Without subband coding, all frequency combinations would be coded identically, so the technique achieves high perceived quality with fewer total bits.

Another approach relating to humans' handling of frequency is transform coding. This usually involves spatial frequencies, as in single images. The most common approach applies the *discrete cosine transform*, which is related to the fast Fourier transform. Rao and Yip cover DCT approaches thoroughly.[32] Lower spatial frequencies must be carefully coded, while higher frequencies need less detailed coding. If we think of a block (say, an 8 x 8-pixel section) of a two-dimensional image as a square with rows and columns numbered from the top-left corner, then the DCT of that block will also be a similarly numbered square. Consider a zigzag sequencing of the values in transform space, starting at the top-left corner and covering the nearest cells first. Run-length encoding and coarse quantification of cells later in the sequence both lead to good compression. The encoder applies DCT in the forward direction, and the decoder uses an inverse mapping from transform to image space.

Importance-oriented Compression

Other characteristics of images besides frequency are used as the basis for compression. The principle is to consider as more important those parts of an image that humans are better attuned to. An example of this approach is to filter images, getting rid of details that cannot be perceived, as in the low-pass filtering done for real-time video with DVI systems. Another technique is to allocate more bits to encode important parts of an image, such as where edges occur, than to encode large homogeneous regions, such as those depicting clouds.

Color lookup table use, as in CD-I and DVI, applies the principle of indirection. Instead of letting the bits that describe a pixel refer to a location in color space, the bits identify a table location, and the table entry refers to color space. Color spaces often cover a palette of size 2^{24}, which means 24 bits are needed. On the other hand, lookup table size may be only 256 (2^8). The reduction is 24 to 8 bits per pixel. The challenge is to select for each lookup table the most important colors to be accessed by the display processor.

Subsampling, also based on characteristics of human vision, was discussed in an earlier section. It involves using fewer bits for chrominance than luminance. Interpolation, which can be carried out in hardware,[40] results in a full but approximate reconstruction of the original. We can think of this process as that of taking one matrix and generating from it another matrix four or 16 times larger — by interpolating values horizontally, vertically, and diagonally. Related to interpolation is line doubling, used in some DVI systems to go from the 256 lines that result from video decompression to 512 lines.

Importance also relates to patterns in an image representation. Clearly, higher level descriptions where symbols refer to large structures can take much less space than raster forms. In coding theory, this translates into the fact that vector quantization can lead to higher compression than scalar quantization.[39] Scalar quantization is often just called quantization, and was discussed in an earlier section in connection with pulse code modulation and audio encoding. It takes values and maps them into a fixed number of bits.

Vector quantization, on the other hand, usually takes two-dimensional vectors of values — for example, 4 x 4 — and maps them into a code symbol. Thus, code books are developed for images, recording the most important vectors, and all data vectors are mapped to the nearest code-book entry, minimizing mean square error. Decoding involves fast table lookup to replace coded entries with vectors from the code book.

Vector quantization is discussed in depth in the literature.[41,42]

There are many algorithms and some VLSI implementations. Encoding usually takes a good deal of computation, so near optimal code books can be developed.

Hybrid coding

Various compression approaches can be combined, for example, DCT and differential pulse code modulation, subband coding and DCT, or differential pulse code modulation and vector quantization. Generally, subband coding is coupled with vector quantization. Systems and standards for video compression often apply motion compensation for temporal compression, transform coding for spatial compression, and Huffman or arithmetic coding for statistical compression.

Standards

Initially, standards for digital multimedia were established by fiat. Thus, Philips and Sony developed CD-I, with its formats for images and audio.[8] Similarly, as a step toward CD-I and a way to incorporate audio more easily into CD-ROM applications, the companies specified CD-ROM XA. It uses ADPCM, with three different sample rates (levels A, B, C). Since the specification of CD-ROM XA, manufacturers have produced interface boards for CD-ROM-based playback. Very widespread use of CD-ROM XA is expected, such as through joint efforts involving Philips and Nintendo systems.

Recently, important new international standards for images, audio, and video have been accepted by electronics, computer, and communications organizations through consensus, with the standards groups actually pushing the limits of state-of-the-art research. Table 2 presents summary details; explanations follow in subsequent sections. Two types of standards are particularly important: low-level coding or compression standards for data streams and hardware processing, and higher level standards for network and software operation.

Coding

The first standard listed in Table 2 is JPEG,[43] named for the Joint Photographic Experts Group, which developed it. This work

Short Name	Official Name	Standards Group	Group Designation	Approval Status
JPEG	Digital compression and coding of continuous-tone still images	Joint Photographic Experts Group	JTC1/SC2/WG10	Committee draft balloting in 1991
H.261	Video coder/decoder for audio-visual services at $p \neq 64$ Kbps	Specialist Group on Coding for Visual Telephony	CCITT SG XV	Approved Dec. 1990
MPEG	Coding of moving pictures and associated audio	Moving Picture Experts Group	JTC1/SC2/WG11	Video committee draft balloting in 1991
MHEG	Coded representation of multimedia and hypermedia information	Multimedia and Hypermedia Information Coding Expert Group	JTC1/SC2/WG12	Working document
HyTime	Hypermedia/Time-Based Structuring Language	Standard Music Representation Work Group	ANSI X3V1.8M	Committee draft balloting in 1991

Table 2: Standards for multimedia and hypermedia

is technically complete. The committee draft was sent for balloting early in 1991, and it will be approved as ISO/IEC (International Electrotechnical Commission) Standard 10918 by 1992. Processing usually involves sequential encoding using forward DCT scalar quantization, and either Huffman or arithmetic coding for compression. The decoder simply reverses the process. Applications control the quantization and Huffman tables.

JPEG also includes optional modes of compression and decompression. Progressive encoding is supported, where the image is encoded in multiple scans and the viewer can see the image build up in successively more detailed versions. This operation is important when communication bandwidth is low, or users need to browse through an image collection. Hierarchical encoding is also specified, where lower resolution images can be accessed before higher resolution images, again useful for browsing or low-resolution displays. JPEG also specifies a lossless encoding scheme, which involves a predictor and entropy coder.

A second international standard, CCITT Recommendation H.261, is referred to as p x 64.[29] The p is a parameter since the standard can be used to produce compressed video streams at rates of p x 64 Kbps, with p ranging from 1 to 30. Given CIF or QCIF input, p x 64 codecs (coder/decoders) will support video telephony. For $p = 1$ or 2, only QCIF and videophone applications at low frame rates will be possible, but for p over 5, use of CIF and video conferencing is possible.

The coding is a hybrid of DCT using 8 X 8 blocks, and differential pulse code modulation with motion estimation[29] involving 16 X 16 luminance blocks, using picture memory for macroblock comparisons. Spatial coding involves DCT followed by scalar quantization. The loop filter removes high-frequency noise. Depending on the fullness of the output buffer, the quantizer step size can be varied to decrease or increase the bit rate. Statistical coding takes place in the multiplexer.

A third important standard is referred to as MPEG, for the Motion Picture Experts Group.[44] The ISO/IEC committee draft was assigned standard number 11172. There are actually three parts to the effort: MPEG-Video, MPEG-Audio, and MPEG-System. The first refers to work with video compression of television resolution — 360 x 240 pixels — down to a bit rate of approximately 1.2 Mbps. This rate is suitable for use with CD-ROM, digital audio tape, and T1 communication channels. All MPEG decoders should be able to operate with a "core" bit stream that has the following upper bounds[44]: resolution of 720 x 576 pixels, speed of

30 frames per second, bit rate of 1.86 Mbps, and decoder buffer of 46 Kbytes. Another MPEG project is to investigate compression for CCIR Recommendation 601 video at bit rates up to 10 Mbps.

While there is overlap between p x 64 and MPEG capabilities, and some of the VLSI components involved can be used for both, p x 64 has a goal of broad coverage for varying channel capacity, while MPEG has the goal of high-quality coverage at an important but narrower range of bit rates.

MPEG-Video specifies a layered bit stream that consists of a

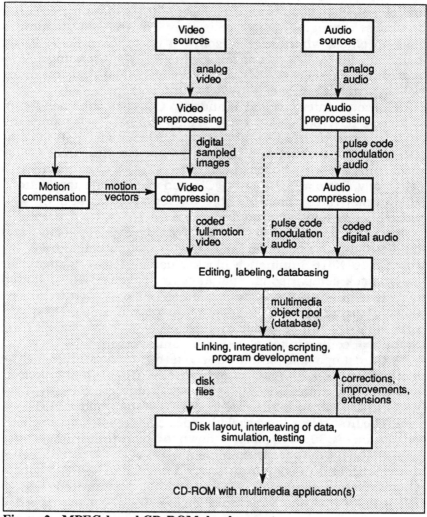

Figure 2: MPEG-based CD-ROM development

video sequence header and layers for sequence, a group of pictures, pictures, slices, macroblocks, and blocks.[44] The lower two levels include motion compensation and DCT data. The algorithm ensures features desirable for a range of applications: random access, fast forward and reverse searches, forward and reverse playback, audio/video synchronization, robustness against errors, delays limited to 150 ms, and editability.

The MPEG-Video algorithm uses motion compensation on 16 X 16 blocks and DCT coding of 8 X 8 blocks, followed by quantization and entropy coding. Motion compensation involves predictive and interpolative coding. As in JPEG, reference frames are fully coded using DCT-based methods. Predicted (interpolated) frames are determined on the basis of the nearest reference or predicted frame (on both sides). Finally, the motion information is statistically coded.

The MPEG-Audio standard[45] is being fully specified in 1991. While CD-quality audio requires two channels of 706 Kbps, the compressed bit rate will be two channels of 128 kbps or possibly 64 Kbps — that is, a reduction from 1.412 Mbps to 0.256 Mbps. Input sampling rates of 32, 44.1, and 48 kHz with 16 bits per sample will be supported; delays will be no more than 80 ms; and addressing will be to units no longer than 1/30 second. Sound quality close to the original is expected.

Ultimately, MPEG-System work will produce a complete approach to encoding television-quality audio and video into a single stream operating at about 1.5 Mbps. Figure 2 shows how this may lead to development of digital multimedia applications for CD-ROM. Video will be converted to digital form and then compressed using motion compensation and other processing specified in MPEG-Video. Audio will be digitized. While limited amounts of pulse code modulation audio can be stored, most will be coded according to the MPEG-Audio standard. Application development will then proceed, involving editing, labeling, and cataloging of the audio/video resources into a pool of "objects." Higher level activities of linking, integrating media streams, scripting interaction, and developing programs all lead to stored files. For CD-ROM, disc layout of possibly interleaved data allows simulation to ensure proper real-time operation of finished applications. After enough cycles of testing and refinement, a finished CD-ROM master can be used for replication.

With these several standards, it is imperative that headers and descriptors for video streams be created so coding methods can be easily distinguished.[14] This is particularly important for multimedia electronic mail.[46] These standards will certainly be further developed to better support users of digital multimedia.[26]

High level

In addition to coding, standards are needed for higher layers of the multimedia application development process. This work is just beginning, and it will require a few years to reach maturity. One effort is coordinated by the Multimedia and Hypermedia Information Coding Expert Group, or MHEG, whose aim is to allow bit-stream specifications for multimedia and hypermedia applications on any platform, leading to good real-time performance drawing on object-oriented methods. Version 2, July 1990, of the MHEG Working Document S includes useful definitions regarding multimedia and hypermedia. It gives a partial object hierarchy of both basic and composite objects, covering input, output, interaction, and linking. Methods include editing, operating, and presenting, with a state model including combinations of not ready versus stopped ready, running versus suspended, and exposed versus concealed. MHEG covers synchronization (between objects, or using marks or conditions), buffer memory, input objects like buttons or menus, and interactive objects like prompts.

A higher level but related effort involves extending ODA (Office Document Architecture) standards to include hypermedia. Further along, however, is work in applying the Standard Generalized Markup Language (SGML, ISO 8879) to multimedia and hypermedia. This approach led to HyTime,[47] balloted in 1991 as ISO/IEC Committee Draft 10744. HyTime allows a complete digital multimedia application to be encoded in a linear stream, including all details regarding "document" structure, hypermedia linking, synchronization, and timing. For interchange, Abstract Syntax Notation 1 (ASN.1, ISO 8824) allows bit string representation. A pool of multimedia objects can be referenced from the main part of the document. Also, there are series of events and "batons" to control the timing, with mapping from virtual time units to real time. The Text Encoding Initiative has drawn on HyTime for describing multimedia and hypermedia documents and performances.

Further standards work will facilitate interchange and transcoding of multimedia,[14] integration of object pools with scripting languages, interoperability of applications on heterogeneous platforms connected by fiber networks, conversions between storage units, and other requirements called for by a growing community of users.

Systems

Interactive multimedia computing systems must support application development and use. At present, there is a tight coupling of hardware, software, and applications, but that coupling will gradually loosen. Here, I deal with a variety of platforms and related software.

Next

Next systems with a Nextdimension board support 32-bit color (24-bit color plus an alpha channel). The board was designed to include an i860 processor for graphics and a JPEG compression chip[48] from C-Cube Microsystems. While 640 x 480-pixel image compression in software requires almost 10 seconds using the Motorola MC68040 microprocessor, the special board must do that in 1/30 second. This allows full-motion compression and decompression, using the 600-Kbps speed achieved by some hard disks to achieve moderate-quality playback.

MediaView is a digital multimedia communication software system built with Nextstep, the interface used on Next systems, to handle graphics, audio, video, animations, mathematics, and so on.[49] It uses an object-oriented approach to documents. Searching is supported for text, and digital darkroom methods are used for images. Annotations include Draw-it and Hear-it notes, as well as object- or image-based animations. Full-motion video will be supported using the Nextdimension board.

CD-I, CDTV

Compact Disc-Interactive was the first interactive digital multimedia technology targeted for the consumer market. First announced in 1986, CD-I is defined in a proprietary standard, the "Green Book," which Philips provided to developers under a license arrangement.[8] The first prototype disks were prepared in 1987. The official commercial launch of CD-I was delayed until fall of 1991, reflecting the complexity of software and application development. Each unit includes a compact disc player, a Motorola M68000 family microprocessor, an audio processing unit, audio and video decoders, a clock, a pointing device, and an operating system, CD-RTOS, derived from OS-9, with real-time capabilities. There will be optional MPEG-compliant full-motion video support. The minimal system, the CD-I Base Case Decoder, will connect to an external monitor and external speakers. The decoder supports a variety of visual effects, including single-plane effects like cuts, scrolling, mosaics, and fades, as well as two-plane effects like transparency, chroma key, matte, dissolve, and wipe.

The challenge of CD-I has been to build a carefully defined hardware, software, and storage environment for interactive multimedia computing that can be sold as a package for under $1,000. Such systems would serve the needs of consumers and the low-end education/training marketplace. Careful design is required, since "hit" CD-I discs, selling for perhaps $40, might establish a large consumer electronics market, as did compact disc players and Nintendo units. Toward that end, Optimage Interactive Services Company has developed tools to help developers, and there is Starter System software that works with the standard decoder, allowing previously captured materials to be reorganized for presentations. However, full application development currently calls for PC-, Macintosh-, and/or Sun-based networks and a variety of software tools and programming expertise.

Bruno gives a short introduction to CD-I.[27] Brewer describes CD-ROM XA, which specifies the use of various levels of CD-I audio in an open hardware environment.[24] Philips' work with MPEG compression and related details on the video decoder are discussed by Sijstermans and van der Meer.[38]

In the spring of 1991, Commodore announced CDTV (Commodore Dynamic Total Vision), with pricing and an approach similar to those of CD-I. Commodore uses CD-ROM with proprietary representation schemes rather than the CD-I format, so CDTV is positioned as a related but competing technology, building on Commodore's experience with real-time operating systems and the Amiga 500 computer.

DVI

Intel's Digital Video Interactive is a more open approach than CD-I or CDTV, emphasizing digital video and audio compression, chip sets, and machine-independent audio/video software environments. Luther gives an excellent short introduction[50] and the best overall description.[20] Included in a series of articles in a special section in *Communications of the ACM*[51] is an overview of

the technology and applications, a short history of the development and graphics-based prototyping, a description of parallel
encoding, and details of an exciting application to training.
Elsewhere, Harney et al. described the new "B" chip set,[40] and
Green described the new software design.[52]

Current DVI technology uses a 25-MIPS pixel processor, the
82750 PB. Although in some ways it is like a conventional
microprocessor, the 82750 PB is five to 10 times faster because
of its specialized architecture. It is programmable and can support various standards.[40] The 82750 PB can

- perform graphics operations rapidly;
- use special effects to highlight image or video transitions;
- decode a 640 x 480-pixel JPEG compressed image in less than
  a second;
  compress or decompress images using a proprietary format at up
  to 768 x 480-pixel resolution in a fraction of a second;
- compress 128 x 120-pixel resolution motion video at 30 frames
  per second with fair quality into a special representation (RTV,
  or real-time video) on hard disk; and
- play back video compressed on a 64-processor Intel computer
  into another special representation (PLV, or production-level
  video) at 30 frames per second with good quality at 256 x 240-
  pixel resolution.

Combinations of these operations are fast and effective for
such effects as warping textures selected from an image database
onto graphic objects selected from a wireframe database.

Intel has published a bit-stream specification. DVI will support
MPEG standards when they are fully specified, and Intel has an
even faster pixel processor planned for 1993.

The companion display processor, the 82750 DB chip, supports pixel interpolation, genlocking, an alpha channel, reconfig-
urable color lookup tables, conversion from YUV to RGB, and
triple 8-bit digital-to-analog converters, for resolutions at least
through 640 X 480 pixels. Intel provides the ActionMedia 750
board set for AT or Micro Channel Architecture 80386-based
computers. Boards using the chip set have been developed for
Macintosh computers as well.

The present DVI audio/video subsystem software, called AVSS,
will be replaced by AVK, the audio/video kernel.[52] Instead of the
current single environment for DOS, AVK has been designed to

work with at least Microsoft Windows, OS/2, and Unix. Instead of implementing only the simple VCR metaphor supported by AVSS, AVK uses the metaphor of a digital production studio, managing a variety of streams with sampling, mixing, and effects. More attention is given to interfacing with the host operating system and handling real-time operations. Saturation of processors, memory, and I/O is avoided with flexible buffering. Scheduling is handled by the pixel processor instead of the host system, streams are synchronized into groups, and windows are supported.

Third-party developers have provided higher level software support. For example, Mediascript[20] is a high-level language interpreter that eliminates much of the need for programming in C. Other tools support painting (for example, Lumena), animation building (Authology: Multimedia), and hypermedia. Our efforts at Virginia Polytechnic Institute and State University (VPI & SU) have led to a "hot spot" tool for managing buttons and a prototype "integrator" that uses the metaphor of a musical score and concepts covered by the MHEG and HyTime standards as the basis for direct manipulation to develop interactive multimedia applications.

Prospects

Clearly there are opposing forces in the future of digital multimedia systems: closed versus open systems, low cost versus high cost, performance versus flexibility, and stand-alone systems versus distributed systems. Table 3 illustrates two key dimensions of systems: components and power. Companies like Microsoft and Tandy have promulgated multimedia PCs (MPCs), but these are fairly minimal systems. As the table shows, most serious offerings go beyond these minimal specifications, possibly adding Ethernet or token ring networking.

The next generation of digital multimedia systems will be at the level shown in the last column of Table 3. Not only CD-ROM but also large-capacity writable local storage will allow capture and development as well as use of applications. Faster host processors and full support for the MPEG standard will be required. Networking will provide access to image, audio, and video servers at high speeds. Tools like our integrator or systems building on the Athena Muse system at MIT[3] will provide flexible support for a variety of application classes.

Component	Multimedia PC	Typical Current System	Typical Advanced System
Storage	CD-ROM, 30-Mbyte disk	CD-ROM, 100-Mbyte disk	CD-ROM, gigabyte disk
Host processor	80286	80386 or MC68030	80486 or MC68040
Display	VGA	768 X 480	1,024 X 768
Extra board	Audio board	Nextdimension, CD-ROM XA, DVI	MPEG system
Networking	None	Ethernet, token ring	Fiber Distributed Data Interface
Software	Windows 3.0	Authology: Multimedia, Mediascript, MediaView	Athena Muse, Integrator

Table 3: Classes of multimedia systems

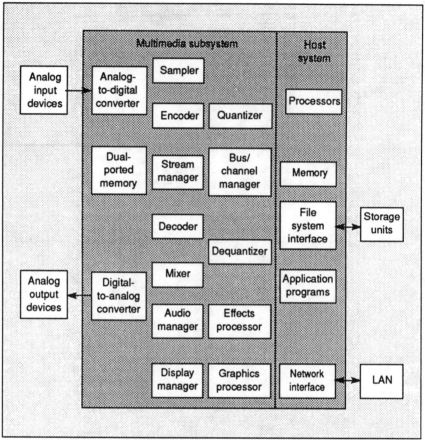

Figure 3: Logical components of a future multimedia workstation

Figure 3 illustrates one type of future workstation. Access to network and storage units as well as analog input and output devices must be supported. Inside the workstation (the workstation itself may be physically distributed) will be the standard host system components and a comprehensive multimedia system. The multimedia system may be part of the host motherboard, but we can think of it as logically separate. Hardware and software components must carry out the multiple functions shown for the multimedia subsystem.

Table 4 illustrates how these advanced workstations might relate to current views of interoperability. Above the bottom layer shown here, which represents the lower levels of the Open Systems Interconnection reference model, are four layers related to multimedia and hypermedia, followed by the usual three top

Layer	Description/Contents
Application	Hypertext, hypermedia, interactive multimedia
Presentation	Devices: keyboard, mouse, speakers, windows
	Media: animations, audio, graphics, images, video
	Operations: accessing, editing, sequencing, transforming
Session	History management, user identification, versioning
Base	Searching and inferencing with data, information, and knowledge bases
View	Frames, graphs, lists, relations
Link	Labels, link identifiers, types
Anchor	Anchor identifiers, span descriptions
Node	Basic and composite media objects, object identifiers
Communication	File systems, messages, processes

Table 4: Reference model, upper layers

layers of the OSI reference model. Thus, the view layer provides convenient abstractions that support data, information, and knowledge bases, which fit into the next layer. In our work at VPI&SU on the Large External Network (object-oriented) Database, we have implemented parts of these top five layers. Altogether, Table 4 provides a partial conceptual framework for digital hypermedia systems, emphasizing how they must fit into the overall picture of open networks, information processing, and flexible access.

The future for digital multimedia systems is bright, but calls for thoughtful discussion and planning.[14] Already, there have been demonstrations of how hypermedia news services can construct and deliver overnight issues in all-digital format.[23] Based on successes of prototypes at MIT, we can conclude that electronic magazines, manuals, and movie services will be developed. Hypermedia publishing and computer-supported cooperative work will use digital multimedia.

Hardware costs will continue to decline, standards will evolve and become more widely adopted, software systems and tools will mature, and publishers and end-users will learn to work creatively with a range of new capabilities.[53] Interactive computing will benefit from the development of the audio and television industries, leading to exciting new possibilities for interactive digital multimedia computing.

Acknowledgments
The anonymous reviewers provided helpful comments. NCR Corp. supported some of our work on interactive digital video. Gregory Fox and Mahesh Ursekar provided secretarial assistance. I extend special thanks to Deborah Hix, Edward Schwartz, and the many students working with us on digital video at VPI&SU.

References

1.   *Managing Interactive Video/Multimedia Projects*, Educational Technology Publications, R. Bergman and T. Moore, eds., Prentice Hall, Englewood Cliffs, N.J., 1990.
2.   *Learning with Interactive Multimedia*, S. Ambron and K. Hooper, eds., Microsoft Press, Redmond, Wash., 1990.
3.   W. Mackay and G. Davenport, "Virtual Video Editing in Interactive Multimedia Applications," *Comm. ACM*, Vol. 32, No. 7, July 1989, pp. 802-810.
4.   *CD-ROM, Vol. 2: Optical Publishing*, S. Ropiequet, J. Einberger, and B. Zoellick, eds., Microsoft Press, Redmond, Wash., 1987.
5.   *The CD-ROM Handbook*, C. Sherman, ed., McGraw-Hill, New York, 1988.
6.   J. Nadler and R. Wiesenberg, "CD-ROM Hardware," in *The CD-ROM Handbook*, C. Sherman, ed., McGraw-Hill, New York, 1988, pp. 79-106.
7.   J. Einberger and B. Zoellick, "High Sierra Group Format Description," in *CD-ROM, Vol. 2: Optical Publishing*, S. Ropiequet, J. Einberger, and B. Zoellick, eds., Microsoft Press, Redmond, Wash., 1987, pp. 195-216.
8.   Philips International Inc., *Compact Disc-Interactive*, McGraw-Hill, New York, 1988.
9.   D. Traub, "An Historical Perspective on CD-ROM," in *The CD-ROM Handbook*, C. Sherman, ed., McGraw-Hill, New York, 1988, pp. 17-50.
10.   D. Davies, "Future Possibilities of CD-ROM," in *The CD-ROM Handbook*, C. Sherman, ed., McGraw-Hill, New York, 1988, pp. 209-239.
11.   *Proc. First Int'l Workshop on Network and Operating System Support for Digital Audio and Video*, Tech. Report TR-90-062, D. Anderson et. al., eds, Int'l Computer Science Inst., Berkeley, Calif., 1990.
12.   R. Sansom and E. Cooper, "The Impact of Broadband Integrated Services on the Structure of Systems and Application Software," *Proc. First Int'l Workshop on Network and Operating System Support for Digital Audio and Video*, Tech. Report TR-90-062, Int'l Computer Science Inst., Berkeley, Calif., 1990.

13. D. Wybranietz, R. Cordes, and F. Stamen, "Support for Multimedia Communication in Future Private Networks," *Proc. First Int'l Workshop on Network and Operating System Support for Digital Audio and Video*, Tech. Report TR-90-062, Int'l Computer Science Inst., Berkeley, Calif., 1990.

14. M. Liebhold and E. Hoffert, "Toward an Open Environment for Digital Video," *Comm. ACM*, Vol. 34, No. 4, Apr. 1991, pp. 103-112.

15. R. Steinmetz et al., "Compound Multimedia Objects — Integration into Network and Operating Systems," *Proc. First Int'l Workshop on Network and Operating System Support for Digital Audio and Video*, Tech. Report TR-90-062, Int'l Computer Science Inst., Berkeley, Calif., 1990.

16. D. Anderson, R. Govindan, and G. Homsy, "Design and Implementation of a Continuous I/O Server," *Proc. First Int'l Workshop on Network and Operating System Support for Digital Audio and Video*, Tech. Report TR-90-062, Int'l Computer Science Inst., Berkeley, Calif., 1990.

17. P. Momtahan and R. Kamel, "PX Connection Architecture," *Proc. First Int'l Workshop on Network and Operating System Support for Digital Audio and Video*, Tech. Report TR-90-062, Int'l Computer Science Inst., Berkeley, Calif., 1990.

18. H. Katseff et al., "An Overview of the Liaison Network Multimedia Workstation," *Proc. First Int'l Workshop on Network and Operating System Support for Digital Audio and Video*, Tech. Report TR-90-062, Int'l Computer Science Inst., Berkeley, Calif., 1990.

19. C. Yu et al., "Efficient Placement of Audio Data on Optical Discs for Real-Time Applications," *Comm. ACM*, Vol. 32, No. 7, July 1989, pp. 862-871.

20. A. Luther, *Digital Video in the PC Environment*, second edition, McGraw-Hill, New York, 1991.

21. J. Bottoms and L. Helgerson, "The First Step Toward Publishing on CD-ROM," in *The CD-ROM Handbook*, C. Sherman, ed., McGraw-Hill, New York, 1988, pp. 269-307.

22. A. Adkins, "Data Preparation and Premastering," in *The CD-ROM Handbook*, C. Sherman, ed., McGraw-Hill, New York, 1988, pp. 343-396.

23. E. Hoffert and G. Gretsch, "The Digital News Systems at Educom: A Convergence of Interactive Computing Newspapers, Television, and High-Speed Networks," *Comm. ACM*, Vol. 34, No. 4, Apr. 1991, pp. 113-116.

24. B. Brewer, "Using Audio," in *CD-ROM, Vol. 2: Optical Publishing*, S. Ropiequet, J. Einberger, and B. Zoellick, eds., Microsoft Press, Redmond, Wash., 1987, pp. 169-183.

25. G. Doherty and R. Apperson, "Displaying Images," in *CD-ROM, Vol. 2: Optical Publishing*, S. Ropiequet, J. Einberger, and B. Zoellick, eds., Microsoft Press, Redmond, Wash., 1987, pp. 121-168.

26. A. Lippman, "Feature Sets for Interactive Images," *Comm. ACM*, Vol. 34, No. 4, Apr. 1991, pp. 92-101.

27. R. Bruno, "Compact Disc-Interactive," in *The CD-ROM Handbook*, C. Sherman, ed., McGraw-Hill, New York, 1988, pp. 131-185.

28. B. Haskell, "International Standards Activities in Image Data Compression," *Proc. Scientific Data Compression Workshop*, NASA Conf. Pub. 3025, NASA Office of Management, Scientific and Technical Information Division, Washington, DC, 1989, pp. 439-449.

29. M. Liou, "Overview of the px64 Kbit/s Video Coding Standard," *Comm. ACM*, Vol. 34, No. 4, Apr. 1991, pp. 59-63.

30. A. Fleig, "The EOS Data and Information System," *Proc. Scientific Data Compression Workshop*, NASA Conf. Pub. 3025, NASA Office of Management, Scientific and Technical Information Division, Washington, DC, 1989, pp. 73-83.

31. E. Fox, "Guest Editor's Introduction: Standards and the Emergence of Digital Multimedia Systems," *Comm. ACM*, Vol. 34, No. 4, Apr. 1991, pp. 26-29.

32. K. Rao and P. Yip, *Discrete Cosine Transform — Algorithms, Advantages, Applications*, Academic Press, London, 1990.

33. *Proc. Scientific Data Compression Workshop*, NASA Conf. Pub. 3025, H. Ramapriyan, ed., NASA Office of Management, Scientific and Technical Informa- Division, Washington, DC, 1989.

34. *Proc. DCC 91, Data Compression Conf.*, J.A. Storer and J.H. Reif, eds., IEEE CS Press, Los Alamitos, Calif., Order No. 2202, 1991.

35. M. Barnsley and A. Sloan, "Fractal Image Compression," *Proc. Scientific Data Compression Workshop*, NASA Conf. Pub. 3025, NASA Office of Management, Scientific and Technical Information Division, Washington, DC, 1989, pp. 351-365.

36. A. Blumer, "Noiseless Compression Using Non-Markov Models," *Proc. Scientific Data Compression Workshop*, NASA Conf. Pub. 3025, NASA Office of Management, Scientific and Technical Information Division, Washington, DC, 1989, pp. 367-375.

37. M. Cohn, "Performance of Lempel-Ziv Compressors with Deferred Innovation," *Proc. Scientific Data Compression Workshop*, NASA Conf. Pub. 3025, NASA Office of Management, Scientific and Technical Information Division, Washington, DC, 1989, pp. 377-391.

38. F. Sijstermans and J. van der Meer, "CD-I Full-Motion Video Encoding on a Parallel Computer," *Comm. ACM*, Vol. 34, No. 4, Apr. 1991, pp. 81-91.

39. A. Lippman and W. Butera, "Coding Image Sequence for Interactive Retrieval," *Comm. ACM*, Vol. 32, No. 7, July 1989, pp. 852-860.

40. K. Harney et al., "The i750 Video Processor: A Total Multimedia Solution," *Comm. ACM*, Vol. 34, No. 4, Apr. 1991, pp. 64-78.

41. R. Gray, "Vector Quantization," *Proc. Scientific Data Compression Workshop*, NASA Conf. Pub. 3025, NASA Office of Management, Scientific and Technical Information Division, Washington, DC, 1989, pp. 205-231.

42. R. Baker, "AVLSI Chip Set Real-Time Vector Quantization of Image Sequences," *Proc. Scientific Data Compression Workshop*, NASA

Conf. Pub. 3025, NASA Office of Management, Scientific and Technical Information Division, Washington, DC, 1989, pp. 419-437.

43. G. Wallace, "The JPEG Still Picture Compression Standard," *Comm. ACM*, Vol. 34, No. 4, Apr. 1991, pp. 30-44.

44. D. Le Gall, "MPEG: A Video Compression Standard for Multimedia Applications," *Comm. ACM*, Vol. 34, No. 4, Apr. 1991, pp. 46-58.

45. H. Musman, "The ISO Audio Coding Standard," *Proc. Globecom 90*, IEEE, New York, 1990.

46. N. Borenstein, "Multimedia Electronic Mail: Will the Dream Become a Reality?" *Comm. ACM*, Vol. 34, No. 4, Apr. 1991, pp. 117-119.

47. S. Newcomb, N. Kipp, and V. Newcomb, "HyTime: The Hypermedia/Time-Based Document Structuring Language," to appear in *Comm. ACM*, Vol. 34, No. 11, Nov. 1991.

48. G. Cockroft and L. Hourvitz, "Nextstep: Putting JPEG to Multiple Uses," *Comm. ACM*, Vol. 34, No. 4, Apr. 1991, p. 45.

49. R. Phillips, "MediaView: A General Multimedia Digital Publication System," *Comm. ACM*, Vol. 34, No. 7, July 1991, pp. 74-83.

50. A. Luther, "Digital Video Interactive," in *The CD-ROM Handbook*, C. Sherman, ed., McGraw-Hill, New York, 1988, pp. 187-207.

51. Special section on interactive technologies, E. Fox, ed., *Comm. ACM*, Vol. 32, No. 7, July 1989.

52. J. Green, "The Evolution of DVI System Software," to appear in *Comm. ACM*, Vol. 35, No. 1, Jan. 1992.

53. M. Liebhold, "Hypermedia and Visual Literacy," in *Learning with Interactive Multimedia*, S. Ambron and K. Hooper, eds., Microsoft Press, Redmond, Wash., 1990, pp 99-110.

The author can be reached at the Department of Computer Science or the Computing Center, Virginia Polytechnic Institute and State University, Blacksburg, VA 24061-0106; e-mail fox@vtopus.cs.vt.edu.

Chapter 2

Multimedia Distributed Computing

IBMs Directions for
Multimedia Distributed Systems

IBM Corporation

Multimedia combines the interactivity of a computer with a natural user interface that includes audio, video and real images. Over the past decade, multimedia has proven its worth as a uniquely powerful set of technologies when used to support applications such as training, business presentations and marketing kiosks.

Most of these applications have been standalone, because of limitations of communications technologies needed to manage and transport multimedia information. Our customers have told us that in this "information age," standalone applications may be valuable, but do not optimize the competitiveness of their organization. Today's organization generates traditional information consisting of text, numbers and graphs more productively than ever before; stores and retrieves that information more efficiently through the use of databases; and shares that information more effectively through the use of electronic mail, facsimile transmissions and telephone communications. These same organizations believe their applications will be even more valuable by adding multimedia content and expect no less flexibility and transportability.

IBM's vision is to extend multimedia capability across the existing infrastructure of distributed computing. The result for our customers will be the ability to deliver information through natural media to people anywhere in the distributed enterprise, around the world. Organizations will be able to maximize the value of information by communicating more effectively and efficiently than before through the use of audio, video and images. Our customers have told us this will give them a competitive edge.

IBM intends to provide both new systems enabled with multimedia, and enhancements to the traditional framework for distributed computing. We will support many complementary models for multimedia computing, from personal workstations to workgroup systems to enterprise distributed systems. To achieve this vision, IBM will provide innovations in the following areas:

- Multimedia workstations
- Operating system services and presentation services
- Application tools and application services
- Data services
- Networking application support, transport network and subnetworking
- Systems management
- Server solutions
- Standards

This chapter describes IBM's vision of the innovation and technologies required to enable distributed systems for multimedia.

Special Notices
The following terms, denoted by an asterisk (*) in this publication, are trademarks of International Business Machines Corporation in the United States and/or other countries:

Ultimedia	ES/9000
PS/2	OS/400
Common User Access	SAA
CUA	DFDSM
OS/2	Audio Visual Connection
Presentation Manager	ImagePlus
AIX	HPTS
AIX/6000	Person to Person
RISC System/6000	LinkWay
POWERstation	Storyboard
AS/400	

The following terms, denoted by a double asterisk (**) in this publication, are trademarks of other companies as follows:

Apple	Apple Computer, Inc.
Windows	Microsoft Corp.
Kaleida	Kaleida Labs, Inc.
Unix	Unix System Laboratories, Inc.
Novell	Novell, Inc.
Netware	Novell, Inc.
Sound Blaster	Creative Labs, Inc.
DVI	Intel Corp.
ActionMedia	Intel Corp.
PhotoCD	Eastman Kodak Company
Bento	Apple Computer, Inc.

Multimedia Distributed Computing - Directions

Today, information systems support only a fraction of communications and information within a corporation. Distributed, multimedia-enabled systems are the next generation of information systems that significantly increase the value of corporate information through the processing and the distribution of new forms of information.

Multimedia increases the effectiveness of communications by combining many data forms: text, graphics, image, sound, animation and video. (See Figure 1.) Future systems will allow users to combine natural communications, such as listening and watching, with the power of information technology to capture, search, edit and store audio/video recordings...and to interactively control media presentations...and to share media with others. Sharing, distributing and collaborating through multimedia will significantly contribute to the improved efficiency, effectiveness and quality of communications.

Distributed Multimedia Applications

Over the past several years, IBM has worked extensively with its worldwide customer base to understand key business needs that can be satisfied with multimedia-enabled information systems. Simply stated, IBM customers believe that networked multimedia information systems will improve productivity through more effective internal and external communications. A personal workstation with

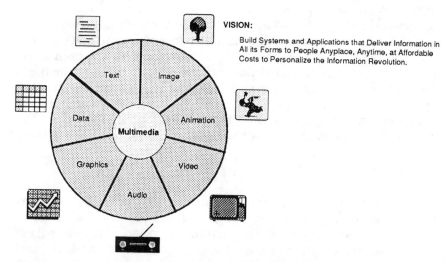

Figure 1: Multimedia Data Forms and Multimedia Vision

network and database access, and enhanced with multimedia capability, becomes a versatile communications system.

For example, companies can communicate product information to customers in the format and location that the customers prefer. In advertising, creative designers can share ideas for video commercials with colleagues and customers through audio/video-enhanced electronic mail and multimedia documents. In manufacturing, a plant floor worker can communicate from his or her station with a development engineer to show a defective part via a videoconference. Medical professionals can collaborate by sharing diagnostic images or videotaped procedures across the world using multimedia distributed systems. In educational settings, multimedia's power of interactive visualization is already augmenting traditional lectures and laboratories. There are strategic applications across all industries in which multimedia can improve competitiveness through increased efficiency, effectiveness and quality of communications.

In addition, entrepreneurs are developing revolutionary products in personalized information and entertainment, and a proliferation of personal organizers and advanced electronic home games have resulted. These technologies are merging with more traditional information technologies to allow interoperability of new products with information systems.

IBM's vision is to build systems and applications that deliver information in all its forms to people anyplace, anytime and at affordable costs to personalize the information revolution. IBM is investing in personal workstations, multimedia workgroup systems and open multimedia distributed systems involving enhancements to networking, data management and storage management. In parallel, IBM is making multimedia distributed computing easier to use, understand and manage by improving tools and human interfaces. The application and system requirements that are the basis for our technology initiatives and decision to invest are being driven by customer input. A consolidated scenario of what a number of customers described to us as their vision for multimedia will set the stage for the discussion of technology directions.

Scenario

One of the most significant lessons learned from customers was the magnitude of the impact and benefits of multimedia on traditional business processes. IBM customers' vision of multimedia is not to use multimedia in isolated applications for standalone merchandising or training. Instead, they believe that multimedia will become the core communications vehicle within extended businesses. (See Figure 2.) As an example, a large manufacturer of consumer products is described below.

With multimedia-enabled systems, communications are improving between research, development, manufacturing, marketing, sales and service. The company more effectively delivers information to employees and customers.

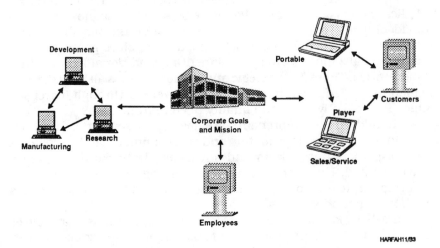

HARFAH11/83

Figure 2. Business functions impacted by multimedia

• Research and Development

In the development of a complex product, engineers work independently to design segments of the product and transfer the design to development engineers for integration. They continuously change and update the design and the manufacturing process throughout the product life. The design consists of drawings, images, text and prototypes, and the process includes meetings and conversations, both within product segments and across product segments. With multimedia-enabled, networked systems, researchers could send voice-annotated notes with images or video clips of prototypes. Developers could videoconference across multiple manufacturing sites to ensure integrated quality product development. This multimedia collaboration solution reduces the R&D cycle and improves quality.

• Manufacturing

The R&D collaboration described above also reaches into manufacturing. When a manufacturing problem occurs, the worker or supervisor can videoconference with a development engineer in another location to solve the problem. The engineer can actually see the defective part and make recommendations instantly. The worker might also reference training videos or a central database of common video problem solutions from his or her workstation. Training on demand and video information on demand are requirements cited by many IBM customers to enable workers to solve problems quickly or learn new techniques on the job.

• Sales and Service

A high-priced, complex product often requires a specialized sales force and extensive customer support. The sales cycle is often long and expensive. A manufacturer can reduce the sales cycle by equipping the sales force with multimedia presentation and training systems, and by providing information/transaction kiosks in stores and sales offices. A multimedia presentation system and kiosks add videotaped testimonials, product demonstrations, competitive comparisons and interactivity. Customers can request more information from a technical database and provide valuable feedback to the company. They can dial up and videoconference with an expert at the company's headquarters. Because multimedia gives the critical information to the customer at the right place and time, businesses can increase service and enhance the company image.

• **Goals and Vision**

Communicating company goals and vision to company employees and customers is often difficult. The CEO cannot easily visit every manufacturing and sales site frequently. And often the corporate message gets distorted when disseminated through the organization. Companies now show videotaped speeches, but multimedia technology can enhance the delivery process. Instead of viewing a two-hour videotaped speech, an employee can access an interactive application that includes clips of the speech filed by topic, plus related information such as a response form. The one-way message now becomes a two-way interactive communication.

These are some of the application requirements found through extensive customer meetings. Each one extends multimedia from a standalone application to a networked, strategic solution for fundamental business problems. This document defines technical solutions to these application requirements.

Enabling Distributed Multimedia Computing

For multimedia to reach its fullest potential within an organization, it must move beyond the limits of standalone technology. Multimedia content should be considered a corporate asset and a vital competitive edge — both of which are best maximized when multimedia is shared across the enterprise. Achieving this vision requires a framework for distributed multimedia computing.

Today, IBM multimedia system solutions can be configured as standalone personal workstations or as workgroup systems consisting of workstations interconnected via local area networks (LANs) to a host system or a server. To enable enterprisewide distributed multimedia computing, IBM recognizes the need to invest in enhancing its strategic system platforms to support multimedia applications. These enhancements will result in an open distributed system enabled for multimedia. (See Figure 3.)

IBM has already announced the first Ultimedia* integrated workstations enabled for multimedia, the PS/2* Ultimedia models M57, DV M57 and M77. IBM intends to extend the workstation family to include low-cost multimedia player models and multimedia portable models. In addition, various workgroup systems enabled for multimedia can be configured using existing products. Several

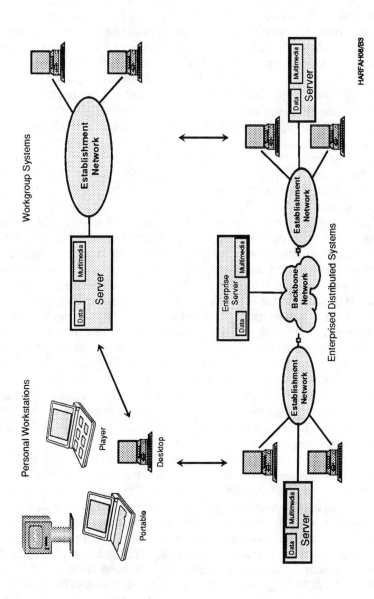

Figure 3. Multimedia Systems Solutions

examples are briefly described in a later section of this paper.

Distributed Computing Framework

Because of the large size of multimedia objects, their transmission as continuous streams of data (datastreams) when played or captured, and the need to control and synchronize them require key elements of distributed computing to be enhanced to support workgroup and enterprise distributed systems. In order to map the development of distributed multimedia computing solutions, this paper will use a "distributed computing framework" to describe the key elements of distributed computing that will be enhanced to support multimedia. This framework is targeted at heterogeneous computing — ensuring interoperability, data interchange and Common User Access* across many dissimilar systems, with selected and emerging international *de facto* standards as the foundation. A version of this framework was used to describe IBM's "Networking Blueprint" (GC31-7057) earlier this year.

An important objective of open distributed systems is to make a network of heterogeneous systems appear as a single system to users. All computing resources and services that a user is authorized to access, local and remote, appear as local resources and services.

Many facilities are required to implement location-transparent, distributed computing —including application development tools, presentation management facilities, data management facilities (which use the services of interprocess communications), directory services, networking and subnetworking. (See Figure 4.) These facilities process a service request using the client/server computing model. In addition, they use relevant international and *de facto* standards to ensure interoperability across multivendor systems. The figure above represents a system framework that outlines the *generic facilities* needed to support both collaborative and client/server computing.

Two characteristics unique to multimedia drive extensions to existing systems — object size and datastreams. Multimedia data objects such as digital video or high-quality digital audio require large storage facilities. Most systems are designed to handle kilobyte data objects, not the gigabyte objects employed for a full-length movie of VHS quality. Storing many such data objects easily requires terabytes. Thus, the automated storage management facilities that catalog, backup, migrate, relocate and archive files must be upgraded to handle large multimedia data objects. As the number of multimedia objects increases, users need the ability to classify,

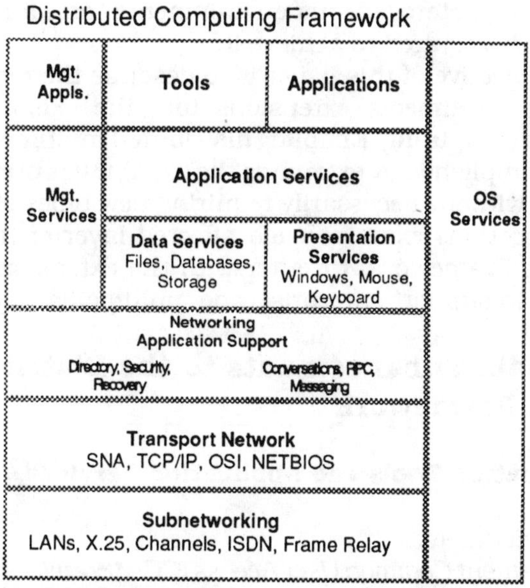

Distributed Computing Framework

Mgt. Appls.	Tools	Applications	
Mgt. Services	Application Services		OS Services
	Data Services Files, Databases, Storage	Presentation Services Windows, Mouse, Keyboard	

Networking
Application Support

Directory, Security, Recovery   Conversations, RPC, Messaging

Transport Network
SNA, TCP/IP, OSI, NETBIOS

Subnetworking
LANs, X.25, Channels, ISDN, Frame Relay

Figure 4. Distributed Computing Framework. (Facilities needed by a client/ server to support distributed computing)

abstract and index the objects —functions best controlled by a data management facility. Therefore, existing data management facilities must be enhanced to manipulate and deliver multimedia data objects.

Multimedia data objects are unique not only in size, but in nature. Multimedia data objects such as audio and video are time-based, continuous datastreams of information that must be delivered at a constant rate with bounded delay between source and target in order to preserve human perception. For example, digital audio from a compact disc results in two continuous datastreams, each flowing at about 706 kilobits per second (a total of about 1.4 megabits/sec). Compressed VHS-quality digital video played off a CD-ROM results in a composite datastream flowing at 1.2 megabits per second. To manage datastreams, the lower four layers of the distributed computing framework require continuous datastream handling capabilities to provide realtime control and synchronization of the audio stream and the video stream that together form a movie clip.

As previously mentioned, current IBM PS/2 Ultimedia models are being networked to host systems and servers in customer establishments. IBM's vision is to extend this capability across the enterprise for heterogeneous environments, and a comprehensive framework is required to achieve it.

The objective of this paper is to describe the requirements for integrating multimedia extensions into the existing facilities of distributed computing. Enabling distributed multimedia computing can be accomplished by extending the capabilities of existing system platforms, without necessarily requiring new types of systems. The following sections examine each affected layer of the Distributed Computing Framework, together with the extensions required for each layer to support enterprisewide multimedia.

Multimedia Enhancements to the Distributed Systems Framework

Application Tools and Application Services

IBM intends to:
• Implement Common User Access (CUA*) services such as virtual volume buttons, virtual slide bars and other graphical data objects for controlling multimedia datastreams. CUA services are currently available in OS/2's* MMPM/2.

Supporting multimedia requires new tools and application services. Tools will be provided through the new Ultimedia Tools Series, an interoperable family of application development tools from IBM and independent software vendors. Application services should include extensions to Common User Access services, object management facilities and data conversion services.

To increase multimedia application development productivity, multimedia extensions to Common User Access services are required. Such CUA extensions will provide standardized graphical screen controls for interacting with multimedia applications, including icons representing virtual volume control buttons, virtual slide bars and other graphical data objects. When CUA services are standardized across multimedia applications, programmers can learn consistent methods

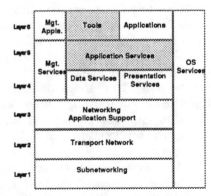

Distributed Computing Framework

Figure 5. Application Tools and Application Services

Text   Graphics

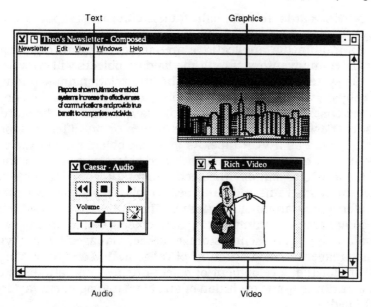

Audio   Video

Figure 6: Example of Common User Access for a Multimedia Application
Common User Access (CUA) interface is a graphical, window-based user interface consisting
of visual representations and interaction techniques. The goal of CUA is to provide a
consistent method for organizing and manipulating multimedia data objects.

for interacting with multimedia content —such as touching a media
control icon with a mouse or touch screen. The Multimedia Presentation Manager/2* toolkit includes the first implementation of multimedia extensions to the CUA services. For a sample screen, see Figure 6.

Multimedia technologies are enabling a major shift toward
natural user interfaces. Examples of natural interfaces include
audio and video help functions, as well as speech recognition capable
of accepting spoken commands and oral queries for help and
application navigation. IBM is investing in research to develop a
next-generation interface with more natural function. Software
developers can build applications based upon this standardized,
natural interface.

IBM sees a requirement for an object-oriented programming
interface to supplement the current low-level media and datastream-
control C programming interface. An object-oriented programming
interface for multimedia applications will evolve based on the
experience derived from using current programming interfaces.

Color images, audio clips, animation sequences and video
segments are all media objects that need to be organized in related
collections, specifically, in a hierarchy of related object classes. For
comparison, consider traditional media, which have been organized

using index cards, folders, light tables, albums, scrapbooks, video switches, etc.

As multimedia applications are employed by an organization over time, an inventory of multimedia data objects will grow across various systems on the network. The interrelationships among the data objects will become more complex, and the types of data objects will increase. In addition, multimedia data objects will be stored as files, entries in databases, in byte spaces or on different types of storage, such as a VCR tape. As a result, object management will become very complicated. A distributed object management facility will be needed to simplify the access to multimedia data objects by application programs and multimedia tools. This facility will provide a uniform programming interface to applications. It should handle the complexities of manipulating data objects stored on any system or on any type of attached storage device, managed by any type of data manager. The work product of Taligent, IBM and Apple**'s joint venture for the development of object-oriented operating systems, will contribute to the evolution of an object management facility for multimedia.

Currently, there are multiple data formats for each type of digital medium. Data interchange among multimedia tools, as well as application programs, can be difficult to achieve. There is now a concerted effort in the information industry to define a unique data format for each type of digital medium. Once the standards for representing digital images, videos, audio and animation are accepted and supported, data conversion services will be needed to convert old data formats to new data formats (and possibly vice versa). IBM is currently making multimedia conversion services available in MMPM/2. IBM sees the requirement to add similar function on other systems and natively support other popular data formats. The Resource Interchange File Format (RIFF) implemented by MMPM/2 and Windows** is an example of the generic data structure, or wrapper, that will be used for standardizing multimedia data formats to allow data interchange between systems.

Critical to the success of multimedia is the emergence of an integrated set of easy-to-use tools for developing and managing multimedia applications and content. IBM has two initiatives underway in this area. The first involves Kaleida** Labs, Inc., a company formed by IBM and Apple to develop; a "standard" object-oriented scripting language (ScriptX), data standards to enable interoperability between differing systems and runtime environments, for script and data portability across various systems. The runtime environments will allow transparent playback of ScriptX-created applications

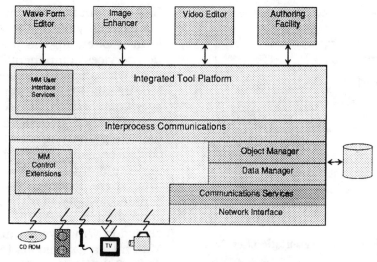

Figure 7. Integrated Tool Platform for User Productivity

across OS/2, Apple's System/7, Unix**, Windows and DOS. These runtime environments will provide portability of playback for ScriptX-developed applications and titles across a number of different hardware and software platforms. Kaleida Labs, Inc. is investigating distributed ScriptX capability to allow the development of distributed applications based on the ScriptX language.

The second initiative is the development of the Ultimedia Tools Series architecture, specified jointly by IBM and its partners to guide the development of a family of multimedia tools for OS/2 and for DOS and Windows running under OS/2, where all tools can share media content, are interoperable and share a common user interface. (See Figure 7.) IBM sees the requirement to extend this family to ensure that tools can work cooperatively, can interoperate and can access multimedia data objects stored on other remote systems, such as multimedia file servers.

Presentation Services

IBM intends to
• *Support multimedia programming interfaces in OS/2 and AIX*/
6000*

In distributed multimedia computing, client systems perform the important role of presenting multimedia and datastreams to the user. The primary client platforms are the PS/2 (including its derivatives) and the RISC System/6000* PowerStation* families.

Distributed Computing Framework

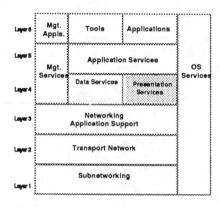

Figure 8. Presentation Services

IBM has enhanced the multimedia capability of the PS/2 platform by extending the presentation services component of OS/2 2.0 with a new set of facilities, Multimedia Presentation Manager (MMPM/2).

MMPM/2 provides a common programming interface to control both multimedia devices and the datastreams that flow from these devices. MMPM/2 contains a superset of the media control interface (MCI) APIs included in Windows 3.1 and the Multimedia Extensions to Windows 3.0. However, exploiting the multitasking capabilities of OS/2, IBM has gone further to introduce stream management and stream handling to the MMPM/2 extensions to OS/2. As a result, OS/2 application programs not only can control multimedia *devices* (through "play", "record" and similar commands), they also can control and synchronize the datastreams themselves.

The figure below is a high-level depiction of how MMPM/2 controls multimedia devices and datastreams. Stream handlers come in pairs, a source datastream handler and a target datastream handler. Their task is to drive the multimedia datastreams flowing from the input device driver to the output device driver with a minimum of delay. To accomplish this, the operating system (OS/2) must schedule the datastreams at highest priority. The source datastream handler recognizes whether the stream is originating from a physical device, for example a CD-ROM drive, or in a data manager (file system). Similarly, the target datastream handler recognizes whether the output device is a physical device or data manager. In addition, an application program can request notification by the datastream management component when a certain event has occurred — at which time the application program can request a certain media control action be taken at a specific time. For example, an application may want to increase the sound volume after playing an audio recording for 10 seconds, or turn on the sound after a video has been playing for 5 seconds.

To support multimedia across open distributed systems, all system platforms must have appropriate client and/or server facili-

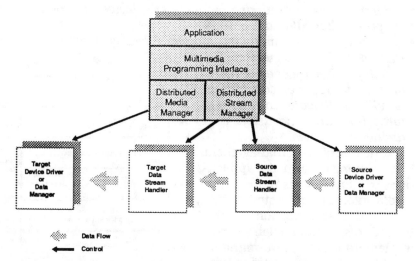

Figure 9. Functional Representation of OS/2's MMPM/2

ties. IBM recognizes the following requirements to support open distributed systems:

- Extend MMPM/2's media control interface to provide media device control support for the most common types of multimedia equipment, both analog and digital.
- Provide compatible multimedia extensions to the RISC System/ 6000 — specifically by providing a compatible media control interface for AIX platforms that allows AIX/6000 application programs to control and synchronize datastreams in a distributed environment.
- Allow OS/2 systems and AIX/6000 systems to interoperate as either multimedia clients or servers.
- Provide *server* datastream management facilities across PS/2, RISC System/6000, AS/400*, ES/9000*.
- Provide media control interfaces with the AS/400 server platform to access host-attached analog devices and to play, edit and author digital files.
- Evaluate providing media control interface extensions to the ES/ 9000 system.

Data Services

IBM intends to:
- *Develop client/server multimedia platforms with distributed data management capabilities on PS/2, AS/400, ES/9000.*

- *Extend relational database products in selected environments to support multimedia data objects.*
- *Extend the system-managed storage facilities available on IBM system platforms to support a hierarchy of heterogeneous multimedia storage devices and to handle multimedia data objects with backup, migration and archiving facilities.*

The role of data management in developing multimedia applications will increase as more multimedia information is stored digitally and as applications evolve toward distributed client/server implementation. Data management includes three major components:

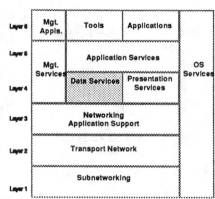

Distributed Computing Framework

Figure 10. Data Services

- File Systems
- Database Management Systems
- System-Managed Storage

The ability of these three components to support multimedia data is critical to the success of Multimedia Distributed Computing. Since multimedia content (video recording, animation sequence, etc.) is typically time-consuming and expensive to produce, it frequently represents a valuable corporate asset that would be costly either to replace if lost, or to duplicate for several users. Data management technologies become key to protecting these assets and maximizing their use by sharing, saving, cataloging, archiving and recovering multimedia content as they have done for more traditional information assets.

File Systems

Existing file systems provide the basic ability to "store and forward" blocks or files of multimedia data, and can be used to develop a number of client/server multimedia applications, such as distributing a video training course to an employee's workstation or updating video content for use by a kiosk application.

IBM supports multiple mechanisms for accessing file data across the network. The OS/2 High Performance File System (HPFS), in conjunction with LAN Server software, transparently directs client requests to the files stored in a server environment. The Network File System (NFS), which is a *de facto* standard for distributed byte stream file structure support in the UNIX environment, has client and server functions available on OS/2 and AIX platforms. The NFS server function is also available on MVS and VM, and IBM intends to make it available on OS/400*. OSI's File Transfer, Access and Management (FTAM) is available on OS/2, AIX/6000, OS/400, VM and MVS. Distributed Data Management (DDM) has been defined across all SAA* platforms and is already used by other products, such as Data Facility Distributed Storage Manager (DFDSM*), for distributed access to data. IBM is also evaluating other alternatives, such as Distributed Computing Environment / Distributed File System (DCE/DFS), which provides a rich set of functions and good performance for byte-level file access across a network.

However, because of the time-based, stream-oriented nature of multimedia data, file systems by themselves cannot effectively deliver such data to multiple users in real-time, unless the number of users on the network is severely restricted. In order to accommodate the time-based nature of multimedia data, additional client, server and communications components must be developed. For a further discussion of these technologies, see the "Multimedia Server Solutions" section later in the document.

Database Management Systems

As the numbers of stored multimedia data objects increase, and as they become more important to an enterprise business, efficient data services will be required to organize, manage, search and deliver these objects to one or more users. These capabilities, provided by Database Management Systems (DBMS) for more "traditional" data, are equally important to application developers and end users dealing with multimedia data.

DBMSs simplify and facilitate application development and operational procedures by providing functions that support:

- Data definition, organization, storage and navigation
- Search and retrieval
- Consistent user/application interface
- Data security, integrity, recovery
- Concurrency control for access from multiple users
- Distributed data, client/server application topologies
- Specific view of data to each application without physical data

redundancy
• Consistency of all data related to the same object

Utilizing databases will allow multimedia application developers to focus on addressing unique *application* requirements, rather than on solving data management problems.

Relational Database Management Systems

Many traditional applications can be enhanced when multimedia is used as a "front end" interface between computers and humans. For example, a spreadsheet application can use audio and animation interface to enhance its help facilities. In addition, there are many applications in which multimedia data itself becomes an important information resource that is often used in conjunction with other customer data. For example, if an insurance claims processing application is enhanced with audio annotation capabilities, recorded audio interviews with claimants and witnesses will have to be integrated with other data in a single "claim folder". In both scenarios, but especially in the latter, the ability to preserve multimedia information for as long as necessary and to integrate it with other customer data will become critical requirements.

To meet these requirements, so that as multimedia data is added to an enterprise, a customer can manage it with the same DBMS that manages existing data, IBM intends to extend relational database products in selected environments to support multimedia data objects.

Object-Oriented Databases

Object-oriented databases (OODB) are another promising technology that can store, retrieve and manage multimedia data objects and support multimedia applications. The strengths of OODB lie in its abilities to support object-oriented programming languages and related data models, efficiently manage complex objects, and work with a wide variety of user-defined data types. By supporting data classes, inheritance and encapsulation, object-oriented programming languages and OODB facilitate code re-use during application development. However, taking full advantage of these strengths is only possible after the development of multimedia class libraries.

New multimedia application development that will benefit from object-oriented programming techniques can use OODB as a persistent storage manager of multimedia data, especially until RDBMS

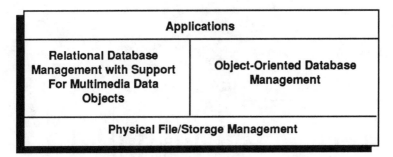

Figure 11. Multimedia database alternatives

products implement support for multimedia data objects. As such support becomes available, multimedia applications can be developed using either OODBs or RDBMSs, depending on specific customer requirements. (See Figure 11.)

System Managed Storage

Storage Subsystems. Multimedia has a significant impact on storage requirements, because of the size of media objects. Figure 12 illustrates the storage implications of large media objects. For a reference point, a 500-page textbook requires 1 megabyte of storage. Ten fax-quality images require 640 kilobytes, whereas ten color or detailed images require 75 megabytes. Five minutes of uncompressed voice-quality audio requires 2.4 megabytes of storage, and 52.8 megabytes of storage are required for premium-quality audio (compact disc, digital audio, CD-DA).

Digitized video requires the greatest storage capacity of all data forms. Without compression techniques, practical storage of digital video is impossible. For example, animation-quality video requires 147 megabytes per minute for a 1/4 screen size video — but with today's compression techniques, this animation-qualtiy video can be compressed to 1.44 megabytes (3.5 inch diskette). A two-hour television-quality video can be compressed to about 2 gigabytes of storage.

Early multimedia applications introduced analog storage devices —such as audio tape recorders, VCRs and laserdisc players — as workstation peripherals. These peripherals have been typically single function, low cost and positioned in a standalone environment. However, effective use of multimedia content requires shared access across the enterprise; this shared access requires networked storage systems.

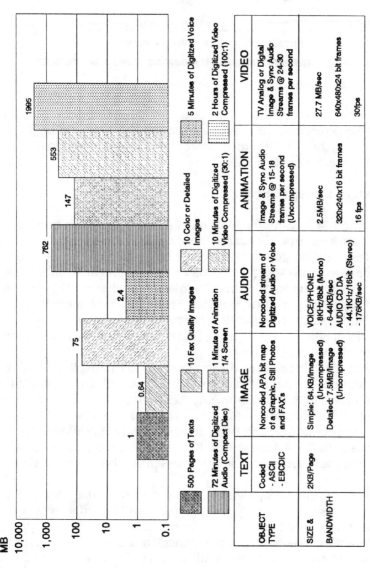

Figure 12. The Impact of Multimedia on Storage Technology

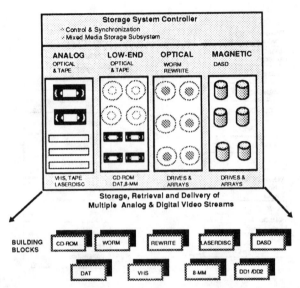

Figure 13. Storage Systems for Multimedia

Distributed multimedia applications demand storage devices and libraries that include both analog and digital devices. These applications will benefit from the flexibility of *digital media* storage — including not only traditional hard disks, but also such optical devices as CD-ROM players, WORM (write once read many) rewritable optical drives and optical "jukebox" libraries. IBM sees the need to support the installed base of multimedia devices — such as consumer analog devices (including VCRs) and digital audio/video devices (including CD-ROM players) — while traditional data storage devices (including magnetic DASD arrays) will evolve to support digital audio/video. (See Figure 13.)

As support for various types of multimedia storage devices develops, the scope of the storage hierarchy needs to be extended (see Figure 14). High-quality digitized images, audio and video data stored on these devices will require automated data management to store, retrieve, back up, archive, restore, relocate, protect and control access to data. The data files will be independent of the storage device. System-managed storage now offers these facilities.

Storage Management Software. Today's computing environment embraces distributed personal computers, workstations, local area networks and larger systems — and within these categories, mixed-vendor systems. This heterogeneous environment increases both flexibility and complexity in network management, data access and data storage. Multimedia data types such as audio and video add

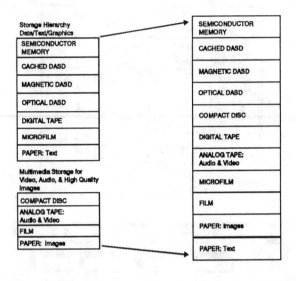

Figure 14. Storage Hierarchy Extended with Multimedia based on access time

to the complexity, because multimedia content involves very large objects and continuous, time-based delivery.

There are two major aspects of managing multimedia storage: **Distributed Data Storage Management** and **Storage Hierarchy Management**.

Distributed Data Storage Management is required for the following functions:

1. To manage backup and archiving of data stored locally on workstations.
2. To share data among various applications and users.
3. To access heterogeneous servers, workstations and local area networks using multiple communication protocols and operating systems.

In this highly heterogeneous environment, IBM sees the requirement to support access and sharing of remote data as if the data were local. IBM's strategy will preserve customers' investments in existing systems while exploiting the flexibility and benefits of the open systems approach.

IBM has announced the Data Facility Distributed Storage Manager (DFDSM) Release 1. DFDSM manages the backup and archival between servers (currently MVS and VM systems) and

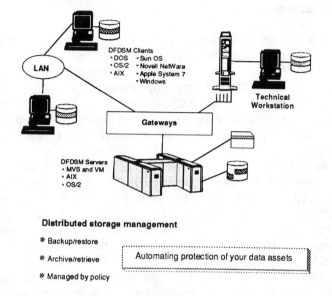

Distributed storage management

❈ Backup/restore

❈ Archive/retrieve   Automating protection of your data assets

❈ Managed by policy

Figure 15. DFDSM Storage Management Services

clients (currently DOS, OS/2, Windows, Apple's System 7, Novell**
Netware**, AIX/6000 and SunOS systems). Clients may be used as
servers for their own applications. (See Figure 15.) In addition, IBM
sees the requirement to extend the DFDSM capabilities to support
additional IBM and non-IBM platforms, and provide DFDSM server
support for AIX/6000 and OS/2. DFDSM addresses the needs for
asset protection and data availability in the distributed environment. It allows users to define backup and archive needs, and
improves productivity by allowing the automation of labor-intensive
processes.

Users are able to access file data archived by DFDSM via a client
with a different operating system than the one used to archive the
data, subject to limitations on operating system compatibility.
DFDSM Release 1 supports such "cross-client" data retrieval for the
following workstation clients:

• DOS or Windows to OS/2
• OS/2 to DOS or Windows (for files compatible with the DOS naming
  convention)
• AIX/6000 to SunOS
• SunOS to AIX/6000

DFDSM clients can, in turn, be used as servers by their own

client applications.

Storage Hierarchy Management manages the many different storage devices capable of storing multimedia data.

Storage devices are divided among various types, have various capacities and have different price, performance and media removability characteristics. Because of the large size and stream-orientation of multimedia data, it is critical to balance available storage resources with user requirements for data availability, performance and capacity.

Multimedia data objects will differ in the type and frequency of access. Moreover, the type and frequency of access to the same object are likely to change during its life cycle. Manually keeping track of multimedia data objects and managing their storage and migration across physical media individually, will become increasingly difficult, especially considering the distributed nature of today's computing environment and the use of removable media.

IBM sees the requirement to automate these functions in a distributed environment and make them a system responsibility. Based on user-specified policies, the system will manage and track all data — including multimedia objects, regardless of where they are stored. From the time of data creation, the system will stage the data through a hierarchy of devices to the most effective and efficient storage media. This hierarchy management will improve space utilization, reduce storage costs by making the most efficient use of available storage resources, and simplify installation of new devices. Hierarchy management will also increase productivity, as users no longer have to manage the data manually.

Currently DFDSM supports distributed data backup and archiving between MVS and VM servers and DOS, OS/2, Windows, Apple's System 7, Novell Netware, AIX/6000 and SunOS clients, managing the magnetic DASD, optical drives and libraries, and tapes. In addition, IBM sees the requirement to extend storage hierarchy management capabilities to AIX/6000 and OS/2 systems.

Networking Application Support, Transport Network and Subnetworking

• *Networking Application Support*

IBM intends to:
- *Provide multiparty communications services for workgroup collaborative computing to distribute and synchronize multimedia streams in realtime.*

- Provide multimedia stream-handling capabilities to support communications from a server to a client.

• *Transport Network*

IBM intends to:
- Provide extensions to networking protocols as appropriate to support multimedia communications.

• *Subnetworking*
IBM intends to:
- Exploit existing LAN wiring: unshielded twisted-pair, shielded twisted-pair and fiber.
- Enhance the ability of existing LAN subnetworking to support the transmission of continuous datastreams.
- Support existing and emerging multimedia networking interfaces.
- Provide high-speed interconnections between intelligent hubs that support multimedia datastreams.

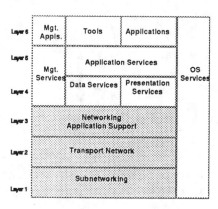

Distributed Computing Framework

Figure 16. Networking Application Support, Transport, and Subnetworking

The *networking application support, transport network* and *subnetworking layers* of the distributed computing framework together form the "arteries" of distributed systems. The IBM "Networking Blueprint" (GC31-7057) describes these facilities in greater detail. The *networking application support* layer consists of components supporting program-to-program (or interprocess) communications, directory services and such systems services as security, transaction management and recovery management. The *transport network* includes the support for SNA/APPN, TCP/IP, NETBIOS and OSI. The *subnetworking* layer includes the physical network support and network attachment.

In a multimedia-enabled network, the *networking application support* component expands to include both simplex (one-way) datastream communications and multiparty communications. The former was described in the Presentation Services section and is represented by the datastream handler components of MMPM/2. The latter, multi-party communications, is undergoing extensive

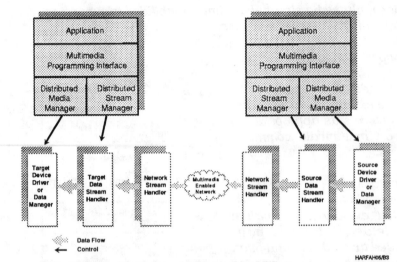

Figure 17. Network Datastream Handling. Network datastream handling is required to achieve distributed media and datastream control services.

prototyping and testing. IBM recognizes that for conferencing to become ubiquitous, standards must be developed encompassing a programming interface, communications protocols and control mechanisms. IBM is working to this end.

A common function of Multimedia Distributed Computing is the delivery of audio/video datastreams from IBM's server platforms to clients in response to a media control "play" request or a request to videoconference. The "play" request is serviced transparently; the application or user need not know whether a network was used or not.

Accomplishing this transparently can be done using existing transport networking facilities coupled with careful network configuration design. However, to ensure a very robust quality of service, a new capability, *network datastream handling,* will be required in the *transport network layer,* plus extended subnetworking services that include bandwidth management and new physical network interfaces. IBM researchers are prototyping network datastream handling for AIX/6000 and OS/2 for a digital video server application. Figure 17 is a high-level representation showing how the network datastream handling may be incorporated into OS/2 and AIX/6000 to support the flow of a datastream across a network from a server to a client. The network datastream handler implements an enhanced version of the multimedia datastream extension of the Internet Protocol (IP), the Experimental Internet Stream Protocol

Version 2 (ST-II). It represents one of several promising multimedia networking activities within IBM.

IBM recognizes the need to support network datastream handling on its strategic system platforms and to ensure that such a facility is based on widely supported standards.

IBM recognizes the need for client/server video applications that utilize local area networks efficiently while maintaining an acceptable level of service. This can be accomplished by a digital video server that uses a scalable digital video compression algorithm to adaptively control video datastream parameters such as frame rate based on feedback about transport network performance. The client system receiving the video datastream decompresses it and presents the video at a quality commensurate with what could be handled by the network without seriously degrading every other network user. IBM is evaluating how LAN performance monitoring can be optimally coupled with scalable video compression to maintain acceptable quality of service to the maximum number of concurrent users.

While some applications require the realtime video transmission facilitated by scalable video, others require only conventional store-and-forward transmission of multimedia data objects. For example, multimedia objects will need to be uploaded and downloaded between clients and servers or accessed while under the control of a distributed file management system. IBM understands the requirement to provide extensions to networking protocols as appropriate to support the store-and-forward transmission of large objects that accompany multimedia.

Multimedia demands changes to the *subnetworking layer* of the framework—the physical transmission network. There are primarily three primary types of high-speed physical networking technologies under active development and applicable to multimedia:

- Local area networking
- Fiberoptic channel switching
- Fast-packet switching

IBM is actively involved in each of these technologies and the corresponding standards bodies. As a result of our research, IBM is making contributions to these bodies and submitting proposals for their consideration.

High-speed circuit switched networking is supported across all IBM platforms. It is the ubiquitous wide area networking technology and for this reason will play an important role in multimedia. As an example, IBM recognizes the growing need for desktop videoconferencing and that this need can be satisfied by the emerging videoconferencing compression standard (e.g., CCITT SGXV H.261) and IBM's comprehensive product support for digital circuit switched networks.

Local Area Networking

LAN technology (encompassing Ethernet, Token-Ring, FDDI, intelligent wiring hubs, bridges, routers and concentrators) is critical to the continued success of distributed computing. LANs and their supporting interconnect products were designed to meet the needs of high-speed data networking applications where the data packet traffic is sent in bursts. Integrating multimedia into distributed computing requires that LAN technology be enhanced to support the transmission of continuous datastreams of data packets. However, any enhancement must attempt to protect customer investment in LANs, including Ethernet, Token-Ring and FDDI.

Ethernet is intrinsically limited by its access protocol and transmission speed to supporting fewer VHS-quality digital video datastreams than a 16 Mbps Token-Ring LAN, which can support approximately 10 video datastreams. IBM intends to enhance the capabilities of existing LAN subnetworking to transmit multimedia datastreams.

IBM, along with its business partners, is evaluating an isochronous transmission enhancement to Ethernet LAN products. Isochronous communications deliver a signal at a specified rate and time interval making it desirable for delivery of continuous data such as voice and full-motion video. This enhancement requires an intelligent wiring hub that employs a time division multiplexing scheme to deliver both 10 Mbps Ethernet service and wideband circuit switched service to a personal workstation over the same physical network interface (in this case, unshielded twisted-pair copper cable).

Token-Ring LAN technology incorporates unexploited access control mechanism capability (in the form of priority scheduling for frame transmissions) that can support multimedia applications. Assigning a high priority to the frames that make up the multimedia datastream will ensure they are among the first to transit the LAN. IBM sees the requirement to develop Token-Ring adapters and the necessary network control software for managing priority assignments. This will allow voice, video and data packets to flow over Token-Ring LANs.

Along with evaluating how best to enhance Ethernet and Token-Ring LANs to support multimedia, IBM is evaluating an alternative approach to delivering high-speed multimedia communications to the desktop. This alternative is based on the observation that limiting the number of attached systems can ensure multimedia support on the LAN. Optimizing this approach requires an intelligent wiring hub capable of a high-performance bridge, which in turn supports *many* LANs, each incorporating one or only a few attached systems. This approach will provide the maximum LAN data transmission rate to each system and confine all LAN changes to the intelligent wiring hub.

In summary, IBM is in the process of evaluating various promising LAN enhancements and understands the requirement to develop LAN products that best meet the customer need to support multimedia while protecting the existing LAN infrastructure investment.

Fiberoptic Channel Switching

Fiberoptic channel switching originally emerged as a solution for the high-speed connection needs of high-performance computer applications. IBM has contributed to the specification of the Fiber Channel Standard. Fiber channels transmit in the 120 Mbps to 1 Gbps range over a distance of several kilometers and are typically used to connect either engineering and scientific workstations to "supercomputers" or host computers to such high-performance storage subsystems as disk arrays. Electronic channel switches dynamically set up and take down fiber channel connections in microseconds. A connection usually lasts for milliseconds (enough time to transmit a burst of several megabits of data) but can stay set up indefinitely if needed. IBM sees the requirement for making fiber channel switching one of the local area networking options available to client/server multimedia applications implemented on the high end of its personal workstations and ES/9000 system platform.

Fast-Packet Switching

The transmission capacity demands (bits-per-second) of digital voice, data, compressed image and compressed video are extremely varied. Controlling the performance of a multimedia network can be achieved by accepting only fixed-length packets (cells) into the network for transmission. This approach has led the telecommunications industry to explore a new mode of network access, Asynchronous Transfer Mode (ATM), in which a 53-byte cell consisting of 5

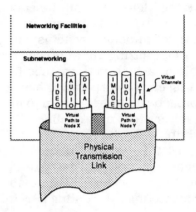

Figure 18. Multimedia Network Interface. A generic multimedia network interface supports multiple virtual paths each consisting of multiple virtual channels.

bytes of header and 48 bytes of data is presented to the network for transmission. The design of the header assumes intelligence exists in the network to interpret it. The header specifies routing and network control information. It allows related multimedia connections to be set up as virtual channels that make up a multimedia conversation. These channels are grouped together into a virtual path so they may be routed and controlled by the network and synchronized at the end points. In addition, the header allows the transmitter at the origin to indicate which cells are candidates to be discarded by the network when there is a problem (see Figure 18).

Private and public ATM networks, whether local area, metropolitan area or wide area, require a new type of switch, based on fast-packet technology. IBM is making an extensive investment to determine how fast packet/cell switching and LAN technologies can be employed to develop the next generation of multimedia networking products.

Networking Cabling Infrastructure

Another aspect of protecting customer's investments in a networking infrastructure includes determining how existing cabling systems can be used to deliver multimedia networking services. Today, VHS-quality digital video requires about a 1.2 Mbps transmission rate. Motion Picture Experts Group (MPEG), MPEG-II compressed broadcast digital video will require 4 to 8 Mbps; advanced digital TV will require 30 to 130 Mbps. On this basis, IBM has concluded that for the foreseeable future it will not be necessary to use fiberoptic cable to deliver video to the desktop and that copper cabling system installation is viable for most multimedia applications.

Impressive digital signal processing advances have recently occurred that make it possible to achieve high-speed digital transmission over unshielded twisted-pair (UTP) cable. In fact, UTP cable can be used to deliver digital video to the desktop. IBM is investigating how to achieve reliable transmission in the range of 25 to 45 Mbps over typical UTP cable lengths (100 meters) found in the office and factory. If successful, UTP cable would be useable for most networked digital multimedia applications. Alternatively, shielded twisted-pair cabling, which provides a bandwidth of 500 Mhz, offers excellent flexibility for broadband transmissions. Using frequency multiplexing techniques, different types of transmission services can be delivered simultaneously over STP cabling, including LAN services and CATV.

IBM intends to exploit existing LAN cabling: unshielded twisted-pair, shielded twisted-pair and fiber. For new installations, IBM provides the consulting services needed to identify the cabling system to meet customers' future communications requirements.

Systems Management

Distributed multimedia applications will introduce the systems management requirements for new devices, object classes and resource managers to be supported by IBM systems management products. As intelligent multimedia equipment (digital VCRs, audio/video storage libraries, digital cameras, etc.) proliferate across distributed systems, centralized management will become very important. IBM sees the requirement to use the the Distributed Management Environment (DME) framework to standardize the systems management support for multimedia equipment.

Networked kiosk applications have already identified the need for centralized systems management to control the distribution of multimedia content to the kiosks and to perform problem determination. Multimedia-based training and education applications will become networked, allowing courses to be taken on demand or delivered "just in time". It is essential that systems/network management products meet the systems management requirements of distributed multimedia applications.

Initially, IBM is investigating the required directory extensions for multimedia support. Directory services store information about the capabilities of systems attached to the network. These services are required to enable heterogeneous systems to interoperate as clients, servers or collaborating/conferencing personal workstations.

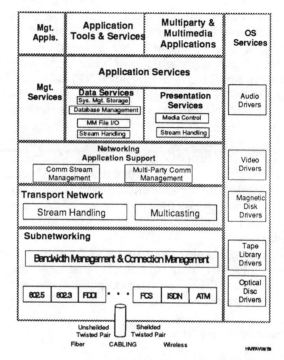

Figure 19. Distributed Computing Framework Enabled for Multimedia. The extensions required to integrate multimedia support into distributed computing.

Summary to the Distributed Systems Framework Enabled for Multimedia

The goals of Multimedia Distributed Computing are twofold: open computing and the integration of multimedia extensions into strategic platforms. Toward these goals, IBM understands the customer requirements to integrate multimedia extensions into its systems platforms to support such distributed computing as collaborative computing and client/server computing. The figure above shows all the extensions discussed in the context of a Distributed Computing Framework.

The fundamental new systems concept that multimedia introduces is the management, control and synchronization of datastreams. These datastreams flow through a user's personal workstation system when the user is participating in a videoconference, navigating through a hypermedia document, viewing a stored digital video or watching and listening to multimedia E-Mail.

IBM understands the requirement to provide stream handling capabilities to support datastream communications between client and server. In addition, IBM sees the requirement to support a common media control interface on OS/2 and AIX/6000.

IBM is working to make multimedia application development more productive. IBM intends to work with leading multimedia tools developers to produce a set of integrated tools on OS/2; we understand the requirement for these tools to operate in a client/server environment to enable sharing of content and tools among collaborating creators. In addition, IBM is investigating application development needs for a multimedia object management facility, data conversion services and an object-oriented programming interface tailored for media and datastream control.

Several significant technological challenges are posed in storing and managing multimedia data objects in a distributed client/server environment. Data management products must provide the abilities to manipulate:

• Time-based data, such as audio and video, that require isochronous presentation to users
• Objects varying in size from several hundred bytes to gigabytes
• Large numbers of very long data objects, stored across a hierarchy of heterogeneous storage devices

Clearly, multimedia poses unique challenges to traditional database management. IBM intends to develop facilitating technologies that extend IBM's relational database management systems to organize, store and retrieve multimedia data. These technologies will enable our customers to build distributed multimedia database applications. Such applications will deliver synchronized audio and full-motion video data to users for local presentation. In addition, storing multimedia data in a RDBMS will ensure robust security, integrity and recovery of data and facilitate new applications that need to integrate multimedia with existing stored business data.

Many existing multimedia applications already use a file system to store and retrieve multimedia data objects. These file systems are easily adapted to provide distributed file management services. IBM is working on extending its file systems and the underlying data access methods to support interactive recording, retrieval and delivery of time-based data to multiple users. This will enable our customers to start building highly interactive applications that deliver audio and full-motion video data to multiple users in realtime.

The storage management needs of multimedia applications are similar to those that exist for more traditional distributed applications. The large size of multimedia data objects, however, makes it impractical to store aging multimedia on disk if not regularly used. Therefore, multimedia applications need a comprehensive set of automated systems management procedures to stage, back up, recover, archive and restore multimedia data objects across multiple heterogeneous clients and servers. IBM intends to enhance its systems-managed storage facilities and systems components to meet these needs.

The communications, networking and subnetworking facilities currently available on IBM's strategic systems platforms are able to support client/server multimedia applications. Relative performance will vary. While LANs were not originally designed to handle multimedia datastreams, each LAN type can handle some specific number of concurrent audio or compressed video datastreams. For this reason, customers can start developing networked applications today.

IBM has made and will continue to make major investments in multimedia networking. These investments include extending key IBM communications products to support multimedia datastreams; such products include LANs, routers, intelligent wiring hubs and communications managers/access methods. In addition, IBM is a leader in fiber channel switching, fast-packet switching, multiparty conferencing, and network management and control. In order to advance the "state of the art", IBM is making technical contributions to the appropriate multimedia networking standards committees in these areas. IBM believes that fast-packet switching will be the basis

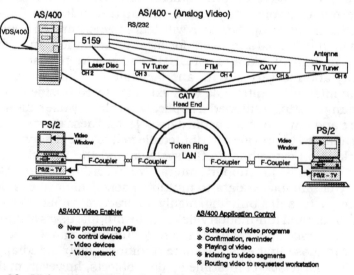

Figure 20. Ultimedia Video Delivery System/400

HARFAH01/83

for multimedia networking in the future. By enhancing existing products and ensuring that these products work with tomorrow's fast-packet switching networks, IBM intends to help its customers exploit the full potential of multimedia.

Multimedia Server Solutions

Sharing multimedia content in a distributed computing environment poses unique challenges to the capabilities of traditional servers. New multimedia server solutions are now emerging that optimize the server's support for sharing multimedia data.

To facilitate shared access to data, multimedia servers need to control very large volumes of continuous datastreams, the media devices that store these datastreams, and the networks and communications that distribute the datastreams to and from the users in realtime. Multimedia servers also have to control and manage the request admission process, so that each data request is accepted only if the server can guarantee that the request can be satisfied without adverse impact on the execution of other requests.

Because multimedia data can be represented and stored in either analog or digital form, multimedia servers should be able to manage both data forms. Analog servers control the *devices* that store the data, such as laserdiscs or TV tuners. Digital servers control the *data* itself, retrieving it from the files or databases. The Ultimedia Video Delivery System (VDS/400), developed for the AS/

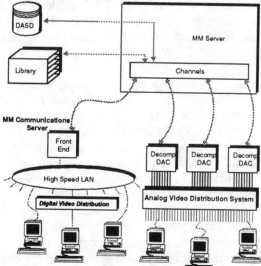

Figure 21. MM Server. Analog and digital distribution

400, is an example of an analog multimedia server (see Figure 20). The Workstation LAN File Services/VM (WLFS/VM) product developed for the ES/9000 is an example of a large-scale digital multimedia server as shown in the figure.

The VDS/400 controls various analog devices (such as laserdisc players, TV tuners, CATVs), schedules user sessions and broadcasts analog TV signals to requesting client workstations. It uses the F-Coupler technology to distribute analog TV signals over shielded twisted-pair Token-Ring cable, exploiting its high bandwidth and frequency multiplexing techniques. F-Coupler technology supports up to 70 simultaneous multimedia sessions on a Token-Ring LAN without any impact on LAN-based applications running in the same environment.

IBM is also developing *digital* multimedia server capabilities. Digital servers offer a number of advantages to organizations — including the ability to incrementally add, delete or edit stored multimedia content on an ongoing basis, often through the use of digital video editing techniques. Digital servers also allow multiple clients to have concurrent interactive access to the same media devices.

For many interactive multimedia applications, digital multimedia servers will also require *digital communications* of multimedia content between the server and clients. But for some applications it might also be desirable to use digital servers together with *analog* distribution, in order to exploit the 70-channel available bandwidth on existing shielded twisted-pair Token-Ring cable using F-Coupler technology. In this scenario, the data must be decompressed and converted to analog form prior to distribution. During distribution, F-Couplers merge analog TV signals and digital LAN data on the same network cabling. (See Figure 21)

Synchronization and management of multiple audio and video datastreams is a rather challenging task even in a standalone environment, where a single system encompasses the datastream handlers, the data they operate on, file devices and the playback devices. (OS/2 , for example, devotes a special multimedia subsystem, MMPM/2, solely for multimedia datastream management.) In a *distributed* multimedia configuration, a server owns the stored data and file devices that are remote from the clients. Client systems and respective playback devices must connect to the server via a network, introducing the potential for delays and interruptions in the continuous delivery of datastreams for playback.

Further complicating delivery, the server and its data concurrently support more than one client on the network. Several clients

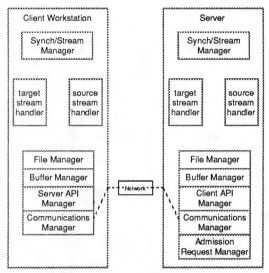

Figure 22. MM Client/Server Functional Structure

can make simultaneous requests for the same or different datastream, located on the same or different storage device — thus increasing the potential for server resource contention and datastream interruptions.

Therefore, in addition to developing the isochronous network support capabilities, IBM is evaluating the development of other components that will ensure the end-to-end isochronous delivery of multimedia datastreams between server and multiple clients. These components include sync/stream management, buffer management, request admission management, file management and communications management components. (See Figure 22.)

IBM is evaluating various technical design and implementation alternatives for some of these components. For example, the sync/ stream subsystem with its stream handlers can be developed as part of the client environment that works with remote files, "pulling", streaming and synchronizing them across the network. IBM is using this approach in developing the PS/2-based multimedia server and the ES/9000 multimedia server. The ES/9000 server will take advantage of such existing products as the Workstation LAN File Services/VM (WLFS/VM) and the OS/2 Presentation Manager Multimedia Extensions running in the client workstations. The WLFS/ VM product, announced in April 1992, will be the basis for the development of a server that can serve hundreds of multimedia datastreams concurrently. (SeeFigure 23.) WLFS/VM allows OS/2 LAN Server requesters and TCP/IP NFS clients to share multimedia

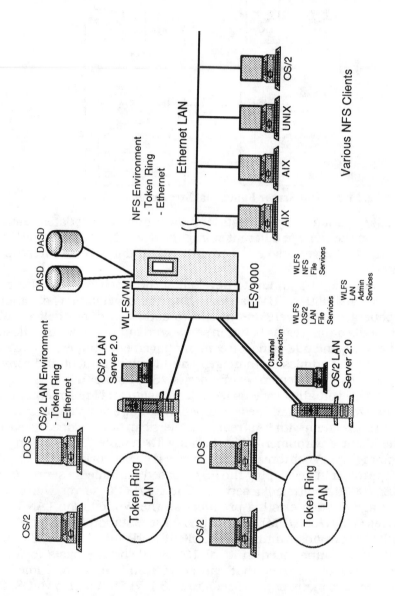

Figure 23. Workstation LAN File Services/VM

files stored on the ES/9000. No additional coding is required to access files stored on the ES/9000. The large system capacity of an ES/9000 with WLFS/VM will facilitate enterprisewide implementation of storage-intensive multimedia applications.

The stream handling functions can also be *distributed* between a client and a server, so that the stream handler is located where the data storage device is, "pushing" the requested data to the client workstation and the target stream handler. IBM is using the latter design in developing the RISC System/6000-based multimedia server.

IBM is investigating several technologies that will increase the number of datastreams that a digital multimedia server can process, record and retrieve simultaneously — thus increasing the number of clients that can be attached to a single server. These technologies include:

- Optimization of the logical and physical data layout
- Improvements in sustained data rate and latency time of storage devices
- Better exploitation of multitasking capabilities of the operating systems and I/O subsystems
- Development of efficient stream management and synchronization capabilities
- Minimization of data movement in a server environment
- Exploitation of unused network bandwidth and optimization of communication protocols for continuous data

IBM understands the requirement to enhance the PS/2 and ES/9000 digital multimedia server functions, and provide similar functions in the AS/400 environment.

Multimedia Standards

IBM intends to:
- *Lead the development of a broad set of multimedia standards that will enable open distributed multimedia computing.*
- *Support selected, emerging international standards across IBM platforms.*

The growth of multimedia applications is being hampered by a lack of widely supported standards. IBM is committed to taking a leadership role both in offering technology for standards and in supporting approved international standards.

Multimedia Standards: Background and Impact

Standards Impact on the Multimedia Environment. Standards are one of the critical success factors in the widespread acceptance and growth of multimedia applications and products. A significant inhibitor to growth has been the "alphabet soup" of multimedia data formats —vendor-proclaimed and industry-developed multimedia standards that continue to proliferate and even compete against each other. At the same time, widely accepted international standards to guide developers in creating applications are lacking. The result is incompatibility and complexity in data exchange among multivendor platforms. The lack of widely accepted standards has also resulted in system-specific multimedia tools and authoring systems that produce applications that "play" only on specific platforms.

This leads to obsolescence as technology evolves. Application developers and information owners need standards that will accommodate new technology as it emerges.

The growth of multimedia can be accelerated greatly through unifying standards. Envision the possibilities: an industry with a set of common standards specifying data formats, multiplatform application development tools and universal (system independent and network independent) content servers. The result will be:

- An increased willingness to invest in the production of digital multimedia content, knowing that applications developed using that content will be "playable" on future systems.
- A rapidly expanding set of multimedia applications.
- A large number of PCs and workstations able to *play* many varieties of content.
- New, innovative applications enabling enhanced levels of personal and group productivity.
- A business expanding at near double-digit growth rates.

That's a business environment IBM wants to be a part of and help stimulate.

The Standards Process

In the information technology industry, standards emerge from three primary sources:

1. Proprietary technology/specifications which gain market accep-

tance based on their success in meeting customer needs. For example, Sound Blaster** audio cards.

2. Consortium or partnership efforts which gain support from vendors. For example, Digital Video Interactive (DVI** - technology from IBM and Intel), Musical Instrument Digital Interface (MIDI - a digital representation of music) and CD-ROM/XA.

3. National, regional and international accredited standards organizations. For example, the Organization for International Standardization (ISO) is working on or has agreed to the following standards:

- Joint Photographic Expert Group (JPEG) for still image compression/decompression.
- Motion Picture Expert Group (MPEG) for motion video compression.
- Standard Generalized Markup Language (SGML) and Hypermedia Time-based Document Structuring Language (HyTime) for text and multimedia augmentation of text.

Multimedia Standards Positioning

For multimedia-enabled systems, standards are most important at certain boundaries. The following template can be used to position multimedia standards requirements:

1. Content Capture and Recording
- Data format standards are needed to simplify the exchange of content among tools, applications and systems. Data types such as graphics, sound, music, text, video, animation and still images have unique characteristics and need identification.
- Data compression and decompression standards are required for more efficient storage of video, sound and images. JPEG, MPEG and Joint Bi-level Image Expert Group (JBIG) are examples of emerging international standards for algorithms used to encode and efficiently compress multimedia content.
- Media storage standards for CD-ROM, CD-ROM/XA, optical data files, digital tape and other devices are needed for better exchange of data on portable media across vendor platforms.

2. Edit and Assembly
- Content description and container standards act as *wrappers* surrounding *chunks* of often dissimilar data types. Standards are needed for the exchange of media content clips and other data among tools, applications and platforms. .*** <CFG> "tagged"

changed to "structural tagging, identification tagging,"
- Scripted, structural tagging, identification tagging and other language technology is required for the most effective development of applications that can be played on a variety of platforms. Examples of language technology include the ISO standard, HyTime and AVA, IBM's scripting language for the Audio Visual Connection* (AVC).

3. Transport Network
- Today's LAN and WAN systems are marginally adequate for transporting multimedia data objects and datastreams. New technology is being explored to support realtime traffic with minimal delay over Ethernet and Token-Ring LANs, which is expected to enhance current network capabilities for multimedia.
- New networking standards tailored to support multimedia applications are needed. Among them, Asynchronous Transfer Mode (ATM) and Fiber Distributed Data Interface (FDDI) will have the effect of increasing the available bandwidth to 100 Mbps and beyond.
- Intelligent communications subsystems should minimize network congestion by negotiating and guaranteeing bandwidth for attached devices that have the capability to scale their bandwidth requirements.

4. Playback and Presentation
- The ability for a single platform to play back a wide variety of titles and applications, as well as interoperate with data stored across the customer's enterprise, is a key factor for industry growth.
- Presentation and interface standards will assist the user in understanding the information content the application is presenting. One size does *not* fit all, but consistency between development tools, for example, will make the authoring job much easier.
- Device-independent programming interfaces such as those contained in MMPM/2 (MCI, MMIO, Stream Handler) will greatly assist the application developer in dealing with the wide variety of multimedia input and output devices.

5. System Services
- Multimedia extensions to basic operating system functions are required to accommodate new data types and their unique characteristics.
- Extensions to relational database standards and object-oriented database standards are needed to support the large size and complexity of multimedia data objects.

It is against this framework that IBM has positioned its multi-media standards strategy and activities. The following section describes IBM's current actions in the various standards areas, together with IBM's strategy for enabling multimedia computing across the distributed enterprise.

IBM Standards Leadership and Strategy

IBM Standards Activities. The following are specific examples of IBM's participation in developing international multimedia standards and industry *de facto* technology and products: Accredited National, International Standards Organizations.

These organizations develop the standards and specifications that gain U.S. and international stature as official standards. These standards and specifications can then be used by developers to create products.

- ISO/CCITT Activities
  - JBIG (Joint Bi-level Image Expert Group) has developed a lossless image compression standard for still images. IBM has contributed the technology used in JBIG and has active technical representation on the committee.
  - JPEG (Joint Photo Expert Group) has developed a lossy compression standard for still images. Algorithms developed by IBM are central to the JPEG standard, and IBM has chaired the U.S. representation to JPEG and has been editor of the standard.
  - MPEG (Motion Picture Expert Group) has developed a standard for motion video compression and is at work on a follow-on that will enable enhancements such as scalable video. IBM has offered much of the compression technology, and IBM chairs the systems subgroup.
  - SGML (ISO 8879) is the most widely used standard for textual information structuring and identification of content elements. It extends IBM's text-based GML to general information structures. IBM is the inventor of SGML, editor of the standard and chair of the ISO/IEC Special Working Group on SGML.
  - HyTime (ISO/IEC 10744) has recently been approved as a full ISO standard. It extends SGML into the realm of hyperlinked and time-based multimedia. IBM is the inventor of HyTime, editor of the standard and chair of the ISO/IEC Special Working Group on Multimedia Languages.

- MHEG (Multimedia and Hypermedia Experts Group) is developing the future international standard for final-form (not requiring restructuring before presentation) multimedia and hypermedia objects. IBM leads the editing of the group's work.
- Joint Technical Committee 1/Subcommittee 24 (JTC1/SC24) is developing a graphics presentation standard for multimedia and hypermedia documents as well as the specifications for toolkits needed to develop multimedia documentation. IBM chairs this subcommittee.
- JTC1/SC18 (Multimedia/Hypermedia Model and Framework) is developing a framework and standards development strategy for multimedia and hypermedia. IBM chairs this committee.

- American National Standards Institute (ANSI)
  IBM is active in defining the following:
  - T1E1.4 — HDSL and ADSL (High-speed/Asymmetric Digital Subscriber Line.
  - X3T9.5 — FDDI 1, 2 extended for multimedia data.
  - .X3T9.3 — Fiber Channel Standard.
  - .T1S1 Committee - Broadband ISDN architecture and signaling.
  - ABIC (Adaptive Bi-level Image Compression) — this algorithm and its chip implementation were developed by IBM and are used in the ImagePlus* HPTS* banking system. ABIC is being proposed as a U.S. ANSI standard for banking.

- Institute of Electrical and Electronic Engineers (IEEE)
  IBM is active in defining the following:
  - Integrated voice/data LAN capability merged into 802.9.
  - Wireless LAN — 802.11.

Consortiums and Partnerships

These organizations are not sanctioned to develop accredited standards, but develop specifications, technology and products required by customers. In many cases, their products will be based on international standards or standards in process.

- Interactive Multimedia Association (IMA)
  - The IMA's mission is to promote the development of interactive multimedia applications and reduce barriers to widespread use of multimedia technology. IBM is a corporate sponsor and sits on the Board of Directors.
  - The IMA Compatibility Project has the goal of multimedia interoperability. The group accomplishes their work by issuing

RFTs to fulfill critical technology areas. Several are currently in process:
- Scripting languages
- Data exchange
- System services
- The IMA is sponsoring an Intellectual Property Project where, in an open forum, participants will address IP issues that inhibit multimedia growth.

• Kaleida Labs, Inc.
- Kaleida Labs is the Apple and IBM joint venture formed to develop advanced multimedia technology. Among Kaleida Lab's first offerings will be:

1. ScriptX — an object-oriented scripting language.
2. Specifications for the exchange of media-rich data between heterogeneous systems.
3. Runtime environments — code to allow the transparent playback of ScriptX-created applications across OS/2, Apple's System/7, Windows, DOS and UNIX.
4. Distributed ScriptX — an extension to ScriptX that will enable the development of networked multimedia applications.

• ATM Forum
- IBM is actively participating in the ATM Forum and considering several technology submissions.

IBM Multimedia Offerings. The following illustrates IBM's support for international and industry de facto standards within selected current IBM products and applications:

1. Ultimedia PS/2 M57, DV M57 and M77
• Supports the IMA Recommended Practices for Multimedia Portability.

2. OS/2 2.0 - MMPM/2
• MMPM/2 contains a superset of the Media Control Interface (MCI) APIs that are also in Windows Multimedia Extensions and were jointly developed by IBM and Microsoft.
• MMPM/2 supports industry-standard file formats
- MIDI file formats type zero and one
- PCM, ADPCM waveform audio files
- Synchronization/stream manager

- CD-DA, CD-ROM, CD-ROM/XA compact disc formats

3. ActionMedia** II digital video adapter card
- ActionMedia II supports Digital Video Interactive (DVI), an industry standard for motion video and still-image capture, compression and playback. Developed by IBM and Intel, DVI is available across a wide range of industry platforms.

4. Person to Person* videoconferencing solution
- Person to Person has ISDN capability. ISDN enablement will occur in mid-1993.

5. The IBM Ultimedia Tools Series brings together multimedia application development functions under a common set of data structures and services based on selected international and industry standards.

6. The PS/2 TV, the Ultimedia Video Delivery System/400 and M-Motion software support both NTSC and PAL television broadcast standards.

7. ImagePlus HPTS banking systems use the ANSI ABIC algorithm for image compression.

IBM Multimedia Standards Strategy. To be successful in expanding the industry and advancing the acceptance of multimedia-enabled products, IBM sees a requirement to:

1. Offer selected IBM multimedia technology to the industry through sanctioned standards bodies, consortiums and partnerships as appropriate. A primary focus will be on technology that supports data interchange, interoperability and distributed computing.

2. Support formal international standards across our product lines. Based on customer and industry demand, IBM will consider support of proposed standards from consortiums and partnerships. A primary focus will be on technology that supports data interchange, interoperability and distributed computing.

3. Develop a broad family of open, interoperable platforms for both authoring and playback of multimedia content, titles and applications.

Standards Strategy Requirements. Based on customer

input, IBM understands requirements for the following standards activities. These are examples of areas IBM is investigating to meet customer needs and should not be considered a complete list nor a commitment to deliver products.

Content Capture
1. Data formats
- Support a set of common multimedia data formats
- Data compression
    - Support a software codec for full-motion video. Evaluate using a software implementation of DVI Real Time Video (RTV) and evaluate other compression technologies as selectable software codecs.
    - As it evolves to a formal standard, support MPEG and its derivatives for coding/decoding technology.
    - For still imagery, support international standards such as JPEG and JBIG.
- Media storage
    - Support industry-standard CD-ROM formats (such as XA and multisession).
    - Support WORM, read/write optical, digital tape and other devices for hierarchical storage of multimedia data.
    - Support Kodak PhotoCD**, as well as other imaging standards (JPEG, JBIG).

Edit and Assembly
1. Content description
- Support RIFF, Bento**, SGML and HyTime specifications for data exchange between platforms.

2. Multimedia language technology
- Implement a toolkit for developing HyTime-encoded documents.
- Evaluate incorporating ScriptX, a scripting language for interactive multimedia applications under design/development by Kaleida Labs, Inc., into our multimedia tools such as the Audio Visual Connection (AVC), LinkWay* Live! and Storyboard* Live! Evaluate adopting ScriptX as a standard for the Ultimedia Tools Series.

Transport Network
1. Investigate 10Base-T (Ethernet) isochronous communication enhancements to support high data rates over unshielded twisted-pair copper cable.

2. Investigate priority scheduling and bandwidth reservation for

multimedia frame transmission over Token-Ring.

3. Support emerging standards such as Fiber Channel Standard (FCS) and Asynchronous Transport Mode (ATM).

Playback and Presentation

1. Support playback of the QuickTime Movie File Format.

2. Implement playback software for HyTime-encoded documents

System Services

1. Enhance MMPM/2 to support additional data types and multimedia devices common in the industry.

2. Extend relational database products in selected environments to support multimedia objects.

3. Work with the IMA, and other groups as appropriate, to agree on data exchange standards to facilitate multiplatform interoperability.

Conclusion

Enabling open distributed systems with multimedia is a challenging goal that spans many of IBM's core technologies and includes many evolving technologies from information systems, telecommunications and consumer electronics. Over the next two years, IBM intends to announce and deliver networked multimedia application solutions that incorporate international standards, and associated systems integration services that span multimedia workgroup systems, enhanced desktop conferencing and networked kiosks. IBM intends to continue to work with our customers to discover new applications for multimedia, and to develop application solutions that meet their needs.

Notice

This document is intended to present IBM's vision and supporting infrastructure for multimedia in distributed computing.

In producing this document, IBM has worked with its worldwide customer base to understand key business needs, strategic directions and constraints. All efforts have been made to listen and develop technology plans in order to produce the needed solutions.

Customers should understand that all information contained in this document represents IBM's intent, is tentative and subject to change, and represents goals and objectives. This document makes references to the

Multimedia Distributed Computing Statement of Direction Announcement issued on 11/10/92.

References in this publication to IBM products, programs or services do not imply that IBM intends to make these available in all countries in which IBM operates.

Chapter 3

Starworks™ - A Video Applications Server

Fouad A. Tobagi
Joseph Pang
Barbara A. Baker
Starlight Networks, Inc.

There is a growing interest in supporting digital video applications over local area networks. These applications fall into two main categories: (i) stored-video applications which involve the sharing of digital video information stored in a server through a local area network, and (ii) live-video applications which involve use of the video medium for interactive communication among humans, as seen in video conferencing and collaborative computing applications. The characteristics of digital video files and traffic differ substantially from those encountered with data applications: (i) video files are quite large (a single video file may be comparable in size to a complete data base); (ii) video traffic is continuous in nature (data traffic is bursty); and finally (iii) the data rate of a video stream is relatively high (larger than the mean data rate of a single data traffic source.) Accordingly, conventional file servers are not well suited to support video services over local area networks; instead, new servers capable of handling the specific characteristics of video files and traffic are needed. In this chapter, we describe StarWorks, a video applications server software designed to support a wide range of digital video applications.

Digital Video Applications

The demand for networked digital audio/visual systems is expected to grow considerably over the next few years as businesses, government and other institutions increasingly turn to digital networks to distribute audio/visual information for education, presentations and reference applications. These users expect systems that will allow a number of people to be able to view audio/visual information from a server simultaneously, while fully retaining their other network functions. For example, in business computing, networked video training applications must support classroom environments with 20 to 50 workstations as well as training distributed to the desktop to support a larger workgroup population. In addition, most of the major productivity software developers see networked video as an effective means of training and supporting users. Many of these developers have begun including digital video for online help and training with their software. Centralizing that support in a video server reduces the cost and ensures that the media are properly maintained by the MIS department or network managers.

Networked video communications and presentation systems in business can allow corporate resources, such as sales videos, employee information, and video-based communications to be available immediately to all employees at their desks. Similarly, networked video documentation systems can allow institutions of all kinds to maintain multi-user audio/vidual databases. Such databases can be used for on-the-job reference such as revisiting a complex procedure on the manufacturing floor, or creating on-line archives of TV commercials for an advertising agency.

Video teleconferencing is a fast growing segment in the communications arena. However, most of today's video teleconferencing installations are dedicated, standalone facilities set aside for that purpose. While the price tag for such systems is dropping (a system that operates over switched 56 Kbps networks is now below $20,000), it remains an expensive facility that needs to be shared. Extending these services to the desktop over local area networks will make video teleconferencing services more widely available at a lower cost.

Finally, the ultimate goal is to be able to provide computer-supported collaboration, whereby users at different locations can share data and files and work on problems simultaneously, using multimedia workstations linked by local- and wide-area networks. Users of such desktop conferencing systems will be able to access stored video and audio from a central server, hold conferences with remotely based colleagues via the PCs on their desks and work simultaneously with them on files in a shared electronic workspace.

These examples clearly show that the support of digital video services must include the communication of video information over digital networks as well as the sharing of video information stored in a server on the network.

Characteristics of video files and traffic

The characteristics of files, file access and network traffic in digital video applications differ substantially from those encountered in data applications. With data applications, whenever a user makes a file access request to a server, or requests that data be transmitted on a network, the user expects fast response time —fast compared to the time it takes it to place the next request. As a result, the capacity of a server as well as the overall network bandwidth must both be large compared to the average demand placed by a single user.

Accordingly, the design of a file server aimed at supporting data applications and the design of a network to support data traffic have been based on the principle of bandwidth sharing and statistical time multiplexing. For example, local area networks of the Ethernet type (10 Mbps) and of the Token Ring type (4 and 16 Mbps) serving tens to hundreds of users have proliferated. Furthermore, file servers have taken advantage of the property of locality in file access, and incorporated appropriate caching mechanisms. In all cases, as the overall load placed on the shared resources increased, the average response time experienced by all users also increased.

Let us now examine digital video. A video signal is analog in nature and continuous over time. It is digitized by first sampling it at regular intervals, and then by quantizing each sample. This digitization process results in a data stream which is relatively constant and of a very high rate. For example, standard television (NTSC) signals result in data rates in the neighborhood of 100 Mbps, and HDTV (high definition TV) signal, 600 Mbps. However, given that the sampled data exhibits a great deal of redundancy, compression is applied, thus significantly reducing the stream's rate. Depending on the bandwidth of the original analog signal, the sampling rate, the quantization step, the encoding method, and the desired image quality, the resulting data rate for a digital video signal can range from 64 Kbps to tens of Mbps. For example, CCITT Recommendation H.261 specifies video coding and decoding methods for audio visual services at the rates of p x 64 Kbps, where p is in the range 1 to 30 (i.e., 64 Kbps to 2 Mbps). Intel's PLV (Production Level Video) video streams have a data rate of 1.2 Mbps; the MPEG (Moving Pictures Expert Group) standard specifies a coded representation that can be used for compressing video sequences to bit rates around 1.5 Mbps, and its successor, known as MPEG II, is currently under development to provide a wider range of functionality and image quality at rates in the range of 4 to 8 Mbps. Advances in compression techniques and in their VLSI (very large scale integration) circuit implementations are among the important reasons why video services over LANs are becoming practical.

Two important observations may be made. The first is that the volume of bits corresponding to a digitized video segment of useful duration (even compressed) is large. A 10 minute PLV video segment requires 90 MB of storage; 10 hours require over 5 GB. Thus video servers, where shared video information is to be stored, must have relatively large storage capacity.

A second observation is that the communication of digital video data between two nodes on a local area network (a server and a desktop station, or two desktop stations) requires that data be transmitted in a stream fashion. This means that data packets must be delivered to the destination on time; failure to deliver data on time would result in video quality degradation. (This characteristic has earned this type of traffic the attribute "synchronous" or "isochronous.")

This has two main implications: (i) from a network's point of view, one requires the availability, on a continuous basis, of a bandwidth at least equal to the signal's data rate; (note that the data rate associated with a digitized video signal, even compressed, is larger than the average traffic rate for a typical data application user); (ii) from a file and storage system point of view, one requires streaming capabilities which guarantee the continuity of each stream being retrieved or stored. Thus, in order to support multiple independent video signals, (i) the network must have the necessary aggregate bandwidth as well as the means to guarantee the bandwidth required for each video signal, and (ii) the file and storage system must be of the streaming type and must have a capacity sufficient to handle all video streams. Also, there is a maximum number of video streams of a given data rate that a network and a server can support. Means must exist to prevent additional requests from overloading the system. While in data applications an overload results in higher response time, with video applications, any additional load beyond the maximum possible would result in degraded video quality.

It is thus clear that the characteristics of video traffic differ substantially from those of traditional data traffic to the point that servers and local area networks designed primarily to support data applications are not appropriate to effectively support video services. New capabilities in servers and networks must be offered.

Starworks And Its Operating Environment

StarWorks design philosophy

There are three basic approaches to the design of servers aimed at supporting multimedia applications. One approach is to retrofit a file server in such a way as to allow it to handle video traffic. For example, a Novell server may be equipped with a "Network loadable module" which provides the streaming capability needed for video. While it is expected that with this approach a single server can support both video and data applications simultaneously, the performance may be compromised for both.

Another approach is to design a fully integrated server which is capable of both transactional data and streaming video services in a well coordinated and dynamically optimized fashion. While this approach may make good sense in the future, for the time being, it cannot be entirely justified.

A third approach is to design a server entirely dedicated to video applications; such a server would then be designed and optimized specifically for streaming, and could thus offer the best performance in video service. To support both video and data services simultaneously, such a video server would have to coexist and interoperate with other data applications. To achieve the best performance at the lowest price, and to take the most advantage of existing data applications servers (e.g., data base servers), this last approach is by far the most sensible one. This is precisely the philosophy behind StarWorks. (See Figure 1.)

StarWorks is a digital video networking software based on a client/server model aimed at supporting many simultaneous video users. It consists of software which is installed in a PC (equipped with a 50 MHz i486 microprocessor and an EISA backplane bus) rendering it a dedicated video server (which we call the "StarWorks Server") capable of supporting at least forty 1.2 Mb/s PLV streams for a total of at least 50 Mb/s. StarWorks also consists of client software which renders the video application running on the client to become networked. StarWorks coexists with today's network

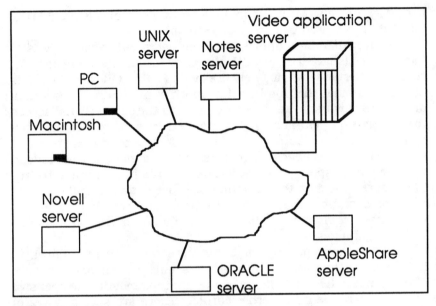

Figure 1: StarWorks video networking solution

operating systems such as NetWare, AppleShare, NFS, LAN Manager, and VINES. Accordingly, video networking services can be used by video applications at the same time that networked data applications are running over the network. We provide a description of the client's software and the server's software later in this chapter.

Network environment

For most data applications which are currently supported by local area networks, bandwidth has traditionally not been a major limitation. With the addition of video applications however, the bandwidth requirement becomes a predominant factor. A network segment which currently supports hundreds of data users can support simultaneously only a few video streams. For example, a 10 Mb/second Ethernet segment can support between 5 and 7 PLV streams simultaneously. Thus only a few video-capable stations may be active sources or destinations of video at the same time. As long as the number of video-active stations per segment remains very small, the current network structure may remain adequate; but as the number of video-active users in the network increases, some restructuring has to take place. A fundamental question is then how to modify the network structure in order to economically provide the bandwidth required by each video stream.

To provide more bandwidth to the users, one possibility is to increase the (shared) bandwidth of network segments. (For example, replace Ethernets and ring networks with FDDI.) One benefit of this approach is that the number of network segments remains small, and the user workgroup structure remains the same. Thus, access to shared resources (namely, the video server) is easily accomplished by placing these resources on the network. However, this approach has one major drawback. It requires all stations to be re-equipped with new high-speed network interface cards (which are substantially more expensive than existing interface cards), despite the fact that not all stations may be video capable. And even when a station is, it never requires more than a mere fraction of the card's bandwidth capabilities.

Another approach is to maintain the same segment bandwidth, but decrease the number of users per segment. One major benefit of this approach is that clients can retain their existing inexpensive interface cards (e.g., Ethernet cards). There are several ways of providing clients access to the server. One way is to connect the maximum number of video users directly to the StarWorks Server via multiple Ethernets. These users can be connected to the multiple Ethernets using standard Ethernet hubs; video users are connected to the wider corporate network through the StarWorks MAC-level bridging capability (see Figure 2). Another way is by means of a switching hub (see Figure 3). This configuration provides access to the StarWorks Server system for a larger number of users. When configured with several connections to a StarWorks Server, hundreds of users can have video-capable access. At any time, however, the actual number of simultaneous users is still limited to the StarWorks Server streaming capacity.

Starworks Client Software

A StarWorks client is a desktop computer such as an IBM-compatible personal computer (DOS 5.0 or higher, or Windows 3.1) equipped with an NDIS-compatible network card (e.g., 3Com Etherlink 16 (3C507), Intel EtherExpress, MediaShare Samba), or a Macintosh (System 7.0 or higher) equipped with a LAP Manager-compatible network card (e.g., Macintosh external and Quadra Internal; Asante MacCon+). The desktop computer may also be a UNIX workstation. To play audio/video, the client must have audio/video hardware and the necessary software drivers. In addition, since the client (personal

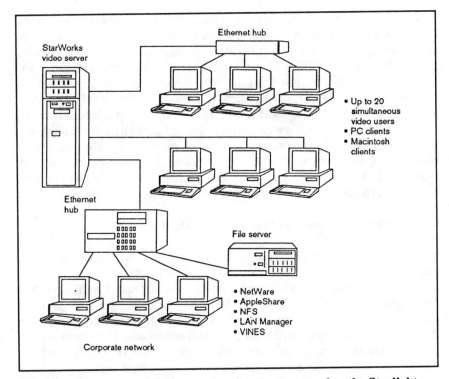

Figure 2: Video-capable users can be directly connected to the Starlight video server

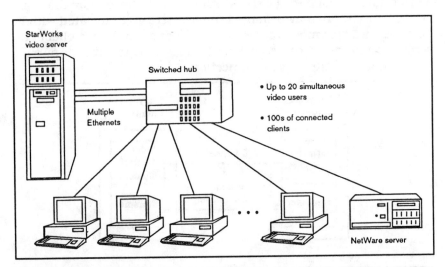

Figure 3: Switched hubs can be used to connect hundreds of video-capable users

computer) will be almost certainly manipulating compressed video data, the client must have the necessary compression/decompression capability. This may be provided by either software or hardware, depending on the CPU's processing power. The actual video compression/decompression format and algorithm are irrelevant to StarWorks. At the application level, the client needs video control software, such as Microsoft Video for Windows or QuickTime, to manage video objects, as well as a movie application to provide a user interface to manipulate/view one or more movies. Finally, the client must be equipped with StarWorks client software. The StarWorks client software provides all the functionalities for the client to access digital video data on the StarWorks server across a LAN.

StarWorks client/server communications

StarWorks clients (PCs) access digital video data from a StarWorks server based on the stream concept. A stream is essentially an ordered byte sequence with the following characteristics: (i) a stream data flow has a rather high but relatively constant rate, (ii) a stream data is accessed sequentially, and (iii) a stream data must be delivered in a timely fashion (meeting the continuity requirement). A major accomplishment of StarWorks is providing timely flow of the stream data from the server to the client, and vice versa.

Figure 4 depicts the communications between a StarWorks client and the StarWorks server. A stream connection is used to deliver data for each movie track. A movie may have more than one track, hence there may be more than one stream associated with it. To access and/or modify movie and stream attributes, a client can send commands to the server by issuing remote procedure calls (RPC) on a separate logical connection.

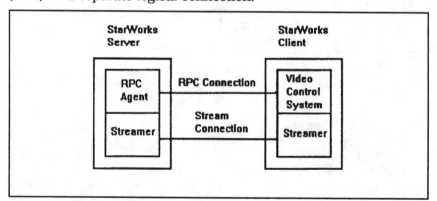

Figure 4: StarWorks client/server communications

Starworks Services And Client API

From the client's point of view, the StarWorks server provides a set of movie and stream control services. These services can be invoked by calling the appropriate library functions provided by the StarWorks client application programming interface. The StarWorks client software translates the function calls to the appropriate RPCS. Typical movie control services include movie name services, as well as various movie manipulation routines like open/close, play/stop/record, and read/write. Typical stream services include connect/disconnect, event post/release, and event handle register.

Coexistence with other network service

Besides providing the necessary functionality for accessing digital video data over a LAN, the StarWorks client software is designed to co-exist with other network services. If the video control system makes direct calls to the StarWorks API, then StarWorks will coexist with the existing networked transactional file system as shown in Figure 5. If the video control system operates under the local file paradigm, StarWorks provides a video redirector to intercept video file requests and dispatches to the StarWorks transport protocol, as shown in Figure 6.

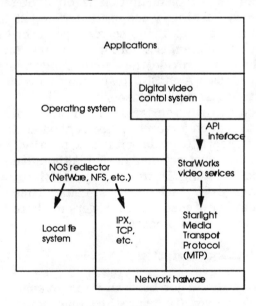

Figure 5: Using StarWorks through its API

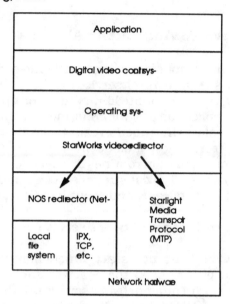

Figure 6: Using StarWorks through a redirector

StarWorks Server

A StarWorks server can be implemented on different hardware platforms. The current implementation is on a 50 MHz 486 PC and supports twenty 1.2 Mbps video users, totaling 25 Mbps. The amount of memory required at the server depends on the number of users; a typical installation is 24 MB for 20 users. Multiple LAN cards are installed to provide the required aggregate network bandwidth of 25 Mbps. A SCSI-II disk array subsystem is also provided for multi-access digital video storage.

StarWorks software runs on a real-time multi-tasking operating system that provides such features as fast context switch, efficient shared memory support, threads, and task priority. StarWorks software is based on object-oriented design, although conventional C language is used for coding. During execution of the code, multiple processes are created for each movie stream. These processes interact with a number of resource managers to share the system resources with other stream processes.

Functional block description

Figure 7 shows the major hardware and software functional blocks in StarWorks server. There are three main control units that

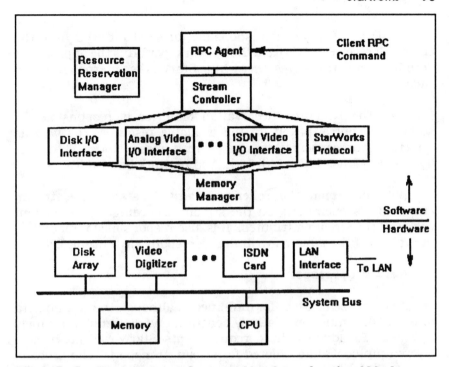

Figure 7: StarWorks server software and hardware functional block diagrams

are of interest to the clients: (i) the RPC Agent, (ii) the Resource Reservation Manager, and (iii) the Stream Controller. They reside more or less at the top level of the software hierarchy. There is the StarWorks multimedia protocol suite which provides network transport for streams and RPCS. There is the Memory Manager, which allows multiple streams to share the available memory efficiently. Various specialized I/O units can fit into the StarWorks architecture. Of interest are the disk I/O unit for stored video applications, the analog feed for live broadcast applications, and the ISDN interface for video teleconferencing applications.

Control units

Although there are numerous control units within the StarWorks server software, most of them are transparent to the clients. Of relatively greater interest to the clients would be (i) the RPC Agent, (ii) the Resource Reservation Manager, and (iii) the Stream Controller.

(i) The RPC Agent is responsible for servicing RPC from the clients. It receives RPCs from the network, performs the appropriate decoding, and translates them into StarWorks internal function calls.

(ii) The Resource Reservation Manager is responsible for admission control based on the available resources, as well as system resource reservation. System resources include CPU capacity, memory, disk I/O bandwidth, and network bandwidth.

(iii) The Stream Controller maintains the state of the stream, and controls operations on the stream according to the current values of the stream attributes. It is also responsible for modifying the values of the stream attributes in response to a client RPC.

Network protocol

As discussed earlier, for multimedia, although the stream data rate is high it must be relatively constant and delivered in a timely fashion. To address these requirements StarWorks provides a layered protocol suite tailored for stream transport. The protocol suite includes (i) a presentation layer, (ii) a session layer, and (iii) a transport layer; it can reside on different network layers or directly on a LAN media access control sub layer.

(i) The presentation layer allows various open presentation encoding standards, and also provides a default format that can be encoded quickly in real time.

(ii) The session layer manages the RPC connection of a movie and the associated stream connections.

(iii) The transport layer is modeled closely after the Express Transport Protocol (XTP).

The whole protocol suite is designed to be "light weight " with minimal overhead, and it executes very efficiently. The suite is also designed to minimize data movement inside the server. In essence, data are copied to memory only once. The selective retransmission strategy in the transport layer, coupled with the choice of large packet size, makes the protocol very bandwidth efficient. Furthermore, tight rate control on each stream reduces the burstiness of data delivery, hence reduces inefficient contention of network resources.

Memory management unit

Memory management is an important aspect of the server design. It must be simple but provide efficient sharing among multiple streams; it must minimize memory copies of bulk data. Central to StarWorks' memory management is the concept of "pipe." A pipe is a linked list of memory chunks that provides a logical FIFO (first in first out) queue. A "producer" and one or more "consumers" are associated with each pipe. A producer may be a disk I/O interface and a consumer may be a stream connection to a StarWorks client. The production/consumption state of the pipe is maintained by a number of producer/consumer pointers. Many algorithms exist for multiple pipes to share memory. We have chosen a fairly simple and yet efficient sharing algorithm that involves partitioning a single memory pool into fixed size chunks allowing multiple pipes to allocate/free memory chunks on a demand basis. The chunk size is currently optimized for stored video applications.

I/O interfaces

Various I/O interfaces are needed to adapt to different forms of video I/O, e.g., video data on magnetic disk, analog feed, video coded on ISDN, etc. These different I/O interfaces can be implemented as separate modules that co-exist under the StarWorks architecture. Due to space limitations, we discuss only the disk I/O interface.

The disk I/O interface, called the Storage Chunk Manager (SCM), manages video I/O between the disk array and memory. The major design goal is to maximize the number of simultaneous streams while maintaining continuity requirements for each stream. For simplicity, consider the case where all streams are of fixed and equal rates, and that all I/Os are data retrievals from the disk array. By examining the continuity requirement, we were led to consider a cyclic scheduling scheme. In this scheme, time is divided into contiguous cycles of fixed length. Within a given cycle, a fixed amount of data is fetched from disks for each stream; the amount is determined by the product of the stream rate and the cycle length. It is clear that this scheme satisfies the continuity requirement.

Under the cyclic scheduling scheme, the design problem becomes that of maximizing the number of stream I/Os from the disk array within a cycle. We employ the techniques of "striping" and "sorting." Striping involves distributing the data being retrieved for each stream in a given cycle evenly across all disks in the disk array. This balances the load on all disks. Sorting involves ordering all the disk I/Os in a given cycle according to disk location among all streams. This minimizes the impact of long seek times. Sorting is also known as the "Elevator Algorithm" in the literature.

The cycle length is an interesting design parameter. A long cycle length can increase the number of simultaneous streams, but it also increases the memory requirement since memory usage is linearly proportional to the cycle length. Furthermore, a long cycle also implies a long startup latency for new streams. Various interesting techniques for reducing memory requirement exist but it is beyond the scope of this paper to discuss these techniques.

Applications Support

StarWorks digital networking software is the foundation for networked-based video applications. Designed to be used in support of other systems, the StarWorks system will allow existing network applications, such as databases and groupware applications, to add video support. These applications can take advantage of the video application services to support the real time demands of streaming data. In addition, StarWorks can support existing standalone video applications without modifications to the applications. In this case the video is moved to the StarWorks server, and the client application accesses the video through the StarWorks client redirector.

Video applications today fall into three main categories: training, information delivery, and video databases. Training applications are found in both the education and the corporate market. StarWorks is being used to network video in support of interactive video-based curriculum at the K-12 level as well as in higher education. Video information is stored on a StarWorks server and courseware is stored on a file server, both accessed over Ethernet by PCs and Macintoshes. Interactive training using video is also found in the corporate world. Here applications can be generic, such as how to use PC-based productivity applications, or specific to the industry or company, such as how to handle customer service situations. These applications can be confined to a training room or lab that is networked, or are available to employees at their desktop via the network.

Information delivery video applications include kiosk and point-of-sale stations which provide a wide range of information. Kiosk applications can be found in museums where the visitor can select video clips that support the museum exhibits. Corporate kiosk applications include providing corporate news bulletins and company product or event video from a kiosk located in the cafeteria, lobby, or factory floor. Advertising kiosks are found in many retail locations. Here networked video applications provide a way to better manage the video information and reduce the amount of storage required at each location.

The last category, video databases, consists of applications that manage databases of video information. In the education environment, networked video applications are used to catalog multimedia information in libraries or laboratories. Video production environments such as film production, corporate media production, and advertising agencies are converting to digital video and using networked video servers to manage their content. This provides timely access to anyone needing to review video work-in-progress, or collections of video.

Future Video Applications

The next generation of video applications will provide support for live video information in addition to stored video. Networked video applications will include broadcasting a live feed over the network for users to "tap" into the broadcast when they desire. This capability will be used by corporate environments to broadcast the address by the company president, or video of an important event in a different location. Other uses will include distance learning applications where remote classrooms can view the lecture being presented in another place. Support for two-way video conferencing will facilitate many different applications. Group meetings, user support applications in remote areas, and performance support systems that link suppliers with their customers for video "troubleshooting" are examples of applications that will be possible with networked video support for both stored and live video information. With video being a more natural method of communication, we believe that video applications will become pervasive throughout corporate and education markets.

For Additional Reading:

Mark J. Bunzel and Sandra K. Morris. *Multimedia applications development using DVI technology*, McGraw-Hill, Inc., 1992.

Fetterman, Roger and Gupta, Satish . *Mainstream multimedia:*

applying multimedia in business, Van Nostrand Reinhold, 1993.

IEEE Communications Magazine, Special Issue on Multimedia Communications, Vol. 30 No. 5, May 1992.

Communications of the ACM, Special Issue on Digital Multimedia Systems, Vol. 34, No. 4, April 1991.

Communications of the ACM, Special Issue on Hypermedia, Vol. 35, No. 1, Jannuary 1992.

Section 2

Application/ Benefits Focus

Chapter 4

Multimedia Computing
An Overview

**K.K. Athappilly, Chris Durben
and Steven Woods
Western Michigan University**

When he arrives at his job each morning at Olivetti Research Laboratory in Cambridge, England, Turner clips on an electronic badge that links him to the lab's experimental video and audio communication system known as "Pandora." The badge emits infrared signals that allow his fellow research engineers to find him whenever they want to chat. Once paged, Turner can sit down at the nearest computer terminal and begin a conversation with up to five other people whose faces show up in different windows on the screen.

Thanks to Pandora's "video news server," Turner can also click an icon on his screen to catch recorded BBC news and weather reports. He can even send video mail. "I might send a message to Ian downstairs - 'Are we going out for a beer this lunch time?' - that he's going to read when he gets back to his workstation in 15 minutes." (Brittan, 1992, pp.43)

The underlying development allowing the technology used in the "Pandora" work environment rests with multimedia technology. The purpose of this chapter is to introduce the reader to this rapidly growing technology and to discuss its manifold applications.

Opinions vary widely on the usefulness of multimedia, ranging from stark skepticism to overwhelming support. John Sculley, the CEO of Apple Computer says, "I love the technology, but nobody has figured out how to make money on it" (Flynn, 1992, pp. 31). However, the abundance of literature on multimedia testifies that it is one of the more frequently used buzz words in today's rapidly changing computer industry. In fact, there is little doubt that multimedia technology has ignited the personal computer marketplace. To fully grasp the essence of "multimedia," it is necessary to discuss each of the following five issues:

- What is multimedia computing? (Note: the terms, multimedia and multimedia computing are used interchangeably in this paper.)
- How has multimedia developed?
- What are the applications of multimedia?
- What are the benefits of multimedia?
- What are the drawbacks to multimedia?

What is Multimedia Computing?

Multimedia, in the past, consisted of only a simple mechanism - a device which incorporated a slide show with sound, using one or more slide projectors. The whole presentation was preprogrammed by an audiovisual technician. Today, according to Charlie Morrison, Director Of Communications for the Association for MultiImage International (AMI), this same technology is called multi-image slide presentation (Filipcziak, 1991).

Although AMI defines multimedia as a computerized device that can generate sound and image, many believe that a strict definition only limits its scope (Filipcziak, 1991). IBM defines multimedia computing at two levels. "At its simplest," it is "the addition of sound and video to personal computers. At its grandest, it means a melding of technologies such as personal computers, television, and telephones, as well as the melding of the computer, consumer electronics, and telephone industries. ... Multimedia is the sum of all these revolutions wrapped into one, a revolution in communication that combines the audio/visual power of television, the publishing power of the printing press and the interactive power of the computer" (IBM Ultimedia: The Ultimate, 1991, P. 1). IBM's attempt is commendable. However, driven by multimedia's potential in the consumer market, application developers continue to add newer elements into the existing technology to produce even more useful applications. Subsequently, the definition undergoes constant change. From a pragmatic point of view, we are better off attempting to have a clear notion about the basic structure and working of multimedia rather than struggling for an accurate definition.

Essentially, multimedia computing consists of using four elements of communication technology - (i) television/video, (ii) personal computers, (iii) audio, and (iv) laser storage systems (i.e. videodisc and compact disc) to bring about the synchronization of text, animation, sound and video to convey information. Through proper integration of those elements, multimedia technology (dis)plays text, music, voice, animation, images, and video on a computer at home or at work. Thus today, a multimedia computer can be any device whose sophistication ranges from that of a talking chalk board to that of a space shuttle simulator .

Regardless of the magnitude and sophistication, all multimedia devices must perform three key functions. They are; (i) natural presentation of information through text, graphics, audio, images, animation and full motion video, (ii) some type of graphical user interface (i.e., a mouse, light pen, or touch-sensitive display), and (iii) nonlinear navigation through applications for access to information on request.

No matter how one defines this technology, its most central feature is the personal computer. Whether it is an Amiga, IBM, or Macintosh, it is the personal computer that coordinates the sound, images, text, graphics, and video clips used in multimedia applications. Today, a common configuration of multimedia includes a high performance PC with a CD-ROM player, a sound board, and stereo speakers. Often, a sophisticated video playback peripheral device is also added to the configuration.

How has Multimedia Developed?

Perhaps, it is the computer industry which has played the most significant role in the development of multimedia computing. To foster an interest in, and to advance the state of multimedia computing, the computer industry needed to promulgate a set of technical standards for this disparate set of technologies. With strong support from Microsoft Corporation, in 1989 the Multimedia Personal Computer Marketing Council (MPCMC) was formed as a subsidiary of the Software Publishers Association (Polilli, 1992). By 1991, AT&T, NEC, Philip's Consumer Electronics Corporation, Tandy, Zenith, and more than a dozen other manufacturers eagerly joined the MPCMC (Winkler, 1992). In July, 1993, IBM announced its membership. Two critical factors influenced the formation of the organization: (i) the multimedia market lacked direction, and (ii) the cost of multimedia computing became affordable (Polilli, 1992).

No standards existed for multimedia manufacturers before the MPCMC was created. In addition, no market standards for this new technology emerged from the manufacturers as there had been very little scope for product selection. While some computer experts criticize the MPCMC, most industry experts support its objectives. Application developers are now able to plan their proposed multimedia products targeting for standard platforms. Even though the MPCMC has been in existence for a short time, the benefits have been substantial. In addition to benefits for developers and manufacturers, the MPCMC's trademark provides a clear route for potential customers of multimedia products.

The MPCMC had defined a minimum configuration to be used in multimedia applications. Currently this standard, called MPC Level 2 consists of:

- 808486X/25 MHz CPU
- 4 Megabytes of RAM
- 160 Megabyte hard disk
- 3.5" Floppy disk drive
- Serial/Parallel/Joystick/MIDI-In/MIDI-Out Ports
- 16-Bit VGA graphics adapter with support for 65,000 colors
- A double speed and double session CD-ROM drive with a minimum data transfer rate of 300 KBS
- Mouse
- Windows 3.1

It is important to note that the MPCMC did have an earlier and more minimal standard than Level 2. But since "true" multimedia applications require extensive memory and computing power capabilities, that standard was upgraded to provide a higher level of hardware support for the evolving applications.

Since MPCMC was launched, 34 vendors have licensed the MPC trademark, each for a fee of $35,000, and 85 vendors have been producing multimedia applications for the standard. The standards created by the MPCMC have already helped achieve its desired objectives. The value of the U.S. multimedia market (excluding home computing) was $4.7 billion in 1991. Industry experts estimate sales to reach $22 billion by 1994, and more than $25 billion by 1995.

Although the MPCMC enjoys success in the marketplace, it is worth noting that, Apple Computer has not participated in the organization. Interestingly, IBM and Apple have pursued the multimedia market with individual product lines as well as with a joint venture called Kaleida. The purpose of the venture is to promote and develop multimedia applications which can be used across different platforms (Zurich & Liebowitz, 1992).

Since the late 1970's, IBM has committed extensive resources to the development of multimedia technologies for education and industry. With a unified vision, IBM offers a variety of multimedia products and services which go beyond using text and graphics, to include images, animation, full-motion video, stereo sound, and touch-screen interaction. The IBM PS/2 Model M57 SLC was the first integrated multimedia computer which the company used to launch its most recent brand of "Ultimedia" PCs.

IBM's Ultimedia applications have received favorable reviews for their unique features. For example, "Columbus: Encounter, Discovery, and Beyond" was a recognized state-of-the-art multimedia application developed for the education market (Amthor, May, 1992). This application explores Columbus' voyage commemorating the 500th anniversary of his discovery of America. The application is not just an exploration of the Renaissance and the Age of Discovery. It examines the breakthroughs in science, mathematics, art, music, philosophy, and literature of that time. One can safely assert that this application is well on its way to realize the ultimate objective of multimedia applications in education, namely, to motivate students to take possession of their own learning abilities. Now, students reading about the first moon walk, can, with the click of the mouse, see Neil Armstrong take that first big step for mankind!

Apple Computer also has a strong foundation in multimedia technology. Apple executives envision the multimedia revolution as an opportunity to gain domination in the consumer electronic industry. In 1991, Apple introduced QuickTime, a multimedia technology for its Macintosh operating systems. QuickTime allows developers to integrate video, sound, and animation within software applications (Mann, 1992). The company has also developed multimedia products related to CD-ROM, video compression, and networking. Many different software and hardware vendors support QuickTime, including Aldus, WordPerfect, and Radius. Not far behind Apple's QuickTime is Microsoft's Video For Windows, based on Intel's DVI (Digital Video Interactive) technology for PCs. Although there are some differences between Apple's and Microsoft's approaches, both make possible the digitization, editing, and playback of motion video images.

Commodore Computer has also established itself in the multimedia marketplace with the introduction, in 1985, of the Amiga personal computer (Strothman, 1992). The Amiga has become particularly popular among developers who regale in the system's ability to produce and edit high quality audio, animation, and video.

What are the Applications of Multimedia?

Researchers have found that people retain only 20% of what they hear, 40% of what they see and hear, and 75% of what they see, hear and do (Fletcher, 1990). Those findings reveal that multimedia technology is a far more direct and complete communication method than a single channel of communication using only text or only voice. As an effective communication technology, multimedia computing has significant value in the applications of (i) training, (ii) education, (iii) kiosk-based product presentations, and (iv) business communications.

Training Applications

Multimedia technology can be used to train personnel better, at lower cost, resulting in improved worker productivity. The following discussion focuses on multimedia training which resulted in more effective and more efficient company operation.

Federal Express. In 1988, Federal Express, the overnight air freight delivery organization, began to implement multimedia employee training programs to improve customer service and overnight delivery sceduling (Janson, 1992). A commitment to employee training was made by Federal Express to use interactive videodisc instruction (IVI) to expand employees' knowledge of their jobs.

Federal Express' program for employee training and multimedia technology was a success. The firm won the Malcolm Baldridge National Quality Award in 1990. With this award, the U.S. Government's National Institute of Standards and Technology cited the company as an exemplar for excellent customer service and for outstanding training programs.

Federal Express is one of the world's largest user of interactive video combined with knowledge testing. The company has IVI installed on 1,200 PCs in 800 offices nationwide, and it uses CD-ROMs as a distribution medium to provide monthly updates of the 25-disc curriculum. These CDs contain an average of 150 audiovisual training material updates concerning the company's products and services. During the three years after the systems' installation in 1988, it was estimated that each workstation cost the company $25 per day compared with the prior $400 per day cost of sending employees to regional headquarters for instructor-led courses.

Holiday Inn. At the end of 1992, Holiday Inn Worldwide announced a new international employee training program that would be the largest single corporate multimedia computer installation to date (Amthor, 1992). The plan called for more than 1,600 Holiday Inns to install IBM Ultimedia PS/2 computers equipped with the latest multimedia capabilities. The motel chain planned to use IBM's video compression technology, Photomotion. With this technology the Ultimedia PS/2 can play video clips directly from a CD-ROM with no additional video decompression equipment. The reasons for the company to employ multimedia training seemed obvious.

Holiday Inn is a decentralized organization with facilities throughout the world. To deliver consistent training to over 1,600 locations in a cost-efficient and timely manner is a difficult task. Besides, due to high employee turnover, there is even a greater urgency for training new employees.

Fred Meyer. Multimedia computing as a training tool is also used by Fred Meyer, a $2.7 billion general merchandise retailer (Baratto, 1992). With 225,000 items in stock, and with each store the size of five football fields, training employees at the 123 retail stores located in the Pacific Northwest had been a personnel nightmare. However, this challenge was met by using multimedia technology in an innovative manner. Fred Meyer's objective of using multimedia computing has been to provide important information about product quality, about why the company carries products, and how consumers can use their products.

The company uses multimedia training in three categories; (i)product education, (ii) job skills training, and (iii) corporate information. Product education also incorporated information regarding the manufacturing of products. The manufacturers and vendors themselves fund some of the multimedia course development, and they teach retail employees how to sell their products. For job skillstraining, Fred Meyer's goal was to develop instructional consistency for employees who perform various on-the-job duties. The multimedia training program guarantees that all employees receive and complete the same training. Multimedia also helped to disseminate corporate information, such as the company's history, its retail philosophy, and the role of the employee in Fred Meyer's success.

Similar to Holiday Inn, Fred Meyer also uses IBM's Ultimedia products. With Ultimedia, senior management can review training for particular products, they can assess how employees are trained, and determine how this training affects sales. The course takes about 30 minutes to complete. It utilizes a mixture of photographic images, audio voice-overs, text, and graphics with an animated character to guide the user through the tutorial program, all without using a keyboard. Fred Meyer's 20,000 employees who are spread across the Northwest United States and Alaska, underwent the multimedia training and were able to retain about 85 % of the key information three months after the training.

Caterpillar. Multimedia technology has also found its way into the earth moving industry (IBM, 1992, November/December). Caterpillar is developing multimedia training programs in hydraulic engines, electrical systems, drive-train systems, and failure analysis using IBM's PS/2 Ultimedia Model M57 SLC and other Ultimedia equipment. Abstract objects are made vivid by blending high resolution images, animation, full motion video graphics, voice-overs and text.

Caterpillar's "Cat Basics" was created to help its dealers' new-hires improve their technical background. In the past, mechanics working at Caterpillar's dealers had a high level of troubleshooting skills, but eventually, their skills began to decline. To combat this trend the corporation developed a cost-effective, interactive multimedia training system for dealers and for the 15,000 worldwide mechanics who are responsible for repairing heavy construction and mining machines.

Team leaders at Caterpillar believe the key element to the success of "Cat Basics" is the level of interactive multimedia training. Interactive multimedia enables an instructor to determine what a trainee does and does not understand. If an issue of concern does arise, the proper instruction can be provided. Mechanics review sections when they want, at their own pace, in a one-on-one tutorial environment. Caterpillar has found that other employees, besides dealers and mechanics, are also enthusiastic about "Cat Basics." Sales personnel at Caterpillar use the system because it improves their knowledge of the products that Caterpillar sells. According to Caterpillar management, in the future the use of multimedia technology will become more popular in areas such as communications and job performance support.

Du Pont. Like Caterpillar, Du Pont also tries to achieve its goal of becoming a great global company by people's use of multimedia training programs (Baratto, 1992, pp. 4). One of the leading global chemical companies in the industry, Du Pont has organized its multimedia training into four segments. These include (i) government-mandated compliance training, (ii) plant process skills and technical training, (iii) major policy awareness, and (iv) personal development training.

In order to meet the U.S. Federal Government's training requirements under the Resource Conservation and Recovery Act, Du Pont and IBM jointly created a multimedia program called "Managing Waste: Your Role." Developing a multimedia training program in this area is challenging because of continuous modifications in legislation by the U.S. Environmental Protection Agency.

Another multimedia training program developed by Du Pont is (BESPA (Basic Electrical Safety Personal Awareness). BESPA assists employees in creating a high level of safety for any task by allowing them to recognize safety hazards, to plan tasks with respect to those hazards, and then to perform the planned tasks. These multimedia training programs and many others developed by Du Pont provide important guidelines needed by employees. Workers have increased their knowledge about 50% more than by traditional, seminar-based methods.

The use of multimedia training has not been limited to large U.S. businesses. Government agencies are also using multimedia computing in their employee training programs. Analysts predict that government expenditures for multimedia software and hardware will grow from $900 million today, to $2.4 billion by 1995 (Liebowitz and Zurier, 1992).

Police Officer Training. In California, the Commission on Police Officer Standards and Training developed an 80 hour multimedia training program to help police and sheriffs learn how to make quick decisions in "touchy" situations (Frandzel, 1991). The computer responds to learners' decisions, instructing them on choices that they make. At the end of the training program, the multimedia users will have covered community relations, arrest and control techniques, laws of evidence, the care of firearms, and other basic aspects of law enforcement. Users can progress at their own pace, mistakes are not made public, and success is acknowledged immediately. Most important of all, the users like it.

U.S. Coast Guard Training. Another governmental agency,

the U.S. Coast Guard, has also incorporated multimedia technology as a training tool (Janson, 1992). Their in-house computer-based flight training simulator for its HH60J helicopter is one such example. In the past, the U.S. Coast Guard has had to rely on the U.S. Navy or third party equipment vendors for this training. However, by developing an in-house computer based training (CBT) program, the organization has saved over $11 million in total training costs since its implementation in 1989. The Coast Guard's Aviator Technical Training Center has developed a multimedia CBT program which allows up to 23 students to work simultaneously on one CBT course. Most of these training programs are designed and developed with the help of Aldus Corporation's SuperCard, an application development tool sold by Aldus. The Coast Guard has found the return on investment of this training program quite significant. Users of the program learn faster and are able to return to the field more quickly.

Education Applications

The educational field too, like training can benefit substantially from multimedia. A recent survey by the Software Publishers Association revealed that U.S. schools spent $2.7 billion on PC hardware and software in 1992 (InfoWeek, 1992). Of this, 70% was spent on high-technology hardware and software such as that used in multimedia computing.   An IBM brochure entitled *Multimedia Solutions for Education* (1992) cites the following classroom applications of multimedia:

• Leading medical schools use multimedia simulations to present symptoms of pathology for medical student diagnosis, reducing the risk of malpractice.

• A Harvard Law School interactive video series simulates hypothetical client cases, without the risk and cost of damaging a real client.

• A comprehensive Chemistry curriculum developed at the University of Illinois allows introductory Chemistry students to simulate reactions without danger to themselves or the lab.

• Social Studies and French classes use interactive video to explore Paris, without chartering an airplane.

• Interactive video simulations marketed by Modern Talking Picture

Service help students develop skills for coping with peer pressure. One simulation explores drug and alcohol issues; another explores AIDS issues.

The classroom has not been the only place where multimedia applications are used. Encyclopedia publishers have also developed multimedia applications. Britannica Software, Inc. markets a product called Compton's Multimedia Encyclopedia (CMME) designed for DOS, Windows, and Macintosh systems. CMME contains the text of the 26 volume Compton's, plus 15,000 illustrations, 45 fully animated sequences, 60 minutes of sound, and a 65,000 word dictionary. Students can select information in eight unique ways that best suit the individual's style of thinking and learning.

Multimedia software manufacturers find a unique niche in the education market. According to one recent advertisement, IBM developed an educational multimedia application which sells for about $140. The application, "The President: It Started With George" offers an in-depth perspective on the personal and political lives of the first 40 presidents of The United States. This application includes more than 1,000 photographs, famous speeches, a multimedia timeline giving a historical perspective, and commentary on each president.

IBM has introduced other multimedia applications for the education market. In addition to one about Columbus mentioned earlier, there is "The Illuminated Books and Manuscripts" which provides five classic literary works to help users gain an in-depth understanding of the publications; *Letter from Birmingham Jail* , *Ulysses* , *The Declaration of Independence* , *Hamlet* , and "*Black Elk Speaks.*"

Kiosk-Based Product Presentation

Multimedia kiosks are a popular tool for providing efficient and effective communication for clients and the public. Kiosks are interactive display units placed in high traffic areas such as malls, airports, hotels, restaurants, and tourist attractions. These usually contain a keyboardless personal computer (with MPC-level performance), a touch-sensitive screen, and optical storage. Increasingly, kiosks are locally or remotely networked.

Shell Canada. Shell Canada has created the multimedia kiosk, InfoCentre, to promote tourism, thereby helping to set Shell apart from competitors. InfoCentres at gas stations and at restaurants provide customers instant access to maps, hotel and restaurant recommendations, and special attractions such as shopping malls and historical landmarks. This kind of application is a "win/win" situation for both the seller and the consumer. Sellers are always looking for productive means of marketing at lower costs, while consumers continue to become more time and value conscious in choosing goods and services.

Mannington Mills. Mannington Mills, Inc. is a manufacturer of sheet vinyl flooring. The company offers a multimedia kiosk that allows a customer to gather information about sheet floor surfaces, installation, yardage and price estimates, and product warrantees (Schlax and Wiegner, 1991). The most popular feature of the kiosk is that it allows users to choose a room similar to one of their own, and to view hundreds of floor colorations. This shows how stunning or ugly the room would look after the manufacturer installs a particular vinyl floor.

Other. In department stores, a multimedia touch-screen-based kiosk can help shoppers to purchase items by asking detailed questions about their hobbies, lifestyles, and price range. Kiosks can show and/or suggest items that might make a perfect fit with the input information; a printed map can lead the shopper right to the suggested item, or even let the customer place an order. Examples described by IBM (1992) are:

At the "World of Coca-Cola" Pavilion in Atlanta, Georgia, multimedia kiosks in the shape of a large can of Coca-Cola, document world events since 1886, and produce matching tales of the development of Coca-Cola which began operation in that year. At the Chicago Mercantile Exchange, patrons visiting the exchange can use a multilingual multimedia kiosk to learn about the frantic work environment of the trading floor. Multimedia kiosks were also used in the 1992 Winter and Summer Olympics, to provide historical and biographical information on Olympic events and current updates of the day's events. Over 1,000 touch-screen multimedia kiosks at 40 venue sites supported journalists in four languages in Barcelona in the 1992 Summer Olympics.

In Los Angeles County, California, the Long Beach Municipal Court lets violators pay for traffic tickets with a credit card attached to a multimedia kiosk. Health, human services, and employment information are offered to Hawaii's citizens in another multimedia kiosk application. Driver's tests administered by multimedia kiosks complete with full motion video in English, French Canadian and several Asian languages are used in British Columbia, Canada, and are now also operating in Oregon. Thus, multimedia kiosks offer users many benefits, including instant information, feedback, as well as communication to remote computing sites.

Business Communications

Multimedia technology can be used by many small and large organizations as a powerful communication tool to get closer to clients thereby gaining a distinct competitive advantage. Two interesting applications in this area include business presentations, and video monitoring.

Presentations. Presentations, an important area of business communication, can be enhanced with multimedia computing. Presentations, enhanced with full-motion video, photographic imagery, high-resolution graphics, animation, stereo music and voice-overs can excite the audience and deliver messages in a convincing style. With multimedia presentation systems, speakers have control over message delivery throughout the presentation. They can pause, back-up, and even branch from one section to another in response to input from the audience. One of the most important aspects of multimedia business presentations is their capability of demonstrating a high degree of professionalism. The professionalism displayed through multimedia presentations can be very persuasive and can lead to strong business relationships.

Video Monitoring. Video monitoring requires the installation of a PC card that allows the computer to receive television broadcasts. Using this capability, network and cable news broadcasts can be monitored on a personal computer screen. This function provides PC users with current information on worldwide events; access to such timely information is essential among journalists and stock traders. Employees can continue to perform their assigned tasks while a small window on the PC can display video broadcasts. When an item of interest arouses the user's attention at the workstation, the TV window can be enlarged to fully display the item of interest.

Applications of video monitoring can be applied to other areas where workers need to receive company-broadcast programs at their desktops. Closed circuit, PC-based TV monitoring and/or security systems can be used, for example, by deskbound manufacturing supervisors to watch assembly line functions. Store clerks can attend to customers, while at the same time they can keep an eye on store operations. Bank employees too can use such systems while continuing to work at a PC instead of having to accompany customers into the vault.

Multimedia computing has also helped many other businesses to communicate information about the service or products they offer to their clientele. In the travel industry, shoppers using a multimedia workstation can explore the sights and sounds of exotic destinations to select the vacation of their choice.

Multimedia applications are also bridging the information gap between patients and physicians (Wilson, 1992). The goal of such applications is to assist patients in making informed decisions about their own medical treatment. These applications allow patients to explore the details of medical problems thereby reducing the physician-patient contact time for question and answers. The cost of developing each individual program can range from $250,000 to $700,000, depending on the context and the amount of copyrighted material included in the application. Patients usually use the program in confidentiality after consultation with the doctor. Each program explains a particular disease, and attempts to estimate the probability of the patient's recovery from disease.

What Are the Benefits of Multimedia?

In the previous sections we saw an overview of what multimedia is, and some of its many applications. We will now focus on the three areas which substantially benefit from the use of multimedia. These are education, training, and business communications. In general, such benefits are realized through (i) lower training costs, (ii) more effective instruction, and (iii) improved employee productivity. A discussion of each of these follows.

Lower training costs. Many of today's multimedia applications demonstrate the benefit of lower training cost. For example, Atmos Energy, a gas utility corporation headquartered in Dallas, Texas, chose a CBT program utilizing multimedia technology (Janson, 1992). CBT, a forerunner of today's multimedia computing training applications, covers a broad range of computer-based training methods. While not all CBT applications incorporate multimedia computing, many of them now use the full range of features that are almost identical to those of multimedia computing.

Atmos' CBT program was created to instruct employees in time management and other computer based applications. With the program, the firm eliminated the need to send a trainer to more than 80 locations in Texas, Oklahoma, and Kentucky. In October, 1989, Atmos started its CBT program with employee training using 15 minute, on-site sessions that were available at the employees' convenience. Atmos' employee development division planned for a positive return within two years.

Bell South Corporation also uses multimedia to reduce training expenses (Sullivan, 1991). The corporation planned to save 20,000 training days and $5 million in travel expenses in four years using interactive training systems (ITV) for its field offices. Formerly, Bell South employees were required to attend a seven day course offered only in Atlanta, but that requirement has been reduced to a seven hour training session completed in the employees' own offices. Attracted by the examples portrayed by Atmos Energy and Bell South, many other corporations have begun to employ multimedia computing in an attempt to control employee training expenses. This trend is encouraged today, thanks to the rapidly decreasing cost of multimedia hardware and software. No doubt, owing to the attractiveness of multimedia technology, the corporate training market will continue to grow, making its most valuable resource, employees, more knowledgeable and more productive.

More effective instruction. Multimedia programs have been received with enthusiasm by educational institutions across the nation. School administrators are convinced that the tools offered by multimedia technology will help students to become more creative, more knowledgeable, and more curious about learning.

The University of Virginia, Curry School of Education, after receiving a grant from IBM, concluded that multimedia computing has the "...potential to radically transform how teaching and learning occur in the public schools." (Ashburn & Cilley, pp. 32)

Educators find that multimedia relieves instructors of many of the administrative trivia assigned to them. Also, it greatly contributes to the effectiveness of classroom management by facilitating the arrangement of the content of information as well as the method of delivery. Instructors can use multimedia features such as animation and sound together with immediate feedback to enhance their instruction delivery, thereby increasing their teaching effectiveness.

Integrated Learning systems (ILS), a form of multimedia that computerizes the classroom curriculum, has greatly contributed to improved academic performance in classrooms. For example, The Education Systems Corporation has developed more than 1,800 lessons covering mathematics, reading, and language arts. A school choosing this program sends its textbooks to the corporation which then prepares weekly computerized lessons according to the textbook objectives. This facility relieves teachers from their routine administrative obligations and allows them to assume new roles as academic coaches, group leaders, and innovators.

With improved classroom delivery through the use of features described above, students achieve improved academic performance. Studies show that the average student receives only one minute of individual teacher attention per day (Van Horn, 1991). However, by using multimedia programs, the students' "individual" attention increases considerably and they are able to continuously develop their own learning abilities. Students can also work at their own pace and receive consistent and appropriate feedback.

Improved employee productivity. Improved productivity is the end result of a multimedia program. When AT&T Network Systems embarked on a program to improve quality throughout its national sales division, it developed a multimedia program to use as a delivery method, hoping to increase the effectiveness of the company's quality campaign (Strothman, 1991). AT&T's goal was to disseminate key quality issues among the employees, and at the same time to motivate employees to take action according to the principles underlying the quality issues. The message was portrayed using multimedia. The program achieved its goal of employee-driven quality.

The possibility of improved employee productivity through multimedia has also attracted other corporations. Ford Motor Company's Service Bay Diagnosis System offers dealers updated car manuals containing as many as 30,000 pages in a multimedia application (Sullivan, 1990). With such a system Ford substantially reduces the cost of supporting new car warranties.

What are the Drawbacks of Multimedia Computing?

Although the benefits derived from multimedia technology are promising, three issues detract corporations and consumers from considering multimedia as a feasible technology. They are; (i) high costs, (ii) lack of standards, and (iii) uncertainty of its relevance.

High costs. Though the hardware and software costs for multimedia computing continue to decrease, they are substantially higher than what is required for a traditional computer configuration. Also, this decrease in hardware and software costs is often offset significantly by increases in personnel cost.

Typically, the consulting fee for developing an interactive multimedia application ranges from $35,000 to over $150,000, not including software, hardware, and customizing expenses (Sullivan, 1990). If multimedia technology is used for training, the expense required to pay experts to assemble the program is far more than for a typical training course. In addition, the cost for a multimedia program increases dramatically when rewrites or updates are required.

The hardware needed to run multimedia programs may also turn out to be surprisingly expensive. Upgrading a PC to multimedia standards can cost from $800 to more than $1,300, depending on the number of adapter boards that need to be added and the memory capacity of the current system (Mann, 1992). The boards and adapters needed to facilitate the video compression/decompression are a major economic liability. Incorporating video technology into applications can range from $500 to over $3,000, with CD-ROM players costing about $500 (Miller, 1992). For example, some models of IBM's Ultimedia system cost about $6,000.

High quality multimedia applications may also be expensive to purchase. "Columbus: Encounter, Discovery, and Beyond" cost IBM almost $5 million in operational and programming expenses to develop (Elmer-Dewitt, 1991). A multimedia program produced for teachers in St. Louis, Missouri, to supplement biology, ecology and conservation classes cost more than $30,000 to develop (Schlax and Wiegner, 1991).

Lack of standards. In spite of the work of the MPCMC, there is still controversy regarding multimedia equipment standards, particularly in the area of video compression and decompression. Even in areas where *de facto* standards had already seemed to have emerged controversy can prevail. For example, at the end of 1992 Microsoft began shipping a new product called the Sound System. Surprisingly, the Sound System did not meet MPC standards. Given this kind of environment, potential buyers become less enthusiastic about investing in the technology until they witness substantial progress in this direction (Mann, 1992). Because of the many different components involved in multimedia computing, the standardization and compatibility of components becomes critical. Many different pieces of hardware, including video compression and decompression boards, sound recording tools, and the PC itself must have the exact configuration in order to operate properly. When discussion moves on to CD-ROM, the question of incompatibility becomes very crucial.

Uncertainty of its relevance. Confusion about multimedia's relevance still exists. Most users focus on software programs using text, graphics, images, and spreadsheets. The general perception is that multimedia can be used only for training. Corporate personnel have not yet internalized how multimedia technology fits into their overall corporate strategy of providing better information for employees, decision makers, and customers. However, as this area is more vigorously researched, before long, people will be more certain about its relevance.

Future Trends of Multimedia Computing

There is clear indication that multimedia technology will evolve into more than just training and education or kiosk-based or business communications applications. As consumers become more comfortable with multimedia technology, more and more they will demand the kinds of multimedia applications described in this chapter.

Corporations, in order to bolster their marketing strategies, have already begun to explore new multimedia applications based in fields such as expert systems. For example, Eckerd Drug Corporation recently installed a multimedia expert system entitled "Expert Advisor" (Vecchione, 1992). This application incorporates voice annotation, animation, and colorful graphics to provide Eckerd's 38 help-desk employees with answers to questions from pharmacists and other personnel who phone them from throughout the Southeast United States. "Expert Advisor" assists help-desk associates answer a range of questions, from as simple as how to fix a printer malfunction, to more difficult questions posed by pharmacists and other Eckerd personnel. When the pharmacist attempts to repair an item such as a broken printer, a help-desk associate can track the process and provide technical support because they are able to see the needed information which is displayed by "Expert Advisor."

As multimedia help-desk expert systems like "Expert Advisor" become more common, other industries will begin to use multimedia expert systems. The financial services industry today faces a great challenge as customers seem harder to satisfy because of their increased level of expectations. However, by using applications of expert systems linked with multimedia, employees at financial service institutions will become better trained to meet these increasing demands.

IBM, as it continues to develop its Ultimedia products, seems to be one of the most forward-looking corporations committed to the promotion of multimedia technology. Recently, the company began working with General Electric Corporation's NBC television network to transfer and digitize video (Hooper, 1992). In the future, this development will allow corporate computer screens to receive television transmissions via satellite from NBC News, its cable-affiliated operator CNBC, and possibly the local NBC station. Because personal computers have difficulty in handling the large amounts of data used in multimedia computing, IBM is claiming its mainframes can handle the task in a much shorter period.

In the field of education, multimedia technology has already proven that it can reshape the way students learn and teachers teach. Computer experts feel multimedia will transfer the focus of education from the teacher to the student. Already, many universities have developed multimedia classes for various science and arts subjects. In the future, multimedia classes may replace or supplement many large lecture courses. Students will be able to attend class in dorms, or even miles away in their homes.

It is a certainty that the number and variety of multimedia applications will continue to increase. For example, Microsoft has developed an interactive multimedia movie guide called "Cinemania" (Sprout, 1992). This program contains photos and recorded dialog from over 19,000 films produced from 1914 to 1991. By selecting "Casablanca," one can see a picture of Bogart and hear his famous line, "Here's looking at you, kid." Biographies, articles on movie topics, and movie reviews are other added features of "Cinemania."

Conclusion

Multimedia computing is a fascinating field with tremendous potential. Currently, some skeptics do not expect the technology to become a household item even though more applications of it are appearing in the marketplace daily. It sometimes seems that very sophisticated technological specialization is required for everyday users to derive the full benefits offered by multimedia.

However, in the future this situation will change. Before long, we will come to expect sound and video as a standard part of computer applications. Even now it is possible to insert animation into word processing documents and to provide voice annotations in spreadsheets and electronic-mail messages. The need for multimedia applications will expand with production efficiencies and increased consumer awareness.   But those looking for the "killer app" to dramatically increase the public's awareness will be sorely disappointed. Unlike the one-dimensional spreadsheets and word processing applications of today, multimedia is a multi-dimensional tool that can enhance existing applications; multimedia *per se* is not an application.

Multimedia computing is a blend of sight, sound, and animation which can be used to enhance existing applications thereby increasing their impact and effectiveness. To truly understand the technology's potential one might consider the analogy of a deaf person's viewing of a movie. Although the person may well be able to follow the general plot, bereft of their sense of hearing, the nuances, hence the excitement may be missed. Suppose that same person can suddenly hear. The plot becomes more interesting, perhaps more memorable, and even more personally relevant.

Advances in the telecommunications field and industry will also have a strong impact on multimedia computing. The traditional boundaries between the telecommunications and computing fields are now beginning to blur. Advances in networking technology now allow large amounts of data to be transmitted quickly over large geographic distances and the telecommunications industry is trying to capitalize upon these advances. A study completed by the Insight Research Corporations indicated that by 1997, 77% of educational and corporate workstations will have telecommunications facilities and 21% will have multimedia capabilities, compared to only 4.8% today (Booker, 1992). The effect of this trend is yet unknown, but the authors believe that in the future multimedia computing will become a daily part of people's lives, at their homes and in their offices.

Today, there is a plethora of alliances taking place among interexchange carriers, local telephone companies, and cable television companies to bring interactive multimedia-computing into the home. The impact on multimedia itself, coupled with the on-going technological changes occurring in telecommunications field cannot yet be calculated. It is the authors' dream that these events will help to democratize our information society and bring about a new world order. Distances will be reduced, time will be shortened, and quantity will be exchanged for quality. The concept of the global village can become an exciting reality consisting of tele-learning centers, tele-business centers, and other governmental and social tele-organizations. Sitting in their own homes, in their own countries, with communication links enhanced by multimedia, students all over the world will be able to attend any university and receive foreign degrees and diplomas; businesses large or small will be able to function globally, and world leaders will be able to communicate with anyone on the globe. Time and distance will be a barrier no more. The world you want to contact will be its virtual reality, right before you on the screen, in your home or office.

Endnote
[1]   Koffman, Gail. "Strike Up the Band", *LAN Magazine*, November 1992, pp. 50.

References

Amthor, G. (1992, May). Multimedia in education: An introduction. *T.H.E. Journal.* pp. 36.

Amthor, G. (1992, Nov/Dec.). Training distributed workforce. *Multimedia Solution.* pp. 3.

Baratto, L. (Ed.). (1992,July/August). *Multimedia Solutions.* pp. 7-09.

Baratto, L. (Ed.). (1992, Nov./Dec.). *Multimedia Solutions.* pp. 4-8, 15.

Booker, E. (1992, April) Multimedia seen as a spur to growth. *Computer World.* Vol. 26 n17. pp. 63-64.

Brittan, D. (1992, May/June). Being there: The promise of multimedia. *Technology Review.* pp. 43-50.

Compton's Multimedia Encyclopedia. pp. 7-9.

Dahmer, B. (1992, Jan.). Climbing the tower of technobabble. *Training & Development.* pp. 44-46.

Doyle, J. (1991, Jan./Feb.). Innovations in training. *Credit Magazine.* pp. 10-12, 14.

Elmer-Dewitt, P. (1991, Oct. 21) The world on a screen. *Time.* pp.80-82.

Executive Summary. (1992, Sept. 28). *InfoWeek.* pp. 10.

Filipcziak, B. (1991, May). Multimedia: Tilting at windmills? *Training.* pp. 73-74.

Fletcher, J.D. (1990, July). Effectiveness and cost of interactive video-disk instruction in defense training and education. *Institute for Defense Analysis.* pp. 2372.

Flynn, M. (1992, January 27). Multimedia must display maturity to sway buyers. *PC Week.* pp. 79.

International Business Machine Corporation.(1992,November/December) Multimedia in training. *Multimedia Solutions.* pp. 4-8

International Business Machine Corporation. (1991). *Multimedia solutions for business communications: Personalizing the way we present.*

International Business Machine Corporation. (1992). *Multimedia solutions for education: Personalizing the way we educate.*

International Business Machine Corporation. (1992). *Multimedia solutions for merchandising: Personalizing the way we sell.*

International Business Machine Corporation. (1992). *Multimedia solutions for public access: Personalizing the way we inform.*

International Business Machine Corporation. (1992). *Multimedia solutions for training: Personalizing the way we train.*

International Business Machine Corporation. *The Presidents: It all started with George.*

International Business Machine Corporation. (1991). *Ultimedia: Illuminated books and manuscripts.*

International Business Machine Corporation. (1991). *Ultimedia: The ultimate in multimedia solutions.*

Koffman, G. (1992, Nov.). Strike up the band. *LAN Magazine.* pp.55-57.

Mann, M. (1992, April 20). Authoring software is making strides toward maturity. *PC Week.* pp. 95, 101.

Miller, M. (1992, March 31). Multimedia:PCs and upgrad hist, MIDI software, authoring software. *PC Magazine.*

Polilli, S. (1992 January/Febuary). Multimedia PC (MPC) snowballing. *Computer Pictures.* pp. 63-65.

Schlax, J., & Wiegner, K. (1991, July 22). Showtime. *Forbes.* pp. 294-296.

Sprout, A. (1992, November 2). Multimedia movie guide. *Fortune.* pp. 94.

Strothman, J. Commodore Amiga, multimedia vet, aids in presentations, training. *Computer Pictures.* pp. s-14-s-16.

Sullivan, E. (1990, Dec. 10). High costs make multimedia feasible only with many users. *PC Magazine.* pp. 39-40.

Sullivan, K. Multimedia's impact blunted by expenses. *PC Magazine.* pp. 20.

The college of tommorrow. *U.S. New and World Report.* (1992, Sept. 28). pp.110,112.

Van Horn, R. (1991, March). Educational power tools: New instructional delivery systems. *Phi Delta Kappan.* pp. 521, 533.

Vecchione, A. (1992, Nov. 2). Expert system: Help is coming off the shelf. *Information Week.* pp. 78.

Wilson, J. (1992 Oct.). New tools for the informed patient.*NewMedia.* pp. 33.

Winkler, C. (1992, April 27). Multimedia Mania: Time for a reality check? *Electronic Business.* pp. 96-99.

Chapter 5

Guide to CD-ROM and Multimedia Publishing

Dataware Technologies, Inc.

CD-ROM and Competitive Advantage

In virtually every industry leading corporations are looking at CD-ROM (Compact-Disc-Read Only Memory) as a powerful business tool. For example:

- A leading computer manufacturer significantly improves the delivery of documentation, training materials, and maintenance releases by bundling a CD-ROM drive in its latest product line.
- A Baby Bell company publishes 300 telephone directories— covering every published listing in a six-state area on a single CD-ROM disc, with room to spare.
- A farm equipment supplier significantly improves its dealer communications by publishing its parts and price catalogs on CD-ROM.
- A major software company provides better technical support by distributing technical bulletins and help desk information on CD-ROM, increasing the effectiveness of telephone support and distinguishing their products in the process.
- A U.S. government agency converts its 20,000 page loose-leaf

procedures manual to CD-ROM. Monthly distribution to field offices saves time and reduces staff requirements.

• A major oil company publishes product and competitive information on CD-ROM for use by sales representatives with portable CD-ROM readers.

Why have these organizations made major commitments to CD-ROM? Why is there so much talk about CD-ROM lately, particularly when the technology has been available for over seven years?

There are two reasons. First, technological developments have substantially lowered the barriers to cost-effective use of CD-ROM. In the '80s, CD-ROM technology was still too expensive and applications too difficult to develop for many corporations. These conditions have changed dramatically. A technology that was once only potentially beneficial is now affordable, easy to use, and widely employed.

Second, CD-ROM has demonstrated clear benefits for business. More than 5,000 CD-ROM titles are now in print for a broad range of applications, including over 3,000 commercial products. One CD-ROM can hold the equivalent of 1,500 floppy disks, 250,000 pages of text, or 12,000 scanned images at an incremental media cost of only $2 per disc. This tremendous data storage capacity and low cost have led many people to focus on the media costs savings alone. Yet even greater benefits of the technology lie in the cost reduction and revenue generation it provides by delivering products and services more efficiently.

CD-ROM technology is a powerful tool that can:

• Improve sales performance
• Lower costs of sales
• Improve product and service quality
• Differentiate products in the marketplace
• Strengthen third-party distribution channels
• Dramatically improve customer service

For companies looking for a competitive edge, these are compelling benefits.

Three areas are emerging as key competitive advantages for business in the '90s: knowledge, time, and information. CD-ROM can enhance improvement activities in these areas, and often serves as the core of a competitive solution.

Knowledge

With expanding product lines, boutique manufacturing operations, and increasing pressure to customize products, businesses today are faced with providing a bewildering array of product possibilities and options. Retail, distributor, and support personnel are increasingly expected to attain more in-depth knowledge about a broader product line. Often simply finding the correct information is difficult. CD-ROM can not only provide correct and current product information, but assist in training personnel in the sales and use of products as well.

Newly emerging self-contained portable CD-ROM and multimedia players are revolutionizing the sales process. Salespeople can now carry an electronic reference that includes complete product catalogs, specifications, sample product applications, and sales and marketing promotions. Sales training time for complex products is reduced, a consistent and professionally prepared product presentation is delivered, and customer questions can be answered on the spot. The competitive advantage gained by organizations employing these technologies is substantial.

Time

Decisions are being made in increasingly complex environments, where any delay can cost lost revenues and customers. Measured through the parameters of market presence or response, time is emerging as a key competitive advantage. CD-ROM can assist in providing up-to-date information in a readily searchable format. Precious time isn't wasted searching for pertinent facts, and all appropriate details can be quickly assembled at once.

A major manufacturer of industrial heating and cooling systems identified the response time to answer product questions as a key competitive advantage. A target of one minute or less to respond to all customers' questions about any of the company's products established the overriding objective. In light of over 60 product catalogs dating back more than 50 years, a complete re-engineering of the company's information systems was required. The re-engineering included CD-ROM delivery of product information. Rather than using information technology simply as a productivity enhancement tool, it was identified as a way of re-engineering the company's customer communications.

Information

Corporate America today captures significantly more data than can be integrated for decision making. Distilling this data to a set of information useful for guiding the business requires both a business and technical perspective. The information challenge isn't how much data can be captured, but how to make the best decisions with the available data. CD-ROM is used to provide databases from which knowledge can be extracted by managers using sophisticated access software and "what-if" analysis.

CD-ROM Technology Today

A Technology Takes Off

CD-ROM has been a fortuitous technological development. It emerged through the coincidental convergence of several developments: the appearance of CD Audio in the mass market entertainment industry; the proliferation and standardization of personal computers in business; and the need for information providers of all types to find alternatives to distributing increasingly higher volumes of information on paper.

CD-ROM derives its low price and manufacturing availability from the consumer audio marketplace. CD Audio is the most successful consumer electronics product in history and has created a stable worldwide standard and manufacturing base. The success of CD Audio has fostered spin-off technologies such as CD-ROM.

CD-ROM is well on its way to becoming the preferred media for electronic distribution. Today there are over 3,000 commercial CD-ROM titles and in excess of 2,000 corporate in-house titles.[1] Figure 1 illustrates representative subject areas.

Besides technological advantages, CD-ROM owes its success to three key advantages it provides to *users*—multimedia, multiplatform, and multiple language applications.

Multimedia means delivering text, data, graphics, audio and video to end users. CD-ROM facilitates delivery of all of these information types in an integrated package. Information sets can be accompanied by audio and video clips describing significant areas. For example, a service manual could contain, along with the written text and diagrams, a video or animation sequence showing a critical procedure. Multimedia will play an increasing role in the way information is distributed and used in the '90s. Because multimedia

---

Over 3,000 Commercial CD-ROM Titles

Structured Data	**Text**
• Bibliographic Data	• Books
• Corporate Directories	• Government Regulations
• Credit Data	• Legal/Tax Information
• Financial Data	• Loose-leaf Publications
• Geographical Data	• Manuals
• Patent Information	• Medical Information
• People Directories	• Reference Collections
• Statistics	• Standards Information

Over 2,000 Corporate CD-ROM Applications

Structured Data	**Text**
• COM Replacement	• Audit Procedures
• Customer Data	• Contracts
• Forms Catalogs	• Engineering Standards
• Inventory	• Maintenance Releases
• Monthly Statements	• Policy Manuals
• Parts Catalogs	• Research
• Purchasing Data	• Technical Documentation
• Service Orders/Reports	• Training Manuals
• Spec Sheets	
• Transaction Histories	

Figure 1: CD-ROM Titles Today

presentations and interactive sessions require significant amounts of storage space for digitized images, sound and video. CD-ROM is uniquely positioned as the medium of choice for these new information formats.

Multiplatform refers to the use of one disc in different computer platforms. A formal CD-ROM standard, developed by an ad hoc industry group known as High Sierra, was approved by the International Standards Organizations (ISO) in 1987. By laying out the CD-ROM files in ISO 9660 format, a publisher insures that the CD-ROM will play on any standard CD drive attached to a computer with appropriate software.

The ISO 9660 standard was developed to be operating system independent. If access software that provides for multiplatform support is employed, a correctly formatted CD-ROM disc can be used in any of a number of computer environments—PC, Macintosh, UNIX, and others. This has allowed CD-ROM producers to publish discs not just for the PC, but for whatever workstation is on the end user's desk. CD-ROM can now replace paper because it's accessible on every desktop.

Multilingual usually implies a user interface that contains operations, hints and help text in different user-selected languages. An initialization parameter determines the start-up language displayed, with an option for the user to change the operating language interactively. The content of the CD-ROM is often only in one language, although a number of emerging applications include multiple versions of the source content in different languages. Multilingual applications help circumvent communication and training issues for international organizations.

The Software Challenge

A CD-ROM disc often contains 100 times more information than a typical personal computer database, but the rate at which the CD-ROM drive can get to various locations on the disc is at least ten times slower than a magnetic disk. The challenge for CD-ROM retrieval software is to reach a much greater volume of information quickly despite an inherently slower hardware technology.

To create applications for CD-ROM, two kinds of software are required: software to build and prepare an application to be put onto the disc (known as authoring software); and software for users to retrieve the information from the disc through their desktop computer (commonly referred to as retrieval software).

Because of CD-ROM's large capacity for data and slow access speed, software originally designed for magnetic media is ineffective when applied to optical media. CD-ROM software must be optimized to minimize disc access rather than use the multiple seek access assumed for magnetic media. There are now several vendors offering software that has been optimized for optical media and the best of these can equal or exceed magnetic media performance, even while searching several hundred megabytes of data.

CD-ROM drives are increasingly attached to computers other than DOS-based PCs, such as Windows, Macintosh and UNIX machines. The newest generation of CD-ROM development systems allows development of discs on one platform that can then be accessed from a variety of hardware platforms and network environments. This new breed of software is often referred to as multiplatform retrieval software.

The next generation systems will be required to prepare and deliver multimedia presentations in addition to data and text applications. The software challenges of the '90s will include not simply delivering multimedia, but integrating multimedia objects with corporate information collections and delivering these integrated databases at exceedingly high performance on a variety of computer platforms.

CD-ROM Advances - More for Less

These software improvements are among the most important developments to change the immediate outlook for cost-effective use of CD-ROM.   Five years ago the creation of a single CD-ROM application through a service bureau cost $50,000 to $100,000. For less money today, corporations can install a complete internal CD-ROM publishing capability, including both the software and premastering hardware.   Installations like these are capable of turning out more than 50 applications per year.

Other recent advances include:

- The cost of mastering and replicating 100 disc has fallen from $5,000 to $1,500.   Incremental discs can be purchased for less than $2 each.
- Capacity has increased from 550 megabytes to 700+ megabytes per disc.
- Stand-alone drive prices have fallen from $1,500 to under $500. Half-height drives for IBM PCs are available under $400. Volume purchases yield even lower prices.
- Recordable CD-ROM systems now available support complete in-house production of CD-ROMs for low volume or security-sensitive applications.   Blank media in low quantities cost less than $30.

Real Problems - Real Solutions

CD-ROM is solving real business problems today. Here are a few examples:

Problem -   **How can a rapidly expanding product line be supported cost-effectively?**

Solution -   Take a cue from several computer manufacturers and improve the effectiveness of sales and service personnel by publishing broad-based and/or constantly changing product information on CD-ROM.   This enables customers to help themselves when they might otherwise call for support. Not only is the need for direct staff involvement reduced, but customer satisfaction is improved.

Problem - **How can a product be supported in the dealer channel?**

Solution - Leading companies, from farm equipment suppliers to airlines, are taking advantage of this technology in the competitive dealer environment. Comprehensive catalogs for all products, including prices and specifications, are distributed on CD-ROM. This makes it easier for dealers to locate the right product.

Problem - **How can products be sold internationally without getting snarled in regulations and rising administrative costs?**

Solution - Follow the lead of an international consumer products manufacturer operating in more than 50 countries that has converted import/export databases to CD-ROM. The system reduces costly mistakes made by personnel who must search among 50,000 products for shipping codes and regulations and saves over $2 million per year.

Problem - **How can sales training and efficiency be improved?**

Solution - Adopt the strategy of a leading oil company that puts product and competitive information on CD-ROM and equips field salespeople with portable CD-ROM systems. Salespeople use the systems to identify the correct product and point out competitive advantages.

Problem - **How can the productivity of professional staff be increased?**

Solution - Learn from a major drug company that scanned chemical analysis reports to create a database of more than 100 years of research. The information had previously been accessible only in paper files and was therefore seldom used. The company has recov-

Reduce Costs and Improve Efficiency
- Lower information distribution costs
- Save information retrieval time
- Avoid duplicaiton of efforts
- Reduce errors and mistakes
- Improve learning rates
- Share knowledge
- Reduce network overload

Increase Productivity
- Deliver information when, where and how it is needed
- Make better decisions due to timely information access
- Increase product support capability

Increase Revenues
- Broaden product scope
- Improve sales and channel performance
- Present/Differentiate products
- Sell information

Improve Corporate/Product Image
- Satisfy customers
- Gain a reputation for technological leadership
- Increase channel loyalty

Figure 2: The Strategic Benefits of CD-ROM

ered the cost of the effort by eliminating the cost of duplicating previously performed tests.

A summary of the potential benefits of CD-ROM information integration and distribution is shown in Figure 2.

CD-ROM and Other Distribution Technologies

Many years ago the computer revolution promised the elimination of paper. We now know that the computer is the most prodigious producer of paper since the printing press. Paper has distinct advantages as an information distribution medium—it is completely portable requiring no additional hardware for access, and updates are simple (although incorporation of update pages can often be complex and time consuming). Paper also has disadvantages—it's cumbersome, hard to search, and environmentally unfriendly.

Virtually every large corporation and most small businesses are now producing, editing and updating information electronically. The next natural step in this process is electronic distribution. The benefits are not simply improved access and increased efficiency. Corporations and government agencies alike are embarking on significant efforts to reduce the amount of paper produced and distributed for efficiency, cost and environmental reasons.

Electronic distribution includes: telecommunications and local area networks; magnetic, floppy and cartridge disks; computer output to microfiche; facsimile; and CD-ROM. Each is appropriate for different types of information and distribution objectives.

Telecommunications is best for smaller amounts of information that have a short life span or must be updated frequently. The significant cost of creating and maintaining a telecommunications capability and the inherent bandwidth limitations reserve this alternative primarily for high-priority information.

Magnetic media are most appropriate for small databases requiring fairly frequent updates. Much of the information created by work groups on local area networks will be stored magnetically. As this information accumulates, storage becomes increasingly unwieldy.

Computer output microfiche and microfilm are used for high frequency distribution to multiple locations and for archival information where search requirements are minimal. Although these are mature technologies, this technology doesn't see wide use today due to dissatisfaction with the media and delivery system. Today there are fewer than one million microfilm readers compared to more than 100 million business and personal computers.

Facsimile is ideal for fast delivery of small amounts of paper-based information.

CD-ROM has broad areas of application due to the following unique advantages:

- Digital-based medium capable of delivering text, data, graphics, sound, and/or video
- Compatibility with personal computers and local area networks
- Can be shared over local/wide area networks
- Information can be exported to other computers and software programs
- Very high capacity at a significantly lower cost than other distribution alternatives
- Searching, sorting, and retrieval capability superior to:
    - paper
    - computer output microfiche[2]
    - microfilm
    - on-line[3]
- Low cost for volume distribution

CD-ROM has limitations that make it inappropriate for some applications and not a viable substitute for traditional storage.

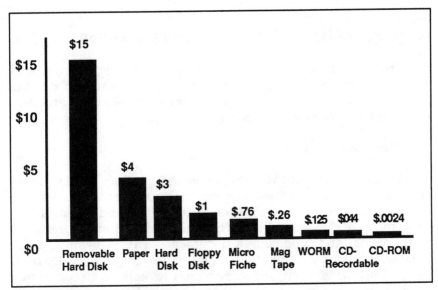

Figure 3: Cost Per Megabyte

These limiting factors include:

- CD-ROM is read-only without the ability to modify the data on disc. However, there are some emerging technological approaches that will allow appending data to an already existing data set on CD-ROM.
- A mastering step is required to create the master and replicas. Mastering costs $1,500 and takes 3 days with faster turnaround available for an extra charge. CD-Recordable technology allows in-house mastering for low volumes of discs, but the blank media are more expensive than mastered CD replicas.
- The slow speed and large capacity of optical discs require special software to provide application performance comparable to magnetic disk.
- The drive must be added to the typical desktop workstation at a cost of $400 to $800. Many of the latest generation of PCs now come with a CD-ROM drive already installed.

CD-ROM's strengths make it most appropriate for applications with any of the following requirements:

- Information distributed to multiple locations
- Mixed test, data, graphic, and/or audio/video information
- Large data volumes
- Fast access time
- Extensive searching, sorting, and retrieval

A Value Multiplier for Information Systems

Four current information management technologies are emerging as high priorities for most organizations over the next decade: electronic publishing, local area networking, client-server architectures, and transaction processing.

Electronic Publishing

To remain competitive, businesses that produce large volumes of paper-based information are moving to electronic publishing. Various types of information, such as text, data, and graphics, can be combined electronically, saving substantial time in revising, reformatting, and producing a document. These advantages are great as far as they go, but they usually stop just short of distribution. Converting electronic information to non-electronic format when there are more than 25 million potential electronic readers on the desks of corporate America does not make sense for many applications. This is a large area for cost savings and productivity improvement.

Local Area Networks and Work Group Computing

The CD-ROM standards were established with networks as an expected requirement. The ISO 9660 standard incorporates the basic hardware and media specifications required to make a CD-ROM network compatible. Once a network is equipped with drives and appropriate software, virtually any CD-ROM disc—assuming appropriate network license agreements and use of the ISO 9660 standard —can be shared on the local area network. Each attached drive provides over 700 megabytes of read-only information to the network nodes. By placing one or more CD-ROM drives on each local area network or in each department, an organization provides ready access to internal information and externally purchased information relevant to that department or work group. Examples of typical work group information requirements are shown in Figure 4.

Downsizing and Client-Server Architectures

Corporations and government agencies are rapidly replacing centrally located, monolithic information systems with distributed architectures. Driving forces include high maintenance on centrally

Service
- Documentation
- Maintenance Releases
- Service Call Reports
- Trouble Shooting Guides
- Maintenance Histories
- Parts Lists
- Inventory
- Warranty Listings

Marketing and Sales
- Catalogs
- Specification Sheets
- Parts Lists
- Prices
- Inventory
- Purchase History

Operations
- Inventory
- Parts Lists
- Stock Number Cross Reference
- Bill of Materials
- Order Data
- Engineering Standards
- Parts Where Used
- Facility and Equipment Registers

Procurement
- Inventory
- Bill of Materials
- Cumulative Order Data
- Vendor Cross Reference Data
- Index of Suppliers

Research and Development
- Research Reports
- Standards Information
- Bibliographic Databases

Figure 4: Work Group Information Requirements

located mainframe systems, long lead times for new application developments, and the increasing need for organizations to provide flexible and responsive information systems. Client-server architectures allow a decentralized information enterprise, allowing local control and maintenance of information pertinent to the work group.

CD-ROM is often a vital component of downsizing efforts. While a new decision support application for a centrally located information system may require lengthy lead time, extracting a copy of the information, committing it to CD-ROM and using fourth generation access tools for decision support is proving successful. This newly emerging use of CD-ROM is helping to accelerate many corporations' downsizing efforts.

Transaction Processing Systems

Some of the best examples of information as a competitive tool are found in those industries that have been transformed by electronic transaction processing such as banking, brokerage and travel. Other examples include the pharmaceutical and auto parts industries, and a variety of other retail businesses where transaction information is essential to the successful operation of the business.

The leaders in transaction processing are now taking the next step in strategic information delivery: CD-ROM. Purchasing activity in corporate and government organizations is converted to CD-ROM for trend analysis. Retailers in the auto, trucking, and appliance replacement parts business are using CD-ROM to find the right part and make the sale.

Using CD-ROM systems to augment point-of-transaction information, improve customer service, and boost sales is widely applicable to other industries. The two technologies work in partnership: on-line transaction processing delivers accurate and time-sensitive information while large volumes of related but less time-sensitive information is delivered on CD-ROM.

How CD-ROM Can Benefit Your Organization

Existing Content

CD-ROM can have a significant impact on an organization's bottom line, but identifying where in an organization to start with CD-ROM applications can be difficult. Most organizations that see an immediate impact with CD-ROM base their initial applications on pre-existing content. CD-ROM is used to improve and expand existing information sources. As these organizations integrate CD-ROM into their business systems, they introduce new content sources to further leverage the investment in CD-ROM development platforms and readers.

Information Used and Produced

To determine if optical information distribution is appropriate for an organization, it's appropriate to analyze the sources and uses of information. One recommended approach divides the organization's major activities between serving the customer and supporting infrastructure. Figure 5 illustrates a typical manufacturing company's primary and infrastructure activities. For each major activity, the information produced and the information used in performing critical functions is identified.

CD-ROM Applications Portfolio

After the information used and produced is arranged according

Primary Activities	Operations	Marketing & Sales	Service	Customer
Information Used	Orders Engineering Standards Purchasing Information	Inventory Orders Parts Lists Design Specifications Market Information Sales Information Inventory	Training Parts Lists Customer Information Inventory	Documentation Maintenance Parts Catalogs
Information Produced	Parts Lists Inventory Ship to Lists Bill of Materials Parts Where Used Facility & Equipment Registers	Parts Catalogs Customer Database Prospect Database Purchase Histories Spec Sheets Pricing Contracts	Service Call Reports Trouble- Shooting Guides Maintenance History Training Service Orders Warranty Listings	Warranty Information Product Improvements Service Requests Customer Information Orders
Infrastructure Activities	Research & Developmet	Purchasing	Human Resources	Financial & Admin.
Information Used	External Research Patent Information Standards Information Bibliographic Research	Inventory Orders Bill of Materials Vendor Information Price Lists Product Information	Government Regulations Recruiting Information	Accounting Standards Government Regulations Accounting Input Budget Input
Information Produced	Internal Research Engineering Standards	On Order Reports Vendor Information Product Information Price Lists	Training Manuals Personnel Records	Policy & Procedure General Audit & Record Retention Budget Information Accounting Information

Figure 5: Information Used and Produced

to priority, it can be organized into an applications portfolio for the organization. The applications portfolio identifies high return activities by classifying information according to mission/activity critical, management/support, and archival. CD-ROM will have the greatest impact on mission and activity-critical information. Figure 6 illustrates the applications portfolio for an insurance firm.

This applications planning process results in a list of high priority applications where CD-ROM distribution yields substantial benefits. This application portfolio becomes the focal point in the technology acquisition process. Those applications that will serve as prototypes to test the technology warrant additional planning to create a complete profile of the user, the information, and the anticipated benefits.

Value Multiplier	Agency Info	Marketing & Sales	Operations
Electronic Publishing		Renewal & Policy Changes	
Database Publishing		Policy Holders File	Claim Payment History
Product & Service Info	Rate Books	Rate Books	
Policy & Standards Info	Policy Manuals		Cumulative Policy Register
Customer & Transaction Info		Renewal & Policy Changes	Transaction Register

☐ **Activity Critical** ▨ **Management Support** ☐ **Archival**

Figure 6: CD-ROM Applications Portfolio-Insurance

Multimedia Applications Portfolio

Multimedia typically implies adding new content through additional data types (such as audio and video) to existing applications. Adding multimedia is reasonable only where it provides significant productivity or communications improvement. Starting with existing content is recommended, as multimedia production costs can quickly accumulate. As with CD-ROM applications, those selected for development should be the high value/activity-critical applications in an organization.

Like the CD-ROM applications portfolio, a portfolio of multimedia applications will pinpoint those areas where applications development will have the greatest impact. Figure 7 illustrates a representative multimedia applications portfolio.

It's important to note that multimedia delivery is immature today. Hardware, software, and data standards are just emerging. While traditional CD-ROM data types (data, text, and graphics) have arrived at platform-neutral standards, multimedia sources, such as audio and video, have not. A CD-ROM application today with traditional content can be portable across numerous end-user computer platforms (assuming appropriate multiplatform software has been employed). A multimedia application must be designed for a specific computer platform.

	Operations	Marketing & Sales	Service
Multimedia Publishing		Product Catalog w/ Sound or Video	Tech Doc. with Sound
Multimedia Database	Employee Databases		Parts Catalog with Sound
Multimedia Presentations	Management Presentations	Sales Presentations	
Multimedia Training	Personnel Training		Service Training
Multimedia Sales Systems		Multimedia Kiosks	

Figure 7: Multimedia Applications Portfolio

Selecting the Right CD-ROM Approach

Once CD-ROM has been identified as a viable technology for existing requirements, the next step is to determine the best approach for developing applications. This entails both a technical and business evaluation. As with most computer applications, software is the key component. Before considering the business options, it's important to understand the match of data type to software support.

Matching Content With Software

When evaluating CD-ROM application software, the type of information supported becomes critical. A brief explanation of the key information types—structured data, text, graphics, audio, and video—is provided below.

Structured data is the most prevalent data type on CD-ROM. Examples of structured data are information from computer databases, bibliographies, directories, catalogs, and numeric data (as illustrated in Figure 1). Structured information may contain text fields, but unlike full text, structured data does not have to be exclusively in the form of sentences, paragraphs, and chapters. It can also be partially or entirely in phrases or fields.

Text includes information derived from books, journals, reports, and documentation. Textual information is often structured by an outline for browsing purposes. Users can select chapters, sections, and headings as convenient access points, provided they know that the material of interest is located within that part of the text.

Key word searches provide another way of accessing text. Users can find information when its location is not obvious, or when its occurrence is so frequent that looking through a book index becomes tedious or impractical. Key terms may be combined to find unique "and," "or," and "not" related documents.

Many text retrieval systems are enhancing search capabilities through the addition of hypertext. Hypertext describes different ways of linking related items to each other. In its simplest form, known as "sideways browsing," the user selects a displayed word or phrase and, with a single keystroke, finds all documents that contain that word. More sophisticated systems search for related terms as well, or provide for item linking created by the publisher or user.

Graphics includes pictures, charts, illustrations, and page images. These can exist as bit-mapped images or structured graphics (vector). Graphics are normally associated with either structured data (such as a parts catalog with part diagrams) or text (such as a maintenance manual with illustrations).

One of the most common types of graphics found in CD-ROM products today is bit-mapped page images. A scanner is used to capture an entire document page as a grid of black and white pixels. Text, as well as drawings, pictures, and tables are represented as part of the same image. Captured this way the text is not machine-readable and therefore not searchable. Only the whole page can be indexed and accessed. This approach is useful where the arrange-ment of the text on the page is complex and meaningful, where graphics appear with regularity, and when the user can find the desired page by means of a key word or hierarchical index that points to the page image.

Audio includes voice, music, and sound clips. While the CD disc was originally developed for audio, using audio on CD-ROM is relatively new. Hardware and format standards are just now emerging, and often are computer-platform specific. Developers who choose to add audio content to CD-ROM applications today must select from several emerging standards.

Video can range from animation sequences to full screen, 30 frame-per-second display. Animation sequences are usually gener-ated with a computer graphics package while video is typically sampled from video tape or video disc. Using CD-ROM for video is also new and immature. Hardware and media standards for rudimentary animation, much less video, are just emerging and several standards are competing.

Many CD-ROM applications use graphics, audio, and video, and are developed with authoring software optimized for video graphics and sound, instead of data and text. Applications that also require sophisticated data and text searching must be merged with these multimedia "front ends."

Because standards have not emerged for multimedia delivery, adding multimedia content to a CD-ROM title today typically limits the title to a specific target computer platform. Some publishers elect to replicate the multimedia information on the CD-ROM, producing multimedia content specific to each target platform. This option requires substantial space on the disc for the multimedia objects.

Application Development Options

The business alternatives for developing CD-ROM applications range from complete in-house development to complete service bureau contracting. Figure 8 illustrates some of the tradeoffs. However, the right approach for your organization also depends on the software development path selected. Discussion of the four common development paths follow.

In-House Software Development. Writing customized CD-ROM software is the least popular option, because of the high development and maintenance costs. Keeping custom products updated in a rapidly changing multiplatform environment is also difficult. Many of the commercial publishers who opted to write their own software in the mid-'80s are now abandoning this approach and licensing software from vendors focused on multiplatform CD-ROM software development.

In those cases where the software developed in-house has been successful, the product was typically written for a single application of limited scope and duration. Unfortunately, when additional applications emerge, the original software frequently cannot be

	Services	In-House
Short Term Issues:	Prove Concept Overcome Data Prep Ensure Optimal Launch Learn from First Project	Data Availability Staff Availability Systems Availability Up Front $$ Availability
Long Term Issues:	Technology Infrastructure Keep Expense variable Assignable Responsibility Insure Technical Response Avoid Up Front $$	Internalize Learning Curve Development Close to Users Lower Per Application Costs Increase Enhancement Control Avoid Priority Problems

Figure 8: Services or In-House Development

readily adapted or modified. Consequently, the development process must begin all over again.

As a result, writing custom software is almost never cheaper than licensing. The cost of writing a simple program for CD-ROM access with documentation is a minimum of two person-years of senior programmer time. The best packages available today have at least ten times that much investment in programmer time, and their developers have more resources to add features and enhancements.

Commercial Software. Over 20 commercial CD-ROM software products are available today for building databases and retrieving information from those databases. These packages range from simple and inexpensive text-only packages to highly flexible "tool kits" for programmers, to multi-function authoring systems.

Organizations developing CD-ROM titles have several options. While the authoring software and retrieval engine must be acquired from the same vendor, there are various ways in which the user interface can be developed. Most (but not all) CD-ROM development systems provide a "standard" user interface. This interface is performance tuned to the retrieval engine and should allow substantial customizing without programming.

Some advanced systems allow development of custom user interfaces by writing software. Dividing the retrieval software into user interface and retrieval engine is a useful differentiation—it allows corporations that wish to develop highly customized user interfaces to capitalize on the advanced technology available in CD-ROM-based retrieval engines. This approach involves more time and personnel than a standard user interface, but results in a custom product tailored to the organization's needs. Figure 9 illustrates the tradeoffs in user interface development.

User interface development systems are emerging that attach to

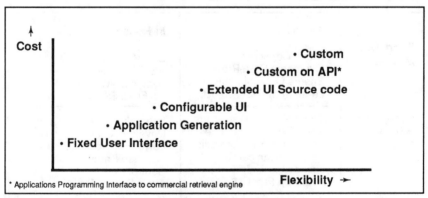

Figure 9: Application Development Approaches

retrieval engines through linking mechanisms such as Dynamic Linked Libraries in Microsoft Windows. These allow CD-ROM developers to attach a third party user interface to a CD-ROM retrieval engine, but generally require some programming. With the increasing popularity of client-server applications, development systems that support this architectural approach are expected to gain popularity in the future.

The PC software industry has produced several text retrieval products not originally designed for CD-ROM. While many of these products offer good to excellent support for small collections of text stored on magnetic disk, they may be inadequate for CD-ROM. Some of the most important differences between mission-critical retrieval software and these low-end packages lie in the range, flexibility and sophistication of searches that may be performed. Without more powerful searching it's difficult to capture the needed information without being overwhelmed with unneeded material as well. Figure 10 illustrates some of the differences in the types of searching that may be performed with software designed for CD-ROM.

Applications vary by the demand they place on the retrieval engine, and the engine's performance is only as good as the authoring software used to create the data structures. Before purchasing commercial software, it may be prudent to develop a product with a service bureau to evaluate the technology.

Service Bureaus. The early CD-ROM service bureaus became successful by creating CD-ROM products that provided them a built-in opportunity for repeat business. In the beginning very little was known about making a good CD-ROM product, so publishers were captive customers, willing to pay high fees to avoid costly mistakes.

The biggest disadvantage of working with a traditional service bureau is the loss of control over the product. There is little flexibility to prototype or enhance a product quickly or easily. More importantly, the investment in a service bureau does not allow expertise in the technology to be leveraged within the corporation.

CD-ROM Publishing Platform. A new type of company has emerged that is effectively a "hybrid" service bureau/software development company. This new generation of companies provides a transition strategy for organizations that would like to use CD-ROM but have not yet developed expertise in the technology. These new hybrids will both develop applications as well as license their CD-ROM development software in the form of a "publishing platform."

The hybrid service bureau/development company creates the first application working closely with a company's technical staff. The technical staff learns how to create an application and can then

Type of Search	CD-ROM Software	Typical Text Retrieval
Keyword	X	X
Wildcard-Trailing Truncation	X	X
Wildcard-Leading Truncation	X	
Wildcard-Within Word	X	
Multiple Wildcards Per Word	X	
Phonetic	X	
Line/Entry	X	
Numerical	X	X
Vector	X	
Date	X	
Binary	X	
Pop-Up Browse of Any Index	X	
Stopword Lists	Many	1
Cross Reference Search	X	
Adjacency-Word Level	X	Maybe*
Adjacency-Sentence Level	X	
Adjacency-Field Level	X	
Order Required	X	
Order Not Required	X	
Boolean and Wildcards	X	
Boolean and Adjacency	X	
Multiple Search Screens	X	
Encryption/Password Protection	X	
Graphics-Link to File	X	Maybe**
Graphics-Decompress & Display	X	
Graphics- Zoom, Size & Pan	X	

* If there is any adjacency it is probably slow and limited. True adjacency requires complex indexing of the location of every word in the file. To avoid this, low-end software simply searches for all occurrences and then checks each occurrence to locate occurrences together. This is very slow, especially on optical media.

* Most PC software has no graphics display functions and simply allows a link to an external graphics file. Programs which display graphics often don't zoom and size images, making it difficult to read detail on most PC screens.

Figure 10: CD-ROM Software vs. Low Ended Test Management Software

bring the software platform in-house for subsequent titles. A publisher can acquire a license to both the authoring software and the retrieval software it will distribute with the discs to its users.

The advantage of this approach is that control of the product development is in the hands of those most knowledgeable about the customer. In addition, software specifically designed for CD-ROM lowers the internal product development costs and time required. CD-ROM expertise is developed internally, and as expertise increases, the costs are reduced further.

The major disadvantage of the in-house publishing platform is the investment required for software, hardware and support staff. These can be kept to a minimum in the early stages by creating a pilot application using the preferred publishing platform vendor as a service bureau. The vendor's product can later be brought in-house so that the investment is not made until the software has proven successful and the applicability of the technology to the entire applications portfolio has been evaluated. While it may be required to educate the vendor on the data types and information usage profile of your industry, the pilot program is often the optimal means of determining if the software is suitable. Staff can be added as needed and the system brought in-house when ready. This provides a smooth transition without disrupting existing customers.

Generally speaking, the more products, enhancements and updates planned, the more in-house publishing platform makes sense. A publishing platform that can be leveraged across a wide variety of applications is the most cost-effective way to introduce CD-ROM technology into an organization.

Successful CD-ROM Publishing In House

Assuming potential applications justify in-house development and that the publishing platform approach is preferable, the next step is to select appropriate hardware and software. First choose software that meets the application portfolio requirements, then choose hardware that can support it.

The applications portfolio drives requirements for the software. By combining identified requirements for all applications, the ultimate needs for an authoring capability are derived. Figure 11 is an example. Most organizations will identify, at a minimum, a requirement to integrate text, data, and graphics. A vendor's retrieval software engine should be able to demonstrate its viability in commercial use. Concentrating on vendors that have published titles and have licensed software for in-house use will result in a short list of finalists to evaluate. A list of commercial CD-ROM

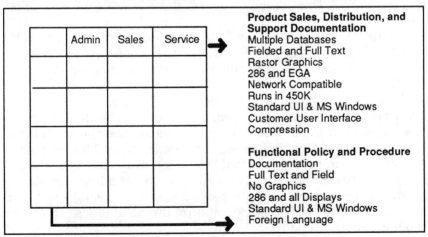

Figure 11: Applications Portfolio Defines Requirements

products produced using the vendor's retrieval engine is a good indicator of credibility. Seeing a demonstration of published CD-ROM applications is even better.

Other Software Considerations

Once software that meets the application requirements has been identified, several other factors should be considered before a decision is made.

Performance. Users familiar with applications on personal computers have developed certain performance expectations, with most actions requiring not more than a few seconds. Actions that take longer must give the user some feedback that the action is in progress and optionally, how much is complete.

CD-ROM applications generally involve searching hundreds of megabytes, with drives that are much slower than magnetic drives. To solve the problem, the software must be optimized for both CD-ROM and data type. Vendors should be able to demonstrate CD-ROM applications with the number of records and megabytes of information similar to your planned applications. CD-ROM optimized software should meet user expectations for magnetic based searching, even when searching hundreds of megabytes.

Multiplatform. With appropriate software the same CD-ROM disc can be used in different computer platforms, such as DOS, Windows, Macintosh, and UNIX. However, the development software must support this multiplatform authoring, and provide retrieval software for each desired environment. Many commercial products are available for developing Windows or Macintosh applications only. They preclude using the CD-ROM in any other environment.

Limiting the application to a single platform may limit the benefits gained. This is especially true when replacing paper because printing must continue until every user is supported with CD-ROM.

Normally developers focus on a single area, such as word processing, numerical databases, or graphics. The CD-ROM software developed must push the technological envelope in all three dimensions. Multiplatform and multimedia add additional dimensions. This multi-dimensional challenge must be met without sacrificing performance and ease of use on an inherently slower hardware technology. Given these challenges, choosing a software partner requires careful consideration of the capabilities of both the product and the vendor.

Application Development

In addition to the functional capabilities of the software, the level of software support for creating applications is a consideration. One of the main impediments to CD-ROM use has been the level of programming and effort required to develop applications. For most organizations only a few of the potential applications justify programming. The broad base of applications must be implemented by non-programmers. In evaluating CD-ROM authoring software, development capabilities that aid application creation without coding should be considered. Authoring software can aid applications development, thus saving valuable time and avoiding programming.

Some advanced software authoring systems have front-end programs for reading and converting data from a variety of formats, including electronic publishing systems or on-line databases. These data reading programs provide a broad funnel for capturing information. Photocomposition, database, and word processor formats can be supported by answering menu prompts, saving several person-weeks of conversion programming for each application. Publishers planning a CD-ROM product using a database that is already on-line can usually format the database directly by using the authoring system.

Interface design and development determines how the end user will interact with the information. Query, display, print, export and other capabilities are executed via the interface.

The most common model is a fixed interface. This option is popular with many text-only products because the query options are limited. Products that integrate text, data and graphics generally require a more sophisticated approach than is available in this model.

The preferred approach borrows from the "application generator" techniques developed for DBMS access. The authoring software provides a model interface. Customizing is done by non-programmers through screen layout and painting, with the authoring software generating the code required in the background. Multiple user interfaces, including search screen, data views, and print options, are possible through switching and editing screens.

The more flexible this approach is, the less programming will be required. Even when custom work is required, the first complete application can be tested using the "standard" interface to insure the information and user requirements are met. The testing process also demonstrates the size of data and indexes, the amount of compression, the memory required, and performance if simulation capabilities are available (See Appendix B: Selecting Hardware—Authoring System). The test application can be used to obtain valuable feedback and determine if the "standard" approach is in fact acceptable.

Other authoring software considerations include facilities for testing and debugging, end user application creation, and creation of foreign language versions of applications.

A robust authoring system contributes value in many ways. It increases the number of applications that can be produced, while improving the quality of each application. It increases learning throughout the organization and puts the technology in the hands of the people who best understand the user and the data. It saves time and money during development and minimizes ongoing support and maintenance costs. Finally, it ensures that a majority of applications can be developed with a single system so that multiple systems need not be supported.

Staffing Requirements

A single application engineer can develop and update a significant number of applications using a properly designed development system. The steps in the first table in Figure 12 indicate the staffing required to develop a typical CD-ROM application using commercial authoring software. The second table indicates the staffing required as the application is updated. (*Note:* Use of a programmer's tool kit requires higher skill levels and generally more time.)

Given the time involved in indexing and developing a full application, the ideal approach is to prototype a complex application using a small subset of data. This ensures up front that the data and software will work together.

Organizational Requirements

For in-house CD-ROM publishing to be a success, there must be an organizational commitment to optical publishing. In some cases one division or group within the organization has taken the lead in successfully demonstrating the utility and cost-effectiveness of using CD-ROM for information delivery. In other organizations, a coordinated corporate-wide effort has been launched simultaneously in many areas of the company.

Publishing corporate data on CD-ROM can be a high profile activity. Discs in the hands of customers and distributors create

Steps and Staffing Requirements for Application Development

Step	Skill Level	Time
Data Conversion and Filtering	Developer*	1 day plus
Database Definitions	Developer	1/2 day - 1 day
Screen Layout	Developer	1-2 days **
Indexing Specification	Developer	1/2 - 2 days
Indexing and Binding	None	10 Megabytes/hr.
Debugging and Texting	Developer	1-2 days
Help Screen	Skilled User	1/2 -3 days
Install Program	Developer	1/2 -1 day
Creation of Premaster Tape	Developer	1/2 - 1 day

• PC DBMS Developer
** Assumes screen painting interface design with no programming.

Steps and Staffing Requirements for Updates to Applications

Step	Skill level	Time
Index and Bind	Skilled User	Set up, then machine time @ 10 Megabytes/Hr.
Quality Assurance	Skilled User	1 hour-1 day
Creation of Premaster Tape	Developer	1/2 - 1 day

Figure 12

positive exposure for the company. Internal information takes on a high profile when it appears on the same medium as Mozart or Madonna.

Publishing Partner

When making the commitment to optical publishing, make sure your technology partner is equally committed.

In a new and emerging industry, it is sometimes difficult to determine who the successful, long term players will be. The credentials of the management team, the financial resources of the company, the reputation of the investors and the company's track record become critical considerations. A history of software development companies suggests that during the early stages of a new technology, a focused product strategy is a key ingredient for ultimate success. For example, most of the leading software products in the PC arena were originally developed by companies whose business was dedicated to one category, such as presentation graphics or word processing.

Finally, because of the high profile nature of optical publishing, leading organizations have already taken the step and have bet their reputation on the vendor they selected. The software developers most likely to be the long term winners should already have a list of demanding and satisfied customers.

Summary

In an age suffering from "information overload" and "drowning in paper," CD-ROM technology is positioned to deliver substantial benefits. CD-ROM provides a means for solving certain information problems when applied to critical activities and undertaken with a clear sense of how information is used by the knowledge worker. CD-ROM fits naturally into corporate computing strategies and leverages major trends, including electronic publishing, work group computing, and transaction processing.

Successful CD-ROM applications integrate knowledge about the information user, information content, software and hardware technology. The ideal CD-ROM publisher is the group that best understands the user and information content. The publisher resides within the organization and must control the software and hardware technology to effectively serve the user.

Technology solutions are available from companies that have focused their business on creating CD-ROM technology for in-house use. This focus is critical because of the challenges in CD-ROM development, ranging from performance, to multiple information types, to indexing gigabytes of data on multiple discs.

Those organizations that have acquired the technology and delivered applications are the greatest proponents of CD-ROM. Their experience suggests that CD-ROM will become a major competitive tool in the hands of information managers. Organizations that use this technology creatively will reap substantial benefits.

Appendix A - Optical Publishing Industry Overview

Optical publishing is a term that describes the result as well as the process of distributing information on optical media. This is similar to the term "electronic publishing" which refers to the distribution of information in digital form over telecommunications or broadcast systems, and to print publishing, which includes books, magazine, and reports on paper or microfiche. Estimates put print publishing at more than 90% of the publishing universe, with electronic at 10%. Optical publishing today represents about 5% of the electronic publishing share, or 0.5% overall.

The term "optical publishing" generally refers to information distributed on CD-ROM. Broadly speaking, it can also be used to refer to laser video disc and interactive video disc (used primarily for merchandising and training). Optical storage (versus optical publishing) refers to the use of write-once and erasable optical discs. The technologies are quite different—a critical distinction being that optical publishing involves the idea of volume production and distribution.

The traditional publishing industry —book publishing houses, magazine publishers, and educational textbook providers—are increasingly involved in optical publishing as the industry becomes more established. The publishers who took the initial risk to adopt the medium and get it established, however, are not household names with popular properties. They are publishers selling into library and technical markets with specialized information, new publishers with no prior publication history, and companies from the computer industry moving into publishing.

A majority of the first CD-ROM titles were transferred from the on-line publishing world, adapted from files already available by modem from remote host database services. since then, content has broadened to include numerous application areas, as indicated in Figure 1. Most observers agree that this is just the tip of the iceberg for potential use of CD-ROM.

Libraries were among the first CD-ROM customers. The technology was a good fit for several reasons. A CD-ROM product has a known cost like a book or magazine subscription, and can be budgeted and made accessible to all patrons without charging back variable on-line fees. Libraries are a known market that enable publishers to target customers with needs and purchasing power. Librarians also had a great deal of experience with on-line searching. They were eager to learn about CD-ROM and share their experiences with others in their field.

Corporations are the next major market for CD-ROM—and they have significantly surpassed libraries in volume use. Like libraries, corporate users benefit from broad familiarity with computers and on-line searching techniques. Corporations are customers for reference products in resource centers; business, financial and directory products at the departmental level; technical and scientific reference products at the research and engineering level; and desktop publishing and related products at the individual level. Corporations are also the leading producers of in-house titles for documentation, database distribution, corporate records, and other internal applications.

Computer software producers have become publishers and distributors. An increasing number are using CD-ROM to distribute software products, particularly where distribution on floppy disk is too unwieldy. In some products content becomes integrated with the application, such as Lotus 1-2-3 and Apple Macintosh Hypercard. Microsoft Corporation, the largest PC software producer, has made invaluable contributions to the optical publishing industry with numerous CD-ROM products, CD-ROM conferences, books about CD-ROM, and the MS-DOS extensions for CD-ROM.

Government is another major market. There are both commercial and in-house training applications in this market. Documentation for military equipment, training programs, standards, and administrative information are among the applications. Many government agencies are taking a commercial publishing role with government collections that are distributed to the Federal Depository Library network and have markets in the private sector, such as patents, social, economic, agricultural and business data, and technical reports.

Other market sectors that are primarily vertical and commercial today include the professions such as law, medicine, health, education, and the emerging consumer market. CD-ROM has also been attractive to publishers and users in niche markets where very specialized information is used by a very specific group of customers.

Optical publishing is the subject of a major annual survey conducted by InfoTech, an international consulting and research firm specializing in optical disc and information technology markets. The most recent results are published in the *Optical Publishing Industry Assessment 1992*, which is available from InfoTech, Woodstock, VT (802-257-1038). To create this report, InfoTech interviewed hundreds of publishers worldwide and applied a sophisticated methodology, drawing on over eight years of direct experience in the optical disc industry.

InfoTech established a tracking system in 1987 allowing it to measure the impressive growth in the industry from 1988 on. The aggregate data from this report is high-lighted here for total titles in Figure A1, installed base of CD-ROM readers in Figure A2, and total industry revenue in Figure A3. Titles in print have grown from fewer than 100 in 1986 to an estimated 5,000 in 1992. The installed base of readers has grown from 9,000 in 1986 to an estimated 4,000,000 in 1992. Total revenue, which includes titles and reader hardware for commercial and in-house applications, has increased from $31 million in 1986 to $3.9 billion worldwide in 1992.

InfoTech estimates that the commercial market shipped 3,256 titles valued at nearly $2 billion in 1992 and forecasts growth to nearly 8,000 titles valued at over $4 billion by 1995. Commercial revenue is calculated at retail prices and based on confidentially reported unit sales data collected from over 80% of the publishers.

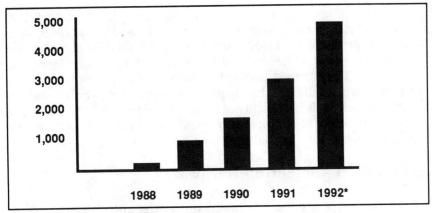

Figure A1: Worldwide Titles in Print

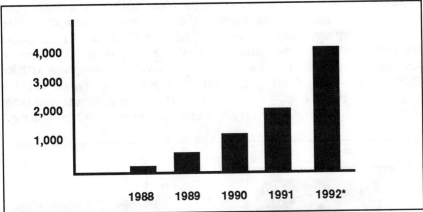

Figure A2: Worldwide Installed Base (in thousand units)

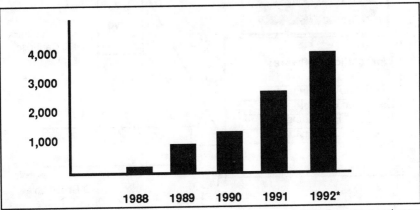

Figure A3: Worldwide Revenue

* 1992 figures are estimates
Source: InfoTech

The in-house market is estimated to have released over 2,000 titles in 1992, roughly 40% of all titles released. By 1995, it is forecast to grow to over 3,500 titles. Titles published for in-house are not directly counted because of the great difficulty in identifying producers. They are estimated by the vendors serving that sector with software, media and hardware. Although the in-house data is not statistically valid, it is still a strong indicator of what the in-house sector represents to the optical publishing industry and is widely regarded as the best available estimation of output.

Appendix B - Selecting Hardware

Hardware is needed to support authoring and delivery.

Authoring System. Hardware systems used for authoring are typically called premastering systems. Most authoring system vendors assume that development will take place on PCs, although there are authoring systems available for other platforms. The highest performance authoring hardware available is recommended due to its higher indexing/processing throughput, for example a UNIX/RISC based workstation. Processing of very large databases will also require additional hardware, such as nine track tape drives and large disk drives. Although the finished application often takes less disk

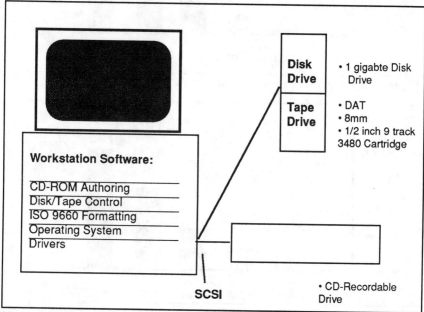

Figure B1: Typical Authoring Systems

space than the original data files (due to compression algorithms in the authoring software) disk space requirements during processing are often five times the raw data file size to accommodate indexing and sorting.

IBM-compatible PC class machines are the most popular premastering hardware system, typically a 486 platform today. UNIX platforms are gaining attention as premastering platforms due to their increased throughput, multitasking capabilities, and sophisticated systems for handling large and numerous files.

Integrating tape drives, large disk drives, and workstations is not a trivial task, so a popular solution is to purchase a CD-ROM premastering system. These systems have integrated tape drives and magnetic disks with gigabytes of storage if necessary. They attach to the workstation through the industry standard SCSI interface.

Premastering software facilitates data conversion and verification. Most premastering systems also include simulation software that slows the faster magnetic disks to emulate CD-ROM access speeds. This enables the actual performance of the application to be tested prior to pressing the CD-ROM disc.

CD-Recordable drives can also be included in these premastering systems for recording low quantities of discs in-house. CD-Recordable drives are attached through the same premastering system, with software support usually included in the premastering software. CD-Recordable drives employ commercially available blank media, which are recorded in "real time." Once recorded, these discs may be read with conventional CD-ROM readers.

A large majority of the CD-ROM titles created to date have been prepared on commercially available premastering systems. Premastering systems are more expensive than buying the individual components, but eliminate system integration labor and support costs.

Authoring of multimedia applications will require additional hardware. Depending on the type and level of multimedia required (audio, animation, video) various digitization, storage and playback devices will be necessary.

Delivery Systems. There are two hardware components to the CD-ROM delivery platform —a computer and a reader or drive.

Computer. The cost and performance parameters of a CD-ROM drive make it a good fit for personal computers or personal computer networks. The IBM PC/XT/AT is the dominant CD-ROM platform although CD-ROM drives are increasingly attached to Macintosh computers and UNIX workstations.

Multimedia applications will require some additional hardware in PC platforms—at a minimum a "sound board," which converts digitized sound files to audio. Macintosh computers will support most multimedia formats directly. Multimedia is getting significant attention in the press and industry today, so numerous multimedia CD-ROM titles can be expected in the future. This will give extra incentive to users to upgrade PCs to support multimedia.

CD-ROM Reader. A CD-ROM drive or reader is very similar to a CD Audio player except there is an additional error-correction chip instead of a digital to analog conversion chip. The servo mechanism is also improved to support the random access of a CD-ROM versus the linear nature of CD Audio. The reader is attached to the computer via an interface board, and driver software is used to communicate with the CD-ROM reader as with any computer peripheral. All CD-ROM drives conform to the "yellow book," a standard promulgated jointly by Philips and Sony. Because of this standard, all drives are essentially interchangeable.

Within the confines of the industry standard, readers are evolving. Single seek access times of one second or more in the first models have now dropped to a fraction of a second. Higher end models may have SCSI interfaces that allow attachment to Macintosh and other platforms. Data transfer from the disc, 150 kilobytes-per-second in the earliest and most current models, is increasing. There are now 300 and even 600 kilobyte-per-second readers. These readers are primarily employed in multimedia applications where data streams can represent encoded video and audio. Following the introduction of multi-disc players for CD audio, multi-disc CD-ROM readers are also available. Units holding up to six discs are common, while some "jukebox" products are available which accommodate as many as 250 discs in a single unit. Readers may be daisy chained, linking up to seven readers at a time to one PC interface board. Local area network servers with CD-ROM drives are supplied by numerous vendors, using off-the-shelf hardware and unique software. Most CD-ROM retrieval software and titles may be used on such a configuration with good performance and no modifications required.

Appendix C - Estimating Costs

When considering CD-ROM, costs must be viewed relative to alternative means of organizing, distributing, and retrieving information. Cost analysis is not complete without factoring performance and competitive advantages that result from the availability of information on CD-ROM, such as ease of updating, accuracy of searching, ad hoc query capabilities, and inexpensive distribution.

Application Development Costs

Service Bureau. The various steps of data preparation, indexing, interface creation, etc., require appropriate software and resources. This varies depending on the actual amount of data in the application, the complexity of the project, and the sophistication of the authoring software.

It is impossible to predict the costs of a CD-ROM application from a distance. For simple projects, a price of $10,000 to $40,000 would not be uncommon from a service bureau. This would include the use of their software, reading and "cleaning" the data, indexing, creating the user interface, pressing the discs, and licensing the retrieval software. Custom applications will cost more.

Publishing Platform - Software. Software should be specifically designed for CD-ROM applications. It should be optimized to achieve maximum performance while minimizing the space requirements for the data and related indexes. Mature software specific to CD-ROM will offer substantial benefits including sophisticated data import capabilities, high throughput indexing, and rich features and functionality in retrieving data from CD-ROM. Less sophisticated software sometimes costs more in the long run because it requires more data conversion prior to indexing or more program development to add required features to the retrieval facilities. Worse still is the case where significant time is invested and the CD-ROM application is unacceptable because of slow performance.

Software specifically designed for the organization, indexing and retrieval of information on CD-ROM can range from a few hundred dollars to $50,000. Cost differences lie in the type of information your application entails, the range of organization and indexing options available, the flexibility inherent in the software and its performance.

Costs may also depend on the reliability and credibility of the vendor. Value is closely related to how complete the software is and how much custom development is required to create your CD-ROM application. A system that saves three person-months of programming per application is worth a significant premium over a programming tool kit.

Software for multimedia authoring can also range from a few hundred to thousands of dollars. The options and differences in costs here relate primarily to the types of information the authoring system supports.

Publishing Platform - Hardware. Costs for the hardware for an in-house development capability vary. A minimum 486-based PC with extended memory is recommended to achieve adequate index build performance. A price range of $2,000 to $4,000 is typical, not including disk drive, tape drive, or CD-Recordable drive. Complete premastering systems range from $10,000 to $50,000 depending on features, memory, throughput, and vendor support. If you already have an installed 386 or 486 with sufficient magnetic disk space, a CD-Recordable drive can be added for under $10,000.

An increasing trend is indexing on high performance UNIX/ RISC based machines. These machines offer substantial price/ performance advantages if the throughput requirements warrant the higher processing speeds.

The major cost advantage of an in-house publishing platform is the ability to leverage the investment in software, hardware, and staffing across a number of applications. With as few as five applications, the fully-loaded cost per CD-ROM disc falls below $20. In this chapter is a summary cost calculation for creating a complete application development capability. Costs per PC, per disc, and per megabyte are included in this cost analysis.

If you are contemplating developing multimedia applications, the required components can usually be added to a publishing platform as needed. Depending on the type of multimedia (audio, video, etc.), various sound and video capture boards, video disk players, cameras and sound equipment may be necessary. Costs for these components vary greatly depending on quality, throughput, and features.

Staffing. Personnel requirements for an individual project using an authoring system with no custom programming are summarized in Figure 12. Projects which require custom interface development are more labor intensive.

A single application engineer can develop and update a significant number of applications using a properly designed authoring system. Experience suggests that compared with a "tool kit," an authoring system increases application production by three to ten times.

Retrieval Software Costs

Retrieval software licenses are offered in one or more of the following ways:

CPU Basis. Primarily for internal applications, this pricing method is similar to PC software that is licensed for use on a particular machine forever. Regardless of how many CD-ROM's your organization creates, the cost for the retrieval software for that PC doesn't change. Charges for this "pay once" CPU license vary by vendor and quantity. Pricing tends to parallel mass market PC software -- $250 to $500 per CPU for low volumes and roughly half that for quantity purchases.

Per Disc or Per Subscription. For applications where the publisher doesn't know or control the end user (e.g., discs distributed outside the organization), retrieval software is charged on a per disc or per subscription basis. Per disc pricing is usually tied to volume-based plateaus and will vary from vendor to vendor. For a 200 disc volume, a price range of $25 to $50 per disc is typical. For a volume of 5,000, a range of $10 to $20 per disc should be expected. (*Note:* It's important to ascertain how "volume plateaus" are computed by the software vendor. Ideally all licenses can be grouped together so an organization can quickly reach and remain at the highest discount level.)

Annual subscription pricing, while somewhat higher, offers the option of updating the users' product without limitation during the year. At a 200 subscription volume, prices in the range of $75 to $100 should be expected. At 5,000 subscriptions, the price per year should be $25 to $50.

Pricing outside these ranges usually indicates an organization that is under-funded and/or a new entrant to the market, complete with the associated risks. Software companies that have survived the ups and downs of an emerging industry and are providing quality products and services generally offer their products in the price ranges identified above. To survive in the PC software business, companies typically need to reach and sustain sales in the $10 million range in their third or fourth year. This can be illustrated by reviewing the few survivors in word processing, spreadsheets, or graphics from the early '80s. A good "going concern" viability test is dividing the vendor's price into $10 million, which indicates the number of new customers they must attract each year.

Media Costs - Mastering the Disc

If only a small number of replicas are required (less than 50 in today's economics), or if a prototype of the completed disc is desired, CD-Recordable technology may be employed. Blank CD-Recordable media today cost $30 in low quantities and less than $25 in high quantities, in addition to the costs for the CD-Recordable drive.

Once a complete application exists, a premaster tape is created and sent to the pressing house. The first cost in this process is the setup charge (currently $1,000 - $2,000). On the low end, five day turnaround is typical. Higher prices can achieve one day turnaround. The next cost is a disc charge, which is volume related. Prices of $1.50 to $2.50 each are typical today. Because of the setup charge, companies normally produce the maximum number of discs likely to be required from each pressing.

In-House Cost Summary

The cost of bringing a complete CD-ROM application development capability in-house is summarized below. Costs are broken into logical groups and summarized in the final section. Organizational overheads have not been included as these will vary from case to case.

1. Initial Investments
These costs are one-time outlays for hardware and software which are assumed to have a useful life of 3 years (although actual life may be longer).

A. Hardware
- Premaster System (1 gigabyte + tape drive) $11,000
- 486 personal computer   4,000
  SUBTOTAL $15,000

B. Software
- Authoring Systems $30,000
  SUBTOTAL $30,000
TOTAL INITIAL INVESTMENT   **$45,000**

2. Annual Costs
These are average annual outlays for personnel, office space and supplies. Experience suggests that these costs and manpower levels are sufficient to produce up to five different applications with an average bimonthly update frequency. More applications or more frequent updates may require more resources.

A. Personnel
- Applications Developer $60,000
B. Office Space   10,000
C. Supplies   5,000
    TOTAL ANNUAL COSTS   **$75,000**

3. Investment per Workstation

These costs assume that 500 PCs in the organization are outfitted with CD-ROM drives and retrieval software. Higher volumes result in somewhat lower per workstation costs due to volume discounting. These investments are also assumed to have a useful life of 3 years.

A. CD-ROM Drive with interface $ 500
B. Retrieval Software (perpetual) 200
TOTAL PER WORKSTATION INVESTMENT $ 700
TOTAL WORKSTATION INVESTMENT **$350,000**
  (Q 500)

4. Costs per CD-ROM Application Update

All steps in the application development process, from acceptance of raw data on magnetic tape through generation of pre-master tapes ready for the mastering/pressing facility, can be accomplished by the above personnel using the listed facilities. The pre-master tapes are then forwarded to the mastering/pressing facility where a set up charge is incurred for each master disc, and a per-disc charge applied for the replication. Documentation can be prepared as a slip-insert to the CD-ROM jewel case packaging.

A. Mastering (per application/master disc) $ 1,500
B. Replication (per CD-ROM disc) 2
C. Documentation (per CD-ROM disc) 1

5. Software Maintenance Cost

Software maintenance is assumed at 15% annually, the industry norm.

6. Cost Summary

This section assumes the organization is producing three CD-ROM applications: one updated quarterly, one monthly, and one every six months. The volumes are 200, 500, and 300 units respectively.

	Annual Total	Annual Per PC	Per Disc	Per Megabyte[1]
Initial Investment (3 year life)[2]	$ 15,000	$ 30.00	$ 2.03	$ 0.01
Annual Costs	75,000	150.00	10.14	0.03
Workstation Costs (3 year life)[3]	116,667	233.34	15.77	0.05
Application Update Costs[4]	49,200	98.40	6.65	0.02
Software Maintenance [5]	19,500	39.00	2.64	0.01
TOTALS	$275,367	550.74	37.23	0.12

1. Assumes discs contain average 300 megabytes.
2. 45,000/3 = 15,000
3. 350,000/3 = 116,667
4. ((4 + 12 + 2) * 1500) + ((200*4 + 500*12 + 300*2) * 3) = 49,200
5. (30,000 + 500*200) * 15% = 19,500

If the number of workstations in the organization increases to 1,000 and the number of applications increases to five (two updated quarterly at 300 units, two monthly at 800 units, and one every six months at 300 units), the following cost summary emerges:

	Annual Total	Annual Per PC	Per Disc	Per Megabyte[1]
Initial Investment (3 year life)[2]	$ 15,000	$ 15.00	$ 0.68	$ 0.00
Annual Costs	75,000	75.00	3.38	0.01
Workstation Costs (3 year life)[3]	216,667	216.67	9.75	0.03
Application UpdateCosts[4]	97,550	97.55	4.39	0.01
Software Maintenance[5]	34,500	34.50	1.55	0.01
TOTAL	$438,717	438.71	19.75	0.06

1. Assumes discs contain average 300 megabytes.
2. 45,000/3 = 15,000
3. 650,000/3 = 216,667; assumes per workstation costs drops to $650
4. ((4*2 + 12*2 +2) * 1400 + ((300*4*2 + 800*12*2 + 300*2) * 2.25) = 97,550; assumes mastering set up drops to $1400 and replica plus documentation drops to $2.25.
5. (30,000 + 1000*200) * 15% = 34,500

Conclusions

A few simple conclusions can be drawn from this cost analysis:

- Total annualized costs for a typical in-house investment in CD-ROM technology are in the low six figures; certainly under $500,000 per year.

- The annual cost per end-user workstation is less than $600.

- The cost per CD-ROM disc or per megabyte distributed declines dramatically as CD-ROM gets adopted more widely in the organization.

- The initial investment for in-house CD-ROM development capability is a relatively small percentage of the total cost. Therefore the quality of the initial software and hardware is much more important than their relative costs.

Appendix D - Dataware's Family of Authoring and Retrieval Software

Providing text, data, graphics, sound and video requires software that is designed to integrate different content and is optimized to deliver superior performance on slower CD-ROM media. Designing around either the data or text model allows each authoring system to make application generation easier and faster and eliminates the need for programming during application generation.

The information structures used for performance optimization are different in data and text applications. Structuring and optimizing information for database retrieval requires the exclusion of certain text retrieval features. Structuring and optimizing text information eliminates certain database capabilities. Dataware's family of products recognizes the need to maximize performance, functionality and integration at the same time. The result is two types of products, one optimized for data and the other optimized for text. Graphics may be associated with either data or text. But selecting either a data or text solution from Dataware doesn't imply giving up the features of the other solution. All of Dataware's products have been developed to maximize the retrieval software feature set, regardless of the type of data for which they are optimized.

Dataware has developed two of the leading CD-ROM authoring and retrieval software product families available today: CD Author® and ReferenceSet®. The CD Author product family includes CD Author/CD Answer®, which is software optimized for structured data, and CD Author HyperText/CD Answer HyperText, optimized for text. The ReferenceSet product family includes Record ReferenceSet, which is optimized for data, and Text ReferenceSet, which has been optimized for text.

CD Author and *CD Answer* are the market leaders for application development and retrieval of structured data from CD-ROM. CD Author builds applications incorporating structured data, text and graphics. It is optimized for high performance retrieval of data from optical disc. CD Answer is the high performance information retrieval and display software for data prepared with CD Author.

Record ReferenceSet has been extensively employed in corporate and government applications involving structured data. Record ReferenceSet prepares data and builds CD-ROM applications primarily containing data and graphics. The user interface and functionality of the companion Record ReferenceBook retrieval software may be thoroughly modified by developers without writing software through an application generator interface.

Typical CD Answer Record ReferenceSet applications include:

Publishing	**Corporate**	**Government**
Bibliographic Data	COM Replacement	Accounting
Corporate Directory	Customer Data	Bibliographic Records
Credit Data	Forms Catalogs	Indexes
Financial Data	Inventory	Inventories
Geographic Data	Monthly Statements	Parts Lists
Newspaper Articles	Parts Catalogs	Patents
Patent Data	Parts Lists	Transactions
People Directory	Purchasing Data	
Statistics	Service Orders/Reports	
	Transaction History	

CD Author HyperText and *CD Answer HyperText* provide sophisticated textual capabilities integrated with a broad range of database and graphic capabilities optimized for searching text. CD Answer HyperText combines traditional full text searching and six different types of hypertext searching and browsing for extensive analysis of textual information on optical disc.

Text ReferenceSet is a leading software product for text organization and access on optical disc. Text ReferenceSet prepares data and builds CD-ROM applications primarily containing text and graphics. The user interface and functionality of the companion Text ReferenceBook retrieval software may be thoroughly modified by developers without writing software through an application generator interface.

Typical CD Answer HyperText/Test ReferenceSet applications include:

Publishing	**Corporate**	**Government**
Books	Audit Procedures	Instructions
Government Regulations	Contracts	Procedures
Legal/Tax Information	Engineering Standards	Regulations
Loose-leaf Publications	Maintenance Release	Research
Manuals	Policy Manuals	Standards
Medical Journals	Research	Statutes
Microform Conversions	Technical Documentation	Technical
Reference Collection	Training Manuals	Reference
Standards Information		
Technical Reference		

ENDNOTES

[1] Source: Infotech.

[2] Com fiche is generally searchable only on a single field. CD-ROM software permits every field to be indexed and searched in multiple ways.

[3] CD-ROM information retrieval is 3-5 times faster than on-line retrieval for large volume databases.

Chapter 6

CD-Recordable Applications Guide

Dataware Technologies, Inc.

CD-ROM and Competitive Advantage

CD-ROM has created significant benefits to business and government today. CD-ROM naturally fits into corporate and government computing strategies and leverages major information management trends including electronic publishing, work group computing and client-server architecture. Publishers use CD-ROM as a new distribution solution allowing them to add value, capture new markets, and increase customer awareness of their information products. Corporations and government agencies also use CD-ROM to strategic and competitive advantage. For example:

- 3M, a major manufacturer of consumer products, eases import/ export administration processes by producing specific information for the distribution work-group on CD-ROM. Shipping requirements, tariffs, and export restrictions are included.
- Independence Blue Cross saved hundreds of thousands of dollars in productivity by transferring ten years of claims history from microfilm to CD-ROM.

• The United States Department of State cuts telecommunication costs by producing a resident mainframe database of policy statements, book references, documents, calendar of events, transcriptions of talk shows and newspaper articles on CD-ROM.

The benefits of CD-ROM technology lie in the cost reduction, revenue generation, and efficiency improvements gained through effective introduction of CD-ROM into business activities.

CD-ROM technology is a powerful tool that can improve sales performance, lower cost of sales, improve product quality, differentiate products in the marketplace and improve both customer service and customer perception of support.

CD-ROM Today

There are over 3,500 commercial CD-ROM titles today, as well as over 2,000 corporate and government titles. There are over four million CD-ROM drives installed primarily as attachments to PCs or PC-based networks, as well as growing numbers of CD-ROM drives attached to Macintosh and UNIX workstations. Additionally, portable PC/CD-ROM Systems (Bookman, CD-I, etc.) have recently been introduced in the United States. This wide availability and acceptance of CD-ROM has been made possible through a combination of factors. Among them:

• Source information digital format is widely available because of the advent and wide acceptance of desktop publishing systems; the increasing sophistication of digital, audio and video production systems; and the increasing amount of historical information being converted into electronic formats through scanning and OCR technology.
• Sophisticated software for searching and access to information on CD-ROM. Although a CD-ROM disc can contain over 600 megabytes, access to the information on CD-ROM is typically some ten times slower than a PC-based hard disc. Software systems that have been optimized for this slow access have been developed and widely employed.
• Development software for CD-ROM, including conversion, indexing, authoring and CD-ROM formatting (ISO 9660) can now be operated by non-technical personnel. This allows for CD-ROM development at the department or work group level, without the involvement of technical staff.
• CD-ROM is accepted and familiar to end users through the

consumer CD Audio industry. In fact, CD-ROM owes much of its current success to CD Audio. Production plants for CD discs, volume manufacturing for CD Audio drives, and consumer acceptance have allowed CD-ROM to capitalize on the existing economies of scale and production facilities of CD Audio. For example, CD-ROM discs can be mastered for $1,500 and replicated for $2 each. CD-ROM drives are commonly available for less than $500.

Three Key Advantages

There are three key advantages that make CD-ROM particularly attractive in today's complex computing and information environment.

Multimedia

CD-ROM offers a distinct advantage over alternative electronic information delivery media. The ability to deliver unlimited end user access to over 600 megabytes using only first class postage means this medium can be used for text, graphics, data, audio and video in one simple package. Forward-thinking companies are using CD-ROM for product catalogs containing not only product names and descriptions, but color pictures, verbal descriptions, and video sequences using the products.

Multiplatform

CD-ROM is also the first truly system independent medium. With appropriate software, CD-ROM allows equal access to information regardless of the computer hardware or software platform employed by the end user. The organization and indexing of the information on CD-ROM can be independent of the eventual environment in which it will be used. In fact, the development of CD-ROM discs is often performed without knowing the computer environment in which they will ultimately be used. This makes CD-ROM an appropriate technology for today and the future.

This system independence can offer substantial benefits to organizations with disparate computing environments and personnel skill levels. For example, technical documentation can be delivered to each user independent of their computer environment or geographic location.

Multilingual

Besides computer system independence, sophisticated software systems today allow for language neutral CD-ROM applications. These applications allow the end user to select the operating language of choice and even change it on-the-fly. For example, the British, French, and German Standards Institutes have combined to produce PERINORM, a multilingual CD-ROM of international standards information with user interface and content searchable in any of three European languages.

Traditional CD-ROM Applications

CD-ROM has traditionally been employed where multiple copies of a stable information base are required. CD-ROM mastering has been performed in multi-million dollar mastering facilities where the set-up charge for each master disc has typically run in the $1,500 to $2,000 range, and required 3-5 days for turnaround. As a result, CD-ROM was traditionally used only where multiple copies were required. Appropriate applications have generally followed one of three tracks:

- Information products from profit-oriented commercial ventures. These are often produced by publishers with established information products and distribution channels. They see CD-ROM as a way to increase revenue from existing products distributed in another form, or expand market share by creating new information products.

- Information bases produced by government organizations to allow a greater dissemination of public information. These serve to increase international competitiveness and domestic efficiency, and lower government operating costs.

- Information bases produced for use within corporations. These products are used to better sell and support products, improve communication and responsiveness to customers, and make available company or work group specific information to appropriate employees.

An Enabling Technology: CD-Recordable

CD-Recordable technology provides the benefits of CD-ROM while improving the economics and turnaround of production and distribution. With CD-Recordable technology, users can avoid mastering costs and turnaround time normally required in CD-ROM production. For sensitive information, nothing is sent outside, ensuring data integrity. Once the appropriate CD-Recordable equipment is installed, a CD-Recordable disc can be produced locally for media costs only, and this disc can be played in any of the millions of CD-ROM drives installed today.

CD-Recordable technology allows a user to produce CD-ROM replicas in low volume quantities. The technology employs a CD-Recordable drive (with a blank CD-Recordable disc) attached to a workstation such as a PC. Data are organized and indexed the same way as if they were to be produced on conventional CD-ROM.

Many early adopters of CD-Recordable technology use the CD-Recordable disc for prototyping their CD-ROM application, sending the recorded disc to the CD-ROM mastering facility for mastering and replication. Data for recording on CD-Recordable discs must be formatted with software specifically designed for CD-ROM production and are typically packaged along with the CD-Recordable drive. The data are then written to the blank CD-Recordable media in "real time" (the playing time of an audio CD disc, about 60 minutes for a full disc) or faster.

CD-Recordable media are the same size as CD-ROM, and although have a different physical appearance (they typically contain a gold reflective layer rather than the silver used in most CD-ROM discs), once installed in a CD-ROM drive, are indistinguishable from a CD-ROM disc. Publishers may pre-print a label on the blank media without affecting disc operation.

Once a section of a CD-Recordable disc has been written it cannot be changed. It becomes "ROM" media. The first generation of CD-Recordable drives, introduced in the United States in late 1989, was capable only of writing the entire disc in one session. Additionally, these devices recorded the disc in "real time," requiring over an hour of recording time for a full disc.

The latest generation of CD-Recordable drives allows multiple-write sessions on a single disc. As before, once a section of the disc is written, it cannot be changed. However, the newest generation drives allow for appending information to already recorded discs. Additionally, these new drives record at a faster rate, typically twice as fast as "real time." Effectively then, a full disc can be recorded in a little over half an hour. Many of today's CD-Recordable drives also double as CD-ROM readers, so they can be used as a standard CD-ROM drive when not employed in the recording process.

These engineering enhancements to the CD-Recordable drives allows application in new areas, but the real advantage of the new generation drives is their price point. The price for these next generation systems, which can be attached directly to a 386-based

workstation, is under $10,000 versus $30,000 for the prior generation. Additionally, blank media, which currently sell for $25 each,
are projected to drop under $10 in the next several years.

The desktop laser printer was the final link in a series of
technologies which enabled desktop publishing. Complementary
advances included high performance workstations, high resolution
display monitors, and sophisticated page composition software for
workstations that allowed users to produce quality printed publications in their own facilities. CD-Recordable drives offer a parallel
solution. When coupled with high performance search and retrieval
software, they allow a whole new class for applications to benefit from
CD-ROM. These personal, work group, or enterprise publishing
applications are cost justified without multiple copies. Users can
produce sophisticated and high quality applications for electronic
distribution by employing the latest generation of CD-ROM preparation software.

For example:

- A company-specific information base which is updated weekly is
  entirely appropriate for CD-Recordable technology whereas this
  application couldn't justify the mastering costs of CD-ROM.
- A mainframe database, previously accessible only through expensive telecommunications and systems experts, or in large volumes
  of printed reports, is migrated to CD-ROM. CD-Recordable technology allows these data to be distributed to appropriate users,
  regardless of where they are located.
- Work group-specific information can be produced on CD-ROM and
  recorded on an as-needed basis. CD-ROM replicas can be made in
  small quantities for the required members of the group insuring
  current and locally accessible information.
- Users of secure or sensitive information can realize the benefits of
  CD-ROM access without releasing it outside the organization.
  Local production using CD-Recordable technology allows this
  information to be produced and accessed locally.
- Historical, archival, and research data previously stored in inaccessible tape farms can be made locally accessible through CD-
  Recordable media. Instead of finding, loading on the mainframe,
  and writing queries, this information on CD-ROM is locally accessible. Coupled with appropriate search and retrieval software, it
  can be searched at any time.

A Value Multiplier for Information Systems

Businesses have invested significant resources in streamlining the collection and maintenance of critical information. High return CD-Recordable applications are those that enable immediate access to this information by users. These applications multiply the value of the intrinsic information by making it immediately available to the appropriate user. Sophisticated search and retrieval software leverages the initial investment in gathering information by enabling users ad hoc query capabilities.

Four current information management technologies are emerging as high priorities for most organizations over the next decade: electronic publishing, local area networking, client-server architectures, and transaction processing. CD-ROM can broaden the application of these systems and enhance their value to the corporation.

Electronic Publishing

To remain competitive, businesses that produce large volumes of paper-based information are moving to electronic publishing. Various types of information, such as text, data, and graphics, can be combined electronically, saving substantial time in revising, reformatting, and producing a document. These advantages are great as far as they go, but they usually stop just short of distribution. Converting electronic information to non-electronic format when there are more than 25 million potential electronic readers on the desks of corporate America does not make sense for many applications. This is a large area for cost savings and productivity improvement.

Local Area Networks and Work Group Computing

The CD-ROM standards were established with networks as an expected requirement. The ISO 9660 standard incorporates the basic hardware and media specifications required to make a CD-ROM network compatible. Once a network is equipped with drives and appropriate software, virtually any CD-ROM disc— assuming appropriate network license agreements and use of the ISO 9660 standard—can be shared on the local area network. Each attached drive provides over 700 megabytes of read-only information to the network nodes. By placing one or more CD-ROM drives on each local area network or in each department, an organization provides ready access to internal information on CD-Recordable discs and externally purchased information relevant to that department or work group. Examples of typical work group information requirements are shown in Figure 1.

Downsizing and Client-Server Architectures

Corporations and government agencies are rapidly replacing centrally located, monolithic information systems with distributed architectures. Driving forces include high maintenance on centrally located mainframe systems, long lead times for new applications development, and the increasing need for organizations to provide flexible and responsive information systems. Client-server architectures allow a decentralized information enterprise, allowing local control and maintenance of information pertinent to the work group.

CD-ROM is often a vital component of downsizing efforts. While a new decision support application for a centrally located informa-

---

Service
- Documentation
- Maintenance Releases
- Service Call Reports
- Trouble Shooting Guides
- Maintenance Histories
- Parts Lists
- Inventory
- Warranty Listings

Marketing and Sales
- Catalogs
- Specification Sheets
- Parts Lists
- Prices
- Inventory
- Purchase History

Operations
- Inventory
- Parts Lists
- Stock Number Cross Reference
- Bill of Materials
- Order Data
- Engineering Standards
- Parts Where Used
- Facility and Equipment Registers

Procurement
- Inventory
- Bill of Materials
- Cumulative Order Data
- Vendor Cross Reference Data
- Index of Suppliers

Research and Development
- Research Reports
- Standards Information
- Bibliographic Databases

Figure 1: Work Group Information Requirements

tion system may require lengthy lead time, extracting a copy of the information, committing it to CD-ROM and using fourth generation access tools for decision support is proving successful. This newly emerging use of CD-ROM is helping to accelerate many corporations' downsizing efforts.

Transaction Processing Systems

Some of the best examples of information as a competitive tool are found in those industries that have been transformed by electronic transaction processing such as banking, brokerage and travel. Other examples include the pharmaceutical and auto parts industries, and a variety of other retail businesses where transaction information is essential to the successful operation of the business.

The leaders in transaction processing are now taking the next step in strategic information delivery: CD-ROM. Purchasing activity in corporate and government organizations is converted to CD-ROM for trend analysis. Retailers in the auto, trucking, and appliance replacement parts business are using CD-ROM to find the right part and make the sale.

Using CD-ROM systems to augment point-of-transaction information, improve customer service, and boost sales is widely applicable to other industries. The two technologies work in partnership: on-line transaction processing delivers accurate and time-sensitive information while large volumes of related but less time-sensitive information is delivered on CD-ROM.

Estimating Costs

When considering CD-Recordable, costs must be viewed relative to alternative means or organizing, distributing, and retrieving information. Cost analysis is not complete without factoring performance and competitive advantages that result from the availability of information on CD-ROM, such as ease of updating, accuracy of searching, ad hoc query capabilities, and inexpensive distribution.

Cost analysis must also consider the complete requirements of a CD-Recordable application. While the necessary hardware subsystems are available from a number of vendors at various price points, a complete analysis will also include the costs for fully executing an application. This includes hardware, software, training, personnel, and on-going update costs. A significant portion of the overall application costs will be related to personnel and software used rather than the specific hardware.

Primary Activities	Operations	Marketing & Sales	Service	Customer
Information Used	Orders Engineering Standards Purchasing Information	Inventory Orders Parts Lists Design Specifications Market Information Sales Information Inventory	Training Parts Lists Customer Information Inventory	Documentation Maintenance Parts Catalogs
Information Produced	Parts Lists Inventory Ship to Lists Bill of Materials Parts Where Used Facility & Equipment Registers	Parts Catalogs Customer Database Prospect Database Purchase Histories Spec Sheets Pricing Contracts	Service Call Reports Trouble- Shooting Guides Maintenance History Training Service Orders Warranty Listings	Warranty Information Product Improvements Service Requests Customer Information Orders
Infrastructure Activities	Research & Developmet	Purchasing	Human Resources	Financial & Admin.
Information Used	External Research Patent Information Standards Information Bibliographic Research	Inventory Orders Bill of Materials Vendor Information Price Lists Product Information	Government Regulations Recruiting Information	Accounting Standards Government Regulations Accounting Input Budget Input
Information Produced	Internal Research Engineering Standards	On Order Reports Vendor Information Product Information Price Lists	Training Manuals Personnel Records	Policy & Procedure General Audit & Record Retention Budget Information Accounting Information

Figure 2: Information Used and Produced

Application Development Costs

Publishing Platform - Software

Software should be specifically designed for CD-ROM applications. It should be optimized to achieve maximum performance while minimizing the space requirements for the data and related indexes. Mature software specific to CD-ROM will offer substantial benefits including sophisticated data import capabilities, high throughput indexing, and rich features and functionality in retrieving data from CD-ROM. Less sophisticated software sometimes costs more in the long run because it requires more data conversion prior to indexing or more program development to add required features to the retrieval facilities. Worse still is the case where significant time is invested and the CD-ROM application is unacceptable because of slow performance.

Software specifically designed for organization, indexing and retrieval of information on CD-ROM can range from a few hundred dollars to $50,000. Cost differences lie in the type of information your application includes; the range of organization and indexing options available; and the flexibility inherent in the software and its performance. See Appendix A for a more detailed discussion of the various software options.

Costs may also depend on the reliability and credibility of the vendor. Value is closely related to how complete the software is and how much custom development is required to create your CD-ROM application. If you do not require indexing capabilities (for example, if you are using a CD-Recordable drive for network backup) you may only require the basic CD-ROM formatting software. This software is often referred to as "ISO formatting software" for the ISO 9660 format in which data are produced prior to writing on CD-Recordable. ISO 9660 is the standard for CD-ROMs.

Publishing Platform - Hardware

Because the new generation CD-Recordable drives record at a faster rate, they also require data during the recording process at a faster rate. A 386-based workstation, even when equipped with high performance magnetic disk drive, may not be able to sustain the required data transfer requirements. Many solutions-based resellers of the CD-Recordable drives today package them with additional hardware to collect and smooth the transfer of data to the drive. These solutions can range from additional controller cards (CD-Recordable drives are based on the Small Computer System Interface (SCSI standard) to wholly dedicated 600 megabyte magnetic disk drives. Installed costs for a successful system may be higher than "drive-only" prices that appear in trade publications.

Dataware has arrived at a CD-Recordable system solution guaranteed to produce "good" discs based on an additional controller card and sophisticated disc caching techniques. These techniques overcome the potential problems associated with fragmented mag-

Step	Skill Level	Time
Data Conversion & Filtering	Junior Programmer	1 day plus
Database Definitions	Skilled User	1/2 day-1 day
Screen Layout	Skilled User	1-2 days*
Indexing Specification	Skilled User	1/2 - 2 days
Indexing and Binding	None	10 Megabytes/ hour
Debugging and Testing	Skilled User	1-2 days
Help Screens	Skilled User	1/2-3 days
Install Program	Skilled User	1/2-1 day
Record Discs	None	Set up, then 30 minutes

* Assumes screen painting interface design with no programming.

Figure 3: Steps and Staffing Requirements for Initial Application Development

Step	Skill Level	Time
Index and Bind	None	Set up, then machine time @ 10 Megabytes/ Hour
Quality Assurance	Skilled User	1 hour-1 day
Record Discs	None	Set up, then 30 minutes

Figure 4: Steps and Staffing Requirements for Updates to Applications

netic disk files or slow access drives. CD-Recordable development platforms vary in price depending on the development capability. A 386- or 486-based PC with extended memory, 600-1200 megabytes of hard disk space, and CD-Recordable drive will range from $20,000 to $40,000.

Staffing

Recent advances in the software development systems for CD-ROM have allowed less experienced users to develop sophisticated and high performance CD-ROM information bases. Software development experience is no longer a prerequisite for developing a CD-ROM application. Neither is extensive database development experience or systems level configuration knowledge required. Of course you may undertake a wider variety of application modifications if you have access to such capabilities.

Alternatively, you may contract with a service bureau for development services. Once the application is developed, the service bureau releases the capability for updating the application to you.

A single application engineer can develop and update a significant number of applications using a properly designed development system. The steps in Figure 3 indicate the staffing required to develop a typical CD-Recordable application. Figure 4 indicates the staffing required as the application is updated.

Getting Started

You can benefit from CD-Recordable and CD-ROM technology today. First identify high value application areas in your organization. Mission and activity critical information will yield the highest returns on your investment in hardware and software systems.

When evaluating CD-Recordable systems, the entire application requirements should be considered. Solutions that accommodate your source data and result in a complete and ready-to-use application are preferable to components. Likewise, the fit of your requirements to the solution can be judged by the experience of the vendor in providing similar applications.

The application areas you define will determine the preparation and retrieval software requirements. Two kinds of software are required—software for preparation of information prior to record and software for retrieval and access to information after the disc has been recorded. Software systems available today normally include both components.

Because of CD-ROM's high capacity and the slow performance of CD-ROM drives, you should select software specifically intended for CD-ROM production, such as the CD Author® or ReferenceSet® authoring systems from Dataware. Software systems for CD-ROM development and retrieval vary greatly depending on the type of information you have and your requirements. Dataware works directly with each customer to understand application requirements and recommends the best software and service alternatives.

The CD-Recordable systems today are sold as PC, Macintosh, UNIX and network attachments. These systems normally come complete with required interface card, cabling and software for recording discs. Blank media are available from the same vendor as the CD-Recordable drive, and are expected to be available through numerous channels in the future.

With installed hardware and appropriate development and mastering software, you can begin to realize the benefits of CD-ROM in your organization today. By focusing on high value applications, CD-Recordable systems can pay for themselves in a matter of weeks or months. A complete solution will encompass the CD-Recordable system and CD-ROM development and retrieval software. Sophisticated software systems are available today that don't require programming, allowing you to quickly put CD-ROM to use in your organization.

Dataware Technologies Corporate Qualifications

Choosing a software partner during the early stages of a market is a challenging and critical decision. The reality is that most software companies entering a new market will not be in business in three to five years. Learning from the history of other software markets, the key requirements for a successful company in an emerging market are:

- Partnership with quality customers, and the ability to listen and enhance products.
- Delivery of innovative products to meet customer needs.
- Marketing capability to get the products to customers.

- Quality technical support.
- Financial resources to build the company and assure its long-term viability.
- Skilled management team.

Dataware is based on innovative quality products developed in partnership with innovative customers. The success of our customers has led to industry-wide recognition, including the section of CD Answer® as the "Best Retrieval Software" by the Optical Publishing Association. But the most important recognition is from the leading organizations who have selected Dataware.

More publishers and corporations have created more CD-ROM products with CD Author and distributed more titles with CD Answer than any other CD-ROM software in the world. (*Source:* "The CD-ROM Directory" disc from TFPL.) The power and flexibility of Dataware's software is exemplified by the range of applications developed by Dataware publishers and distributed to over ninety countries worldwide. In a global high tech market, the fact that half of the CD-ROM titles using CD Answer were developed outside the United States indicates Dataware's worldwide strength.

Given rapid changes in technology, Dataware's software has

been designed for portability. Dataware has also unveiled application programming interfaces for MS-DOS, MS-Windows, Macintosh, UNIX, MMCD and Compact Disc Interactive (CD-I) systems. Dataware also produces authoring tools for MS-DOS, UNIX, VAX/VMS and MVS to accommodate the heterogeneous computing needs of our clients.

Appendix A - Software for CD-ROM Applications

As with most computer applications, software is key to a successful implementation. Although CD-ROM is computer system independent, access software must be available from the vendor in the various targeted platforms. A key consideration of any solution should be the ability to operate in multiple computer platforms and, if required by your user community, ability to operate in multiple languages.

A complete product for CD-ROM publishing and retrieval must incorporate capabilities normally provided by several different programs (database, word processing, graphics, etc.) into a high performance retrieval system. The authoring system should provide the application developer with a complete range of development options ranging from a non-programming application generator to a configurable user interface or fully customizable application programming interface.

The value of a complete product is measured not only by the satisfaction of users and customers as well as the range of content that can be delivered, but also the ease with which applications can be developed and the flexibility to integrate CD-ROM technology with existing computing strategies.

Currently available options are briefly detailed below.

In-House Software Development

Writing customized CD-ROM software is the least popular development approach today. Custom software entails high development and maintenance costs and is usually only justified for commercial CD-ROM titles where the development costs can be amortized over a number of titles. Writing custom software is never cheaper than licensing, and the results often don't rival those readily available in commercial software due to the extensive development already devoted to commercial packages.

Commercial Software

Commercial software vendors divide the functions of CD-ROM development into a series of steps. Because the preparation of data is a separate and distinctly different step from access to data on CD-ROM, commercial CD-ROM development software products tend to supply both a preparation facility, typically called authoring and software to access the prepared discs, typically called retrieval. Most authoring software available today goes hand-in-hand with retrieval software, since the arrangement of data by the authoring software is proprietary to the vendor.

Authoring software can be further divided into a number of steps, included among them are data capture, conversion, indexing, compression, and formatting the data into the format specific for CD-ROM called ISO 9660. Most CD-Recordable applications can benefit from the use of CD-ROM specific search and retrieval software, which has been optimized for finding and using relevant information in a large collection.

Software for ISO 9660 formatting is often packaged with the CD-Recordable drive. Backup applications, such as network backup, require only this formatting software since there are typically not sophisticated search requirements for the resultant discs.

Commercial retrieval software systems are normally complete with "standard" user interface for typical applications. In many applications, particularly CD-Recordable where a sophisticated but non-customized user interface is desired, this standard user interface is sufficient. Some systems include extensive user interface configuration options, without programming. These user interfaces allow for rapid application development.

For even more flexibility, some development systems provide a programmer interface, called an Application Programming Interface (API). Use of the API allows development of CD-ROM based applications without developing the database specific technology necessary for high performance CD-ROM retrieval. While development using an API will take longer than a standard user interface, it is still considerably faster than developing database access technology from scratch.

CD-ROM development software today tends to divide CD-ROM applications into five categories of data types, and often accommodates one data type only. The five are data, text, graphics, audio and video.

Directories on CD-ROM, searching 10,000,000 names in less than a second.

WTV (Germany) - The NATO PCO disc covers over 20 years of non-military scientific and technical meetings and publications sponsored by the NATO Science Committee.

Ziff Desktop Information - Produces the Computer Select* database of computer industry and product information.

Corporate and Government
3M - Multiple applications including import and export regulations, material safety data and sheets, purchasing histories and product catalogs for more than 50 subsidiaries worldwide. Replaces both mainframe and microfiche databases.

Bosch Siemens (Germany) - The household appliances group is using CD Author internally for the dissemination of internal financial information.

Ciba Geigy AC (Switzerland) - Bibliographies on disc of its 80,000 scientific publications concerning its own pharmaceutical and chemical products.

Eastman Kodak - Is producing internal corporate information on CD-ROM, including inventory information and technical documentation.

Ford New Holland - 300,000 parts plus images for agriculture and industrial equipment for use by more than one thousand dealers in North America.

GEM Part - Repair and replacement parts for appliances.

Independence Blue Cross - Ten years of claims history and membership information moved from microfilm to CD-ROM.

NEC - CD-ROMs containing technical documentation.

The National Statistical Agency and Optim Corporation (Canada) - Statistical databases on CD-ROM.

R.R. Donnelley & Sons - Technical information on CD-ROM for

leading semiconductor manufacturers.

Siemens A.G. - Multiple applications including technical manuals, import and expert regulations, phone directory, etc., for distribution worldwide in multiple languages.

U.S. Army Corps of Engineers - Numerous applications of engineering manuals, forms, and bibliographic records.

U.S. Geological Survey - Multiple titles including the Aerial Photography Summary Record System (two million plus records describing 12 million frames of photography on file) and State Water Data Reports (tabular and textual information from state stations tracking water statistics).

U.S. Government Printing Office - Provides comprehensive CD-ROM applications for federal government clients.

U.S. Information Agency - The PDQ (Public Diplomacy Query) disc provides U.S. embassies worldwide with policy statements as well as documents, book references, a calendar of events and newspaper articles.

U.S. Navy - Purchasing history and account reconciliation information produced on CD-ROM, along with logistical and administrative data.

U.S. Patent and Trademark Office - CASSIS CD-ROM (2) ASIST Multiple discs of patent and trademark information, including over five million patent records on a single disc.

U.S. Social Security Administration - Produces the *Program Operations Manual System* for Social Security field operations.

Woodward Governor - Publishes repair and replacement part information on CD-ROM.

Section 3

Application Development Focus

Chapter 7

Total Quality Management of Multimedia Development Projects

Donald A. Carpenter
University of Nebraska at Kearney

Marc Schniederjans
University of Nebraska-Lincoln

Enlightened information systems professionals have discovered and incorporated methodologies to insure quality as information systems are developed. Similarly, software engineers have created and applied methodologies to insure quality as computer software is developed. The two sets of methodologies are compatible and gaining in acceptance.

Advances in computer technologies have enabled sophisticated multimedia capabilities to be affordable and usable by an increasingly broad spectrum of individuals. The majority of those individuals embark on the development of information systems and computer software that include multimedia features in an unenlightened manner. That is to say, the typical multimedia system developer does not apply proper information system development or software engineering methodologies.

This chapter argues for the use of enlightened methodologies in the development of all multimedia-based systems and software. Special attention is paid to those multimedia systems that are instructional in nature. The argument is made that computer assisted instruction techniques should be used in such projects.

Application of multimedia capabilities has added a new dimension to the design and creation of information systems. As is the case when any new technology is introduced, multimedia presents additional challenges with which information systems managers must deal. It is highly likely that those information systems managers who have been effective in their management of other technologies will also be successful in their management of system development projects which include multimedia technologies.

Unfortunately, not all multimedia projects will be managed by seasoned and successful managers. Many less-skillful project managers, as well as many inexperienced end users, are in charge of information systems development projects. The number of information systems projects which were not well managed is staggering. Delays and cost overruns in completing the projects, plus flaws and excessive maintenance in the resulting systems are a few common symptoms among many which are indicators of poor information systems project management.

Multimedia technologies and hypertext authoring software have substantially increased the attractiveness of personal computing. As CD-ROM and related devices become more prevalent in homes, schools and businesses, more applications will be conceptualized by end users. As a result, many end users will be involved in the design and construction of multimedia applications.

The advantages and disadvantages of end user computing have been thoroughly discussed in the literature. The advent of multimedia computing has the potential to significantly spread the advantages of end user computing. Unfortunately, the potential also exists for multimedia computing to spread the disadvantages of end user computing. Many of the common problems with end user computing culminate in diminished quality of both software and systems. This seems to run contrary to the increasing emphasis presently being placed on improving quality in all aspects of organizations.

One approach to improving quality throughout the organization is total quality management (TQM). TQM is widely seen as the means to improve organizational, national and international productivity. It is inconsistent with the goals of total quality management to allow any information systems projects—including those which feature multimedia technologies—to be managed poorly.

In order to assure the quality of information systems development projects, the information systems industry has created and successfully applied many methodologies. Those methodologies can and should readily be used for projects which include multimedia technologies. The methodologies are applicable to the development of entire multimedia information systems. Furthermore, the methodologies are applicable to the development of the various media themselves. For example, as audio and video presentations are planned, scripted, recorded and edited, the concepts and techniques described in this chapter can also be applied.

One of the purposes of this chapter is to bring a few of the more popular system and software development methodologies to the attention of managers and end users of multimedia development projects. Such enhanced awareness ought to result in increased usage. As more of the prescribed methodologies are applied to multimedia information systems and software projects, the general quality of the projects as well as the quality of the systems and software created by those projects ought to increase.

Another purpose of this chapter is to highlight one specific category of multimedia systems which is analogous to the genre of educational software known as computer assisted instruction (CAI). There are many specific considerations relating to the development of such CAI systems, which are unfamiliar to many seasoned, novice and end-user managers of information systems development projects. This paper seeks to explain the nature of those systems and will present methods to assure their quality.

Background Concepts

This section presents several background concepts as the basis for subsequent sections' discussions on applying appropriate methodologies to multimedia systems development projects. The first concept presented is total quality management and its application to information systems development projects. Next are general discussions to introduce the reader to the information system development life cycle and software engineering. Those are followed by a discourse on the phenomenon of end user computing. The section concludes with a comparison of the categories of multimedia applications, with particular attention paid to the type that involves computer assisted instruction.

Total Quality Management and Systems Development Projects

Total quality management (TQM) has become a major focus for many organizations (Berry, 1991). TQM provides the prescription for success in the increasingly competitive global market place. In the twenty-first century, it will be difficult for any organization to ignore the basic principles of TQM. Even service organizations will feel pressure from consumers and competitors to adopt a plan for insuring quality of delivered services. Government agencies will also be held more accountable by the public to incorporate quality awareness into all its programs and activities (Deming, 1986).

The focus on quality has gained unparalleled worldwide momentum. As evidence, one only needs to consider that the quality movement is so pervasive that the International Standards Organization has considered and adopted five standards for procedures to incorporate quality into organizational activities (ISO, 1993). The ISO 9000-9004 standards provide models for quality assurance in the aspects of design/development, production, installation, final inspection/testing, and servicing. The American National Standards Institute has adopted equivalent standards, Q90-Q94 (ANSI, 1987). Table 1 presents both sets of standards.

The intent of the ISO and ANSI standards for quality is to provide a means to describe and measure quality in all aspects of designing and supplying products and services. The standards can be used in contract negotiations between supplier and consumer. The standards can also be used as a model for an organization-wide quality assurance program. As such, the standards can guide the process of developing information systems including those which feature multimedia technologies.

Specifically, the ISO and ANSI quality standards call for each stage of the development of a product or service—design, development, installation, etc. — to be based on the verified and validated input specifications. The processes within each phase will be verified for quality and will be staffed with capable workers. The standards also specify that the output of each stage shall meet predetermined

ISO #	ANSI #	Topics Addressed
9000	Q90	Quality management and quality assurance standards—guidelines for selection and use.
9001	Q91	Model for quality assurance in design/development, production, installation and servicing
9002	Q92	Model for quality assurance in production and installation
9003	Q93	Model for quality assurance in final inspection and test
9004	Q94	Quality management and quality systems elements—guidelines

Table 1: ISO and ANSI Quality Standards

design requirements and acceptance criteria.

The information industry has strived for many years to create and use methodologies that would yield quality information systems and software. If properly applied, those methodologies should also allow systems and software development projects to conform to the ISO and ANSI quality standards. Specifically, the systems development methodologies are applied within the phases of the information systems development life cycle. Similarly, the quality assurance practices relevant to software development projects fall within the domain of software engineering. Both the information systems development life cycle and software engineering principles are discussed in subsequent sections.

Information System Development Life Cycle

Classically, information system development projects follow the linear phases of the information system development life cycle (ISDLC). There is minor disagreement as to the number, names and content of the ISDLC phases. However, there is a general consensus that system analysis activities are to be accomplished before system design activities, which in turn need to be completed before system construction and implementation activities. All those steps need to be accomplished before operation of the system can commence (Ahitiv & Neumann, 1994; Davis & Olson, 1985). Table 2 and the following discussion explains those ISDLC stages in more detail.

Stage	Activities
Analysis	Feasibility study
	Formation of project team
	Preliminary investigation
	Needs assessment
	Data gathering and analysis
	Information requirements determination
Design	Conceptual design
	Physical design
Construction	Programming
	Acquisition
Implementation	System testing
	Data Conversion
	Operator and user training
Operation	Performance monitoring
	System maintenance and enhancement

Table 2: Information System Development Life Cycle Stages and Activities

It is in the analysis stage that the system development project is formulated. A feasibility study is done to determine whether the project can be accomplished efficiently and effectively and whether to engage in the project further. The initial project team is formed and tasks are assigned. The team members set about to assess needs and determine the information and processing requirements that the completed system must meet. Users, managers and other relevant parties are interviewed to discover their perceptions of needs. Documentation is consulted. Data are collected and analyzed. The ultimate outcome is a needs and requirements specification document.

Systems design activities encompass two broad categories. First, the conceptual design must be performed. That includes specifying the environment in which the system will operate, the conditions it must meet, and the general flow of the system. Second is the physical design. The result of the second set of activities is a document which outlines specific hardware and software components which will comprise the system. In each design stage, multiple alternative designs should be discovered. Those are weighed against each other and against cost and other organizational constraints to choose the best one.

System construction activities include the coding, debugging and testing of application programs that are part of the complete system. In the next section on software engineering, those activities will be discussed in more detail. The system construction stage also includes the activities involved with procuring, assembling and testing hardware and software components which will comprise the completed system.

In the implementation stage, the final assembly and testing of the complete system is performed. Data are converted from any previous automated or manual system. Users and operators are trained on their aspects of the system.

Following successful implementation, the system is operational. Proper quality assurance procedures dictate that the performance of the system be monitored and evaluated. Periodically changes will be required. The need for change is two-fold. First, the system is a model of the real world. As such, when changes in an organization's operations or environment occur, corresponding changes need to be made to the system. Second, occasionally system and programming errors are found which had not previously been detected. Those bugs must be fixed. System and program maintenance is so prevalent that it is common for the project team to continue on assignment to that system well after the initial project is installed. In many organizations, such an assignment is permanent.

The phenomenon of system maintenance also justifies the use of the terms "life" and "cycle" in the "information system development life cycle" label. The growth and rejuvenation that results from system maintenance causes one to think of the information system almost as if it was a living entity. Furthermore, as a system maintenance project unfolds, the steps of analysis, design, construction and implementation are reapplied. Consequently, the ISDLC steps are applied in a cyclic manner to the system.

Excessive system and program maintenance is one of the severe problems that has plagued the information systems industry. It has been reported by many sources that system and program maintenance accounts for as much as 70% of the total time spent by information systems workers. Of course, that means only 30% of their time is left over to divide between creating new systems and many other organizational activities. That resulting low productivity level is alarming.

There are several factors which lead to excessive maintenance. Perhaps the most prevalent of those is that systems analysis, design and construction activities are not accomplished thoroughly enough. Sometimes that is in response to pressure from management and users to get to the implementation stage as quickly as possible. Such pressure is often due to the unenlightened practice of not involving management and end users early and often enough in the ISDLC. Consequently, it is often not until the installation stage that managers and end users see evidence that something worthwhile really is being created.

There are other reasons for not performing analysis, design or construction thoroughly. One is that information systems personnel might be unaware of the many tasks that should be performed. Another is that the projected completion schedule was set without enough slack or that the project has fallen behind schedule for some other reason. Of course, there is also the possibility that inferior workmanship is being applied. All of those reasons are also symptoms of an unenlightened approach to ISDLC.

Excessive maintenance time is also an indicator that proper TQM practices are not being followed. Decades before TQM became a widely accepted notion, the information systems industry began to address the issue of quality in information systems and software. That was, to a large degree, in response to the severe problem of excessive time being spent maintaining information systems and software, as explained above. Many ISDLC and software engineering methodologies have been developed to ensure that system analysis, design and construction are handled properly.

An enlightened approach to ISDLC should result in a higher level of quality both in the project and in the resulting system. As ISDLC methodologies are utilized, the enlightened approach will probably require more time to complete than the unenlightened approach. The pay off, of course, is that the system constructed using an enlightened approach will require less maintenance. If the system is in operation for a sufficiently long period of time, the savings accrued by minimizing system and program maintenance will more than justify the cost of the additional time required to use proper ISDLC methodologies.

Figure 1 illustrates a stereotypical relationship between the enlightened and unenlightened approaches to ISDLC. The logistics of a particular system development project could result in significantly different curves. The portions of the curve for the maintenance phase is considerably longer than for the other phases to represent the on-going nature of that stage of systems.

One popular alternative approach to the classical ISDLC is rapid system and software prototyping. Creation of a working prototype of the system relatively early in the information system development project provides many advantages. The eventual users and managers of the system can view a working prototype and can be able to

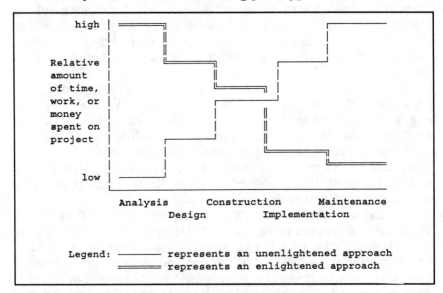

Figure 1: Stereotypical Relationship Between Enlightened and Unenlightened Approaches to the Information Systems Development Life Cycle

Category	ISDLC Phase	Sample Methodologies
Single phase methodologies	Analysis	SOP, BIAIT, BICS, SPM
	Design	IPC, PLA/PSA, SODA, Structured analysis, Entity-relationship & Bachman diagrams, System charting
	Construction	System flow diagrams, Structured programming
Two phase methodologies	IRD and system design	ADS
	Conceptual & physical system design	BISAD, TAG, PLA/PSA II DFD, SADT, HIPO, VTOC, Jackson diagrams, Warnier/Orr diagrams
Multi phase methodologies	Design, construction, implementation, and operation	HOSKINS, PLEXUS
	IRD, design, construction, implementation, and operation	ISDOS

Table 3: **Information Systems Development Life Cycle Methodologies**

conceptualize how the complete system will appear and operate. As a result, the prototype can greatly facilitate communications. Furthermore, given proper design of the prototype, it can become the system by adding missing features. Therefore, the time and effort to create the prototype is not an additional developmental cost.

Some contend that rapid prototyping is a contradiction to the ISDLC approach as it encourages system construction without sufficient prior analysis and design. Most agree, on the other hand, that prototyping simply changes the linear ordering of the ISDLC stages, by allowing iteration through the analysis, design and construction stages.

Whether the classical rigid ISDLC approach or the more flexible prototyping approach is used, the system development team has many tested and proven ISDLC methodologies at its disposal. Some methodologies address one phase of the project while others are integrated across several phases. A subsequent section will discuss the application of a few of the most popular ISDLC methodologies to multimedia system development projects. Table 3, which is adapted from Colter (1982) and Couger (1986), presents a few of those methodologies.

The ISDLC stages and methodologies discussed in this and subsequent sections are not explained in great depth herein as they are well-documented in a number of other sources. Rather the purpose is to introduce the topics in preparation for the discussions in the next section. For more detailed explanations, the reader should refer to any one of several system analysis and design textbooks (Burch, 1992; Fertuck, 1992; Jordan et al., 1992; Kendall, 1992; Kendall & Kendall, 1992).

Software Engineering

Software engineering is a term originally coined to clearly differentiate the practices of proper computer programming with those of undisciplined hacking. Today, software engineering has become a label for two phenomena. First, it refers to a set of principles and practices used by individuals who are purposefully engaged in proper computer programming activities. Second, software engineering has become a field for scientific study —complete with a theoretical basis—within the domain of computer science and information systems.

Software engineering has many characteristics in common with the concepts of the information systems development life cycle. The focus of software engineering is quality assurance as it is with ISDLC. The birth of software engineering as a discipline for study was, to a significant extent, a response to the dilemma of excessive software maintenance. Software engineers and scholars, like information systems practitioners and scholars, have created many methodologies to use in the development of software systems. The methodologies are typically applied in a asynchronous manner with each step

Software Development Phase	Methodology
Macro program design	Modular Diagrams, also known as: Visual Table of Contents (VTOC), Yourden or Constantine diagrams, or Structure Charts Jackson Diagrams Warnier-Orr Diagrams
Micro program design	Classical Program Flowcharting Pseudo Code Nassi-Schniederman Charts Input-Processing-Output Charts

Table 4: Software Engineering Methodologies

closely tied to the preceding and succeeding steps. Some of the software engineering methodologies are shown in Table 4.

Some contend that software engineering is a subset of the ISDLC focused on the portion of the design and construction stages that pertain to the creation of computer programs. Others would insist that software engineering is directly parallel to the entire ISDLC. The disagreement can be reduced to the notion that the terms "system" and "software" are often used interchangeably. Regardless, software engineering is a critical element in the development of multimedia systems and software.

The seasoned, successful information systems project manager will apply the principles and practices of software engineering, even to those projects which incorporate multimedia technology. Conversely, novice information system development project managers and the end user who is managing a multimedia system development project will not be aware of and will not apply software engineering. The purpose of this section is to make the novice and the end user project managers aware of the existence of software engineering.

A subsequent section will describe two of the more popular software engineering methodologies. Those are the concepts and principles of: 1) modular program design; and, 2) structured program design. To some, those two topics are one in the same. Indeed they do share the same goal, proper program design. Nonetheless, to the software engineer they are distinctly different. Modular program design is applied at the macro or overall program level, while structured program design is applied at the micro level, usually to design the contents of modules.

Just as with ISDLC, the concepts and methodologies of software engineering are well documented in a variety of sources. Hence they will not be explained in great detail herein. For more detailed explanations, the reader should consult any one of several good software engineering textbooks (Ghezzi et al., 1991; Pfleeger, 1991; Schach, 1993; Sommerville, 1989).

End User Computing

Some would argue that the day of the monolithic mainframe computer has passed. Others insist that the mainframe computer will always have a niche as it is the most appropriate platform for certain applications. Regardless of their position on that issue, none can argue that smaller computers have accounted for the largest growth in numbers of units sold during the past several years.

There are many reasons for the rapid growth in the number of small computers installed in organizations. In some instances, small computers are used to augment a larger corporate mainframe. In other instances, small computers have replaced a corporate mainframe as an organization has down-sized its information systems operation. In still other instances, an organization has opted for smaller computers because they fit the applications at hand. In addition to economic justification such those just given, there are other reasons for adopting smaller computers. Often users find the operating systems on smaller systems to be friendlier than those on larger platforms. There are also pride of ownership, power and status issues.

Very often, smaller computers—including both personal and mini computers—are housed in departments under the control of the managers of those end user departments rather than the manager of information systems. This phenomenon—known as "end user computing"—has rapidly gained in popularity for all the reasons given above. Unfortunately, in many instances, the reason that end user computing got a start in an organization is because the information systems professional staff was not as responsive to end user requests as the end users might have preferred.

Regardless of the reason for the existence of end user computing, a common complaint from information systems professionals is that end users do not take advantage of the many proven information system development life cycle and software engineering methodologies. The net result is a proliferation of systems and software that have not been analyzed, designed or constructed properly. Often it defaults to the information systems professionals to maintain such systems and software. The cost of maintaining systems and software which are not written to meet normal information systems department standards is typically prohibitive.

Therefore, it is commonly recommended that the information systems professionals within an organization serve as consultants to the end users, advising them as to the proper procedures to follow in developing their own systems. Often organizations will establish enterprise-wide standards which must be followed regardless of whether it is the end users or the information systems professionals who develop the system or software. Such consultation and standardization can contribute substantially to the improvement of all information systems development in an organization.

The attractiveness of multimedia technologies is causing an even greater increase in end user computing. At the same time, the complexity of the technology and the programs which use the technology has escalated. As a result, the problems associated with end users developing their own applications have also increased dramatically. Therefore, it is even more imperative that end users follow sound ISDLC and software engineering methodologies.

As with other topics in this section, the goal is to make the reader aware of end user computing rather than to explain it in great depth. For more complete discussions of the end user computing phenomenon, the reader can consult any one of several good textbooks on information systems concepts (Ahitiv & Neumann, 1994; Davis & Olson, 1985).

The Nature of Multimedia Projects

There are many applications wherein multimedia technology is used to augment computerized information systems which are otherwise fairly classical in nature. For example, software with multimedia capabilities can be used to manage a topical knowledge base such as a medical handbook (Frisse, 1988) or a complete organizational knowledge base (Akscyn et al., 1988). The use of multimedia software to manage a knowledge base is analogous to the use of a classical database management system to manage an enterprise database.

Another application of multimedia to augment a classical application would be in the aspects of a user interface. For instance, multimedia can be used to provide a more exciting means to access a database or information service (Raymond & Tompa, 1988) or to a computer assisted software engineering (CASE) package (Smith & Weiss, 1988).

On the other hand, multimedia could be applied to less classical information systems applications equally well. For example, multimedia technologies have been applied to create a media space, which is an electronic setting in which groups of people can engage in collaborative work even though they are in geographically separate locations (Bly et al., 1993; Fish et al., 1993). That is an extension of the concepts of telecommuting and group decision support systems. Another example is the use of hypertext to manage collections of ideas to foster the creative process for authors, researchers and other intellectual laborers (Halasz, 1988).

When multimedia technologies are applied to such classical or non-classical information systems applications as discussed above, proper ISDLC and software engineering methodologies must be employed in the development processes. The seasoned and successful manager of system and software development projects might recognize how to apply those techniques. On the other hand, the intrigue of the technology might cause even seasoned professionals to rush into the construction and implementation stages without paying proper attention to analysis and design.

The risk is extremely great that novice managers of system or software development projects will not be aware of the existence of proper ISDLC and software engineering methodologies. That will also be true where the project manager is an end user engaging in the creation of a multimedia project. The next section is intended to explain the need to use and the existence of such ISDLC and software engineering tools.

On the other hand, seasoned and successful managers of system and software development projects might be equally unaware as the novice of the special ramifications of a particular class of multimedia applications. The nature of many multimedia projects —arguably the majority—is to apply that technology to enhance instructional processes. Multimedia and hypertext technologies are being used on a widespread basis for such educational purposes.

Multimedia based instructional systems and software are a form of enhanced computer assisted instruction (CAI). CAI software without multimedia capabilities is used extensively in traditional primary, secondary and post-secondary educational environments, as well as in training environments in industry. CAI software with multimedia capabilities is gaining rapidly in popularity in those arenas.

Multimedia technologies have the potential to revolutionize our approaches to teaching (Bruder, 1991; Marchionini, 1988; Trotter, 1989). The technology alone is fascinating (Kennedy & Wright, 1990; Salpeter, 1991). When applied to an appropriate learning application, the results can be very impressive (Dede, 1987; Mendrinos, 1990). However, without the proper skills to build instructional applications, the technology alone is not effective (Bosco, 1984). An alternative is to buy prewritten or packaged software, assuming that the proper evaluation is done to ensure a good fit with the instructional task at hand (Dede, 1989; Watt, 1982).

CAI software which incorporates multimedia and hypertext provides considerable advantages over CAI without those capabilities. Hypermedia can give the learner the ability to navigate through a knowledge base. It allows the user to be in control rather than to be controlled (Megarry, 1988). Of course, teaching and learning functions also have a home in the corporate environment. Multimedia technologies are being applied extensively for a variety of instructional purposes in corporate and governmental settings. Multimedia can be used as a tool for employee training. It can also be used to instruct consumers, as in pre-sales and post-sales activities.

Multimedia-based CAI can motivate a learner—whether student, employee or consumer—to use the software and explore it more fully, thereby creating a more effective learning environment (Swensen & Anderson, 1983). However, multimedia-based CAI is not appropriate for all learning experiences, especially if more traditional educational processes can be equally (or more) effective and less costly (Salisbury, 1984). It has also been noted that CAI tends to be more effective when applied to analytical rather than intuitive situations (Dreyfus & Dreyfus, 1984).

When developing a CAI type of information system or software, there are unique considerations to be made. Specifically, the system and software must be centered on sound instructional principles and objectives. Those will be explained more thoroughly in the next section.

Improving the Quality of Multimedia Projects

As mentioned previously, the purpose of this discussion is to explain—especially to the novice manager of a system or software development project—how some specific methodologies can and should be applied to projects which include multimedia technologies. Application of the tools and concepts presented in this section should result in higher quality of multimedia system development projects and the systems and software produced by those projects.

To that end, a few of the most popular concepts and techniques will be briefly presented. It should be noted that the popularity of these chosen techniques is due to the significant return on investment that typically can result from applying the techniques. That pay-back is in terms of either the efficiency of the technique in its use to get the job done initially, or the effectiveness of the technique in building systems which can be maintained most readily.

Project Planning and Initiation

Prior to commencing an information systems development project, an organization must engage in deliberate and thorough planning. Much of the quality of the resulting system and software will be directly related to the quality of the project itself. The more time that the project managers spend in planning the project, the more likely that a quality project will result.

The purpose of this section is to highlight a few aspects of a multimedia system project. Most of the aspects of planning for information systems development projects will not change substantially just because the project includes multimedia technologies. However, inclusion of that technology does add some new planning elements that should be considered.

In the feasibility study, for instance, the project planner needs to estimate costs of developing a system and weigh them against the benefits the installed system ought to produce. It is often a challenge to quantify all the benefits of every aspect of an information system. The benefits of some aspects can be quantified directly and the benefits of other aspects can be quantified by evaluating the costs that would be avoided due to those features. However, it is quite difficult to place a monetary value on factors such as increased satisfaction of end users.

If multimedia is to be incorporated in the system, costs and benefits related to that technology will also need to be included. In some systems, the benefit of multimedia will be considerable and quantifiable in a relatively straight forward manner. However, often the justification for including multimedia is primarily to enhance the user interface to the remainder of the system. If such enhancement leads directly to increased user productivity, then it can be readily quantified. On the other hand, if such enhancement is intended only to improve user satisfaction, it might be questionable as to whether the cost of applying multimedia technology is justifiable.

There are other details of initial project planning that might be altered due to the inclusion of multimedia in the project. For example, it is widely prescribed that the project activities as well as the resulting system and software be thoroughly documented. That documentation provides considerable benefits to the project team during the development life cycle, and to management and users when the system and software is installed. Perhaps the greatest value of documentation is as an aid to future information systems professionals as they maintain the system and software, months and years after it has been installed.

Much of the documentation is external to the system and software. That is to say, the documentation takes the form of user manuals, systems descriptions and activity reports during the various stages of the development process. Conversely, some of the documentation is internal to the software being developed. Most programming languages allow the programmer to include comments within the programs to explain what each portion of the program is supposed to accomplish.

The problem is that some of the languages that are used to

incorporate multimedia technologies do not allow for internal program documentation. Of course, even if the language does allow for comments to be included in the program, a novice multimedia programmer might not realize the importance of including such documentation. The challenge to the initial project is to insure that documentation of the use of multimedia is not overlooked due to lack of capabilities within multimedia programming languages or lack of experience of multimedia programmers.

Another initial project planning activity that is complicated by inclusion of multimedia relates to staffing the project team. One or more members of the project team must have a sufficient level of expertise with multimedia technology in order to derive the greatest benefits of that technology. The need is for multimedia programmers as well as multimedia designers (Van Dam, 1988). Unfortunately, that expertise is not yet widely distributed (or even available) in many organizations.

The problems become even more complex if the multimedia project includes the production of audio/video materials. It is safe to assume that the information systems professional who has experience with audio/video production is a rare individual. Integration of such capabilities in a multimedia information systems project will greatly complicate all ISDLC activities.

The implications are threefold. First, an organization might need to invest in formal multimedia training before the project can commence, causing delays in completing the project. Second, if multimedia expertise is limited within an organization, the opportunity to engage in more than one multimedia project at one time would be seriously jeopardized. Third, quality walkthroughs in which the project team frequently engages might be less effective and efficient if some of the project team members are not conversant in the details of the multimedia technologies addressed in the meeting.

Some educational institutions have found a partial solution for the shortage of trained multimedia professionals. Students, working under the supervision of an instructor in a multimedia course, have been assigned team projects to develop multimedia-based computer assisted instruction systems for other instructors in the school (Shaw & Farnsworth, 1993). Other industries could learn from that model by conducting multimedia training sessions. End users attending those sessions would be closely supervised as they develop their own multimedia applications in compliance with corporate standards. Information systems professionals attending those sessions could design and create portions of future systems as their class assignments.

Incorporating Instructional Objectives

The development process for systems that are intended for instructional purposes can serve as a model for the development of all multimedia-based information systems. That is due to the intensive user-orientation of both instructional-based and multimedia-based information systems. This section focuses on the intersection of those two classes of systems, i.e. on instructional-based systems which incorporate multimedia technologies. The advice can readily be applied by developers and project managers of other kinds of multimedia-based information systems as well.

Construction of multimedia systems that are intended for instructional purposes presents a challenge for which information systems professionals are typically not trained. The challenge is to create a system so that it properly addresses instructional objectives. The nature of the system becomes that of a computer assisted instruction (CAI) package. That greatly changes the nature of planning for the systems development project, as there are many considerations pertinent to CAI projects that are not present in the typical ISDLC project.

Fortunately, there is a well-developed body of literature which addresses the planning of CAI projects and the creation of CAI software. It draws heavily on the even more well-developed body of literature pertaining to learning theory, proper instructional design and instructional objectives. In several ways, it ties in well with research on human computer interaction.

Information regarding learning theory, instructional design and objectives are described in many sources. In particular, the relationship of those topics to computer assisted instruction is explained in a number of good textbooks (Hannafin & Peck, 1988; Walker & Hess, 1984). The reader is referred to such works for more complete information.

There is unanimous agreement in the CAI literature that effective instructional or tutorial software must be based on sound instructional objectives and proper instructional design. That is true regardless of the specific technology used. The designers of CAI software, as well as other information systems, which incorporated multimedia or hypertext technologies should follow that premise as well.

The process of planning for projects which incorporate multimedia technologies in an instructional or tutorial manner should also reflect the need to address learning objectives. Several aspects of the classical system development life cycle need to change. Those include the feasibility study, needs assessment, system design, and system testing activities.

For example, before the conclusion is drawn that a particular system should be of a multimedia-based computer assisted instruction design, the feasibility study should focus on assessing whether a multimedia CAI approach is appropriate. That decision should be based on an examination of the objectives and cost effectiveness of the training that is intended to be accomplished. One must also consider whether some other media or instructional approach might deliver the training more effectively or efficiently.

Computer assisted instruction—with or without multimedia—has the potential advantage of providing individualized instruction that keeps the learner's attention and provides increased motivation. That is similar to the attractiveness, improved productivity, and reduced error rates that a graphical user interface might create as a front-end of an otherwise traditional information system. That is due, to a large extent, to the immediate feedback provided by the technology and the sense of control over the learning process that the learner perceives. CAI software can also track the learner's progress and provide feedback to the administrator of the instructional process, if the appropriate features are included.

On the other hand, CAI applications can have disadvantages. For example, CAI can be a more expensive instructional delivery mechanism than other more classical instructional approaches, such as classroom instruction or video tape. CAI also requires more development time and is more of a challenge to update, especially if the subject of the lesson changes frequently. Another disadvantages of CAI is that it limits interaction with other human learners, thus reducing the incidental learning that is not programmed into the software. Furthermore, the learner must be able to operate the hardware and software platform before the CAI software can be utilized. All those potential disadvantages of a CAI system are exacerbated within multimedia systems.

Scholarly research indicates that CAI is, on the average, no better or worse than traditional instructional techniques (Hannason & Peck, 1988). Bearing that in mind, an organization should weigh carefully the advantages and disadvantages of CAI when considering the feasibility of applying CAI concepts to the project at hand. Determination of whether multimedia-based CAI is the best approach must be a key part of the feasibility study.

Needs assessment must focus on the determination of one or more appropriate instructional objectives. The objectives will guide the development of the lesson and the software that delivers the lesson. The objectives will also be the basis for evaluation of the effectiveness of the CAI system and software. Well-written instructional objectives must include statements that indicate the measurable behaviors which should be the outcome of the lesson, the conditions for delivery, and criteria for judging the success of the lesson. Focusing on objectives is, of course, important for non-CAI-based multimedia systems as well.

The following are three examples of instructional objectives which might be found in multimedia CAI packages. 1) "When you have completed viewing the images presented by this software, you should be able to discuss in an essay the important Greek artists of the early twentieth century with the art works they produced." 2) "After you have completed the lesson contained in this software package, you should be able to move to the welding lab and, under the supervision of the lab proctor, correctly perform three spot welds on materials supplied to you in the lab." 3) "Once you have viewed this presentation, you will understand four reasons why your company should buy our product and will sign and return the attached order form."

Each of the three preceding instructional objectives illustrates a different purpose for the multimedia CAI package. The first is a classical classroom type of objective. The second is for an on-the-job training situation. The third is a pre-sale illustration. In each case, the objective states a measurable behavior as the outcome of the lesson. Each also specifies the delivery conditions and criteria for judging success.

A rule of thumb for the designer is to consider the advantages and disadvantage of CAI systems and software, as presented above. The designer should try to incorporate features that maximize the advantages and minimize the disadvantages of CAI. For example, the software ought to be designed so that it is tutorial and extremely easy to operate. That would reduce the disadvantage associated with the learner's need to master the hardware and software platform prior to using the CAI software.

Furthermore, the packaging of the lesson must adhere to sound instructional design principles. Those include incorporating mechanisms to keep and focus the learner's attention, to provide feedback and reinforcement, and to evaluate the learner's performance. The CAI system should inform the learner of the instructional objectives addressed by the system before the learner commences the lesson.

The CAI designer should keep several other factors in mind. The designer should include methods to individualize the CAI package to various levels of backgrounds and achievement. The software should not include material or references that would be disadvantageous or offensive to any specific demographic groups or that would date the presentation. Many of the above points should also be applied to multimedia systems which do not include CAI characteristics.

After the multimedia CAI system has been designed and constructed, it needs to be tested. System testing of CAI packages also takes on a different dimension than testing of more traditional systems. To be considered effective, CAI software must be tested in actual operation with a number of learners, as is the case with all information systems. The learners' performance must be measured in order to assure that the software is achieving its goals, namely meeting its instructional objectives.

Data Flow Diagrams and Document Analysis

Many activities of the analysis stage of the systems development life cycle remain much the same whether or not multimedia technologies are to be included. Analysts still need to interview users and managers to determine their requirements. Data flow diagrams, as illustrated by Figure 2, still need to be drawn to gain a clear understanding of the flow of the existing and proposed systems.

A data flow diagram (DFD) is unique in its ability to capture details about the flow of information through a system without concern for the control which causes the flow. Moreover, DFDs are

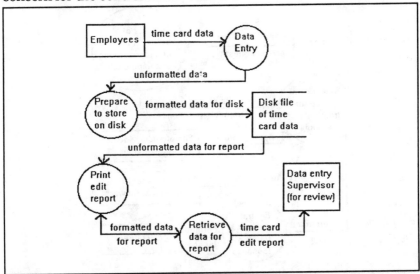

Figure 2: Sample Data Flow Diagram for Employee Time Card Batch Data Entry

easily understood by non-technical individuals. In that sense, a DFD can be a valuable analysis tool for use in communicating about the system with users and managers. Furthermore, a DFD can be the basis for an easy transition to the design stage of the information system development life cycle.

The squares in a DFD indicate the sources and destinations of information. In the case of Figure 2, the sources of information are the employees who submit their time card data, while the destination is the data entry supervisor who examines the edit report for errors. The lines represent flows of information, where each flow is different. The circles are points where the data are transformed from one form to another. The points where the lines and circles intersect indicate user views, e.g. unique reports, screen layouts, etc. An open rectangle represents a data storage facility, usually a disk file.

Figure 2 depicts a classical business application example. Data flow diagrams can and should also be applied to multimedia systems. An illustration of a data flow diagrams for a multimedia systems is shown in Figure 3. That is an illustration of a multimedia computer assisted instruction session which pre-tests a trainee and customizes an audio/video training session based on the trainee's level of understanding.

When dealing with multimedia technology, data flow diagrams ought to be used as well. The flow of information within a multimedia system is the essence of that system. Depicting the multimedia

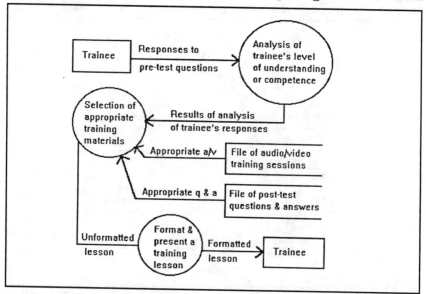

Figure 3: Sample Data Flow diagram for a Multimedia Application

information flows using DFDs will enhance the level of understanding about the system. The quality of the system under design will be enhanced as a result.

One activity should be added to the analysis stage of the ISDLC when the project involves multimedia technology. Most multimedia projects will intertwine many multimedia documents, which might include sound tracks, still images and motion pictures. It is important to perform an analysis of those documents to gain an understanding of what is to be included (Perlman, 1989). Data flow diagrams can be applied to document analysis as well as system analysis.

A key part of document analysis is document selection. Documents should be chosen for inclusion only if the documents relate to the task at hand or to the central theme of the system and software under development. Documents should complement each other and should be comprehensible to the ultimate users of the system. Other considerations relate to how the documents should be linked, what kind of links should be used and where the links should be located (Glushko, 1989).

Modular and Structured Program Design

Two proven techniques for use in the ISDLC design stage are modular program design and structured program design. Both are used in the detailed design phase in preparation for writing programs. Modular design is typically used to design programs at the macro level, while structured design is used to design the contents of the program modules at the micro level.

The goals of both modular design and structured design are to produce software that is of a higher quality, and software that will be easier to maintain. The use of each technique will result in more time spent in the program design phase. Often the use of each technique will result in more lines of program code being generated than if the techniques were not used.

Structured program design and modular program design should both be applied to the design of multimedia software. Multimedia authoring tools—including those generically referred to as hypertext—are indeed programming languages (Canning, 1992; Fersko-Weiss, 1991). As such, the hypertext program designer ought to use the standard techniques for applying computer languages, i.e. modular and structured design.

Modular Program Design

Modular design can be accomplished by using any of several specific methodologies, as shown in Table 4. The most frequently used technique is a block diagram. Although there are subtle differences among the methodologies, each can be used equally effectively.

Regardless of the methodology used, the basic approach is the same. As the program designer examines the potential design, the program is conceptualized as several logical units. Each logical unit accomplishes a specific task. The program design is then divided along the lines of those logical units into relatively small modules. Each module will eventually be developed into a cohesive set of program instructions.

Each module is designed so as to not be too highly dependent or tightly coupled to any other module. Each module should have only one entry point and one exit point.

Figure 4 illustrates the use of a block diagram to modularize a typical business application program. The program is one which will produce a report from a previously entered data file.

Block diagrams and other modular design tools can and should be applied to multimedia program design as well. An illustration of the use of a block diagram to modularize the design of a multimedia program is shown in Figure 5. It illustrates a computer assisted

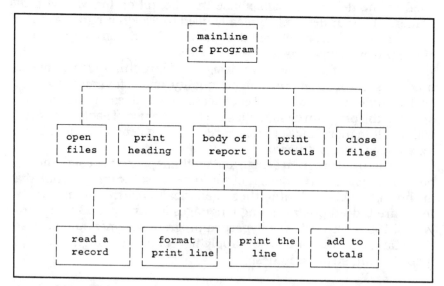

Figure 4: Modular Programming Example Using a Block Diagram

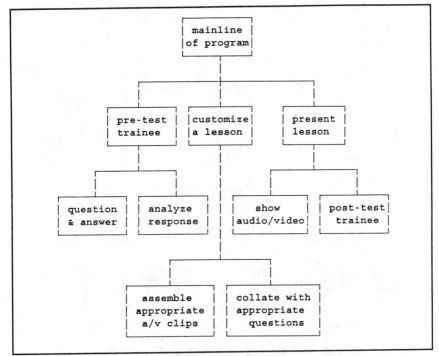

Figure 5: Modularized Multimedia Application Program Using a Block Diagram

instruction program that pre-tests a trainee, assembles an appropriate audio/visual presentation based on the outcome of that pre-test, then presents the lesson and post-tests the trainee. That illustration corresponds to the system depicted in the data flow diagram in Figure 3.

Structured Program Design

As with modular program design, there are many methodologies for use in structured program design. One of the most popular techniques is called pseudo code. The oldest technique is flow charting, which, due to its more visual nature, is used in Figure 6 to illustrate structured programming.

The focus of structured programming is the detailed design of the content of each of the modules created in the modular design phase. The basic principal of structured programming is that each module can be designed as one—or as a combination—of three unique control structures. The use of only those three control

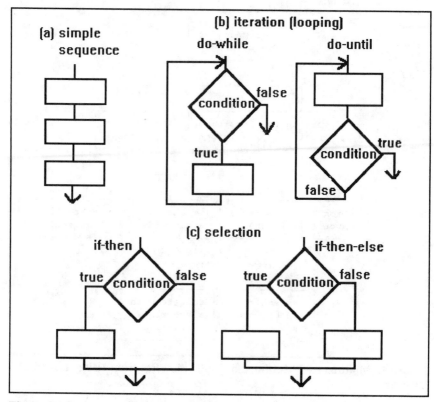

Figure 6: Structured Programming Control Patterns

patterns will produce software that is reliable and easy to maintain. The use of any other pattern will produce improper code, often called "spaghetti code" by professional programmers.

The three control patterns are illustrated in Figure 6. First is the "simple sequence." In this pattern, one program instruction is followed by the next, and the next. Although the illustration only shows three program instructions — represented by rectangles — any number of instructions can be included in a simple sequence.

The second control pattern is the "iteration" or "looping" pattern. There are two variations. In one, the controlling condition is evaluated prior to execution of the loop. In the other, the controlling condition is evaluated after a pass of the loop has been completed. The former is called the "do-while" pattern and the latter is the "do-until" pattern. The choice of patterns is dictated by the needs of a particular module.

The third control pattern is called the "selection." Two variations on the selection are shown. One is typically implemented by an "if-then" set of language commands. The other is implemented by an "if-then-else" language construct. A third variation of the selection control pattern, called the "case structure," is not shown. It is usable in many but not all programming languages and differs from the other two variations in that multiple paths are allowed based on the outcome of the evaluation of the condition.

Both the selection patterns and the iteration patterns involve branching to a non-sequential point in the program. In each instance the branching is based on the evaluation of a condition. The set of program instructions that is executed as a result of the branch —indicated in each diagram in Figure 6 by a single rectangle—can be one instruction or several. Furthermore, the set of instructions can take the form of a simple sequence or a selection or an iteration.

Spaghetti code is caused by the programmer designing a branch that is not based on a condition. Such unconditional branches are usually implemented by use of a "go-to" language construct. Hence the indiscriminate use of the go-to construct should be avoided. Unfortunately, many hypertext languages allow and even encourage the use of the go-to construct. Consequently, many multimedia applications are written in a spaghetti code fashion (Van Dam, 1988). Awareness of and adherence to proper modular and structured program design techniques should foster improved quality of multimedia software.

Summary

This paper has related the concepts of total quality management to the development of information systems which integrate multimedia technology. The prescribed methods to bring total quality management to information system and software development projects involve applying the tools and techniques of the information systems development life cycle and software engineering.

Unfortunately, the popularity of end user computing suggests that not all multimedia system and software development projects will be managed by an individual who is knowledgeable or skilled in the use of ISDLC or software engineering methodologies. Hence, this material has presented several such considerations. In the project initiation activities, attention should be paid to justifying the use of multimedia technology, to insuring that proper documentation will occur, and to the staffing of the project team to include workers with multimedia expertise.

In the analysis stage of the ISDLC, data flow diagrams should be used to conceptualize and illustrate the flow of information in a multimedia system. The analyst should also focus on the analysis of documents and the interrelationship of the documents that are to be included in the multimedia system. In the ISDLC design stage, proper modular and structured program design techniques should be applied to multimedia projects.

Development of systems and software which incorporate multimedia technologies for instructional purposes presents a different scenario than most information systems professionals and end users have previously encountered. Effective instructional software must be based on well-written instructional objectives and on proper instructional delivery methods. That changes the nature of the system development project. The system developers need to receive training in such topics in order to build quality systems.

Adherence to all of the concepts and techniques described above should foster a higher level of quality in multimedia systems and software as measurable in several manners. First, one acid test of information system and software quality is whether the system and software is relatively easy and less time consuming to maintain. Improved maintainability is the logical outcome of following the methodologies described above.

A second test of software and system quality is end-user satisfaction with the utility of the system and software. User involvement in all the stages of the information system development life cycle is a critical success factor in achieving user satisfaction. Following the methodologies decribed herein will result in more user involvement and greater satisfaction.

A test of quality of computer assisted instruction systems is improved learner performance and comprehension of the material at hand. Basing multimedia-based CAI on valid learning objectives is critical to that end. Designing and constructing CAI using the proven techniques discussed in this chapter will result in designed level of quality.

References

Ahitiv, N., & Neumann, S. (1994). *Principles of Information Systems for Management*, 4th Ed. Dubuque, Iowa: Wm. C. Brown Publishers.

Akscyn, R., McCracken, D., & Yoder, E. (1988). KMS: A distributed hypermedia system for managing knowledge in organizations. *Communications of the ACM*, 31(7). 820-835.

American National Standards Institute [ANSI]. (1987). *Quality Systems - Model for Quality Assurance in Design/Development, Production, Installation, and Servicing*. Milwaukee: American Society for Quality Control.

Berry, T. H. (1991). *Managing the Total Quality Transformation*. New

York: McGraw-Hill Company.

Bly, S. A., Harrison, S. R., & Irwin, S. (1993). Media spaces: Bringing people together in a video, audio, and computing environment. *Communications of the ACM*, 36(1). 28-47.

Bosco, J. J. (1984, April). Interactive video: Educational tool or toy. Educational Technology. 27-31.

Bruder, I. (1991, Sep). Guide to multimedia: How it changes the way we teach and learn. *Electronic Learning*, 11(1). 22-30.

Burch, J. G. (1992). *Systems Analysis, Design, and Implementation.* Boston: Boyd & Fraser Publishing Company.

Canning, J. (1992, Mar 9). Multimedia authoring tools. *Infoworld.* 76-96.

Colter, M. A. (1982). Evolution of the structured methodologies. In Couger, J. D., Colter, M. A., & Knapp, R. W. (Eds). *Advanced System Development/Feasibility Techniques.* New York: John Wiley & Sons.

Couger, J. D. (1982). Evolution of system development techniques. In Couger, J. D., Colter M. A. & Knapp, R. W. (Eds.). *Advanced System Development/Feasibility Techniques.* New York: John Wiley & Sons.

Davis, G. B., & Olson, M. H. (1985). *Management Information Systems: Conceptual Foundations, Structure and Development.* New York: McGraw-Hill.

Dede, C. J. (1987, Nov.). Empowering environments, hypermedia, and microworlds. *The Computing Teacher*, 15(3). 20-26.

Dede, C. J. (1989, Apr). Planning guidelines for emerging instructional technologies. *Educational Technology.* 7-12.

Deming, W. E. (1986). *Out of the Crisis.* Cambridge, MS: Massachusetts Institute of Technology Center for Advanced Engineering Study.

Dreyfus, H. L., & Dreyfus, S. E. (1984). Putting computers in their proper place: Analysis versus intuition in the classroom. *Teacher's College Record*, 85(4). 68-75.

Fersko-Weiss, H. (1991, May 28). 3-D reading with the hypertext edge. *PC Magazine.* 241-282.

Fertuck, L. (1992). *Systems Analysis and Design With Case Tools.* Dubuque, IA: Wm. C. Brown Publishers.

Fish, R. S., Kraut, R. E., Root, R. W., & Rice, R. E. (1993). Video as a technology for informal communications. *Communications of the ACM*, 36(1). 48-61.

Frisse, M. E. (1988). Searching for information in a hypertext medical notebook. *Communications of the ACM*, 31(7). 880-886.

Gheezi, C., Jazayeri, M., & Mandrioli. (1991). *Fundamentals of Software Engineering.* Englewood Cliffs, NJ: Prentice-Hall.

Glushko, R. J. (1989). Design issues for multi-document hypertexts. *Proceedings of Hypertext '89.* 51-60.

Halasz, F. (1988). Reflections on notecards: Seven issues for next generation of hypermedia systems. *Communications of the ACM*, 31(7). 836-852.

Hannafin, M. J., & Peck, K. L. (1988). *The Design, Development, and Evaluation of Instructional Software.* New York: Macmillan Publishing

Company. International Standards Organization [ISO]. (1993). ISO 9000. Boston: Allyn and Bacon.

Jordan, E. W., Machesky, J. J., Matkowski, J. B. (1990). *Systems Development: Requirements, Evaluation, Design, and Implementation.* Boston: PWS-KENT Publishing Company.

Kendall, K. E., & Kendall, J. E. (1992). *Systems Analysis and Design,* 2nd ed. Englewood Cliffs, NJ: Prentice-Hall.

Kendall, P. (1992). *Introduction to Systems Analysis and Design: A Structured Approach,* 2nd ed. Dubuque, IA: Wm. C. Brown Publishers.

Kennedy, W. P., & Wright, G. (1990, Apr). Desktop video. *InCider.* 44-49.

Marchionini, G. (1988, Nov). Hypermedia and learning: Freedom and chaos. *Educational Technology.* 8-12.

Megarry, J. (1988). Hypertext and compact discs: The challenge of multimedia learning. *British Journal of Educational Technology,* 19(3). 172-183.

Mendrinos, R. (1990, Jan). CD-ROM: A technology that is steadily entering school libraries and classrooms. *Electronic Learning,* 9(4). 34-36.

Perlman, G. (1989). Asynchronous design/evaluation methods for hypertext technology development. *Proceedings of Hypertext '89.* 61-82.

Pfleeger, S. L. (1991). *Software Engineering: The Production of Quality Software,* 2nd ed. New York: Macmillan Publishing Company.

Raymond, D. & Tompa, F. (1988). Hypertext and the new Oxford English Dictionary. *Communications of the ACM,* 31(7). 871-879.

Salisbury, D. F. (1984, Mar). How to decide when and where to use microcomputers for instruction. *Educational Technology.* 33-38.

Salpeter, J. (1991, Feb). Beyond Videodisks: Compact discs in the multimedia classroom. *Technology & Learning.* 33-67.

Schach, S. R. (1993). *Software Engineering,* 2nd ed. Homewood, IL: Richard D. Irwin, Inc.

Shaw, H. J., & Farnsworth, B. J. (1993). The academy of multimedia: A quest for new destinations. Technological Horizons in Education *(T.H.E.) Journal,* 20(7). 87-88.

Smith, J. B., & Weiss, S. F. (1988). Hypertext. *Communications of the ACM,* 31(7). 816-819.

Sommerville, I. (1989). *Software Engineering,* 3rd ed. Workingham, England: Addison-Wesley.

Swenson, R. P., & Anderson, C. (1983, Spring). The role of motivation in computer assisted instruction. *The Journal of Computers in Mathematics and Science Teaching.* 43-49.

Trotter, A. (1989, Mar). Schools gear up for hypermedia — A quantum leap in electronic learning. *The American School Board Journal.* 35-37.

Van Dam, A. (1988). Hypertext '87 keynote address. *Communications of the ACM,* 31(7). 887-895.

Walker, D. F., & Hess, R. D. (1984). *Instructional Software: Principles and Perspectives for Design and Use.* Belmont, CA: Wadsworth Publishing Co.

Watt, M. (1982, May). Making a case for software evaluation. *The Computing Teacher,* 9(8). 27-31.

Chapter 8

Practical Issues in Multimedia User Interface Design for Computer-Based Instruction

J. Morgan Morris
G. Scott Owen
M.D. Fraser
Georgia State University

Computer systems using information components of diverse media such as text, hypertext, static and animated graphics, still photographs, and motion video hold great promise as information tools in many diverse areas. The designer of a multimedia system faces many challenges in both design and evaluation of the system. Thus, a methodology for producing a multimedia application is needed, as well as understanding of evaluation techniques for both textual and non-textual media components. A design methodology is presented that encapsulates appropriate use of diverse media and a media production plan, as well as other typical user interface issues. Then evaluation techniques are discussed, followed by practical experiences in applying the methodology to educational systems.

Multimedia systems represent the synthesis of several longstanding technologies including computers, video, print, and audio. In recent years multimedia technology has become available for affordable personal computer systems. These technologies should prove to be powerful tools in many areas, including learning, persuasion, documentation, and visualization (Bunzel and Morris, 1992). Multimedia systems are flourishing, and it is expected that they will soon be used at all levels of education. Trends towards small, sophisticated, and powerful computers, represented today by notebook computers and personal communicators, will open the market for these technologies to larger segments of the general population.

Computer-based instruction (CBI) is rapidly emerging as the education and training medium of choice for many schools and businesses. Advantages typically mentioned for CBI include lower costs, increased student achievement, better handling of individual differences, and an increase in student motivation (Shlechter, 1991). Multimedia systems are capable of realizing the full potential offered by CBI. The primary challenge, then, is the design of the information content and the appropriate use of diverse media to provide an advantageous learning environment.

The quality of an instructional multimedia system depends on the integration of technology, information, and personnel. Many problems associated with the development of a quality instructional system cannot be solved merely by piecing together existing media components. An effective CBI system must exploit the interactive aspects of the system in order to provide full advantages to the user. For example, teacher training is often cited as a barrier to the widespread use of computer systems at all levels of education. Using a proper design methodology, multimedia systems can provide documentation and other user assistance appropriate for those who will be teaching with them.

The goal of this chapter is to present a set of recommendations for multimedia training systems based on the literature and experiences in the design and implementation of such systems (Owen, Morris, and Fraser, 1992). Training goals for such a system include the following:

- The information in the system is correct and complete.
- The information is presented using appropriate media.
- Multiple representations of the information are used to take advantage of the diverse media.
- The information is easy to learn, retain, and reference.
- Users know how to interact with the system.
- Users perceive the system to be beneficial and enjoyable.

Two broad needs are implied by these goals. The first is a multimedia user interface design process intended to capture all of the necessary information. This is presented in the first section titled Multimedia User Interface Design. The second need is for guidance in evaluating platforms and the diverse information components contained in such a system. Together, these insure that the interactive features of the system are molded to the characteristics of the intended user audience. This information is presented in the section titled *Multimedia User Interfaces for Computer-Based Instruction*. Experiences in applying these methods of design and evaluation are collected and described in the section named *System Development Experiences*.

Multimedia User Interface Design

The design of a high quality human-computer interface should take the user into account during early phases of design. To do this properly, the target audience for the system must be identified and described so that their physical and cognitive characteristics are understood. This information may be obtained from existing data and specially constructed surveys. Such information is critical for behavioral evaluations and for provision of special interaction strategies to accommodate population differences.

The implementation plans for the system should feature iterative design, to allow input from the potential users in the early stages of development. Frequent behavioral evaluations during implementation with representative users must be planned to keep the information components relevant and easy to learn.

The following process describes the crucial components of a user interface design process as applied to the use of multimedia technologies. Figure 1 is an overview of the major components of the design process. It consists of components selected from a number of sources, including Shneiderman (1992), Spencer (1985), and Whiteside, Bennett, and Holtzblatt (1988), then tuned to the needs of multimedia design.

Although these components and their subcomponents are presented sequentially, many of the actions involved within each component may be performed concurrently. For example, most of the components of the Initial Analysis phase are independent of one another, and need not be conducted in sequence.

No mention of personnel is made, since the makeup of design teams varies widely for organizations and individual projects. For a

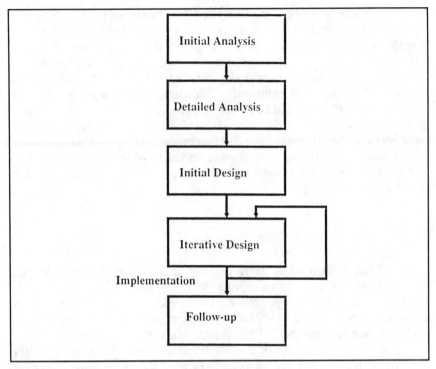

Figure 1: Multimedia Interface Design Process

large-scale high quality effort, specialists are needed in the areas of graphics design, technical writing, video production, and sound engineering. Contrast this with a system intended for a single recurring class, where the instructor captures information for the benefit of his or her class. The quality of the media is less of a concern since the instructor can control when and where the information is presented within a course and accompany it with additional material.

The formality of the components may vary according to the specific needs of a design. In a large-scale design effort, there may be a need for formal reports to ensure that the information is communicated to all designers and that a common vision of the result is maintained. For a smaller effort, many of the components may be assumed or omitted.

Initial Analysis

The Initial Analysis phase of user interface design involves

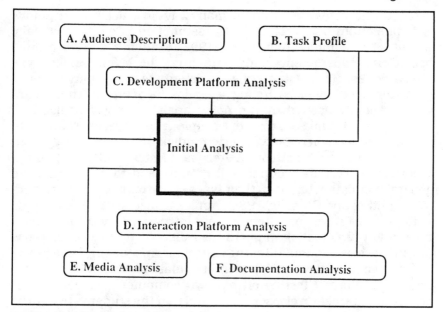

Figure 2: Initial Analysis Overview

collecting all of the information that may influence design decisions. The composition of the user audience, the tasks they will perform, and the hardware and software they will use all affect the way that the system should be shaped to fit the users' needs.

The Initial Analysis consists of several components, as shown in Figure 2:

    A.   Audience Description.
    B.   Task Profile.
    C.   Development Platform Analysis.
    D.   Interaction Platform Analysis.
    E.   Media Analysis.
    F.   Documentation Analysis.

This section describes each of these components.

Audience Description. The primary axiom of user interface design is to "know the user." This is necessary in order to plan the interface design to accommodate the user's needs and to evaluate the resulting design using representative subjects.

It is often tempting, whether intentionally or unintentionally, to assume that users are well represented by those who are designing the software. Given the many ways in which human beings can differ from one another, this assumption is often drastically wrong. For example, Tognazzini (1992) examines several groups based on temperament using data from the Myers-Briggs Type Indicator Test. This test attempts to determine personality types by detecting the tendencies among several pairs of types. (These pairs were originally posited by the noted analytical psychologist Carl Jung.) For example, introverted people tend to prefer solitude to recover energy, whereas extraverted individuals draw energy from their encounters with others (Keirsey and Bates, 1984). Tognazzini reports that certain occupational groups tend to differ from the general population based on their types. For example, programmers (50%) (Sitton and Chmelir, 1984), Apple engineers (42%), and Apple writers (39%) were consistently more introverted than the general population (25%). Programmers also differed on the other types (intuition vs. sensation, thinking vs. feeling, and judging vs. perceiving) in comparison with the general population. One of the authors has done informal testing on his own computer science human-computer interaction classes and found that the students tend to be more introverted, more intuitive, more thinking, and more judging than the general population. Thus, programmers' ways of communicating and thinking may be quite different from that of the general population.

The differences exhibited by people have been studied in fields such as psychology, sociology, and education. Many of these differences can affect the interaction between a human being and a computer system (Egan, 1988). For example, aging can change many interaction characteristics (Czaja, 1988; Morris, 1993). A user's individual aptitudes and abilities may influence the degree to which the use of visual technologies are beneficial. For example, spatial abilities have been linked to other areas of computation (Gomez, Egan, and Bowers, 1986), and it may be the case that those with below average spatial abilities benefit most from an animation. Blake (1977) found that subjects with low spatial aptitude benefited from motion sequences more than those with high spatial abilities. A system featuring visual displays of information would certainly benefit those with below average reading abilities.

Age has proven to be an important factor in several studies involving animated graphics. Research has shown that younger students rely on images more often than do older students (Pressley, 1977). Rieber (1990) found significant performance differences in a study involving fourth- and fifth-graders, while in a similar study involving adults no performance differences were found.

The technical, educational, and domain-specific background of the user population must be considered. Many concepts taught in school or in educational computer systems assume certain knowledge and abilities that are necessary to grasp the new concepts. For example, in the domain of computer programming, searching and sorting algorithms are important for programming any realistic system, and these core concepts are often taught early in the curriculum. A multimedia instructional system for teaching these algorithms could feature textual descriptions and animations of the algorithms to allow students to view the process described by static code. Understanding many of these algorithms requires certain prerequisite knowledge. For example, in order to understand the heap sort, a student must be familiar with the concept of a binary tree, and have a programming background in order to understand the use of sorting routines.

Given the diversity of characteristics of computer users, software designers must be made aware of the differences so that they can construct the interface to fit the user population. Additionally, it is quite difficult for the creator of any product to be objective about its usability. Thus, a method is required to determine the characteristics of the target user audience so that (1) the designers will be aware of the differences, (2) the characteristics of the user audience can be accommodated by the user interface design, and (3) the resulting interface design can be tested using representative users.

The steps to take in developing an audience description include the following:

1. Determine which characteristics are needed.
2. Gather precompiled data from existing sources.
3. Collect the remaining data.

The interaction environment helps to determine which characteristics are needed. An instructional system intended for the general population should accommodate a wider range of characteristics than one intended for a selective audience. For example, the textual components of an interface should be written for a tenth or eleventh grade level for the general population, while a system developed for a college class need not be as restrictive.

Some of the characteristics that are appropriate for most user interface design efforts include:

• Demographic: Age, Gender, Handedness, Socio-economic status.

- Education: Level, Type.
- Individual Aptitudes: Reading Level, Reading Rate, Spatial Ability, etc.
- Physical Abilities/Impairments: Visual, Auditory, Motor.
- Skills: Job skills, Typing.
- Computer Experience: Operating Systems, Programming, Devices, Terminology.
- Familiar Technology: Telephones, VCRs, FAX, etc.
- Familiar Software: Word Processing, Spreadsheets, Programming Languages, Communications, Database, etc.
- Familiar Information Sources: Reading Habits, Viewing Habits.
- Attitudes: Motivations, Attitudes Towards Computers.
- Cultural Factors: Languages, Symbols, Conventions, Colors.

The choice of characteristics to gather and analyze must be made carefully to determine whether there is justification for committing to the potential cost and difficulties associated with data collection. For example, some individual aptitudes may require specific tests and be difficult to administer to large populations. Some characteristics, such as handedness and color deficiencies, may be assumed to conform to established percentages. For example, left-handers are usually considered to make up from 8 to 10 percent of the world population (Barsley, 1970). Approximately 8 percent of the male population of European descent exhibits some form of color deficiency; the percentage of females with color deficiencies is believed to be less than 1 percent (Hurvich, 1981). Most other characteristics, including experience, skills, attitudes, familiar software and technologies, and languages and conventions specific to a particular environment, do not correspond to established percentages. In such cases there are two choices: either gather data pertaining to them, or else design the system to be flexible enough to accommodate the potential range of values.

Before beginning the time-consuming and perhaps expensive process of questionnaire construction, other existing sources of information should be considered. External sources for user characteristics, marketplace and user environment information include (Spencer, 1985):

- Independent, specifically contracted surveys or market studies.
  - Various industry survey and analysis report publishing services.
- Business and technical society or organization special studies and reports.

- Government standards, codes, and regulations.
- Franchised business and services surveys and feedback.
- Trade and technical society journals and publications.
- Business magazines and papers.
- Newspapers and news magazines.
- Books (industrial, business, human factors, etc.).

Once the set of characteristics has been identified, existing sources are surveyed for compiled data. When characteristics are needed but unknown, the designers must either make an assumption about the characteristics or use interviews and surveys to gather the needed data. There are numerous sources of survey and questionnaire construction guidelines, e.g. Berdie et al. (1986) and Labaw (1980).

One frequent educational situation which simplifies this process is that in which the author of the system is the instructor of a recurring course. This provides the author with intimate knowledge of the users and the interaction context. It also allows an ideal situation for data collection, since data can be collected on a long-term basis. Instructors can often assume a certain background based on the prerequisites of the course, then focus on obtaining more detailed information. For example, an instructor may make assumptions about age, reading level, and educational background based on past experiences, and obtain data regarding attitudes and preferences when presenting new versions of the system to students.

Not all situations are as simple as the above scenario. In many cases, the developers may not be familiar with the needs of the users, and the full process must be used. When collecting data for external environments, knowledge of the following characteristics is often critical for the success of the instructional system:

- *Reading Abilities and Habits.* Instructional systems will continue to depend on text to impart many forms of knowledge. It is important to identify the range of reading levels so that text can be written at the appropriate readability level. If the audience has common reading habits, i.e. they read some of the same magazines, newspapers, or other materials, then the text can be tailored to a familiar style.

- *Education.* The type and level of education can influence the wording and design of the system. For example, those with technically oriented educations will generally have backgrounds more compatible with understanding computer technologies. If the audience is from a liberal arts background, then the computer technologies should be transparent to the user.

- **Computer and Technical Background.** Devices and concepts that are familiar to developers, e.g. mice and windows, may be completely new to many users. Special training sessions may be necessary before beginning instruction.

- **Familiar Computer Software.** Users may be accustomed to certain user interfaces; if so, the new system should be as consistent as possible with the familiar systems. If not, the differences should be emphasized during initial training.

- **Age.** Many skills and abilities vary with age. If a wide age range is noted, then the system must be flexible enough to allow users to continue using the system as their abilities change.

- **Visual, Auditory, and Physical Impairments.** All impairments should be anticipated. For example, synthesized speech could cause problems for some with hearing impairments, since most synthesized speech is distorted. Any action communicated in one modality should be duplicated in another in case of impairment. For example, screens should be designed assuming monochrome to ensure that color coding does not hinder those with color deficiencies.

- **Attitudes.** Attitudes toward using a computer-based instructional system can influence its success. Attitudes toward existing documentation can often carry over to the electronic system.

The final outcome of the audience description should be a set of characteristics, data corresponding to these characteristics, and an analysis of the data. The analysis should describe the implications of the data on the proposed system design. For example, the text should reflect the reading abilities of the audience. The computer and technical background will often determine the nature and extent of documentation.

Task Profile. The second basic tenet of user interface design is to know the user's tasks. The user performs tasks within an environment, and this environment shapes the functionality of the system. An instructional system may be designed as a "standalone" system, i.e. the material is complete and there is no "teacher" or "class." In contrast, the system may be designed to augment a teacher's lessons. Each context poses a unique set of problems for the system designers. For example, a standalone system must provide more detailed guidance for the user, while a lecture-augmentation system generally must provide more flexibility for change. Thus, the beginning of the task profile may be to provide a statement of purpose for the proposed system that makes mention of the interaction context. It may also mention several interaction scenarios, i.e. contexts featuring specific user segments and their interaction needs.

Next, the full range of functionality should be identified. One starting point is to arrange all of the system actions and system objects into tabular form. This action/object table will typically be presented with the actions labeling the rows and the objects labeling the columns. A check is placed in each cell where the action is permitted on the object.

In order to design from the user's perspective, the action/object table must be reorganized to reflect the user's goals. Once identified, the actions and objects can be structured by arranging them hierarchically. The task profile is a high-level description of the tasks that the user will perform while using the system, from the user's perspective. Many of the tasks can be stated as a hierarchical combination of action/object pairs, such as the following example from a word processing environment:

- edit document
  - insert paragraph
  - delete paragraph
  - insert word
  - delete word
  - etc.

At this level of design, the syntactic details of the actions, e.g. keystrokes and mouse movements, should be omitted, concentrating only on the semantic level. This semantic ordering of tasks should reflect the user's goals in using the system. For example, a user's top-level goal in revising a document is "edit document," even though there is no such command in the system. Approaching the task profile from the user's perspective will be beneficial when developing the detailed task analysis in the Detailed Analysis Phase. It is important that the profile be an exhaustive one, as this profile will directly affect the features and functionality of the proposed system.

Frequent tasks in using instructional multimedia systems include browsing or reading, and searching for particular pieces of information. In order to browse a particular article, chapter, or section, a user must get into the system, then navigate to the correct location using the system's user interface. The following example uses this scenario. This is a general example; the "A" in brackets is used in place of the name of the article. Each of the following examples will follow this structure.

- Browse article <A>
  - Enter the system
  - Navigate to article <A>
  - Process article <A>
  - Exit the system

Exploring the information chunk may involve reading, viewing a diagram, or watching a video depending on the layout of thechunk.

- Process article <A>
  - Read text <A.text>
  - Examine diagram <A.diagram1>
  - View Video <A.video1>
  - Listen to Audio <A.audio1>
  - etc.

Searching is a feature of electronic systems not found in printed materials. Most authoring systems provide some sort of search facilities so that keywords can be located quickly. String searching, history mechanisms, and indices are all useful tools when searching. Consider an example where a user wants to search for the string *task analysis*, then read the article that contains it.

- Search for string <task analysis>
  - Enter the system
  - Use system's search facilities to search for <task analysis> until found
  - Process article
  - Exit the system

A feature-analysis list is useful for comparing existing designs and in identifying the tasks to be included in the profile. Many popular computer magazines use feature lists to compare products. For example, one (Fersko-Weiss, 1991) lists the features of several popular hypertext/hypermedia systems including Guide, Hyperties, SmarText, and several others. Such summaries are useful for avoiding the needless repetition of collecting and comparing information.

If there are data available concerning the frequency of use of the functions in related software or in previous versions of the current software, then those data should be presented in the Task Frequency Analysis. If possible, the frequency of use should be broken down into a table composed of audience segments and their associated use frequencies.

Once tasks have been identified from the user's perspective, appropriate metaphors may be identified to encapsulate the cognitive requirements of the task domain. Metaphors provide electronic counterparts for familiar objects. For example, the desktop metaphor is used extensively in many personal computer user interfaces, and it affects the objects presented to the user and the way in which they interact to provide the functionality of the system.

Appropriate metaphors for many instructional hypermedia systems include the notebook, the encyclopedia, and the classroom. Many authoring systems come equipped with graphical backgrounds appropriate for a particular metaphor. For example, one of the graphical backgrounds available in several current authoring systems is a notebook. This analysis should present all potential metaphors and their corresponding matches and mismatches (Carroll, Mack, and Kellogg, 1988).

To summarize, the task profile analysis consists of several components:

1. System Functionality Description.
2. Action/Object Table.
3. Task Profile.
4. Feature Analysis List.
5. Task Frequency Analysis.
6. Metaphor Analysis.

The System Functionality Description should be a concise statement of the intended functionality of the system, stating the interaction context and describing several interaction scenarios. The Action/Object Table is merely a table with actions labeling the rows, and objects labeling the columns. A check is placed in each cell if the action is valid for that object. The Task Profile should be the hierarchical list of action/object pairs organized from the user's perspective. The Feature Analysis List is a list of all of the features found in similar designs, with comparative ratings assigned. The

Task Frequency Analysis, if available, summarizes the percentages associated with specific tasks and specific audience segments. Finally, the Metaphor Analysis describes potential metaphors on which to base the design.

Development Platform Analysis. The system will be developed using particular hardware devices and software products. Many software tools are necessary to develop sophisticated features of an interface such as graphics, video, etc.

All hardware devices and software tools should be identified. Often, new devices or tools must be acquired to meet the needs of the design. These should be identified and costs assigned to each acquisition.

The components of this analysis are:

1. Hardware Platform.
2. Hardware Needs.
3. Software Platform.
4. Software Needs.

Interaction Platform Analysis. The user often interacts with different devices and software tools than does the developer. The user's platform should be identified, and differences noted that may result in oversights by designers. For example, development platforms are often state-of-the-art and extremely fast, while those platforms produced as products may be less sophisticated in order to reduce costs.

If particular software products form the basis of the proposed interface, then any usability data corresponding to that software should be identified. The feature analysis lists can be a good source of information for comparison of features of existing hypermedia products. Usability assessments using particular authoring systems also are good sources of information, such as Nielsen and Lyngbaek (1990) for Guide, a widely available authoring system for personal computers.

Additionally, usability considerations for hardware should be noted. For example, some situations may require a larger screen than usual. Some environments are better suited for a touchscreen, others for a mouse or keyboard. The usability characteristics of the interaction devices should be analyzed and described. Many of these characteristics can be found in the literature or in guidelines documents.

The components of the Interaction Platform Analysis are:

1. Hardware Platform.
2. Hardware Usability Assessment.
3. Software Platform.
4. Software Platform Usability Assessment.

Media Analysis. Media forms including text, hypertext, static graphics, photographs, animations, video, speech, music, and sound may be used to communicate in multimedia user interfaces. Each media form should be used appropriately and to fit an intended purpose.

Text remains the most pervasive form of instructional media, due to the established use of printed materials. In order to provide a basis for the use of text, several text structures have been identified that correspond to the underlying purpose for the text (Anderson and Armbruster, 1985). A *description* attempts to describe, define, or list the characteristics or features of an action, concept, or physical entity. A *temporal sequence* traces the steps over time of an action. An *explanation* may explain causes, effects, or describe conclusions, and even predict what will happen. *Comparing and contrasting* states how two entities are alike or unlike, perhaps by listing their similarities and differences, or advantages and disadvantages. A *definition-examples* structure defines an entity, then gives several examples of it. Finally, a *problem-solution* structure traces the development of a problem and provides a solution.

All of the above structures may be presented using text. Each structure may be enhanced, or in some cases presented exclusively, with other media. Descriptions can be enhanced by graphics or photographs when the referent can be represented visually. Static graphics and photographs can be used to indicate temporal sequences, but they can be presented most effectively with animation or video. Animations are useful for the above structures when the referent is abstract or otherwise impractical to video. For example, an animation can show the details of a building by lifting the roof off a building; filming such a scenario would be an unlikely and unwanted occurrence.

In some cases, the addition of graphics or other visual information may be superior to the exclusive use of text. For example, Kamman (1975) found that two flowchart formats were superior to printed instructions for comprehension accuracy and speed. Bauer and Eddy (1986) compared two representations for command language syntax. One used meta-characters (Backus-Naur Form) and the other used a flowchart-like representation. In all three experiments, the graphic method resulted in lower learning times and error rates. Booher (1975) compared several formats for comprehension of instructions: print, pictorial, pictorial-related print, print-related pictorial, pictorial-redundant print, and print-redundant pictorial. Of these, the pictorial-related print and the pictorial-redundant proved best for comprehension. These studies all indicate the need for careful, task-related integration of text and static graphics to enhance performance.

Animations and video may also provide new ways of presenting information. One such use is that of providing interface agents. An interface agent, as defined by Laurel (1990), is "a character, enacted by the computer who acts on behalf of the user in a virtual (computer-based) environment." The agent can be helpful in many ways: navigation and browsing, reminding, scheduling, tutoring, and many others. For example, Oren et al. (1990) discuss the use of guides, interface agents to assist users in navigating through a hypermedia system. Several guides are presented in an interface, each interested in particular topics. Video clips are used to present the guides to users. When the guide is uninterested in the current topic, it "sleeps." When the user chooses something that a guide is interested in, the guide "wakes up" and becomes available to be selected. The guide then may speak and present other related topics.

Speech, music and other sounds are useful in many situations. The use of speech to provide narrative during a video, for example, is a common and expected use in multimedia systems. McConkie (1983) proposes that allowing the system to pronounce an unfamiliar word may cause users to read at higher levels. Music is useful as background for videos and other media elements, and as a medium unto itself, e.g. in a music instruction system. Audiolization refers to the presentation of information by combinations of sound. For example, Brown and Hershberger (1991) use sound to convey information about algorithm animations, often using pitch-weighted values to indicate items involved in comparisons and switches. They list several uses of audio in a user interface:

- Audio reinforces visual cues.
- Audio conveys patterns.
- Audio replaces visual views.
- Audio signals exceptional conditions.

Blattner et al. (1991) provide an example of scientific audiolization for the representation of information concerning turbulence in fluids. Gaver (1989) describes a direct manipulation environment in which sounds indicate an object's size and type.

Hypertext is a medium available only on computers, although

some aspects of other media have hypertext-like features. Rather than featuring a linear structure that typifies a text, a hypertext is organized into nodes and links, with the navigation through the information space under control by the user. The author of a hypertext must attend to the structuring of information and facilities for navigation within the system.

In a multimedia instructional system, the challenge is to integrate a variety of media to present a message that can be received and decoded effectively by the user. Table 1 summarizes the appropriate uses of the different media forms. Frequently documents form the basis of the system. For example, a hypermedia system may be built from existing documents such as manuals, textbooks, and other printed materials. Other media forms, e.g. photographs and video clips, often are available for interface construction. Thus, at

Media form	Uses
Text	• Good for description, temporal sequences, explanation, compare-contrast, definition-examples, problem-solution
	• Necessary for abstract, nonvisual information
	• Good for labels, titles, caption
Static Graphics	• Good for description, location/spatial information
	• Can be used for temporal sequences (cycle charts); compare-contrast (histograms)
	• Good for depictions of objects, data organization, and visualization
	• Used as background for text, other displays
Hypertext	• Useful when links, associations are important
	• Shneiderman's Three Golden Rules
	(1) Large body of information organized into numerous "fragments)
	(2) The fragments relate to each other
	(3) The user needs only a small fraction of the fragments at any time
Animation	• Useful for simulating physical processes
	• Good for depicting "invisible" or impractical processes and actions
	• Useful for temporal sequences
	• Useful for providing interface agents
	• May be used as an attention mechanism or for entertainment.
Still Photography	• Can show people, places, things
	• Can enhance descriptions, explanations
	• Can be used to illustrate temporal sequences or to provide examples
Motion Video	• Powerful communication tool
	• Useful for documentary-style presentations
	• Useful for providing interface agents
	• Can provide for learning by modeling
Music	• Good for background for displays, etc.
	• Can be used to indicate temporal changes
	• Potentially useful for scientific audiolization
Speech	• Useful for systems messages in some situations
	• Pronunciation of words can help low ability readers
	• Useful for narration of video

Table 1: Media Uses

this phase, it is important to determine (1) how media will be used, (2) what exists, and (3) what must be prepared. Plans must be made to develop media components that must be prepared and to ensure that appropriate hardware and software are available to facilitate the process.

The sections of a Media Analysis include:

1. Media Use Analysis.
2. Media Base Analysis.
3. Media Preparation Analysis.

The sections cover the proposed uses, the existing media base, and the preparation needs respectively.

Documentation Analysis. Users have information needs as they interact with computers. They may require help for unfamiliar actions and concepts. Frequent forms of assistance include quick references, user manuals, and on-line assistance. This analysis should identify the appropriate forms of documentation to be included with the system.

Most multimedia systems should feature on-line assistance, since the capability exists to match the user's information needs with information presented in an ideal modality. Many uses for hypertext help have been cited (Campagnoni and Ehrlich, 1989), and multimedia help has been explored (Sukaviriya, 1991; Sukaviriya et al., 1992). For example, Sukaviriya (1992) states that traditional textual help provides little support for visualization of tasks, especially in systems with a strong visual component such as graphical user interfaces. A prototype was developed to explore the use of multimedia technology for on-line help. The system which she described supports context-sensitive animated help by showing animated input devices operating on screen objects. Other media forms may be used to support on-line assistance needs. For example, a video of a user using the system can enhance initial training by providing for learning by modeling.

Detailed Analysis

Once the initial data have been collected, a more detailed analysis can be conducted. This detailed analysis provides all of the information needed to actually begin the design.

The Detailed Analysis phase consists of several components, as shown in Figure 3:

A. Usability Guidelines Analysis

B. Usability Specification Analysis
C. Detailed Task Analysis

Usability Guidelines Analysis. Although a wealth of empirical data regarding human-computer interaction issues have been collected, not everyone is capable or even interested in examining the literature to extract recommendations for design. To meet the need of the non-empirical user interface designer, numerous guidelines documents have been developed.

Additionally, many corporations wish to promote a common "look, touch, and feel" for application interfaces. In these cases, corporate standards and guidelines are developed to enhance consistency and provide guidance in many design issues regarding menus, interaction devices, and many other screen design issues.

The first phase of developing the Usability Guidelines Analysis is to analyze existing guidelines to determine whether they are appropriate for the current design. Some existing sources for guidelines include the following: Apple Human Interface Guidelines (1987), Brown (1988), Galitz (1988), Marcus (1992), and Smith and Mosier (1986). There are many others. For a more complete listing, see Shneiderman (1992). Smith and Mosier (1986) provides a wealth of general guidelines and is an excellent starting point for any guideline development effort. More specific guidelines are available for particular interface platforms, such as the Apple Human Interface Guidelines (1987).

The analysis should result in a guidelines document that is readable and easily referenced. A consistent organization strategy should be used for the sections and subsections so that each entry may be assigned a unique number. There should be major sections pertaining to, but not limited to, the following:

- General interface design.
- Graphical user interface issues (scrollbars, buttons, metaphors).
- Screen design (color, wording, use of graphics).
- Menu design.
- Window design and manipulation.
- Interaction devices (mouse, keyboards, etc.).
- Dialogue design.
- Data entry.
- Error messages.
- Documentation and online assistance.

For hypermedia development efforts, there should also be sections pertaining to the following:

- Navigation.
- Hypertext usability.
- Media.

Each entry should be comprised of a brief title, the guideline, an example of its application, and a reference stating the source from which it was obtained.

Although numerous guidelines documents are available, e.g. Smith and Mosier(1986), most were written with interfaces other than multimedia instructional systems in mind. In fact, there are very few guidelines specifically intended for hypertext applications with diverse media. Specific guidelines for the development effort can be derived from the Interaction Platform Analysis and the Media Analysis. Navigational needs and hypertext usability guidelines can be based on the usability information contained in the Interaction Platform Analysis. The media guidelines can be based on the information gathered in the Media Analysis.

Usability Specification Analysis. "Ease of use" is a vague term. The purpose of the Usability Specification Report is to state in precise terms exactly what usability is for a given design. The attributes used to specify usability will be useful for evaluation during iterative design, and in measuring how well the system meets the specifications upon release.

Usability attributes should be selected that are important for the current design. Common attributes in user interface design correspond to installability, initial use, learning rate, errors, user evaluations and attitudes, comparisons to other products, etc. Whiteside, Bennett and Holtzblatt (1988) provide a technique for specifying attributes. There are several components associated with each usability attribute. For example, using the attribute   of "installability:"

Attribute: installability.

(1) Measuring Concept: installation task.
(2) Measuring Method: time to install.
(3) Worst Case: one day with media.
(4) Planned Level: one hour without media.
(5) Best Case: 10 minutes with media.
(6) "Now" Level: many can't install.

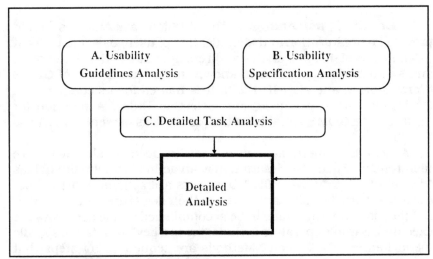

Fgure 3: Detailed Analysis Overview

The *Measuring Concept* and *Measuring Method* components describe what activity is performed as the attribute is measured, and the particular response variable to analyze. Given a particular response measure, thresholds should be set realistically that determine success or failure for each attribute. The *Worst Case* corresponds to the lowest acceptable level for the metric, i.e. a lower bound on "what counts as a success." The *Planned Level* represents a "success," and the *Best Case* should be an agreed-upon state-of-the-art limit for the attribute. The "*Now*" Level corresponds to the present level of the attribute in current systems. There is no definite technique involved in setting the thresholds. If a system already exists, the thresholds may be set according to its level. If a similar competitor's product exists, it may be used to determine the levels. Otherwise, the values must be estimated.

Some typical attributes that are relevant to a multimedia design include:

- Readability of text.
- Initial subjective evaluation.
- Long-term subjective evaluation.
- Browsing efficiency (the ratio of nodes visited to total nodes).
- Retention of information.
- Directed search effectiveness.
- Ease of navigation for first-time users.
- Visual components evaluation.

Detailed Task Analysis. The Detailed Task Analysis should provide an organization and identification of user goals and tasks at a detailed level, i.e. this analysis will encapsulate both the semantic and syntactic levels. One well-known technique is that of GOMS (Card, Moran, and Newell, 1983). It is named for its components: Goals, Operators, Methods, and Selection Rules. A notation for conducting a GOMS suitable for task analysis is presented in Kieras (1988).

A goal is something a user tries to accomplish. Goals are hierarchical. Each goal description is an action/object pair such as "delete a file" or "move a file." Operators are actions that the user executes. They look similar to goals in their structure, but they differ in that goals are something to be accomplished, while operators are executed. Sample operators include "press a key" and "find a specific menu item on the screen." Methods are sequences of steps that accomplish goals. Describing methods is the main focus of the detailed task analysis. The general form of a method is:

Method to accomplish goal of <*goal description*>

Step 1. <*Operator*>
Step 2. <*Operator*>
   ...
Step n. Return with goal accomplished.

If there is more than one method for accomplishing a goal, then a selection rule is required. For example, there may be different ways to move to a certain place in a text, using cursor keys or a built-in "find" function.

The general form for selection rules is:

Selection rule set for goal of <*goal description*>

If <*condition*> Then accomplish goal of <*specific goal description*>
If <*condition*> Then ...
   ...
Return with goal accomplished.

The bottom-level operators are those elementary physical or cognitive actions that are performed during an interaction sequence. By estimating times for each bottom-level operator, a GOMS can be

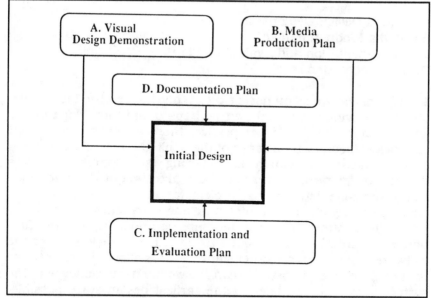

Figure 4: Initial Design Overview

used to predict user performance. A GOMS is also a useful starting point for documentation development, since it views the functionality of the system from the user's perspective and breaks it down into sequences of steps.

There are many actions in a GOMS that are difficult to specify for prediction when multimedia applications are considered. Primitive actions such as keystrokes and mouse movements have been studied extensively, and their estimated times are available. Complex actions such as examining graphics, animations, and videos currently are difficult to predict.

Research has been conducted into the perception and processing of graphs (Lohse, 1991), and into contexts involving visual and auditory information (John, 1990). More research is needed in order to obtain appropriate prediction values for instructional multimedia contexts.

Initial Design

Once all data have been collected and analyzed in the necessary detail, the system and user interface may be designed. The Initial Design phase consists of several components, as presented in Figure 4:

A. Visual Design Demonstration.
B. Media Production Plan.
C. Implementation and Evaluation Plan.
D. Documentation Plan.

Visual Design Demonstration . While the detailed task analysis may provide a detailed and perhaps quantitative look at the design from the user's perspective, there is nothing in it that provides someone with a sense of the "look and feel" of the design. Multimedia systems usually have a strong visual component that is difficult to communicate verbally. Several techniques exist for providing someone with the visual elements of the design. Common techniques include rapid prototyping and storyboard design.

With prototyping, a brief (perhaps nonfunctional) representation of the interface is prepared using either a basic form of the software system or some other software. This allows a viewer to see the design in true context, and can allow limited interaction with the system to provide feedback at the earliest design stage possible. Wilson and Rosenberg (1988) cite several advantages of rapid prototyping, including the ability to test questions that cannot be answered specifically by guidelines, and the provision of a common reference point for the designers. Disadvantages cited include the ability to ignore limitations and constraints that apply to the real product and the potential for creating unrealistic expectations with an oversold prototype. The use of rapid prototyping can speed development and reduce costs by condensing the transition from design to implementation. Multimedia platforms using existing authoring packages provide an excellent base for rapid prototyping, since skeletal outlines of the complete system can be provided, with some of the more important information components filled in.

Storyboards are useful when prototyping is not possible, and for augmenting incomplete components of the prototype. In this form, paper or cardboard representations of screen sequences are prepared with narratives to depict common use scenarios. Storyboards have been used extensively in the creation of video and animations, and may be used for the development of static and dynamic images, including screen representations in a user interface. Storyboards offer many of the advantages of prototyping in that they can present the visual sense of the system and allow designers to share a common reference point. The lack of an interactive dimension is a major disadvantage, since it precludes feedback from potential users.

Regardless of which technique is used, it should provide the viewer with a sense of "what is done" and "what it looks like" for common situations.

Media Production Plan. Development of media components that are to be a part of the user interface are often developed using several hardware devices and software systems. For example, an animation may be developed on a workstation, stored in one file format, downloaded to a personal computer, then converted to a file format suitable for animations. All such loops should be identified, along with the nature of the media to be developed. Flowcharts are useful for identifying the major steps involved in production.

Once all production loops have been identified, storyboard designs for all visual elements and scripts for all vocal elements should be prepared, along with plans for any other media. Flowcharts are also useful for plotting the flow of action within a component of the system.

Implementation and Evaluation Plan . The interface development effort should be broken down into meaningful chunks, with evaluation corresponding to the usability attributes mentioned in the Usability Specification Analysis taking place. A project time-line should be developed which includes all deadlines for development and evaluation.

Two useful techniques to meet this purpose include Gantt charts and PERT charts (Wiest and Levy, 1977). A Gantt chart typically is labeled with time periods on the x-axis and project components on the y-axis. Horizontal bars are used to indicate the beginning and ending times for each component of the project, as well as the entire project. A PERT chart is a graph with nodes corresponding to states, and arcs corresponding to activities. PERT charts are useful for showing all of the dependencies among the tasks of a design effort, as well as for identifying critical paths for completion of the project.

Documentation Plan. The plans for developing user documentation should be stated in the Documentation Plan. In some cases, the user manual is developed before the system is constructed in order to ensure that the system behaves appropriately and that all design issues have been considered. In most cases, the iterative design of the system leads to many hazy intermediate states that preclude advance preparation of the manual. The documentation may be developed in lock-step with the system, or it may be developed after the system is completed.

If the system features on-line multimedia help, then plans should be included in the Visual Design Demonstration and the

Media Production Plan. In most cases, additional documentation will be needed to explain basic operation of the system, and its development plan should be provided to augment the Implementation and Evaluation Plan.

Iterative Design

A system can be developed according to usability principles and guidelines without anyone ever using it. However, there are too many complexities and intricacies in any computer system to plan for them all, and it is necessary to allow representative users to provide feedback and to discover any problems.

Once a portion of the system has been developed, observational studies are useful for discovering problems and oversights. These studies need not be meticulous in design, but should involve users unfamiliar with the system. For example, using system designers as test subjects will not usually lead to the discovery of new problems. Once problems and oversights have been corrected, then a more rigorous approach is necessary.

The usability attributes developed in the Usability Specification Analysis should be tested in accordance with the Implementation and Evaluation Plan. Representative subjects should be used to measure the attributes. For example, questionnaires could be developed to measure a user's attitudes towards the system, and performance measures such as time to complete a task or percent task completion can be evaluated. Given the measured attributes, should any fail to meet successful levels, the problems should be corrected and re-evaluated.

Once all user feedback has been incorporated, another portion of the system can be developed and tested. This process continues until all of the system has been developed and it successfully passes the established thresholds for the usability attributes.

Follow-up

Once implemented, there should be techniques for gathering data. An on-line monitor can capture interaction-level information, and a log can be kept of questions for the interface. If there is a technical support line, the calls can be tracked to determine where most of the problems lie. Surveys and questionnaires are useful for determining user attitudes once the system has been developed and used for a period of time. This information is useful for developing new versions of the same system, and for developing similar systems.

Summary

The design of a multimedia user interface poses many problems that a purely textual interface does not. Once implemented, the media components must be evaluated in isolation and in combination with others. The following section provides information regarding anticipated platforms for the next century and for the evaluation of diverse media components.

Multimedia User Interfaces for Computer-Based Instruction

Development and Delivery Platforms in the 21st Century

Hardware and Software Requirements. A computer system to support multimedia requires substantial computer capability in terms of processing power, main memory, mass storage, and graphics display. The processor capability is needed for the rapid display of computer animations and video and for processing hypertext data accesses. A large main memory is necessary to hold the multimedia engine as well as the information. A large (500 - 1000 Mbytes) and fast mass storage device is also required, in order to hold the hypertext lessons, static images, computer animation, and stored audio and video. Suitable mass storage devices include a fixed disk drive, a CD-ROM drive, an optical disk drive, or some combination of these.

The ideal system should have a large screen monitor (17-19 inch) with high resolution (1280 x 1024) graphics. The graphics displays need 24-bit color plus a z-buffer for showing realistic color images. Experiments have shown that increasing the quality of the screen improves the speed and comprehension of reading text from a computer (Gould et al., 1987).

There are currently three ways to display live video in a single-screen multimedia system. The first is using a special video card to display video from a source such as a VCR or a Laserdisc player. This gives the highest quality but requires a Laserdisc player, a special video card, and production of the Laserdisc. The second is to use digitized video with hardware supported playback, such as the DVI system from Intel/IBM. The gives a smaller image but reasonably good quality. The third is to use software-only playback, such as the Apple QuickTime format or the Microsoft Windows AVI system. A disadvantage of software-only playback is lower quality playback of about fifteen frames per second (half of the normal videotape rate of thirty frames per second), and smaller windows for the video. The advantage is that the user need not buy any additional equipment other than the PC, whereas the DVI board set for replay currently costs up to $2,000. Rapid progress is being made in the performance of the software replay systems and they are approaching hardware playback quality.

The most rapid advances are being made in digital technology; it is clear that the future lies with an all-digital system, i.e., one that does not use an external analog device such as a videodisc player. While software-only playback, as in the Microsoft AVI system, is currently primitive and unsatisfactory, in a few years increasing CPU speeds will lead to systems that are capable of full-screen full-speed digital video replay that will be superior to today's VCR technology.

The above hardware requirements for an ideal system are expensive using today's technology. The rapid pace of computer hardware and software developments will make such systems available inexpensively in the near future. Capabilities of such systems will include photorealistic image display, real time graphics processing, sound generation, the ability to play stored video, and will have extensive hypertext capabilities. A typical inexpensive ($3,000) computer system to support multimedia in 1993 has a 66 MHz 80486 processor (about 20 MIPS and 2 MFLOPS), eight Mbytes of RAM, a 210 mbyte disk drive, an audio board, and a 15-inch color monitor with 1024 x 780 pixel resolution displaying 256 colors. By the year 2000, a similarly priced system will have a processor capable of about 500 MIPS and 100 MFLOPS, 128 Mbytes of RAM, two gigabytes of disk space, and a 17 to 19 inch color monitor displaying 1280 x 1024, 24 bit graphics (16.7 million colors).

The hardware requirements for powerful multimedia systems will be met in the next few years. As usual, the more difficult problem will be the software. The software requirements include a hypertext authoring system plus a good program development environment, e.g. C++ for the demonstration programs. There are a number of hypertext products currently available for IBM PC compatibles or the Apple Macintosh. These systems vary in their capabilities and user interaction style. The following discussion will present characteristics of some current multimedia authoring systems, along with an indication of the needs for the future.

Current Multimedia Authoring Systems. The current hypertext systems tend to be either card-based or file- and window-based. The card-based systems, such as HyperCard for the Macintosh or Toolbook for the IBM PC are limited in that only one card at a time can be displayed whereas the user might want to look at two different topics simultaneously. Another problem with card-based systems is that the card size is fixed and is usually given in terms of the number of horizontal and vertical pixels, e.g. 640 x 480. The card can be larger than the actual screen and the extra material can be viewed by scrolling, but the entire card is stored, whether there is information on it or not. If additional information is added to a card, it might overflow and a new card must be created.

Fixed card sizes hinder portability. For example, an application might be developed for a Macintosh with a small screen size, e.g. 512 x 340 pixels. When this is moved to a Macintosh II or an IBM VGA system the card no longer fills the screen. This becomes even more of a problem if the application is moved to a workstation with 1240 x 1024 resolution. The card systems do have some advantages, e.g. it is easier to define fixed areas for data base entries or links.

File- and window-based systems, e.g. Guide (1990) for the Macintosh and IBM PC, allow one or more scrollable windows to be opened. Each window can contain an entire file of text and graphics. The windows can be dynamically resized and are easy to port to systems with different screen resolutions. This offers many advantages to users familiar with window manipulation. Unfamiliar users, however, may get lost with a large group of open windows.

Problems with Current Multimedia Authoring Systems . Current authoring systems are inadequate for building and using the large multimedia systems of the future. One of the primary areas of weakness is in tools for navigation of the information space. The author needs these tools to help develop the system, and the user needs them to search the system for needed information. A valuable tool to remedy this situation is a conceptual map to display the nodes and links in the system. The authoring system should automatically construct this map.

Another useful feature would be the maintenance of hypertext links independent of the source material (Van Dam, 1992). This would allow for easy modification of the material and for the ability to have several different sets of links for the same material.

One needed requirement for authoring systems is greater interoperability,i.e. the ability of the final system to run on different platforms. These systems will not be fully successful if they require educators to be limited to a particular hardware vendor. This means that the systems should run on a Macintosh, IBM (under Windows or OS/2) and an X-Windows UNIX workstation. There are currently some systems that run on both IBM's and Macintoshes, as noted above, but these don't run under X-windows. Commercial hypertext authoring systems are just being developed for UNIX workstations.

The Book vs. the Computer

The use of computer technology to present multimedia information invites the comparison with the traditional medium, the book. Books have been in widespread use since the development of the printing press. Recent improvements in technology have made the computer a realistic alternative to the book as a source of information. Nielsen (1990) lists the following advantages of hypertext/hypermedia as compared with the book:

- Can show moving images, animations, film.
- Easier to update— can permit automatic downloading of changes.
- May be shipped over networks.
- Making single copies is easy.
- Can be shared by several people.
- User-oriented reading.
- Potentially: the whole world's literature a click away.

Nielsen also lists several disadvantages:

- 30% slower reading speed on current displays.
- Lower resolution graphics.
- Not portable.
- Overhead in having to learn system and setting up computer.
- No user interface standard.
- No standard for data transfer.
- No regular publishing channels, bookshops, libraries, ISBN, etc.
- No "romance"— first editions, leather binding, etc.
- Computer text "homogenized".

Clearly the presentation of text on displays must improve if users will be expected to read large quantities of information from CRT displays. Shneiderman (1992) lists several disadvantages for reading from displays. Poor fonts and low contrast between the characters and the background can hinder a reader. Lighting also causes several problems not found in a book. For example, glare can cause many problems for computer screens, particularly if the screen is difficult to adjust. If the displays are small, the pages will be small and the reader will be forced to turn the page frequently. Some users, such as those requiring bifocals, may experience problems in maintaining the correct reading distance. There is also a greater chance of layout and formatting problems, for postural changes which lead to fatigue, and for increased stress levels. There are many variations in posture where a book is comfortable, such as lying in bed, where a computer screen is currently impractical.

These disadvantages explain the reduction in reading speed for electronic displays. Several of the disadvantages are dependent on current technologies, and should disappear as the technologies improve. Gould et al. (1987) found that reading speeds increase to levels near that associated with paper with the use of high resolution displays, dark characters on light background, fonts that resemble those found on paper (rather than dot-matrix fonts), and anti-aliased fonts. Use of high-resolution displays also allows higher resolution of text. The trend toward more sophisticated display technologies will benefit those trying to read or view displayed information.

Another trend is the reduction in size and mass of computers available to the general population of computer users, making the market broader for many applications. It has long been the dream of computer researchers to produce a small computer that was powerful and portable enough to function as a "dynamic book," or Dynabook (Kay and Goldberg, 1977). Recently notebook computers and personal digital assistants (PDA's) have been promoted in sales literature, and it is only a matter of time before this dream is realized. Once widespread, portability will no longer be a disadvantage of multimedia systems. Other difficulties associated with electronic displays, such as glare and postural distortions, will be alleviated.

Many of the other disadvantages cited above are either irrelevant or only vaguely related to the needs of the learner. User interface and data transfer standards could enhance many aspects of computer use, but have no direct bearing on a specific scenario. Eventually publishing channels for multimedia systems will exist, and the "romance" of the book will be replaced by some other characteristic of the electronic information package.

Of those disadvantages mentioned above, only two are expected to be significant for future efforts. While many methods have been advocated to enhance consistency for user interfaces, there will always be some overhead associated with learning the user interface. For example, learning how to manipulate windows can pose problems for those new to them (Tombaugh et al., 1987). The other disadvantage cited by Nielsen that should remain an issue is the homogeneity of text, i.e. it looks the same visually regardless of where it occurs. In a large information space, orientation and navigation are important issues. The more distinct the information components, the easier it is for a user to orient himself based on visual qualities.

Since all text looks similar, some strategy is needed to help users orient themselves. The use of unique visual backgrounds and maps can help users to orient themselves in large information spaces.

Although hardcopy manuals and books currently have the advantage in resolution and portability (Crane, 1988), the ability to provide successive levels of detail through hypertext links at the choice of the reader, and to augment the information with figures, photographs, animations, and video provide many advantages for implementing textual information using multimedia. Readers have been shown to read above their instructional level by having unfamiliar words pronounced by the system (McConkie, 1983). The use of hypertext allows elaboration and definition of terms while retaining much of the original context. There are many proven benefits of static and dynamic graphics.

Previous attempts to implement traditional print forms in electronic form have led to mixed results. As reported in Shneiderman (1987), a comparison of TIES, a hypermedia system, with a printed document resulted in slower task times for TIES subjects, except when a task required a search in more than one article. Sixteen of 20 subjects preferred TIES to the paper version. Marchionini (1989) found that students using an electronic encyclopedia usually were able to adapt their long-standing print mental models to the new medium, often at the expense of efficiency. Thus, new users to the system should be introduced to the features of the system that are particular to interactive electronic media, such as searching, in order to gain efficiency.

Some research is promising for developing electronic systems that compare to or even exceed the capabilities of printed text, assuming that iterative design is used to improve the electronic system. The facilities available exclusively for the electronic document, such as fast search and indexing, should be designed to maximize user efficiency. In one case, revisions to a hypermedia system based on behavioral evaluations led to performance improvements, in comparison to printed media. Superbook (Egan et al., 1989), a system which takes text as input into a structured browser, offers search and navigation enhancements in comparison with printed text.

Initial studies featuring search tasks resulted in lower performance for Superbook. By enhancing successful user strategies in the user interface, Superbook was superior to printed text in further evaluations. In order to allow for such a progression in improvements, usability evaluations should be planned at distinct implementation phases to gain input into needed revisions.

Very often, a system is implemented based on an existing book, manual, or combination of several textual sources. If based on a single book or manual, a beginning point for the design of the system is the book metaphor. Since the book is familiar to nearly everyone, the overall organization of the material should be accessible to all who can read. The chapter, section, table of contents, and index are all highly ingrained concepts for readers. Thus, when planning a multimedia CBI system based on a textbook or manual, the overall organization of the book may be adhered to when developing the initial version of the system. When the system is based on several existing documents, Glushko (1989) recommends using the task analysis process to determine which portions of which documents to include in the system. The task analysis should also guide the extent, locus, and the type of integration.

Evaluating Information Components of Diverse Media

The appropriate use of media is important for the overall effectiveness of the system for instruction. Text is irreplaceable in many circumstances, since it is familiar for many types of users. However, for many users who read poorly, the use of visual technologies can enhance communication tremendously. Images can be used to depict physical objects and some abstract concepts. Animations can be used to represent physical and abstract processes and to provide other information in the user interface. Videos can be used to facilitate learning by modeling. Each media component must be evaluated separately to ensure that it communicates successfully. For example, text must be written for the appropriate reading level and contain the correct information. All images must portray the referent correctly and convey no misleading messages, and must communicate correctly without misleading (Morris, 1993).

In evaluating a multimedia system of any kind, the designer must ensure that all components communicate effectively. The text must be "readable," the visual components must be "watchable," and the aural components must be "listenable." The following sections describe evaluation of diverse media components. The Readability section discusses previous attempts at identifying the difficulty of text. The Watchability section examines the evaluation of visual components and presents a taxonomy for computer animations. Finally, the Listenability section discusses briefly the evaluation of aural components.

Readability. Text will remain an important communication medium for multimedia training systems. The readability of any text intended for training or education must be considered relative to the information needs of the intended user audience. Readability can be viewed as consisting of three components: comprehension, fluency, and interest (Gilliland, 1972). Comprehension is concerned with the understanding of words and phrases, and is the basis of most readability formulas. Fluency is the ability of a person to read at their optimal rate; it can be limited or enhanced by the size and type of characters and several environmental factors. Finally, interest and motivation play a strong role in determining choice of reading materials and how the information is assimilated.

Many factors can affect the readability of a printed text. Aesthetic factors include the size of the book, the design of the cover, the use of illustrations and color, and the "feel" of the pages (Gilliland, 1972). Multimedia interfaces can provide many aesthetic benefits, some comparable to and some exceeding the capabilities of printed text. Static and dynamic graphics, use of color, and video can all enhance the visual appeal of an electronic document. Portability of a book or magazine remains an advantage of printed text, but this is expected to vanish as small, powerful computers are developed and refined that can fit in a shirt pocket. The size of an electronic book will no longer be a factor, since a disk will be a negligible size and weight. Multimedia training systems should provide high motivation levels associated with use of the system if the media are used to proper advantage.

Several formulas have been developed over the years to assess readability. Most deal with word difficulty, i.e. percentage of long or multi-syllabic words, and sentence length. The argument favoring this approach is that (1) many difficult words are three or more syllables long, and that (2) long sentences are often composed of several dependent and independent clauses and are thus difficult to learn.

Numerous techniques have been used to assess readability based on word and sentence difficulty. The Flesch Reading Ease Score (RES) is calculated as follows:

RES = 206.835 - (.846)(syllables per 100 words) - (1.015)(average sentence length)

This formula is cumbersome when performed manually, due to the need to count all of the syllables in the text being considered. A formula that is simpler to apply is the Gunning FOG index, stated as follows:

GFI = (.4)(average sentence length + percentage of words with more than three syllables)

One technique is to select a sample of 100 words, compute the average sentence length, and count all words with three or more syllables. This is simpler than counting all syllables, as is required by the RES. It must be noted, however, that the GFI may overstate the difficulty of a text relative to other measures (Gilliland, 1972). Another, even simpler readability assessment method is to select 30 sentences from the target text in the following way: select 10 from the beginning, 10 from the middle, and 10 from the end. Using these thirty sentences, count the number of three or more syllables. Add three to the square root of this count, and this yields the McLaughlin SMOG Grading. Although simple to apply, the SMOG grading yields similar results to other methods (Gilliland, 1972). Ease of manual calculation should not be the primary factor used for assessing readability, but many systems can be assessed manually to yield a quick indication of difficulty.

Use of readability formulas yields an important assessment of textual information. There are critics of readability formulas who note that the formulas fail to provide a measure of how readers will comprehend the text (Duffy, 1985). Duffy proposes a more extensive model to predict the comprehension for a particular text:

P(comprehension) = a + b(reading skill) + c(subject matter knowledge) + d(prose factor) + e(format factor) + f(graphic factors)

To date, no such comprehensive formula based on this model has been developed. It is also unknown how such a measure, or any of the other readability formulas are affected by a hypertext system where an unfamiliar phrase can be selected, then explained by linking to a node and examining its contents.

Another possible resource to guide the development of readable text is the use of guidelines. Hartley (1981) makes several recommendations for the development of effective text. These were combined with a few other situation-specific guidelines for the HyperSludge (Owen, Morris, and Fraser, 1992) project to form the following set of recommendations:

• Use simple wording.
• Define terminology before it is used.
• Avoid sentence lengths in excess of 25-30 words.
• Avoid technical jargon.

- Avoid using more than two subordinate clauses in a sentence.
- Avoid excessive use of passive voice.
- Keep paragraphs short, probably no more than nine lines long.
- Avoid words with three or more syllables whenever possible.
- Use advance organizers (e.g. goal statements) for each of the major sections to orient the reader.
- Present questions at the end of major sections to give the reader the opportunity to review.

Application of these guidelines and the corresponding reduction in reading difficulty resulted in 30% higher exam scores.

Other tools have been developed in recent years to allow particular writing styles to be enforced. Computer software can assess readability levels, and, as an added feature, contrast the writing style of one document with an established style. For example, a technical report style can be established, then contrasted in terms of readability and sentence types with a document. Portions of the text falling outside of the style can be
identified and modified. Such analysis is useful for systems designed to fit a particular audience's need. If their reading interests can be identified, then a style can be developed to guide the structure of training materials.

Watchability Images, whether filmed or generated, static or dynamic, are attractive features of existing and envisioned multimedia systems. While assessments of readability have been developed and refined since the 1920's, there is currently nothing comparable for assessment of images. Evaluating visual information is a more difficult task, given the variety of images and a lack of a common visual language as a basis for construction of more complex images. Further, many of the qualities of images are abstract, and cannot be measured as discrete units.

As with text, designers must be concerned with comprehension, fluency, and interest of images. The interest and motivation associated with images is believed to be higher than for text alone, given the enthusiastic response to computer graphics, video games, and multimedia systems featuring visual media. The comprehension of an image involves how effectively it communicates its intended message, while the fluency refers to the rate of comprehension.

The watchability of a multimedia system can be viewed as consisting of several components:

- An attractive, compelling initial screen.
- An attractive, non-distracting background for text.

- Effective use of static generated images, diagrams, charts, etc.
- Effective use of animations.
- Effective use of photographs.
- Effective use of video.
- Effective integration of these media.

Each image should be visually interesting; however, this is subjective and will often depend on the context. Questionnaires and surveys can be developed to assess the subjective aspects of a particular image.

More difficult to assess is the efficacy of the image in communicating its intended message. When used properly, visual technologies are beneficial to learners in many ways, especially for those with poor verbal or spatial abilities.

Evaluating Animations. The use of static and animated graphics in education have been found to aid those with poor spatial abilities (Blake, 1977), to provide for incidental learning (Rieber, 1991), to promote faster learning (Rieber, Boyce and Assad, 1990), and to provide other advantages (Rieber, 1990).

The use of animations has been explored previously in educational contexts. Animations can communicate movement, changes in status, and various other temporal changes more effectively than static images. Computer animations are especially useful for visualizations of abstract and concrete processes, allowing perceivable manifestations of actions, motions, and status changes which otherwise must be imagined by the user.

It is difficult to determine the degree to which an animated graphic display communicates its intended message. The diverse collection of characteristics present can affect the message that is received by the user. In order to fully characterize the effects of an animation on understanding and comprehension, the interaction scenario, the static graphic displays, and the use of animation must all be characterized effectively.

Several studies have explored the effectiveness of animations in educational contexts. Rieber (1990) contains an excellent review of empirical studies involving animated visuals. He states that animations have served one of three purposes in education: attention-gaining, presentation, and practice. An empirical study investigated the effects of using animations to teach children science (Rieber, 1990). Fourth- and fifth-grade students were presented with three levels of visual elaboration—static graphics, animated graphics, and no graphics. Animated graphics were found to be superior to static graphics and no graphics under certain conditions. In another study (Rieber, 1991) fourth-graders were able to extract incidental information from animations without detriment to intentional learning, but were also more likely to develop misconceptions. The work of Rieber et al. (1990) examined the effects of different visual presentations on adult learning in the context of Newtonian mechanics. Students were again presented with three levels of visual elaboration — static graphics, animated graphics, and no graphics. They found no performance effects for adding static and automated visuals to text, but they reported that response latency effects suggest that the use of animation supported encoding and retrieval tasks.

One area of computer animation which has benefited from extensive development is that of algorithm visualization (London and Duisberg, 1985; Duisberg, 1986; Brown, 1988; Stasko, 1990). Understanding the algorithms common to many programming efforts is essential for a programmer to acquire the knowledge necessary for development of large, complex programs. Algorithm animation systems have been developed to present the actions of an algorithm in visual form, with the goal of facilitating acquisition of algorithmic concepts.

Recent work (Badre et al., 1991) was devoted to the difficult process of quantifying the effectiveness of algorithm animations in the teaching of algorithms. Many suggestions were made that would apply to a formal study. It was noted that performance results are difficult to relate to the effects of an animation, and that the following factors should be controlled carefully: academic and technical background, spatial abilities, and prior experience with visual technologies. It was also noted that particular algorithms may be inherently visual; thus, some algorithms may yield performance results more readily than others. Future plans included a study of performance for several algorithms, emphasizing long-term retention of concepts.

A Taxonomy for Evaluating Animations. In order to fully understand how comprehensible an image is, it must be broken down into its components just as text is often assessed by the difficulty of its words and sentences. To meet this need, a taxonomy was developed (Morris, 1993). An evaluator must consider elements of program development, graphics design, and cognitive psychology in order to grasp the overall effectiveness of communication of an animation view. The complexity of view components must be crystallized into a form permitting design, evaluation and experimental control decisions. The taxonomy suggested in Morris (1993) contains the following elements:

I. Interaction Scenario
   A. Goal and Intended Use
   B. Visualization Style and Interaction Capability

   C. User Attributes
   D. Use With Other Media

II. Views
   A. Objects
   B. Icon Styles
   C. Structures
   D. Lifetime
   E. Graphical Attributes
   F. Interaction Attributes
   G. Animations

The Interaction Scenario. The interaction scenario, the environment in which an animation is viewed, plays an important role in designing the view, and in the interpretation of the view by a user. Thus, all of the factors at play when a user interacts with a computer animation must be considered. These factors include goals, uses, user characteristics and interaction capabilities.

Most of these components of the interaction scenario can be identified by applying the interface design process discussed earlier. Baecker (1991) provides the following 10 basic ways that animation may help a user within the context of a conventional user interface. Thus, the goals and intended use may be identified using these concepts.

1. Identification: What is this?
2. Transition: Where have I come from and gone to?
3. Orientation: Where am I?
4. Choice: What can I do now?
5. Demonstration: What can I do with this?
6. Explanation: How do I do this?
7. Feedback: What is happening?
8. History: What have I done?
9. Interpretation: Why did that happen?
10. Guidance: What should I do now?

Three kinds of visualization have been reported (Brown and Cunningham, 1990). The first is *postprocessing*, where the display is of a finished product, and all data are known and complete. The second is *tracking*, where the knowledge is under development and the user watches the display of information as the system processes information. The third, *steering* places the user in the loop so that the user's input affects subsequent displays. Animation is an effective technique to allow tracking and steering.

The interaction capability is closely related to the visualization style, and will determine how the user is allowed to interact with the animation. The lowest capability is no capability: the user is merely a *passive* viewer. For example, a videotaped presentation of an algorithm animation presented to a classroom of students allows no effective interaction on behalf of the viewers. The next level is termed *endpoint interaction*, where the user can only start and stop the animation. *Multiple function interaction* allows the user several alternatives in addition to starting and stopping the system. For example, the user might be able to pause, unpause, fast forward, and rewind the animation, similar to the functionality on many videocassette players. The user does not alter the content of what can be presented to him in any way. In *reactive interaction*, the system contains many possible presentation paths, and chooses a path according to user input.

User attributes are important in determining how the animations may be interpreted. The earlier section on audience descriptions provides a basis for selection of attributes to gather. Additionally, use of other media can affect the way an image is interpreted. Use of legends, for example, can provide cues for interpreting coded visual elements.

Views. Displays involve a diverse collection of components, including icons, text, and other visual elements. Each display object must be well understood in order to determine its contribution to the effectiveness of the view. Additionally, many properties of these objects may change with time.

A frame consists of any number of display objects. Display objects can take many shapes and forms. For the purposes of this taxonomy, any basic display element with a meaning relevant to the display is considered to be an icon. This includes lexical elements such as letters and characters, elements excluded from some classifications (Lodding, 1983). Since an animation can be viewed as a sequence of frames, the characteristics of a frame will first be considered independently of animation.

An icon is an image used to convey information in a nonverbal manner (Lodding, 1983); for the purposes of this taxonomy it will be further restricted to be a static image. There is a tremendous historical precedent for the use of images for communication.

Humans communicated with images long before the development of textual languages, and many early languages were based on pictograms (Gittins, 1986). The use of images has been studied extensively (Shepard, 1967; Standel, 1973; Mandler and Ritchey, 1977) and has been found to benefit retention and recognition.

Several classifications of icons developed to support iconic interfacing have been proposed. Lodding (1983) proposed three styles of icons: representational, abstract, and arbitrary. Each has a characteristic relationship with its referent, the physical object or concept that it stands for. Representational icons serve as an example of a general class of objects. They have many of the features that an instance of this class of objects would have, without the detail. For example, a gas pump icon has many of the physical characteristics of an actual gas pump. An abstract icon represents a concept associated with the physical object, rather than features of the object itself. Lodding (1983) uses the typical icon for fragile— a cracked glass— as an example of this icon style. Finally, there are arbitrary icons, which are created and assigned a meaning. Nothing about them conveys any physical or conceptual features of the referent. Representational icons tend to be the easiest to learn, while arbitrary icons are the most difficult to associate with a referent, since there is nothing familiar about the image.

Gittins (1986) classifies icons into three broad categories: color, type, and form. Color consists simply of monochrome and color. For the purposes of this study, color is considered to be a graphical attribute, and something distinct from the icon itself. Another broad category is type, which consists of static and dynamic. Dynamic icons change over time. For the purposes of this study, icons are considered to be static display objects within a frame. The main category, form, has many characteristics similar to Lodding's classification. Form consists of two subcategories, Associative and Key. Associative icons feature characteristics of the object, and are either literal or abstract. Key icons may be mnemonic, where the icon provides a cue to the associated referent. Key icons also consist of those icons termed arbitrary and invented in Lodding's scheme.

The styles of icons for the purposes of this taxonomy are adapted from Gittins (1986) and Lodding (1983). The names in Lodding's scheme are considered to convey more information, so those names are used where the categorical content is similar. The icon design styles used for this taxonomy are:

1. Literal: The icon represents itself, e.g. a numeral or a digit.
2. Representational: The icon contains features similar to the

physical features of the referent.
3. Abstract: The icon conveys a conceptual feature of the referent.
4. Arbitrary: The icon is invented, and contains no features related to the referent.

An icon may depict a single isolated object, but more often depicts a class of objects. For example, the document icon for the ubiquitous desktop metaphor represents the class of documents. Relationships may exist among object instances in a class. For example, an animation may use height-weighted rectangular bars to represent data values in a sorting algorithm. Thus, the rectangular bar is an icon for the class of data values, and the relationship among the elements is usually the fact that they belong to the same array of elements. The depiction of the relationship may be explicit, e.g. the use of marked slots to represent array locations, with the icons contained inside them. The depiction may also be implicit, with no markings to indicate a relationship except for physical proximity. In the case of explicit depiction of relationships, an icon is necessary as a structural marking.

A display object may exist as a permanent feature of the display, appear only briefly to indicate a change in status, or appear intermittently upon activation of special conditions. The pattern or conditions under which the object appears is termed its lifetime. This temporal condition is closely related to the use of animation, and should be carefully specified for any temporary or intermittent object.

Many aspects of the graphical design of an object can affect how it is perceived by a user. Changes in graphical attributes can imply relationships, provide coding, or cause an object to stand out from other objects in the display. McCleary (1983) describes six basic graphical elements: size, value, form, color, direction, and texture. Size, appropriate for ordinal, interval, and ratio scale data, may be appropriate to represent varying physical sizes or values. Choices for graphical depictions of size must be made carefully: a circle twice as large in area as another may not be perceived by a viewer as being twice as large, but somewhat less than twice as large (McCleary, 1983).

Value is restricted to ordinal, interval, and ratio scale data. It involves varying the tone in a unit area of space. The user must be able to discriminate among different tones for this to be appropriate. McCleary suggests that differences in tone tend to be overestimated.

Form is associated with two important factors: (1) the number of different symbols that are used in its construction, and (2) the discriminability of different symbol forms. Thus, one constituent of an icon's form is its complexity, defined as the number of elementary graphical components used to compose it. Many user interface guidelines have suggested that icons be simple and consist of only a few components. However, these recommendations were made in the context of user interfaces for computer systems, not for the purposes of visualization. In many visualizations, complex icons may be necessary to render more effectively the nature of the referent. The discriminability of symbol forms is also necessary if the message is to be conveyed correctly by the icons. For example, McCleary reports that if a circle and a square have equal areas, the square will be perceived as being larger. It is also necessary to add dimensionality to the constituents of form. A display object which appears to be three-dimensional appears to be more representational of a physical referent, and potentially can communicate more information with the added dimension.

Color is useful for representing qualitative (nominal) data. Color is useful for coding schemes, and its use and perception are well-documented (Murch, 1984). The appropriate use of color can have a dramatic effect on the effectiveness of an icon and, in turn, an animation. Tufte (1990) provides several uses of color. It may be used to label, to measure, to represent or imitate reality, and to enliven or decorate. In addition to a well-defined purpose for the use of color, there are many conventions that must be followed within a task environment. For example, the color red may mean "hot" in one context, "stop" in another, and "on" in yet another. Any use of color that conflicts with these well-established conventions will pose difficulties for the user. A change in color may also indicate that an object has changed status, or merely function as an attention mechanism. Direction (orientation) can be used for representing both qualitative and quantitative data. For example, the use of horizontal lines across the display object can provide a sense of upward or downward directionality. McCleary (1983) remarks that "there is potential for the graphic use of this variable, but that many confusing results often occur if it is used." Texture involves display of a pattern on an object that is coarse enough for an observer to detect the pattern. For example, textures include dots, line screens, grid patterns, textured patterns, and special dot patterns. McCleary (1983) presents a classification scheme for textures that involves manipulating a grid. Variations in texture result from manipulating the contents of the grid, the location of the elements within the grid, or both.

In addition to these attributes, an indication of position is necessary to provide a basis for movement of a display object. An object may appear in many different positions during its lifetime. Movement is one of the principal uses of animation, so the specification of position is especially important for display objects. For fixed objects, a permanent location may be provided; for movable objects, the range of positions and conditions causing a change should be specified.

Each object or class of objects may be classified by the degree with which a user may interact with them. In many algorithm animations, the user cannot manipulate any of the objects. Thus, one scale is whether it can be manipulated. If so, the complete set of operations should be specified. Many operations are possible for display objects depending on the task environment. Each use of animation should be specified by (1) the purpose of the animation, (2) the type of animation, and (3) the graphical attributes involved in the animation.

The use of animation for a set of objects can be used for a variety of purposes. It can be used to simulate a physical process, such as an animation of the flow of influent through a centrifuge. It can be used to depict an abstract process, as is the case with most algorithm animations. It can be used as an attention mechanism, to separate a set of objects visually from the others. For example, one view of a Shell sort used in XTango, a version of TANGO (Stasko, 1990) that runs under XWindows, uses animation to separate a subarray that is currently being sorted. Within the same view, elements of the current subarray being sorted are moved away from the rest of the data set, to bring attention to the subarray. The type of animation depends on whether it involves a change in positional attributes or graphical attributes. A change in positional attributes is movement of some form. Other types of animation include metamorphosis (change in form), change in color, etc.

The transformation dimension (Brown, 1988) is determined by the transition from one frame or display to another. A discrete transformation abruptly replaces the old display with the new one, with no sense of continuous change. An incremental transformation shows a smooth transition, and if displayed with sufficiently small increments of change, yields the perception of continuous change.

The persistence of the animation (Brown, 1988) involves display of the history of previous states on the screen. If all previous states are displayed, then a complete history is maintained. Many animations show only the current state.

General Guidelines. The above classification scheme may be applied to dynamic images, and to static images by omitting the section on animations. More work is necessary to assess the comprehension and fluency of images. In the meantime, designers are left with general guidelines, such as those found in Tufte (1983):

- Show the data.
- Induce the viewer to think about the substance rather than about methodology, graphic design, the technology of graphic production, or something else.
- Avoid distorting what the data have to say.
- Present many numbers in a small space.
- Make large data sets coherent.
- Encourage the eye to compare different pieces of data.
- Reveal the data at several levels of detail, from a broad overview to the fine structure.
- Serve a reasonably clear purpose: description, exploration, tabulation, or decoration.
- Be closely integrated with the statistical and verbal description of a data set.

Still Photographs and Motion Video. In addition to developing assessment procedures for generated images, guidelines and techniques should be developed for the assessment of photographs and video segments. As with generated images, properties of static images (photographs) can be determined and then augmented with a time dimension to classify video segments. In general, photographs should be of high enough quality so that the viewer can distinguish critical elements. The primary objects of interest should generally appear in the middle section of the photograph, since that is where a user's attention will be directed initially. Videos should use high quality images, and use effects such as cuts and fades appropriately so as not to draw attention away from the images. An additional concern with video are the media biases that accompany the medium. Laurel, Oren, and Don (1991) cite two major biases with the use of video. First, the information contained in a video may be questionable, since it looks like what is seen on television, and much of what people view on television is fictional. Second, viewers may expect high production values similar to those used on television and in the movies.

Listenability. Most guidelines and recommendations regarding sound in human factors literature refer either to generated speech or to warning tones. Michaelis and Wiggins (1982) provide general guidelines for situations in which the use of speech generation is desirable for system messages:

1. The message is simple.
2. The message is short.
3. The message will not be referred to later.
4. The message deals with events in time.
5. The message requires an immediate response.
6. The visual channels of communication are overloaded.
7. The environment is unsuitable for transmission of visual information.
8. The user must be free to move around.
9. The user is subjected to high G forces or anoxia.

Most of these items do not apply to current instructional contexts. While short, simple messages may be preferred due to storage requirements, generated speech for instruction may be any practical length. For example, speech accompanying a video need not be simple or short. Since selection of topics is frequently under user control, i.e. the user can select a button to play a video or have the system pronounce unfamiliar words, the third recommendation also does not apply. Thus, the fact that speech may be under user control makes items one through three unnecessary. Items four, five and six may apply to system messages in specialized settings. For example, auditory icons were proven useful in a complex simulation of a plant for providing auditory feedback (Gaver, Smith, and O'Shea, 1991). Item seven will not occur unless the instructional system is in an aircraft.

Speech in instructional systems should sound like human speech. When using speech as a pronunciation aid, special attention must be paid to ensuring that all inflections are correct, i.e. that the original speaker pronounces the word correctly. Music can be used in many ways in an instructional interface. Its most frequent use is as background sound to set a mood. When music is the subject of instruction, high-quality sound may be achieved through use of MIDI interfaces.

The use of sound to represent data, termed audiolization, associates characteristics of sound such as duration and pitch with data (Blattner, Greenberg, and Kamegai, 1991; Yeung, 1980; Lunney and Morrison, 1981; Bly, 1982; Mezrich, Frysinger, and Slivanovski, 1984). Most results are promising in that users have been shown to perceive differences in sounds as intended.

More work is needed to provide a set of guidelines for speech, music, and audiolization appropriate for use in multimedia interfaces.

System Development Experiences

Introduction

The Hypermedia and Visualization Laboratory (HVL) at Georgia State University (GSU) has several on-going research projects to develop hypermedia systems for education and training. The discussion in the following sections will focus first on general software engineering issues and then concentrate on the technological issues introduced by the use of multimedia. First, a brief description of the hypermedia projects will be presented. These hypermedia application systems use commercially available tools and are delivered on relatively low-end systems. All of the projects have been developed for IBM PC-compatible systems in order to meet client requirements.

Hypermedia Projects

The projects discussed below are being developed using the Guide authoring system, from OWL International. Guide runs under Microsoft Windows on IBM PC-compatibles. It is a window-based system, as opposed to a card-based system like Hypercard or Asymetrix Toolbook. Guide supports four types of buttons or links. The first is a "pop up" button. When it is selected, a block of text pops up and remains only so long as the mouse button is depressed. This feature is useful for short text segments such as definitions or image annotations. The second type of button is an expansion button. When clicked, an in-place text expansion occurs. The expansion can consist of text and images. This is useful for showing a superficial view of a topic and then a more detailed, expanded explanation. The third type of button is a "goto" general hypertext button which opens a window displaying another document. The last type is a command button, which is used to launch external commands to display images, animations, or interactive programs.

Four projects are described in the following sections. HyperCase is a relatively old system and did not incorporate any computer animation or video. HyperGraph and HyperSludge are on-going projects and incorporate computer animation and video. For these two projects we are using digital technology, i.e., both animation and video are digitized, and stored and replayed from a fixed disk, and the system has only a single monitor. The U. S. Army Corp of Engineers project involves a more complicated system, using two Laserdisc players with a separate monitor for display of the animation and

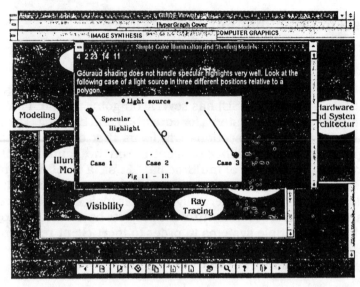

Figure 5: Hypergraph Screen

video and a touch screen/trackball combination for textual and static graphical display and control purposes.

HyperGraph. This project, with initial support from ACM SIGGRAPH plus some support from the National Science Foundation (NSF), is to develop a hypermedia system for teaching computer graphics (Owen, 1992). Development of HyperGraph was begun on a VGA-based system and then moved to a super VGA system. An extensive set of notes was created for the computer graphics courses. These notes were made available to the students, who were encouraged to annotate their copies. The initial phase of development of HyperGraph consisted of transferring text from the notes into the Guide system. The next phase consisted of converting the linear text into a non-linear hypertext form, using the different types of buttons described above. Thus far, HyperGraph incorporates static images, digitized video, and computer animation. There are also jumps to interactive graphics programs so the students can run demonstrations at appropriate points. Figure 5 shows a screen from HyperGraph.

HyperSludge. The Bureau of Pollution Control for the city of Atlanta, Georgia is responsible for four water pollution control plants. A hypermedia training system is being developed that is intended to be used by supervisory, operational and maintenance personnel who control the water treatment facilities at the plants (Owen, Morris, and Fraser, 1992). The primary objective of this

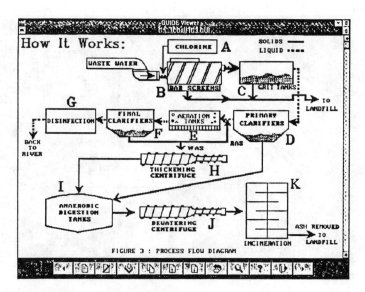

Figure 6: HyperSludge Process Flow Diagram

research effort is to develop an effective combination of text, figures, photographs, computer animations, and live video connected via hypertext links that motivates and communicates with the plant personnel. The methodology used to accomplish this goal is iterative design, which allows constant feedback from potential users of the system and emerging technologies and media to be gradually incorporated into the system. The initial version of HyperSludge was based on a manual, and the initial efforts in system development involved transferring the manual into Guide format and evaluating the understandability of the text. The current system incorporates text, static images, photographs, animation, and video. Figure 6 shows a process flow diagram used as an entry point to the information content in HyperSludge.

HyperCASE. This was a project for the U.S. Army to develop a prototype tool for explaining how phases of the software life cycle are supported by different Software Engineering methodologies (Conger et al., 1990). It was also to show how various Computer Aided Software Engineering (CASE) tools supported the different methodologies. The Army was particularly interested in methodologies that supported MIS applications so the project was a cooperative effort between Computer Science faculty and Information Systems faculty (from the College of Business Administration at GSU).

U. S. Army Corp. of Engineers WES ITL Project (COE-WES)

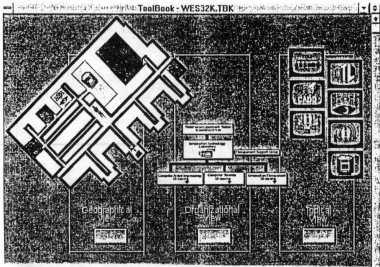

Figure 7: Introductory Screen for WES System

. This is a new project to develop an information kiosk system which contains a complex set of information spaces. For testing purposes we will develop a system that will display three different views of the Information Technology Laboratory (ITL) at the U. S. Army Corp of Engineers Waterways Experiment Station (WES) in Vicksburg, Mississippi. The first view is that of the physical facilities, the laboratories and offices of the ITL. This view will be presented using two Laserdisc players displaying video and computer animation on a set of three large screen TV monitors. The second view will be an organizational view of the ITL. In this view there will be brief textual descriptions of the organizational structure and duties of different individuals with photographs and short videos of some of the people. The third view is a topical or content view, i.e. the types of research carried out by the different components of the ITL. The users of the system will be people who are touring the ITL. Thus, this is a "walk up and use" type of system and must be very simple.

We expect the users to search for information in two ways: either by browsing or by searching for specific information. The users may wish to move back and forth among the different views. For example, a user might look at the organizational chart, then want to know what type of research a certain person does, and then want to look at that person's laboratory. Then they might want to look at the physically adjacent laboratory or "walk down the hall" to another laboratory, query the system regarding the research performed there, and determine where it fits in the organizational structure. Thus, the users should have the capability to jump between information spaces easily using links provided by the system. The challenge will be to structure the system so that the users can obtain the information they want and not get lost.

Figure 7 shows the introductory screen for the WES system.

Usability Engineering Issues

The foremost issue is to be sure that the end users are intimately involved in the design, implementation, and testing of the system, in accordance with the multimedia interface design process presented in an earlier section. This ensures that the system does what they want it to do, they share the pride of authorship, and will be much happier with the end result. For example, the HyperSludge project was thrust upon the manager of the water treatment plant. At first the plant manager was skeptical of the project. Then we worked very carefully with him, using weekly visits to go over all of the textual material describing the plant operations. He made numerous changes, suggested what images we should use, and what figures to incorporate. He became a very enthusiastic supporter of the system and made sure that it was used since he had invested a major part of his own time and energy into creating the system.

A second issue is to be sure the system is tested by the target audience and not just by the experts. When we tested HyperSludge with new employees they had difficulty understanding the material incorporated into the system from the manual. This was because the plant manager had so much knowledge of the system that many things were obvious to him but obscure to others. After the test we changed several aspects of the system, as mentioned earlier in the section on readability.

A third issue is to use the multimedia components of the system only when necessary, i.e., they should add to the understanding and not get in the way of understanding; avoid gratuitous displays of flashy media. The first computer animation we did for HyperSludge was of the operation of a centrifuge pump. This is a giant pump, about ten meters long and its function is to separate out solids from the water. It is housed in a large opaque box and so its inner workings are not visible. Thus, no video could be taken and computer animation was the only possible way to illustrate the action of the pump. Students who have taken the graphics course have done much of the work on HyperGraph so they were both potential users as well as authors. Also, the HyperGraph system, although not yet in full use, has been used by some students and modified according to their comments.

User Interface Issues

One of the fundamental principles of Human-Computer Interaction methodologies is consistency of interaction methods. Many inconsistencies can only become evident during iterative testing. In an early version of HyperSludge, the mouse was used for all interaction except when pressing the enter key on the keyboard to remove a displayed image. Due to space limitations at the plant, some of the computers at the plant had their keyboards in retractable drawers underneath the system units. Thus, pulling out the keyboards just to press a single key was irritating to the users. We promptly changed the system by replacing any program called from Guide that required keyboard input with one that would accept mouse input. This meant that a user need never use the keyboard to interact with the system.

Another issue is the tradeoff between complexity of interaction and flexibility of use. Ideally, a system would be both simple to use and extremely flexible, but generally, the more options a system has, the more it is potentially confusing to the user. The optimum trade-off point will vary with the sophistication of the users. An example of this is the method used to display computer animations or digitized video. Computer animations are converted into Autodesk .fli or .flc files and then displayed using AAPlay, the Autodesk Animator program to play animations. This gives the users several options in modifying the display and animation playback. But the presence of these options may be confusing to a naive user. For HyperSludge, we wrote a short program that automatically loads the correct animation, displays a window with the first frame of the animation and has two buttons labeled "Run" and "Stop." The user clicks on "Run" to start the animation and on "Stop" to end the animation. The animation continues to recycle until the "Stop" button is clicked. This very simple interface has been proven to work well with naive users. For the HyperGraph system, where the users are primarily Computer Science majors or others who are quite computer literate, the full AAPlay program is used so the students can change the animation settings.

Windows can pose problems for both naive and experienced users. A problem we noticed with the use of the digitized video and animation was that many users would run the video, then click on another video to run it without closing the first video. In Guide, the window for the first video remains open but is hidden when the user clicks on another full screen window or another video. This also happens with text windows but is not a problem since text windows require fewer system resources. To solve this problem, we had our animation/video players check to see if there was already an active player program. If so, then the new program terminated the previous program before it started playing.

A general problem with a window-based system, such as Guide, is that the user may open a large number of windows, never close any, and run out of system resources and/or get very confused. A card-based system does not have this problem since opening a new card automatically closes the previous card. Guide does offer a capability similar to cards (frames) in which opening a new frame automatically closes the previous frame. Thus, any system using window-based authoring systems should contain tutorial information alerting users to the problem, or else be outfitted with special software to remove extraneous windows.

Technological Issues

Choice of Delivery Platforms. In each of our projects we have not had the option of choosing the delivery platform, since it has been mandated by the external funder or by other circumstances. The HyperSludge project had to be delivered on IBM PC-type equipment to be compatible with the current City of Atlanta systems. Similarly, for the HyperGraph project, since most students own or have access to PC-compatible machines, we were limited in our options.

Technology Advances. When designing these systems, rapid advances in technology must be anticipated. For example, originally HyperGraph and HyperSludge were developed for a standard VGA graphics system with 640 x 480 pixel resolution. The current systems are either 800 x 600 pixels or 1024 x 780 pixels. This is not a problem for window-based authoring systems, such as Guide, where the windows can all be resized, and text and even some graphics images will adapt to the different window sizes. It would be a major problem with a card-based system where the developer defines a fixed size card.

We did experience some difficulties with images. Our images were originally developed at a resolution of 320 x 200 pixels, which is the 256 color mode for a standard VGA adapter. The newer systems display 256 colors at the higher resolutions. Using the VGA we had to do a graphics mode switch from the 640 x 480 16 color mode to the 320 x 200 256 color mode whenever we displayed a color image. With the newer adapters we can remain in the high resolution mode and display the color images in a window. However, a problem is that the images were created at 320 x 200 which appears rather small on a 1024 x 780 pixel screen. Simply enlarging the image by pixel replication works, but aliasing artifacts rapidly become apparent. A better solution would be to use algorithms that display high quality images on displays with differing resolutions. One such solution uses fractals to do this, and collectively these algorithms are called the fractal iterated function compression and decompression techniques. Thus, as the systems continue to increase in resolution, the image size can be easily changed to accommodate the increased resolution.

A problem with 256 color graphics boards is that the color palette switches when displaying more than one color image. This occurs since only one image at a time can have the correct palette. When the user switches between images the other image has a very strange appearance featuring unusual colors. True color 24-bit graphics boards will solve this problem and they are rapidly becoming available. For example, a 640 x 480 24-bit board can now be purchased inexpensively.

Live Video. As mentioned in an earlier section, there are currently three ways to display live video in a single-screen multimedia system. The first is using a separate monitor or special video card to display video from a source such as a VCR or a Laserdisc player. This gives the highest quality but requires the production of the Laserdisc, the acquisition of the Laserdisc player, plus the special video card. The second is to use digitized video with hardware-supported playback, such as the DVI system from Intel/IBM. The gives a smaller image but reasonably good quality. The third is to use software-only playback, such as the Apple QuickTime format or the Microsoft Windows AVI system. This gives lower quality slow playback of about fifteen frames per second (half of the normal videotape rate of thirty frames per second). The advantage is that the end user does not need to buy any additional equipment other than the PC, whereas the DVI board set for replay is currently rather expensive. Rapid progress is being made in the performance of the software replay systems and they are slowly approaching hardware playback quality. We are currently using the AVI replay system.

Conclusion

Multimedia computing systems will be important in educational settings in the next century. Regardless of the paradigm shifts associated with changes in technology, the quality of these systems will depend on the ability of the system to communicate with users effectively using diverse media. This effectiveness can be assured only with a systematic approach to design and evaluation, and with a design process that features user characteristics in the original design and the implementation.

Computer systems are becoming smaller and faster. Integrated multimedia systems featuring full media capabilities should soon be available in portable form, realizing the dream of the dynamic book that was envisioned years ago.

The technology will be in place, and research is necessary to bridge the gap between the relatively primitive multimedia systems of today and those of the next century. Suggestions to the developers of new multimedia authoring systems include the following:

- The authoring systems should include an automatic readability and style text analyzer.
- The authoring system should support both the window and the card based paradigm.
- The methods of displaying images, animations, and video should be easily variable in terms of the complexity and capability presented to the user.
- The display of static images, video, and computer animation should all be scalable.
- The output of the authoring system should be portable to other systems and hardware platforms.

Further research is needed in several key areas to provide support for design and evaluation. Detailed studies of human perception of static and dynamic images are needed to provide time estimates suitable for a task analysis. Metrics similar to readability formulas for static graphics and animated graphics are needed; if this is not possible, then guidelines must be developed.

Finally, user interface guidelines are needed that specifically address multimedia interfaces.

The next century should provide more educational opportunities for more people than any other. This goal can best be achieved by merging methodology with technology and pursuing the necessary research.

References

Anderson, T. H. & Armbruster, B. B. (1985). Studying strategies and their implications for textbook design. In T. M. Duffy and R. Waller (Eds.), *Designing Usable Texts*. Orlando, Fla.: Academic Press, Inc.

Apple Human Interface Guidelines: The Apple Desktop Interface. (1987). Reading, MA.

Baggett, P. (1984). The role of temporal overlap of visual and auditory material in forming dual media associations. *Journal of Educational Psychology*, 76(3),408-417.

Berdie, D. R., Anderson, J. F. & Niebuhr, M. A. (1986). *Questionnaires: Design and Use* (Second Edition). Metuchen, N. J.: The Scarecrow Press, Inc.

Barsley, M. (1970). *Left-handed Man in a Right-handed World*. London, U. K.: Pittman.

Badre, A., Beranek, M., Morris, J. M., & Stasko, J. (1992). Assessing program visualization systems as instructional aids. ICCAL'92 (Fourth International Conference on Computers and Learning), In I. Tomek (Ed.) *Computer Science Lecture Notes #602* (pp. 87-99), New York:Springer-Verlag.

Brown, J. R. & Cunningham, S. (1990). Visualization in higher education. *Academic Computing*, 4(6), 24-45.

Bauer, D. W. & Eddy, J. K. (1986). The representation of command language syntax. *Human Factors*, 28(1),1-10.

Bieger, G. R. & Glock, M. D. (1985). The information content of picture-text instructions. *Journal of Experimental Education*, 53(2),68-76.

Blattner, M., Greenberg, R. M., & Kamegai, M. (1991). Listening to turbulence: An example of scientific audiolization. In M. Blattner and R. B. Dannenberg (Eds.), *Multimedia Interface Design* (pp. 87-102). New York: ACM Press.

Brown, M. H. & Hershberger, J. (1991). *Color and sound in algorithm animation*. (Technical Report 76a). Digital Systems Research Center, Palo Alto, California, August 30 1991.

Blake, T. (1977). Motion in instructional media: Some subject-display mode interactions. *Perceptual and Motor Skills*, 44,975-985.

Bly, S. A. (1982). Presenting information in sound. *Proceedings of the ACM SIGCHI '82 Conference on Human Factors in Computing Systems*, 371-375.

Bunzel, M. J. & Morris, S. K. (1992). *Multimedia Applications Development Using DVI Technology*. New York: McGraw-Hill.

Booher, H. R. (1975). Relative comprehensibility of pictorial and printed words in proceduralized instructions. *Human Factors*, 17(3),266-277.

Brown, M. H. (1988). Exploring algorithms using Balsa-II. *Computer*, 21(5),14-36.

Brown, M. H. (1988). Perspectives on algorithm animation. *Proceedings of the ACM SIGCHI '88 Conference on Human Factors in Computing Systems*, 33-38.

Brown, M. C. (1988). *Human-Computer Interface Design Guidelines.* Norwood, NJ: Ablex.

Baecker, R., Small, I., & Mander, R. (1991). Bringing icons to life. *Proceedings of the ACM SIGCHI '91 Conference on Human Factors in Computing Systems,* 1-6.

Campagnoni, F. R. & Ehrlich, K. (1989). Information retrieval using a hypertext-based help system. *ACM Transactions on Office Information Systems,* 7(3),271-291.

Conger, S. A., Fraser, M. D., Gagliano, R. A., Kumar, K., McLean E. R., & Owen, G. S. (1990). The intelligent testbed: A tool for software development and software engineering education. *Proceedings of the Eighth Annual National Conference on Ada Technology,* 408-418.

Carroll, J. M., Mack, R. L., & Kellogg, W. A. (1988). Interface metaphors and user interface design. In M. Helander (Ed.) *Handbook of Human-Computer Interaction* (pp. 67-85). Elsevier Science Publishers B. V. (North-Holland).

Card, S. K., Moran, T. P., & Newell, A. (1983). *The Psychology of Human-Computer Interaction.* Hillsdale, NJ: Lawrence Earlbaum Associates, Inc.

Crane, G. (1988). Redefining the book: Some preliminary problems. *Academic Computing,* February, 6-11,36-41.

Czaja, S. J. (1988). Microcomputers and the elderly. In M. Helander (Ed.), *Handbook of Human-Computer Interaction* (pp. 581-598). Elsevier Science Publishers B. V. (North-Holland).

Duffy, T. M. (1985). Readability formulas: What's the use? In T. M. Duffy and R. Waller (Eds.), *Designing Usable Texts.* Orlando, Fla.: Academic Press, Inc.

Duisberg, R. A. (1986). Animated graphical interfaces using temporal constraints. *Proceedings of the ACM SIGCHI '86 Conference on Human Factors in Computing Systems,* 131-136.

Egan, D. E. (1988). Individual differences in human-computer interaction. In M. Helander (Ed.), *Handbook of Human-Computer Interaction* (pp. 543-568). Elsevier Science Publishers B. V. (North-Holland).

Egan, D. E., Remde, J. R., Gomez, L. M., Landauer, T. K., Eberhardt, J., & Lochbaum, C. C. (1989). Formative design-evaluation of superbook. *ACM Transactions on Information Systems,* 7(1),30-57.

Fersko-Weiss, H.(1991, May 28). 3-d reading with the hypertext edge. *PC Magazine,* pp. 241-282.

Gould, J. D., Alfaro, L., Finn, R., Haupt, B., Minuto, A., & Salaun, J. (1987). Why reading was slower from crt displays than from paper. *Proceedings of the ACM SIGCHI '87 Conference on Human Factors in Computing Systems,* pp. 7-11.

Galitz, W. O. (1985). *Handbook of Screen Format Design.* Wellesley Hills, MA: QED Information Services, Inc.

Gaver, W. (1989). The sonicfinder: An interface that uses auditory icons. *Human-Computer Interaction,* 4(1),67-94.

Gomez, L. M., Egan, D. E., & Bowers, C. (1986). Learning to use a text editor: some learner characteristics that predict success. *Human-Computer Interaction,* 2,1-23.

Gilliland, J. (1972). *Readability.* London, UK: University of London Press Ltd.

Gittins, D. (1986). Icon-based human-computer interaction. *International Journal of Man-Machine Studies, 24,519-543.*

Glushko, R. J. (1989). Design issues for multi-document hypertexts. *Proceedings of the ACM Hypertext'89 Conference, 51-60.*

Gorman, D. (1973). Effects of varying pictorial detail and presentation strategy on concept formation. *AV Communication Review, 21(2),337-350.*

Gaver, W., Smith, R., & O'Shea, T. (1991). Effective sounds in complex systems: The arkola simulation. *Proceedings of Human Factors in Computing Systems CHI'91, 85-90.*

Guide Hypermedia Information System Version 3.0. (1990). 2800 156th Avenue Southeast, Bellevue,WA, 98007.

Hartley, J. (1981). Eighty ways of improving instructional text. *IEEE Transactions on Professional Communication,* 24(1):17-27.

Helttula, E., Hyrskykari, A., & Raiha, K. (1989). Graphical specification of algorithm animations with Aladdin. *Proceedings of the 22nd Hawaii International Conference on System Sciences, 892-901.*

Hurvich, L. M. (1981). *Color Vision.* SUnderland, MA: Sinauer Associates Inc.

John, B. E. (1990). Extensions of goms analyses to expert performance requiring perception of dynamic visual and auditory information. *Proceedings of the ACM SIGCHI '90 Conference on Human Factors in Computing Systems,* 107-115.

Kamman, R. (1975). The comprehensibility of printed instructions and the flowchart alternative. *Human Factors,* 17(2),183-191.

Keirsey, D. & Bates, M. (1984). *Please Understand Me: Character & Temperament Types.* Del Mar, CA: Prometheus Nemesis Book Company.

Kieras, D. E. (1988). Towards a practical goms model methodology for user interface design. In M. Helander (Ed.), *Handbook of Human-Computer Interaction* (pp. 135-157). Elsevier Science Publishers B. V. (North-Holland).

Labaw, P. J. (1980). *Advanced Questionnaire Design.* Cambridge, MA: Abt Books.

Laurel, B. (1990). Interface agents: Metaphors with character. In B. Laurel (Ed.), *The Art of Human-Computer Interface Design* pp. 355-365. Reading, MA: Addison-Wesley.

London, R. L. & Duisberg, R. A. (1985). Animating programs using Smalltalk. *Computer,* 18(8),61-71.

Lunney, D. & Morrison, R. C. (1981). High technology laboratory aids for visually handicapped chemistry students. *Journal of Chemical Education,* 58(3),228-231.

Lodding, K. L. (1983). Iconic interfacing. *IEEE Computer Graphics and Applications,* 3(3),11-20.

Laurel, B., Oren, T., & Don, A. (1992). Issues in multimedia interface design: Media integration and interface agents. In M. Blattner and R. B. Dannenberg (Eds.), *Multimedia Interface Design* (pp. 53-64). New York, NY: ACM Press.

Lohse, J. (1991). A cognitive model for the perception and understanding of graphs. *Proceedings of the ACM SIGCHI '91 Conference on Human Factors in Computing Systems,* 137-144.

Marchionini, G. (1989). Making the transition from print to electronic encyclopedia: Adaptation of mental models. *International Journal of Man-Machine Studies,* 30(6),591-618.

Marcus, A. (1992). *Graphical Design for Electronic Documents and User Interfaces.* New York: ACM Press.

McCleary, G. F. (1983). An effective graphic vocabulary. IEEE Computer Graphics and Applications, 3(3),46-53.

McConkie, G. W. (1983). Computer-aided reading: A help for illiterate adults. Paper presented at the meeting of the National Reading Conference.

Mezrich, J. J., Frysinger, S., & Slivjanovski, R. (1984). Dynamic representation of multivariate time series data. *Journal of the American Statistical Association,* 79(385),34-40.

Mandler, J. M. & Johnson, N. S. (1976). Some of the thousand words a picture is worth. *Journal of Experimental Psychology: Human Learning and Memory,* 2(5),529-540.

Morris, J. M. (1993). Computers and the older adult learner. Submitted to Interacting With Computers.

Morris, J. M. (1992). Evaluation of educational animations: Taxonomy and recommendations. *Computer Science Education,* 3(3),233-249.

Mandler, J. M. & Ritchey, G. H. (1977). Long-term memory for pictures. *Journal of Experimental Psychology,* 3(4),386-396.

Murch, G. M. (1984). Physiological principles for the effective use of color. *IEEE Computer Graphics and Applications,* 4(11),49-54.

Michaelis, P. R. & Wiggins, R. H. (1982). A human factors engineer's introduction to speech synthesizers. In A. Badre and B. Shneiderman (Eds.), *Directions in Human-Computer Interaction.* Norwood, NJ: Ablex.

Nielsen, J. (1990). *HyperText & HyperMedia.* Boston, MA: Academic Press.

Nielsen, J. & Lyngbaek, U. (1990). Two field studies of hypermedia usability. In C. Green and R. McAleese (Eds.), *Hypertext: State of the Art* (pp. 64-72). Oxford, England:Intellect.

Owen G. S., Morris, J. M., & Fraser, M. D. (1993). The development of a hypermedia training system, *Computers and Graphics,* 17 (3),243-249.

Oren, T., Salomon, G., Kreitman, K., & Don, A. (1990). Guides: Characterizing the interface. In B. Laurel (Ed.) *The Art of Human-Computer Interface Design* (pp. 367-381). Reading, MA: Addison-Wesley.

Owen, G. S. (1992) Hypergraph — a hypermedia system for computer graphics education. In Cunningham and Hubbold (Eds.), *Interactive Learning Through Visualization,* pp. 65-78, Springer-Verlag.

Palmiter, S. & Elkerton, J. (1991). An evaluation of animated demonstrations for learning computer-based tasks. *Proceedings of Human Factors in Computing Systems CHI'91,* 257-263.

Potter, M. C. (1976). Short-term conceptual memory for pictures. *Journal of Experimental Psychology: Human Learning and Memory,* 2(5),509-522.

Pressley, M. (1977). Imagery and children's learning: Putting the picture in development perspective. *Review of Educational Research*, 47(4),585-622.

Rieber, L. P., Boyce, M. J., & Assad, C. (1990). The effects of computer animation on adult learning and retrieval tasks. *Journal of Computer-Based Instruction*, 17(2),46-52.

Ranskowsi, C. A. & Galey, M. (1979). Effectiveness of multimedia in teaching descriptive geometry. *Educational Communication and Technology Journal*, 27(2),114-120.

Rieber, L. P. (1990). Animation in computer-based instruction. *Educational Technology Research and Development*, 38(1),77-86.

Rieber, L. P. (1990). Using computer animated graphics in science instruction with children. *Journal of Educational Psychology*, 82,135-140.

Rieber, L. P. (1991). Animation, incidental learning, and continuing motivation. *Journal of Educational Psychology*, 8(3),318-328.

Sitton, S. & Chmelir, G. (1984, October 15). The intuitive computer programmer. *Datamation*.

Sylla, C., Drury, C. G., & Babu, A. J. B. (1988). A human factors design investigation of a computerized layout system of text-graphic technical materials. *Human Factors*, 30(3),347-358.

Shepard, R. N. (1967). Recognition memory for words, sentences, and pictures. Journal of *Learning and Verbal Behavior*, 6,156-163.

Shlecter, T. M. (1991). Promises, promises, promises: History and foundations of computer-based training. In T. M. Shlechter (Ed.), *Problems and Promises of Computer-Based Training* (pp. 1-20), Norwood, New Jersey: Ablex.

Shneiderman, B. (1987). User interface design and evaluation for an electronic encyclopedia. In G. Salvendy (Ed.), *Cognitive Engineering in the Design of of Human-Computer Interaction and Expert Systems* (pp. 207-223). Elsevier Science Publishers.

Shneiderman, B. (1992). *Designing the User Interface: Strategies for Effective Human-Computer Interaction* (Second Edition). Reading, MA:Addison-Wesley.

Sukaviriya, P., Isaacs, E., & Bharat, K. (1992). Multimedia help: A prototype and an experiment. *Human Factors in Computing Systems: CHI'92 Conference Proceedings*, 433-434.

Smith, S. L. & Mosier, J. N. (1986). *Guidelines for designing user interface software*. (Technical Report ESD-TR-86-278), Electronic Systems Division, the MITRE Corporation, Bedford, MA.

Spencer, R. (1985). *Computer Usability Testing & Evaluation*. Englewood Cliffs, New Jersey: Prentice-Hall.

Standing, L. (1973). Learning 10,000 pictures. *Quarterly Journal of Experimental Psychology*, 25,207-222.

Stasko, J. (1990). TANGO: A framework and system for algorithm animation. *Computer*, 23(9),27-39.

Stern, K. R. (1984). An evaluation of written, graphics, and voice messages in proceduralized instructions. *Proceedings of the Human Factors Society*, 314-318.

Chapter 9

Cognitive Issues in the Development of Multimedia Learning Systems

Richard G. Feifer
United States International University

In this chapter I focus on the cognitive issues that should be considered in the design of multimedia learning environments. My goal is to answer the question: how do we design software that best uses multimedia technology to enhance learning? I propose case-based learn-by-doing environments (CaBLE). A simulation allows the student to learn in the most natural way, by attempting to accomplish a meaningful task. A hypermedia system and videotaped experts provide guidance. The multimedia element helps the learner bridge the gap between reality and the simulated task. Instead of reading computer generated text telling him that he is wrong, the learner sees a real person describing a real event in which a mistake similar to the learner's was made.

The technology combining video, animation, sound and computers allows us to produce visually appealing computer programs. Particularly to a generation weaned on television, seeing a live video image integrated with a computer program is compelling. It seems natural, then, to use multimedia technology to help motivate the users of tutoring systems. But this attraction will be short lived if the technology only enhances conventional computer-based instruc-

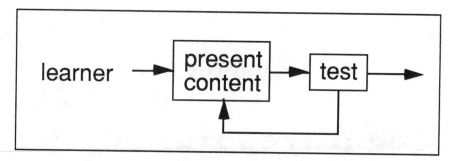

Figure 1: Learner interaction with some instructional software

tion. The question is: how do we design software that best uses this technology to enhance learning?

Interaction with conventional instructional software is often some variation on Figure 1. In this type of software the learner is presented with content and is then tested on that content. The content may be presented in any of a number of forms ranging from expository text to a film segment of a dramatization.

After some portion of the content is delivered, the learner is tested for comprehension. The test may take the form of multiple choice, true-false, or matching items. If the learner answers a test item incorrectly, he* may receive feedback saying it is wrong, a re-presentation of the content, or new information that will help him get it right. Better instructional software might present the new information in multiple modes, branch to special modules based on the type of wrong answer, or both.

One advantage of the learn-then-test design is that the learner is motivated to carefully read the content because he does not know what information will be tested. The disadvantage to this is that learners are often asked to recall irrelevant facts. The more trivial the facts, the more motivated learners will be to read carefully. In many systems the learner cannot continue until he somehow achieves a passing score.

Even given the best of implementations, this design has the following problems:

1. the learner's motivation for reading the content is to pass the test;
2. the learner is exposed to the content often without an understanding of the context in which it would apply;
3. the approach asks the learner to apply the right label to a concept, rather than to use that concept in an appropriate situation.

Delivering the content in a multimedia format, or presenting content in multiple modes, will do little to ameliorate these basic flaws. The design still relies on artificial techniques for inducing someone to learn, rather than exploiting the natural ways in which we learn in the real world.

A more natural way to learn how to do something is by trying to do it and then learning from your mistakes. Schank describes one of the simplest cases of this kind of learning (Schank & Jona, 1991) . Children learn to walk by watching adults, trying to walk, failing, trying again, getting gentle assistance from adults, failing, and trying again. This first example is the most natural form of learning because the teacher (in this case a parent) rarely intends to give a lesson until the student (the child) demonstrates interest or ability. Furthermore, there is no such thing as a test in this example, rather there is merely practice and more practice, and mastery is indicated by success at the goal task.

Apprenticeship is a similar model of learning. While traditionally applied to vocational tasks, there is current work applying the apprenticeship model to more cognitive tasks (Collins, Brown, & Newman, 1989) . As described by Collins, apprenticeship consists of three stages; the master modeling a skill, coaching the student as he attempts the skill, and then reducing her coaching (fading) as the student gains competency. This is a more intentional mechanism for learning than the previous example. Similar to the previous example, however, there is no need for formalized testing during apprenticeship. Demonstration of competence at the skill can be seen as coaching decreases and the student begins to complete the task without assistance.

These more natural learning models are based on the premise that it is best to learn knowledge in a context that is close to the context in which the knowledge will eventually be needed. This helps the learner see the relevance of the learning, thus possibly increasing motivation. Using knowledge, as contrasted with just hearing it, is also believed to make knowledge more usable in the future. In the ACT* model of cognition, for example, practice leads to what Anderson calls *proceduralization* (Anderson, 1983).

Proceduralization is the process that transforms declarative knowledge into procedural knowledge. When you first learned how to drive a car you were probably given a very long list of steps and rules. Everything from, "Look in the rear-view mirror before you pull out," to, "Always steer into the skid." But knowing all of these steps and rules does not really mean that you know how to drive. You learn how to drive by driving enough that the process becomes almost automatic. You know what to do at any given moment, without having to access the specific fact, step or rule that you originally learned.

Despite the advantages of the apprenticeship model of learning, it is time consuming, labor intensive, and, for some tasks, too dangerous. Historically, a master had but one apprentice, and would take years to help the apprentice learn all of the skills associated with a trade. Further, it is sometimes just too dangerous to allow a learner to learn from his own mistakes. When learning to dismantle a bomb, for example, a mistake might be fatal. If not physically dangerous, mistakes might be too costly in a business setting.

Computer simulations, however, can provide an environment for tasks that might otherwise be too dangerous or costly. Steamer, for example, allows students to perform fault diagnosis of a simulated steam power plant (Govindaraj, 1988; Williams, Hollan, & Stevens, 1981). Sherlock provides a "supported practice environment" for learning to troubleshoot a test station whose malfunctions are rare enough to make on the job training unrealistic (Lesgold, Lajoie, Bunzo, & Eggan, 1991). Schauble's simulation of an electronic circuit system represents subtle processes visually so that novices can master concepts in electronics (Schauble, Glaser, Raghavan, & Reiner, 1991).

Two factors, however, limit the use of computer simulations in teaching:

1. good simulations are hard to build;
2. learners can flounder with just a simulation.

Good simulations are hard to build. In non-trivial domains, the representation of objects and of relations among objects is a complex task. Allowing the user a wide range of actions, (e.g. from shutting down a nuclear power plant to maintaining that plant just below the danger level), and simulating the results of any combination of those actions requires a complete model of the domain. In most domains, particularly any domain involving people or even complex machinery, complete models do not exist.

Even if we could build a simulation that sufficiently reflected the real world, it is difficult to learn from mistakes without some guidance (Kuhn, 1989; Kuhn, Schauble, & Garcia-Mila, 1992). In a simulated world a student may experiment freely, following his own model of logic and inference, in the process of discovering how the simulated world works. It is easy for incorrect rules to be discovered but not disconfirmed, because nothing forces the student to follow a rigorous research path (diSessa, 1993)

Furthermore, failure may lead the student astray, eating up time that is better spent experimenting further.

Schauble's studies of how students use their causal models in experimentation with electrical circuits showed that effective learners can make good use of available information (Schauble, et al., 1991). They make better plans, and therefore learn more in their experimentation. Poor learners, in contrast, fail to make good use of information available from their own research. Schauble's results indicate that failure only teaches students what not to do. To many students in unfamiliar domains, it is not obvious why they failed, in what range of circumstances the actions they took would lead to failure, or what they should have tried instead.

One solution to the floundering problem is the addition of a computer-based coach to watch over the learner's shoulder, and advise. In WEST, an early intelligent tutoring system, a coaching module advises learners on the best strategy for winning an arithmetic game (Burton & Brown, 1976; Burton & Brown, 1979). The system compares each learner move with the move an expert model within the program would have made. The system tries to establish what missing strategies would account for any discrepancies between the expert move and the learner's move. These strategies are then put on the queue for the coach to discuss with the learner.

A similar approach to coaching has been used in many intelligent tutoring systems since. The drawback to all of these systems, however, is that even if we could model a learner's misunderstandings in a simulation, we still have the problem of generating a dialog to ameliorate those misunderstandings. In Sherlock, for example, a great deal of work was devoted to diagnosing why the learner had made a mistake (Feifer, 1989a; Feifer, Dyer, & Baker, 1988) . Unfortunately the coach used the diagnosis to do little more than say, "You believe X, but X is not true." Feifer, 1989b).

I propose case-based learn-by-doing environments (CaBLE) Feifer & Soclof, 1991; Schank, 1991). In a CaBLE tutor, instead of the computer generating instruction, good story tellers, that are experts in the domain, tell their stories on video tape. These stories are then indexed to the kinds of failure for which they are relevant. This enables the system to react to the learner's failures as a good teacher might, by recalling a real and personal story containing the principles to be learned from the failure.

These stories make teaching through simulations more practical in three ways:

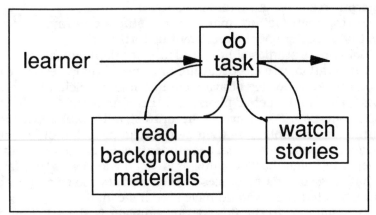

Figure 2: Learner interaction with a CaBLE Tutor

1. the simulation need only provide a context and motivation for the story, and the stories make up for any lack of depth or fidelity in the simulation;
2. it is easier to index failures than to model the learner sufficiently to provide intelligent coaching;
3. it is easier to show a video than to generate instruction, and it is more compelling to the learner.

What is a CaBLE Tutor?

The interaction with a CaBLE tutor is illustrated in Figure 2. The functionality of the test in Figure 1 is replaced in a CaBLE tutor with the simulation of a real-world task. There is no test in the conventional sense of the word; successfully completing the task is evidence of mastery. In addition, the order from Figure 1 is reversed. The task comes first. The learner is only exposed to background material later, whenever he wants or needs it.

If the learner does not know what to do, he can ask questions. If the learner attempts the task but experiences some failure, the tutor will present a story. The tutor chooses a story that will either help the learner explain the failure, or discover a strategy for avoiding the failure in the future, or both.

In a CaBLE tutor, multimedia technology strengthens the connection between reality and what is being taught. If a learner makes a mistake in a conventional tutoring system and the system merely tells him that he has made a mistake, it will have little impact. The learner may not even believe that it was truly a mistake. Maybe the computer did not understand what he did.

If we wait for the mistake to lead to a failure within a simulated world and then tell the learner that the mistake led to the failure, there is a better chance that the learner will see why it is a mistake. The learner will at least see why, in the tutor's opinion, it is a mistake. He may still, however, doubt that the linkage between the mistake and the failure would occur in the real world.

In a CaBLE tutor we go one step further. After the mistake has led to a failure in the simulated world, the system presents a video of a person describing a first person experience with a similar mistake and the real-world failure that it led to. We have found nothing to match the impact of a real person describing a real example of what has just happened in the simulated world.

HeRMiT: An Example CaBLE Tutor

HeRMiT is one of 15 modules of a business practices course (BPC) designed to teach the principles of human resource management (HRM). The course was built for Andersen Consulting to be used by their consultants after one year with the firm. HeRMiT was designed and built over a six month period by a staff of six people.

HeRMiT is written in SmallTalk and runs on IBM-386 compatible computers. The remainder of BPC was written in Authorware. The video for the entire business practices course is stored in DVI format and is delivered on 3 CD-ROM disks.

Andersen wrote their own drivers to interface to the CD-ROM from both Authorware and SmallTalk. The entire BPC consists of 15 modules, each module covering a basic business area. All of the video for any one module is contained on one of the CD-ROM disks. This eliminates disk swapping while within a module, and reduces disk swapping while going through the course.

In HeRMiT the learner is asked to accomplish the following task Bell & Feifer, 1992; Feifer & Hinrichs, 1992).

> You are the manager of the human resources department of Perrin Printing & Publishing (PP&P). You must make human resource decisions for the next four years, without destroying the company. To make your job easier, you will only make decisions for three employees. The computer will generalize your decisions to the rest of the staff.
>
> You can monitor the health of the company by watching the productivity and morale meters. If either of these meters goes into the danger zone, you will be fired.

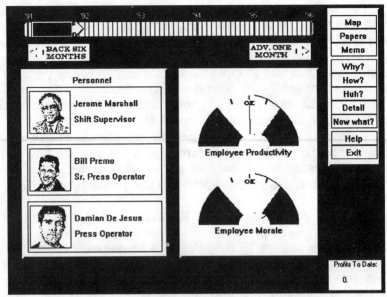

Figure 3: Top-level view of simulated company

The learner begins with a top-level view of the company (see Figure 3). At the top of the screen is a time line representing the current point in the task. This particular time-line indicates that the learner is in January of 1992, the beginning of the game. The game is over when the marker gets all the way to the right.

Immediately below the time-line are the buttons for controlling time. When the learner thinks that he has taken the appropriate actions, he clicks the Adv. One Month button. If he thinks that he has made some mistakes, he can click the Back Six Months button. Pictures of the three employees upon which the learner is currently focusing are displayed on the large buttons down the left side of the screen. Clicking on any of these employees will open the employee's personnel folder. The personnel folder provides both information on the employee's status and an interface for taking actions on that employee (see Figure 4).

The two meters on the right of Figure 3 indicate the learner's success in accomplishing the top level goals; keeping productivity and morale high. If either of these meters falls into the red danger zone, the learner is fired. After being fired, he is sent back in time nine months, to try again. On the right-hand side of the screen is a column of buttons. The top three buttons (Map, Papers, and Memo) give the learner access to the rest of the Business Practices Course. Learners can temporarily leave this module at any time to try something else, returning later to continue from where they left off.

The next five buttons are the basic question buttons. These

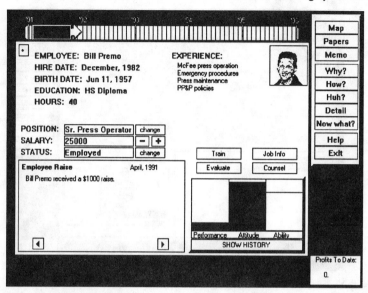

Figure 4: Personnel folder

buttons allow the learner to ask a content question at any point in the game.

One last interface item is the Profits To Date box in the lower right corner. The learner's performance in this game is not timed or rated; he continues until the time bar reaches the end. If he does not learn from his mistakes, he will keep getting fired, going back nine months each time. This success-based design assures that the learner knows or learns the principles we are trying to teach. The learners at Andersson, however, want to know how they stack up against everyone else. Thus the game begins with an arcade game-style high score list. The Profits To Date box is a constant reminder of how efficiently and effectively they are accomplishing the task.

At this point the learner would probably open each of the employee folders, by clicking on their pictures, to see who is responsible for the low productivity. Bill Premo seems like a likely culprit (Figure 4).

The first thing that the learner will notice is the bar chart at the lower right indicating Bill's current performance, attitude and ability. The learner can see in this case that his attitude is high, his ability is relatively high, but his performance is very low. If he wants to see if Premo's performance has always been low he can hit the show history button and see a graph showing performance, attitude, and ability plotted over time (Figure 5).

The lines in this graph are color-coded to match the bar chart. Thus, the top line corresponds to the attitude bar, and shows that

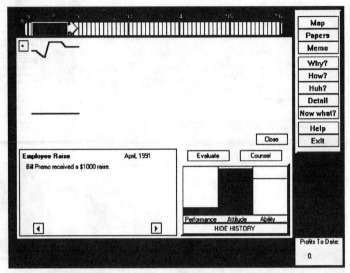

Figure 5: Employee history

Bill's attitude has had its ups and downs, but has always been relatively high. The second line down corresponds to the ability bar, and shows that his ability has always been at the level it is now. The bottom line corresponds to the performance bar, and shows that his perfomance has always been this low.

The learner's job is to figure out what it means when an employee's attitude and ability are high, but performance is low.

There are only six actions that a learner can take to affect an employee. These actions are made clear to the learner on the interface (in Figure 4). He can:

1. change the employee's position (promotion or demotion);
2. change the employee's salary (raise or pay cut);
3. change status (put on probation or fire);
4. train the employee;
5. evaluate the employee (initiate a formal performance review of the employee);
6. counsel the employee (his or her supervisor will have an informal chat with the employee).

The job info button on the middle of the right side of this interface accesses a minimal description of the PP&P's personnel policies. By clicking on a particular Position the learner can investigate the normal salary range, requirements, and job description for that position. This is all of the case specific information the

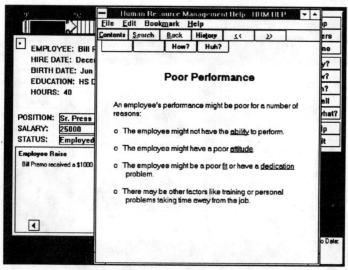

Figure 6: Advice to the learner

learner will need to make a decision in the simulation.

Let us assume in this particular case that the learner has no clue why Bill's performance is low. If the learner selects the why? button, he would see the advice shown in Figure 6. Notice that this does not provide the specific reason that Bill's performance is low. Rather, it is a list of possible causes for a low performance. If the learner does not understand an item, he can click on that item and get more detailed information. The learner can also ask follow-up questions. For example, clicking the How? button at this point would suggest strategies for fixing any of these performance problems.

The learner is motivated to understand each of the items on the poor performance list well enough to decide if it applies to Bill's situation. If the learner believes that Bill does not have the ability to perform (a bad guess given how high his ability bar is), the employee could be given some training. After assigning him to a course, the learner closes Bill's folder and hits the advance one month button.

The meters on the top level (Figure 7) would now show the new values for productivity and morale. The solid line represents the new value, and the dotted line is last month's value. This makes it easier to see what changes have occurred. To see what part Bill plays in these changes, however, the learner opens Bill's folder again and sees how his characteristics have changed.

Proceeding in this way, the learner can try any series of actions or just wait to see if Bill gets better. Bill, unfortunately, is one of those characters who cannot be fixed. He just does not want to work

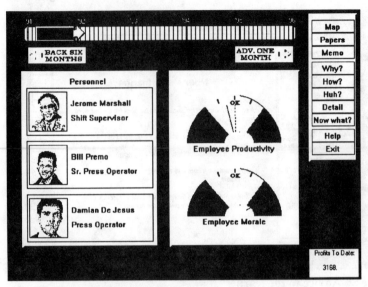

Figure 7: Top-level after one month

harder. The learner should have picked this up from the fact that his attitude and ability were high. If he fires Bill, he has an opportunity to experience another aspect of human resource management: hiring.

Let us assume now that while working on Bill, the learner has failed to check on Damian De Jesus (the employee on the bottom button). By about August 1992 in the simulation, the learner will receive a memo indicating that Damian has resigned. After closing the memo window, the learner is shown Damian's folder to determine why Damian quit, and, if possible, to try and get him to change his mind. In looking at Damian's personnel folder (Figure 8), we can see the immediate cause of his resignation was a low attitude. If the learner decides that this attitude is low because Damian has not received a raise in some time, he can raise Damian's salary and close the folder to see if it is accepted. The learner will then receive a note from Damian saying, in effect, "That was part of my reason for leaving, but your offer comes too late."

The tutor will then pop up with the box shown in Figure 9. This box lists any errors the tutor has noticed that could have led to Damian resigning. For each error, the learner can either click on the detail button or the story button. The detail button will jump the learner into the hypermedia at a point appropriate to the error. The story button will find a videotaped story about someone who experienced a similar failure.

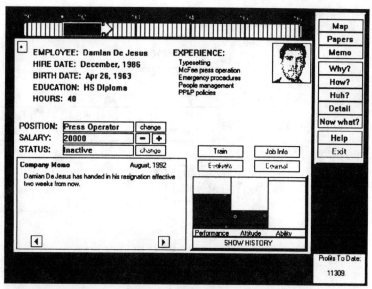

Figure 8: Damian's personnel folder after he quits

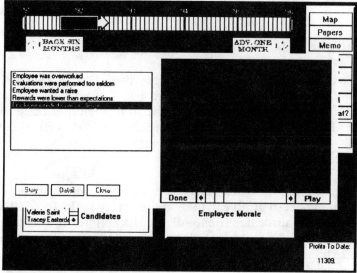

Figure 9: Tutor suggesting reasons that the learner failed

The learner uses these resources to understand his mistakes. Any information the learner hears or reads at this point is in context, as he has just experienced a failure, and information pertains to the mistakes that led to that failure. The learner is motivated to understand what went wrong since he will probably be fired soon, and have to go back and do a better job.

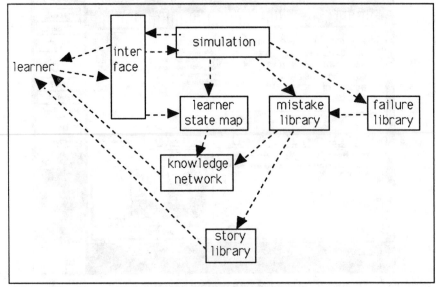

Figure 10: Flow of information in a case-based tutor

Components

To enable the interaction just described, CaBLE tutors contain the components illustrated in Figure 10. The arrows in this figure indicate the flow of information. The role of each of these components and the nature of the information flow is described below:

Interface

The interface provides the learner with the means to take actions he might expect to be able to take in the actual task. In addition, the interface communicates the results of the actions as determined by the simulation. The interface also contains generic question buttons that are interpreted by the current learner state to provide access to the knowledge network.

Simulation

The simulation of the task indicates the probable results of any learner action, if that action had occurred in the real world. The CaBLE tutor checks after each learner action to see if the mistake library recognizes that action as a mistake. The simulation then calculates what the results of this action would have been in the real world. The simulation then checks the failure library to see if any of the resulting events or states are recognized as failures.

Learner State Map

The learner state map allows the CaBLE tutor to recognize the context in which the learner asks a question. This allows the tutor to provide more relevant information in response to the question. The learner's current location in the learner state map is updated when key interface actions occur and when key events occur in the simulation.

Knowledge Network

The knowledge network contains the declarative knowledge the learner would have to have to be successful at the task. When the learner asks a question, the CaBLE tutor will bring him to an appropriate piece of information in the network.

Failure Library

The failure library contains a list of events that would be considered failures in the domain (i.e., a plane crashing or a patient dying). Any time an event occurs in the simulation that matches one of these failure events, the CaBLE tutor will check to see what mistakes have occurred that could have led to that failure.

Mistake Library

The mistake library contains a list of the common errors made in the domain. For each mistake there is a set of conditions that would allow the CaBLE tutor to recognize that the error occurred. In addition, each mistake is associated with a list of failures that could occur if the learner made the particular mistake. Each mistake is linked to appropriate stories and/or information in the knowledge network so that these can be offered to the learner after a failure.

Story Library

The story library contains explanations, positive examples, and negative examples for the domain being taught. When a failure occurs, the CaBLE tutor finds and tells a relevant story.

Designing The Task

What Do We Want to Teach

The first step in designing any instruction is to ask, "What do I want the learner to be able to do?" We will refer to this as the goal task. Being able to do the goal task implies at least four sub-goals:

1. knowing how to do the task, that is, knowing the steps, process, strategy or procedure involved;
2. having the necessary skills;
3. knowing the facts, concepts, and principles necessary to carry out the task;
4. believing that the task should be done and that the process being taught is a good way to do it.

These four sub-goals are similar to the classification of possible goals included in most instructional design theories (Gagne & Briggs, 1979; Reigeluth, 1983b). Instructional design has been defined as, "... the process of deciding what methods of instruction are best for bringing about desired changes in student knowledge and skills for a specific course content and a specific student population (Reigeluth, 1983a)"

What instructional design theories generally omit, however, are any criteria for deciding which goals are important or relevant. While it is important to teach each of these subgoals, the primary goal of instruction is to empower the learner. We want to enable the learner to do something he could not do before. In schools, for example, we might want to enable the learner to write, read, make decisions or use scientific methods to solve problems. In a training situation we might want to enable the learner to sell, manufacture, or manage.

Any skills or facts are meaningful only to the extent that they enable the learner to accomplish a real world task. By starting with the goal task, we have a clear criterion for the inclusion of other knowledge goals.

When we began designing HeRMiT we were told that the goal was to teach the key functions of HRM (i.e., hiring, training, benefits, retirement, legal compliance). What does it mean to teach these key functions? It could mean that the learner has to memorize an official list of functions. Or it might mean that the learner has to know everything that goes on in each function.

The point is that if you start with a knowledge goal, you have no clue how appropriately to teach that knowledge.

The question is, "Why?" That is, what do we want the learner to be able to do that requires that he has the knowledge? If there is no answer to this question, then do not teach the knowledge. If there is a capability we want to give the learner that requires this knowledge, then that capability should drive our design.

In the case of HeRMiT, the goal was to enable a consultant to recognize a company's potential HRM problems. While this goal task requires some knowledge of the functions of HRM, it does not, for example, require memorization of an official list of twelve functions. Rather, this goal task requires that the learner know that there are some standard issues that any company has to face in managing its human resources. Further, it is important that the learner believe that the HRM decisions affect the company's bottom line.

Choosing a Teaching Task

The second step is to choose the computer-based teaching task that the learner will attempt. The teaching task should require the same knowledge needed for the goal task, but the two tasks need not be identical. In HeRMiT, for example, any of the following tasks might have required the same knowledge as the goal task:

- become a successful employee of the case company (get yourself hired, trained, promoted and retired while dealing with the HRM bureaucracy);

- manage the HRM function of the case company;

- supervise someone who is managing the HRM function of the case company (evaluate his or her decisions);

- create HRM policies for the case company;

- observe and critique the HRM policies used in the case company.

The last task listed above is probably the closest to the goal task. However, similarity should not be the only consideration in choosing a learning task. Other considerations include:

1. How easy would it be to simulate the dynamics involved in this task on the computer?
2. How wide a range of actions would the learner expect to be able to take in carrying out the task?

3. Would the results of mistakes be clear and concrete?
4. How engaging would the task be?
5. How many extraneous choices, not related to the goal task, would the learner have to make?
6. How real will the learning task feel on the computer?
7. How much time will the learner have to accomplish the task?

How each of these considerations affects the choice of a learning task will become clear in the remaining sections.

Designing the Interface Inputs

The first step in defining the interface is determining how the learner will indicate actions. The goal is to create an interface that does not have to be learned. Once the learner has chosen a course of action, he should not have to spend much time figuring out how to communicate that decision to the simulation (Norman, 1986).

One answer is to allow the user to type his intentions in natural language. Unfortunately, our ability to parse natural language is limited at the present time. In the best of situations the tutor will be able to understand, and know how to execute, only a small subset of the possible actions a learner could choose. Thus the learner would have to spend time figuring out which words and actions the tutor can recognize. Since the range of allowable actions is always going to be limited, the limits should be clearly specified to the learner.

At the other extreme, we could present a multiple choice question at every point in the simulation. Multiple choice questions pose the opposite threat. The learner does not have to spend any time choosing an action, he merely has to recognize the best alternative in a limited set.

In the ideal situation the learner independently generates an action choice that is within the range allowed by the simulation, and then intuitively knows how to communicate the choice to the computer. To approach this ideal we have adopted the following standards:

1. Provide a fixed set of actions that remains constant throughout the simulation (so that the learner does not have to learn a new set at every point).
2. Have actions correspond to choices that the learner would have in the real world (if the role can limit the actions possible then the learner does not have to learn the artificial boundaries imposed

by the simulation).
3. Label actions with terms that will be understood by the learner (no domain dependent jargon).
4. Actions should be neutral, their rightness or wrongness determined by the context and or the order in which they are taken.

In HeRMiT, the interface allows the learner to take any of a set of actions that remains constant throughout the simulation (see Figure 4). The actions represent the primitive actions the learner would expect an HR department to be able to make: change position, change salary, provide training, evaluate, counsel, change status.

Contrast this with offering more specific choices such as: promote, give merit raise, make the employee feel appreciated or comply with government regulations. The specificity of each of these choices might allow learners to complete the activity with little understanding of what they were doing or why they succeeded. It would seem obvious, for example, that you should make employees feel appreciated. The hard part is to determine the action that would make the employee feel appreciated in a particular context.

Outputs

We try to avoid feedback that sounds like, "Wrong, try again." If an action is wrong it is wrong because it would have some undesirable consequence in the real world. There are numerous ways that we get feedback on our actions in the real world:

1. Data — we see some data ("Last month's profits - $50,000");
2. Events — we hear about a resulting event ("Bob just quit.");
3. Feedback from other agents— someone tells us what she thinks of our actions ("I did not like the way you handled that situation.");
4. Body language— we sense how people feel as a result of our actions ("hmm...Bob seems happier.");

The learner should receive the same type of feedback in the simulated task that he would receive in the real world. The question is, how hard should the learner have to work to interpret the feedback? At one extreme we can be very direct. Give the learner only the feedback that we want him to attend to, and make the implication clear and concrete. At the other extreme we can give the learner access to a wide range of information, relevant and irrelevant, that is couched in subtleties.

How hard the learner should work to interpret the feedback is dependent on the goal task. If the real world task requires that the learner will be able to sift through extraneous data or make inferences from the data, then the learning task should require the learner to find the relevant data or make the inferences. On the other hand, if we can assume that the learner in the real world would be able easily to determine the relevant data, that the challenge is knowing the right action given the data, then we do not have to hide the relevant data.

In HeRMIT, for example, the learner needs only look in an employee's folder to get a graphic representation of the employee's current ability, attitude, and performance (Figure 4). This type of direct feedback would probably not be available to the learner in the real world. However, the learner's goal task, recognizing HRM problems, does not require the skills involved in assessing an employee. The goal task only requires that the learner be able to diagnose an employee's problem, given an accurate assessment of that employee. Thus, presenting ability, attitude, and performance in such a direct form avoids forcing the learner to learn and use extraneous assessment skills.

We now look at examples for each of the above types of feedback: data, events, feedback from other agents, and body language.

Data

To use data in the real world we may first have to find the data or ask the right questions to get the data we need, sift through irrelevant data, understand the data, or interpret the data. How much we use technology to aid any of these processes is contingent upon the aspects of the goal task we want to emphasize.

In terms of accessibility, we can hide all data from the learner until they are specifically requested. The learner can request the data by asking to see the current value of a variable or by reading a simulated report.

If it is important for the learner to develop the skills to understand and interpret data, we can just display the raw values that are relevant to the situation. We can also provide scaffolding by showing the learner the results of calculations on the raw data to make trends or significance clearer. For example we can show ratios or compute the difference between the current and previous value for a variable.

We can further help the learner interpret data by showing the data graphically in a chart or a meter to make it more concrete.

Events

The challenge in using the information implied by events in the real world can be either discovering that the event has occurred, or discovering the significance of the event, assuming that we would know that it had occurred. Thus we can require that the learner work to discover an event by imbedding it in simulated reports or requiring the learner to ask a simulated agent to discover the event.

The difficulty in interpreting an event can be varied by adjusting the directness of the experience. The learner can experience the simulated event (i.e., a plane crashing) directly or a memo can pop up on the screen describing the event. The directness of events can also vary in terms of the number of irrelevant events to which the learner is exposed, and the degree to which the cause of the event is indicated.

Feedback From Other Agents

When interpreting feedback from other agents in the real world, we must consider the agent's personality and role. Feedback from other agents can be biased or wrong. By using this mechanism, the CaBLE tutoring system can give the user hints that the user must work to evaluate. Care must be taken, however, to keep each agent internally consistent (Laurel, 1991).

In addition to these special considerations, we can vary the parameters listed above for other data sources. We can wait for the learner to initiate the feedback by asking another agent for her opinion or asking that he be evaluated. The feedback can provide an explanation for an event or data that the learner has already seen. Or the feedback can be immediate and direct. For example, the learner could receive a simulated note from his boss saying, "I just heard that you fired John. I don't think that was a good thing to do."

Body Language

A more subtle form of feedback in the real world are the non-verbal reactions of other agents. Providing the learner with opportunities to practice skills used in interpreting body language can be a major challenge to the designer of a computer-based tutor. In situations where these skills are important, the system must provide a functional replacement for body language. Some functional replacements have included: video clips of agents showing different reactions, stills or cartoons to illustrate reactions, and meters or other quantitative indicators to represent aspects of an agent's mood.

Designing the Simulation

Simulating the real world on a computer is certainly a formidable task. Fortunately, a true simulation is not necessary in a CaBLE tutor. All that is required is to simulate aspects of the world, or at least the external behavior of those aspects, that have an impact on the learning goals.

Objects

Building the simulation begins with defining the objects that inhabit the simulated world. In HeRMiT these include: employees and the company. It is important to teach the learner that personalities and characteristics will vary from employee to employee, and that taking the same action with two different employees may have very different results. Thus, each employee is a separate object in the system. All of these employee objects share certain characteristics, but they each have individual values for dedication, flexibility, ambition, etc.. An object is defined by set of variables and the relationships among those variables. The simulated world, in turn, is described by the relationship among variables belonging to different objects.

Variables

To determine which variables are needed, we trace a path from actions to outcomes. We need to simulate the causal chain from the actions we want the student to learn to the outcomes that would reflect the learner's success. For example, in the real world we can directly manipulate an employee's salary. In HeRMiT the outcomes that measure whether we do that appropriately are the company's productivity and the employee's morale. The effect of salary on the employee's morale is determined by comparing the current salary to the employee's expected salary. Each simulated employee begins the game with a hard-wired expected salary. The expected salary is then adjusted each month using variables such as last salary earned, time since last raise, ambition, and current responsibilities. Thus, in order to teach a student the relationship between salary and morale, all of these variables must be represented for each employee.

Also notice the variables that need not be represented. We observe a certain representational efficiency by representing only those variables that affect what the learner should be learning. For example, fixed overhead is certainly a part of current cost. Since the learner cannot directly affect overhead in the simulation, and since it does not affect the ratio of costs to work, it is not represented. Similarly, the actual value of work is based on sales. Since we are not teaching inventory or pricing skills, however, sales variables are not represented.

Relationships

The relationships between objects are determined by formulas which state how the variables of any one object affect the variables of any other objects. For example, the value of the goods produced by the company is calculated by summing the productivity of all of the employees. Each employee's productivity is calculated as the product of that employee's performance and what we call the employee's nominal salary. An employee's performance is stated as a percentage of some theoretical optimum performance possible for someone in that employee's current position. The nominal salary is the average of the minimum and maximum recommended salary for the employee's current position.

Nominal salary is factored into an employee's productivity to insure that the more responsibility an employee has, the greater the impact of that employee's perfomance will be on the bottom line of the company. This assumes that there is a positive correlation between responsibility and salary. Therefore, a poor performing junior pressman will not hurt the company as much as a poor performing supervisor.

Events

Events cause objects to change over time. An event specifies the variables that change when the event occurs. There are three kinds of events:

1. automatic;
2. learner initiated;
3. ad hoc.

Automatic events happen periodically independent of any learner actions. For example, in HeRMiT whenever a month passes, all employees are paid. How much they are paid, and the effect of being paid, are determined by the salary that the learner has set. But the actual event of paying an employee happens whenever time advances a month, without the learner even looking at an employee, let alone explicitly initiating the payroll event.

Automatic events allow objects to change over time without the learner managing, or perhaps even being aware of, low level details. This allows the learner to focus better on the issues we are trying to teach.

Some events are initiated by the learner. The learner using HeRMiT can fire, train, evaluate or counsel an employee at any point. The actual impact of that action will be determined by the current values of the variables representing that employee. The learner-initiated actions give the learner a sense of control, and thus responsibility, for the outcomes of the simulation. The actions kept under learner control are chosen to allow the learner to express, in operational terms, his understanding of the important issues.

Thirdly, there are ad hoc events that happen randomly, just as in real life, to keep the learner on his/her toes. An employee might suddenly find themselves in the middle of a divorce. This would obviously not result from any action the learner has taken, but the learner will have to become aware of this situation and consider it when taking actions. Ad hoc events are used sparingly. Random events remind the learner that the real world (especially a social world) is not totally deterministic. Too many random events, however, can convince the learner that he cannot control the outcomes. This would lead to what Seligman called "learned helplessness" (Seligman, 1975).

Designing the Tutoring

The simulation and the interface provide a context in which learning can take place. To capitalize on this context the tutoring system must be capable of answering learner questions, pointing out mistakes and explaining misunderstandings. The story library and the knowledge network contain the knowledge necessary to support the learner and provide scaffolding. Interfaces must be designed to make the knowledge available at appropriate times. Let us consider two types of situations in which knowledge is shared:

1. learner initiated, in which the learner interrupts the flow of action to ask a question;
2. tutor initiated, in which the tutor interrupts to offer some information.

Learner Initiated Tutoring

The most efficient method of tutoring is often to wait for the learner to specify what he does not understand. It would be nice if we could allow the learner simply to express a question in natural language. Lacking natural language capability, the question becomes, how does the learner express his misunderstanding in a way that the computer-based tutor can understand?

One answer is to keep track of the context the learner is in, and then to use that context to limit the possible relevant questions the learner might be asking at any given time. If we can sufficiently limit the number of possible questions, the learner can use a simple interface to indicate which of these questions he wanted to ask.

All of the learner contexts possible in a CaBLE tutoring system are represented in the learner state map. Each learner state includes a definition of the context the learner is in, and a list of questions the learner may have given this context. We define the learner's context by:

1. what the learner is looking at;
2. the learner's last action;
3. what has changed since the last action.

In addition, the transitions between learner states are defined by a set of actions that would indicate that the learner is in a new state. As an example, consider the HeRMiT main screen shown in Figure 11. In this context, the learner might sensibly ask:

1. what an object on the screen represents ("What is productivity?").
2. why an object is in its current state ("Why is productivity low?").
3. why an object has changed its state ("Why did employee morale fall?").
4. how to influence the state of an object ("How can I improve productivity?").
5. how he should respond to developments in the simulation ("What should I do now?").
6. how to use the interface ("How do I advance time?").

The goal of the interface is to allow the learner to ask any of these questions as intuitively as possible. We provide the why?, how?, Huh?, Detail and Now What? buttons on the right side of the screen. Since each of these buttons represents an utterance typical of those likely to be expressed in instructional interactions, the hypothesis is

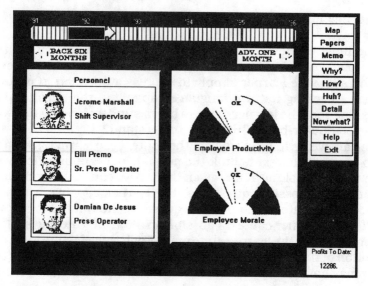

Figure 11: Top-level view after seven months

that there is a clear mapping to the types of confusion a learner may be experiencing (Jona, Bell, & Birnbaum, 1991). Each button thus corresponds to a subset of the questions that have been defined for a particular learner state.

In Figure 11, for example, the why? button would indicate that the learner either wanted to know why something is in its current state, or why a state has changed. This is disambiguated by having the learner click on a screen object. If the learner clicks on employee productivity the tutor concludes that the learner wants to know why productivity is low, since that is the salient characteristic of employee productivity in the current learner state.

HeRMiT's learner state map, then, reflects the interface objects that are on the screen, the states of those objects, the changes in state over time, and the learner questions that might arise from this context.

Tutor Initiated Tutoring

The first step in providing tutor initiated tutoring is to define the types of mistakes a learner could make in the domain. There is no need to represent every possible mistake, just the mistakes that matter in terms of the goals. The mistake library can be further simplified by defining mistake types at a sufficiently general level. Generalizing mistake types not only simplifies the representation, it also forces the learner to generalize lessons learned.

In the human resources domain, for example, a learner may make the following kinds of mistakes pertaining to training an employee:

1. not training a new hire who lacks any starting skills;
2. not training someone after a promotion that requires new skill;
3. not training the work force when technology changes require new skills.

In HeRMiT all three are represented at a more general level:

- not training someone who is missing a needed skill.

Thus if the learner fails to train a new employee, he might see a story about a company that neglected to keep their work force current on the new technologies being used on their shop floor. In order to use this story, the learner must generalize the principle: train anyone who is missing needed skills.

Each mistake type in the library is described by a set of conditions that would indicate that it has occurred. Sins of commission are recognized when the learner takes a certain action or series of actions when the object is in some particular state. Sins of omission are recognized when some negative state, that could have been changed, leads to a negative outcome.

In order to tutor, each mistake type is linked to appropriate knowledge and stories in the knowledge network and the story library.

Designing the Knowledge Base

The facts, concepts, principles and processes that the learner needs to know to accomplish the task are contained in the knowledge network. The information is broken into bite-size pieces. Each piece of knowledge is a node in the knowledge network. Each node is written to be a straightforward answer to a question that a learner might ask.

Structure

The nodes in the knowledge network are kept short, so that there is a better chance that they answer a specific question that the learner had. The nodes should not contain long lectures or sermons from the expert. If the learner wants or needs further information, he can ask follow-up questions. By giving a direct answer to the learner's original question, while leaving the door open for further questions, the knowledge network allows the interaction to feel more like a conversation between an expert and the learner.

To provide this functionality, we look at each node in the knowledge network and try to anticipate any questions that this node might raise in the learner's mind. Much as was done at the top interface level (see above), these possible follow-up questions are mapped to the question buttons: why?, how?, huh?, more detail and context. In addition, questions about a specific word (i.e., "What do you mean by benefits?"), are mapped to that word. The word appears in green when the node's text is displayed, to let the learner know that he can ask follow-up questions on that word.

Each of the question buttons and green words are then linked to other nodes in the network that would answer the follow-up questions implied by those buttons and green words. This process results in a richly connected network of pieces of knowledge which comprise the domain knowledge of the tutoring system.

Content

The hypermedia nature of the knowledge network allows one knowledge base to be collected and viewed from three very different perspectives:

1. the expert's model;
2. common sense model;
3. learner's model.

The Expert's Model. When the expert considers her domain from the outside, it may look very different from when she is trying to operate within it. This is the result of long experience and the opportunity for reflection — from her experience, the expert is able to make an explicit model of how her domain operates. A good abstract model of a domain has the benefits of being concise, of being well organized, and of being immediately understandable, given enough schooling in the domain being modeled.

The problem is that the expert's model is often not very useful for the novice in a domain. There is too much cognitive overhead required to understand the model because of the distance from theory to practice. However, in a conversation that is informed by the model, a good teacher can communicate some sense of the way she understands the domain in terms that the learner can understand,

and relate to the learner's context and prior knowledge. This is the way that HeRMiT uses the expert's model of human resource management.

For example, learners in HeRMiT are confronted with a situation in which employees are complaining about a new evaluation policy. The old policy was: rate each employee based on concrete number like attendance, volume, and errors. The new policy is: together with employee, agree on subjective assessment of the employee's contribution to the company. Employees are complaining that the new evaluations are too "fuzzy," the old evaluations gave them something clear to shoot for. The learner must decide whether to advise that the company stick to the new evaluations, or go back to the old evaluations.

If the learner were to ask the knowledge network for information on evaluations, he would see the following text:

Evaluate

Evaluation is a way of communicating with an employee and recording his or her progress towards clear performance goals. The elements of evaluation are:

- Deciding what areas of performance are most important in each job's *design.*
- Using a formal *performance review* to recognize and document the employee's progress in those areas.

While our subject matter experts recognize this as a valid description of the evaluation process, it is hard for a novice to use it to decide what to do in the above case.

Common-Sense Model. On the other hand, learners can see the following story, by hitting the get advice button:

There was a situation in one company that had a policy that said that if you were late three times, you got written up. One clerk was excellent. But she was a single mother who took the bus to work. As a result, she was a little late several times. It wasn't a problem, but McKee (the HR director) being a by-the-book kind of person wrote the clerk up.

A second clerk was never late. But she also never got up from her desk, never did anything she didn't have to do.

Bonus time came around, and the policy was that you only got a bonus if you weren't written up. The second clerk got a bonus, the first clerk did not. The first clerk stormed into McKee's office and slammed down her bonus rejection letter. She said, "I see what's important around here. It's not the quality of your work, it's just being here on time. Well, you can guarantee that I will be on time from now on. But, do not ask me to do a single thing that is not in my job description."

Although not even about evaluation, learners found this story far more useful in helping them recognize and apply the general principle: make sure that you reward the things that are truly important to the company.

The above story is part of the second kind of knowledge that the knowledge base tries to capture, the expert's common-sense understanding of his/her domain. This comes out of the stories that the expert tells about the domain, including his/her greatest failures, biggest successes, and other, more idiosyncratic events. When operating in the domain, the expert reasons from cases: recognizing elements in the current situation that resemble elements in a past situation, and adapting the plan used in the past case to deal with the present.

Most experts do this unconsciously. They are unaware of any system that makes a new problem remind them of a past case. This doesn't stop them from being good teachers — from using their stories to help illuminate a problem for a novice in the domain. It is harder to program a computer to simulate this interaction.

Fortunately, common-sense knowledge is not just piecemeal. The stories that experts tell about their domain always illustrate something. If a story is about something terrible that happened, it illustrates one or more mistakes that the expert will know to avoid the next time. A mistake is the violation of some larger principle. If the expert tells a story about a company whose payroll was so large that it went bankrupt, the mistake might be "paying employees too much" and the principle might be something like "pay employees what they are worth." A list of mistakes in human resource management, linked to stories that illustrate them and to the principles they violate, is basis for the organization of the common-sense wisdom in the knowledge network.

HeRMiT's knowledge network tries to communicate the expert's common-sense knowledge of the domain by explaining the stories in the story library. These explanations point out in general terms the elements of the stories that are applicable to the learner's situation in the module.

The Learner's Model. The third point of view that the knowledge network addresses is the learner's. We try to anticipate the learner's questions and answer them in terms that the learner can relate to both his/her work within the module and to the real-world 'goal task.' This often requires extra "buffer" nodes that serve as a transition from the kind of questions that novices initially ask to the kind of questions that experts are comfortable answering. These buffer nodes are intended to be both direct, simple answers, understandable by a novice learner and advance organizers for the expert's view of the world. Ideally, then, these buffer nodes will stimulate follow-up questions.

The content in HeRMiT's knowledge network is surrounded by access points — pieces of knowledge that serve as transition between what the learner wants to know and the relevant knowledge that the expert can provide on the topic. These pieces of knowledge insure that every question the learner might want to ask at any point in the simulation can be answered. They answer questions like "What should I do now?" or "Why did that happen?" - the most common types of questions, and exactly the kind of question that abstract models fail to address. HeRMiT's strategy for answering these questions is to give the most straight-forward, direct answer possible — but to leave the door open for the learner to ask further questions if he wants to know the principles upon which the answer is based.

Collecting Stories

The success of a CaBLE tutor is contingent on its ability to tell good stories. Multimedia technology allows the story to be told in a natural manner. The simulation provides a meaningful context for using the story. But all of this is meaningless if the system doesn't "know" any good stories. Critical to success are the very non-technical steps of finding the right story teller, and eliciting good stories.

The use of stories is based on the notion that what makes an expert an expert is having good stories at his/her disposal. When something anomalous occurs, he or she is reminded of a similar previous experience. The expert then attempts to apply whatever he or she learned in the previous experience to the present situation. It is these appropriately indexed cases that separate an expert from a novice. For the purposes of collecting stories in a CaBLE tutor, one cannot be considered an expert in a domain by merely knowing all of the facts and rules. He or she must have actually lived within the domain and had opportunities to apply those facts and rules.

To help experts remember appropriate stories, we have employed the following strategies:

- ask the expert to recall any interesting stories in the domain;
- have the expert describe the process used in accomplishing the task, stopping them at each step to ask if anything interesting has ever happened at that step;
- have the expert describe one particular time he or she did the task;
- ask the expert to recall the most important lessons learned during her first year doing this task, and the experiences that taught her those lessons;
- have the expert recall her most brilliant "save;"
- have the expert describe her most memorable near-miss;
- have the expert recall any situations he or she would handle differently today.

We suggest the following story outline to our story tellers:

context — how I know this story, what my role was, where this took place;

symptoms — build some drama with the first symptoms or events as they led to the interesting situation that eventually developed;

problem — a clear description of the disaster I eventually found myself in, and why it is a problem;

principle — any thoughts about the principles involved in this type of problem;

resolution — what happened at the end, or after, this story. What was the solution? or, what would I do differently next time.

Experiences With HeRMiT

HeRMiT is one of 15 modules designed and built to replace an instructor-led course on basic business. The previous course required 60 hours of individual study and then 40 hours in class, regardless of the student's background. The new course requires 38 to 45 hours total, depending on the learner's background.

HeRMiT represents, in a sense, the minimal approach to CaBLE tutoring. It was built to run on a realistic platform, within real-world constraints, and developed within a business-driven time frame. It is only a suggestion of what this technology and design approach make possible. Between August of 1992 and April of 1993, 700 students have used the HeRMiT module (400 in the US, 300 internationally).

A formal learner test of HeRMiT was conducted in April of 1992 with five subjects (Feifer & Hinrichs, 1992). Four subjects had no previous exposure to human resource management. Subjects were video-taped and observed using the program. After using HeRMiT, subjects were interviewed on issues ranging from enjoyment of the program to understanding of HRM concepts.

All learners expressed a new appreciation of the importance of human resource management to the health of a company, and were able to demonstrate an understanding of the basic issues (through written and oral debriefing). At least as important, all subjects found the program engaging.

In addition to the formal learner test, we have observed and conducted follow-up interviews with 40 HeRMiT learners. Through our observations we have identified three different learner interaction styles with the program. These correspond to the following learning styles and/or background:

1. learners with some previous knowledge or experience in the domain — they will use approximately 40 minutes to finish the module. They ask almost no questions during the simulation. They experience few or no failures in the simulation. When a failure does occur, they will read the list of mistakes but ask no follow-up questions;
2. novice learners who hate to fail — they will use approximately two hours to finish the module. They will read all information on each employee each month, ask all possible questions, and consider every option before acting. They will experience few failures. They will ask follow-up questions on all mistakes for each failure;
3. novice learners who aren't afraid to learn by failing — they will use approximately two hours to finish the module. They will ask very few questions in the beginning, and only read the minimum information on each employee. They will just jump in, experimenting, often letting several months pass without re-checking on an employee. They will fail often, asking sufficient follow-up questions to understand the cause of the failure.

These learners who hate to fail, may be the kind of learners Elliott and Dweck call performance goal oriented (Elliott & Dweck, 1988). In a non-supported learn-by-doing environment, they might be too intimidated to try. By providing the tools to avoid failure, we avoid the negative effects on motivation. On the other hand, these learners who aren't afraid to fail, seem to be the kind who like to jump right in and experiment. They might be bored if the tutor began with any information. HeRMiT allows them the option to jump right in.

Despite the different approaches used by each type of learner, each type reports a similar understanding of the material after using HeRMiT. In addition they report the same perception of the program as being engaging and enjoyable. HeRMiT is thus able to provide a learning environment that allows learners with a range of learning styles and background to master the original pedagogical goals.

CABLE Tutors in the Next Century

HeRMiT's importance is not as a technological leap in the use of multimedia for learning. What it does represent, however, is good use of existing technology. We applied cognitive research to provide an effective learning environment. HeRMiT was built in a reasonable time frame to run on reasonable platforms that currently exist in the business world.

The current technology clearly has its limitations. A long list of desired enhancements was not implemented because we wanted a real system that taught real people. Further, although we designed for what was considered a reasonable platform, many offices around the world had to upgrade their equipment to run HeRMiT. Many machines needed faster CPU's, more RAM and hard disk space, and a CD-ROM player. Lastly, though a CaBLE tutor is built in a modular fashion, updating the video is difficult and expensive.

The Technology

With the multimedia technology that we can expect in the future, however, these limitations will go away. We can expect computers that are much more powerful. This will make many of today's issues of speed, limited screen real estate, and capacity for storing and manipulating information less significant. Systems far more sophisticated than HeRMiT will be able to run on any desk top. The networks will be able to deliver video and other media almost anywhere, on demand. Updating systems such as HeRMiT will then become trivial as we will be able dynamically to add new media sources with links.

These technological advancements will lead to the potential for rich interaction with multimedia in our home, school or work place. These advancements and their potential are all safe predictions not only because the technology is already close, but also because there is much commercial competition to get us there.

What is less clear is what kind of information will be distributed through this technology. Assuming that we will have the means to store and deliver large amounts of information, what information should we store, and how should we organize it so that the end user can easily find what he or she wants? There is far less competition to develop a cognitively based approach to storing and retrieving information.

CaBLE tutors are one example of a class of designs for using multimedia content. The designs are based on principles of how people learn and use information.

The Need

Learning by doing has always been a good idea. Originally people learned by some form of apprenticeship or trial and error. It is only in the last century that it has become common and accepted to separate learning from the context in which the learning is used. The modern school has allowed society to mass produce learning.

In the traditional classroom, the teacher is the gate keeper of knowledge. If the learner wants or needs to know something, he or she must get the new knowledge from the teacher. Books help, but finding the right book, accessing the right information within that book or understanding the information once it is found, are themselves non-trivial tasks that require the teacher's help. This is why the traditional classroom has a teacher lecturing in front of 30-200 students. A lecture is the least labor intensive means of delivering knowledge. It is also, unfortunately, one of the least effective.

We can imagine far more effective learning environments in which all teaching is individualized and interest based. Every learner would be involved in a project that naturally integrates all of the skills and concepts that need to be learned. In the work place this would imply projects that present the learner with the kind of goals they would have on the job, but within an environment where it is safe to make mistakes and learn from failure. In school this might mean projects that are driven by the individual student's interests. In the course of these projects, if the learner needs more knowledge, or help developing a skill, he gets appropriate help on demand.

Providing these types of learning environments, however, is labor intensive. Multimedia technology, if properly organized, can remove the teacher from the role of knowledge gate keeper. Learners can interact with each other, and the teacher, and can directly interact with the knowledge. The technology will make it possible to ask questions of, and receive answers from, the best experts regardless of how far away, or dead, that expert might be.

As we build CaBLE tutors in new domains we have been able to generalize principles described in this chapter, as well as to define situations that require new architectures and approaches. To make these learning environments more available, our next step is to build tools to help people build CaBLE tutors easily. These tools include: brainstorming aids to help design learning tasks, indexing tools to organize the knowledge and link it to meaningful events in the simulation, media manipulators to create and edit multimedia objects, and simulation builders to create the worlds in which the learner accomplishes the learning task. These tools will eventually enable a teacher, instructional designer or subject matter specialist to create systems similar and superior to HeRMiT, in shorter time, and without a whole team of specialists.

Acknowledgments

This research was supported in part by the Defense Advanced Research Projects Agency, monitored by the Air Force Office of Scientific Research under contract F49620-88-C-0058 and the Office of Naval Research under contract N00014-90-J-4117, by the Office of Naval Research under contract N00014-J-1987, and by the Air Force Office of Scientific Research under contract AFOSR-89-0493. The Institute for the Learning Sciences was established in 1989 with the support of Andersen Consulting, part of The Arthur Andersen Worldwide Organization. The Institute receives additional support from Ameritech and North West Water, Institute Partners.

In addition to the authors, the following people were involved in the development of HeRMiT: Larry Langelier, Donna Fritzsche, Wayne Schneider, Michael Korcuska, Tom Hinrichs, Joshua Tsui, Leena Nanda, Cheryl Jindra, Matt Greising, Alan Nowakowski, and Don Jastrebsky. Thanks to George Marcolides for reading the early versions of this chapter and to Laura Allender for editing the many versions that followed. Special thanks to the HeRMiT storytellers: Bill Braemer and Tim Coan.

References

Anderson, J. R. (1983). *The architecture of cognition*. Cambridge, Ma: Harvard University Press.

Bell, B. L., & Feifer, R. G. (1992). Intelligent tutoring with dumb software. In C. Frasson, G. Gauthier, & G. I. McCalla (Eds.), *Intelligent Tutoring Systems* Berlin: Springer-Verlag.

Burton, R., & Brown, J. S. (1976). A tutoring and student modeling paradigm for gaming environments. *ACM SIGCSE (Computer Science and Education) Bulletin*, 8, 236-246.

Burton, R., & Brown, J. S. (1979). An investigation of computer coaching for informal learning activities. *International Journal of Man-Machine Studies*, 11, 51-77.

Collins, A., Brown, J. S., & Newman, S. E. (1989). Cognitive apprenticeship: Teaching the crafts of reading, writing, and mathematics. In L. B. Resnick (Eds.), *Knowing, learning, and instruction: Essays in honor of Robert Glaser* (pp. 453-494). Hillsdale, NJ: Lawrence Erlbaum Associates.

diSessa, A. A. (1993). Toward a knowledge level theory of learning. In Fifteenth annual conference of the cognitive science society.

Elliott, E. S., & Dweck, C. S. (1988). Goals: An approach to motivation and achievement. *Journal of Personality and Social Psychology*, 54(1), 5-12.

Feifer, R. G. (1989a). An intelligent tutoring system approach to teaching people how to learn. In *Proceedings of the Eleventh Annual Conference of the Cognitive Science Society,* . Ann Arbor, Michigan:

Feifer, R. G. (1989b) An intelligent tutoring system for graphic mapping strategies. Doctoral dissertation, University of California, Los Angeles.

Feifer, R. G., Dyer, M. G., & Baker, E. L. (1988). Learning procedural and declarative knowledge. In *Proceedings of the Intelligent Tutoring Systems Conference - 88*, Montreal, Canada.

Feifer, R. G., & Hinrichs, T. R. (1992). Using stories to enhance and simplify computer simulations for teaching. In *Proceedings of the Fourteenth Annual Conference of the Cognitive Science Society,*. Indianapolis, Indiana: Lawrence Erlbaum Associates.

Feifer, R. G., & Soclof, M. S. (1991). Knowledge-based tutoring systems: Changing the focus from learner modelling to teaching. In Proceedings of the International Conference on the Learning Sciences, (pp. 151-157). Northwestern University, Evanston, IL: Association for the Advancement of Computing in Education.

Gagne, R. M., & Briggs, L. J. (1979). *Principles of instructional design* (2nd ed.). New York: Holt, Rinehart & Winston.

Govindaraj, T. (1988). Intelligent computer aids for fault diagnosis training of expert operators of large dynamic systems. In J. Psotka, L. D. Massey', & S. A. Mutter (Eds.), *Intelligent tutoring systems: Lessons learned* (pp. 303-321). Hillsdale, NJ: Lawrence Erlbaum Associates Publishers.

Jona, M., Bell, B., & Birnbaum, L. (1991). Button theory: A taxonomy of student-teacher communication for interface design in computer-based learning environments. In *Proceedings of the Thirteenth Conference of the Cognitive Science Society,*. Chicago, IL.:

Kuhn, D. (1989). Children and adults as intuitive scientists. *Psychology Review*, 96(4), 674-689.

Kuhn, D., Schauble, L., & Garcia-Mila, M. (1992). Cross-domain development of scientific reasoning. Cognitive Instruction, 9(4), 285-327.

Laurel, B. (1991). *Computers as theater*. Reading, Mass.: Addison-Wesley Publishing Company.

Lesgold, A., Lajoie, S., Bunzo, M., & Eggan, G. (1991). SHERLOCK: A coached practice environment for an electronics troubleshooting job. In J. H. Larkin & R. W. Chabay (Eds.), *Computer assisted instruction and intelligent tutoring systems: Shared goals and complementary approaches* (pp. 201 - 238). Hillsdale, NJ: Erlbaum.

Norman, D. A. (1986). Cognitive engineering. In D. A. Norman & S. W. Draper (Eds.), *User Centered System Design* (pp. 31-61). Hillsdale, NJ:

Lawrence Erlbaum Associates.

Reigeluth, C. M. (1983a). Instructional design: What is it and why is it? In C. M. Reigeluth (Eds.), *Instructional-design theories and models: An overview of their current status* (pp. 335-381). Hillsdale, New Jersey: Lawerence Erlbaum Associates.

Reigeluth, C. M. (1983b). *Instructional-design theories and models: An overview of their current status.* Hillsdale, N.J.: Lawrence Erlbaum Associates.

Schank, R. C. (1991). *Case-based teaching: Four experiences in educational software design* (Technical Report No. 7). The Institute for the Learning Sciences, Northwestern University, Evanston IL.

Schank, R. C., & Jona, M. Y. (1991). Empowering the student: New perspectives on the design of teaching systems. *The Journal of the Learning Sciences*, 1(1), 7-35.

Schauble, L., Glaser, R., Raghavan, K., & Reiner, M. (1991). Causal models and experimentation strategies in scientific reasoning. *Journal of the Learning Sciences*, 1(2), 201-238.

Seligman, M. E. P. (1975). *Helplessness: On depression, development, and death.* San Francisco: Freeman.

Williams, M. D., Hollan, J. D., & Stevens, A. L. (1981). An overview of STEAMER: an advanced computer-assisted instruction system for propulsion engineering. *Behavior Research Methods and Instrumentation*, 13(2), 85-90.

Author's Note: * Due to the lack of appropriate gender neutral pronouns, I will consistently refer to the learner with male pronouns and the subject matter experts with female pronouns.

Chapter 10

Script-Coding Multimedia Applications

Sorel Reisman
California State University

The intricacies of underlying technologies often preclude subject matter experts from playing a more active role in the development of multimedia computing applications. The Multimedia Computing Presentation System (MCPS) was developed to permit subject matter experts to design, script, and code, modern multimedia PC applications. The system has been designed to enable developers to code their applications, even as they script them, hence the term "script-code." MCPS, which is a Fourth Generation Language running under Microsoft Windows 3.1, has enough features of procedural languages to give script-coders the flexibility they need to produce real, production-level multimedia applications. MCPS is so easy to use that developers can easily test their coded scripts as if they were prototype applications. A completed "prototype" will usually be a fully operational, production-level multimedia application.

The development and implementation of multimedia computing applications has traditionally been a complex undertaking. The intricacies of underlying technologies have often precluded subject matter experts from playing a more active role in the actual development of such applications. The Multimedia Computing Presentation System (MCPS) was developed to permit subject matter experts to design, script, and code, modern multimedia PC applications. MCPS allows developers to focus on the content of the application by providing a powerful, yet easy-to-use application scripting language. MCPS can be used to script multimedia-rich information presentation applications such as computer assisted instruction, kiosk data retrieval, and desktop presentation systems. The system has been designed to enable developers to code their applications, even as they script them, hence the term "script-code." MCPS is a Fourth Generation Language with enough features of procedural languages to give script-coders the flexibility they need to produce real, production-level multimedia applications. At the same time, MCPS is so easy to use that developers can easily test their coded scripts as if they were prototype applications. A completed "prototype" will usually be a fully operational, production-level multimedia application.

MCPS-coded scripts are interpreted by the MCPS Interpreter (MCPSI). During execution, 1) MCPSI outputs scripted information on a frame-by-frame (screen-by-screen) basis using either script-defined or MCPS default output formats, 2) it collects and stores user inputs, and 3) executes flow-of-control logic based on collected end user inputs.

The MCPS interpreter was programmed in Microsoft Visual Basic Professional under Windows 3.1. MCPSI was designed to "protect" the subject matter expert from the technologies of multimedia. MCPSI uses Windows I/O libraries, DLL's (dynamic link libraries), and Multimedia Extensions to (dis)play text, graphics, audio, and video at the workstation. As a result, as Windows evolves, obsoletes old multimedia technologies and incorporates new ones, previously written application scripts should not become obsolete.

Figure 1 illustrates the overall architecture of the MCPS system. MCPSI interprets and executes the contents of the Subject Matter Application Script. MCPSI also collects end user input and stores it in ASCII files on a hard disk. Data collected in this manner can be processed by application-specific utility programs (Data Processing Utilities) to produce customized (Transaction) reports.

The Application Scenario

The characteristics of applications script-coded in MCPS will vary, depending upon the creative skills of the application develop-

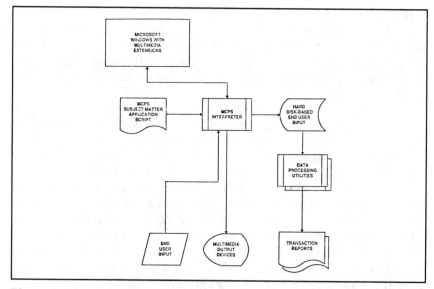

Figure 1: MCPS System Architecture

ment team. In general, applications will likely follow the pattern described here. MCPSI interprets and executes user/application interactions in terms of "frames." When MCPSI begins to execute, it displays information defined in the script's first frame. Although MCPSI treats all frames equivalently, the first frame of most applications will likely contain information that introduces the user to the current application. That frame may contain text, a graphics image, or an audio/video sequence displayed either within a window on the screen, or in a full screen. Figure 2 illustrates an introductory frame displayed in a full screen. The end user is prompted to continue the

Figure 2: The Introduction Frame

application.

MCPSI then clears the screen and displays the next frame. Figure 3 illustrates the display of information within a window. User-selectable option "buttons" are also displayed. In addition to the menu options, the user may obtain help, or an explanation of the contents of that frame.

If the user seeks help, MCPSI displays a window that overlaps the current frame's information (Figure 4). The help window may contain text, graphics, audio and/or video information. The user must select the return button to remove the overlapping help window to return to the original information screen (Figure 3).

After the user selects from the options shown on the screen, MCPSI branches to another frame. The next frame that is displayed is determined from script logic. When MCPSI executes the last frame, an application termination screen is usually displayed.

The appendix at the end of this chapter contains an MCPS script that illustrates the commands that generate a number of screens, including the ones illustrated in Figures 2, 3, and 4.

Application Scripts

Application scripts are designed and coded by application or subject matter experts. Scripts consist of a series of frames. Frames

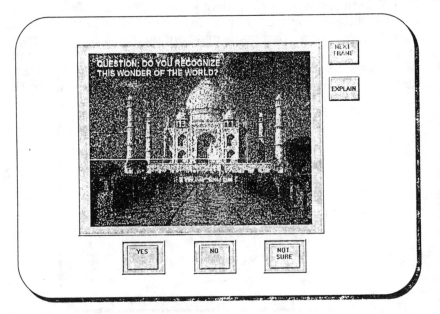

Figure 3: An MCPS Frame Presentation

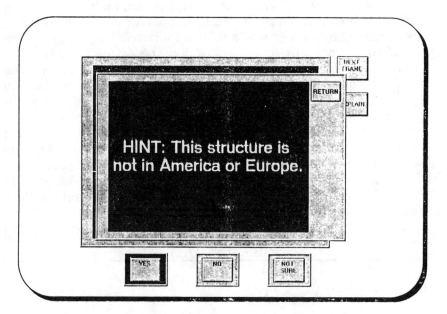

Figure 4: Overlapping Help Window

define the stimuli and acceptable responses for each screen of presented multimedia information.

Script Structure

Figure 5 illustrates the logic flow of every MCPS script. A script is a set of sequentially numbered frames. A frame consists of a Display Definition and of Frame Logic. Display Definition a) defines the information to be output on the multimedia workstation, and b) specifies the menu options selectable for the frame. Frame Logic defines the conditions that determine the next frame to be presented on the workstation.

Frame Structure

Frames contain commands for the application developer to:

a) Display information.
b) Define menu options.
c) Define help information.
d) Specify the next frame to display (branching conditions).

a) Display information. Script-coders may display information in the form of text, graphics images, or video, any of these accompanied by background audio. Information may be presented in default formats, or script-coders may use MCPS commands to alter most default settings. Text is displayed in "windows." The number and placement on the screen of these windows is determined by the "template" selected by the script-coder (Figure 6). The font size, font type, and font color of text may be set (and reset) by the script-coder. Window colors and screen background may also be set (and reset) by the script-coder. The positioning of windows on the screen and of all text within buttons is determined by MCPSI.

b) Menu options. In general, the script-coder may define up to five user-selectable responses (menu options) for each frame. MCPSI positions the response option text within option buttons. MCPSI determines the size and screen location of the buttons, depending on the number of options specified by the script-coder.

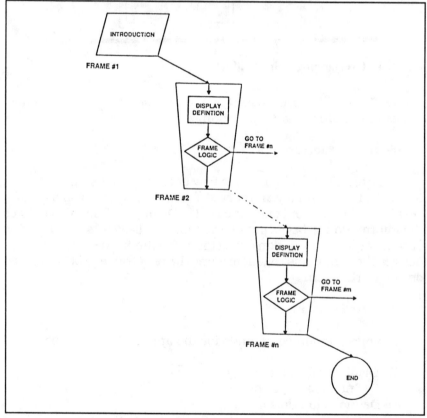

Figure 5: MCPS Script Logic

c) **Help.** The script-coder may define user-selectable "help" information for each frame. Help is displayed on the screen within an overlapping window. Help windows may contain;

1. Text, with or without background audio, or
2. A graphics image with or without background audio, or
3. A video sequence with or without background audio.

d) **Branching conditions.** The script-coder can alter the default linear flow of control after a frame is displayed. This is done by defining Boolean relationships based on combinations of previously selected user responses.

MCPS Frame Command Syntax

In the list below, *TextStrings* define the legal arguments of MCPS commands. If the commands enclosed by "curly" brackets {} are not used within a frame, MCPSI uses default values. The character **S** represents one space.

The following illustrates the commands that may appear within a frame:

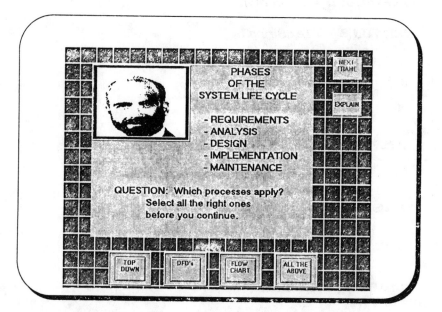

Figure 6: Video Window Within an Information Window

[**F**number] **S** *TextString1*

{**FONT** = *TextString2*}

{**FONTSIZE** = *n*}

TEMPLATE = *m*

WINDOW*p* = *TextString3* or *TextString4*
 or *TextString4* **S** *TextString7*
 or *TextString8* **S** *TextString7*

{**BACKGROUND** = *TextString5 or TextString6*}

{**FONTCOLOR** = *TextString6*}

{**WINDOWCOLOR** = *TextString6*}

{**WINDOWFRAMECOLOR** = *TextString6*}

DEFAULTS

PLAYSOUND = *TextString7*

BUTTON(S)1 = *TextString3*
•
•
(s)5 = *TextString3*

HELP = *TextString3* or *TextString4*
 or *TextString4* **S** *TextString7*
 or *TextString8* **S** *TextString7*

PAUSE = *q*

{**NEXTFRAME** = F*number*] or **END** or
 IF S *Conditional Statement*}

TextString Definitions

TextString1 - Any string of alphanumerics (maximum of 70)

contained within quotation marks.

TextString2 - Any legal type-font installed in the operating version of Windows.

TextString3 - Any string of alphanumerics (maximum of 256) contained within quotation marks.

TextString4 - Any legal DOS file name defining a file with the following contents and extensions:

       Text - A maximum of 256 ASCII characters with file extension .TXT.
       Image - A graphics image with file extensions .PCX, BMP, DIB, or RLE.
       Video - A video file with a file extension .AVI.

TextString5 - Any legal DOS file name containing a graphics image and a file extension .BMP, DIB, RLE or PCX.

TextString6 - One keyword selected from the color palette, - **RED, BLUE, WHITE, GRAY, BLACK, MAGENTA, CYAN, YELLOW, GREEN, LIGHTGREEN, LIGHTBLUE, LIGHTRED, LIGHTGREEN, LIGHTCYAN, LIGHTMAGENTA, LIGHTYELLOW, DARKBLUE,** or **DARKGREEN**.

TextString7 - Any legal DOS file name defining an audio file with extension .WAV or MID.

Frame Labels

Each frame begins with a frame label. Frame labels must be enclosed by square parentheses (i.e., - [ ]). Frames may be numbered as an integer, or as two integer numbers separated by a period. This numbering scheme allows script-coders to insert new frames after a script has been completed. Frame numbers must be consecutive in a script. Examples of frame labels are F1, F2, F2.1, F2.2, F4.0 and F27.65.

Each frame label may be followed by at least one space, and on the same line, an optional comment (usually used to describe the frame) - *TextString1*. *TextString1* is ignored by the interpreter, MCPSI. The inclusion of any frame within a script will cause a "continue" (or "next screen") button to be displayed.

The FONT Command

The **FONT** command sets the font type of script-defined text. If **FONT** is not used, MCPS sets the default font type to Helvetica. The **FONT** command may be used anywhere in a script to set or reset font types of the font used within windows and option buttons. Examples are:

FONT = ARIAL

FONT = CENTURY GOTHIC

The FONTSIZE Command

The **FONTSIZE** command sets the font size (specified by the integer value n) of script-defined text. If **FONTSIZE** is not used, MCPS sets the default font size to 10. *This command does not alter the font size displayed in buttons.* The **FONTSIZE** command may be used anywhere in a script to set or reset font sizes. An example is:

FONTSIZE = 20

The TEMPLATE Command

The **TEMPLATE** command is used to define the template that will be used in a frame. The selected template determines the output format of a screen. Each template has one or two windows. Each template automatically displays a "continue" option. If the script-coder does not use the **WINDOW** command(s) in a frame, the appropriate window will not be displayed. All templates do <u>not</u> implicitly display help or option buttons. If **TEMPLATE** is not used in a frame, the most recent template definition is assumed. At least one **TEMPLATE** command must be used initially for MCPSI to display the first frame.

In general, each template provides one or more of the following screen formats in which text, image, or video is displayed:

a) A full screen with no border.
b) A full screen with a centered, bordered window.
c) Two side-by-side windows in one screen.
d) One large window and one small, inset window.

e) A numeric data entry keypad, with two windows.

f) A date entry keypad with two windows.

g) A time entry keypad with two windows.

h) An alphanumeric data entry keyboard with two windows.

i) A multiple choice selection screen with two windows.

The integer value *m* defines the template to be used. In the following example, Template # 7 is defined:

TEMPLATE = 7

The WINDOW Commands

The **WINDOW** commands may be used to display a) text, b) text with background audio, c) a graphics image, d) a graphics image with background audio, e) a video sequence, or f) video with "dubbed" audio. There may be one or two **WINDOW** commands in one frame, depending on the **TEMPLATE** that has been defined. For frames using templates with only one window, **WINDOW1** may be used; for templates with two windows, **WINDOW1** and **WINDOW2** may be used. When a template is defined in a frame, MCPSI reserves space on the screen for one or both of the windows defined by that template. If the script-coder chooses not to use the **WINDOW** commands, the portion of the screen that would display the window(s) will be blank. In all templates, **WINDOW1** is either the largest window, or if both windows are the same size, it is the window displayed to left of the other window.

a) Display text. Text may be defined locally (i.e., within the frame) using *TextString3*, or in an ASCII text file defined by *TextString4*.

In the following example, the **WINDOW** command displays locally-defined text in an information window:

WINDOW1 = "What is the probability of selecting 3 black balls from a hat containing 70 black balls and 40 white balls? Before you answer, reread pages 55 to 60 in your textbook."

b) Display graphics images. MCPSI can display a graphics image that has been prepared using a draw or paint program that stores files in one of the graphics formats defined by *TextString5*. For example:

    WINDOW2 = C:\PAINT\OCEAN.PCX

c) Play video. A prerecorded video sequence using the .AVI file format defined by *TextString4* may be played. The audio played with this command *will have been recorded at the same time as the video.* An example is:

    WINDOW1 = C:\MOVIE\SURF.AVI

d) Display text with background audio. A prerecorded audio sequence using the .WAV or .MID file formats defined by *TextString7* may be played as background to displayed text. If this format is used, the two files must be separated by at least one space in the command line.

In the following example, a text file (BILL.TXT) is displayed in WINDOW1 and background audio is played from the file C:\AUDIO\TALK.WAV.

    WINDOW1 = C:\BILL.TXT C:\AUDIO\TALK.WAV

e) Display a graphic image with background audio. A prerecorded audio sequence using the .WAV or .MID file formats defined by *TextString7* may be played as background to a displayed image. If this format is used, the two files must be separated by at least one space in the command line.

In the following example, an image file (BEACH.BMP) is displayed in WINDOW2 and background audio is played from the MIDI file C:\MOVIE\SURF.MID.

    WINDOW2 = BEACH.BMP C:\MOVIE\SURF.MID

f) Play video with background audio. MCPS allows script-coders to simultaneously play video (from .AVI files) that have been recorded with or without interleaved audio, together with back-ground audio that has been recorded separately (in .WAV or .MID files). This may be done by using an .AVI file together with a .WAV or .MID file as a parameter. If this format is used, the two files must be separated by at least one space in the command line.

In the following example, video is played (from file MOTION.AVI) in a window while background audio is played from file NOISE.WAV. If the file MOTION.AVI had been recorded with interleaved (embedded) audio, that audio is completely suppressed by the dubbing of the audio recorded in NOISE.WAV.

    WINDOW2 = MOTION.AVI   NOISE.WAV

The BACKGROUND Command

The **BACKGROUND** command may be used to set the background of the display. If *TextString5* is used, windowed information will be surrounded by "wallpaper" whose image is defined by the contents of the file name specified in *TextString5*. If *TextString6* is used, the background color of the display is specified by the color palette keyword. **BACKGROUND** may be used in any frame, to set and reset displayed background images or colors. If, in a particular frame, the script-coder uses a template that contains no bordered window, then the **BACKGROUND** command serves no useful purpose.

Examples of the **BACKGROUND** command are:

    BACKGROUND = D:\IMAGE\CARS.BMP

    BACKGROUND = BLUE

The WINDOWCOLOR Command

The **WINDOWCOLOR** command may be used to set and reset the background color of the display window. In templates that contain no bordered windows, the **WINDOWCOLOR** command essentially sets the screen background color.

An example of the **WINDOWCOLOR** command is:

    WINDOWCOLOR = BLUE

The DEFAULTS Command

The **DEFAULTS** command may be used anywhere in a script to reset the text font and size to the MCPS default settings. The **DEFAULTS** command also resets all user-defined colors to their default values.

The PLAYSOUND Command

PLAYSOUND is used to play background audio when either text or a graphics image is displayed on the screen. **PLAYSOUND** uses prerecorded audio files defined by *TextString7*. For example:

PLAYSOUND = C:\NOISE\DRUMS.WAV

PLAYSOUND = C:\MUSIC\TONE.MID

In any frame, if a **PLAYSOUND** command is followed by any command that plays video (or vice versa), the second command will not begin until the first is complete.

The BUTTON(S) Command

BUTTON commands may be used to display up to five user-selectable menu options. The exception to this limit of five buttons is the multiple-choice template which may contain up to 10 buttons. **BUTTON** commands cause text (contained in quotations) to be placed within user-selectable buttons that are displayed on the screen. MCPSI determines the font size, centers the text, and sizes and positions each button, depending on the number of button options defined in the frame. The type-font and the text color of buttons may be set (and reset) by the script-coder.

There are two versions of the **BUTTON** command, 1) **BUTTON**, and 2) **BUTTONS**. A selected **BUTTON** option is automatically deselected if any other **BUTTON** or **BUTTONS** option is selected. A selected **BUTTONS** option remains selected unless the user explicitly reselects it in order to "deactivate" it, or if a **BUTTON** option is selected.

In addition to the defined **BUTTON** options, MCPSI displays a button at the bottom of every screen to allow the user to proceed to the next screen. If buttons are present on a screen, the "continue" button remains inactive until the user selects a **BUTTON(S)** option.

If buttons are not present, the "continue" button is always active in that frame. When a button is selected, its color and shading change to indicate that it was selected. Buttons may be deselected before "continue" is selected, causing them to return to their original color and shade. When a user is satisfied with the selection(s), the user selects the "continue button" to proceed to the next frame. Button selections are saved to disk.

The following example causes MCPSI to display three buttons. The user may select only one of the three options.

```
BUTTON1 = "YES"
BUTTON2 = "NO"
BUTTON3 = "I DON'T KNOW"
```

The following example causes MCPSI to display three buttons. The user may select all three options.

```
BUTTONS1 = "Green"
BUTTONS2 = "Sofa"
BUTTONS3 = "Peanut Butter"
```

The following example causes MCPSI to display four buttons. The user may select Button 1, or Button 2, or Button 3 and Button 4.

```
BUTTON1  = "YES"
BUTTON2  = "NO"
BUTTONS3 = "Green"
BUTTONS4 = "Blue"
```

The HELP Command

A frame may contain the definition of the contents of a Help window. A Help window is displayed when the user selects the Help (or Explain) button. When a Help window is displayed, it overlays the displayed frame information, and all buttons (option buttons, the continue button, and the Help button) become inactive. The current status of the active frame is saved (i.e., all selected option buttons remain selected).

Help windows may contain a) text b) image c) a video sequence, d) text with background audio, e) an image with background audio, or f) video with "dubbed" background audio.

The user exits from the Help window by selecting the help/continue button. When the Help window is cleared, the status of the active frame is restored (i.e., previously selected option buttons are highlighted.)

Examples are:

HELP = "Remember that Newton's First Law
           does not apply to objects that are
           traveling close to the speed of sound.
           Use Einstein's work to answer this
           question."

HELP = C:\PHYSICS\NEWT.TXT

HELP = C:\PAINT\OCEAN.PCX

HELP = C:\DRAW\WATER.BMP

HELP = C:\MOVE\SURF.AVI

In the following examples text (from the file NEW.TXT) is displayed in a Help window while background audio is played; an image file (OCEAN.PCX) is displayed while background audio is played; a video (SURF.AVI) is played, first with a MIDI file (MOZART.MID) playing in the background (replacing any audio that may have been recorded when SURF.AVI was recorded), then with the dubbed audio file, SOUND.WAV.

HELP = C:\PHYSICS\NEW.TXT TALK.WAV

HELP = C:\PAINT\OCEAN.PCX SURF.MID

HELP = C:\MOVIE\SURF.AVI MOZART.MID

HELP = C:\MOVIE\SURF.AVI SOUND.WAV

The PAUSE Command

The **PAUSE** command can be used anywhere within a frame to delay the execution of the commands that follow the **PAUSE**. The integer parameter q specifies the duration of the delay, in seconds. In the following example MCPSI displays an image, waits 5 seconds, then plays background audio.

```
WINDOW1    = C:\DRAW\AUTO.PCX
PAUSE      = 5
PLAYSOUND = A:\TALK\MUSIC.WAV
```

The NEXTFRAME Statement

The **NEXTFRAME** statement may be used to alter the linear execution of frames. If the **NEXTFRAME** statement is absent from a frame, MCPSI executes the next consecutive frame. If **NEXTFRAME** is present, it can be used for either unconditional or conditional transfer of control.

In the following example, execution after Frame 1.2 will unconditionally continue at Frame F2.5.

```
[F1.2]
  •

  •

NEXTFRAME = F2.5
```

In the next example, execution of the application will terminate after Frame F1.2; the application then returns to the Windows environment.

```
[F1.2]
  •

  •

NEXTFRAME=END
```

NEXTFRAME may also be used for conditional transfer of control. In this case, the syntax of **NEXTFRAME** is:

$$
\text{NEXTFRAME} = \text{IF } F_a \quad = r \text{ \textbf{AND/OR}}
$$
$$
F_{a+1} \quad = r \text{ \textbf{AND/OR}}
$$
$$
\bullet
$$
$$
\bullet
$$
$$
F_{a+n} \quad = r \text{ \textbf{THEN} } F_b
$$

F_a and F_{a+1} are the frame labels of previously executed frames. r is the integer value of the button selected by a user in Frame

F_a, F_{a+1}, etc.

F_b is the next frame to execute if the AND/OR conditions are true.

If the AND/OR conditions are false, the next consecutive frame in the script is executed. AND/OR conditions are evaluated by MCPSI in the order in which they are listed in the **NEXTFRAME** command.

In the example shown in Figure 7, Frame F1 is shown first, F2 next, then F3 is shown. In F3, if the user had decided to "SELL" a "RED" "CAR" or "BOAT" then MCPSI transfers control to Frame F9. Otherwise MCPSI continues with Frame F4.

Using Comments Within a Script

Although MCPS scripts are relatively easy to read, in many ways they resemble conventional, procedural computer programs. As with any procedural program, it is important for program writers (script-coders) to properly document their programs (scripts). Script-coders can insert one-line comments anywhere in a script by placing an asterisk (*) in the first column of a line. When MCPSI detects the asterisk, it ignores the remaining text on that line. (Note: comments can also be placed in the **FRAME** command.)

Application Development

The development of multimedia applications is a complex process. MCPS has been designed to simplify the computer-related components of that process. The MCPS application development environment contains a set of tools to facilitate testing of application scripts. The tools are the a) Script Preprocessor and b) Script Execution Module.

a) The script preprocessor. This module parses an application script and checks the syntax of each frame label and each reserved word in the script. The module also verifies the syntax and validity of each command parameter. The Script Preprocessor produces a list of all disk files referenced by commands in the script, sorted by file type (i.e., text, image, audio, and video). The list is created as an ASCII file on disk.

b) The script execution module. This module is the interpreter MCPSI. MCPSI executes an application script in two stages. First it verifies that every file (text, image, audio, and video) that is referenced in the script is actually present on the disks, directories, and sub directories specified in the script. A list of files that cannot be found is displayed on the screen and execution halts. If no errors are found, the Execution Module begins execution of the application script.

Media Preparation

The version of MCPS described in this chapter does not contain functions or utility programs that would enable developers to prepare text, images, audio, or video material that might be used in a script. This was not an oversight, but a deliberate strategy to keep application content independent of changing multimedia tools and technologies. For example, since text used in MCPS must be ASCII, script-coders can use any ASCII text editor they prefer; as new and improved editors become available, those too may be used. A similar case may be made for draw and paint programs. Future versions of MCPS will provide an integrated Windows-based work environment in which Microsoft Windows tools will be easily accessible by script-coders.

```
[F1]  This is the first frame in the script
•

•
BUTTON1 = "RED"
BUTTON2 = "GREEN"
BUTTON3 = "BLUE"


[F2]  This is the second frame in the script
•

•
BUTTONS1 = "CAR"
BUTTONS2 = "BOAT"
BUTTONS3 = "NOTHING"


[F3]  This is the third frame containing the logic example
•

•
BUTTON1 = "BUY"
BUTTON2 = "SELL"
BUTTON3 = "DO NOTHING"
IF  F1 = 1 AND
    F2 = 1 OR
    F2 = 2 AND
    F3 = 2 THEN F9


[F4]  This is the fourth frame
•

•
```

Note: Reserved words are shown in boldface type.

Figure 7: Example of Conditional Branching

One of the advantages to making MCPS a Windows-dependent environment is that Microsoft has defined a set of multimedia standards that separates multimedia technology from applications running under Windows. As multimedia products and methodologies (e.g., data capture, editing, compression) evolve, MCPS script-coders will easily be able to integrate them, usually by simply changing the extension of referenced files. If changes need to be made to MCPSI, these will be transparent to the script-coder.

A Final Note on Multimedia Application Design

The design of multimedia-based computer applications has traditionally been a complex and expensive process. Multimedia PC application development projects are usually team efforts in which subject matter experts work together with media and computer experts. MCPS was designed to simplify this process by allowing the subject matter expert to work logically, directly, and independently with both media and computers.

However, MCPS is merely a tool to facilitate the *development* and *implementation* of applications. MCPS is not a *design* tool. Effective MPC applications require significant planning of program content, format, and logic. Designers must decide what information to present, when to present it, and the best media formats to use. It is only after these decisions are made that the real value of the Multimedia Computing Presentation System will become apparent.

Appendix: An Example of an MCPS Multimedia Application Script

[F1.0] This is frame #1- Figure 1 and Figure 2.

*
* This frame generates "Figure 2. The Introduction Frame"
* The asterisk in column 1 makes these comment statements non-executable.
* This frame uses Template # 0; in this template, there are no bordered windows.
* The only "window" is the whole screen which is defined by WINDOW1.
* Because this is the introductory title screen, it is appropriate to use font sizes
* bigger than the default of 10.
* The font type is set to "domcausul" for a "theatrical" effect.
* The default window color is gray; it is set to white.
* Note that the command WINDOWCOLOR is used here instead of the

command
* *BACKGROUND.* That is because Template # 0 does not have a background.
* The full screen is considered to be *WINDOW1.*
* The last command *NEXTFRAME* is optional. Without it, the script would proceed to the next frame automatically.
* Note, that except for text strings, MCPSI treats upper and lower case
* equivalently. If this were a fully functioning demonstration, it would be
* appropriate to play introductory, background audio with this screen. Hence,
* the *PLAYSOUND* command might be operational. In this script it is
* commented out.

```
template      = 0
fontsize      = 40
font          = domcasual
windowcolor   = white
window1       = "MULTIMEDIA COMPUTING: PREPARING FOR THE 21ST
                 CENTURY  DEMONSTRATION SCRIPT"


* PLAYSOUND    = C:\SICK\APPLAUSE.WAV
*

nextframe      = F7.0

*
++++++++++++++++++++++++++++++++++++++++++++++++++++++++++++++++++++++++++++++++++
*
```

[F2.0] This is frame #2 - Figure 3 and Figure 4.

*
* This frame generates "Figure 3. An MCPS Frame Presentation" and
* "Figure 4. Overlapping Help Window."
* It uses Template #1 which is a single window in the screen.
* *WINDOW1* displays the .BMP file which contains an image of the Taj Mahal
* together with the question that is asked.
* Defaults are reset from Frame #1.
* Background color of the screen can be defined in this template and is set to white.
* The *BUTTON* command is used in this template because the user can only select one of the options.
* A "help" or "explain" screen is provided. It contains the local-text shown
* between the pair of quotations.
* The background color of the "help" window is reset from the default, to
* red, and the font color is reset from the default to white.

* The *NEXTFRAME* command is not used in this frame. Execution *
continues automatically to frame F3.0.

```
template       = 1
defaults
background     = white
window1        = c:\book\wk-sp-46.bmp
button1        = "YES"
button2        = "NO"
button3        = "NOT SURE"
fontsize       = 25
windowcolor    = red
fontcolor      = white
help           = "HINT: This structure is not in America or Europe."
```

*

++

*

[F3.0] This is frame #3 - Figure 6 and Figure 8.

*

* This frame generates "Figure 6. Video Window Within an Information
* Window."
* Template # 2 automatically generates a small window within a larger
one.
* The text displayed in *WINDOW1* is in an ASCII text file (F3.TXT) prepared
* with Microsoft Windows Notepad.
* The image displayed in *WINDOW2* was scanned as a .BMP file. It is
displayed
* with a black window frame color.
* The background of this screen (or its "wallpaper") is set from the file
* rivets.bmp.
* In this screen, the *BUTTONS* command is used because users may
choose as
* many commands as they wish. However, if they select *BUTTON4*, that
* precludes *BUTTONS1* or *BUTTONS2* or *BUTTONS3*.
* Help is provided in this template. It contains some simple text.
* Unlike the font size of *WINDOW1*, the font size of the help window has
been
* set to 25; the font-type is set to TMS Roman; the background of the (help)
* window is set to white.

*

```
defaults
template       = 2
fontsize       = 15
window1        = C:\BOOK\F3.TXT
```

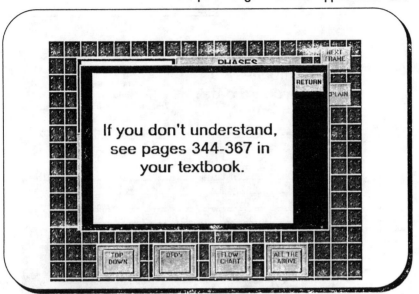

Figure 8: Help Window in Frame #3

windowframecolor	= **black**
window2	= **C:\SOREL.AVI**
background	= **c:\windows\rivets.bmp**
fontsize	= **25**
font	= **TMS Roman**
windowcolor	= **white**
help	= **"If you don't understand, see pages 344-367 in**
your	**textbook."**
buttons1	= **"TOP DOWN"**
buttons2	= **"DFD's"**
buttons3	= **"FLOW CHART"**
button4	= **"ALL THE ABOVE"**

*

━━━

*

[F4.0] This is frame #4 - Alphanumeric Keyboard (Figure 9).

*

*   This frame illustrates the alphanumeric keyboard with two windows.
*   All default values are reset. *WINDOW1* displays the text shown between the parentheses in the default font with a size of 25.
*   *WINDOW2* displays the text shown on a white background, in default

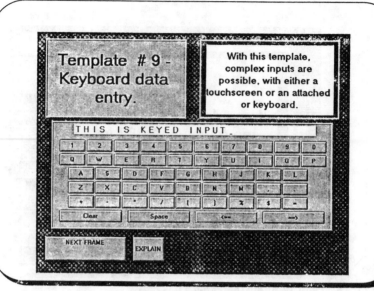

Figure 9: Keyboard Template in Frame #4

    font, size 15, surrounded by a black window frame color.
* The help window has a red window frame color and contains the same .AVI
* image as *WINDOW2* in Frame 3.0

```
defaults
template            = 9
fontsize            = 25
window1             = "Template  # 9 - Keyboard data entry."
fontsize            = 15
windowcolor         = white
fontsize            = 15
windowframecolor    = black
window2             = "With this template, complex inputs are possible,
                        with either a touch screen or an attached or
                        keyboard."
windowframecolor    = red
help                = c:\sorel.avi
```

*

*

[F5.0] This is frame #5 - Audio Samples (Figures 10,11,12,13).

*

* This frame illustrate the use of audio played as background to a text file and,
* in the explain/help window, as background to an image file.
* In this frame, Template # 1 is used with wallpaper from the file weave.bmp.
* *WINDOW1* contains the text shown between the quotation marks.
* The *PLAYSOUND* command plays background audio when *WINDOW1* text is displayed.
* If help/explain is selected, an image file (CARS.BMP) is displayed with audio
* in the background, played from the file NONE.WAV.
* Audio played from within both *WINDOW1* and the help/explain window is interruptable by the user. Note that there are no *BUTTON* commands in this frame.

```
defaults
template       = 1
fontsize       = 12
background     = C:\WINDOWS\WEAVE.BMP
window1        = "THIS IS A FULL SCREEN OF TEXT WITH
                 BACKGROUND AUDIO. IF 'PAUSE' IS PUSHED,
                 THE BUTTONS 'PLAY AGAIN' AND 'KEEP
                 PLAYING' APPEAR. IF, AFTER 'PAUSE' HAS BEEN
                 SELECTED, THE USER SELECTS 'EXPLAIN',
                 MCPSI GOES TO THE HELP/EXPLAIN WINDOW.
                 WHEN IT RETURNS, IF THE USER SELECTS 'KEEP
                 PLAYING', THE AUDIO CONTINUES FROM
                 WHERE IT WAS ORIGINALLY INTERRUPTED. IN
                 THIS FRAME, IF 'EXPLAIN' IS SELECTED, THE
                 .BMP FILE IS DISPLAYED ACCOMPANIED BY
                 BACKGROUND AUDIO. THAT AUDIO TOO MAY
                 BE INTERRUPTED IN THE SAME WAY AS THE
                 AUDIO IN THE MAIN WINDOW IS
                 INTERRUPTABLE."
playsound      = C:\gary\welcome.wav
help           = C:\CARS.BMP C:\gary\none.wav
```

*

++

*

[F6.0] This is frame #6 - Date Entry Keyboard (Figure 14).

*

* This frame illustrates the date entry keyboard with one window, Template # 7.

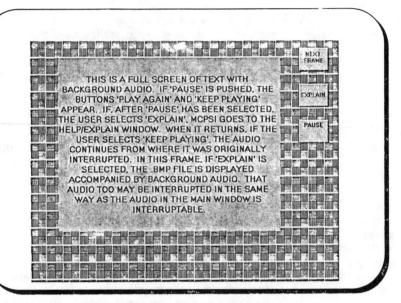

Figure 10: Screen Capture While Audio is Playing in Frame #5

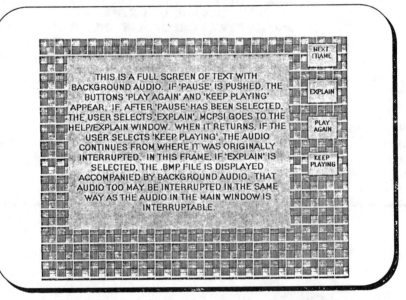

Figure 11: Screen Capture While Audio is Paused in Frame #5

Figure 12: Help Screen in Frame #5 With Audio Playing

Figure 13: Help Screen in Frame #5 With Audio Paused

* All default values are reset. *WINDOW2* displays the text shown in Courier font
* of size 15 surrounded by a black window frame color.
* A help window is defined with local text.
* Although 2 windows are permitted, only *WINDOW2* is defined here. The space
* normally used for *WINDOW1* is left empty by MCPSI. *BUTTONS* are illegal in this template.

*

defaults
template   = **7**
fontsize   = **15**
font   = **Courier**
windowframecolor = **black**
window2   = **"ONLY LEGAL DATES CAN BE ENTERED."**
help   = **"THIS IS TEXT FOR A HELP FRAME."**

*

+++

*

[F7.0] This is frame #7 - Multiple Choice Keyboard (Figure 15).

*

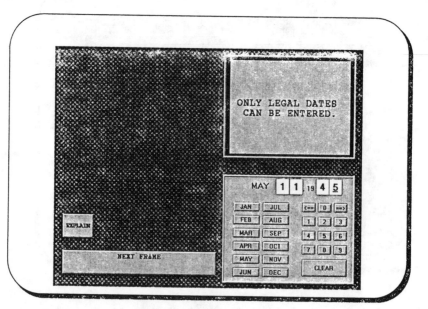

Figure 14: Date Template in Frame #6

* This frame illustrates the multiple choice template with two windows, Template # 6.
* In this example, 8 multiple choice buttons are defined. The first 7 use the *BUTTONS* command because all options are selectable. The eighth uses
  BUTTON which, if chosen, invalidates any other selected option.
* Font size of 15 was chosen for the first 7 buttons but the font, font size, and font color of the eighth button has been completely redefined. This
* would probably not normally be done in a real multiple choice quiz, but
* has been done here to demonstrate MCPS features.
* This frame also illustrate conditional transfer using the *NEXTFRAME*
* command.
* If Button #3 is pushed in Frame 2.0, or
* Button #1 or Button #3 in Frame 3.0, or
* Button #3 and Button #6 in Frame 7.0   then
* execution continues at Frame 1.0   else the application terminates.

```
defaults
template            = 6
fontsize            = 25
window1             = "Template  # 6 - Multiple Choices"
fontsize            = 15
windowcolor         = white
windowframecolor    = black
window 2            = "Which countries are in Europe?"
buttons1            = "France"
buttons2            = "England"
```

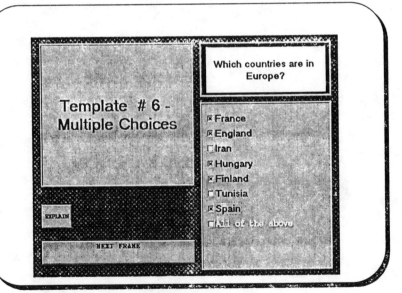

Figure 15: Multiple Choice Template in Frame #7

buttons3	= "Iran"
buttons4	= "Hungary"
buttons5	= "Finland"
buttons6	= "Tunisia"
buttons7	= "Spain"
fontcolor	= white
fontsize	= 15
font	= courier
button8	= "All of the above"
help	= "You may choose as many as you like. If you choose 'All of The Above' all your other choices will be invalidated."
nextframe	= IF F2.0 = 3 OR
	F3.0 = 1 OR
	F3.0 = 3 OR
	F7.0 = 3 AND
	F7.0 = 6 THEN F1.0
nextframe	= end

Chapter 11

Cinema Theory, Video Games, and Multimedia Production

J. Christopher Westland
University of Southern California

This chapter describes extensions of cinema theory for multimedia production. Multimedia has been relatively accessible for around a decade, and promises to be made more accessible with the push toward digital and high definition TV by industry giants such as Sony and Philips. Various approaches and perspectives have been suggested as organizing principles for multimedia implementations. To gain insight to the appropriateness of these approaches, the chapter surveys current applications of multimedia. Based on the expected market for multimedia, features from video game production and cinema are combined to construct a theory of editing which provides a place for user interaction. The final section discusses the market potential for multimedia productions.

Multimedia Technology

What makes a multimedia presentation effective? How can an author effectively organize and integrate the diverse modes of information offered by multimedia technology to provide compelling productions? What can be communicated through multimedia that cannot be communicated through film or television? These and other questions face authors wishing to convey their message through the new and uncharted technology of interactive multimedia.

The concepts and capabilities offered by multimedia technology have existed in one form or another for centuries. But the flexibility and integration of these components on a computer platform have engendered a decidedly different medium — one offering dramatic improvements in communication.

Think about the modalities offered by currently available multimedia information technology. A typical list might include:

- Still Pictures
- Cinema and Animation
- Sound (Narration, Dialogue, Music, Sound Effects, Ambiance)
- Text

Some modalities are unlikely to be supported by current technology — tastes, smells, touch, and kinetic senses — although they are exceedingly important in negotiating the physical world. The four modalities listed are already supported in cinema, and it is to this field that the current chapter looks for guidance.

Although modalities offered by currently available multimedia technologies duplicate those in cinema, the use of computer platforms offers flexibility and the potential for significantly different contributions to communication from each modality. The computer platform provides potential advantages of:

- Speed
- High volume capacity
- Flexibility
- Flawless, efficient processing without human intervention
- Interaction and two-way communication

Multimedia technologies themselves provide an interface between *computer information processing* and *human information processing*. Because computers and the human mind operate and perceive information in different manners and locations, multimedia must provide two functions for interaction and communication to occur:

• Information Transfer
• Information Translation

Transfer and translation existed prior to the advent of computers and information technology. Information transfer has at various times been accomplished by postal letters, Pony Express (US), Marathon runners (Mayan, Greek, Roman City-States), and smoke signals (Native Americans). Information translation has been accomplished by translators, services, or official languages. Table 1 summarizes the manner in which information transfer has been supported by strictly personal means prior to the advent of information technology.

As new technology becomes available, and more efficient and effective substitutes appear for traditional media, the uses of traditional media can change radically. For example over the past decade, paper which was once the long-term storage medium of choice, has been superseded by magnetic and optical recording

Human	Manual (Paper)	Information Technology
Two-way, Interactive Communication		
Marathon Runners, Pony Express (Fast Long-distance)	Letters	Electronic-Mail (E-Mail)
Shouting, Fog or Alpenhorns, Smoke Signals (Faster Long-distance)	Express Mail, memoranda	Telephone, Data Communications, Client-Server LAN
Pow-wow (Tribe, Group)	Agenda-Minutes of the Committee	Groupware, Group Decision Support Systems
One-way Broadcast Stentors	Sales & Distribution of Books, Newspapers, Phonograph Records, etc.	TV, Radio, Software Distribution, Read-only databases

Table 1: Information Transfer

media. These media offer cheaper, more compact storage, with faster access. But the advent of compact, inexpensive laser printing has given paper a new role — the pervasive display medium.

Table 1 compares and contrasts the manner in which information is transferred between individuals given the availability of differing technologies. At particular stages of history, only certain technologies have been available. Throughout most of human existence, the only vehicle for information transfer was speech. Even today, some types of knowledge — particularly esoteric knowledge — are conveyed only through an oral tradition. Human information transfer is labor intensive, and requires that people traverse distances (as in the case of marathon runners and bards) or expend great deals of energy (as with shouting) at precisely the time the listener is available to receive the information. But conversation has an important benefit — it is interactive. This gives it warmth, flexibility and vibrancy which makes it attractive as a medium.

With the development of paper, and later the printing press, longer-lived, less labor intensive information transfer was possible. The information in a book did not have to be repeatedly spoken for every new recipient. Paper based information was asynchronous — the author did not have to be present, or even alive, to convey the intended information. Information transfer became lighter and less intrusive — books could be read at one's leisure, and did not have to be fed, as did bards and other conveyers of information. Paper based media eliminated the potential biases which arose through the retelling of "facts," a feature that made them desirable for minutes of committee meetings.

The trend begun by paper based communication has been carried further with the availability of low-cost networked computing. Multimedia on low-cost networked computing platforms has no human or paper-based predecessor as an integrated vehicle for transfer of information. Multimedia provides a new functionality — a two-way, interactive vehicle for communication on media that have traditionally been used for one-way broadcasts of information (e.g., TV, Cinema, and so forth). The interactivity of conversation, and the storage and bias elimination of paper are both benefits of multimedia.

Evolution and change of media dictate a change in message content and in "language" — notions broached repeatedly by McLuhan [1964]. Table 2 attempts to elucidate the nature of some of these changes by looking at ways that individuals from different backgrounds might bridge the "language" gap and convey their message. For example, to convey a message, individuals may adopt a common

Human	Paper (Manual) Equivalent	Computer (Automated) Equivalent
Adopt Common Language (Latin—Math for Science, English for Commerce)	Standard Forms, Standard Operating Procedures	Software and Hardware Standards (OSI, Unix, Open Systems)
Speak a Foreign Language	Copy information on one document to another	Translate Functions (Excel, Lotus 123, Word, more other microcomputer packages)
Pidgin, Creole	Communicate only the essential information to complete the contract or transaction	ASCII translation for distribution of information
Hire a Translator	Common task of book-keepers and auditors in practice	Systems integration
Sign Language	Draw pictures (e.g., US Army using Comic Book format to describe weapons operation and maintenance)	Screen Icons, Graphical User Interfaces (GUIs)

Table 2: Information Translation

language specific to their message (e.g., Latin for scientific work as was done in medieval Europe) while speaking their colloquial language with friends and family. Or they may learn and speak the language of their listener, as might be done when traveling. Similar tacks are taken in paper based communication. For example, standard forms provide a common language for precisely those items covered by the form. Standard database formats (e.g., an ASCII format) provide a common language to communicate between differing software packages. Table 2 lists five different approaches to bridging the "language" gap.

The issue of translation has become especially important in computer markets, where interoperability and connectivity are catchwords. The challenge of multimedia production arises from the novelty of functions offered by multimedia information technology (Laurel 1992). Table 2 shows the manner in which information translation has been supported by strictly personal means prior to the advent of information technology.

Multimedia integrates benefits from prior approaches, while presenting new challenges. Multimedia provides the ability to interactively act out the development of a story line, but does not yield to one unique story line. Rather it demands an infinite number of possible story *paths.* The unique path taken by a given multimedia session will be determined by the *control events* input by the user during the session, and by the software underlying the display and delivery of the multimedia session.

This short comparison should convince one that computer-based multimedia provides a qualitatively different vehicle for communication and expression of ideas. To what end should one apply multimedia? It is not enough to provide a new and different technology. There must also be a demand for the functions provided by that technology, and those functions must be provided cost effectively.

Applications and objectives for multimedia production are the subject of the next section. This explores the history of cinema production while suggesting applications and design for multimedia presentations.

Cinema's Contribution to Multimedia Production Theory

Multimedia provides a vehicle for authoring. The term "author" includes traditional authorship functions of writing the script, narrative, and dialogue. These functions meld into the interpretive functions provided by a film director. In the 1950's, so-called *Auteur Theory* promulgated by Alexandre Astruc (1948 Le Caméra Stylo) and François Truffaut (A Certain Tendency in French Cinema, *Caheirs du Cinéma*, January 1954) promoted the idea of director as author.

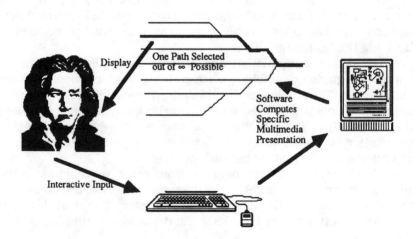

Display

One Path Selected out of ∞ Possible

Software Computes Specific Multimedia Presentation

Interactive Input

Modern Hollywood filmmaking favors a segregation of duties, with the director providing cinematic vision to and implementation of a script that has already been circulated. Multimedia software programmers extend this segregation of duties allowing an infinite number of story line paths. They have no direct counterpart in traditional filmmaking. This section explores the cinematic constraints and possibilities of multimedia as they influence the message that the multimedia author wishes to communicate. There are two objectives to this exploration:

- Normative: Hollywood film techniques reflect the culmination of many years of filmmaking extensively critiqued. They may be considered to provide a highly efficient (perhaps optimal) vehicle for communication. Thus cinematic theory from Hollywood's mainstream school of film production, integrated with new developments in video game technology, can establish the parameters of a normative theory of multimedia production.

- Positive: New multimedia applications appear daily, the result of fertile development efforts. This paper will survey trends in television, film and video games and how they impact information consumption and tastes. These trends will be compared with current features of multimedia to surmise future features and uses. The positive objective asks the McLuhanesque question: if the medium is the message, then what kinds of messages are facilitated by multimedia?

Multimedia has been relatively accessible for around a decade, starting with experimental systems at Xerox PARC. In the 1990's it has received additional emphasis with the push toward digital and high definition TV by industry giants such as Sony and Philips. Various approaches and perspectives have been adopted as organizing principles for multimedia implementations. At least four different approaches have been taken to multimedia implementations — novelty, montage, video game and layered film script.

Multimedia as Novelty

Most new technologies start as novelties. The reason for this is straightforward — a technology is not desirable until it is integrated into a complete system of tools, methodologies and standards to meet the objectives of the user. This has to be worked out and widely accepted. The working out of standards, methodologies and tools is usually the task of "hobbyists" who like the technology's novelty.

The cinematic predecessors of multimedia — from which current perspectives on multimedia draw heavily — were themselves novelties for many years. Zoetropes, Stroboscopes, Phenakistoscopes and other novelty predecessors of cinema appeared to whet the public's appetite. Similarly, there are many novelty applications of multimedia which demonstrate some of the technology but do not really offer anything useful.

Multimedia, in its most economically significant incarnation, is a melding onto microcomputer platforms of various consumer electronics technologies that grew in importance throughout the 1980s. Technology development has outpaced the development of complementary usage methodologies. As a consequence, multimedia productions often suffer from the same defects that were seen in desktop publishing in its nascency — too many options applied in a confusing, contradictory and self-defeating fashion. This is the result of multimedia authors becoming enamored of the novelty of technology (the medium), and ignoring the message.

Multimedia as Montage

Montage was a dominant cinema production theory prior to the advent movie sound in 1928. Audio technology has outpaced video technology in digital computers, due to lower bandwidth requirements and effective compression algorithms. But production theory for sound has lagged that for video in multimedia; other modalities such as taste and touch have been almost completely ignored. This probably reflects a bias toward text and visual representation of information by designers of software. Thus the best constructed multimedia presentations still seem substantially different from film and television. This is only partially due to the interactive nature of multimedia. It most greatly reflects the heavy emphasis on *visual* aspects of the message.

Current implementations of multimedia parallel films developed in the 1920's. These early films were guided by the theory of *montage* promulgated in the silent films of Sergei Eisenstein (the "collision" theory of montage). Montage emphasized the dynamic juxtaposition of individual shots that called attention to themselves and forced the viewer consciously to come to conclusions about the sequence and interplay of images. Although useful, this is so greatly at variance with modern film and TV editing that even the best "montage" multimedia presentations communicate poorly.

Multimedia as Video Game

Perhaps the highest quality multimedia implementations, and certainly the most economically successful ones have been in the area of video games. The arcade games made popular by Nolan Bushnell at Atari have evolved and have been downsized to the pervasive microcomputer-based video games of Sega and Nintendo in the 1990's. These do not involve a complete use of available modalities, since narrative and dialogue are typically missing in video games. This also causes their implementation to diverge significantly from cinematic models which use narrative and dialogue as organizing themes around which visual material is presented. In the best video games, music, sound effects and visual action are linked to human controls with subsecond response time in a compelling and challenging production.

Multimedia as Layered Film Scripts

Recent theories of multimedia production have been put forth in attempt to get multimedia out of the lab — or off the microcomputer — and into the theater where the public can pay. *Interfilm* , a New York film production group, is producing films in which traditional scripting concepts of parallel editing — intermingling of two perspectives or story lines in a series of questions and answers — have been expanded to three or more story lines which may be selected with a switch on the patron's theater seat. Because interaction is very rudimentary, production costs can be economically controlled. For example, *Interfilm's* 20 minute film "I'm your man" (which at the time of this writing is showing in New York) incurred production costs of $360,000 in six days of shooting. In addition, they have levied a $65,000 one-time charge to install controls in each theater (Today Show 1992). On the negative side, restrictions on interaction make *Interfilm's* undertaking inherently less appealing than one inspired by, say, video games.

The ideal implementation of multimedia would seem to be one that adopted the subtleties and polish of current video games combined with the Hollywood style of effective story-telling which has evolved over the past 40 years. The next section provides the rudiments of a cinematic multimedia theory that accomplishes such a combination.

The Grammar of a Language for Multimedia

Multimedia, despite its numerous communication possibilities, incumbent complexities, and specialized knowledge required for programming, must be for the author only a registering mechanism, such as the pen or typewriter. Far more important to the author is the ability to apply and convey ideas and concepts — to tell a story. Once these ideas have materialized in graphics files and program code, they must be assembled. The thesis of this chapter is that the multimedia author should rely on "parallel editing" — the alternation of two or more centers of interest — to organize the components of a multimedia production.

Parallel editing is frequently used in cinema editing. It serves to present clearly conflicting or related story lines. The technique is so common that film audiences take it for granted in every film or television show. Productions that avoid use of this technique irritate the viewers, although viewers may be hard pressed to say exactly why they are unsatisfied with the production. Since Hollywood refined parallel editing in the 1940's and 1950's, two generations have grown up accustomed to parallel editing and invisible cutting in film and television.

These concepts have carried through to video games, whose objective is to be as interesting and challenging to players as possible. So successful have they been that some concern has arisen that younger players may abandon reality for a video game world. In video games, two parallel "perspectives" (story lines) are usually taken. The player with the control takes the perspective of the protagonist, and the machine takes the part of multiple antagonists, only occasionally revealing enough of the antagonists' actions and intentions to make the game challenging. In two-controller games, the opponents each choose their own protagonist.

The novelty of video games is software-driven. Instead of two or more determinisitically recorded story lines or perspectives as in cinema, video games lay out rules, planned responses, and actions in their supporting software. The particular path that a story line takes, then, depends upon the particular sequence of controller inputs provided to the software that then unfolds the story onto the screen.

Because of the added complexity contributed by interactive controllers, story lines must necessarily be kept simple. Just as the stories told in a two hour film must be simpler than those told in a 500 page novel, so the stories told in interactive multimedia must be simpler still. In video games, narrative and dialogue are dropped; sound effects, music and stereotyped action are all that remain. This

Human Interaction	Modality				
	Formatted Data	Text	Image	Audio	Video
Meaning determined by format and definition	Yes	No	No	No	No
Meaning requires time dimension	No	No	No	Yes	Yes
Richness in representing reality	Low	Low	Higher	Higher	Highest
Degree of summarization	High	High	Low	Low	Lowest
Time required to use these types of data	Low	Low	Medium	Medium	Highest

Table 3: Characteristics of Multimedia Modalities

also simplifies the job of coding multimedia software. The next section discusses the role of multimedia's diverse modalities in production.

Basic Tools

Information richness is a qualitative measure of the amount and informativeness of a given medium. Multimedia offers a varied palette of modalities for communication — images, animated video, sound and text. Multimedia is particularly rich because it combines diverse modalities and presents them simultaneously. Table 3 summarizes various communication strengths and weaknesses of the modalities supported by multimedia, on various parameters requiring human interaction. Traditional text based information can be seen to be more information rich than is often supposed. Even though time is not an integral part of the information presentation, summarization of information is high, and the time required to use it is low, allowing efficiencies of use. For example, an hour television show on allosauruses is likely to be the product of a script which can be read in five minutes.

In practice there will be a trade-off between information richness and the effort required to use a given modality. Additionally, information-rich modalities will have a tendency to overload the user, with resulting loss of attention, or understanding of the underlying story line. The modalities presented in table 3 do not cover the full range of human senses, only the modalities currently offered in multimedia. Additional columns could be added as

Modality	Function	Editing Conventions	Multimedia Implementation
Text:			
• Subtitles	Substitute for narrative where audio would be awkward.	Bottom of frame, relatively bold, but not overpowering screen.	Because of extensive development of special effects in packages such as Video Toaster, multimedia provides many possibilities.
• Signs	Cues reinforcing some event or action	Cues reinforcing some event or action.	Because of extensive development of special effects in packages such as Video Toaster, multimedia provides many possibilities.
Audio: • Dialogue/ Narrative	Unifying stream on to which attention is directed. Most important component of a multimedia production; it tells the story.	Unifying stream to which attention is directed. This is the most important component of a multimedia production.	Underdeveloped in multimedia.
• Ambiance (Generic elements that set mood, e.g., wind)	Attempts to put user in correct mood, draw attention to appropriate subject or reinforce the narrative.	Background sound, not even noticeable, but attempting to put user in correct mood, draw attention to the appropriate subject, or reinforce the narrative.	Underdeveloped in multimedia.
• Sound effects	Cues reinforcing some event or action.	Cues reinforcing some event or action.	Extensive libraries of digitized sound effects exist, which can be filtered and modified to achieve the precise effect desired.
• Music	Powerful cues reinforcing events, action, point of view (leitmotif), and narrative	A very powerful tool to put user in correct mood, draw attention to the appropriate subject, or reinforce the narrative	Well-developed in video games and electronic music; no effective theory for application in multimedia; should be implemented in the form of leitmotifs.

Table 4a: Form and Function of Multimedia Components

Modality	Function	Editing Conventions	Multimedia Implementation
Still Image:			
• Photo "Frames" (Stopped Action)	May substitute for video.	Use sparingly; also an alternative when you have no animated material; or for MTV-style editing.	Due to bandwidth constraints, many multimedia applications fall back on stills.
• Static Objects	Can be used to reinforce narrative, or as a "for example."	Can be used to reinforce narrative, or as a "for example."	Due to bandwidth constraints, many multimedia applications fall back on stills.
Video: • Characters (e.g., Protagonist, Antagonist)	Provides point of view, and the nature of user interaction; extremely important component of multimedia production.	Defines the point of view of a scene, thus must support the dialogue, and determines what other components are communicated.	In video games, characters are often constructed as software objects.
• Background	Defines where the user is located.	Defines the point of view of a scene, thus must support the dialogue, and determines what other components are communicated.	Potential for libraries of locales.
• Ambiance (Generic elements that set mood, e.g., city street)	Subtle cues reinforcing some event or action.	Attempt to put user in correct mood, draw attention to the appropriate subject, or reinforce the narrative.	Extensive "photoshop" editing capability on computer platforms should allow this to become a much more powerful tool for supporting the narrative.

Table 4b: Form and Function of Multimedia Components

computer support becomes available for other modalities. There should be great demand for taste and odor "display" (e.g., computer enhancements of "scratch and sniff") for the conveyance of information on cookbook recipes, perfumes, air fresheners, and other consumer products. Readers would benefit greatly from being able to sample the wares before investing ingredients and time in the actual cooking.

It is insufficient for a technology such as multimedia simply to provide specific vehicles for conveying information — there must also be methodologies for using these. Tables 4a and 4b survey the ways that these modalities may be employed in a production, drawing heavily on the methods for employing them in cinema and television. These methods, because of their familarity to viewers, provide a basic but incomplete set of methods for multimedia. Subsequent text will detail the methods needed for completion.

Story line is central to cinema and television production. Story line is likely to be important in multimedia production also — though the character of this story line is likely to differ significantly from cinema, just as cinema differs from books. The story line is typically defined in the narrative or dialogue. In multimedia, though, the option exists to develop this story line dynamically, with user interaction providing the inputs to define the various twists and turns of the plot.

This formula is not constrained to fiction — concepts of story line and plot are just as important for demonstrations, lectures, travelogues, and other factual multimedia presentations. But these unifying themes usually go by other names. For example, a demonstration of the operation of a computer would require a script which might pose 1) the question "What do you want to do?" and 2) an interaction providing a number of possible answers leading to the next question, more answers and on and on. This is precisely the nature of plot and story line in fiction. The purpose of this format is to keep the production interesting — not to let the viewer's attention wander from the production. This concept is discussed below in the analysis of components and production of "Sonic 2" the Sega video game.

The following sections discuss the application of the various components in Table 4 to multimedia production.

Narrative and Invisible Editing

The theory of *invisible editing*, which builds visual scenes around sound tracks, was initially adopted in the films of German director G. W. Pabst, and developed in the studio system of Hollywood throughout the 1940s. This ultimately developed into the modern style of editing — a.k.a. invisible cutting, editing for continuity, and invisible editing. Video games, e.g. those offered by Sega and Nintendo, effectively use a variant of this approach, relying on music punctuated by sound effects rather than dialogue. Yet except for video games, most multimedia applications ignore sound, and at best use something corresponding to montage editing developed under Sergei Eisenstein in the Soviet Union. Montage technique evokes viewer responses by the obvious cutting from frame to frame, which juxtaposes and relates a series of separate images. It tends to be weak in conveying a story line.

A basic rule of invisible editing is to cut on action so that viewers are sufficiently involved with what is happening to be unaware of transitions from shot to shot. Normally this is done by overlapping action when one perspective is employed, invoking two perspectives ("cameras") simultaneously or consecutively, and joining the action in editing. Examples of cutting on action occur when a character begins to move across a room to a window and the camera suddenly focuses on him through the window itself; or a character is seen in a medium shot from the rear reaching for something on a shelf and suddenly we see her close-up from the side taking a specific item off the shelf. In dialogue, the cuts focus individually on the speaker and the reactions of the listener, alternating these shots with a master two-shot.

These cinematic techniques assume that *people* are involved in action or dialogue. But people are often left out of microcomputer-based multimedia presentations. This may be a severe mistake in multimedia production. Without a perspective to adopt, the viewer is left confused, and multimedia fails where it should be strong — in communicating a clear and explicit message or body of information.

Invisible editing allows both space and time to be significantly compressed. This is used with great effect in video games, where constant pace of rhythm and interaction are needed to keep the game challenging. Space and time compression are indispensable when addressing an audience raised on and inured to MTV videos, action cinema, and video games (Konigsberg 1987).

Parallel Editing and the Story Line

The task of relating two or more story lines, or two characters, or two different events, or a larger number of story lines, characters and events, is assigned to parallel editing. This relating of lines generally takes one of two forms:

• The lines of interaction are close together, in the same space.
• The lines of interaction are far apart, in different places, and only a common motivation provides the link.

The former interaction is most common, and is always used in video games where there is no dialogue to provide a common motivation. The latter requires an involved narrative, and may not work well in the information-rich space provided by multimedia. The remainder of the chapter will presume the first form for multimedia, although it recognizes the successful application of the latter form in cinema.

To be suitable for multimedia, parallel editing must be modified to allow user interaction in the following way. Using an object oriented paradigm, let individual characters in the story be objects that are provided specific behaviors (methods) and modes of communication (messaging). Since characters, behaviors and modes of communication all have corresponding constructs in object oriented software, the use of object oriented languages such as C++ might be used to facilitate writing the "rules" which determine how the story line progresses, based on user interaction.

Sega's highly successful video game "Sonic 2" provides an excellent example of how parallel editing, point of view, and object oriented behavior and communication may be integrated in a multimedia presentation.

The following script starts by establishing the "behaviors" of the two protagonists — Sonic and *Tails*. In the single-player game, the user controls only one of the protagonists — Sonic — and *Tail's* actions are automatically generated from the interactive input for Sonic (Sega 1992).

> Miles *Tails* Prower, the Fox, can't sit still when
> Sonic's around. Ever since Miles was a baby fox,
> he's dreamed of being like Sonic. He loves to run
> after Sonic, waving his 2 tails behind him, trying
> to keep up with his hero!

Mostly, Sonic lets him trail along. But sometimes, just to show off, Sonic explodes in a burst of super speed and leaves him behind. But Miles doesn't give up. He whirls his tail like a helicopter rotor and takes off flying until he catches up!

All the animals call Miles by his nickname, *Tails*, because of his 2 special tails. And one day they saw an astonishing feat ...

They were all together in the forest, watching Sonic perform. Sonic would run, spin and jump in his Super Spin Attack. Then *Tails* would whirl like a turbo engine and blast off in his Super Dash Attack. What a showoff!

Suddenly, *Tails* just couldn't help himself. He took a running start, curled up his tails, and — whoosh — he was spinning like Sonic!

But now something frightening is happening. Sonic's friends are disappearing. In their place, nasty metal robots are popping up all over the island. The mad scientist Dr. Robotnik is at it again!

This time Robotnik's planning a global disaster. He needs workers to create a doomsday machine that can take over the world. So he's trapping all the animals, turning them into robots, and forcing them to build his ultimate weapon, the Death Egg!

Robotnik now rules the factories, refineries and cities! He's grabbed control of everything— except the 7 Chaos Emeralds. These magnificent gems are believed to hold exceptional powers. With them, Robotnik could have the entire world in his grasp. And he'd never let go!

The Chaos Emeralds are buried somewhere on the island. Only one tough dude with spiky hair has the speed to find them first!

Help Sonic stop the devious scheme of the demented
scientist! Spin like a speedball through space.
Grab Power Sneakers and loop 'til you're dizzy.
Twirl over twisting speedways and rocket through
tunnels. Balance and blast across a bubbling ocean
of oil!

Find the Emeralds, free the animals, and squash
Robotnik forever! (Sega 1992)

The last two paragraphs establish the objective of the game — they provide an overall direction for the story line. This objective must be stated explicitly in multimedia productions, because the path of the story line may change due to user interaction. Contrast this with cinema, where the objective or statement made by the film may purposely be left vague, as was often the case in films of the 1970's.

The narrative opens by strongly establishing the relationship of *Tails* to Sonic. and describing the characters of Sonic and *Tails*. The subsidiary relationship of *Tails* is important, since it describes the rules through which user-control of the behavior of Sonic (through the joystick) influences the behavior of *Tails* (i.e., he is always flying around helping Sonic).

The existence of an unpredictable opponent — Dr. Robotnik —

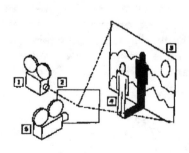

provides uncertainty and challenge necessary to keep the user's attention. The antagonist Dr. Robotnik is clichéd and unidimensional — an evil scientist with ambitions of global domination. Since the computer interaction is with Sonic, and little is revealed of the antagonist, it is necessary to make the antagonist as familiar to the user as possible — even to the point of hack writing.

Robotnik's actions are revealed one-by-one through the game, and they provide the series of "questions" that Sonic must "answer" through his actions. Although these are not the script- or dialogue-based questions and answers of cinema, they achieve the same effect. Robotnik's and Sonic's lines of interaction provide the two parallel lines of attention needed for parallel editing in the production of this video game.

Multimedia Space

Background is established —factories, refineries and cities. Because of the object oriented construction of the game, activities and pathways through each of these background are analogous. But they establish a new point of view, without massive reprogramming to define new characters and behaviors.

Multimedia space can be distinguished from real space in at least two ways:

- The space that exists in multimedia is two-dimensional, altering our perception of sizes and relationships of objects. In multimedia space, frame "camera" movement and editing must be used to recapture an image of "real" space.
- Editing can move instantaneously through space, seeing the same object from different perspectives, distances and angles.

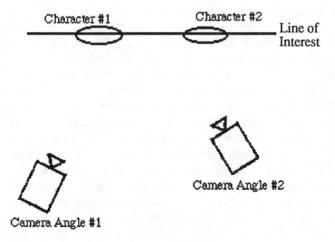

The Triangle Principle

In the Sega game "Sonic 2," space and background are established as a set of separate locations —factories, refineries and cities— but where characters have the same or analogous behaviors. Because of the object oriented construction of the game, activities and pathways through each of these background are analogous. But they establish a new point of view, without massive reprogramming to define new characters and behaviors.

The process of manipulating action forces a selectivity process in working out a story line. Only the peak moments of a story are shown on a screen, and all of the events or action which delay or do not add new, significant information are deleted from the script. Thus even if some of the multimedia material provides additional information, it should not be included in a production if it disrupts the "rhythm" of the story line as it unfolds. If the user's attention is to be kept, a delicate balance must be maintained between the demands for answers or interaction, and the pace at which challenges, actions and questions are presented to the user.

In comparison to the real world around us, the multimedia author is always compressing or expanding time and yet giving the illusion of supplying the entire real time of the event. The users are moved from here to there, from the present to the past, without warning. The viewer accepts this naturally, because the mind itself compresses or expands remembered time based on intensity of attention—mental time is almost never real time. Thus story telling must similarly compress and expand time based on the amount of information that must be conveyed. As long as a succession of actions and reactions—questions and answers—is maintained, the interpretation of that visual language does not demand of the viewer an understanding of its physical construction. For the multimedia producer, this action-reaction pattern dictates all the formulas for perspective and construction of multimedia space.

Because multimedia, and indeed our visual perception of the world, requires a projection into two-dimensional space, certain special organizing principles dictate the placement of characters and objects of interest on the screen. The cinematic principle commonly used — "Triangle Principle" — places characters on one side or the other of a "line of interest." Whatever scene changes and movement take place, the positions, direction, camera angle and so forth need to remain consistent. Otherwise the viewer will be confused; in a multimedia production already threatening overloading the viewer with information, confusion can severely hamper the effectiveness of the production. There are many ways that the Triangle Principle can be implemented. Arijon (1976) provides an excellent text on application of the Triangle Principle in cinema — a major subset of his suggestions can also be applied to multimedia.

In multimedia there is no real camera, rather the "camera" is a metaphor for the user (audience) perspective on a particular multimedia scene. Every scene has a perspective: it may be that of an individual in the presentation, or of the narrator, or (less desirable) of a disinterested observer.

The triangle principle, as it is applied in cinema, can provide standard formulas for enhancing visual action, reaching visual climaxes, time expansion and compression, follow focus, and so forth. Because of the extreme flexibility of multimedia editing, these can and should be used to great effect in multimedia.

Dialogue

As was seen in the analysis of "Sonic 2," dialogue needs not involve speaking — rather the visual nature of multimedia provides "action oriented" alternatives to dialogue. However implemented, though, motion is achieved and user interest maintained through dialogue — the sequence of "questions" and subsequent "answers." In multimedia, these are often silent, or responses are reflected in screen objects (or perhaps sound objects). An explicit or implicit menu system usually provides the main vehicle for the dialogue. Recently, models promulgated by Brenda Laurel (Laurel 1992) have sought to expand the scope of computer-based dialogues.

Still Images

Current multimedia presentations are often presented as series of stills, rather than as computer-based cinema. Although not as compelling as full animation, considerable reduction in production difficulties and demands for computing power make it cost effective for many implementations — especially one-of-a-kind customized productions. The reason that still images are attractive is their low cost and fast processing compared with multimedia animation (especially color and full-screen). They have been used very effectively in cinema. For example, Arnold Schwarzenegger's blockbuster "The Terminator" was inspired by a 1955 French film "La Jetée" shot entirely as black and white stills with a powerful voiced-over narrative.

Sound

It is in sound that multimedia most diverges from the Hollywood editing style. It is also, unfortunately, the aspect of multimedia production that is least developed in theory and in practice. Once again, it is important to review the work that has been performed in video game technology.

There are four basic soundtracks provided in cinema — dialogue, effects, ambiance and music. Dialogue provides the basic story line, and as has been shown, may often be non-verbal in multimedia. This may be as much a result of poor facilities for sound handling as anything else.

Effects, on the other hand, are well developed. The microcomputer platform provides exceptional facilities for modifying sound effects to fit the production. Effects provide emphasis and punctuation of the action; they are also used to announce events of importance. Because of their discrete, punctuated nature, implementation of effects is simple and unproblematic. Effects are tightly coupled to the action sequence in multimedia.

Ambiance (i.e., background sound, room presence) creates a sense of a particular time or place. These sounds include both the echo and noise that naturally occur in the background of dialogue recording. Just as main events, dialogue and story line should be seen as tightly coupled, ambiance and background images should also be tightly coupled, since they both provide a sense of location and a mood.

Music in video games is typically conceived in terms of the *leitmotif* — a distinguishing theme or melodic phrase representing and recurring with a given character, situation or emotion. The use of leitmotifs was developed by Richard Wagner, applied in a seamless manner in his operas. The leitmotifs of video games are more akin to those found in studio orchestras which allow a very quick change of mood, interruption for commercials and so forth.

Whereas ambiance and background may remain constant for long periods of time, user interaction and control of action force story line, character behavior and music to be conceived in terms of "snippets" that can be quickly and seamlessly linked. There is need to develop the concept of sound along object oriented lines — just as characters in video games have received such development — in order to fully use the power of music to support multimedia story telling.

Multimedia Punctuation

Multimedia punctuation — separations between sequences, pauses in narration, stress of a passage — is the most *abused* feature of multimedia. Dissolves, wipes, titles, props, cuts and so forth each has a specific meaning in multimedia, and must be used properly for maximum communication with the user. Again, the Hollywood editing style has set the standard with which most users will be accustomed, and it is these standards that should be adopted in multimedia.

Misuse of punctuation results from the vast array of special effects options at the multimedia author's disposal on the computer. Yet special effects fades and wipes should be used sparingly, and only when they contribute to the message being communicated.

The standard punctuation in transition from one scene to the next is a straight cut, where one scene ends, and the other begins. When synchronized properly with the dialogue, it is essentially invisible. The straight cut should be used wherever there is no additional information to be provided by the scene change. Notice that in video games, there is almost never a cut in the middle of a particular scene — there is no dialogue to keep the continuity. Thus the "camera" just appears to pan across the background following the character controlled by the interactive user.

Fades and wipes can be used to indicate a larger transition to a distant location or time. Iris effects are most closely associated with cartoons (e.g., Warner Brothers *Porky Pig*, and the TV series *Batman*). Fades to a solid color may be used to set a mood, although they can be problematic. Special-effects such as diamond, picture-in-picture, and so forth are standard fare in multimedia production packages. But they are not often used in film, and may appear amateurish if not used properly. They should generally be avoided unless they address a particular cinematic problem.

As with all other components of multimedia, story line is the deciding factor dictating the type of punctuation to invoke is the story line. Multimedia's novelty is in the ability of user interaction to dynamically alter the story line. Yet for users growing up, inured to Hollywood film and television, the devices of Hollywood filmmaking are expected, and must be applied to multimedia if the user is not to be overloaded by the information richness of multimedia.

The Market for Multimedia Productions

Multimedia is still a technology in development. Experience with digital TV suggests that processors of 500 MIPS need to be economically available before multimedia will be widely used. The prior discussion suggests that multimedia editing theory and practice probably need to advance before multimedia production will be widely accepted. Filmmaking went through around 50 years of development — from the end of the 19th century to the 1940's — in developing the Hollywood style of editing. Multimedia editing will probably develop much more quickly, because it can borrow heavily from film.

The development of cinema required a parallel development of technology and markets to provide a source of income for production. Multimedia will have much less of a challenge in this regard, because the markets exist, waiting for adequate technology and programming. For example, interactive videotex has been tried off and on for two decades. Poor technology has generally doomed prior videotex implementations. But broadband cabling and digital TV promise to change that, perhaps within a decade.

And this is only one channel for the sale of multimedia programming. A review of the industry by Sautter (1988) describes numerous outlets for traditional programming material: cable, home video, industrial, educational and training films, public broadcasting, daytime serials, news, magazine and interview shows, game shows, animation, children's programming, documentaries, radio, playwriting, commercials, alternative television, and so forth.

If, as Sony's chairman Akio Morita says, digital TV unites personal computer and TV technologies into a single technology available in every home, then interactive TV (i.e., multimedia) can be expected to gain the same audience that TV commands today. With broadband cable, there would be three choices for procuring multimedia software:

• purchase
• rental at, e.g., Blockbusters Video Stores
• rental from a "host" computer owned by the cable company.

With luck, by the time we see this technology in our homes, multimedia production will have reached the polished state of editing and production we see from Hollywood today.

References

Arijon, D., *Grammar of the Film Language*, Los Angeles:Silman-James, 1976.

Laurel, B., *Computers as Theater*, Reading, MA:Addisson-Wesley, 1992.

Cassill, R.V., *Writing Fiction*, New York: Prentice-Hall, 1975.

Goldstein, L. and J. Kaufman, *Into Film*, New York: E.P. Dutton, 1976.

Hawes, W., *Television Performing: News and Information*, Boston: Focal Press, 1991.

Kongsberg, I., *The Complete Film Dictionary*, New York: Meridian, 1987.

McLuhan, M., *Understanding media: The extensions of man*, New

York:McGraw-Hill, 1964.

Sautter, C., *How to Sell Your Screenplay: The Real Rules of Film and Television,* New York:New Chapter Press, 1988.

Sega, Sonic the Hedgehog 2, Hayward, CA:Sega, 1992.

Today Show, report on *Interfilm* 's "I'm your man," 7:40AM EST, December 26, 1992.

Chapter 12

Multimedia Computing and Intellectual Property Law:
What Developers and Users Should Know

Cherie Sherman Werbel
Ramapo College of New Jersey

During the past decade, a new product category has surfaced, the interactive multimedia system (Grogan, 1991). Such systems can retrieve text information from large databases and simultaneously associate and display this text with audio and visual images. For example, a new media product would enable the user to search the full text of a scholarly article on the Watergate affair, for all references to meetings between John Dean and President Nixon, and to simultaneously play the audio from the White House tape of one of the meetings or the videotape of John Dean's testimony before Congress regarding the meeting (Grogan, 1991). A multimedia work need not be fixed in a tangible medium, however, it can also be a performance in progress which includes music, lights, fireworks, and dramatic readings (Sarnoff, 1992). New media products have had only limited market penetration to date because the hardware and software components of such systems are only now beginning to become standardized across vendors, and the cost of the requisite hardware, such as CD-ROM players, fast computer chips, videodisc players, and VCR's remains prohibitive. However, as these costs continue to decline and standards for products develop, new media products will become an exciting resource as well as a concern for businesses and educational institutions (Grogan, 1991). Multimedia will replace the overhead projector and the slide show (Sarnoff, 1992).

A remaining impediment to the growth of the multimedia market is the expense and difficulty of creating and acquiring the audio, video, and text which constitute the subject matter of the multimedia creation (Grogan 1991). The authors of a new media product must acquire the rights to create their products by converting or adapting an existing product (such as a text encyclopedia) or negotiate with the numerous owners of the information they need and build the product from scratch. In some cases, the information may be in the public domain or may be provided as part of a multimedia software editing package. For example, Prosonus MusicBytes provides 27 useful songs for $99 on CD-ROM. These tracks may be used unless the use is in competition with Prosonus (Seymour, 1993). And of course, the author always has the option of writing his own text, taking his own photographs, and making his own videotapes and sound recordings provided that he also has the ability to digitize these components in the appropriate format so that they can be accessed by multimedia software.

Would-be multimedia authors and users must keep in mind, however, that whenever already-existing materials are part of a multimedia production, copyright law, and possibly trademark law, come into play. In fact, multimedia has been described as a marketing manager's dream and a lawyer's ultimate nightmare (Sarnoff, 1992). The goal of this chapter is to apprise developers of their potential liability for copyright and trademark infringement and to present them with suggestions for avoiding liability. A further goal is to explore some of the as-yet unresolved liability issues and to propose some recommendations and solutions to them. The current copyright law does not adequately deal with the ownership issues new media products present, and the legislature must soon assume responsibility for resolving some of these issues (Multimedia Spawns, 1992).

This paper is divided into the following sections: 1) Copyright protection; 2) Trademark protection; 3) New forms of copyright and trademark infringement; 4) The fair use defense to infringement; 5) assembling the rights to create a new media work; 6) Difficulties in determining who owns the rights involved, alternative means for acquiring multimedia; 7) Rights to photographs; 8) Rights to film; 9) Rights to audio; 10) Other; 11) License provisions; 12) Ancillary legal issues; 13) Inadequacy of the current copyright law—proposed changes; 14) Copyright enforcement; 15) Role of libraries; 16) Printing and copying restrictions—a gray area; and 17) Conclusion.

Copyright Protection

Copyright protection extends to literary, musical, dramatic, pictorial, graphic and sculptural works, as well as to computer programs (Kunstadt, 1992). Copyright protection lasts for the author's lifetime plus 50 years. Where a work is made for hire, (created as part of an employee's job, or commissioned), the copyright lasts for the shorter of 75 years from publication, or 100 years from creation.

The copyright laws protect the expression of an idea rather than the idea itself. Accordingly, authors are free to write plays about lovers from different ethnic groups who face family opposition even though this topic has been the subject matter of many plays going back to Shakespeare's time. Conversely, a work which copied the particular selection and combination of characters, sequence of events, and other details of an existing work would infringe upon that work's copyright.

The copyright owner has the exclusive right to reproduce her work, to distribute reproductions of her work, to display and perform her work publicly, and the sole authority to authorize anyone else to do any of the above. Copyright becomes effective without any legal act. Copyright exists the moment the author produces a tangible work. Once the work is taped or written down, it enjoys copyright protection even if it has not yet been published.

Copyright notice (affixing the symbol for copyright, the year of first publication, and the name of the owner) is not mandatory but it reduces the likelihood of innocent infringement as well as enables the author to sue for actual damages or for damages that the copyright law provides. Practically speaking, a work must be registered with the Copyright Office in order to institute an infringement action since an innocent infringer, relying on the absence of a notice would not be liable for actual or statutory damages. Under the Copyright Act of 1976, a court may award between $500 and $20,000 for each act of infringement if a work contains a notice of copyright and has been registered (Copyright Act, 1976). Copyright infringement is defined as the unauthorized use or copying of a copyrighted work. (Kunstadt, 1992). Infringement can be proved by showing the infringer had access to the copyrighted work and that the new work is substantially similar to the old work. The standard for adjudging similarity is whether an ordinary individual would find the works to be similar.

Trademark Protection

Trademark law protects words, names, symbols, logos and devices when they are used to identify the source of a good or service (Gullotti, 1992). Both the Lanham Act and various state acts provide for registration of trade marks. Under federal law, trademarks must be reregistered every 10 years. Some examples of trademarks are "Wonderware" for computer software and "Kodak" for photographic processing.

Trademark infringement actions may be brought in both federal and state court. The infringer may have to pay monetary damages and can be enjoined from using the mark.

New Forms of Copyright and Trademark Infringement

Because multimedia uses digital technology, copies of multimedia products, as good as the original, can be produced cheaply and easily (Dvorak & Somerson, 1992). Copying disks and video tapes is certainly more feasible than copying motion pictures, for example. In addition, large segments of the population have access to networks and bulletin boards and can download digital files which are potential components for multimedia products. For example, some of the information downloadable could be sound files of Captain Kirk speaking famous lines, or files of scanned swimsuit-issue photos (Dvorak & Somerson, 1992). The legion of computer users who enable their machines to say "Beam me up Scotty" upon the click of a mouse, are copyright violators, although their intentions are probably innocent. So in addition to facilitating violation of the copyright law by simplifying the processes of duplicating an entire work (copyrighted disk), digital technology enables the user to easily circumvent the law by including copyrightable components within the disk without paying for the privilege.

The specter of trademark infringement has also appeared on the multimedia horizon. MTV threatened to sue Sut Jhally, a University of Massachusetts communications professor, unless he stopped showing and distributing a video he authored, which incorporated the MTV logo and MTV footage; he was also required to destroy all existing copies of the video (Davis, 1991). The 55-minute video, entitled "Dreamworlds: Desire/Sex/Power in Rock Video," incorporated a stream of images from 165 rock videos shown on MTV interlaced with film footage from the "Accused," a film based on an actual pool hall gang rape which took place in New Bedford Massachusetts. Professor Jhally narrated the video with the intent of showing that suggestive videos based on male adolescent fantasies promote rape.

Ironically, MTV admits that it does not control the rights to the rock videos that comprise most of its programming, so the basis for its suit against Jhally would rest upon his unauthorized use of the MTV logo. Jhally's production came to the attention of MTV after he sent out 3,000 brochures, incorporating the logo, which advertised the video to colleges and libraries for $100 (Newman, 1991.) (The proceeds were to go to the university's communications department.)

Video game rental presents still another realm where copyright infringement takes on a new appearance. In *Red Baron Franklin Part Inc. v. Taito Corp.* (1989), the Fourth Circuit court held that using a video game in a public place constituted a "public performance" and therefore such use was subject to control by the owner of the copyright to the game software. This ruling prohibits game owners from purchasing games on printed circuit boards which would enable games to be swapped in and out of the same machine; it obliges game operators to buy dedicated equipment consisting of a cabinet, monitor, and power supply. Seemingly then, copyright law would also caution against setting up a PC in the student center with pirated games, not merely on the grounds of unauthorized use of copyrighted material, but also because such use would be an unauthorized public performance.

Still another area where copyright infringement issues will surface is in corporate presentations because it is not uncommon for the chairman of the board of a Fortune 100 company to make a video presentation at the annual stockholder's meeting (Burger, 1992). Should the video include unlicensed material, the company would be violating the copyright law. Likewise, the marriage of video and interactive technology will play a strong role in employee training spawning another functional area in which companies must be vigilant to comply with copyright law. Finally, interactive video may eventually make its way into the home as infomercials, "how-to" tapes, and magazines and these too must be in conformity with the law.

The Fair Use Defense to Infringement

Although the copyright owner has the exclusive right to reproduce her work, to distribute reproductions of her work, and to display and perform her work publicly, Section 107 of the Copyright Act exempts educational fair use from copyright infringement. This doctrine provides a limited exception to the copyright owner's exclusive right and allows use and reproduction of copyrighted works under certain prescribed circumstances. The fair use doctrine allows courts to flexibly apply the copyright laws so as to avoid unfairness, to prevent the stifling of creativity, and to foster the production and dissemination of useful works to the public. The fair use doctrine generally applies to news reporting, criticism, teaching, scholarship, and research.

In determining whether the use of a copyrighted work by someone other than the copyright owner or a party he has authorized should be permitted, courts look at four factors: 1) the purpose and character of the use, i.e., commercial or nonprofit educational; 2) the nature of the copyrighted work; 3) the amount of the work used in proportion to the copyrighted work as a whole; and 4) the effect of the use upon the potential market for the copyrighted work or upon its value (Groenewold, 1990). Other sections of the copyright law further clarify what constitutes fair use. Section 108 provides instructions for legal reproduction by libraries and archives. Section 109 permits the owner of a copy of a book or recording to sell or dispose of it as he pleases. Section 110 encompasses performances or showings of copyrighted works by non-profit institutions. Section 111 regulates cable transmission of copyrighted works.

In 1980, Congress enacted Section 117 to regulate copying and use of computer programs. For example, it is not an infringement for the owner of a copy of a computer program to make a copy of the program or to authorize the making of another copy as long as: 1) the copy is necessary for the utilization of the computer program in conjunction with the machine, i.e. an "essential step"; or 2) the copy is for archival purposes. This section permits users to backup programs and to use programs that employ certain copy protection schemes.

The bottom line is that the copyright law allows a certain amount of freedom for teaching and scholarship as long as these activities are part of a nonprofit educational endeavor. This does not mean, however, that educational institutions are free to violate the law with impunity. For example, in 1991, Kinko's Graphics Corporation was fined $510,000 for photocopying material and placing it on sale in college bookstores, (*Basic Books, Inc. v. Kinko's Graphics Corp.* 1991). Professors gave the company lists of material they planed to use in their courses and Kinko copied the relevant extracts from published books. The District Court held that the fair use exemption was not available to Kinko's.

Assembling the Rights to Create a New Media Work

The watchword for creators of new media works, according to Bob Kohn, vice president of corporate affairs for Borland International, Inc., is "when in doubt, you require a license" (Barney 1992). In fact, assembling the rights to create a multimedia CD-ROM product can be a forbidding task. Sarnoff (1992) summarizes what she identifies as the many steps in producing, for Macintosh computer users, a hypothetical CD-ROM on the life and times of William Shakespeare.

The very first task is to identify all of the components which comprise the packages. In this hypothetical they would comprise:

> Macintosh operating system software
> Hypercard programming software
> Other third party application software programs necessary for graphics, sound, and animation
> Copies of historic documents
> Scholarly articles
> Portraits of William Shakespeare
> Portions of films of Shakespeare's plays
> A dramatic reading by Richard Burton
> An interactive question and answer section
> A drawing program students can use to create costumes and sets
> A recording of Elizabethan music by a symphony orchestra.

Since some of these materials will be created in-house, the first step is to have employees sign an agreement specifically stating that the materials they create for the project are the property of the employer. Independent contractors and consultants should execute agreements that expressly assign all rights to the materials created for the project to the employer. These agreements prevent employees and contractors from later claiming that they personally own the copyright to the works they produced and that the employer's inclusion of their work in a commercial product is a copyright infringement.

Although materials in the public domain, for example materials whose copyright has expired, can be used freely, it is not always easy to determine whether or not a material falls within this category. For example, Shakespeare's play Hamlet is in the public domain, but popular films based on the play might not be.

Any third-party software used as an integral, behind-the-scenes component of the project would have to be licensed. The software could not simply be reproduced on numerous CDs or videodiscs because one legal copy had been purchased.

In order to incorporate a recording of Richard Burton's soliloquy into the project, the owner of the copyrighted recording would have to give permission. Also, Richard Burton's estate might have to grant permission due to state laws governing the right to publicity.

An historical document from Elizabethan England would be in the public domain, but not a contemporary work discussing the document. To use the full text of a work may require permission of both the publisher and the author. Similarly, while Shakespeare's likeness is no longer subject to copyright protection, an artist's rendition of Shakespeare would be.

Difficulties in Determining Who Owns the Rights Involved, Alternative Means for Acquiring Multimedia

In addition to the inherent difficulty involved in nailing down licensing and permission arrangements with numerous parties, an additional problem is identifying who can give permission. Some of the complex legal issues that can arise are raised by Grogan in his discussion of how one might go about authoring a CD-ROM version of a recent hypothetical book, *The Baseball Story* (Grogan, 1991). The CD-ROM would include:

- Still photographs, some of which appeared in the book version
- Film clips including interviews with players, footage of key plays and locations, and excerpts of related commercial films
- Music including hit songs about baseball
- A database of baseball statistics.

An initial question would be whether the author of *The Baseball Story* can even grant the right to make a CD-ROM version of the book. Perusing the form agreement the author signed with her publisher might not answer this question. Although such forms determine which rights the author has granted to the publisher and which rights she has retained, many form agreements fail to address or define the new rights which have developed along with new technology.

For example, the terms "electronic rights" and "motion picture and audiovisual rights" often appear in such agreements, and it might not be clear into which category a CD-ROM would fall. Such vagueness has in fact resulted in major lawsuits. Simon & Schuster sued Qintex Entertainment, Inc. for seeking to distribute audiocassettes of the soundtrack to the television mini-series based on author Larry McMurtry's novel, *Lonesome Dove* (Kirsch, 1990). McMurtry assigned "electronic rights" to his novel to his publisher, Simon & Schuster but retained motion picture rights.

Rights to Photographs

Photographs present another sort of stumbling block to the would-be multimedia author. Even if a photograph appeared in a publication, the publisher might not own all rights to its use. In general, publishers have been inconsistent in acquiring rights to photos; policies regarding the acquiring of rights vary from year to year and from photo to photo. Generally, the only way to determine the rights status of a particular photo is to manually search through old and incomplete records.

Furthermore, photo rights can be very restricted and limited in ways unique to the medium. Photographers can grant rights limited to black and white reproduction, a specific size range, a specific resolution (number of dots per inch), or to publication in a specific sort of magazine. Limitations may also be imposed on the number of copies that can be reproduced, the time period during which the copies can be made, or the geographic area in which the copies can be circulated. Sometimes, the photographer is entitled to special fees for the reuse of a photograph.

An alternative to acquiring rights to a particular photograph is to consult a stock house that carries photographs from a number of photographers. The stock house may own a particular photograph outright, or act as an agent for the photographer and negotiate with him for the rights one needs. Typically, for a small flat fee, one can obtain the right to store a particular photo at a specific physical area on the CD-ROM as well as to make the photo visible under certain conditions. For example, each time the CD-ROM user highlights the name of a player, he would be able to bring up the player's picture.

Rights to Film

A wide variety of film footage is also available from stock houses. Some institutions have libraries of film footage available for license. These organizations usually charge a flat fee based on the number of frames of film licensed, and the nature of the use. Licensing film for use in new media products is still novel and fees may have to be negotiated.

Obtaining rights to commercial feature film footage is complicated, expensive and sometimes impossible. The first party to contact to acquire these rights is the film distributor. Usually, the distributor can at least identify who owns the rights. However, the putative owner may not warrant that it has all the rights necessary for a specific multimedia use. For example, to legally use the music incorporated into the film clip and the names and likenesses of actors appearing therein may require the acquisition of additional rights.

Rights to Audio

In comparison with the murky procedure for obtaining film rights, the procedure for obtaining audio rights is well-established. This procedure does, however, involve several steps. Firstly, the owner of the copyright in the underlying musical composition must agree to supply a "mechanical license." This license authorizes the production of material objects which embody the composition. This license does not authorize the manufacture or distribution of a recording of a particular performance by a particular artist. The performer must still grant permission. The Copyright Law requires that the owner of a composition grant a mechanical license at a rate of 5.7 cents per song or 1.1 cents per minute per song. A negotiated license is usually preferable to a compulsory license because it need not include the same restrictions on payment terms and payment certification that the law imposes upon a compulsory license. Many music publishers authorize a clearing house to negotiate mechanical licenses on their behalf.

Where a musical composition will be used in conjunction with visual images, a synchronization license is also required. Usually, consent of the composer and a music publisher are required although some agencies serve as clearing houses for these rights. Synchronization fees may be several thousand dollars or more.

Because synchronization licenses limit the number of seconds a song can be used, they pose special problems when they are negotiated for interactive multimedia works. The number of times that a song will be played will vary with the user.

The composer of a musical composition controls still another right, the right to public performance. "Public performance" is defined by the copyright act as a performance open to the public where a substantial number of persons who are not friends or family are gathered. The transmission or communication of a work to such an audience also constitutes public performance. ASCAP[1], (the American Society of Composers, Authors and Publishers), SESAC[2] (the Society of European Stage Authors), and BMI[3] (Broadcast Music Inc.) are the primary agents for licensing performance rights to music.

Performance rights also include a sub-category, grand performing rights. These rights can be asserted by the copyright owner when the musical composition is incorporated into a dramatic or theatrical production. For example, if a CD-ROM included excerpts from a Broadway musical, both the composer and publisher might have to be consulted in order to obtain grand performing rights.

Other

Despite the piece-meal acquisition of innumerable licenses, the would-be multimedia producer must still obtain additional rights if he wishes to reproduce or distribute a particular performance by a particular artist, for example, a performance by the Beatles of one of their compositions. Usually, a record company that distributes recordings which include that particular performance will own the copyright to it.

Yet another consideration is that copyright protection for databases and other compilations of facts is still a complex and evolving issue. Although facts themselves are not copyrightable, a particular arrangement of them, for example, company names and addresses arranged in a directory by product category or zip code, might be. Therefore, a compilation of baseball statistics could be subject to copyright protection. Probably the best way to deal with this issue would be to do the research on one's own.

Finally, promotion of the multimedia work may require a permission letter or release if logos or trademarks connected with third-party materials are included in brochures or packaging (Sarnoff, 1992). If use of the trademark would lead a buyer to believe a third-party sponsored the multimedia product, or if the multimedia product is effectively part of the distribution chain for a third-party product, a trademark license may be required.

License Provisions

Licenses are familiar to most computer users because they are commonly incorporated into software shrink wrap and they appear on the initial screen of certain popular software packages. However, it is reasonable to assume that when most users "consent" to the terms of such a license, their consent is uninformed. In fact, Mary Kay Duggan (1991) reports that as far as libraries are concerned, signed license agreements are frequently located in inaccessible, locked filing cabinets, and are unknown to both the librarian and the user.

A license is a right granted which gives one permission to do something he could not legally do without such permission (Gifis, 1984). In the case of intellectual property, the copyright owner grants the user a limited right to use the copyrighted work. A boilerplate multimedia license agreement, granting the author permission to include copyrighted material within her project, has been developed by Sarnoff (1992) and should contain the following types of information:

•Identification section— identification of licensor and licensee, identification of the multimedia project and its form of distribution, e.g. CD-ROM.
• Definition section— definition of terms used within the contract, e.g. territory shall mean worldwide.
• Term and termination—length of license, date of commencement, procedure for terminating the license
• Consideration— the cost of the license.
• Nature of license—whether the license is exclusive or other parties may use the copyrighted material concurrently with the multimedia author.
• Required notices on the product —notice of copyright and credits which the multimedia project must contain.
• Warranties of licensor— the licensor certifies the extent of the rights he is granting, e.g.: synchronization rights, releases of all persons whose likenesses appear; the licensor guarantees the legality or quality of the product, e.g. bug-free software, lack of defamatory material.
• Indemnification— the licensor agrees to pay any expenses the licensee occurs if he is sued for using the licensed material by a

third party.
- Insurance— the licensor agrees to secure and maintain an insurance policy payable to the licensee.
- Assignability— a statement that neither party can assign the license without the other's consent.
- Governing law— the state law which a court will apply in interpreting the terms of the contract should there be a lawsuit between the licensor and the licensee.
- Arbitration— a provision that disputes related to the contract will be submitted to arbitration.

Duggan (1991) notes that librarians should be particularly concerned with four areas that sometimes appear in license agreements drawn up by publishers of online information and CD-ROM subscriptions. Publishers may restrict printing, downloading, use on a network, or transmission. Such restrictions may be problematic because of the difficulty in monitoring use of these products by users. However, there are software 'tricks' which can be employed to monitor control and use. (See section on printing and copying restrictions for further discussion.)

Ancillary Legal Issues

In addition to issues of copyright and trademark, further legal ambushes can snare the unwary multimedia author. New media works which contain defamatory material, (false statements which would expose an individual to ridicule and harm his reputation), are illegal. The defamer can be required to pay damages to the individual harmed.

Likewise, invasion of privacy or unauthorized exploitation of an individual's likeness (look-a-likes) can be grounds for a lawsuit. For example, Christian Dior was enjoined from distributing advertisements which included a photograph of a model who closely resembled Jacqueline Kennedy (*Onassis v. Christian Dior*, 1984).

If a multimedia author creates a brochure to advertise her new work, she needs permission to include screens which display an individual's photograph, for example. Similarly, use of photographs or audio recordings which were obtained by violating an individual's private sphere, e.g. through use of a telescopic lens or wiretap, would be illegal. As an example, newsmen who photographed a doctor in his home with a hidden camera and transmitted their conversations with him by hidden microphone to a nearby tape recorder, were found liable for invasion of privacy (*Billings v. Atkinson*, 1973). Even when material is utilized for the benefit of the public, here as part of an investigation into medical quackery, rather than for strictly commercial purposes, a publisher may incur liability.

The multimedia author must also be sure he does not publicly disclose within his production, private, potentially embarrassing facts about an individual. Showing two unmarried teachers in an embrace would be an example of a forbidden disclosure. However, public figures such as well-known actors and athletes, are exempt from this protection.

In the same vein, portraying an individual in a false light, for example implying that an individual receives public assistance when this is not the case, or that the individual was a war hero when in fact she never served in the armed forces, is also illegal. For liability to arise, the author must have an intent to provide false information or be reckless with regard to determining the truth of the information he provides.

To avoid potential liability in these areas, authors of new media works should obtain written releases from anyone whose likeness appears in their production. If an author uses a pre-existing image, he should review all the releases obtained by the original producer of the image.

The nature of multimedia productions conflicts with the ability to supply credits, a precondition that copyright owners often require before they will grant a license. Because traditional media works such as books and movies are linear in nature, the appearance of credits and their precise location are easily negotiated. New media works, subject to the control of the user, may be harmed aesthetically by the frequent and persistent appearance of credits. For example, should credits appear on the screen everyone time Captain Kirk says "Beam me up, Scotty?" This issue has yet to be resolved satisfactorily.

Still another potential legal violation exists in the area of moral rights which protect the distortion or modification of an author's work. An author has the right to be identified as the author of her work and to prevent works from being wrongly attributed to her. Even after assigning a copyright, the author may withdraw his work if it is misused. Moral rights apply primarily to photographs, drawings, paintings, and sculptures, and can become an issue even when modification of the original material consists of excising material because it is suggestive or obscene. Just such a scenario was the basis for a lawsuit involving the British comedy group, Monty Python and it arose when the BBC edited the group's scripts for U.S. network television (Gilliam v. American Broadcasting Co., 1976). In this case, the court held that Monty Python was entitled to an injunction preventing ABC from showing the edited scripts. By offering a mutilated version of the series, ABC impaired the integrity of Monty Python's work and presented a "mere caricature" of the group's talents.

The so-called "look and feel" analysis may also have some bearing on whether a given multimedia work violates the copyright law. This analysis has been applied to computer programs, films, and other audiovisual works. The total combination of camera angle, decor, background, makeup and the like may constitute a particular movie-making style which is the property of a particular artist and therefore copyrightable. Imitation of such a style in a multimedia work might constitute copyright infringement.

In a recent decision, Computer Associates v. Altai Inc. (1992), the Second Circuit Court of Appeals reaffirmed that certain types of screen displays, if copyrighted separately as audiovisual works, would be protectible regardless of the underlying program's copyright status. However, the court went on to say that the non-literal structure of a computer program, i.e. those elements which are incidental to the program's function, may not be protected by the copyright laws.

Another recent decision, Apple Computer, Inc. v. Microsoft Corp. and Hewlett-Packard Co. (1992), indicates that unprotectible elements (such as the concept of overlapping windows) which combine with protectible elements (the Macintosh trashcan for example) to form the "look and feel" of a software package, do not necessarily produce a copyrightable composite. The court held that the notion of a computer "desktop" was not proprietary to the Macintosh interface and that other software packages could employ a desktop graphical user interface and its standardized features without infringing (Being similar, 1992).

Inadequacy of the Current Copyright Law—Proposed Changes

In response to the recognition that the copyright law was not designed with new media products in mind, the Subcommittee on Courts, Intellectual Property and the Administration of Justice of the House Committee on the Judiciary, asked Congress's Office of Technology Assessment (OTA) to prepare a report examining the changes in computer software technology and their impact on U.S. patent, trademark, and copyright laws (Raysman & Brown, 1992). In its 1992 report, *Finding a balance: computer software, intellectual property, and the challenge of technological change,* the OTA noted the factors that have created complexity in the software arena. Firstly, the very nature of software technology does not fit neatly within copyright and patent legislation, legislation which primarily evolved prior to the computer. Amendments to this legislation continue to be inadequate because the rapid pace of technological change in computer software and hardware continues to surpass the speed of legislative development and enactment. An additional issue is the cultural and definitional differences which exist between the legal and technical communities; these communities share neither training nor objectives and such differences make communication difficult.

And finally, the international scope of software markets and technologies has further complicated an already complicated legal dilemma. The United States has bilateral copyright relations with about 80 countries. Sixty of these countries adhere to the Berne Convention which provides for a minimum level of copyright protection without requiring notice or registration. Many countries have also ratified the Universal Copyright Convention (UCC) which requires that foreign works be afforded the same copyright protection as domestic works. However, under the UCC, a published work must bear a notice of copyright in order to receive protection (Kunstadt, 1992).

The portions of the OTA study which focused on computer programs are relevant to multimedia because all multimedia works incorporate software. The OTA study focused on four key elements of computer program development: 1) the program function, 2) its external design, 3) the user interface, and 4) the program code. It studied the technology behind each of these categories of the development process and how the current law would be applied. The OTA noted that for each issue raised in its report, Congress would have to decide whether and when it would take legislative action, and when and how comprehensive it would be. Three policy areas highlighted by the report were: 1) the appropriate scope of copyright protection, 2) patent protection for inventions incorporating software, and, 3) the complications facing libraries and other users of digital information. It outlined possible legislative action in each area.

With regard to the scope of protection for programs, the OTA recommended that copyright protection for computer programs be clarified and extended beyond the code or programming statements which comprise the program. However, such protection might currently run afoul of Section 102 of the Copyright Law which excludes ideas, procedures, processes, systems, and methods of operation from copyright protection. The OTA therefore recommended that Section 102 be amended and that copyright be specifically extended or denied to the following system components: computer languages, algorithms, design specification, and user and other interfaces. The report also noted that software terminology such as "algorithm" would have to be added to Section 101 of the Law, the definitions section.

The OTA also recommended that computer programs should no longer be treated as literary works and subsumed within that category. Instead, a new category, "computer programs" should be added to the Act. Because programs follow a unique economic life cycle and are disseminated differently than literary works, courts need a suitably unique standard by which to adjudge their infringement. Congress could choose to extend only limited protection for the program's code, for example a short time span, and yet develop a very different kind of protection for the design and functionality elements of the computer program.

Alternatively, Congress might replace current copyright protection for computer programs completely. Congress could develop a new law which, in addition to providing for protection which would correspond to the market life and purchase patterns of software, would also specifically address reverse engineering of software (a translation from object code to source code which enables the user to understand how the program works, and to modify it). The law could also specifically include or exclude coverage for software interfaces.

OTA also suggested that the reverse engineering issue could be resolved by clarifying the fair use and exclusive rights provisions of the Act, and amending the scope and subject matter of copyright provisions. Congress might also consider other policies such as: 1) directing the Copyright Office to work with software professionals, educators, and consumers to develop practical guidelines for "fair use" and "essential steps" in the use of programs (exceptions to the Copyright Law which permit copying); and 2) establishing legislative guidelines regarding these terms.

The OTA also addressed the issue of patent protection for software, a new approach to protecting computer programs that is becoming more prevalent (Sumner & Lundberg, 1991). The OTA did not give unqualified approval to such protection because guidelines of the Patent and Trademark Office prohibit patents on "algorithms" and this term has yet to be defined precisely enough that it can be said to exclude computer programs. The OTA also noted that patenting is an expensive process unlikely to be available to the small start-up companies which dominate the software marketplace. Also, the PTO does not have a database of so-called "prior art" which would enable it to evaluate whether a new program was indeed novel and nonobvious and therefore patentable under the guidelines of the existing patent law.

Furthermore, the OTA noted the special problems that libraries face in dealing with information in digital form. For example, although guidelines exist with regard to making archival copies of books and computer programs, the Copyright Act makes no provision regarding the right to make copies of databases. Likewise, the Act makes no provision regarding a library's right to convert copyrighted works it owns into digital form, for incorporation into multimedia databases. The OTA suggested that Congress clarify the fair use guidelines and establish guidelines for differentiating among "copying", "reading," and "using" works that have been copied or borrowed from other libraries. And perhaps most importantly, the OTA recommended that Congress clarify the status of multimedia works with regard to their copyright protection and that it create a royalty-collecting agency to alleviate the difficulty of obtaining permission for including images, text, and other copyrighted works within a multimedia product.

Despite the issuance of the OTA Report, not all the players in the legal and creative community are sanguine that the amendments to the copyright law are the answer. At a recent Digital World conference, David Nimmer, an attorney with Irell & Manella, predicted that the ease of copying digital media would result in technology that continues to "leapfrog" past the law (Multimedia spawns doubts, 1992). Although he agreed that new copyright law would help, he expressed doubts that it would be enacted. In his opinion, it is more likely that artists will band together into a collective licensing operation, like ASCAP or BMI, and will develop a working model outside the traditional frameworks of legislation and litigation.

Yet another alternative to amending the copyright law would be to mimic the recording industry and add a blind royalty to each blank floppy disk purchased, suggest Dvorak & Somerson (1992). (Currently, a blind royalty is added to every blank audio cassette sold.) In this way, every time a disk is backed up or a data file stored, a small amount of money would go to the software publishers. Under this system, publishers who sold more software would be entitled to a larger share of the fees collected.

Somerson also speculates that as multimedia tools become

more widespread, software piracy will increase markedly. Unless Hollywood lobbies for effective reform of the copyright muddle, large amounts of film footage could effectively enter the public domain. Copyrighted material would pass from the control of its owners, and widespread wrongdoing would make enforcement of the copyright law impracticable.

Copyright Enforcement

Although copyright infringement is an old area of the law, software copyright infringement has remained largely unpunished. (Meyer, 1992). This may begin to change now that software developers have formed a trade organization called the Software Publishing Agency (SPA). The Agency maintains an 800 number that informants may call to report software violations. The organization has won each of the 100 enforcement proceedings it initiated and finances itself solely through the penalties the court awarded from these proceedings. Recently published settlements ranged between $75,000 and $300,000 U.S. dollars.

SPA will provide a free disk that shows the programs running on a machine. The user can then compare this list against his purchase record to find out if any illegal programs have been copied onto his machine. So far, 25,000 of these disks have been distributed.

When an informant reports illegal copying to the SPA, the SPA writes to the alleged offender and identifies the programs he is allegedly using illegally and asks to audit his computers. If the alleged offender refuses, the SPA applies for a court order to enter the alleged offender's premises. The informant's affidavit can recite evidence a court will deem sufficient to permit such an entry. In the alternative, the SPA may simply sue the alleged offender without advance notice. The fact that an employer did not know about the illegal programs is not a defense to a law suit. Where more than one program is illegal, an multi-count indictment may be forthcoming.

To stay legal, a software purchaser should generally make no more than two copies of the original program. The program should be backed up to diskette so that if the original is destroyed, the purchaser can go on using the software. The Copyright Act specifically allows this type of copying. In addition, the user can make one copy of the program on his hard disk to enable him to run it from there.

Role of Libraries

Duggan (1991) notes that publishers of electronic information have apparently assigned library professionals a special role in policing copyright violations. Seemingly, library staff are to stand beside the workstations and monitor printing and downloading from electronic databases and CD-ROMS to ensure that there is no violation of license provisions that may restrict these activities. Duggan proposes that as an alternative, a standardized sign, similar to those displayed at photocopy machines, should be posted in the electronic information area. The sign would inform users that some databases are copyrighted and that activities such as downloading, file transfer, and printing may be limited or prohibited. She also suggests that the initial screen of some products could delineate the penalties for copyright infringement, just as many commercial videotapes do, as well as clarify what constitutes fair use. The importance of electronic notification, as opposed to a paper sign, becomes increasingly important as more users begin to access electronic information housed in the library, from remote sites. The AT&T electronic library has coped with the copyright compliance problem by assigning each publication, one of a set of thirteen codes that identifies its copyability status.

Printing and copying restrictions— a gray area

Libraries face some special problems in policing copyright compliance because of the multitude of restrictive licenses that are part and parcel of providing access to online databases and CD-ROM databases. Typically, a license may dictate that no more than a specific number of copies of a printout can be made; in addition, the copies can be distributed only within the licensee-organization. Other licenses forbid reproduction, abstraction, or transmission of the information. Still other licenses only permit the user to download a portion of the licensed database to her own disk if the downloaded material is saved to a temporary file.

A number of philosophical questions arise in attempting to comply with such licenses. Given that fair use permits the non-commercial user to make a limited number of copies of a copyrighted document, can the user incorporate a portion of a database within a wordprocessed document or a database he has created using database management software? Can portions of the database be transmitted across the network to other users, or mounted on a bulletin board accessible to other users? If a database is downloaded to a file for the duration of a three-year grant, is such a file temporary? If a CD-ROM is networked, and more than one user can access the data simultaneously or serially from a number of different workstations, has a "copy" of the data been made; does the database "exist" on more than one workstation?

According to Duggan (1991), some database vendors will reply to these questions with definitive answers; but sometimes the answers are surprising and at other times vendors can provide no real answer. For example, the Ohio College Library Center (OCLC), a supplier of online bibliographic information, views "temporary" as corresponding to a professor's lifetime, an unpredictable length of time. Yet another vendor, SilverPlatter, allows some amount of downloading from their CD-ROM, stating that a year's worth of data is too much to download, yet not stating the amount that would be permissible.

Software does exist to monitor the amount of information downloaded and SilverPlatter, for example, does monitor downloading. Another practical control mechanism for libraries would be to limit the amount of time a user could spend at a CD-ROM workstation and thereby limit downloading. Duggan (1991) also points out that software does exist to monitor network activity and that the network administrator does have the capability to revoke passwords if a user appears to be violating the law. However, to the extent that a license is indefinite and vague, it is unlikely that a court would enforce it anyway (Lieberman & Siedel, 1988).

Conclusion

In conclusion, colleges, universities, libraries and businesses will find it judicious to assume a proactive stance in preventing violation of the copyright law. Multimedia technology will represent a temptation to some portion of computer users and to society at large. Some individuals will seek an outlet for creativity and unknowingly use copyrighted materials without permission. Others may see an opportunity to disseminate vicious, defamatory or provocative material, to create an impact with relatively little trouble or expense.

Because the existing copyright law is difficult to apply to multimedia and because enforcement seems lacking, there has been little incentive for organizations to self-police. Yet the specter of legal action and damages is real, particularly when the offending organization has large resources or the copyright violation results in commercial gain.

For the most part, schools may be able to hide behind the fair use doctrine and to avoid prosecution for copyright infringement. However, if and when an individual sells his illegally produced multimedia creation, even non-profit organizations can be liable. Both business and educational institutions can protect themselves by undertaking to educate potential multimedia users to the rights they have and the practices that go beyond those rights. This can be accomplished through workshops, newsletters and postings. Organizations should act promptly to terminate illegal activity they uncover and to create an environment where the user community feels free to report violations and knows how and where to do so.

However, when the lawbreakers outnumber the lawabiders, it becomes clear that the law must be changed. Congress needs to rewrite the copyright law to reflect the needs of current technology. As long as non-profit organizations or individuals do not use copyrighted material for gain, they should be protected under the fair use exception to the law.

Lawmakers must work with software practitioners as well as those in the arts to devise a means of untangling the copyright morass. The notion of a copyright clearing house which would act as an agent for the innumerable licenses required for a multimedia production would appear to be a tidy solution, but this task might be more efficiently handled by the private sector.

The "information highway" is a new form of interstate commerce. Just as Congress regulated airlines, railroads and the telephone system when they were in their infancy, so it should step in to regulate the electronic networks of this era. Congress needs to define information rights more clearly so that users can know what constitutes a "copy" and can more readily determine where their own rights begin and end.

References

Barney, D. (1992, November 9). You may need a license for the music in your multimedia show. *InfoWorld*. p. 28

Basic Books, Inc. v. Kinko's Graphics Corp., 21 U.S.P.Q. 2d 1639 (1991).

Being similar and copyright may conflict. *Software Law Bulletin*, 5, 214-218.

Billings v. Atkinson, 489 S.W.2d 858 (Tex. 1973).

Burger, J. (1992, May). A funny thing happened on the way to the Renaissance. *Post: the Magazine for Animation, Audio, Film & Video Professionals*, 7, 31-32.

Computer Assoc. Int'l. v. Altai, Inc., 538 F.2d 14 (2d Cir. 1976).

Copyright Act of 1976, 17 U.S.C. 101 et seq.

Davis, W. A. (1991, August 25). Flesh for fantasy. *Boston Globe*. p. F2.

Duggan, M. K. (1991). Copyright of electronic information: issues and questions. *Online*, 15, 20-35.

Dvorak, J. C. & Somerson, P. (1992). Hands off that scanner! The media police are on your trail. *PC-Computing*, 6, 104-105.

Finding a balance: computer software, intellectual property, and the challenge of technological change (OTA-TCT-527). Washington, DC: U.S. Government Printing Office.

Giffis, S. H. (1984). *Law dictionary.* (2d ed.). New York: Barrons.

Gilliam v. American Broadcasting Co., 538 F.2d 14 (2d Cir. 1976).

Groenewold, G. (1990). Rules of the game: roll on, O mighty river; intellectual property. *UNIX Review*, 8, 30-40.

Grogan, A. R. (1991). Acquiring content for new media works. *The Computer Lawyer*, 8, 2-13.

Kirsch, J. L. (1990, April). "Lonesome Dove" and the electronic rights revolution in book publishing. *The Los Angeles Lawyer*, p. 24.

Kunstadt, R. M. (1992). Introduction to copyright law. *"Bright Ideas"*, 1, 6-7.

Lanham Act, 15 U.S.C. 1051 et seq.

Lieberman, J. K. & Siedel, G. J. (1988). Business Law and the Legal Environment. (2d ed.). N.Y.: Harcourt, Brace, Jovanovich.

Meyer, H. (1992). Lawyer software copyright infringers "Flee, All is Discovered!". *New York State Bar Journal*, 64, 18-19.

Multimedia spawns doubts and copyright headaches— seminar. (1992). *Video Week*, 13, 5-6.

Newman, M. The Eye. (1991, June 2). *Billboard.* p. 66

Onassis v. Christian Dior, 122 Misc. 2d 603 (N.Y. Sup. Ct. 1984).

Raysman, R. & Brown, P. (1991 November 10). OTA report: finding a balance for software protection. *New York Law Journal*, pp. 3, 5.

Red Baron Franklin Part Inc. v. Taito Corp., 883 F.2d 275 (4th Cir. 1989).

Sarnoff, J. (1992). Getting a grip: a practical approach to corporate production of multimedia. *International Computer Law Adviser*, 6, 4-17.

Seymour, J. The multimedia copyright swamp. (1993). *PC Magazine*, 12, 99-100.

Sumner, J. P. & Lundberg, S. W. (1991). Software patents: are they here to stay? *The Computer Lawyer*, 8, 8-15.

Chapter 13

New Era Video, Inc.:
A Case Study of Entrepreneurship in Hypermedia Computing[1]

Peeter J. Kirs
Joyce J. Elam
Gary Walter
Florida International University

As any student of information technology history might observe, many of the innovative advances in the development and application of new technologies are attributable not to well planned organizational initiatives, but to entrepreneurial individuals who were guided by their vision of what the technology could, or should, accomplish. Introductory Information Systems textbooks are replete with examples of entrepreneurs who have advanced information technology, from Charles Babbage to Herman Hollerith to Steven Jobs and Steve Wozniak to Bill Gates.

Typically, such textbooks provide accompanying descriptions of the innovator's undertakings, and in doing so delineate the successes and failures experienced along the way. The intent of such an approach is clear: not only does the description of events provide a clearer understanding of the industry growth, but the knowledge gained in hindsight can also provide us with prescriptive strategies for repeating accomplishments and avoiding potential pitfalls.

Even though a number of established organizations have recently recognized that multimedia computing (MMC) has far reaching implications, the relative infancy of the field, the rapidly changing technologies involved, and the myriad of possible applications imply that the area is well suited to entrepreneurship. As we shall see, the major forces driving the MMC industry favor new entrants, but the window of opportunity is rapidly closing.

This chapter provides a case study of entrepreneurship in MMC. Specifically, we examine New Era Video, Inc. (NEVI), a hypermedia computing company established by Mr. Michael Greenberg. The primary focus of the case study is on the entrepreneurial process and how it relates to the multimedia computing industry, but it is recognized that the essence of entrepreneurship is the entrepreneur (Mitton, 1989). We will consider a number of relevant issues which directly contribute to the success of an entrepreneurial venture: the number, strength, and positioning of MMC competitors; the resources, positioning and strategy employed by the venture; and the size, growth and needs of the customers (Bygrave and Hofer, 1991). We will also examine a number of global variables, such as the economics, politics, and prevalent sociological attitudes (see Stevenson, 1987) to aid in developing generalized predictions based on a single case study (Bygrave and Hofer, 1989).

We will first present an overview of our discussions with Mr. Michael Greenberg about New Era Video, Inc., and the experiences he went through in developing the company. After the case presentation, we will provide a brief analysis of where New Era Video, and the MMC Industry in general, can be classified in terms of their development, and what events might be expected in the future. Finally, we will focus on what New Era's experiences might mean to three distinct groups: entrepreneurs, technocrats, and consumers.

Before beginning, however, one distinction needs to be noted, namely, the difference between Multimedia and Hypermedia. Rather than relying on academician provided definitions, we offer Greenberg's own definition:

> I view Multimedia Computing as a medium which provides the technical ability to show moving pictures, and notice I said moving pictures and not video, in conjunction with sound, photographs, graphics, and simulation within a computer-based platform. This presentation media has limited predefined launch and link switches or buttons. Hypermedia includes all the features of multimedia computing and provides full systematic interactive access about the

target, subject, and the topic from any point in any media to all other instances of information.

New Era Video, Inc. (NEVI)

New Era Video, Inc. (NEVI), in Miami, Florida, was founded in 1986. NEVI is a producer of hypermedia 'Surrogate Travel' programs. The programs are CD-ROM or Laserdisc based, highly interactive, and allow the user to transverse between an extensive number of 'layers' of information about the objects appearing on the screen. NEVI products are visually unique in that they provide extremely high quality presentations and offer more objects which can be targeted for additional information than are generally found in interactive programs. Technically, they are unique because producing these features requires highly efficient production and innovative processing of audio, video, and text. Among the products produced to date, which we will refer to throughout the case description, are *The Boliva Hypermedia Expedition*, NEVI's first project which was developed for demonstration purposes; *The NASA/Ames Mars Landing Site Data Retrieval System Video*, a project for which NASA commissioned NEVI to present topographical information about Mars' surface; and *The Coral Reef Hypermedia Expedition*, an elaborate surrogate travel experience of Florida's coral reefs which is just now nearing completion.

In the following sections, we will present (1) some background information about the events leading to NEVI's founding, (2) the underlying premises upon which NEVI operates, (3) a description of some of the successes and failures experienced during the company's start-up, (4) an overview of the procedures followed in developing products, (5) a more detailed description of the products produced, (6) a discussion of how NEVI goes about distributing its products, and (7) Michael Greenberg's goals for NEVI's future.

Company Background

Mr. Michael Greenberg might best be characterized as a 'budding genius.' He is the type of individual who, in his own words, "doesn't listen to people who say *it can't be done* or *I can't do it* because they don't think the same way I do." In fact, even though there is considerable disagreement about whether entrepreneurs truly possess unique traits, Greenberg demonstrates many of the characteristics typically associated with entrepreneurs: risk taking, achievement motivation, knowledge of 'state of the art' technology, perceptions of opportunity, and self-discipline and motivation (see Gartner, 1989).

Greenberg has always exhibited an interest and aptitude in the creative process. He studied science and cinematography at the University of Miami and UCLA, but also had an urge to experiment with alternate presentation media. By the middle-to-end of the 1980's, he had developed an interest in multimedia computing, especially hypermedia, long before there was any general awareness of the topic or before there were tools available to develop multimedia products. He decided

> ... just off the top of my head, with ideas I had formed over the years, on the spur of the moment, to go out and actually create a hypermedia movie map to recreate a location for other people to explore, and to document as much information as possible about it so that they could learn further about that location. I wanted to connect it with a number of different types of media. I had read an article in a video magazine by Russ Gant from MIT who had done an interactive video project on China. I called him out of the blue, and we had an excellent conversation. He suggested that the ideas I had come up with, specifically making movie maps in real time using special production tools, would enable streamlined production, and they could be connected to all other types of information based on visual representations in real space. Although he said no one had done the combination I was attempting to do, he said parts had been done, and certainly some of those things might be possible.

Finding someone who shared his ideas and enthusiasm served to increase Michael's own zeal and commitment.

> I called Russ back a little while later, and he asked me to come to MIT as his guest. Within the week, I was in Boston. It might seem a little impulsive, but I just had a feeling that it was the right thing to do. Anyway, I had some good conversations, and was able to see some of the projects they were involved with. A week after that, I went to an interactive videodisc conference to see what was going on. Not much, as it turned out. Your basic training kind of junk. No one was doing the kinds of things I wanted to do.

Nonetheless, it was at this conference that Greenberg had his first break.

I got a phone call from Russ at MIT and he said, *"We need you to go down to Colombia to shoot some materials for our Spanish Language Project."* This was for a project called *No Recuerdo* (Spanish for *I Don't Remember*) which was part of the Athena Language Learning Project headed by Janet Murray and Doug Morganstern.   It was intended as a university-wide implementation of state-of-the-art technologies to connect interactive multimedia databases and the courses offered. The idea of Project Athena was that the entire university would be connected so that people could communicate and share ideas and materials for learning and research. It was an interesting undertaking; rather than focusing on proven technologies, they made the choice to use leading technologies, with the assumption that in 10 years it would be inexpensive and readily attainable in the mass market. That was MIT's basic philosophy toward new technologies, or at least toward these projects.

Anyway, *No Recuerdo* was to be an interactive video-based narrative with documentary segments. A movie map. It was intended to recreate a situation where the storyline would change, depending on how well the student had learned their Spanish. They faxed me a list of 10 things and said that if I could do any of them, they would be happy. Nothing was pre-produced, nothing was planned, no script, and I had no crew. I told them to book me a ticket out of Miami. I was still in Los Angeles, but I took the next flight back to Miami. Within 24 hour of the phone call, I was on a plane from Miami to Colombia with nothing but the fax list and some ideas on how to implement them.

Greenberg's flexibility and creativity turned out to be his greatest assets in completing the assignment.

The story turned out to be about a microbiologist who discovered a microbe that causes amnesia. Beyond that, it was like a mystery which the students had to solve. If they applied their Spanish well, and used some thought, they could arrive at a solution. It appeared, for example, that the microbe had been lost, but it was possible that it had been stolen. It also wasn't clear if the microbe had affected the scientist, since he came off as absent-minded. There were a lot of subplots, too. His supposed girlfriend might be a terrorist, and as the story progresses, it's not clear if she kidnapped him, or if he's even missing, or lost, or dead. The idea was that the student had to ask a lot of questions and try and track him down. Depending on the questions asked, the story led to a number of different outcomes, or sometimes, dead-ends. The people of whom the questions were asked would also respond differently. For instance, if the student asked where a house was, the response given could either be, '*Oh, yes, it's over there, on that street, just turn left and ...*', or, '*What? What did you say?*', or, '*House? What is a house? I don't know anything. Leave me alone!*' I had to shoot at least three variations of every question. In four days, I shot 15 video tapes, some 4,000 pictures, and gathered much more than the 10 things they asked me to get. They were satisfied, and that gave me an opportunity to be at MIT as a guest, contractor, guest project director, or whatever you want to call it. The folks at the Center for Advanced Visual Studies were very helpful.

The shooting of *No Recuerdo* and working with others who shared his thoughts inspired Greenberg to take a more active role in shaping the products developed. The people at MIT who shared similar visions had given him considerable encouragement, and he felt more confident that he was on the right path. He wasted no time in embarking on his next venture.

Two weeks after the Colombia filming, I put all the equipment I had, which had never been used in combination before, and began *The Bolivia Hypermedia Expedition.* I had been filming in Boliva about a year earlier and I thought it was visually interesting, and it fit within the parameters of what I thought would make an interesting first example. I already had quite a bit of material about it. I also chose it because it was a difficult place to shoot. I didn't want people to say, '*Oh sure, you can do it there, but you can't do it at ...*' I wanted to do something difficult so that people would know that I could. I was also in a hurry. I had six free tickets to Bolivia from an airline, enough to fly me and some of my friends, who could act as my crew, to do this project. I decided, on the spur of the moment, with no pre-planning, to do an interactive moving map for museums based on the Witch's Market in La Paz. I thought the Witch's Market was perfect because they have all these little stalls of things for sale; all sorts of colorful textiles, herbal medicines and religious items. I personally have a love for these textiles, and there has not been much positive information printed about Bolivia lately, so I thought I could do something to change the image, and at the same time, I could practice the skills I needed to develop new products using these media. I had an idea for combining a number of them in a different manner, and I was anxious to try it out.

Although the behaviors which Greenberg demonstrated might be necessary in creative endeavors, from a business and operational sense, his impulsiveness could be counter-productive. His lack of planning had hurt his efforts.

There were a lot of problems with *The Bolivia Hypermedia Expedition.* I had chosen a place which was very unreceptive to photography; the people there just did not want their photos taken. Although some people took some time out to talk to me, most would give me a few minutes, at best, to photograph 50 or 100 items. Sometimes, they just started throwing things at me. There was a lot of conflicting information from the 'experts' on the area. Of the three major languages spoken there - Aymara, Quechua, and Spanish - only Spanish has any written history. The spelling and grammatical conventions for Aymara and Quechua had only recently been agreed upon, and therefore much of the information I received had different spellings in different reference materials. Some of the friends I brought along with me became sick from the altitude, and were of no real use to me. Some of the equipment didn't work, or at least it didn't work like I expected it to. Still, I was able to improvise and get everything working. I was carrying a 60 pound Steadycam, which really gives you a work-out. You need a special vest which connects to the Steadycam, so it is literally strapped onto your body on an articulating arm. It is intended for use in controlled environments; this was anything but a controlled environment. I had been certified to use it a few years earlier, but hadn't used it since. To make matters worse, I was walking up some extremely steep streets in The Witch's Market. I was shooting for long periods of time at altitudes of about 10,000 feet in steep, crowded, everyone pushing and shoving, traffic-congested, cobble-stone streets, with virtually no help, trying not to draw too much attention from the crowd. Additionally, it was winter, and the weather was very bad.

I sent the entire crew back after 10 days. I ended up staying a total of six weeks. All in all, I believe I shot about 10,000 pictures on location. I don't remember how many video and audio tapes I managed to put together, but there were a lot of them. All sorts of stereo recordings of music, different ceremonies, and interviews with people on the street. I also had volumes of notes I made. Comments, logs of the shots I took, time code numbers, exact numbers for the actual frames, and so forth. I had borrowed a portable computer from a friend of mine, and believe it or not, it was the first time I had ever used one. I used a database program to record the time codes.

In retrospect, maybe there were some things I would have done differently. Certainly in terms of researching the project beforehand, I would have done things differently. In terms of the actual shoot, however, there wasn't a lot of pre-planning I could have done. Because the combination of equipment I put together had never been tried before, the only way to really find out how it would work was just to go out and try it. Also, the whole concept was based on a dynamic design, so that it constantly changed as we shot it. As far as the amount of material I had collected, well, that was almost overwhelming. It took an enormous amount of organization and coordination. Even though I admittedly am not as well organized, in terms of work structure, as I would like, I make an effort to arrange all my materials in an categorical fashion. In this line of work, if you don't, you're really in trouble.

Small successes, especially in a highly uncertain environment, can be extremely encouraging. In spite of some of the setbacks, his initial attempts at developing an MMC product were successful enough to encourage him to set out on his own. After a brief return trip to Boston, he decided to start his own production company. Because he believed he needed a corporate structure to protect himself, he founded New Era Video, Inc. (NEVI), of which he was the sole stockholder.

NEVI's Foundations

As might be predicted from the *No Recuerdo* and *The Boliva Hypermedia Expedition* experiences, NEVI was initially created solely to develop educational programs which would offer leading-edge, discovery learning systems. Greenberg's vision was that the programs would recreate a reality experience, called "surrogate travel," using Hypercard and other hypermedia technology. The student would essentially set out on a self-exploration tour of a topic of interest to them, in real time. All the information one might wish to gather along the way would be available in a very knowledgeable, and accommodating, fashion. The media might suggest a direction toward certain points of interest, providing salient sounds and images, and even anecdotal experiences intended to pique the student's interest, but it was intended to be 'self-guided': the pace and direction of the actual tour was determined by the student. If interest was stimulated, the student could pause, and ask questions. For any given topic, comprehensive facts, details, and background associations would be made immediately available in the same engaging fashion as the tour itself.

While this might sound commonplace, it is the level of interaction, the amount of available supporting information, the general philosophy of self-guided exploration, and the manner in which the material is presented which differentiates NEVI's products from the rest of the market. NEVI's products are not reliant on 'buttons' to indicate that additional material for an object is available. As an object transverses the active window, there are clues, such as reverse video and highlighting, to let the user know that more information is available, but the aesthetic value of the presentation is not interrupted. To get further information, the user clicks the mouse on the object of interest and is taken to the next level of interaction.

The problem is the multidirectional seek and launch. If these objects are moving in real time, the trajectories and velocities have to be identified accurately and quickly. Because I provide a lot of objects which frequently overlap each other, the authoring language has to be relatively powerful. I also take into account user inaccuracies in mouse placement.

Because the products are comprehensive, the levels of interaction can be extensive. Aside from the coding complexity, storing information efficiently becomes a matter of considerable concern.

Providing a high quality product only serves to compound the problem.

> There are a lot of platform limitations. A Laserdisc might only hold 54,000 frames, a CD-ROM considerably less. The real trick is to put together the correct material using a combination of technology which makes full use available storage and minimizes retrieval time. There are a lot of tricks which can b⌐ applied here also. I can't tell you what they are, because that is what makes my products unique. I played around with ˋ lot of different combinations, and am still improving on them. However, I think what I've come up with is better than you will find in other products. I provide everything I can for a given presentation platform while simultaneously keeping a high level of sophistication. I can obviously provide more, say, with a Laserdisc than I can with a CD-ROM. I'm also aware that the technology will improve in the future. When it does, I'll be ready.

The philosophy of self-guided versus guided instruction corresponds to Greenberg's own style of learning, but can be troublesome also.

> If the exploration is completely nondirected, the user might never uncover all of the information. There has to be some structure provided, but I believe that exploratory, learning-based, surrogate travel will result in the users actually getting more out of the product because they become more involved. Also, from a home marketing perspective, if people buy this on their own, I don't believe they only want something which looks like a lecture. It has to be interesting *and* fun.

Essentially, it was Michael Greenberg's personal attitudes and experiences with the delivery of educational products, as well as his vision of the future of the educational system, which impelled him towards this specific niche in the hypermedia market. From the aspect of information delivery, no instructor could be expected to be an expert on all aspects of the subject matter they were teaching, nor could they always be expected to be at their 'best.' Similarly, not all instructors were created equal; regardless of individual knowledge, some were better presenters and could readily incite interest. More was also required of the student. Each year, more information was available, and students were expected to master the skills and tools of research as part of their basic education. While films, and later videotapes, as well as televised classroom lectures were all available, none of them offered the real advantage of interactive discussion which takes place in the classroom. With hypermedia, however, students could learn at their own rate, at a depth they felt comfortable at. They could ask all the questions they wished. Not only would they receive stock answers, as well as new and unexpected responses, but they would actually be exposed to additional surrogate travels. Hypermedia programs would allow students to learn advanced topics in ways that both mimic reality and prepare them for a career that will now take place in the global "information age." It also seemed intuitively logical to Greenberg that there would be an enormous demand for such products, especially as the price of the technology needed to present the information dropped. In this respect, even though he was acutely aware of consumer budgetary restrictions, he was guided by the MIT philosophy: Make sure that the products produced are ahead of the 'leading edge' so that when prototypical technologies become commonplace, the products would not become obsolete.

NEVI's Start-up

While Greenberg felt quite capable of managing the creative and production aspects for NEVI, his business experience was admittedly limited. With the help of some friends, one of whom was an industrial/video producer, he put together a promotional video based on *The Bolivia Hypermedia Expedition* to explain and demonstrate NEVI's concepts and philosophy. One acquaintance, John Simpson (not his real name), helped Greenberg promote the video, and convinced him that he needed his assistance. Given Greenberg's recognition of his own lack of organization, and Simpson's apparent business experience, Greenberg readily agreed.

One of Simpson's first actions was to seek out some specialized hardware, since much of the hardware which Greenberg envisioned was not commercially available. He contacted a company in California which had some IBM boards and were in the process of completing an authoring language. He convinced them to give NEVI the boards, at no cost, in order to promote their product. However, upon his arrival in Los Angeles, Greenberg was told that the boards would cost $1,300, and the authoring language would not be available for a few months. Nonetheless, Simpson convinced Greenberg that they should purchase the boards. The boards were never used, and the authoring language never completed in the time frame promised.

It was at this point in time that Greenberg began to suspect problems in his relationship with Simpson.

> That was the first big mistake I made. I needed help getting started, and I didn't know much about the business aspects, but I should have checked this guy out a little better. Simpson convinced me that he was a brilliant businessman and that he could accomplish all sorts of great things. He also convinced me that the products developed should not necessarily be associated with me, but should be viewed as NEVI's products. I should have taken more time to analyze what he was saying and why. But he was a very smooth talker. Extremely confident. He came off like he knew what he was talking about. My family and a lot of my friends saw through him. I should have listened to them.

Throughout the period, Greenberg sought out leading-edge technologies which he could use. After a prolonged period of trying to contact BIGCORP[2], Simpson finally arranged for the head of a BIGCORP group to view NEVI's promotional tape.

> This particular person was extremely happy with what he saw in the videotape. Apparently, BIGCORP had created a film called *The Information Pilot* which was an example of BIGCORP's vision for the future. They had gotten a lot of negative criticism about it, because most people thought it was pie-in-the-sky type stuff. I knew it wasn't. Apparently, this guy believed that a small company like us could create these highly interactive surrogate travel programs, and that we would prove to the critics that BIGCORP's vision was right on the mark. Also, they were about to release, or had just released *Mediacard*, and our products were good examples of how it could be used. Mediacard was not being used to even a fraction of its potential. The idea was that we would stretch the envelope and show how it could be improved, since we were doing things which were beyond its apparent capabilities at the time. Anyway, they asked *'What would it take for us to get you to make your projects using Mediacard?'* I thought about it for a minute, and said, *'If you can make up your mind in 48 hours and give me the hardware and the support necessary, I'll do it.'* So they did. That was how we got started with BIGCORP.

Unfortunately, the relationship with BIGCORP didn't work out as either envisioned.

The big mistake we made with BIGCORP was that we should not have contacted the particular group within BIGCORP that we did. There are units at BIGCORP which do just this sort of thing, but this wasn't one of them. Again, this was mostly due to Simpson, who should have known, but obviously didn't even investigate their corporate structure. There are units at this company that truly are interested in helping individuals. However, the group we were working with was interested primarily in advancing their own platform by distributing the software we created. They really didn't care about what we were trying to do. We could have gotten better support from some of BIGCORP's other areas. In fact we got most of our financial and hardware support from their Latin American Division. They were very helpful.

Another big mistake we made was letting one of the programmers from that group into our lab without signing a nondisclosure agreement. I showed him the ideas and parameters I had come up with for targeting of moving objects, regardless of object velocity or direction. He went back with the ideas, and a little while later BIGCORP claimed the design was theirs. Foolish mistake. I knew non-disclosure forms were standard in the business, but once again, I assumed that Simpson had obtained them. I guess he thought I had obtained them. I later sent BIGCORP the non-disclosure forms, but they weren't interested in signing them. Their reasoning was that it would slow down the entire process because every interaction would have to be approved by their legal staff, and then by ours, and the creative process would be mired-down in bureaucracy. Part of that is true, but it's a necessary evil.

The contract they previously sent us, ready for signing, said nothing about them owning the code we created. All of a sudden, they sent another set of contracts, involving all sorts of things they had taken out of our labs. It was a real mess, and it was never properly straightened out, and ultimately, we severed our relationship with BIGCORP. We got to keep the equipment. *Big Deal*. It was an incompetent business move. If I had contacted the right group there, their User

Support Group is really interested in helping people like me, I might still be working with them.

I have no relationship with BIGCORP, whatsoever, anymore. I was a certified developer for them for a while. The original agreement was that they would give me all the equipment and technical support I needed to create *The Bolivia Hypermedia Expedition* in Mediacard. In return, they would get the rights to demonstrate the project in Latin America. They owned none of it - none of the visuals, none of the code. Not being a certified developer anymore is a problem. Still, I can generally get what I need.

Although BIGCORP was NEVI's most important contact, it was not their only one.

Simpson had also contacted ANOTHERBIGCORP[3], and talked to some marketing guy. Some new guy, who, I don't think, knew an awful lot. According to Simpson, ANOTHER-BIGCORP would give us $50,000, in either products or cash, as well as some hardware and technical support, to use their new authoring tool and computer to work on the Coral Reef project. In return, when the product was delivered, we would give them one year exclusivity, meaning that the product would be available only on their platform for that period of time. I thought we had all of this in writing. Well, this is when one of my contractors called me and said he hadn't been paid. I immediately figured out exactly what had happened, and within 20 minutes, I locked up the entire operation. I contacted the people at ANOTHERBIGCORP, and they told me that the $50,000 agreement was for a loan, and not a grant. I wanted to get this thing straightened out right then and there, so I asked them to send me what they had in writing. It turns out that Simpson had never gotten anything from them in writing. I asked them if they would send me two tickets, one for me and one for the programmer. They said that ANOTHERBIGCORP's policy was never to supply airfare for 'vendors.' Well, at this point, I should have seen the handwriting on the wall. If they weren't willing to send us two measly airline tickets, then something was terribly wrong. Still, and I guess this was also not the smartest thing to do, I went out and purchased two airline tickets to go see them. Needless to say, things just didn't work out with ANOTHERBIGCORP.

It was only then that Greenberg discovered the true extent of his misjudgment in relying on Simpson.

> He completely misrepresented my business. I found that he submitted various copyright forms and hid me in the background and made it appear that he was the creative force behind the products we were producing. People thought that NEVI was Simpson's creation instead of Michael Greenberg's. He created five or six new companies in the time he was with me. I foolishly allowed him to take control of the finances and represent the business while I was doing the work. I had essentially given up a lot of control over NEVI. I found out that he had put together a company called *General Interactive Communications*, of which he was the CEO and President, and I was a minor stockholder. He had been double naming corporations so he could claim credit for all of it. He sent me all sorts of agreements that he drafted. Well, I'm not a lawyer, but I read these papers and I understood instantly that he would still be in charge. I spent about $3,000 trying to get him to be reasonable about things. No luck. His lawyer even tried to get me to pay for his legal fees.

> Well, the man had chutzpa. When he finally left, he just looked at me and shrugged, '*Well, you gave me the power to do it.*' That I did.

> I know that my strengths are in creating products, and I had no experience in dealing with these sort of things. I might not be the best person to negotiate contracts, but I've learned that's what lawyers are for. I've also learned that I can set up basic business deals myself, and I'm not about to get involved with anyone in a partnership unless they can contribute as much as they take out. If they are not capable of exceeding expectations, they don't belong in business with you. I've learned a lot from my mistakes.

Aside from learning to be more selective when choosing business associates and relying solely on his instincts, Greenberg admits that there are a number of other actions he might have taken, from both a strategic and operational perspective.

> First, I would be more selective in the commercial prospects

for the projects I chose to undertake. *The Bolivia Hypermedia Expedition*, even though I thought it was interesting, turned out to be too involved for an initial product. The museum market turned out to be terrible. The project was far too expensive for such a limited market. Whenever you start out, you need to choose a project which can at least bring in enough money to keep you going. This was not it. That's not to say this type of project shouldn't be done. I still have this commitment to educational programs, and I'm not out to make a killing, but I have to make enough to survive. If I simply add up the cost of filming and supplies, *The Bolivia Hypermedia Expedition* might not seem too expensive. But once you add up all the time spent in developing it, the lost income I could have been making, the cost of having to pay others to help, and the amount of money I could sell it for, it was just too expensive. *The Coral Reef Expedition* will cost considerably more to develop than the $50,000 which ANOTHERBIGCORP agreed to *loan* us. I need a way to make a fair amount of profit and then I could almost give the product away to educational institutions.

Another big mistake I made was not being more organized. Even though I have always done things on the spur of the moment, I found that it just doesn't work well in business. I would do a lot more investigation and planning. I could have avoided a lot of the problems I faced in Bolivia if I had researched the location and planned out, in advance, the topics I wanted to include. I wouldn't have gone there in the winter. I would set deadlines for myself. Short term deadlines that I could realistically aim for. I would also manage my time better. I would focus on the activities necessary to meet those deadlines, and I would try to avoid distractions. That may not be easy, but once you set your mind to it, it can be done.

I've also learned not to try and re-invent the wheel. I used to try and create custom software tools and do all the coding in house, even though there were tools available which could have met my needs. I would focus on the product itself, and not the tools necessary to develop the product. Although I think I am a natural programmer, it's not really what I like doing. I like the creative aspects. For me, the computer is just a wonderful tool that lets me accomplish these great things and organize maximum amounts of material. I'm in the business of producing products and not tools.

The Development Process

As might be expected in a creative industry with a limited number of competing firms, especially one depending upon the efforts of a few 'non-traditional businessmen', there exists an informal 'creativity network' of entrepreneurs and academicians who share a common interest in MMC. Starting with the relationships he developed at MIT and BIGCORP and expanded by contacts made along the way, a forum for new ideas has been developed. The network constantly expands as entrepreneurs with similar interests enter the market. Compuserve and Applelink have also provided a platform for discussion of new ideas, introducing interested individuals to one another, and sharing solutions to problems. Network participants act as sounding boards; when a new idea is presented, the others offer advice, suggest modifications, act as devil's advocates, indicate additional contacts, or simply offer support.

Procedurally, Greenberg has changed the manner in which he approaches a product.

When I get an idea, I am much more concerned with who will be interested in the product. That doesn't mean that I have 'sold-out.' There are enough topics that I am interested in and which a lot of people would be interested in buying. I try and focus on those. I am also much more organized in the way I approach a shooting. I don't just go out and create everything off-the-cuff, stringing everything together as I create. I have developed a set of procedures which I try to adhere to when developing products. First, I have to have a good idea of the product intent. By that, I mean what the delivery mechanism will be. Will it be CD-ROM, Laserdisc, or what? This will have a great impact on the scope of the project. Even with the techniques I have developed for information compression, there is only so much that can be included on a CD-ROM.

Next, I concern myself with the spatial dimensions of the project. Aside from the technical limitations, I have to be concerned with the degree of subject coverage and level of detail which I can provide. If I were to do a project on, say refrigerators, well, obviously, that's very simple. Everything is already compartmentalized, there is a lot of technical information available, and I could probably cover everything, right down to the schematics of it. Something like the Amazon Rain Forests, well, that is an entirely different ballgame. Just think of the composition: there are almost countless levels of different forms of life, geographical strata, political implications, etc. You would have to do a whole series on it, and even then, there is always the doubt of whether everything was covered.

Thirdly, I have to break it down in terms of how it will be physically mapped out. This is the start of the planning stages, and I have learned the importance of good planning, in spite of the fact that I still do some things on the spur of the moment. Solid planning can save a lot of time in the long run, however. I work in a top-down fashion, so that I try to identify the major components, and then decompose each one of those until I reach some extremely simplistic level, where further explanation becomes trivial. If I can visualize the basic components, and how they all might fit together, I go onto the next step, which is finding out what reference and supporting material is available and if it can be used. By that I mean copyrights. There is a lot of public domain information available, although the quality is not guaranteed. There is also a lot of copyrighted material for which permission can be obtained at no cost, or very little cost. This also gives me an idea of what sources of information I must create on my own. If it is not too overwhelming, I will go on, but I can't afford to put so much time into tangential sources that it interferes with the delivery of the product.

Finally, I get into the development stages. I tend to develop quite a few intermediate prototypes before I actually deliver the final product. I develop a prototype, test it, refine it, show it, refine, and so forth. There is no set number of revisions, but I will keep going through the process until I feel comfortable with it. In between, I spend a lot of time reviewing the materials I am using, collecting more as needed, replacing it with better material, modifying it as necessary, and recreating if it doesn't meet my expectations. This whole area is the one which I am in the process of automating. Information collection and presentation. It can be very time consuming if you have to start from scratch with each project. You should note, however, that when I say automate, that doesn't mean that I give a 'mechanical' feel to my products. I will not compromise the quality of them. For that reason, it has taken me a lot longer to develop automation procedures and tools.

Again, I can't tell you all the details, because this is what gives me an edge in the market.

One thing I have learned in this testing process is not to limit your tests to the intended market. For example, if I had only tested *The Coral Reef Expedition* on divers, I would have lost out on a large portion of the potential customers. True, I might have been able to complete the project in a shorter period of time. But I don't think that narrowing the focus would save all that much time, and I certainly would not have as good an overall project.

I am also very concerned with the end user of the product. I consider the limitations of their hardware, based on what is generally available, because I don't want them to have to go out and purchase new equipment. Knowing the platform that the product will be used on helps me determine how I will put the material together. Then, working backwards, I can fit the material in the most compact and easily accessible fashion. In this way, I can present the material as flexibly as possible. This is important because it is an interactive product, and the combinations of ways in which the user can manipulate it are almost endless. However, I am also very aware that the technology is improving, and what is available today may be obsolete tomorrow, or, more to the point, tomorrow's equipment will be much more powerful than what is available today. I try to capture more information than people can access right now, say, using a CD-ROM, so that I can later deliver a more robust product as the technology advances.

If I am working for a corporate customer, on a project which they specify, I tend to put in a little more effort than is required to merely meet their demands. In other words, I give them a little more than they ask for. I do this for two reasons: One, I have an image which I not only want to protect, but also enhance. Two, because it provides me with the opportunity to gather information which I can use in later projects. That doesn't mean that I am going to take the product I make for them, reshape it, and sell it to their competitors. There are certain ethics which must be maintained. But it is possible that in the future I can use some of the material for different purposes in different settings and on different platforms.

One of the good things about *The Bolivia Hypermedia Expedition* was it resulted in a lot of R&D which I don't have to go through now. I'm a lot more automated as a result of it. A lot of the designs for targeting moving objects came about as a result of that project. I also use a lot of commercially available hypertechnology entry tools now, in line with the concept of using what is available, and not recreating the wheel. These are presentation tools which allow people to capture interactive entries in the database and present them, re-editing them and reordering them at will according to their presentation needs. One of the things I am proud of is that I stretched the "Mediacard" envelope, the actual working environment, making it work in full screen, wide screen, and touch screen environments.

The Products Produced

NEVI's first product, *The Bolivia Hypermedia Expedition* was never made commercially available. However, since its main purpose was to act as a demonstration of NEVI's capabilities, it can be considered successful. As a result of it, Greenberg has been contacted by a number of individuals and organizations who have been interested in pursuing other projects.

Greenberg is justifiably hesitant about publicizing a list of companies for which he has done work, but he is willing to mention a few organizations for illustrative purposes.

There have been quite a few projects we were contracted for. About five in the past two and one-half years. One interesting one, which came about as a direct result of some of the people who had seen *The Bolivia Hypermedia Expedition*, was a contract for *The NASA/AMES Mars Landing Site Data Retrieval System Video*. NASA had gathered a considerable amount of data on Mars' landing sites. The main problem they had was that they hadn't connected it all together in a medium which would allow for quick retrieval and comparison of information. After seeing what was possible, they contacted me and I went and gave them an overview of some of the things that might be done.

There have also been such projects as a series of movie maps in India and the Florida Keys. Greenberg has tried to develop relationships with corporate clients which would be mutually beneficial to both: the clients pay for a project which they need and

Greenberg develops material which can be used in later, unrelated, projects. As we shall discuss in the following section, Greenberg has been extremely cautious when negotiating these contracts.

> I want to give the companies a product they can use, but I will not give them total rights to the product. In other words, I give them a product which they are free to use for the intended purposes, but I still own the original pictures, sound, and technology which went into it. They can't take anything out of it and reconstruct it for some other purpose or project.

Since *The Bolivia Hypermedia Expedition*, the most involved and time consuming project has been *The Coral Reef Expedition*, which is just now becoming available. Greenberg has tried to overcome some of the obstacles and shortcomings experienced with the Bolivia Project. First, he decided on a topic about which there is considerable reference material already available: coral reefs. Essentially, he put into practice the developmental procedures described in the previous section. Prior to beginning any actual shooting, he gathered as much information as he could and laid out a shooting script of the topics he would cover, making sure that the necessary supporting documentation was available. Another major consideration was who would purchase the product. Having seen that the museum market could not support a venture with the scope of the Bolivia Expedition, Greenberg focused on a project which was directed at a wider audience. *The Coral Reef Expedition* is directed towards the education and home market.

The *Coral Reef Expedition* provides rich video, photos, sound, and information on a topic of concern to ocean scientists, ichthyologists, botanists, geologists, ecologically oriented groups, naturalists, and sportsmen. The market, while diverse, is thus relatively vast. It is intended to incorporate parts of Greenberg's visions of Hypermedia products, and to incorporate all of the refinements he has made along the way. Using video as the primary vehicle, the user becomes a diver through part of a Florida coral reef, the only coral reefs remaining in North America. The reefs have an abundance of coral, plants and animals[4], many of which are visually existent at any given moment. The project typifies Greenberg's achievements to date. Fish swim in schools or individually in front of, or behind, overlapping coral reef formations and aquatic plant life. Considering that each fish, plant, rock formation, and animal form is an object, each viewed in different trajectories, directions, and velocities, the amount of definition required is staggering. Although there are delivery medium constraints, the product attempts to allow as many of these objects to be targeted as possible. The level of decomposition is correspondingly complex. While there is an abundance of related reference material available, this too can present problems. Attempting to integrate all of the material causes a number of logistical and organizational problems. The dilemma is only partially solved by employing Greenberg's proprietary combination of techniques. The organization of materials, manner of presentation, level of quality, abstraction level, and inclusion of invisible buttons becomes of paramount concern.

> *The Coral Reef Expedition* is important, not only because it represents my most significant product to date, but also because it lays the foundation for the materials I want to present in the future. If you ask me about it five years from now, I'm sure I'll have a lot of regrets about it. Still, given the level of technology available today, it sets the tone of the products I am producing, the tone of the products I will produce in the future, and, although this is probably not apparent to the users, has established a lot of the groundwork for the way I will produce products later.

The Distribution of NEVI's Products

Michael Greenberg has no intention of attempting to distribute his products directly, at least not within the foreseeable future. Even though MMC is a relatively new industry, there are already a number of distributors in place. While there are some larger, better known organizations, such as IBM, Apple, EduCorp, Optical Data Corporation, Voyager, and New Media Source, the majority are small, regional companies.

The MMC market, given the limited number of competing producers and proportionately large number of distributors, is a seller's (i.e., creator's) market, at least for the time being. This advantage is magnified if the products produced are viewed as high-quality.

> Everyone I have ever spoken to about distributing my products, especially if they have actually seen them, has been very interested. The real attraction has been the high-quality of the workmanship, and the degree of interaction surpasses that anything else available. I think I also have a real advantage because no one else is doing surrogate travel using the same Hypermedia platforms. Basically, everyone is interested in distributing the products. Picking the right distribu-

tors is simply a matter of cutting the right deals with the right people. I keep an eye on standard industry contracts, and make sure that I do better. Given the quality of the material I produce, especially compared to the rest of the market, I don't anticipate major problems negotiating contracts.

In choosing distributors, there is a distinct trade-off between the size of the distributor, and the per unit profit. Larger distributors may demand a larger percentage of gross sales. But because of their wider distribution channels and greater promotional expenses, they sell considerably more units. The net result is increased profits to the distributor. Nonetheless, in choosing a distributor, Greenberg is careful not to be swayed by exaggerated sales projections.

A lot of these distributors offer projections of sales which are unrealistic. They also conveniently forget to indicate how many complimentary copies will be shipped, how long it will take to meet their sales projections, and what kind of discounts might be available.

One additional alternative available to developers is 'bundling.' Under this arrangement, the producer's product is sold along with other products 'as a bundle', with the price for the entire group typically being considerably less than the sum total of the individual products. Accordingly, the price paid to the producer is less than that which might be obtained if sold separately, but, as with larger distributors, the number of units shipped is considerably larger. An additional advantage of this approach is that the product can reach audiences which might not otherwise purchase the product.

There is one extremely significant caveat which Greenberg offers when dealing with distributors: be careful about ownership rights.

I'm lucky because I learned about ownership rights a long time ago. My parents are entrepreneurs, and neither of them would ever relinquish the copyrights to the products they have produced. I grew up with the belief that you should own what you create. I have seen what can happen if you don't. Some of these distributors, and suppliers, appear to be giving you a good deal if you sell them the products outright. Inexperienced producers sometimes jump at the chance, or they are tricked into signing away the rights to their products. What they don't realize is that when they do, their products can be used in ways they never intended or wanted.

Advertisements, photos taken out of context, all sorts of unintended outcomes. A lot of future profits lost. Unfortunately, that is happening a lot. Quite a few very large, very well endowed corporations, companies which everyone knows, have gotten into this market. A lot of stock photo agencies. It's amazing. They go out and purchase entire libraries of materials, sometimes from large, highly regarded organizations, and tie up distribution. What this means is that they own the rights to every picture, every original image, word, and sound which has been produced. Then, they present it in the most commercially successful format, which might not be the original format on which it was produced, and the end result is that they can be of lower quality. As the technology improves, they might increase the quality, but in the mean time, they reap profits from shoddy workmanship, and the creator gets nothing. I won't mention the names of any of these companies, but the newspapers and magazines are full of stories about them.

For the same reason, Greenberg prefers dealing with multiple distributors. He has never entered into a sole distributor relationship, nor has he any intention of doing so.

Once you sign an agreement for exclusive distributorship, you are signing away your profits. The distributor is under no pressure to sell your product, and basically knows that you are helpless to do anything about it. If they want, they could come back to you and say something along the lines of *'Well, we're having trouble selling your product at this price. We can't afford to sell it for less because of the agreement we have with you, but if we could rewrite it so that we could make a little profit on it ...'* Essentially, they've got you.

Maintaining ownership control may seem like a difficult task, but in fact, given the industry structure, is actually extremely easy. The simple solution is for the developer to manufacture the products they create themselves.

People are amazed when I tell them how much it actually costs to produce the products. After I put together all the material, I have someone produce the master. A master CD-ROM costs about $1,000 to $2,000 to produce. A Laserdisc, well, between $1,200 and $3,400. It costs about $2.00 to

$2.50 to produce each CD-ROM, and about $8.00 to $12.00 for a Laserdisc. This usually includes all of the post-developmental production costs, including the cases, the reproduction of the art work for the cover, which I create myself, the shrink-wrapping, everything. Often, I think, you'll have to check this with the pressers, even the product fulfillment, which means they will fill the orders. I think that some of these pressers will even provide you with an 800 number for orders. Unbelievable. It's just really inexpensive when you consider what you've got to gain.

As a result, Greenberg maintains ownership and product integrity. Contract negotiation consists of the distributors' placing an order for a fixed number at a fixed price. As noted previously, the trade-off is in terms of order size and unit price. Typically, each order by the distributor requires a deposit, which is usually enough to pay the production costs.

Distributor deposits require a little bit of attention. You have to be careful not to get tied into a C.O.D. type relationship, and to pay special attention to the terms of payment. Sixty days can be a long time. Agreements can be worked out with the pressers, but still, you don't want to get into a situation where you can't pay them, or have to dig into your own pockets to pay them. I think it is very important to keep a good relationship with the manufacturer. They appreciate it, and will make sure to give you good service in the future.

Because Greenberg is very concerned with the end user, the purchasers of his product, he also considers the retail price for his products. His interest comes from his concern for eventual sales and the public's perception of his products.

I keep an eye on the prices of hypermedia products, and try and sell my products for slightly less. For example, I have seen some of these travelogue type things, which, by the way, tend to be mediocre at best, and know that they are selling for about $50 to $120 on a CD-ROM platform. I expect the initial offering for *The Coral Reef Expedition* to retail at about $100. You really shouldn't quote me on this; I'm not sure. However, because I am still interested in education, there may be considerable discounting to educational institutions and other non-profit institutions.

While not presently interested in self-distribution, Greenberg will nonetheless accept the direct orders which come in unsolicited. Because many distributors in this area do not heavily promote their goods, the number of requests coming directly from customers is larger than might normally be expected.

> Some people will see my products and, since I don't have a sole distributor, and my products still aren't generally available off-the-shelf in retail outlets, they will contact me directly. The expense involved in selling directly is quite small, and so I can afford to sell wholesale. Almost wholesale. Because I am dealing with very small quantities, it isn't worth my time to sell at the same price I sell it to distributors for. If the number of direct orders were to increase to the point where it interfered with operations, I have no problems with either hiring someone to take the orders, or to contract out one of these order acceptance firms with an 800 number.

NEVI's Plans for the Future

While Greenberg is still committed to producing 'state-of-the-art' surrogate travel projects, his experiences with small markets have made him wary. He intends to keep his focus on the larger, more profitable, home market. In order to achieve this goal, however, he needs to restructure his production processes and develop the automated technologies necessary for mass production. He has been working toward this end for some time, and believes that he has a number of mechanisms already in place.

> I'm not quite at that point yet, but I'm getting close. I already have established procedures for assuring intensity and quality of video presentation. In other words, I can already analyze the lighting available, and have a good idea of the range of brightness required for a given series. Maintaining that range across the entire set of frames is not that difficult. I also have in place a library of tools which will help me in the construction and editing of products. I expect that within the next few years, I will have everything in place to actively enter the home market with a number of products, and to be able to mass produce a number of new titles each year.

Until that time, he intends to keep a relatively low profile.

While not at all shy, he is well aware of the problems associated with premature exposure. Correspondingly, the benefits of promotion have not been lost on him.

> When I do go public, you will know about it. I expect to do everything I can to garner as much national attention as possible. Television, magazine, trade publications, and demonstrations to all the movers and shakers. My goal is to lead the market in this area.

How Far Has NEVI Come?

While not a dominating force in the MMC industry, NEVI has managed to get its foot in the door. In many respects, NEVI's present operating position corresponds to the stage of development of the MMC industry as a whole. Specifically, within the Technology Life Cycle (TLC) (Ford and Ryan, 1981), both might be classified in the Application Launch Stage, where there is a commitment to, and initial distribution of, newly developed products. According to this framework (see Figure 1), technological applications can be characterized along a useful life span much in the same manner as the products produced are. The stages included in this model are discussed in the following sections.

Technological Development

The initial stage of the TLC begins prior to any real production of applications. At this point in time, it has become clear that a potentially valuable technology exists, but is in need of further research and development. Actual product production and subsequent sales, if any, are marginal at best. The vast majority of effort exerted is in finding new ways in which to apply the technology. In NEVI's case, Greenberg's experiments with *No Recuerdo* and initially with *The Bolivia Hypermedia Expedition* represent typical examples of the work done during this stage. The major consideration is whether or not to continue with the project, since the rate of return may be difficult to estimate, investment returns are generally not immediately foreseeable, and the cost of funding tends to be high, as are the risks of success. Should a company continue its efforts, however, the benefits may be substantial. Initial market entries tend to show high profitability at a later period, assuming the industry progresses, and can position the developer as the major force within that segment.

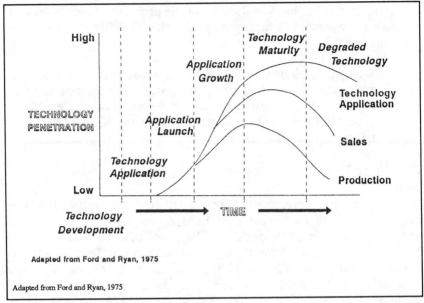

Figure 1: The Technology Life Cycle

It is in this stage of the life cycle that one typically witnesses the greatest number of entrepreneurs and innovators. In established companies, the bureaucracy through which such decisions must pass not only increases the time required before a project can be initiated, but tends to emphasize costs over potential benefits. This might explain why many of the more familiar names in computer and software development are missing from the list of prominent producers. Entrepreneurs, and especially individualists such as Michael Greenberg, seem to take a completely opposite viewpoint, and are more willing to put off immediate gains for long term returns.

Technology Application

This stage begins when a company decides to apply the new technology to a new product. The stage thus indicates a commitment to the product, and correspondingly, generally requires a substantial commitment of capital.

Typically, at this point in time, a number of new organizations emerge into the forefront and, correspondingly, a number of product ideas and individual entrepreneurs fall by the wayside. We have witnessed the emergence of a number of companies, such as Optical Data Corporation and New Media Source, which established themselves in the Technology Development stage. Larger corporations, with few exceptions, are generally not found in the forefront of the industry. As Nabseth and Ray (1974) note, few stockholders of a public corporation will encourage the development of technology that at the outset involves high costs and risks. However, the embodiment of technology into products which involve associated process and product technology costs may necessitate involvement in the emerging technology through either licensing or on a risk-bearing basis (Ford and Ryan, 1981). For example, development of the European Airbus occurred because the costs and risks could be shared by a consortium which included such companies as British Aerospace. Ethernet involved the cooperation of Xerox, Digital Equipment and Intel, all of whom made special arrangements which allowed other manufacturers to license their network system as a way of encouraging use of their protocols and equipment. In MMC, Apple's Hypercard, a preferred tool by many developers, has impelled Apple's entry into the market.

For the individual entrepreneur, the cost of commitment may be overwhelming, especially in industries requiring mass production. As with larger, better established firms, the entrepreneur must also seek out partners, license agreements, or simply sell the technology to the highest bidder. A number of corporations have profited handsomely as a result of the technologies they have purchased from inventors. In some cases the entrepreneur who has held onto product control has prospered. Ray Dolby (see Ford and Ryan, 1981, for a more detailed accounting) initially sought to sell his noise reduction technology for tape equipment to the professional electronics industry. Because of the smallness of the industry at the time, however, he found that any attempt to offer licensing agreements would not justify his investment in product development to date. However, also because of the smallness of the industry, he was able to market his product without enormous investment and without attracting the attention of large rivals. After establishing his reputation, he was later able to position himself well when he entered the mass market for consumer tape-recording equipment. In the MMC industry, we are presently seeing a number of organizations who are also positioning themselves for future possibilities. SONY and Microsoft, for example, have been cited as purchasing multimedia materials from smaller organizations and entrepreneurs, and developing libraries of material.

As we have seen, NEVI has been able to apply the MMC technology to a variety of applications because the transfer costs are relatively small. However, commitment to product development implies much more than mere production costs. A considerable investment in equipment, supplies, and most significantly, time, is required. Given the lack of revenues, Greenberg has accepted a number of side-projects in order to meet expenses. This has delayed the production of new products accordingly.

Application Launch

At this stage, the competing firms are maximizing performance by further developing the technology, either through product modification or through additional or wider ranging applications (Abernathy and Utterback, 1975). This stage might best characterize the present state of the MMC industry. There are a number of factors which may inhibit company growth or even survival. If there are not enough firms in the market with the skill to employ the technology properly, the premature sale of licenses could easily damage the reputation of the technology. Secondly, unproven technologies tend to be suspect, and initial sales are often slow. Thirdly, new technologies frequently require changes in purchaser behavior. Even if the new technology is intuitively superior, such as bar-coding of goods for sale, there may be initial user reluctance and even resistance. Finally, new technologies may require additional investments in associated products, which may be more costly than the original technology. The purchase price of a CD player, for example, even though approaching acceptability, may be beyond the consumer's budgetary limits.

The MMC industry appears to finds itself in a similar situation. There are a limited number of firms with qualified individuals who can fully take advantage of all available technologies. While the technologies which drive MMC applications are not necessarily new, there seems to be consumer reluctance to commit to those applications available. Perhaps the memory of how PCs have evolved, for example the relatively rapid progression of 286-based computers from 'leading-edge' to virtual obsolescence, has served to heighten suspicions that there are newer technologies right around the corner which will replace existing ones, or that the price of MMC systems will decrease as the capability increases concurrently.

NEVI's particular niche within the MMC market also appears to be lagging some of the other applications, such as games and encyclopedias. For example, in a recent issue of *PC Sources* (March, 1993), there were 23 advertisers of CD-ROM titles. In contrast, there were 42 software utilities advertisers. However, perhaps as an omen of future trends, there were 35 advertisers in the section labelled *Video/Audio/Multimedia Equipment.* While obviously not statisti-

cally valid assessment, a quick perusal of the advertisements is informative: of the 23 advertisers, only 10 provided a list of offerings[5]. Approximately 120 titles were uniquely identified, of which approximately 25% of these could be categorized as reference materials (e.g., *Grolier's Encyclopedia, The Guiness Book of World Records*), 15% as games (e.g., *Chessmaster, King's Quest, CD Games*), 12% Books (e.g., *Shakespeare on CD-ROM, Bedtime Stories*), 10% as Atlases/Almanacs (e.g., *U.S. & World Atlas, Sport's Illustrated Almanac*), 10% as Development tools, 10% as Software transferred from disk format (e.g., *Windows*), and about 5% as instructional software (e.g., *Playing with Languages/Spanish*). Although a number of these offer interactive capabilities, only six could clearly be identified as such (e.g., Interactive Stories), and only one clearly identified itself as a travelogue. As might be expected, the vast majority of titles were available from multiple suppliers. The prices of the titles varied from $25 to $949, with a median price of approximately $59.

Indicative of the stage of development is the manner in which most of these titles are sold. While available individually, most are also available at a discount as part of a bundle. Typically, these packages appear to have one or two readily recognizable names, such as the *U.S. & World Atlas*, listed at the top of the bundle, with a larger number of more obscure titles following. Additionally, especially for those advertisers whose primary product is hardware, the bundles or individual packages are given away free, or at greatly reduced prices with the purchase of the hardware. While the prices paid to the developers is not known, it seems reasonable to assume that they are minimal. The main advantage to the developer, as noted previously, is that their products reach customers which they might not otherwise reach.

Application Growth

This stage, as well as the two stages which follow, are included for the sake of completeness. The MMC industry has not reached a period of expansion, although it is conceivable that it will be entering the first of these remaining stages in the relatively near future.

The Application Growth Stage corresponds to Abernathy's and Utterback's (1975) "sales maximization" phase. In contrast to the previous stages, the tendency is towards increased sales and decreased costs. Since competitors prefer to avoid the costs of developing alternative technologies, the market value of the original technology is at its maximum. For the originating company, the improving sales, coupled with their competitor's evident desire for the technology dissuades them from selling the technology. As Ford and Ryan suggest, the critical issue involved in this stage is *timing*. While there is a fear of not taking full advantage of customer demand, there is a concurrent risk of not capitalizing on technology value. If the sale of the technology is delayed until later in the TLC, the value can drastically decrease because of lessened customer interest and development of alternative and perhaps improved technologies by competitors. Firms must make a number of decisions at this point in time based on market size, technological leadership, and degree of standardization.

A. *Market Size.* If the originating company is unable to penetrate a wider market, either because lack of personnel, expertise, or capital, sale or licensing of the technology might be advisable. Should a smaller organization fail to fully take advantage of the profits to be made, it is almost inevitable that larger, better endowed organizations will, and in doing so, weaken or eliminate the originating company.

B. *Technological Leadership.* The originating company must assess whether its strengths are in the development of new ideas or the reduction of old ideas to practical implementation (Ansoff and Stewart, 1967). Should the company share its technology, it might better maintain its leadership position, or perhaps position itself as a leader in a newer technologically-based industry, by investing some of its additional revenues in further research and development. It is also possible that by selling its technology to competitors, it can delay the development of newer, alternative technologies. This becomes a very tricky assessment with respect to MMC products, since their livelihood is in large measure dependent upon related technologies.

C. *Degree of Standardization.* As has generally been the case in technologically-based industries, after the innovations have been accepted by the customer, there is a demand for product standardization, either from within the industry or by governmental decree. The developer has a clear cut edge; the first product on the market *is* typically the standard. The sale of licenses can help in assuring that its design will be incorporated into other's products, and hence assure royalties, which might offset, or even surpass, the profits from proprietary sales. The developer needs to be cautious, however, in pricing and royalty demands, or competitors will be tempted to develop alternative technologies.

Technological Maturity

Sooner or later, every 'leading-edge' technology will approach obsolescence, if not literally, then figuratively. Through modifications and improvements, either by the originator or its competitors, the emphasis will shift toward cost minimization as a means of protecting profit margins. Production levels tend to level as the overall market stabilizes. New markets will depend on technological transfers to developing countries, typically on the basis of standardized turnkey deals. The original developer must consider the impact such transfers could have on their own manufacturing efforts, as illustrated by the competition the Italian automobile manufacturer Fiat faces in Western Europe as a result of its decision to license its automobile manufacturing processes to Eastern European countries (Ford and Ryan, 1975).

Degraded Technology

The final stage in the TLC occurs as exploitation of the technology reaches universal status. Licensing agreements have probably expired, and the technology itself has likely been supplanted by newer technologies. The innovations' most likely strategies are to 'milk' the technology, if possible, sell the technology to third world countries where the technology may still have some value, or retreat from the market entirely.

What Does NEVI's Future Look Like?

Obviously, no one can predict the future with any real accuracy. If the past is any indicator of the future, however, a few patterns have been identified which might be applicable. Porter (1980) has developed a model of technology and industry structure which assumes that there are five fundamental competitive forces which collectively determine the ability of firms to profit within industry (see Figure 2). The forces are:

• *Rivalry among Incumbent Competitors.* As we have already seen, the MMC Industry might best be characterized as an emerging or application launch industry. Accordingly, the industry structure is not well established nor can well defined rivalries among existing competitors be identified. Given a market with a considerable number of creatively oriented entrepreneurs such as Michael Greenberg, a spirit of cooperation, the 'creativity network' described

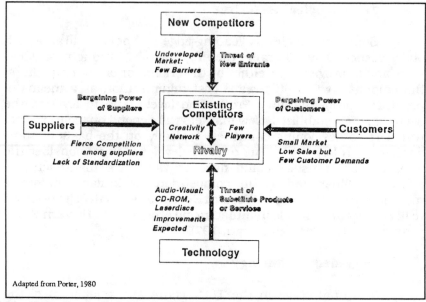

Figure 2: Forces Driving the MMC Industry

earlier, had been commonplace. However, as the industry evolves, total revenues and profit margins increase, and additional larger corporations enter the marketplace, we can expect domination by a few organizations who may dictate the 'rules by which the game is played.' Among the impacts frequently noted in such situations are pressures to cut prices as a result of changes in fixed costs, switching costs, or product differentiation, changes in industry growth as a result of substitution, altered capacity utilization due to increases or decreases in effective capacity or the ability to adjust capacity to demand, and a change in the players as a result of modified entry barriers and exit incentives. However, the main determinants of future industry structure will be (1) the threat of entry, (2) product substitution, (3) the bargaining power of suppliers, and (4) the bargaining power of customers.

• **The Threat of Entry.** In any industry there are a number of barriers which have been established by existing firms to protect their strategic positions from attack by rivals. Typically, firms wishing to enter the marketplace must (a) seek a 'niche' or a segment of the market which has been overlooked or under-exploited, as Digital Equipment Corporation did when it introduced its mini-computers, (b) aggressively challenge the weakest or most vulnerable competitor in the market, or (c) change the rules of competition.

As Porter (1985) points out, technology is a powerful change agent, and can affect the capital requirements for competition, the opportunities for product differentiation, access to distribution, the buyer's fixed costs of changing suppliers, and research and development costs.

There is very little doubt that the MMC industry is still 'wide open,' although as it enters the stage of application growth, an increased cost of entry can be expected, and the window of opportunity can be expected to close. At the present time, there is considerable room for individual entrepreneurs and small firms, especially those engaging in 'leading edge' technologies. However, the industry is also seeing the entrance of some larger, well-known firms. Microsoft already has entered the market by making some of its products, such as Windows, Word, and The Works, available on a CD-ROM format; Apple is apparently perched to make its impact felt on the market; a number of PC manufacturers already offer CD-ROMs and developmental software as part of their standard packages. As already mentioned, a number of firms are purchasing material, or the rights to present material and distribute products.

In NEVI's case, given that it has chosen a relatively small segment of the market, the threat of increased competition is not a major consideration at the present. Nonetheless, it can be anticipated that as the barriers to entry in the larger, more profitable, segments of the MMC industry increase, the Hypermedia surrogate travel niche will become more appealing. NEVI's best strategy might be to firmly establish itself as the leader in this area, and hence raise the entry fees to new entrants.

• **Product Substitution.** Product substitution occurs when the relative price/performance of competing goods outweighs the costs associated with switching from the original product. For industries that rely on new or constantly changing technologies, the affect of substitution is readily apparent. New products or product uses can absolutely or virtually eliminate products or entire product lines, as witnessed by the demise of the slide rule or the practical obliteration of the vinyl Long Play record, or severely reduce profitability, as was the case of the cassette tape industry after introduction of the compact discs.

For the MMC industry, the primary hardware and platforms for presentation *are* substitutions for the older magnetic-based technologies. It can be anticipated that the major players in floppy disk-based technologies will not relinquish their market without resistance. Product improvements, such as increased storage and quicker access times, are already being witnessed, as are substantial decreases in product prices. While the price of CD-ROM hardware and formats has decreased, the rate of decrease has not kept pace with floppy disc-based applications, thereby maintaining the relative cost differential for switching technologies.

It might further be argued that the quality of MMC products, in contrast to their potential, has not yet altered user perceptions to the point where switching to the newer technologies is sufficiently attractive. In scanning the list of available products, the majority (e.g., reference material, atlases, almanacs, games, books) are repackaged offerings in new formats, providing benefits primarily in the form of increased storage capacity and only tangentially taking advantage of the interactive nature of MMC. As shall be discussed later, many of the perceived benefits are not necessarily a result of the MMC technology, but are due to advances in computer and peripheral technology.

Michael Greenberg has been cognizant of product substitution from the outset. The products he develops are directed toward the most popular platforms, but also allow for transfer to as yet undefined technologies as they become available. With respect to quality of products, NEVI is already on the forefront, and is in a prime position to take advantage of improved technologies.

• **The Bargaining Power of Suppliers.** Either through formal or informal channels, suppliers establish agreements with firms in an industry to provide materials, components, or products. Technological change can alter or eliminate the relationships established by obviating the need to purchase from a monopolistic or powerful supplier, or can allow substitution of needed inputs for product development. Such practices were instrumental in enhancing the bargaining leverage of U.S. Auto manufacturers over component suppliers (Porter, 1983.)

It can be argued that the suppliers of MMC equipment are themselves in a stage of application launch or application growth, depending on the specific technology in question, slightly ahead of the MMC industry. For the developer of MMC applications, this situation can be viewed as a mixed blessing. While there are a growing number of suppliers, and the price of components is dropping, there are often no clear-cut standards or generally accepted protocols. The market is fraught with suppliers and distributors, most of them willing to reduce profit margins in order to increase sales. However, a number of newer entrants into the field have not yet developed viable reputations, and while their prices may be attractive, it is difficult to determine if this is due to a desire to increase market penetration, or if the quality of their products is lacking. Even more disconcerting is the lack of standardization and comparability. Given that MMC relies on integration of components, the wrong choice of equipment can be fatal to the application developer. Beyond the choice of the development platform, the application developer must be concerned with the customer's operating platform.

The issue of standardization may be settled in the near future. Kaleida, the joint effort by IBM and Apple, might dictate standardization for interactive tools across platforms. CD-ROM formats appear to be nearing standardization. While this will lend stability to MMC, it may also force the demise of some of the smaller suppliers in the industry, although in general, the costs of equipment should continue to decrease for some time. NEVI feels it is in a good position with respect to standardization, or concurrently, new product introduction. Greenberg's basic philosophy of being prepared to provide improved products as new technology emerges serves this goal well.

• *The Bargaining Power of Customers.* Technological change can also drastically alter the bargaining relationship which exists between a firm and its customers. Such change can vary consumer opinions of product differentiation, either making new products more attractive or minimizing previously existing differences, hence lessening switching costs. For example, IBM's domination of the business oriented PC market has steadily eroded as a result of a variety of clones which have successively incorporated technological advances at correspondingly decreasing costs, effectively eliminating any perceptions of product differences, or, in some cases, creating beliefs in the superiority of the newer product.

As with any emerging technology, the onus to increase sales lies with the producer, and the industry can be characterized as a 'buyers' market.' The issue then becomes "what will sell and what won't." White (1978) suggests that there are three critical questions which the producer must ask with respect to market dynamics:

A. *Does the product incorporating the new technology provide enhanced effectiveness in the marketplace serving the final user?*

It does not appear that MMC has promoted itself well with respect to its enhanced effectiveness. As discussed earlier, much of the so called MMC products are merely repackaged versions of programs available in other formats, and have primarily only taken advantage of increased storage and access speeds. As Greenberg points out, most of the users are impressed with having larger color monitors, faster speeds, mouses, and so forth. A few years ago, everyone was working on PCs and monochrome monitors, so naturally, they feel the products are much better. But for the most part, the presentation is not as good as they could get from television. The potential for MMC products is well beyond anything available either on TV or in most of the commercially available packages today.

MMC products must sell their products based on their innovation; it seems unlikely that the costs associated with MMC technology will be less than the cost of providing such products as games or reference materials on floppy-disk or hard-disk technologies.

B. Does the operation reduce the cost of delivering the product or service?

In conjunction with the above question, these two issues constitute the 'scissors' of supply and demand (White, 1978). If the answer to both is *no*, the producer may as well go back to the drawing board; if the answer is *yes*, there is little market uncertainty. Nonetheless, compounding this issue is the sophistication of the MMC industry. In the stage of Technology Application, a significant amount of resources are expended on product and operation development and refinement. During Application Launch, operational efficiencies can be tolerated given the relatively small number of non-dominant competitors. In the Application Growth stage, however, inefficient operations can hasten a firm's exit from the market.

NEVI, for one, has apparently recognized that in order to remain competitive, it must automate as many of its developmental processes as possible. Greenberg no longer attempts to develop his own authoring tools, and has developed procedures for cataloging and sequencing of objects. With standardization and improvements in third party authoring tools, improved efficiencies seem likely.

C. Does the latent demand expansion, or price elasticity determine the characteristics of the new markets?

Major market expansion is difficult to obtain if the factor driving a market area is lower per unit price. Market expansion is much more likely if demand is driven by changes in product effectiveness. For MMC, there is little question that improved effectiveness and enhanced features will drive the industry. In NEVI's case, product differentiation should improve the likelihood of increased market segment share.

What Can Be Learned From NEVI?

As mentioned in the introduction, case studies provide more than just an interesting description of past events. The successes and shortcomings described can serve as lessons for readers interested in creating MMC products. What is of importance, however, depends in large part on the interests of the reader. There are three groups in this area: (1) Entrepreneurs, individuals or groups of individuals whose primary interests are in profiting from the sale of MMC oriented products, (2) Technologists/Developers, whose main interests lie in the application and extension of MMC technology, and (3) Consumers, or those individuals who are interested in purchasing MMC products for other purposes.

Entrepreneurs

From a business perspective, NEVI offers both encouragement and caveats. The costs associated with market entry remain relatively low, but present profit margins are correspondingly low and risks alternately high. Still, the market remains underdeveloped and a number of market segments unaddressed. The entrance of some larger firms into the market, assuming they are entering the industry based on market projections, would seem to imply increased profitability in the near future. Along with entry by these firms, however, we can expect subsequent increases in entry barriers. Entrepreneurs who have already entered the market hold a distinct advantage. NEVI's experiences provide a number of considerations for entrepreneurs:

A. *Establish a Realistic, Well-Defined Business Plan.*

Entrepreneurs entering the market need to be aware of a number of factors which influence success. The Porter Model serves to focus attention on some these categories, but beyond that, entrepreneurs need to carefully select their market segments in terms of who are the competitors in that segment, who are the potential purchasers of the products, what products are selling, what is the cost of producing products, and, concurrently, what price the products are selling at. The entrepreneur must also be careful not to be shortsighted; improvements in technology and consumer demand, seem almost certain. Once these issues are settled, an operational plan, including personnel required and scheduling of activities must be arrived at.

B. Research Product Costs and Profitability in Advance.

While this consideration is a major component of any business, it merits special attention. Greenberg's efforts on *The Bolivia Hypermedia Expedition* might better have been spent on a similar product directed toward a larger and profitable market segment. The museum market proved to be too small and under-funded to substantiate the time and capital invested. This situation was compounded by the lack of accepted reference material on the subject. While the uniqueness of the project might add to the appeal, it needs to be weighed against the costs associated with product completion.

C. Choose Business Associates Carefully.

Michael Greenberg's business experience might admittedly be lacking in contrast to most business-oriented entrepreneurs, but even accomplished businessmen must realize the need for associates in undertaking such ventures. Development of MMC products, unless the entrepreneur intends to become a free-lance contractor, requires a team effort by a variety of individuals with divergent skills. Since the MMC industry is lacking structure and is still in a period of application launch, selection should be based on success in related industries which have undergone the transition from launch to growth. Because of the preponderance of creatively-oriented innovators, a similar number of individuals whose main interest is in exploitation can similarly be assumed.

D. Clearly Define the Terms of Assistance from Supporting Organizations.

Given the developing nature of the industry and the relatively low profit margins available at the present, financial and technical support from better endowed organizations is generally necessary. Fortunately, there are a number of sources, primarily suppliers, who are willing to provide assistance in order promote their platforms, increase applications, or refine their products. Greenberg's experiences with BIGCORP could have been avoided had he investigated the organizational unit offering the support, and had he defined, and upheld, the terms of the association. While the establishment of legal protocols for behavior might slightly delay product development, in the long run, it serves to protect the interests of both parties. As in selecting business partners, the entrepreneur should not make unwarranted assumptions about the intent of such relationships.

E. Maintain Product Control.

Unlike the previous points, this suggestion is based on NEVI's success. Product developers in MMC, especially smaller organizations which find themselves with cash-flow difficulties, might be tempted to sell the rights to the products produced. As we have seen, even though initial product revenues might be larger, the developer can lose out on later profits and product integrity. While entrepreneurs need to further investigate available arrangements with manufacturers, it appears that the terms of production, as a result of the industry structure, presently favor the developer.

F. Price Products According to Market Segment Position.

NEVI has essentially paid no attention to product pricing and product demand. Pricing strategy is dependent upon a number of factors, including demand, competition, product differentiation, production costs, price elasticity, and price/performance ratios, and is moderated by such factors as product evolution and industry development. NEVI's approach of undercutting the price of similar products is not necessarily unfounded, but is certainly unacceptable if the total revenues fail to exceed total costs, or misguided if product demand would entertain a higher price. While this issue is too involved to adequately cover in this chapter, the interested reader is advised to refer elsewhere for information[6].

G. Research Distribution Channels.

Product distribution, unless the developer intends direct sales, carries a distinct trade-off: extent of distribution and per unit profits. The entrepreneur needs to determine their optimal placement along this continuum. While Greenberg's preferences are toward multiple distributors, a detailed analysis would be required before any commitment is made. Although only briefly mentioned in the case, the issue of bundling is worthy of further investigation, either in terms of offering bundles of proprietary products, or inclusion in packages of multi-developer bundles. The primary distribution tradeoff still remains, but there is the distinct advantage of reaching customers who might not otherwise purchase the developer's products. The approach of direct marketing through third parties established for this purpose might also prove a viable alternative, but again, additional investigation is necessary.

Technologists/Developers

For individuals whose primary concerns are with either the creative process or simply the application of MMC technology, NEVI offers a number of interesting insights. It should be noted, however, that much of these are based on Michael Greenberg's personality. While impulsivity and risk-aversion are traits which frequently characterize innovators, readers should assess their own personality to determine the appropriateness of the suggestions.

A. *Do Not Attempt to Re-Invent the Wheel.*

This is Michael Greenberg's strongest caveat to developers. Greenberg's infatuation with the process of product development and his insistence on perfection almost caused him to lose sight of his primary goal: to produce products. There are a number of development tools available, and developers need to select those which best meet their needs. Prior to developing or modifying these tools, the developer should determine whether or not commercially available products are available. As noted above, suppliers often provide assistance to developers; if it can truly be determined that product alterations are necessary, it is possible that the supplier will provide necessary modifications.

B. *Plan and Organize Projects in Advance.*

In spite of the necessary learning curve, there are a number of developmental aspects which can be planned in advance. Even though Greenberg developed *The Bolivia Hypermedia Expedition* as an exploratory project, he admits that he should have paid more attention to the time of the shooting, the physical conditions he would face, and identification of some of the topics to be included. Research into the availability of supporting material would have saved considerable time in product development. 'Visualization' of what would be involved in the actual shooting has never been one of Greenberg's problems, but the developer should be well aware of the media to be used, how much information can be included given the platform selected, and how the topics will be sequenced in the final product.

C. *Automate those Processes which can be Automated.*

Even though each MMC product is intended to be unique, there are many components which remain constant across products. In Greenberg's case, the cataloging of information, leveling of detail, and identification and targeting of objects vary slightly from product to product. Each developer needs to identify those components of the product which can be transferred between products, determine the best methods to be applied, and adhere to those procedures. As with the first point above, attempting to modify procedures with each new project will merely lead to delay of completion.

D. *Differentiate the Product from the Market.*

This suggestion can be viewed from either a business perspective or a development perspective. As a business strategy, product differentiation, especially in a more populated market segment, can increase market share and profitability if the purchasers of the product perceive it as superior in terms of price/performance, or offers enhanced effectiveness. From a developmental perspective, it would advantageous to determine the techniques and combinations of technologies which will facilitate differentiation. Greenberg's insistence on quality and level of interaction have increased the appeal of NEVI's products and reduced the expected time to product obsolescence.

E. *Allow for Improved Future Technologies.*

One of NEVI's strengths is that it produces products which anticipate improved presentation platforms. However, while there is an awareness of the MIT philosophy of always applying leading-edge technologies without regard to cost, NEVI is acutely aware of customer limitations and preferences. The products produced are directed toward these platforms, but are transferable to improved technologies as they become available and affordable. Additionally, the products are designed to take advantage of the enhancements offered by the new technology both in terms of quality and extent of content.

Consumers

Consumers of MMC products, including those 'hackers' who are interested in applying products for other purposes, have interests separate from entrepreneurs and developers. As previously noted, the primary concerns of this group center around the enhanced effectiveness of the product and the product's price/performance ratio. Although the specific aspects which consumers look for vary extensively, there are some considerations which might be made.

A. Evaluate Products Based on Technological Enhancements and not on Platform.

MMC products have yet to approach their potential. Even for NEVI's products, the degree of sophistication provided is lacking. Just a few years ago, the most likely computer configuration consisted of a monochrome monitor, and a 286-based, or lower, machine. In today's market, 486 and Pentium-based machines with multitasking, and 15 to 17 inch SVGA monitors have become commonplace. Accordingly, the extent and quality of presentation have improved dramatically. The purchaser should evaluate whether MMC products offer enhancements over other products which operate in this environment. As we have seen, the majority of products advertised as multimedia are actuality repackaged programs offered on MMC platforms. Note that this caveat is not intended to discourage customers or developers; it is suggested in anticipation of possible consumer dissatisfaction and subsequent loss of interest in MMC products.

B. Examine Product Quality.

In conjunction with the points above, the consumer should be aware that not all MMC products are created equal. There is some truth to the adage 'you get what you pay for.' In addition to the number of media included, the quality of presentation of each is a consideration. The purchaser should also realize that there is also a trade-off between the scope of topics covered and extent of topic coverage. While the selection of MMC products is solely an individual decision, and hence no suggestions can be made, it behooves the consumer to be aware of these aspects.

Conclusions

This chapter is primarily intended to serve as an anecdotal description of one MMC firm's experiences in developing, manufacturing, and distributing its products. In doing so, we hope that it provides some insight in some of the pitfalls and opportunities which other MMC firms might face. While the generalizability of the events witnessed is limited, we believe that many of the lessons learned can benefit all interested parties.

We have framed our analysis of NEVI's experiences in terms of a variety of conceptual models, most notably Porter's model of forces which drive industry structure, and Ford and Ryan's Technology Life Cycle. We have done so because these models have been well received and because they are useful for organizing discussion and focusing attention on some of the more salient factors affecting industry development. We are not advocating their usage regardless of setting or even implying that they are 'ideal' frameworks, but we do believe that they can add to the reader's understanding of the issues involved.

Finally, we are neither promoting NEVI nor portraying it as an example of what not to do. We believe that NEVI has had considerable accomplishments, but has also faltered along the way. We appreciate Michael Greenberg's frankness in discussing NEVI's achievements and failures, and allowing us to present our analysis without interference. We leave it to readers to come to their own conclusion about NEVI, but we would hope that they allow for our shortcomings in reporting NEVI's experiences.

For additional information on this chapter, contact the first author at 305/348-3401.

ENDNOTES
[1] The authors wish to thank Mr. Michael Greenberg for his time and input into this case study. Any misrepresentations which might be construed are unintentional, and do not reflect the intentions of either the authors or Mr. Greenberg.
[2] At Mr. Greenberg's request, we have disguised the name of the actual company. All references to the company's products have similarly been altered.
[3] As with the previously mentioned corporation, the true company name and company products have been disguised at Mr. Greenberg's request.
[4] Filming for the project occurred prior to Hurricane Andrew; The Hurricane

had a devastating effect on the coral reefs.

[5] While we believe that the summary information presented is representative, categorization based on advertisements is extremely difficult based on size of advertisement and level of detail provided. Some advertisers merged CD software disk-based material, did not provide clear-cut descriptions, or merely referred to available material. In one case, the manufacturer provided only XXX (Pornographic) material.

[6] See, for example, Porter, 1985, or Burgelman and Maidique, 1988.

References

Abernathy, W.J., and Utterback, J.M (1975) "A Dynamic Model of Process and Product Innovation", *Omega*, 3(6), p. 639.

Burgelman, R.A., and Maidique, M.A. (1988) *Strategic Management of Technology and Innovation*. Homewood, ILL: Irwin Publishing.

Bygrave, W.D., and Hofer, C.W. (1991) Theorizing about Entrepreneurship. *Entrepreneurship Theory and Practice*, 13-22.

Ford, D., and Ryan, C. (1981) "Taking Technology to the Market", *Harvard Business Review*, 59(2), pp.

Gartner, W.B. (1989) "Who is an entrepreneur?' Is the wrong question", *Entrepreneurship Theory and Practice*, pp. 47-68.

Mitton, D.G. (1989) The complete entrepreneur. *Entrepreneurship Theory and Practice*, 13(3), 9-19.

Porter, M.E. (1980) *Competitive Strategy: Techniques for analyzing Industries and Competitors*. New York: Free Press.

Porter, M.E. (1983) *Research on Technological Innovation, Management, and Policy*. Greenwich, Conn: JAI Press.

Porter, M.E. (1985) *Competitive Advantage: Creating and Sustaining Superior Performance*. New York: The Free Press.

Stevenson, H.H. (1987) Entrepreneurship Education: Crisis or Opportunity. Presented at the Seventh Annual Meeting of the Strategic Management Society. October.

White, G.R. (1978). "Management criteria for effective innovation", *Technology Review*, MIT Alumni Association, pp.21-28.

Section 4

End User Focus

Chapter 14

The Strategic Use of Hypermedia and Multimedia by the Fortune 1000

J.P. Shim
Mississippi State University

Sun-Gi Chun
Alabama State University

Numerous researchers have come forth with various studies in the areas of hypermedia and multimedia over the past decade. Hypermedia/multimedia technology is a useful tool for corporations because such applications can make an endless range of available information, easy-to-comprehend. Today, the technology can provide strategic opportunities by supplying advanced information retrieval and representation capabilities to management. However, there has not been much empirical research on the strategic use of hypermedia and multimedia technologies even though hypermedia and multimedia technologies have been introduced and used across industry boundaries. This chapter presented i)an overview of hypermedia and multimedia as an instructional, research, and decision making tool for users/managers, and ii)the results of a study (conducted by the authors) to determine whether hypermedia and multimedia technology is being used as a strategic tool in major manufacturing and service firms.

This paper is based in part on a paper: "Living Up to the 'HYPE'" by J. P. Shim, which appeared in the *OR/MS Today*, Vol. 19, No. 1 (1992).

The subjects of hypermedia and multimedia have, over the past few years, received considerable attention from academics and practitioners. Since the results of exploratory studies concerning hypermedia were first presented at the annual meetings of the Association of Computing Machinery (ACM) in 1987 and 1989, numerous seminars and workshops concerning hypermedia and multimedia, as well as special issues of *Communications of the ACM* have clearly indicated an increasing level of research interest in this area. This is well demonstrated when one considers that even the industry trade shows COMDEX '92 and Hypertext '91 both featured a variety of sessions concerning these subjects.

Over the past decade, numerous researchers have come forth with various studies in the areas of hypermedia and multimedia. Among these is Conklin (1987), who has done very comprehensive surveys of these subjects, and who points out that "hypertext," a subset of the more general topic called "hypermedia," is becoming widely used in commercial information systems. More recently, Marchionini and Shneiderman (1988), Minch (1989), Nielsen (1990), Ritchie (1989), and Fox (1991) have echoed this same theme, -- that hypermedia and multimedia are emerging as a very useful information technology. Straub and Wetherbe (1989), in a survey of 12 selected information management experts well known to the information systems and computer science communities, showed that hypermedia and multimedia applications were found to be one of the most promising information technology of the 1990s.

Recently, distinctions between the terms multimedia and hypermedia have become blurred. In this chapter the term "hypermedia" will be used to mean a navigational tool that allows users to explore interrelated materials from large databases of "multimedia" information. For example, hypermedia systems can be used to store, retrieve, and represent information in such varied data forms as text, graphics, images, animation, sound, and motion pictures. Systems that permit such navigation and use of text-only databases are considered to be "hypertext" systems. And the term "multimedia" will mean any other kind of computer based system that uses text with one or more of the media of graphics, images, animation, sound, or motion pictures. Regardless of the specific definition, the use of these systems for decision making is indeed proving to be valuable for professionals in academia, government, and industry.

Hypermedia/multimedia is a useful tool for corporations because such applications can make an endless range of available information, easy-to-comprehend. As we shall see, examples include corporate organization structures, employee-related data files, and portfolios of assets. Many multimedia applications employ hypertext as a means of relating textual components with associated data in a variety of media forms (Anderson *et al.*, 1991).

In the past, hypermedia and multimedia technologies had not provided much incremental information to corporate management because senior executives have traditionally relied upon informal and non-computerized information for their decision making (Jones and McLeod, 1986). Today, multimedia technology can provide strategic opportunities by supplying advanced information retrieval and representation capabilities to management. In 1991, Elofson and Konsynski indicated that multimedia technology was not yet being used to support the environmental scanning process as part of companies' strategy formulation procedures. However, there has not been much empirical research on the strategic use of hypermedia and multimedia technologies even though hypermedia and multimedia technologies have been introduced and used across industry boundaries. The primary objective of this chapter is 1) to present an overview of hypermedia and multimedia as an instructional, research, and decision making tool for users/managers, and 2) to present the results of a study (conducted by the authors) to determine whether hypermedia and multimedia technology is being used as a strategic tool in major manufacturing and service firms.

Overview of Hypermedia

Originally introduced by Vannevar Bush, and extended and refined by Theodore Nelson, D. Englebart, and others, hypertext systems were initially defined as a valuable interactive approach for presenting text and graphic information by allowing users to jump from a given subject to related ideas (Horn, 1989). It is interesting to note that Ted Nelson, who is sometimes considered to be the modern originator of the term (and others in academia), tend to include all media in the term "hypertext." In industry, however, "hypertext" generally refers to text-only-based systems. In general, we can consider hypertext to be a sophisticated approach for interactive use of text-only databases. Figure 1 depicts the evolution of hypertext and hypermedia beginning in 1935 (Horn, 1989). Hypertext is often referred to as "nonsequential" text (Conklin, 1987). The structure of a hypertext database (Figure 2) illustrates how users can quickly follow documents without losing their original context (Horn, 1989). Note that hypertext software creates links among the documents/nodes using four types of links; 1) hierarchi-

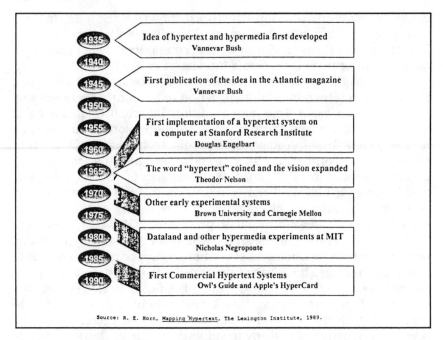

Figure 1: A History of Hypertext/Hypermedia

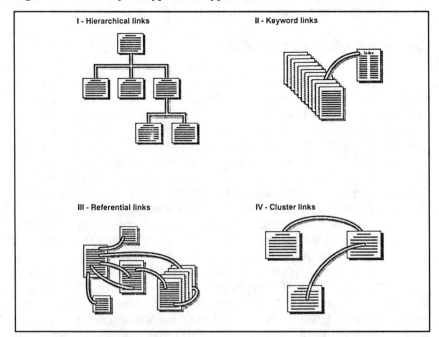

Figure 2: Four Types of Links

cal links, 2) keyword links, 3) referential links, and 4) cluster links (Figure 3).

On the other hand, hypermedia is really much more inclusive than a mere extension of hypertext. It incorporates other media such as video, illustrations, diagrams, animation, and computer graphics. The six major functions that hypermedia products can provide to users are; 1) browsing, 2) training/education, 3) briefing/illustration, 4) learning and analysis, 5) help, and 6) referencing/on-line documentation. With these types of functions, hypermedia systems can play a major role in industry through their ability to access information and provide users with control navigation through data. Recently, it has become important to include, among the functions of hypermedia systems, persuasion and motivation (e.g., sales, marketing, and business presentations). Five concrete benefits have accounted for the recent surge and popularity of hypermedia. Hypermedia can:

1) save time by allowing users to browse through information,
2) offer nonlinear access to information,
3) promote a collaborative work environment by allowing users working on individual pieces of information to be linked together,
4) aid in the discovery of new and relevant information by indicating links to existing information, and
5) present the same information in multiple media formats.

For example, users (e.g., students) can read a John F. Kennedy

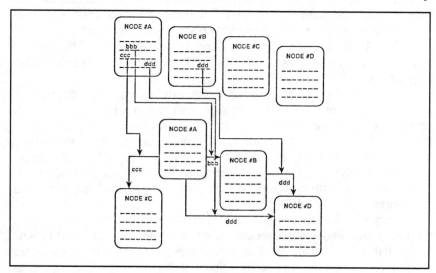

Figure 3: Structure of a Hypertext Database

speech in order to analyze rhetoric; they can also see and hear the speech to grasp emotional content.

Since the late 1980s, there has been an avalanche of microcomputer software packages concerning hypermedia. A mail survey conducted by the first author of this chapter showed that, at that time, there were more than a dozen hypermedia products available. In 1991 the author developed a one-page questionnaire and sent it to 24 different software vendors. Seventeen usable questionnaires (representing 25 different products) were returned— a return rate of 70.8%. This was an excellent return rate considering that some of the vendors had either gone out of business, or relocated and their forwarding address could not be determined. As the results of the survey revealed, there is an increasingly large number of available microcomputer-based hypermedia products, indicating a continued and growing interest in hypermedia technology. Table 1, which contains a summary of the information provided by the vendors, provides product names, vendors, platforms, cost, and system requirements concerning hypermedia software packages.

Strategic Uses of Hypermedia

Over the past decade, information technology (IT) has been viewed as a corporate strategic weapon (Ives and Learmonth, 1984; Porter and Millar, 1985, Wiseman, 1988). Trends regarding the integration of IT and changes in the business environment have influenced companies' proactive use of IT. The technology of hypermedia and multimedia can be integrated into IT and be applied to support management in focusing on strategic decision making. As shown in Table 2, there exists a fairly large inventory of published studies concerning the strategic use of hypermedia and multimedia applications.

Hypermedia can be used strategically as a text or document retrieval and storage tool in business environments. Davis (1989) revealed that Chase Manhattan Bank utilized hypertext capabilities in order for the top management team to get direct access to a number of databases all over the world. Using this technology, executives retrieved critical information directly and quickly from broad areas of information sources, for use in making strategic decisions (Verity, 1990).

Gray (1989) stated that hypermedia would help group work during strategic decision making. For example, certain products or "deliverables" of strategic decision making require the cooperative work of many people. To produce some of these deliverables requires

Software	Feature		Vendor & Address	Phone #	FAX #	Platform it runs on	Minimum hardware required to run	Cost	Educational Price	Any other information
	hypertext	hypermedia								
Aldus SuperCard		*	Aldus Corporation 411 First Ave. S., Seatle, WA 98104-2871	(206) 622-5500	(206) 343-3360	Macintosh Plus, SE, SE30, II Series	2MB for color, hard disk, system 6.04 or above	$299.00	$99.00	Complete toolkit for developing Macintosh applications
askSam V5	*		Seaside Software, Inc., 119 S. Washington Street, Perry, FL 32347	(800) 800-1997	(904) 594-7481	DOS 2.0 or higher	IBM PC, XT, AT, PS/2, or compatible	$395.00	$99.95	Offers educational discounts on network and developer's versions[a]
Asymetrix ToolBook		*	Asymetrix Corp. 110 110th Ave. NE, Suite 700 Bellevue, WA 98004	(206) 637-1500	(206) 454-0672	Windows and OS/2	286 CPU/1.5 MB RAM/VGA monitor	$395.00	$150.00 for single unit	$1,000 for a 10 pack (only valid for a classroom or lab)
AUTHORWARE Professional for Macintosh and Windows		*	Authorware, Inc. 275 Shoreline Drive, Suite 535 Redwood City, CA 94065	(415) 595-3101	(415) 595-3077	Macintosh, IBM PS/2, AT with DOS 3.3/Win. 3.0 or later	20+ Mhz 386 with 4MB RAM, 16 color VGA (256 with VGA+ card)	$995.00	Call	It also provides update support and user education along with its own magazine
Black Magic	*		INTERGAID, Inc.					$99.95	Call	
HyperWriter 3.0	*		2490 Black Rock Turnpike, Suite 337 Fairfield, CT 06430	(203) 380-1280	(203) 380-1465	PC, XT, AT & compatible	Min 384k RAM, DOS 3.00 or later, HD recommended	$495.00	Call	HyperWriter is named as PC magazine Editor's choice product
HyperWriter 3.0 Professional		*						$995.00	Call	
Folio Views 2.1	*		Folio Corporation 2155 N. Freedom Boulevard, Suite 150 Provo, UT 84604	(801) 375-3700	(801) 374-5753	MS-DOS, PC, PS/2	512k RAM, Hard disk	$695.00	$295.00	All Folio software products are licensed on a "per unit" basis, but Folio will provide multi-packs of 5, 25, and 100 licenses.
GUIDE		*	OWL International, Inc. 2800 156th Ave. SE Bellevue, WA 98007	(206) 747-3203	(206) 641-9367	Macintosh, IBM PC, AT, PS/2 or compatible	PC Windows 80286, 1MB free, 640k RAM. Windows compatible, Monitor and mouse	$495.00	N/A	In addition to GUIDE, OWL provides GUIDE Video Toolkit, GUIDE Reader/CD and Interactive Electronic Publications (IEPs)
HyperCARD 2.1	*		Claris Corporation 5201 Patrick Henry Drive Santa Clara, CA 95052-8168	(408) 978-7000	(408) 987-7440	Macintosh	1 MB RAM, Hard disk	$199.00	$99.00 or site license available	
HyperPAD	*		Brightbill-Roberts & Company 120E Washington St., Suite 421 Syracuse, NY 13202	(315) 474-3400	(315) 472-1732	MS-DOS V2.1 or higher	512k of system memory; two 360k disk drives or hard disk	$149.95	10% Educational discount	384k of available memory but 512k of system memory recommended

Table 1: List of Microcomputer Software Packages in Hypertext/Hypermedia

Product	*	Company/Address	Phone	Fax	Platform	Hardware Requirements	Price	Discount/License	Comments
Hyperties 3.0	*	Cognetics Corp. 55 Princeton-Hightown Road Princeton Junction, NJ 08550	(609) 799-5005	(609) 799-8555	IBM PC, XT, AT, PS/2 or compatible	1 Floppy disk/256k minimum, Hard disk/512k recommended	$379.00		In addition, Hyperties 3.0 for Professional($579), Hyperties 3.0 for DVI Technology($1,450), Hyperties 3.0 for Demo($35).
I/C: Intelligence/Compiler	*	Intelligenceware Inc. 5933 W. Century Boulevard Los Angeles, CA 90045	(213) 216-6177	(213) 417-8897	IBM PC/AT, compatible	640k of memory, PC-DOS or MS-DOS 3.0 or later	$490.00	Site license available	Starting at $7500 for SUN and VAX. Automatic hypertext interface generation, object-oriented and rule-based data base.
KnowledgePro DOS		Knowledge Garden, Inc. 473A Malden Bridge Nassau, NY 12123-0861	(518) 766-3000	(518) 766-3003	MS DOS 3.1 or later/Windows	Intel 8088 or better 640k memory	$449.00	$150.00	Educational pricing valid in USA & Canada only Foreign and site license and bulk purchase pricing available
KnowledgePro Windows						Intel 80286 or better, 640k (2MB recommended)	$549.00	$150.00	
LEVEL5 OBJECT for Microsoft Windows	*	Information Builders, Inc. 1250 Broadway New York, NY 10001	(212) 736-4433	(212) 967-6406	IBM PC/AT PS/2 and compatible	RAM 640k or 2MB, Hard disk 2MB, Monochrome/color with EGA & VGA, DOS 3.0 or higher	$495.00	20% Discount	For LEVEL5 OBJECT for VAX/VMS 5.0 or later, FOCUS 6.0 or later. Price ranges from $3,500 to $54,000 for VAX/VMS
LEVEL5 OBJECT for VAX/VMS	*				VAX/VMS	VT 100, 200, 300 series terminal	$54,000	20% Discount	
SmarText	*	Lotus Development Corp., Wordprocessing Division 5600 Galnridge Dr. Atlanta, GA 30342	(404) 851-0007 Ext. 281	(404) 303-7624	Windows 3.0	IBM PC, AT, 1MB RAM	$495.00 for builder / $95.00 for reader	$199.00 for builder / $49.00 for reader	
Spinnaker Plus	*	Spinnaker Software 201 Broadway Cambridge, MA 02139	(617) 494-1200	(617) 494-0173	PC under Windows 3.0 Macintosh	PC 386, 2MB, MAC II or higher	$495.00	$149.00	Runtime also available for schools
Trans Text	*	MaxThink 2490 Channing Way, #218 Berkeley, CA 94704	(415) 540-5508	(415) 548-4686	PC, MS-DOS 2.0 - 5.0	PC 8088 - 80486	$89.00	20% discount	Hypertext ASCII editor construction systems
Hyper BBS							$89.00	20% discount	BBS Hypertext ASCII text
Hyper LAN	*						$89.00	20% discount	NOVELL LAN graphic/text Hypercard
Hyper Rez	*						Free	Free	ASCII file Hypertext
Hyplus	*						Free	Free	ACX file, DOS, ASCII
xText	*	Flambeaux Software 11147 Broadway, Suite 56 Glendale, CA 91205	(818) 500-0044	(818) 957-0194	DOS 2.1 or later	Require 256k RAM	$139.95		PC magazine Editor's choice for on-line DOS help systems

Table 1: List of Microcomputer Software Packages in Hypertext/Hypermedia

	Authors	Applications
Hypertext/ Hypermedia	Jarvis and Tagliarini (1991)	Retrieval of specifications in the apparel industry
	Kimbrough et al. (1991)	US Coast Guard KSS (document oriented DSS)
	Steffey (1991)	Multimedia encyclopedia
	Weaver and McCleary (1990)	Hypertext journal
	Kasavana (1991)	Training system in food service industry
	Slater (1991)	Presentation
	Davis and Deter (1990)	Earth DSS (U.S. Agriculture Dept.)
Multimedia	Schlack (1991)	Cargo booking and tracking in the shipping industry
	Fisher (1991)	Advertising Media in the footwear industry
	Magrath (1992)	Direct Mail Marketing
	Shulman (1992)	Training
	Wilder (1992)	Training sales representatives
	Chain Store Age Executive (1992)	Multimedia kiosk system in the retail industry
	Rouland (1992)	Marketing information system for analyzing consumer activity
	Fuochi (1992)	Desktop publishing tool
	Hillman (1992)	Image processing in insurance industry
	Dwek (1992)	Sales promotion in automobile industry
	Bredin (1992)	Public relations for tourists of New Mexico

Table 2: Literature on the Strategic Use of Hypermedia and Multimedia Applications

group participation in the creation and approval of technical reports, proposals, annual reports, and policies. Traditionally, each participant in the group must change the document by writing in the margin of the current draft. One individual might have responsibility for pulling the document together. Hypertext can support this phase of strategic decision making because hypertext can guarantee the joint authorship and direct document retrieval by executives for accessing information to create new documents. Minch (1989) too claimed that hypertext could be used to support early stages of decision making such as a problem exploration, because hypertext has direct and fast information retrieval capabilities.

Hypermedia also can improve employees' productivity by supporting individually-tailored training methods. In order to improve documentation for an information systems (IS) development project, hypertext-based applications were presented by Garg and Scacchi (1990) for handling the documentation requirements of large scale software development. This documentation could also be used for training end users. SAS Institute Inc. utilized hypertext to document a wide range of software products in a hyperdocument which combined hypermedia with other software applications (Ressler and Stribling, 1990). Such hypertext systems can provide instant job-related help to people during work hours. Thus, hypertext can back up on-the-job training by supplying hyperdocuments well-designed to meet the individual needs of trainees as well as already-trained employees.

Hypertext can be used as a marketing or sales tool. Tiampo (1988) described a hypertext-based system to replace an automotive parts catalog. Hypertext, supported by a built-in text editor, was shown to be useful in supporting telemarketing activities that required fast customer tracking capabilities (Porter, 1988). Hypermedia and multimedia can be used as a tool to introduce new products to the market by attracting customers' attention and responding quickly to customers' queries. Shim (1992) pointed out that hypermedia was important for including persuasion and motivation features for sales, marketing, and for other business presentations. Fidelity Investment Co. utilized living file techniques for a customer support system where manuals with hypertext features were electronically updated and retrieved, allowing sales representatives to respond quickly to customer enquiries. Hypertext capabilities can also be used to easily publish and update a variety of product and service support materials (Doebler, 1990).

Davis (1989) indicated that hypertext is a qualitatively different medium for business communication because it gives readers a feeling of moving effortlessly through a transparent information environment, like a fish in a sea of knowledge. He presented examples of two hypertext applications used in government and business: 1) The Environmental Protection Agency utilized hypertext documents to inform people of underground gasoline storage, and 2) with the aid of hypertext, the Ford Motor Company helped customers diagnose possible causes of malfunctions in cars and search for part numbers required for repairs. Consequently, hypertext can also be used to improve public or customer relations by highlighting the use of high technology as an effective communications and public relations tool.

Hypermedia can be used for research and development projects which require information, represented from a stack of collected documents, to be retrieved, and filtered. A hypertext system was used to allow auditors to access many reference materials such as documents, drawings, and spreadsheets during audits of financial and income statements (Hogg, 1992). Hypermedia was used at the Kennedy Space Center to replace tedious document searches for numerous specifications and process procedures for the Space Shuttle, with the correct interpretation of the vast amount of information, in a timely manner (Hosni et al., 1991).

In summary, hypermedia applications are being widely used strategically as text or document retrieval and storage tools in the areas of individual or group decision making, training, marketing and sales, and public and customer relations.

Strategic Uses of Multimedia

Multimedia has become a useful tool for corporate executives because multimedia applications can make an endless range of easy-to-comprehend information available to them (Mantha, 1992). With the aid of multimedia executives can combine visual, audio, and textual data about corporate organization structures, employee-related data, and portfolios of assets.

Multimedia application areas include training, business presentations, desktop conferencing, kiosk merchandising, and kiosk public access (Borzo, 1992; Fuochi, 1992; IBM Directions, 1991), interactive multimedia electronic mail (Borenstein, 1991), and news systems (Hoffert and Gretsch, 1991). The multimedia features of sound, images, and animation can help people better understand abstract or difficult concepts and complicated facts. Also, during learning and lesson presentation, multimedia features seem to be able to stimulate human curiosity in ways that printed material cannot (Borzo, 1992).

Recently, a U.S. Department of Defense study found that multimedia training was roughly 40% more effective than traditional training, resulted in a retention rate that was 30% greater, and a learning curve that was 30% shorter (Shulman, 1992). Trainees enthusiastically participated in learning while instructors could easily transmit and get trainees to remember important concepts and principles. According to Wilder (1992), training time for a point-of-sale cashier dropped from an average of 8 hours, to between 2 and 4 hours. Other benefits were reduced errors at the point of sale, better retention of skills, and standardization of training across the company.

In order to investigate the current and future use of multimedia, IBM Europe held a meeting where 49 participants and 20 presenters from 17 countries attended. Almost half of the presentations made at the meeting focused on successful multimedia applications in higher education (Jones, 1992). Multimedia applications were also demonstrated in the medical, scientific, and music fields.

Multimedia can be used in the field of education and can complement it in the following three ways; 1) by enhancing communications channels between tutors and students to allow more effective open and distance learning, 2) by delivering knowledge, and 3) by enriching reference and resource documents used for education and research to add all forms of audio/visual media.

Multimedia technology has been used as a direct mail advertising tool to reach target customers with greater brand awareness because this technology can be used as a persuasion tool to reflect the changing nature of lifestyles of customers, time pressures, demographics, and attitudes (Magrath, 1992). For example, Mattel has sold more Barbie fashion accessories and toys than ever before through its database-driven direct mail clubs for Barbie Doll collectors who are 3 to 12 years old. Multimedia was used to advertise footwear focusing on specific segments of potential customers (Fisher, 1991). And in the automobile industry, in order to expand new markets in the U.K., Nissan has used a massive multimedia marketing campaign to convey a dreamy, image-led message concerning its automobiles (Dwek, 1992).

Multimedia has been used by discount retailers to provide information on customers. Coopers & Lybrand used multimedia merchandise decision support systems for retail organizations to capture additional external information on customers, with the aid of multimedia databases and artificial intelligence software (Zimmerman, 1991). VF Corp. with headquarters in Reading, Pennsylvania introduced market response information systems as multimedia communication systems to allow the company to work closely with its retail partners to immediately analyze customers' activities at the store level (Rouland, 1992). The four major benefits of multimedia applications in the retail industry have been identified as; 1) the gathering and synthesizing of information, 2) enhanced decision making, 3) rapid implementation of merchandise decisions, and 4) improvement of customer service.

In many industries, growing numbers of retailers have installed interactive kiosks to place catalog orders, to inquire about service and credit, to check on the status of products being serviced, and to communicate with store managers (Chain Store Age Executive, 1992). For example, Sears, Roebuck & Co. has spent $7 million for 6,000 mini-kiosks to permit customers to place catalog orders and to inquire about services and credit. Also, K-Mart together with IBM has developed a multimedia kiosk pilot program to make shopping easier and more enjoyable for customers (Rouland, 1992). The pilot consisted of five interactive kiosks called Information Centers used in the home electronics, home entertainment, and automotive departments. All K-Mart Information Centers utilized touch-screen technology, high-quality color graphics, and sound. An ostensibly innovative feature of the system was that all multimedia information resided on a large hard disk on each kiosk's computer. This gave K-Mart the capability of easily updating kiosk information from headquarters through its satellite data network. Some criteria used to asses the study's success included the cost of installing and operating kiosk systems, increased sales, and improved customer services.

As described previously in the example of hypermedia systems use by the Ford Motor Company, multimedia information kiosks can also be used for improving public relations. The New Mexico Department of Tourism utilized multimedia information kiosks which employed touch-screens, video monitors, and audio, to provide visitors with tourist information (Bredin, 1992).

Multimedia has been used in the banking industry for dealing with high volumes of check images, even though magnetic ink character recognition (MICR) technology has traditionally been widely used (Radding, 1992). Agency Management Services in the insurance industry has utilized multimedia technology to provide insurance agents with the functions of electronic image management, an electronic camera that produced images for computer display, fax transmission, and full access to reference manuals (Hillman, 1992).

Besides service industries, manufacturing industries have developed multimedia applications because manufacturing industries require better tools to retrieve and represent information on the basis of huge investments made in the development of various types of information systems (Gadre, 1992). Also, multimedia has been used in the transportation industry where customers have access to multimedia-based cargo booking and tracking systems for handling large amounts of shipping transactions (Schlack, 1991). Airline computer reservation systems have also started using multimedia. American Airlines has added multimedia features to the text-only SABRE computer reservation system to improve travel agent productivity and to increase the number of hotel bookings by providing on-line hotel information in the form of text, color, photographs, and maps (I/S Analyzer, 1991).

Multimedia applications are being used as a strategic tool in the areas of training, marketing, sales, decision making, and public relations in the service and manufacturing industries. Most of the literature on the strategic use of hypermedia and multimedia applications comes from trade journals where little empirical research on the utility of the technology has been done. However, the applications of hypermedia and multimedia in trade journals have demonstrated the potential strategic opportunities to support decision making, training and learning, marketing and sales, business presentations, and public relations.

The Strategic Uses of Hypermedia and Multimedia in Industry

In order to assess the degree of usage of hypermedia/multimedia technology as a strategic tool in major manufacturing and service firms, the authors conducted a survey of Chief Information Officers (CIO) and senior information systems (IS) managers of Fortune 1000 companies. This population was chosen because one of their major responsibilities is to use IT to gain a corporate strategic advantage. These people are able to carry out this responsibility based on their knowledge of both the company's business strategy and the field of information technology.

Research Instrument

A two page, seven part questionnaire was designed (and pretested) to assess the degree of use of hypermedia/multimedia technologies as a strategic tool. Each part of the questionnaire was designed to serve a different purpose:

Part 1. The purpose of this part was to examine the computerization phases of hypermedia and multimedia. This part contained four questions concerning 1) the computerization phases of hypermedia and multimedia, 2) whether those technologies are actually used, or 3) investigated, and 4) if those technologies are used, in what stage they are used (Frand and Britt, 1989).

Part 2. The second part of the questionnaire examined company satisfaction with hypermedia and multimedia as a tool in providing competitive advantage and improved decision making. A five point Likert scale, ranging from "strongly disagree" to "strongly agree" was used to collect responses in this part of the survey (Porter and Millar, 1985; Wiseman, 1988; Minch, 1989; Wilkes, 1991).

Part 3. The third part was designed to investigate how hypermedia and multimedia are used strategically for formulating business strategy. "Yes"/"No" and open-ended questions were asked regarding the five stages of the strategy formulation process. These include 1) scanning the external business environments, 2) scanning the internal environments to identify strengths and weaknesses, 3) identifying problems, 4) evaluating strategic alternatives, and 5) making strategic decisions (Gray, 1989; Minch, 1989).

Part 4. The fourth part of the questionnaire was used to determine the strategy that the company is implementing among the following five generic strategies; 1) cost leadership, 2) product/service differentiation, 3) innovation, 4) growth, and 5) alliance. The five generic strategies were used to collect responses in this part of the survey (Wiseman, 1988).

Part 5. The fifth part of the instrument was designed to inquire into how companies use hypermedia and multimedia for implementing strategy. To determine this, "Yes"/"No" and open-ended questions concerning hypermedia/multimedia applications were asked (Wiseman, 1988).

Part 6. This part of the questionnaire solicited respondents' opinions regarding the actual or potential application areas of hypermedia and multimedia. Respondents were asked to select from six application areas on the questionnaire, and were also asked, in an open-ended question, to provide other application areas that they considered important.

Part 7. Finally, the respondents were asked to describe their company according to major industry type.

Results of Study

All returned questionnaires were usable (a total of 110 responses were obtained). Among the 110 respondents, 52 (47.3%) were from the *Fortune* manufacturing 500, and 58 (52.7%) were from the *Fortune* service 500.

Part 1. Five computerization phases of hypermedia and multimedia were employed for this study. The five phases were as follows: 1) not applicable, 2) investigation, 3) startup, 4) growth, and 5) stability (or maturity). The rationale was that most of the Fortune 1,000 companies were in the initial computerization phases of hypermedia and multimedia, such as investigation or startup. As shown in Figure 4, hypermedia had not been utilized by 83% of the respondents. Most of the respondents were at the investigation (43%) and not applicable (40%) stages for this technology, while only 17% of the respondents had been utilizing hypermedia. Similarly, 91% of the respondents had not used multimedia technology; however 55% (60

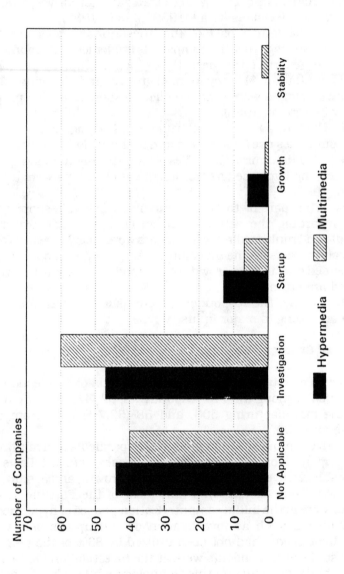

Figure 4: Computerization Phases of Hypermedia and Multimedia

out of 110 responses) of the respondents had been investigating the potential applications of multimedia.

Part 2. About 61% of the responses to the questions concerning "competitive advantage" agreed that hypermedia and multimedia provided competitive advantage in the market. Fifty-five percent of the respondents agreed that hypermedia and multimedia could be used to improve the decision making process. Fifty percent of the responses showed satisfaction with their current use of hypermedia and multimedia. Therefore, hypermedia and multimedia were perceived as a valuable strategic tool by more than half of the respondents.

Part 3. Among the five steps of the strategy formulation process, 43% of the respondents used hypermedia and multimedia for evaluating strategic alternatives and 39% of the respondents used the technology for making strategic decisions.

Part 4. Respondents were asked to order the five generic strategies. Their responses (by frequency) were as follows: 1) innovation (45), 2) cost leadership (32), 3) product differentiation and growth (27), and 4) alliance (9).

Part 5. A number of respondents used hypermedia and multimedia for implementing strategy. Innovation strategy (37%) was chosen by the respondents as most frequently supported by hypermedia and multimedia during the strategy implementation process.

Part 6. As shown in Figure 5, more than 50% of the respondents agreed that the most popular application areas of hypermedia and multimedia were business presentation, learning and training, and sales and marketing, rather than research and development, public relations, and decision making.

Part 7. As shown in Figure 6, hypermedia and multimedia application was used in a variety of industries. One interesting thing was that two companies, i.e., one in the insurance industry and one in the transportation industry, had already been at the mature stage for the computerization of multimedia technology while no company had been at the mature stage for the computerization of hypermedia technology.

Conclusion

The subject of the strategic use of information technology has been one of the top 10 issues chosen by IS professionals and managers over the past decade (Brancheau and Wetherbe, 1987). In the past, hypermedia and multimedia, as one category of information technologies, has not directly provided much information to execu-

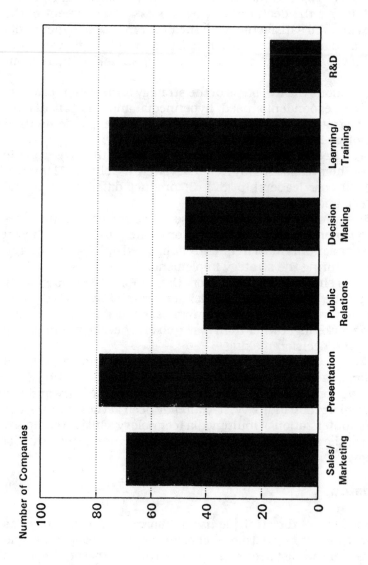

Figure 5: Application Areas of Hypermedia and Multimedia

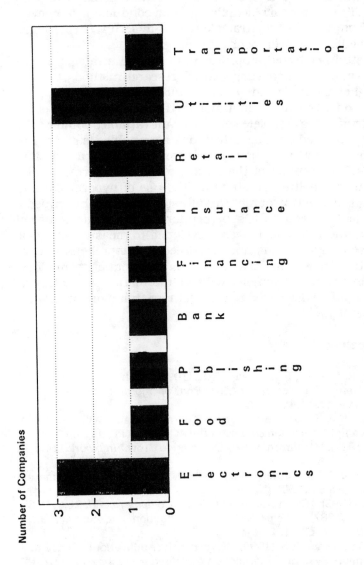

Figure 6: Hypermedia and/or Multimedia Used in Various Industries

tives because senior executives have relied more on informal and noncomputerized information for their decision making. Hypermedia and multimedia can provide strategic opportunities by supplying advanced information storage, retrieval, and representation capabilities. Even though many success stories, anecdotes, and tales about the strategic use of hypermedia and multimedia have been addressed, little empirical research has been conducted. Moreover, research constructs of the strategic use of hypertext/hypermedia and multimedia have been poorly developed.

This study collected empirical data on the strategic use of hypermedia and multimedia using survey research methods, thereby yielding higher external validity than would be possible with experimental methods. Due to the limitation on the number of pages of the survey instrument, a complete set of relevant variables could not be completely examined because other context variables (e.g., organizational characteristics, industry structure) would likely affect CIOs' (respondents') perception of the strategic use of hypermedia and multimedia. A longitudinal study on the use of hypermedia and multimedia is needed to examine the diffusion process of hypermedia and multimedia. Even if CIOs' perceptions of the strategic use of hypermedia and multimedia were developed to measure strategic performance of hypermedia and multimedia, comprehensive constructs for the strategic use of an individual information technology, a group of information technologies, and information technology as a whole, should be developed to conduct research more accurately and consistently.

References

Anderson, R.E. Sallis, P.J. & Yeap, W.K. (1991). "Enhancing a Hypertext Application Using NLP Techniques," *Journal of Information Science Principles & Practice*, 17.1, PP. 49-56.

Borenstein, N.S. (1991). "Multimedia Electronic Mail: Will the Dream Become a Reality?" *Communications of the ACM*, 34.4 PP. 117-119.

Borzo, J. (1992). "Multimedia Uses Expected to Grow," *Infoworld*, 14.6, P. 19, P. 28.

Brancheau, J.C., & Wetherbe, J.C. (1987). "Key Issues in Information Systems Management," *MIS Quarterly*, 11.1, PP. 23-45.

Bredin, A. (1992). "Electronic Tourist Info." *Computerworld*, 26.9, P. 65.

Conklin, J. (1987). "Hypertext: An Introduction and Survey," *IEEE Computer*, 20.9, PP. 17-41.

Davis, J. S., & Deter, R.S. (1990). "Hypermedia Application: Whole Earth Decision Support System," *Information & Software Technology*, 32.7, PP. 491-496.

Davis, K. (1989). "Hypertext for Business Communication: An Introduction and *Bibliography*," The Bulletin of the Association for Business Communication, 53.12, PP. 20-22.

Doebler, P.D. (1990). "The Living File," *Computer Publishing Magazine*, 5.8, PP. 42-51.

Dwek, R. (1992). "Nissan Gears Up for Growth," *Marketing*, PP. 18-19.

Elofson, G., & Konsynski, B. (1991). "Delegation Technologies: Environmental Scanning with Intelligent Agents," *Journal of Management Information Systems*, 8.1, PP. 37-62.

Fisher, C. (1991). "No Amazing Feet: Dropouts Mar Athletic-Shoe Expectations," *Advertising Age*, 62.6, PP. 31-32.

Fox, E. A. (1991). "Standards and the Emergence of Digital Multimedia Systems," *Communications of the ACM*, 34.4, PP. 26-29.

Frand, J. L. & Britt, J. A. (1989). "Fifth Annual UCLA Survey of Business School Computer Usage," *Communications of the ACM*, 32.1, PP. 62-76.

Fuochi, A. (1992). "Lines Blur as DTP Moves to Multimedia," Computing Canada, 18.8, P. 41.

Gadre, A. (1992). "Computer Technology for Manufacturing: The Next Generation," *Manufacturing Systems*, 10.4, PP. 40-49.

Garg, P. K. & Scacchi, W. (1990). "A Hypertext System to Manage Software Life-Cycle Documents," *IEEE Software*, 7, PP. 90-98.

Gray, P. (1989). "Managing the Emerging Information Systems Technologies: The Case of Group Technologies," *The Management of Information Systems*, edited by Gray P., King, W. R., McLean, E. R., and J. J. Watson, PP. 123-155. Chicago: The Dryden Press.

Hillman, B. (1992). "AMS Makes Commitment to Cutting-Edge Tech.," *National Underwriter*, 96.14, PP. 38-39.

Hoffert, E. M. & Gretsch, G. (1991). "The Digital News System at EDUCOM: A Convergence of Interactive Computing, Newspapers, Television and High-Speed Networks," *Communications of the ACM*, 34.4, PP. 113-116.

Hogg, J. D. (1992). "Automating a Procedures Manual," *Internal Auditor*, 49.2, PP. 16-18.

Horn, R. E. (1989). *Mapping Hypertext*, The Lexington Institute.

Hosni, Y. A., Hamid, T.S., & Andrew, A.E. (1991). "Hypermedia Based Application for Space Shuttle Processing," *Computers & Industrial Engineering*, 21:1-4, PP. 241-245.

Ives, B., & Learmonth, G. P. (1984). "The Information System As a Competitive Weapon," *Communications of the ACM*, 27.12, PP. 1193-1201.

Jarvenpaa, S. L. & Ives, B. (1990). "Information Technology and Corporate Strategy: A View from the Top," *Information Systems Research*, 1.4, PP. 351-376.

Jarvis, C. W., & Tagliarini, G. A. (1991). "Garment Specs Using Hypermedia," *Bobbin*, 32.10, PP. 94-98.

Jones, B. (1992). "Multimedia with IBM," *Management Services*, 36.3, P. 28.

Jones, J. W., & McLeod, R. (1986). "The Structure of Executive Information Systems: An Exploratory Analysis," *Decision Sciences*, 17.2, PP. 220-249.

Kasavana, M. (1991). "The Impact of New Technology," *Restaurant Business,* 90.5, PP. 64-66.

Kimbrough, S. O., Pritchett, C. W., Bieber, M. P., and Bhargava, H. K. (1990). "The Coast Guard's KSS Project," *Interfaces,* 20.6, PP. 5-16.

Magrath, A. J. (1992). "The Death of Advertising Has Been Greatly Exaggerated," *Sales & Marketing Management,* 144.2, PP. 23-24.

Mantha, L. (1992). "End-Users Become Power-Users with Multimedia," *Computing Canada,* 18.5, P.42.

Marchionini, G., & Shneiderman, B. (1988). "Finding Facts vs. Knowledge in Hypertext Systems," *IEEE Computer,* January, PP. 70-80.

Minch, R. P. (1989). "Application and Research Areas for Hypertext in Decision Support Systems," *Journal of Management Information Systems,* 6.3, PP. 119-138.

Nielsen, J. (1990). "The Art of Navigating through Hypertext," *Communications of the ACM,* 33.3, PP. 297-310.

Porter, K. (1988). "Choosing DBMS Software for Customer Tracking," *Business Software,* 6.6, PP. 24-27.

Porter, K., & Millar, V. E. (1985). "How Information Gives you Competitive Advantage," *Harvard Business Review,* 63.4, PP. 149-160.

Radding, A. (1992). "A View of Technology in '92," *Bank Management,* 68.1, PP. 28-35.

Ressler, D., & Stribling, D. (1990). "Designing and Prototyping a Portable Hypertext Application," *ACMSIG,* PP. 87-94.

Ritchie, I. (1989). "Hypertext - Moving Towards Large Volumes," *The Computer Journal,* 32.6, PP. 516-523.

Rouland, R. C. (1992). "Multimedia Technology: Systems for the Senses," *Discount Merchandiser,* 32.4, P. 32, P. 35, P. 72.

Schlack, M. (1991). "Plug Your Customers In," *Datamation,* 37.5, PP. 49-50.

Shim, J. P. (1992). "Emerging Information Technology: Hypertext/Hypermedia for Decision Makers," *OR/MS Today,* 19.1, PP. 34-45.

Shulman, R. E. (1992). "Multimedia...A High-Tech Solution to the Industry's Training Malaise," *Supermarket Business,* 47.4, PP. 23-24, P. 77.

Slater, D. (1991). "Presentation Graphics: Razzle-Dazzle, Plain and Simple or in Between?" *Computerworld,* 25.9, P. 35, P. 40.

Steffey, R. J. (1991). "Compton's Multimedia Encyclopedia: Bringing Multimedia to the Masses," *CD-ROM Professional,* 4.3, PP. 13-20.

Straub, D. W. & Wetherbe, J. C. (1989). "Information Technologies for the 1990s: An Organizational Impact Perspective," *Communications of the ACM,* 32.11, PP. 1328-1339.

Tiampo, J. M. (1988). "Update on Retrieval Software Products," *Optical Information Systems,* 8.2, PP. 86-88.

Verity, J. W. (1990). "The Next Frontier is the Text Frontier," *Business Week,* 178.3165, PP. 178-180.

Weaver, P. A., and McCleary, K. W. (1990). "Hypertext: Publishing Method of the Future," *Cornell Hotel & Administration Quarterly,* 31.2, PP. 108-110.

Wilder, C. (1992). "Multimedia Training: For Good Sports," *Computerworld,*

26.18, P. 35.

Wilkes, R. B. (1991). "Draining the Swamp: Defining Strategic Use of the Information Systems Resource," *Information & Management*, 20.1, PP. 49-58.

Wiseman, C. (1988). *Strategic Information Systems*, Homewood, Illinois: Irwin.

Zimmerman, R. (1991). "Technology in the Year 2000," *Discount Merchandiser*, 31.5, PP. 76-80.

Chapter 15

Systematic Evaluation Procedures for Interactive Multimedia for Education and Training

Thomas C. Reeves
University of Georgia

Stephen W. Harmon
University of Houston at Clear Lake

This chapter describes two complementary multi-dimensional approaches to evaluating interactive multimedia programs for education and training. The first approach is based upon a set of fourteen pedagogical dimensions such as "experiential value" and "learner control." The second approach is based upon a set of ten user interface dimensions such as "ease of use" and "screen design." The chapter also describes preliminary efforts to apply the pedagogical and user interface dimensions to the evaluation of two interactive multimedia programs, the Jasper Woodbury Problem Solving Series developed by the Cognition and Technology Group at Vanderbilt University, and the Columbus Encounter: Discovery and Beyond "Ultimedia" program developed by the IBM Corporation. The chapter concludes with recommendations for testing and improving these two sets of pedagogical and user interface dimensions.

Introduction

Sex sells. Even in education! At least that is what some of the designers and producers of large-scale interactive multimedia (IMM) programs seem to believe. The following quote from a video promotion for the IBM Corporation's *Illuminated Books and Manuscripts* multimedia program is typical of the "hype" proclaimed by many in the industry. The speaker is Morgan Newman, a partner in AND Communications, the company that produced this program for IBM:

> Our real competition is not necessarily the books. It's MTV. And so for us to be competitive in that marketplace, we have to be able to embody the sexiness and the passion that's able to be communicated with MTV and those types of mediums, and put that into this educational device. (Newman, 1991)

While there may be nothing inherently wrong with pointing out the "sex appeal" of IMM programs, a question arises about why there is such a lack of emphasis on the user-oriented features and capabilities of interactive multimedia? Why is the majority of advertising space and time devoted to the "sex" and "pizzazz" of IMM rather than the features that empower the user such as "ease-of-use" and "navigation" or the ability of an IMM program to accommodate individual differences among learners? Part of the explanation may simply be based on the long-standing practice in the advertising field of emphasizing surface features over deeper purposes and values.

Consider advertisements used by the auto industry. Despite limits on speed on our highways, acceleration and speed are often highlighted. The sleekness of a car's looks are emphasized over its safety features. Sex appeal is also stressed in car ads, repeating a subliminal message over and over that the car you drive directly affects how appealing you are to the opposite sex. We are so accustomed to these advertising ploys that a straightforward commercial stressing safety, economy, and environmental impact issues comes across almost as an anomaly.

As educators and trainers, we disdain the marketing of IMM programs on the basis of sex appeal and media pizzazz alone. We would prefer to highlight the effectiveness and efficiency of IMM. Reliable and valid evidence of IMM's outcomes and impact would be integral to our ideal marketing "pitch." But it isn't that easy. The problem is that the kind of evaluative information that we would prefer to provide is rarely available, especially in the early stages of a program's development and marketing. Very few IMM programs have been subjected to extensive evaluation in realistic settings (Flagg, 1990; Fletcher, 1990). The dilemma for educators and trainers considering IMM programs is how to invest their often limited resources as wisely as possible. Should they buy into the sex appeal and pizzazz arguments promulgated by commercial interests? Or should they await the results of systematic research and evaluation studies that may never come, and that even when available, are seldom free from controversy? Obviously, some sort of middle ground is needed to guide potential adopters of IMM in education and training.

Purpose

We believe that a clearer explanation of the pedagogical and user interface dimensions of IMM is a middle ground for evaluation of IMM that will benefit all parties engaged in the design, adoption, and use of these systems. Therefore, the first purpose of this chapter is to describe sets of pedagogical and user interface dimensions of IMM that have the potential to provide an improved basis for understanding, describing, and evaluating IMM programs.

In physics, dimensions are used to describe a physical quantity or phenomenon in terms of certain fundamental properties such as mass, length, time, or some combination. For example, velocity has the dimensions of length divided by time as in "the car has a maximum speed of 120 miles per hour." Similarly, the phenomenon we call interactive multimedia can be described in terms of various types of dimensions. The media dimensions of IMM include such factors as color, text, video, and animation. These are the dimensions touted by commercial interests. Pedagogical dimensions are concerned with those aspects of the design and implementation of IMM that directly affect learning. User interface dimensions are concerned with those aspects of IMM that ensure the learner can actually engage in a meaningful interactive with a program.

Systematic evaluation and research regarding instructional hypermedia and multimedia systems have lagged far behind their development (Heller, 1990; Jonassen & Grabinger, 1990; Tsai, 1988). We believe that the pedagogical and user interface dimensions and the accompanying evaluation procedures described below represent an incremental improvement over existing approaches to evaluating IMM. But describing these dimensions is not sufficient; they must be applied to the assessment of actual IMM programs. Therefore, the second purpose of this chapter is to describe our admittedly fledging efforts to utilize these pedagogical and user-interface dimension to evaluate IMM. We invite readers to adopt these dimensions to their own evaluative efforts and thus contribute to the on-going effort to improve the evaluation of IMM in education and training.

Pedagogical Dimensions

Pedagogical dimensions refer to the capabilities of IMM to initiate powerful instructional interactions, monitor learner progress, empower effective teachers and trainers, accommodate individual differences, or promote cooperative learning (Reeves, 1992). The following set of pedagogical dimensions can be used as a basis for evaluating and promoting IMM.

Pedagogical Dimension 1 – Epistemology

Epistemology is concerned with theories about the nature of knowledge. A dimension of IMM important to users of these systems is the theory of knowledge or reality held by the designers. Figure 1 illustrates a dimension of IMM ranging from an objectivist theory of knowledge to a constructivist one. Tobin and Dawson (1992) describe these two theories in relation to interactive learning environments.

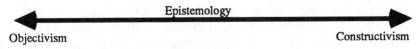

Objectivism   Constructivism

Figure 1. Epistemological dimension of IMM

Objectivist epistemology (cf., Thorndike, 1913) encompasses the following facets:

• knowledge exists separate from knowing,
• reality exists regardless of the existence of sentient beings,
• humans acquire knowledge in an objective manner through the senses,
• learning consists of acquiring truth, and
• learning can be measured precisely with tests.

Constructivist epistemology (cf., von Glasersfeld, 1989) encompasses a different set of facets:

- knowledge does not exist outside the bodies and minds of human beings,
- although reality exists independently, what we know of it is individually constructed,
- humans construct knowledge subjectively based on prior experience and metacognitive processing or reflection,
- learning consists of acquiring viable assertions or strategies that meet one's objectives, and
- at best, learning can be estimated through observations and dialogue.

If the designers and users of IMM lean toward an objectivist epistemology, they will be primarily concerned with assuring that the content of the IMM they create and implement is comprehensive and accurate with respect to ultimate "truth" as they know it. They will seek to establish the definitive structure of knowledge for a given domain based upon the advice of the most widely accepted experts in a field. For example, in science education, they will seek to transmit to students the "immutable laws" of any given field.

Advocates of constructivist epistemology, on the other hand, will be much more concerned with assuring that the content in IMM reflects the complete spectrum of views of a given domain, ranging from the traditional academic perspectives to the views of the most radical "fringe." Above all else, constructivist epistemology calls for a multiplicity of perspectives so that learners have a full range of options from which to construct their own knowledge. In science education, constructivists would provide students with opportunities to rediscover the currently accepted theories of a given science as well as rival theories that may eventually replace the current positions. They might provide coaching or scaffolding to assist students in their discovery, but they would not overly direct the learning process. Constructivist pedagogy is increasing popular in educational contexts today, whereas the training field espouses an objectivist pedagogy in most contexts.

Pedagogical Dimension 2 – Pedagogical Philosophy

Rieber (1992) and others (cf., Duffy & Jonassen, 1992; Papert, 1990) make a clear distinction between instructivist and constructivist approaches to teaching and learning. We prefer to think of these orientations in terms of pedagogical philosophies. Figure 2 illustrates a dimension of IMM ranging from a strict instructivist philosophy to a radical constructivist one.

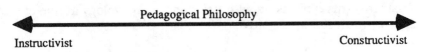

Figure 2. Pedagogical philosophy dimension of IMM

Instructivists stress the importance of goals and objectives that exist apart from the learner. These goals and objectives are drawn from a domain of knowledge, e.g., algebra, or extracted from observations of the behaviors of experts within a given domain, e.g., surgeons. Once goals and objectives are delineated, they are sequenced into learning hierarchies, generally representing a progression from lower to higher order learning. Then, direct instruction is designed to address each of the objectives in the hierarchy, often employing instructional strategies derived from behavioral psychology (Rieber, 1992). Relatively little emphasis is put on the learner *per se* who is usually viewed as a passive recipient of instruction. IMM based on instructivist pedagogy generally treats learners as empty vessels to be filled with learning. Direct instruction demands that the content be sharply defined and that instructional strategies focus as directly on this content as possible.

Alternatively, constructivists emphasize the primacy of the learner's intentions, experience, and metacognitive strategies. Rieber (1992) describes the constructivist view of learning as involving "individual constructions of knowledge" (p. 94). In this view, learners attain a state of cognitive equilibration through reconstruction of concepts, schema, mental models, and other cognitive structures in the face of new information and experience that may conflict with earlier constructions. A major goal in constructivist pedagogy is to assure that the learning environment is as rich as possible. Major emphasis is placed on identifying the unique interests, styles, motivations, and capabilities of individual learners so that learning environments can be tailored to them. Instead of an empty vessel, the learner is regarded as an individual replete with pre-existing knowledge, aptitudes, motivations, and other characteristics that are difficult to assess, much less accommodate. Constructivists often argue for replacing direct instruction with self-directed exploration and discovery learning.

Pedagogical Dimension 3 – Underlying Psychology

At the risk of ignoring a number of other important theoretical perspectives (e.g., developmental psychology), a dimension related to the basic psychology underlying IMM is proposed. Figure 3 illustrates this dimension with behavioral psychology at one end of the continuum and cognitive psychology at the other.

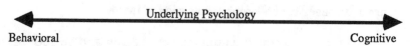

Behavioral   Cognitive

Figure 3. Underlying psychology dimension of IMM

Debunking behavioral psychology has become quite fashionable, despite a few staunch defenders (cf., Gilbert & Gilbert, 1991). Therefore, it seems ironic that behavioral psychology continues to be the underlying psychology for many IMM programs. According to classical behavioral psychology (Skinner, 1968), the important factors in learning are not internal states that may or may not exist, but behavior that can be directly observed. Instruction consists primarily of the shaping of desirable behaviors through the scientific arrangement of stimuli, responses, feedback, reinforcement, and other contingencies. First, a stimulus is provided, often in the form of a short presentation of content. Second, a response is demanded, often in the form of a question. Third, feedback is given as to the accuracy of the response. Fourth, positive reinforcement is given for accurate responses. Fifth, inaccurate responses result in either a repetition of the original stimulus or a somewhat modified (often simpler) version of it, and the cycle begins again.

Cognitive psychology, on the other hand, is quite popular today, and virtually all self-respecting instructional design theorists now claim to be cognitivists (cf., Gagné & Glaser, 1987). Without ignoring behavior, cognitive psychology places much more emphasis on internal mental states than behavioral psychology. Kyllonen and Shute (1989) have proposed a taxonomy that represents the spectrum of internal states with which cognitive psychologists are concerned. Their taxonomy begins with simple propositions (e.g., stating that kangaroos are native to Australia.), proceeding through schema, rules, general rules, skills, general skills, automatic skills, and finally, mental models (e.g., analyzing threats to the ecosystem of Australia based upon competing theories of global warming). The latter type of knowledge seems particularly important because mental models are the basis for generalizable problem-solving abilities. Cognitive psychologists recognize that a wide variety of learning strategies may have to be employed in any given instructional setting depending upon the type of knowledge to be con-

structed. Learning strategies include memorization, direct instruction, deduction, drill and practice, and induction (Schank & Jona,
1990). The latter is most highly valued in that it fosters the
construction of mental models (Jih & Reeves, 1992).

Pedagogical Dimension 4 – Goal Orientation

The goals and objectives of IMM can range from sharply focused
ones (e.g., following strict protocols for handling medical emergency
situations) to more or less unfocused ones (e.g., learning to appreciate modern art). Figure 4 illustrates a dimension of IMM related to
the degree of focus represented in the goals of an interactive
program.

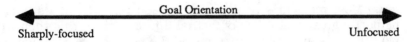

Sharply-focused   Unfocused

Figure 4. Goal orientation dimension of IMM

Cole (1992) clarifies the relevance of different types of goals to the
design of IMM. She maintains that some knowledge "has undergone
extensive social negotiation of meaning and which might most
efficiently and effectively be presented more directly to the learner"
(p. 29). In such cases, direct instruction, perhaps in the form of a
computer-based tutorial, may suffice for learning. Other knowledge
is so tenuous, creative, or of a higher level (e.g., mental models) that
direct instruction is inappropriate. In the latter cases, IMM programs that promote inductive learning such as microworlds (Rieber,
1992), virtual reality simulations (Henderson, 1991), and learning
environments (Hannafin, 1992) are much more appropriate. However, we suspect that most advocates of discovery-based environments for the learning of social studies, science, and even mathematics in schools would probably prefer their airline pilots and surgeons
to be trained via direct instruction!

Pedagogical Dimension 5 – Instructional Sequencing

Instructional sequencing is another important dimension of
IMM. The Cognition and Technology Group at Vanderbilt (CTGV)
(1992) contrast "the extreme reductionist view" with a constructivist
perspective (pp. 72-73). In the former, learning to accomplish a task
(e.g., troubleshoot electronic components) requires that all the
components of the task be mastered independently before they can

be assembled into the final performance. In the latter, instructional sequencing based upon a constructivist view might put novice learners in a realistic context requiring troubleshooting, in which scaffolding and coaching would be introduced as needed by individual learners. Figure 5 presents a continuum of instructional sequencing views ranging from reductionist to constructivist.

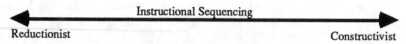

Reductionist   Constructivist

Figure 5. Instructional sequencing dimension of IMM

Bransford, Sherwood, Hasselbring, Kinzer, & Williams (1990) describe the sequencing problem in the context of medical education. Most medical schools follow a sequence whereby students memorize great quantities of factual information during their first two years of training and then spend the next two years in various clinical settings where they may or may not have opportunities to use the memorized knowledge. A few enlightened medical schools have begun to place students in clinical settings from day one while providing them with the pedagogical support to learn basic knowledge and skills as needed. Perelman (1992) describes alternative medical schools in Canada and The Netherlands that employ this innovative approach.

Similarly, IMM can be designed to present a focal event or problem situation that will serve as an "anchor" or focus for collaborative efforts among instructors and students to retrieve and construct knowledge (Brown, Collins, & Duguid, 1989; CTGV, 1992). Cognitive psychologists at the CTGV call this type of instruction "anchored instruction" (Bransford et al., 1990; CTGV, 1992) because the process of constructing new knowledge is situated or anchored in meaningful and relevant contexts. They maintain that events and problems presented in IMM should be purposively designed to be intrinsically interesting, problem-oriented, and challenging. They have evidence that in response to these types of events and problems, students construct useful as opposed to inert knowledge (Bransford et al., 1990; CTGV, 1992).

Pedagogical Dimension 6 – Experiential Validity

The earliest type of systematic learning activity probably involved some sort of apprenticeship whereby a novice worked side by side with a master. Apprenticeships have high, i.e., concrete, experiential value. More abstract learning activities, e.g., classroom lectures, were developed much later in history. A major criticism of many of our current dominant pedagogical schemes is that they are too abstract, removed as they are from "real world" experience (cf. Brown et al., 1989). Figure 6 illustrates an experiential value continuum ranging from abstract to concrete.

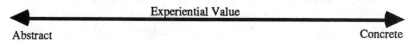

Abstract   Concrete

Figure 6. Experiential value dimension of IMM

A major concern for educators and trainers alike is the degree to which classroom learning transfers to external situations in which the application of knowledge, skills, and attitudes is appropriate. The cognitive theories of Newell and Simon (1972), Anderson (1983), Brown (1985), and others support the fundamental principle that the way in which knowledge, skills, and attitudes are initially learned plays an important role in the degree to which these abilities can be used in other contexts. To put it simply, if knowledge, skills, and attitudes are learned in a context of use, they will be used in that and similar contexts. This is especially important in training for the work place, whether it be a construction site, hospital, bank, or airplane.

In traditional instruction, information is presented in encapsulated formats, often via abstract lectures and texts, and it is largely left up to the student to generate any possible connections between conditions (such as a problem) and actions (such as the use of knowledge as a tool to solve the problem). There is ample evidence that students who are quite adept at "regurgitating" memorized information rarely retrieve that same information when confronted with novel conditions that warrant its application (Bransford et al., 1990; Perelman, 1992).

Pedagogical Dimension 7 – Role of Instructor

Some IMM programs are designed to eliminate pedagogical roles for live instructors. In fact, a hidden agenda of many of these programs seems to be making them "teacher-proof," perhaps because of a belief that earlier instructional innovations have failed as a result of teacher interference with the programs. Alternatively, IMM can be designed in which instructors (whether teachers or trainers) have critical roles. Figure 7 represents a continuum of instructor roles ranging from absolutely non-existent to integral.

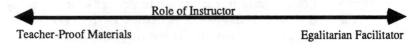

Figure 7. **Role of instructor dimension of IMM**

Authoritarian, teacher-centered approaches and teacher-proof approaches both have fervent contemporary advocates (cf., Hirsch, 1987, for the former, and Winn, 1989, for the latter). The "Egalitarian Facilitator" role is a viable alternative to either of these extremes. The Cognition and Technology Group at Vanderbilt (CTGV) (1992) describe a shift in the teacher's role "from authoritarian provider of knowledge to a resource who at times is consulted by students and at other times can become the student whom others teach" (p. 73). Of course, in some training contexts, it may be appropriate to reduce or even eliminate the need for professional instructors. However, this must be done with caution. Rigorous evaluation should be conducted to assure that the reduction in the human factor in training has not had unexpected ill effects.

Pedagogical Dimension 8 – Value of Errors

The old maxim that "experience is the best teacher" reflects a belief that we learn much in life through trial and error (CTGV, 1992). Although this approach is inefficient and even dangerous in some contexts, experiential learning is highly valued simply because it provides opportunities for us to "learn from our mistakes." On the other hand, some educational theorists, especially proponents of programmed instruction, have maintained that ideal learning involves no errors. These developers attempt to arrange the contingencies of instruction in such a way that learners can only make correct responses. Figure 8 presents a continuum of error values ranging from errorless learning to learning from experience.

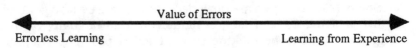

Figure 8. **Value of errors dimension of IMM**

An example of an IMM program that prohibits errors is the Principles of the Alphabet Learning System (PALS) designed for the IBM Corporation by Dr. John Henry Martin (1986). PALS uses interactive videodisc technology to teach basic literacy skills to adolescents and adults. At specific intervals, learners are required to type in letters to form the words that on-screen characters say. However, only those keys that match an acceptable form of spelling the words are enabled. Pressing the wrong keys puts nothing on the screen except more and more refined directions as to the desired response.

Such an errorless approach contrasts sharply with IMM employing simulation as an instructional strategy. In "The Case of Dax Cowart," an interactive videodisc simulation created at the Center for the Design of Educational Computing at Carnegie Mellon University (Covey & Cavalier, 1989), college students are placed in the roles of members of a hospital ethics panel that must decide whether a horribly burned patient can be allowed to die as he has requested or must undergo months of excruciatingly painful treatments. Regardless of a student's decision, he or she is confronted with the negative outcomes of that decision. In this unique simulation, each choice is treated as an "error" from which valuable lessons can be learned.

Pedagogical Dimension 9 – Motivation

Motivation is a primary factor in many instructional models (cf. Carroll, 1963). Rieber (1992) describes five design principles for IMM that can be derived from constructivism. The first is to "provide a meaningful learning context that supports intrinsically motivating and self-regulated learning" (p. 98). Intrinsic motivation has been held forth as the "Holy Grail" to which all IMM programs should aspire (Malone, 1984). Figure 9 illustrates a motivation dimension that ranges from extrinsic (i.e., outside the learning environment) to intrinsic (i.e., integral to the learning environment).

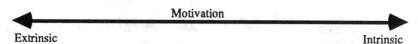

Motivation

Extrinsic   Intrinsic

Figure 9. Motivation dimension of IMM

Intrinsically motivating instruction is very elusive regardless of the delivery system, but virtually every new approach to come along promises to be more motivating than any that have come before. Interactive multimedia (IMM) is the latest type of interactive learning system that is supposed to motivate learners automatically, simply because of the integration of music, voice, still pictures, text, animation, motion video, and a friendly interface on a computer screen. In practice, as Keller (1987) has specified, motivation aspects must be consciously designed into IMM just as rigorously as any other pedagogical dimensions. However, the current state-of-the-art of IMM indicates that extrinsic motivation remains a critical factor in many education and training contexts.

Pedagogical Dimension 10 – Structure

All IMM programs possess some degree of structure, but it can vary from tightly prescribed pathways through a program to widely divergent options that learners can activate in any order they wish. Figure 10 illustrates a structure dimension that ranges from high to low.

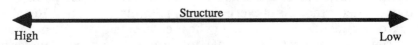

Structure

High   Low

Figure 10. Structure dimension of IMM

Although low structure may seem to promote learner independence and increase individualization, there is a cost for low structure. This is especially true for IMM programs that adapt the "free exploration" structures associated with many contemporary examples of hypertext, hypermedia, and multimedia. The price for this freedom from structure is that learners may become confused or lose track of what is going on, what they can do, and/or where they are located in the program. Screen designs can be crafted to help orient learners "lost in hyperspace," but guidelines for these designs are limited (cf., Laurel, 1990; Marcus, 1992; Mayhew, 1992). The set of user-interface dimensions described in the next section of this chapter describe these aspects in more detail.

Pedagogical Dimension 11 – Accommodation of Individual Differences

Although it might be assumed that the main reason for employing IMM for instruction would be to accommodate individual differences among learners, this is not always the case. Some IMM programs have very little, if any, provision for individual differences whereas others have been designed to accommodate a wide range of individual differences including personalistic, affective, and physiological factors (Ackerman, Sternberg, & Glaser, 1989). Figure 11 illustrates a continuum of accommodations of individual differences that ranges from non-existent to multi-faceted.

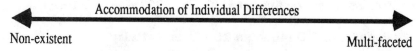

Figure 11. Accommodation of individual differences dimension of IMM

The impact of individual differences is a major factor in the effectiveness of IMM. Learning is a function of the learner, the content to be learned, and the features of the instruction (Sternberg, 1985). Many theoretical models of learning treat individual differences among learners as the major predictor of differential learning outcomes (cf., Carroll, 1963). In most education and training contexts, we cannot be guaranteed that our learners will be homogeneous in terms of aptitudes, prerequisite knowledge, motivation, experience, learning styles, eye-hand coordination, and so forth. Therefore, we must endeavor to provide scaffolding, cognitive bootstrapping, and other types of metacognitive support to promote learning (Cates, 1992; Resnick, 1989).

Pedagogical Dimension 12 – Learner Control

Learner control has been one of the most heavily researched dimensions of IMM in recent years (Steinberg, 1989). Figure 12 illustrates a dimension of IMM that can range from complete program control to unrestricted learner control.

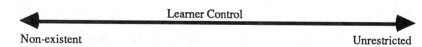

Figure 12. Learner control dimension of IMM

Learner control refers to the options in IMM that allow learners to make decisions about what sections to study and/or what paths to follow through interactive material. The popular wisdom is that learner control makes IMM more effective by individualizing the instruction and making it more motivating, but all too often experimental studies have led to no significant results in terms of the predicted main effects (Williams, 1993). Reeves (1993) describes critical theoretical and methodological flaws in learner control studies. Ross and Morrison (1989) concluded that "research findings regarding the effects of learner control as an adaptive strategy have been inconsistent, but more frequently negative than positive"

(p. 28). Better research is needed before questions about the learner control issue can be answered (Clark, 1992; Reeves, 1993).

Pedagogical Dimension 13 – User Activity

Hannafin (1992) identified another important dimension of IMM, especially those that he and others characterize as "learning environments." He maintains that some learning environments are primarily intended to enable learners to "access various representations of content" (p. 59). He labels these "mathemagenic" environments. Other learning environments, called generative by Hannafin, engage learners in the process of creating, elaborating or representing knowledge. Figure 13 illustrates this continuum of user activity.

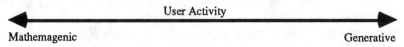

User Activity

Mathemagenic   Generative

Figure 13. User activity dimension of IMM

Generative learning environments are aligned most closely with constructivist pedagogy whereas mathemagenic environments are often based upon instructivist pedagogy, but this is not necessarily always obvious. Contemporary IMM programs such as the ABC News Interactive series (ABC News Interactive, 1991) and the IBM Ultimedia programs (IBM Corporation, 1991a,b) include generative capabilities nested within otherwise mathemagenic presentations of content.

Pedagogical Dimension 14 – Cooperative Learning

Support for the value of cooperative learning is growing throughout education and training circles (Slavin, 1992). IMM can be designed to thwart or promote cooperative learning. In fact, some IMM programs require cooperative learning (cf., IBM Corporation, 1986) whereas others make no provision for its support. Figure 14 illustrates a cooperative learning dimension ranging from a complete lack of support for cooperative learning to the inclusion of cooperative learning as an integral part of IMM.

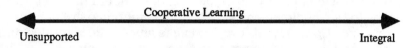

Figure 14. Cooperative learning dimension of IMM

Cooperative learning refers to instructional methods in which learners work together in pairs or small groups to accomplish shared goals (Slavin, 1992). Johnson and Johnson (1987) and Slavin (1990) present evidence that when IMM (and other instructional delivery systems) are structured to allow cooperative learning, learners benefit both instructionally and socially.

User Interface Dimensions

Earlier in this chapter, we noted that reliable and valid data concerning effectiveness, efficiency, and impact would be the ideal basis for evaluating IMM. Given that such data is rarely available, we have presented fourteen pedagogical dimensions that can be used to analyze the potential effectiveness of IMM. Unfortunately, even information concerning pedagogical dimensions, while highly desirable, is difficult to find with respect to many IMM programs. An additional approach to evaluating IMM involves the application of a set of user interface dimensions, i.e., those aspects of IMM that assure that users have a meaningful and purposeful experience with IMM. They represent a middle ground between the media elements promoted in advertisements and the sometimes elusive pedagogical dimensions of IMM. User interface dimensions are necessary, but insufficient, criteria for comprehensive evaluation of IMM.

The literature about user interface design for interactive multimedia ranges from the highly artistic (cf., Laurel, 1990) to the highly technical (cf., Blattner & Dannenberg, 1992). Our description and application of ten dimensions of user interfaces for IMM represents a synthesis of both the artistic and scientific foundations of IMM together with our personal experiences in designing, using, evaluating, and researching IMM programs (cf., Harmon, 1992; Reeves, 1991; Reeves & Harmon, 1991).

User interface dimensions include such factors as ease of use, media integration, and cognitive load. Each dimension can be represented as a continuum with a more or less specified range of values. The ends of any given dimensional continuum represent extremes that few actual IMM programs exemplify. Instead, most

IMM programs can be described in terms of a profile of values across the dimensions described below. Also, it should be noted that the following set of dimensions are neither comprehensive nor mutually exclusive. Considerable overlap exists among the identified dimensions, and some dimensions have yet to be specified.

Laurel (1990) defines user interface as a combination of "the physical properties of the interactors, the functions to be performed, and the balance of power and control" (p. xii). In IMM, the interactors are the human learner and the IMM system itself. According to Laurel, the primary concerns in user interface design are the intentions of the user. From Laurel's perspective, everything about the user interface should serve to empower the learner to accomplish the tasks that he/she has determined (e.g., learn a new language, experience time travel, or find information needed to solve a problem).

In their more technically-oriented volume, Blattner and Dannenberg (1992) refer to interface design in terms of media (e.g., text, audio, and video) and modes of interacting with media (e.g., pointing, speaking, and keying). With respect to media, Blattner and Dannenberg "are most concerned with how the information content of a media is conveyed" (p. xxv). With respect to modes, they "are usually more concerned with the dynamics of interaction" (p. xxv).

User Interface Dimension 1 – Ease of Use

"Ease of Use" is concerned with the perceived facility with which a learner interacts with an IMM program. Figure 15 illustrates a dimension of IMM ranging from the perception that a program is very difficult to use to one that is perceived as being very easy to use. Like many of the dimensions described in this chapter, ease of use is both an aggregate and individual dimension. For example, in the aggregate sense, the Apple Macintosh desktop interface is generally perceived as easier to use than the command line interface of Microsoft disk operating system (MS DOS). However, in the individual sense, some people may perceive the MS-DOS interface to be easier to use because of their own unique experiences and attributes.

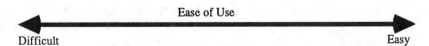

Ease of Use

Difficult   Easy

Figure 15. "Ease of Use" dimension of IMM

We suspect that user interface dimensions are highly correlated with how well users enjoy a specific IMM program. Whether users like a program may be more or less important, depending on the intent of the program and the context for its use. Certainly, not liking an IMM program that is intended to be "edutainment" is a major problem, whereas learners' affect for a program may be less important in a training context in which powerful extrinsic motivational factors exist. Nonetheless, we believe in the long run, improving the user interface dimensions of IMM, such as "ease of use," is a highly desirable goal, regardless of context.

User Interface Dimension 2 – Navigation

"Navigation" is concerned with the perceived ability to move through the contents of an IMM program in an intentional manner. Figure 16 illustrates a dimension of IMM ranging from the perception that a program is difficult to navigate to one that is perceived as being easy to navigate. An important aspect of navigation is orientation, i.e., the degree to which a user feels that he/she knows where he/she is in an IMM program and how to go to another part of it. This is a critical variable because IMM users frequently complain of being lost in a program (Harmon, 1992; Utting & Yankelovitch, 1989). IMM designers use several ways of supporting navigation and maintaining orientation. A popular approach to navigation is the WIMP (window-icons-mouse-pointing) interface.

Navigation

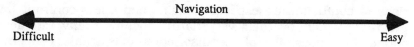

Difficult   Easy

Figure 16. "Navigation" dimension of IMM

It should be noted that not all disorientation in IMM is necessarily bad. Kahn and Landow (1993) present an analysis that indicates that some types of disorientation may be appropriate, even pleasurable, especially when the learner is engaged in dealing with complex, novel material. However, the disorientation to which our navigation dimension refers is related to the stressful disorientation that results from a poorly designed interface.

User Interface Dimension 3 – Cognitive Load

Learning with IMM requires different mental efforts than performing learning tasks via print or other non-print media. To make any meaningful response to IMM, learners must cope with and integrate at least three cognitive loads or demands, i.e., (a) the content of the program, (b) its structure, and (c) the response options available. To learn via IMM, the learner must perceive options, conceptualize a choice, and make some physical action, all while mentally coordinating the demands of these three cognitive loads. The user interface is the vehicle that allows perceptual, conceptual, and physical contacts with the IMM program. In terms of "cognitive load," the user interface can seem unmanageable (i.e., confusing) at one end of the continuum and easily manageable (i.e., intuitive) at the other end (see Figure 17).

Cognitive Load

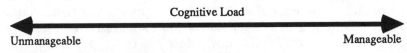

Unmanageable   Manageable

Figure 17. "Cognitive Load" dimension of IMM

Learners acquire and structure information delivered via interfaces, conduct mental operations, and accomplish physical activities during their interactions with IMM. The limited capacity of working memory to hold only five to nine chunks of information simultaneously (Miller, 1956) makes it difficult for users of complexly structured IMM to reason when numerous cognitive load factors must be handled simultaneously. Users may feel overwhelmed by numerous options that increase the cognitive load. The risks of confusion are especially high when users confront IMM programs which by their very nature include many interactive options. The possibility of user disorientation is a major concern in the increasingly popular IMM programs that feature a complex, flexible structure. Successful users possess an adequate "mental model" of the form and function of the program's user interface (Rogers, Rutherford, & Bibby, 1992). Investigating the mental models that learners construct of IMM interfaces represents an important challenge for researchers in this field (Jih & Reeves, 1992).

User Interface Dimension 4 – Mapping

"Mapping" refers to the program's ability to track and graphically represent to the user his or her path through the program. In complex, non-linear IMM programs, user-disorientation can be alleviated if users can see what parts of the system they have examined. Utting and Yankelovitch (1989) discuss user disorientation as referring to, among other things, the user's not knowing "the boundaries of the information space." Harmon (1992) reported that users frequently felt they had seen all of a program after viewing only about a third of it. Having a detailed mapping system gives users an aid in understanding which parts and how much of the information space they have interacted with, and conversely which parts and how much of it they haven't. IMM programs fall in a continuum of containing no mapping function to an appropriately powerful mapping function (see Figure 18).

Mapping

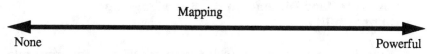

None   Powerful

Figure 18. "Mapping" dimension of IMM

The notion of an "appropriately powerful" mapping function requires some explanation. Just as it is important to possess a map of the most usable scale when taking a road trip, it is important for IMM programs to provide enough, but not too much, detail in showing user paths. An IMM map that shows every piece of its knowledge space might prove to be so tedious or unwieldy as to be of as little value as an IMM program with no map.

User Interface Dimension 5 – Screen Design

"Screen Design" is a particularly complex dimension of IMM that can easily be broken down into many sub-dimensions related to text, icons, graphics, color, and other visual aspects of IMM programs. Shneiderman (1987) maintains that although certain design principles have been established, "screen design will always have elements of art and require invention" (p. 326). We have delineated a separate dimension to deal with the artistic aspects of IMM (see Dimension 9 - Aesthetics below). We define "screen design" as a dimension ranging from substantial violations of principles of screen design to general adherence to principles of screen design (see Figure 19).

Screen Design

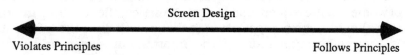

Violates Principles   Follows Principles

Figure 19. "Screen Design" dimension of IMM

We recognize two problems with this dimension. First, as Jones (1992) describes, screen design principles have not kept up with the rapidly changing nature of interactive multimedia technology. Second, creative designers may sometimes intentionally violate screen design principles for effect or to otherwise focus the user's attention. Nonetheless, we think that there exists enough knowledge about the principles of screen design that people, particularly experienced IMM designers, can make meaningful distinctions among poorly and well designed screens in IMM programs.

User Interface Dimension 6 – Knowledge Space Compatibility

"Knowledge space" refers to the network of concepts and relationships that compose the mental schema a user possesses about a given phenomena or topic. Designers of IMM programs are generally perceived as possessing an expert knowledge space with respect to the topics included in the programs they create. This expertise usually is the basis for the structure of the knowledge or information presented in an IMM program. Novice users, on the other hand, often possess an inadequate knowledge space with respect to the topics in a program. The knowledge space of novices may be inadequate because of ignorance, misconceptions, or some blending of ignorance and misconceptions. When a novice user initiates a search for information in an IMM program, the interface should be powerful enough so that the user perceives the resulting information as compatible with his or her current knowledge space (see Figure 20). If the information received is not perceived as relevant to the search strategies used by the user, the system will be perceived as incompatible.

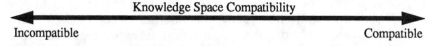

Knowledge Space Compatibility

Incompatible   Compatible

Figure 20. "Knowledge Space Compatibility" dimension of IMM

Admittedly, this is a very difficult dimension to judge. However, if a user initiates a search for information about a topic, e.g., the role of women in the exploration of North America, the resulting information should seem compatible with that search once the information is thoroughly explored. If the information seems arbitrary or irrelevant to the search that was initiated, the knowledge space representation should be judged as incompatible.

User Interface Dimension 7 – Information Presentation

The "Information Presentation" dimension is concerned with whether the information contained in the knowledge space of an IMM program is presented in an understandable form. The most elegantly designed user interface for IMM is useless if the information it is intended to present is incomprehensible to the user. Certainly the user might be able to find all of the information about a subject, but whether the user could then comprehend/understand/learn that information is another matter. Imagine a complicated concept like Kant's categorical imperative presented in textual form, written in a stream of consciousness style reminiscent of James Joyce's *Ulysses*. Or consider a video presentation on surgical techniques for angioplasty, directed and produced by the late pop artist Andy Warhol. In each case the information requisite for understanding may be present, but would probably be difficult if not impossible to comprehend. Information presentation is defined as a dimension ranging from obtuse to clear (see Figure 21).

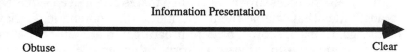

Information Presentation

Obtuse   Clear

Figure 21. "Information Presentation" dimension of IMM

User Interface Dimension 8 – Media Integration

There are two aspects to the "Media Integration" dimension. In the first, media integration refers to how much the IMM program is truly a "multimedia" program. The term "multimedia" is applied in a fast and loose manner these days, and frequently programs touted as multimedia are actually "bi-" or "tri-media" programs. These programs may include text and graphics, or text, graphics and sound, but they often fall short of incorporating text, graphics, sound, animation, and still and motion video. While we do not advocate the philosophy that more is always better, we do feel that so called "multimedia" programs should make the best use of available technology. The second aspect of media integration is the more important of the two. It refers to how well an IMM program combines the different media to produce an effective whole. Do the various media work together to form one cohesive program, or is the program a hodgepodge of gratuitous media segments? Are the various media components necessary to the function of the program or would the program function equally as well without them? We define the media integration dimension as ranging from uncoordinated to coordinated (see Figure 22).

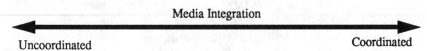

Media Integration

Uncoordinated   Coordinated

Figure 22. "Media Integration" dimension of IMM

User Interface Dimension 9 – Aesthetics

"Aesthetics" refers to the artistic aspects of IMM programs in the sense of possessing beauty or elegance. In the aggregate sense, many people may praise the aesthetics of an automobile design or the elegance of a bridal gown. However, in an individual sense, aesthetics are highly unique and one person's sense of the beautiful may seem grotesque to another. Eisner (1985) described the need to develop "connoisseurs" in education, just as we have connoisseurs in the arts. Connoisseurs have refined tastes and a deep sensitivity to aesthetics that enable them to criticize phenomena (e.g., plays, paintings, musical scores, or IMM programs) in a manner that can be communicated to others. In turn, other people, perhaps less refined and less sensitive, may become more informed by "consuming" the expert reviews provided by the connoisseurs. In the absence of such connoisseurs, we have defined a dimension of the user interface of IMM that ranges from displeasing to pleasing (see Figure 23).

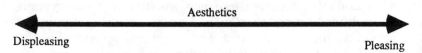

Aesthetics

Displeasing   Pleasing

Figure 23. "Aesthetics" dimension of IMM

User Interface Dimension 10 – Overall Functionality

"Overall Functionality" is an aspect of IMM related to the perceived utility of an IMM program. The perceived functionality of an IMM program is obviously highly related to the intended use of the program. A given IMM program may have multiple uses. For example, a program such as Broderbund's (1992) *Just Grandma and Me* can be used to entertain young children, teach students to read, or provide practice in English, Spanish, or Japanese as a second language. Its overall functionality must be judged in relation to the specific intended use that currently exists in the mind of the user. Figure 24 illustrates a dimension of the user interface of IMM that ranges from dysfunctional to highly functional.

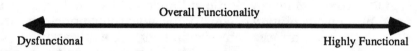

Overall Functionality

Dysfunctional   Highly Functional

Figure 24. "Overall Functionality" dimension of IMM

Preliminary Applications

To illustrate the potential utility of the pedagogical and user interface dimensions of IMM, the next part of this chapter presents an analysis of two IMM programs employing these dimensions. The most successful of our preliminary efforts to apply the pedagogical and user interface dimensions described in this chapter have involved asking experienced IMM developers and users to rate IMM programs. Reeves and Harmon (1993) reported on the application of the user interface dimensions by a group of inexperienced IMM users (undergraduate preservice teacher education students) that was unsuccessful. Based on that study, we have concluded that inexperienced users tend to rate user interface dimensions too highly, perhaps as a result on the overall novelty effect of the IMM experience.

Experienced developers and users of IMM, on the other hand, seem to possess the necessary background and objectivity to provide a reliable and valid assessment of both pedagogical and user interface dimensions. The experienced developers and users of IMM that we have used in our preliminary analyses have been faculty and graduate students in an instructional technology graduate program. We look forward to additional applications of these dimensions involving experienced personnel in other education and training contexts.

The two programs that we report on below are quite different. The first has been created in an academic environment within the context of a long term research and development program, viz., the *Jasper Woodbury Problem Solving Series* developed by the Cognition and Technology Group at Vanderbilt University (1992). The second IMM program, *Columbus Encounter: Discovery and Beyond* (IBM Corporation, 1991a), was created by one of the largest scale multimedia ventures to date, viz., the IBM "Ultimedia" series. In the next two subsections, we report on the assessment of these two programs.

Applying the Pedagogical Dimensions

The *Jasper Woodbury Problem Solving Series* developed by the Cognition and Technology Group at Vanderbilt University (1992) is a notable implementation of constructivist learning principles, and as such provides an excellent example for the application of our fourteen pedagogical dimensions. These programs (which are provided in both interactive videodisc and linear video versions) provide students with opportunities to learn advanced mathematical problem-solving skills within the context of a series of high-interest video adventures. Students discover the need to develop mathematical skills within the context of flying planes and operating motor boats to solve simulated dilemmas. Numerous studies have been and are being conducted using the *Jasper* series of programs (cf., Bransford et al., 1990).

The *Jasper* series is an example of what Hannafin (1992) calls a "generative" learning environment, i.e., a program that requires students to construct or generate their own knowledge as opposed to one that requires them to select knowledge from prepackaged options. Knowledge acquired in generative environments is more likely to generalize than the inert knowledge acquired in traditional passive learning environments (CTGV, 1992).

Figure 25 presents a profile of the *Jasper* programs using fourteen pedagogical dimensions. The ratings have been synthesized from reviews provided by instructional technology faculty and graduate students. They are based on seeing demonstrations of the programs at professional conferences plus reading several extensive reports about the program (cf. Bransford, Vye, Goldman, Hasselbring, & Pellegrino, 1991), rather than first hand experience with the programs themselves. Our analysis reveals that the Jasper programs are grounded in constructivist and cognitivist foundations. Teachers are integral to the implementation of Jasper and collaborative learning is strongly supported. It appears to be an advanced example of a generative learning environment. However, we caution again that this conclusion is not based upon actual use of the *Jasper* programs with the intended middle school student population. Further, an analysis of the user interface dimensions on the *Jasper* programs has not be done.

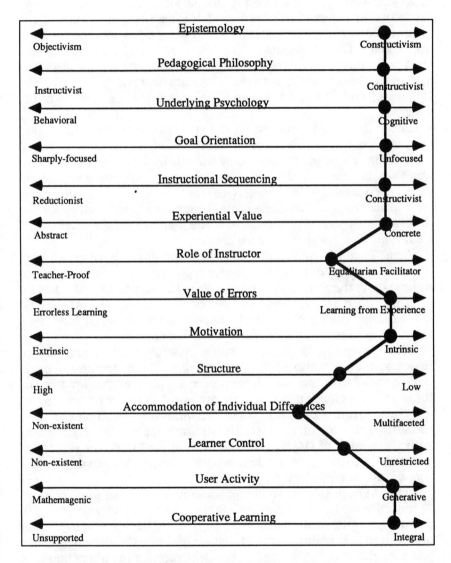

Figure 25. Pedagogical dimensions of the Jasper programs

Applying the User Interface Dimensions

The following critical analysis of *Columbus Encounter: Discovery and Beyond* is based upon the synthesis of the reviews provided by experienced developers and users of IMM. In the case of this program, Wolf's (1975) adversary evaluation model was employed to structure and report the results of the assessment. Half of the graduate students enrolled in a graduate evaluation course were appointed to the "prosecution," and directed to make a case that this IMM program violates user interface design dimensions as described above. The other half of the students were appointed to the "defence," and directed to defend the user interface aspects of the program.

After several weeks of review, the students presented their cases for or against the program at a "trial" presided over by the course instructor. Evidence presented by the students included their own analyses of the program and its accompanying documentation, videotaped sessions with preservice teachers, videotaped interviews with other "experts," and excerpts from promotional videos for the program. Figure 26 summarizes the user interface analysis of *Columbus Encounter: Discovery and Beyond.*

The "ease of use" of the *Columbus* program is rated as very difficult. Graduate student reviewers reported that it took two to four hours before they felt at all comfortable with the interface of this IMM program. Further, what were perceived as long wait times (up to 60 seconds) for media elements to appear once a search had been initiated resulted in considerable user discomfort.

The "navigation" aspects of *Columbus*, while creative, are difficult to learn and sometimes difficult to use. One primary type of navigation is to drag a search term over a topic and to drop it on the topic. This seemed unnecessarily awkward to many reviewers.

The "cognitive load" aspects of *Columbus* are so complex as to be unmanageable for many users, including people relatively familiar with the design of IMM. The "river metaphor" used for display of "articles" in this large scale IMM program sometimes leaves the user "drowning" in complexity.

The "mapping" capability of *Columbus* is marginal at best. Admittedly, with reportedly over 180 hours of interactive material in the program, it would be difficult to provide the user with a clear orientation to how much of the program had been "experienced," but some mechanism to provide better orientation for the user should be available.

The "screen design" aspects of *Columbus* violate some principles of screen design, but in general text, graphics, and video are displayed according to the principles of sound design. However, given the freedom of users to reshape and move windows in the program freely, many of the standard screen design principles created for static displays are not relevant to this program.

The "knowledge space compatibility" aspects of *Columbus* are probably its greatest weakness. Users frequently reported not understanding why certain articles appeared in the "river" when specific searches were initiated. Expected articles sometimes did not appear and articles that did appear sometimes seemed arbitrary or irrelevant to the specified search.

The "information presentation" aspects of *Columbus* are generally clear. That is, once a given "article" is activated, its presentation is understandable. The problem is that, as noted above, it may not seem relevant to the information the user is seeking at that particular time.

The "media integration" aspects of *Columbus* are generally coordinated. However, there are "articles" that seem to have been treated as text primarily because of budgetary or temporal limitations in the production of this enormous IMM program.

The "aesthetics" of *Columbus* are extremely pleasing. This is not surprising given that the program was produced in Hollywood using designers primarily known for the creativity and production values of their music videos and television commercials.

The overall functionality of *Columbus* appears moderate for anyone especially interested in the topics of Columbus and the age of exploration. Such a person would have to be very patient. The functionality of this program with teachers and students remains to be established, but it is not expected to be very high given the problems experienced with the user interface. An analysis of the pedagogical dimensions of *Columbus* has not been done.

Recommendations

In light of our admittedly preliminary investigations into the value of these dimensions, we offer the following recommendations for improving their utility as intermediate steps in the comprehensive evaluation of interactive multimedia. First, the dimensions should be subjected to rigorous expert review by leaders in the design and application of IMM in both education and training. Second, once there is evidence for the qualitative validity of the dimensions, quantitative scales should be integrated into each dimension, e.g., a ten point rating system. We have hesitated to add this quantitative aspect to the dimensions up to now for fear that reviewers might get

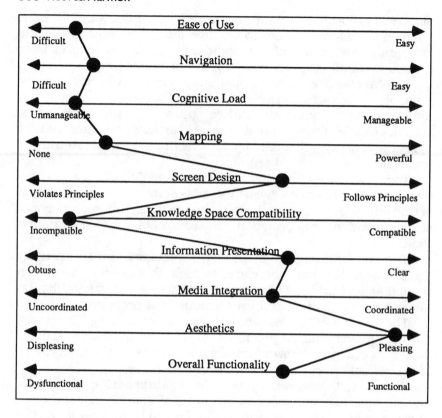

Figure 26. User interface ratings of *Columbus Encounter: Discovery and Beyond*

too distracted by the numerical values to concentrate on qualitative ratings of the dimensions themselves. However, we recognize the value of ultimately grounding the ratings in quantitative values. Third, we recommend that the validated dimensions be applied within a wide variety of education and training contexts to provide evidence for their utility. Fourth, we recommend that research be initiated into the relationships among ratings of the pedagogical and user interface dimensions of IMM and actual data regarding the instructional effectiveness and impact of these same programs.

Although the ten user interface dimensions represent an improvement over the surface features analysis often provided in advertisements and promotional materials for IMM programs, analysis of the user interface dimensions of IMM does not eliminate the need to analyze the fourteen pedagogical dimensions of IMM programs. In turn, analysis of the pedagogical dimensions is not a sufficient alternative to evaluating the instructional effectiveness, efficiency, and impact of these programs. A comprehensive approach to evaluating IMM requires multiple levels of assessment and interpretation.

Is all this evaluation necessary? Each month sees the introduction of new commercial IMM packages promoted to be effective instructional systems. Yet systematic evaluation of the efficacy of these systems is sadly lacking. The ultimate result of the refinement of these dimensions may be enhanced guidelines for developing IMM programs as well as improved procedures for their rigorous evaluation. The need for these design guidelines and evaluation procedures cannot be overemphasized. Developers of IMM programs and/or the commercial interests behind them seem to assume that since IMM *ought* to be effective for instruction, they *are* effective for instruction. Anyone involved in educational evaluation and research or the implementation of instructional innovations knows that such assumptions are usually unwarranted. The cover story of *New Media* magazine for February 1993 illustrates the problem (Stansberry, 1993). On this cover, two grade school students are depicted entering a school carrying IMM hardware and software. The headline reads: "Saved by the Bell: Is Digital Media the Answer for our Failing Schools?" Much work remains to be done before we can even begin to address this question.

References

ABC News Interactive Corporation. (1991). *In the holy land: A history of hatred in the Middle East* [Interactive multimedia program]. New York: ABC News Interactive.

Ackerman, P. L., Sternberg, R. J., & Glaser, R. (Eds.). (1989). *Learning and individual differences: Advances in theory and research.* New York, W. H. Freeman.

Anderson, J. R. (1983). *The architecture of cognition.* Cambridge, MA: Harvard University Press.

Blattner, M. M., & Dannenberg, R. B. (Eds.). (1992). *Multimedia interface design.* New York: ACM Press.

Bransford, J. D., Sherwood, R. D., Hasselbring, T. S., Kinzer, C. K., & Williams, S. M. (1990). Anchored instruction: Why we need it and how technology can help. In D. Nix & R. Spiro (Eds.), *Cognition, education, and multimedia: Exploring ideas in high technology* (pp. 115-141). Hillsdale, NJ: Lawrence Erlbaum.

Bransford, J. D., Vye, N., Goldman, S. R., Hasselbring, T. S., & Pellegrino, J. W. (1991, April). *The design of environments that support meaningful, generative learning: An introduction to the mathematics problem solving series, The adventures of Jasper Woodbury.* Paper presented at the Annual Meeting of the American Educational Research Association, Chicago, IL.

Broderbund Software. (1992). *Just grandma and me* [CD-ROM program]. Novato, CA: Broderbund.

Brown, J. S. (1985). Process versus product: A perspective on tools for communal and informal electronic learning. *Journal of Educational Computing Research, 1,* 179-201.

Brown, J. S., Collins, A., & Duguid, P. (1989). Situated cognition and the culture of learning. *Educational Researcher, 18*(1), 32-41.

Carroll, J. B. (1963). A model of school learning. *Teachers College Record, 64,* 723-733.

Cates, W. M. (1992, April). *Considerations in evaluating metacognition in interactive hypermedia/multimedia instruction.* Paper presented at the Annual Meeting of the American Educational Research Association, San Francisco, CA.

Clark, R. E. (1992). Media use in education. In M. C. Alkin (Ed.), *Encyclopedia of educational research* (pp. 805-814). New York: Macmillan.

Cole, P. (1992). Constructivism revisited: A search for common ground. *Educational Technology, 32*(2), 27-34.

Cognition and Technology Group at Vanderbilt. (1992). The Jasper experiment: An exploration of issues in learning and instructional design. *Educational Technology Research and Development, 40*(1), 65-80.

Covey, P., & Cavalier, R. (1989). *The Case of Dax Cowart* [Interactive videodisc program]. Pittsburgh, PA: Center for the Design of Educational Computing, Carnegie Mellon University.

Duffy, T., & Jonassen, D. H. (Ed.). (1992). *Constructivism and the technology of instruction: A conversation.* Hillsdale. NJ: Lawrence Erlbaum.

Eisner, E. W. (1985). *The art of educational evaluation: A personal view.* London: Falmer.

Flagg, B. N. (1990). *Formative evaluation for educational technologies.* Hillsdale: Lawrence Erlbaum.

Fletcher, J. D. (1990). *Effectiveness and cost of interactive videodisc instruction in defense training and education* (IDA Paper P-2372). Institute for Defense Analysis.

Gagné, R. M., & Glaser, R. (1987). Foundations in learning research. In R. M. Gagné (Ed.). *Instructional technology foundations* (pp. 49-83). Hillsdale, NJ: Lawrence Erlbaum.

Gilbert, M. B., & Gilbert, T. F. (1991). What Skinner gave us. *Training, 23*(9), 42-48.

Hannafin, M. J. (1992). Emerging technologies, ISD, and learning environments: Critical perspectives. *Educational Technology Research and Development, 40*(1), 49-63.

Harmon, S. W. (1992). *On the nature of exploratory behavior in hypermedia environments: Considerations of learner use patterns of hypermedia environments for the design of hypermedia instructional systems.* Unpublished doctoral dissertation, The University of Georgia.

Heller, R. S. (1990). The role of hypermedia in education: A look at the research issues. *Journal of Research on Computing in Education, 22*(4), 431 - 441.

Henderson, J. (1990). Designing realities: Interactive media, virtual realities, and cyberspace. *Multimedia Review, 1*(2), 47-51.

Hirsch, E. D., Jr. (1987). *Cultural literacy: What every American needs to know.* New York: Vantage.

International Business Machines Corporation. (1991a). *Columbus encounter: Discovery and beyond* [Interactive multimedia program]. Atlanta, GA: IBM Corporation.

International Business Machines Corporation. (1991b). *Illuminated books and manuscripts* [Interactive multimedia program]. Atlanta, GA: IBM Corporation.

International Business Machines Corporation. (1986). *Principles of the alphabet learning system (PALS)* [Interactive videodisc program]. Atlanta, GA: IBM Corporation.

Jih, H. J., & Reeves, T. C. (1992). Mental models: A research focus for interactive learning systems. *Educational Technology Research and Development, 40*(3), 39-53.

Johnson, D. W., & Johnson, R. T. (1987). *Learning together and alone* (2nd ed.). Englewood Cliffs, NJ: Prentice Hall.

Jonassen, D. H., & Grabinger, S. R. (1990). Problems and issues in designing hypertext/hypermedia for learning. In D. H. Jonassen & H. Mandl (Eds.), *Designing hypermedia for learning* (pp. 3-26). Berlin: Springer-Verlag.

Jones, M. G. (1992). *Guidelines for screen design and interface design in computer-based learning environments.* Unpublished doctoral dissertation proposal, The University of Georgia.

Kahn, P., & Landow, G. P. (1993). The pleasures of possibility: What is disorientation in hypertext? *Journal of Computing in Higher Education, 4*(2), 57-78.

Keller, J. M. (1987). Strategies for stimulating the motivation to learn. *Performance and Instruction, 26*(8), 1-7.

Kyllonen, P. C., & Shute, V. J. (1989). A taxonomy of learning skills. In P. L. Ackerman, R. H. Sternberg, & R. Glaser (Eds.), *Learning and individual differences: Advances in theory and research* (pp. 117-163). New York: W. H. Freeman.

Laurel, B. (Ed.). (1990). *The art of human-computer interface design.* Reading, MA: Addison-Wesley.

Malone, T. W. (1984). Toward a theory of intrinsically motivating instruction. In D. F. Walker & R. D. Hess (Eds.), *Instructional software: Principles and perspectives for design and use.* Belmont, CA: Wadsworth Publishing.

Marcus, A. (1992). *Graphic design for electronic documents and user interfaces.* New York: ACM Press.

Mayhew, D. J. (1992). *Principles and guidelines in software user interface design.* Englewood Cliffs, NJ: Prentice-Hall.

Miller, G. A. (1956). The magical number seven, plus or minus two: Some limits on our capability for processing information. *Psychological Review, 63*, 81-97.

Newell, A., & Simon, H. (1972). *Human problem-solving.* Englewood Cliffs, NJ: Prentice-Hall.

Newman, M. (1991). *The making of Ulysses* (Video). Atlanta, GA: IBM Corporation.

Papert, S. (1990, April). *Constructivism versus instructionism.* Paper presented at the Annual Meeting of the American Educational Research Association, Boston, MA.

Perelman, L. J. (1992). School's out: Hyperlearning, the new technology, and the end of education. New York: William Morrow.

Reeves, T. C. (1993). Pseudoscience in computer-based instruction: The case of learner control research. *Journal of Computer-Based Instruction, 20*(2), 39-46.

Reeves, T. C. (1992, September). *Effective dimensions of interactive learning systems.* Invited keynote paper presented at the Information Technology for Training and Technology (ITTE '92) Conference, Queensland, Australia.

Reeves, T. C. (1991). Ten commandments for the evaluation of interactive multimedia in higher education. *Journal of Computing in Higher Education, 2*(2), 84-113.

Reeves, T. C., & Harmon, S. W. (1993, April). *Systematic evaluation procedures for instructional hypermedia/multimedia.* Paper presented at the Annual Meeting of the American Educational Research Association, Atlanta, GA.

Reeves, T. C., & Harmon, S. W. (1991). What's in a name: Hypermedia versus multimedia. *Interact Journal, 3*(1), 28-30.

Resnick, L. B. (1989). Introduction. In L. B. Resnick (Ed.), *Knowing, learning, and instruction: Essays in honor of Robert Glaser.* Hillsdale, NJ: Lawrence Erlbaum.

Rieber, L. P. (1992). Computer-based microworlds: A bridge between constructivism and direct instruction. *Educational Technology Research and Development, 40*(1), 93-106.

Rogers, Y., Rutherford, A., & Bibby, P. A. (Eds.). (1992). *Models in the mind: Theory, perspective and application.* San Diego, CA: Academic Press.

Ross, S. M., & Morrison, G. R. (1989). In search of a happy medium in instructional technology research: Issues concerning external validity, media replications, and learner control. *Educational Technology Research and Development, 37*(1) 19-33.

Schank, R. C., & Jona, M. Y. (1990). *Empowering the student: New perspectives on the design of teaching systems* (Tech. Rep. No. 4). Evanston, IL: The Institute for the Learning Sciences, Northwestern University.

Shneiderman, B. (1987). *Designing the user interface: Strategies for effective human-computer interaction.* Reading: Addison-Wesley.

Skinner, B. F. (1968). *Technology of teaching.* New York: Meredith Publishing.

Slavin, R. E. (1992). Cooperative learning. In M. C. Alkin (Ed.), *Encyclopedia of educational research* (pp. 235-238). New York: Macmillan.

Slavin, R. E. (1990a). *Cooperative learning: Theory, research, and practice.* Englewood Cliffs, NJ: Prentice Hall.

Stansberry, D. (1993). Taking the plunge. *New Media, 3*(2), 30-36.

Steinberg, E. R. (1989). Cognition and learner control: A literature review, 1977-88. *Journal of Computer-Based Instruction, 16*(4), 117-121.

Sternberg, R. J. (1985). *Beyond I.Q.: A triarchic theory of human intelligence.* Cambridge, MA: Cambridge University Press.

Thorndike, E. L. (1913). *Educational psychology: The psychology of learning* (Vol. 2). New York: Teachers College Press.

Tobin, K., & Dawson, G. (1992). Constraints to curriculum reform: Teachers and the myths of schooling. *Educational Technology Research and Development, 40*(1), 81-92.

Tsai, C. J. (1988). Hypertext: Technology, applications, and research issues. *Journal of Educational Technology Systems, 17*(1), 3-14.

Utting, K., & Yankelovitch, N. (1989). Context and orientation in hypermedia networks. *ACM Transactions on Information Systems, 7,* 58-84.

von Glasersfeld, E. (1989). Cognition, construction of knowledge, and teaching. *Syntheses, 80*(1), 121-140.

Williams, M. D. (1993). A comprehensive review of learner-control: The role of learner characteristics. In M. R. Simonson (Ed.), *Proceedings of the Annual Conference of the Association for Educational Communications and Technology* (pp. 1083-1114). New Orleans, LA: Association for Educational Communications and Technology.

Winn, W. (1989). Toward a rationale and theoretical basis for educational technology. *Educational Technology Research and Development, 37*(1), 35-46.

Wolf, R. L. ((1975)). Trial by jury: A new evaluation method. *Phi Delta Kappan, 57,* 185-187.

Chapter 16

Implementing Multimedia-Based Learning
Today and Tomorrow

Dennis H. Sorge
James D. Russell
Ginger L. Weilbaker

Purdue University

Because multimedia-based learning provides an environment that is self-paced, learner-controlled, and individualized, it is an increasingly popular instructional delivery system. However, it does not work just by having the hardware and software available for the learner. The success of the technology is related to the effectiveness of its implementation. This chapter reviews the historical background of multimedia-based learning systems. Advantages of these systems are identified as well as major considerations for implementing multimedia-based learning including human support, planning, selecting software and hardware, purchasing materials and equipment, placement of hardware, scheduling and maintaining equipment. With rapid changes resulting from knowledge and technology growth, direct retrieval of text and image will become standard practice; requirements to hold a job will continue to change; re-education will be required more and more often. Through all of the changes, implementation will always be a key to successful application.

Because multimedia-based learning provides a learning environment that is self-paced, learner controlled, and individualized, it is an increasingly popular instructional delivery system. Experiments with programmed learning textbooks in 1960s coupled with advances in computer technology led to computer-assisted instruction (CAI) packages. In the past multimedia has referred to the use of several media (slides, film, audio tape, etc.) simultaneously in a coordinated manner. Today computers integrate these media and others (video, text, graphics, and sound) to allow interaction and control by the learner. Computer-based man-machine interfaces allow for a flexible learning environment wherein multimedia-based learning can take place. Two widely used approaches to multimedia-based learning are hypermedia and interactive video. Hypermedia is a non-linear approach for accessing a wide variety of media; interactive video integrates the computer with vidediscs and sometimes video tapes. Computer software controls learner/system interactions and maintains records of each user's activities. Multimedia systems can be as responsive in self-paced study as a private tutor would be. Multimedia systems can do things that are difficult for an instructor to do, combining images of anything from a video of a human heart to photographs of stars in deep space and integrating them with computer graphics and text for instructional purposes. While multimedia will likely become commonplace, it will be many years before it is readily available for all learners. Because technology is always changing, implementation will always be a major concern.

Over the last six years the authors have been studying and developing implementation strategies for multimedia-based learning technology. One of the objectives has been to develop "wrap around" materials to enhance the overall effectiveness of the instructional system. A second objective has been to develop a delivery system usable at a variety of locations, even at the most technically unsophisticated locations. The objective of this chapter is to help instructors/trainers implement multimedia-based learning systems. The chapter will present information about software and hardware selection, implementation guidelines, special considerations, and future trends. This chapter provides a helpful base of information so anyone can successfully implement multimedia-based learning systems within any instructional setting.

This chapter reviews the historical background of multimedia-based learning systems. Advantages of these systems are identified. Major considerations for implementing multimedia-based learning include human support, planning, selecting software, selecting hardware, purchasing materials and equipment, placement of hardware, scheduling, and maintaining equipment. The chapter concludes with a discussion of future research opportunities and the continued merging of instructional technologies.

Background

Technology, especially multimedia-based learning, offers a new and non-threatening way to learn that differs from traditional school learning. Computer-assisted instruction (CAI) has been found to have beneficial effects on achievement in a wide variety of instructional settings (Dalton, 1986). By utilizing CAI, the learner often avoids the frustration and aggravation encountered in a normal classroom setting. Askov and Turner (1989) provide insight into seven advantages of computer-assisted instruction. The advantages include privacy, individualization, achievement gains, cost effectiveness, control of learning, flexibility in scheduling, and open entry or open exit. These advantages also are relevant to multimedia-based CAI system.

Privacy: Once students learn how to use a computer assisted instruction system, they can work independently of other classmates and even the teacher. Only the student and the teacher know the actual level and pace at which each student is achieving (Askov & Turner, 1989).

Individualization: Multimedia computer-assisted instruction allows lessons to be tailored to a student's needs rather than those of the group. The instructional pace and sequence can match the learning styles of the individual student (Kearsley, Hunter, & Seidel, 1983).

Achievement gains: Instructional computing has demonstrated beneficial effects on learner achievement in a variety of settings. Some researchers have also found a reduction of learning time and an increase in attitudes associated with the beneficial effects of learner achievement (Charp, 1981).

Cost Effectiveness: For many applications involving large numbers of students, multimedia-based learning systems may be more cost effective than other teaching/training formats. The initial costs are high, but by amortizing them over a large number of learners, the cost per student may be equal or lower. During an extensive evaluation of an urban technology literacy center, Turner and Stockdill (1987) found no significant increase in cost between computer-assisted instruction and traditional classroom approaches.

Control of Learning: By allowing the learner to control rate and direction of his/her own learning, multimedia-based learning adds a motivational touch to the instructional situation.

Flexibility of Scheduling: Computers allow users to incorporate instruction within their busy schedules. The adult learner does not have to wait for a scheduled class time in order to learn (Askov & Turner, 1989).

Open Entry Open Exit: One prominent problem in adult education is the transient population which it serves. Mutimedia computing can accommodate the frequent dropping in and out of programs by saving student information on disk and allowing the student to begin where he/she left off (Askov & Turner, 1989).

Of the seven advantages, achievement gains have been of particular interest among researchers. Other research studies have demonstrated better than average gains by using computer-assisted instruction (Kulik, 1983; Askov, 1986; Maclay & Askov, 1987). For example, compared to traditional classroom instruction, CAI has accelerated students' development of mathematics skills (Henderson, Landesman, & Kachuck, 1985; Vickers, 1984). Researchers also have found an increase in students' perceptions of the amount of learning they achieve in relation to their effort. Although many research studies have demonstrated better than average gains by using computer-assisted instruction, some researchers have found the contrary.

Major Considerations

Before adopting multimedia-based learning into education/ training, several aspects of this new technology must be addressed. Four considerations have surfaced: human support, planning, selection of software, and selection of hardware.

Human Support

Regardless of the quality and sophistication of the computer hardware and software, the success of the instruction with many students depends upon the support and encouragement they receive from teachers, facilitators, and other students. The amount of human teaching/intervention needed may vary with the ability of the student. Good learners need less assistance than do weaker learners. A number of researchers have begun investigating the human factors involved in using computer assisted instruction with adult learners. Gayeski (1989) found that even though technology was an effective substitute for classroom instruction, both instructors and learners report that they didn't like learning in isolation. McNeil and Nelson(1991) found that the importance of the instructor was implicated in their meta-analysis of interactive video instruction. The success of the instructional materials depends upon the motivation and enthusiasm of the site coordinator, teachers, and facilitators. Technology itself will not maintain students' attention and interest. They need encouragement from other people.

Multimedia-based learning does not work just by having the hardware and software available for the learner. The administrator and staff must be committed to making it work. Alderman, Appel, and Murphy (1978) state that the impact of computer-assisted instruction is not determined by technology, but by the manner in which the instructors perceive a sense of responsibility for the technology. Someone needs to encourage students to use it. Most adults who are learning basic skills lack sufficient internal motivation to maintain their interest over a long period of time.

In planning to use multimedia-based learning, one needs to provide ongoing support for students in addition to support for the hardware and software. It is important that *someone* be available to provide encouragement and to answer questions. That someone may be a student who has mastered the material, a teacher, or any adult who knows the content of the lesson.

Planning

For successful implementation of multimedia-based learning systems, hardware and software usually are not major problems. Students do learn and enjoy learning using multimedia-based learning. Assuming one has selected appropriate software and hardware, the success of the technology is related to the effectiveness of its implementation. The manner in which this is accomplished often depends on the nature of the organization that plans for the implementation of the system.

A broad range of individuals should be involved in planning for multimedia-based learning. They include teachers/trainers, administrators, students, community leaders, and consultants. For organizations just getting started in the use of multimedia-based learning, consultants can assist during the planning process. Consultants may be personnel from other organizations who have experience using multimedia-based learning for instruction. They may be representatives from the hardware and software companies, consultants from training organizations, or experienced staff from colleges or universities. These individuals can make suggestions on hardware and software purchases, instructional applications, and implementation strategies.

Decisions need to be made about the management of multimedia-based learning systems (hardware and software). The managerial and organizational concerns are very important in the successful use of computers for instructional purposes.

For example, the expectations of the various groups and individuals responsible for planning must be consistent. For successful implementation, the expectations of the teacher/trainer about content, achievement, cost, and role of teachers must coincide with those of the administrators/managers as well as with the needs of the student/trainees. If the expectations of the teachers/trainers differ from those of administrators/managers, then less than full success and perhaps failure can be expected. Conflicting expectations affect interpersonal relations among facilitators and can affect learners' morale in the accomplishment of instructional objectives. Teacher anxiety and over or under expectations toward the technology must also be considered. Gayeski (1989) suggests that slowness in multimedia-based learning implementation results from conservative attitudes towards an unknown entity.

Many of these planning questions can be initially answered by a task force composed of teacher/trainers, administrators, and other stakeholders. The task force can oversee the planning, implementation, and operation for the entire organization and be responsible for macro-management. The task force should address the following question. How will the multimedia-based learning system be used: initial instruction, presentation, remediation, enrichment, problem solving, or a combination? Goals must clearly be communicated to administrators, teachers/trainers and students. One effective way to communicate these goals is through a curriculum guide. A curriculum guide should state the curriculum goals, course objectives, recommended software, instructional activities to be used before and after the multimedia packages and evaluation techniques. Effective instructional implementation demands a convergent and consistent set of goals and objectives for multimedia-based learning to maximize the performance of learners.

Planning involves many phases: 1) pre-planning before software is selected and hardware purchased, 2) on-going planning while the materials and equipment are in use, and 3) future planning to keep the facilities and materials up to date with changes in the organization. If the software and the machines dictate curriculum, it is like the tail wagging the dog! The curriculum should determine what software and hardware are purchased and how they are implemented.

Even if a committee is utilized for pre-planning, on-going planning, and future planning, one person will need to be responsible for everyday decisions and operations of the equipment and facilities. In many cases these tasks are handled by an on-site coordinator. The on-site coordinator handles the day-to-day operations of multimedia-based learning by working with the teachers/trainers and those who manage the learning center. The on-site coordinator should be a member of the task force and handle micro-management concerns. There should be an on-site coordinator for each location.

Selecting Instructional Software

Selecting the appropriate instructional software is a very important component of success when using multimedia-based learning. The needs and characteristics of your learners must be taken into consideration. For a given institution, you may want a variety of multimedia-based learning packages on the same subject. There is no *one* best software package—different software works best for different people and for different purposes. Students who need to review material or who do not need lengthy concept development benefit from one type of software. If concept development and greater detail are needed, a different software package must be considered.

Selection decisions about software should be made by the planning task force, on-site coordinator(s), and facilitators who will be administering the multimedia-based learning lessons. They are the ones who have been involved in the planning and should be the ones to make the final selection decisions.

Before selecting software, the goals and objectives for the instructional package should be considered along with its appropriateness for the learners. Any available field test data resulting from actual use of the specific software in an instructional situation for the target population should be considered. If these data are not available, be sure to preview the materials and try them out with representative learners. Also try to talk with other people who have used the materials which are under consideration. They may point out things you have overlooked. Users manuals, teachers guides, and other documentation are important sources of information for selection decisions. After consideration of these general criteria, a checklist of criteria should be used for determining specific characteristics of the software. Even though the checklist is subjective, it provides a valuable guide for software comparisons.

Selection Criteria. There are several factors which need to be considered when selecting software. They have been grouped into the areas of content, instruction, student, operation, design, package, and other factors (see Appendix A for checklist).

Content. Instructional objectives should be clearly stated. They should identify for students and teachers the purpose of the software package. The stated objectives permit the teacher to determine if the multimedia-based learning package matches the content prescribed by the existing curriculum. The content of the software package must be accurate. Lessons and instructions should be sequenced in a logical and clear manner.

Instruction. It is important that the software package follow sound educational techniques and principles such as frequent practice with feedback for the skills being taught, maintaining interest for the learner, effective feedback for both correct and incorrect responses. Positive reinforcement is more effective than negative reinforcement. The amount of learning should justify the time spent by learners. An important feature of multimedia-based learning is that the system should be learner controlled. Students should have the ability to set the pace at which they work, to repeat material, to branch through the lessons, and to try additional problems. These types of involvement maintain interest and enhance learning. Frequent and meaningful interactions are features of *effective* multimedia-based learning. There should also be valid assesssment instruments, diagnostic tests, achievement tests, and student exercises. Performance summaries should be available for both the student and the instructor. At a minimum the summaries should contain time on task information and results of any assessment (quizzes or tests, etc.). Additional records could contain information about learning paths and response patterns.

Student. The program must relate to the "life" of the learner and include examples that are relevant to the learner. Practical examples that relate to the student's day-to-day life are valuable. Do the images have meaning to the students? People who have lived in large cities might not understand examples related to rural life. Prerequisite skills and learner characteristics should be clearly indicated. This saves much time when determining if a software package is appropriate for a particular student. Text and audio should be presented at a reading level appropriate for the users.

Operation. Even though software should be "user friendly," many multimedia packages are not simple to use. On screen instructions should be simple, clear, concise and consistent. All information that a student needs should be provided on the screen.

If a manual is required, it should contain all instructions that also appear on the screen, but with more detail. This information should serve as support and not as a requirement for system operation. Only a minimal use of operations manuals should be necessary -- preferably none at all. Specific attention should be paid to whether the system will function without requiring the instructor be available to assist users. Instructors should deal with content questions. Students should not need computer knowledge to use the system. Students should be able to review previous frames of information and use the menus at any time. Changes from one screen to the next should be learner controlled. When a student must respond to a prompt, it is important that the format of the acceptable response be clearly presented. Changes permitted in the software, such as rate of presentation, sequence, or selection of lessons, should be explained through clear menu instructions. "Bookmarks," which allow students to go away and come back where they left off, are a desirable feature.

Design. Some software products may have many "special effects" that are in fact more frosting than substance and are not necessary for effective learning. Color, graphics, animation, and sound should maintain student interest without being distractive. The text should be presented using size, color, and screen location that make the words clear. Students should know, without looking them up, what commands are available to use and what key strokes, mouse-usage, or touch screen contacts are necessary to initiate them. On-screen help should be available to students when needed. Incorrect commands should not cause the system to stop working.

Package. Lesson plans, grouping arrangements, student workbooks, interesting follow-up activities, and/or projects may add to the value of a multimedia-based learning package. However, the importance of these items will vary from course to course. The software should be easy to integrate into the curriculum and suggestions for doing this should be included. Certain learning environments require a software package that is very flexible. For example, in some situations, students need to be able to get in and out of different sections very easily. In other situations, students need a structured and more detailed instructional package in which they should not have the freedom to move about. Each instructor must decide which of these options is important for his/her students and then determine if the software package provides the kind of freedom or structure desired. Some software packages have management systems that permit the instructor to provide variations in the order and speed of presentations, and criteria for success (e.g.

scores required for passing quizzes and tests). For instructors, the management system should be easy to use and provide different kinds of reports and permit on-line monitoring.

Other Factors. Many of the current software packages have similar characteristics. They have some type of testing and record keeping. There are introductions and explanations for each topic, sample problems, and practice and feedback for students. There may be practical examples and a glossary of terms. Where the software programs differ is in content, length, depth, and techniques of presentation and screen interface.

If multimedia-based learning systems are reviewed following the guidelines presented here, important information about the products will be discovered. Most multimedia systems are so complex that an accurate appraisal of the programs can be obtained only by testing them with students. Vendors often permit a 90 day preview before purchase. This is an excellent time for students to work with the system. Student input can be a valuable part of the decision-making process. Carefully read the materials, study guides, and manuals supplied with the software. When this is not possible, check with others who have used the multimedia-based learning materials. Vendors should be willing to tell who have purchased their products.

Selecting Hardware

After the learning materials have been identified, hardware acquisition is then in order. Once acquired, the software usually can be installed without major difficulty provided that instructions are followed step-by-step. Often instructors avoid set-up and installation because they think they can not do it. They feel there is someone else better qualified. It is not that instructors try and fail, but rather they do not try at all.

Some critical issues in the evaluation and selection of hardware for multimedia-based learning applications include: examining the requirements of the selected multimedia software, providing a suitable learning delivery platform, and selecting vendors. The use of a hardware evaluation checklist will assist in making these determinations. If hardware already exists, the effectiveness of that hardware must be determined. Instructional materials can easily be limited by compromises resulting from trying to use available hardware that may not have suitable performance. Evaluate needs, review software and hardware requirements, and then determine if the hardware available can be used with the current and future software.

Selection Criteria

To evaluate multimedia-based learning hardware, it is necessary to have a clear perception of the various elements of the system. A multimedia-based learning system consists of the computer, video-disc player, CD-ROM, disk drive, and other peripherals (such as mouse, printer, etc.). The result is a powerful system that uses the audio/video source augmented by the computer's text and/or graphics.

Instructional Software Requirements

The first step in the evaluation and selection of multimedia-based learning equipment is to identify the requirements of the instructional software. What instructional materials will be used on the system? Without identifying specific needs for the hardware to fill, a user may find that a hasty purchase was inadequate.

The selection of instructional software is the most important first step in the selection of hardware. The computer's utility may be limited by an inadequate quantity or quality of available instructional software. A computer may have great features, but it is of little value if there are no materials to take advantage of them. On the other hand, it is difficult for instructional software to overcome limitations of the computer hardware. Media designed for one multimedia system may not run on another system.

It is difficult making selection decisions for the present and an unknown future. To prevent unexpected problems, it is important to look at the past performance of the company from which you intend to purchase. Is the company financially stable? Are other institutions using the same equipment? Is the company committed to support their equipment? Are other firms developing software for the multimedia-based learning equipment in question? What are the update policies? What about costs and availablity of site licenses?

Unfortunately, the computer hardware industry is changing so rapidly that hardware selection decisions cannot be made solely on present needs. One must consider future needs. By purchasing hardware with significant limitations, one is unlikely to be able to take advantage of new advancements without purchasing new hardware.

An Integrated Multimedia-Based Learning Environment

What other computers does the organization currrently have? A factor in selecting an integrated multimedia-based learning system is compatibility with any other equipment that may have been purchased previously. However, do not become trapped by equipment that can never meet identified needs. If a change is required, it is often better to make it sooner than later. What operating system do the other computers use? Is there a need for exchanging files and programs among different applications and/or departments? If so, mixing several different computers will often be difficult. Software designed to run on one computer will generally not work on another type of computer. Additionally, learning to operate, maintain, and effectively use the full potential of a given computer is not a trivial investment of time. If a single model will not meet all of the computing needs, consider different models from the same manufacturer.

In addition to these general compatibility issues, some hardware compatibility features must be considered. Can a monitor from one manufacturer be used with a computer from another manufacturer? Although some feel that it is cheaper to order various computer components from a catalog, the buyer must beware that not all components are necessarily compatible. Just because an item is advertised as compatible does not mean it will always work.

The ease of expansion is important to consider when purchasing a multimedia-based learning system. Rapid advances in computer technology assure obsolescence of a multimedia-based learning system soon after taking it out of the box. Yet, the announcement of a new computer does not reduce the utility of a previous purchase. Even if a computer is not the latest technology, it may still be sufficient. If needed, existing computers can be kept "up to date" by adding new peripherals, new microprocessors or even new motherboards. New peripherals (e.g. modems, printers, and hard disk drives) can easily be connected to existing computers.

Hardware Serviceability

Unfortunately, multimedia-based learning systems are not always as dependable as they are advertised. When selecting a hardware system, one must consider the availability of service. Is there someone to support and maintain the equipment? Is there a local service center and how long has it been established? Is it local or remote? Valuable information can be provided by others who have used such services. Were they satisfied? Was service prompt and speedy? Finding someone to service computers often becomes a difficult and frustrating experience. This is particularly true of multimedia-based learning systems equipped with components made by various manufacturers. Sometimes the computer users have to ship their systems to a service location, thus being inconvenienced for a time. If shipping is required, is there easy access to shipping locations nearby or does the shipping service provide pickup of packages? Are loaners available?

The Hardware Evaluation Checklist

Since each organization has different needs, one person's evaluation will be different from someone else's evaluation. First, compare "apples with apples" and "oranges with oranges." Use the Checklist for Selecting Multimedia-Based Learning Hardware (see Appendix B) to help in this process. Here are some general guidelines.

Memory/Storage

The memory of the computer can be a limiting factor. One must insure that the computer has enough memory to run the multimedia-based learning software. If more than one application will be used at a time, it is recommended that there be at least four and preferably eight megabytes of memory. One megabyte can hold approximately 2,000 pages of text (at about 500 characters per page). The trend is toward requiring more and more memory.

Hard Drives

Today one can buy a hard drive as small as 20 megabytes. One must first consider the size of the programs one plans to install on the computer. The authors recommend investing in at least a 100 megabyte hard disk drive. While some may find it difficult to imagine using a 100 megabyte hard disk drive, most users soon find themselves with not enough space. It is also possible to almost double a hard drive's storage capacity by purchasing one of the many disk compression utility packages that have become popular. In general, the larger the hard disk drive, the smaller the cost per megabyte.

Monitors

A large variety of monitors is available to display text, graphics, or video from the computer. An option for headphones should be considered. It should allow for stereo sound and volume control. The option for a one or two monitor system should be addressed. A one monitor system utilizes a video overlay board. If this is the case, make sure the signal between the video overlay board and the monitor are in sync. These two must be compatible with each other. The two monitor system utilizes the monitor from the computer and another monitor as a television.

Videodisc Players

Videodisc players are usually attached to and controlled by the computer. One can ask a variety of questions when examining videodisc players currently available. Is a player with a bar code reader needed? Bar code readers are similar to the technology which reads the price from the label in a grocery store. In some multimedia-based learning applications, the learner reads a book with bar codes imbedded in the text. If the learner would like to find out more, he/she uses a hand-held wand to scan the bar code. The player automatically goes to the relevant information on the video disc. More and more multimedia programs are being developed using bar code readers.

Should the player play all disc sizes? Today, many videodisc players can play the 12-inch videodiscs and the 120 millimeter compact discs. Does the videodisc player's search speed effect the application? Search speed is the maximum time the videodisc player requires to find a frame on the disc. Vendors often use this characteristic to sell an expensive player. However, the small variation in search speed generally will not affect learning.

CD-ROM Player

To read and display the information on a CD-ROM, a CD-ROM player is required. The computer reads the data from a CD-ROM as if it were a hard drive. Recent advances have seen access times cut in half. CD-ROMs containing motion video clips can now be accessed quickly enough to see the motion smoothly without the jerkiness found in earlier CD-ROM players. Headphones or speakers are required to hear the audio on CD-ROMs. Headphones should be light weight and comfortable.

Other Peripherals

What other peripherals are needed? Is a printer required? Usually one printer can be used for several workstations. Today there is a variety of printers. Do applications require the use of a mouse? Rather than remembering keyboard commands, a mouse allows the user to point and click on menu items. Many users prefer using the mouse over the keyboard. Most instructional software available today can be used with or without a mouse. Another peripheral that may be preferred in certain "keyboardless" environment is a touchscreen. Usually these can be used as direct replacements for mouse input.

Documentation

Documentation is another consideration when purchasing hardware. The documentation must be easy to read and to understand for a novice computer user. It should have an extensive index and table of contents to allow easy access to the information. Diagrams should be included to show the various parts of the system and how to put the system together. Diagnostic information should be provided. A help-line (800 number) is very useful.

Maintenance Contracts

A maintenance contract should be a consideration when purchasing hardware. Such a contract may vary in cost from a few dollars a month for each machine, to many times that amount. Prices are influenced by whether or not the equipment is repaired on-site or has to be taken, by the user, to a repair location. Multimedia-based learning systems tend to be reliable if proper care is taken by users. Failures/problems most often occur during the warranty period. Once through the warranty period, major breakdowns are infrequent with proper care. The actual cost of the repairs may be cheaper than the cost of a maintenance contract. You can use a broken-down irreparable system for spare parts. Check on local repair facilities.

The evaluation and selection of multimedia-based learning hardware is a difficult process even for experts. There seems to be a multitude of models, options, peripherals, and prices. The task becomes even more perplexing because of rapid advances in the technology. What is new today may be obsolete tomorrow. However, the Checklist in Appendix B should help make the job easier. The recommendations listed are general suggestions. Different organizations may require more or less than what is recommended. The minimum requirements of the software must be met.

Funding and Purchasing

In some situations it may be necessary to combine funds from several sources. If funds are allocated to departments, several departments may pool portions of their budgets to purchase multimedia-based learning software and hardware that all can use. Often there are reserves available at the end of the fiscal year. A wise teacher/trainer or department head will have a list of desired software and hardware available at all times. End-of-the-year funds most often need to be spent in a manner of days if not a matter of hours. The "want lists" should be complete with order numbers, vendors, and sources. This listing should be updated continuously to reflect changes in local needs, hardware advances, and new software.

External funding for multimedia-based learning systems may be available for educational institutions from federal or state sources. However, these funds have been on the decline recently. When these funds are available, it is usually easier to obtain support if the local organization has made a financial commitment of its own. Many of the government programs call for matching funds from the educational institutions. Proposals for state and federal funds may be tied-in with existing programs such as education for the handicapped under Public Law 94-142. One concern should be the continued support and maintenance of the equipment after the grant funds are no longer available. Many funded programs in the past have "died" when the funds dried up.

Other sources of external funding include foundations, corporations, software companies, and computer manufacturers. Many computer companies provide up to 50% discounts on both hardware and software for educational institutions. Foundations with local or state tie-ins are more likely to provide funds, but all avenues should be explored. Local corporations may provide computer systems that they no longer need in order to receive tax credits. Before accepting such a gift remember that old and/or used equipment can cost more to repair and maintain than the equipment is worth. Many of the computer manufacturers have their own funding programs, usually in the form of providing equipment.

Purchasing decisions should be based upon the selection decisions previously made by the on-site coordinator and trainers/teachers with guidance from the computer planning task force. The on-site coordinator should be responsible for carrying out the decisions made by the selection committee.

In the case of multimedia-based learning, it is recommended that decisions be made about which software to purchase *before* deciding upon the necessary hardware to run the software. In reality, the hardware may have already been purchased and be in place. Your standard purchasing procedure should be followed. In order to maintain standards and compatibility of materials and equipment, it is best to have the purchase orders approved by one individual. The on-site coordinator is the logical person to be responsible for ordering multimedia-based learning materials.

Many organizations purchase their multimedia-based learning systems from a local dealer who is willing to provide some instruction on how to use the system and who is readily available for service and repair. If the local dealer does not provide the repair, they can assist in getting the equipment to an authorized service center and may even provide loan equipment while the hardware is being repaired.

No one can foresee fire or water damage. Fire or water can instantly ruin electronic equipment. Even a nearby lightning strike may cause a power surge and "fry" the components of the equipment. There is always the possibility of theft. If any of these disasters happen, how will the equipment be replaced? Most institutions do not have enough money to purchase new equipment when a disaster strikes. Insurance is a preventative way to ensure the multimedia-based learning system (hardware and software) will always be available for the users students.

Many institutions may have their equipment already covered with their current insurance company. If the equipment is not covered, many policies can have the new multimedia-based learning systems added to the policy for a nominal increase in premiums.

Placement

In all cases, housing of multimedia-based learning systems should be planned around the personnel involved, the students, the purposes for which it will be used, and best accessibility. The location of the learning systems can impact the utilization and acceptance of multimedia-based learning. The specific set-up will vary from organization to organization and even from department to department within the same organization. In the area of multimedia-based learning for remedial instruction or for use with special needs learners, a few systems in a resource center staffed with teachers or aides may be appropriate. Some instructors use a single multimedia-based learning system in a classroom setting with 15 to 30 students. One student or the instructor does the keyboarding with all students discussing the questions presented by the system. The advantages of using a single multimedia-based learning system in a classroom setting should not be under-estimated. It can be used to introduce topics, try problems, or as an alternative for a group of students to practice. One computer in a classroom can encourage peer tutoring, and reduce computer anxiety. It is also an inexpensive way to experiment with multimedia-based learning before buying many systems.

Factors to be considered in determining where to place multimedia-based learning systems include the type and amount of equipment available, long and short-term instructional plans, physical layout of the building, available personnel, and security. Ease of moving the system should also be a consideration. In some cases there may be a separate networked computer laboratory, computer classroom, or computer resource area that may be used by several different classes. Other cases may require that multiple computers be interconnected on a local area network.

A key concern is ease of access. If the multimedia-based learning systems are to be centrally housed, a location in a high traffic area such as the resource center may be desired. These study centers are usually open the longest hours. Someone with expertise should always be available to assist the students and maintain security. His/her expertise may be nothing more than having gone through the multimedia-based learning program and having mastered the skills being taught. An "expert" should be able to deal with simple problems with the multimedia-based learning hardware. This "expert" can be serving other functions in the center (e.g. lending out videodiscs as required) when not assisting the students with multimedia-based learning.

The placement of the multimedia-based learning system should be determined by the type of use expected. If the preferred mode of instruction is tutorial or problem solving, an individual learning station is necessary. In this case, the student controls the content and the pace of learning. Small groups using the same system simultaneously are appropriate for simulations and educational games. For these applications, a learning station with several chairs is required. Within the group of students cooperation is encouraged. In order to facilitate problem solving and to use the computer system for instruction or as a demonstration tool, a classroom arrangement with video projection is best. The teacher controls the pace and can provide additional explanations in the large group.

If there is just one computer for a classroom or for a series of classrooms, place the computer and videodisc player on a roll-around cart to make it easy to move from classroom to classroom for use by many instructors. (Be aware that because there are so many cables that connect the various components of such systems, you will have to plan to protect those cables from becoming disconnected when the system is being moved. A video projector or a liquid crystal display (LCD) panel used in conjunction with an overhead projector can be used to project the computer and video images for the entire class.

When the multimedia-based learning system is to be used in a classroom where other activities are to be conducted, eliminate distracting the rest of the class by keeping the computer's monitor out of the view of the rest of the class. Headphones will prevent the computer user from being distracted by other noise in the classroom and keep the computer narration from interfering with other activities in the room. Short dividers can be used between the multimedia-based learning system and the rest of the classroom.

Position the multimedia-based learning system away from direct sunlight to prevent eye discomfort from window glare. Also avoid glare from overhead lights. Use the systems in a non-smoking area since smoke can cause serious damage to computers and the disk drives. Tile floors are better than carpets to avoid problems from dust and static electricity. Air conditioning is important. A multimedia workstation draws twice the power and generates twice the heat of a regular 486 PC. A white board with markers should be used in the vicinity of a multimedia-based learning system instead of a chalkboard to prevent chalk dust from damaging the equipment. Use a power strip with surge suppression to eliminate the possible tangle of cords and wires from the computer, monitor, videodisc player, and other peripherals. Comfortable tables and chairs should be used with the computer.

If a computer classroom or learning center is being set up, a room with plenty of electrical outlets and open wall space for posters is desirable. Don't put all the workstations on a single circuit. Should there be a break in the circuit, all operations would be affected. The posters can illustrate the different ways that computers can be used or they can provide instructions on the basics of using a multimedia-based learning system. A book shelf should be available for storing books, magazines, and other reference materials. The references can serve as a stimulas for students and to help answer questions. A noticeboard for announcements should also be considered.

Implementation Guidelines

During implementation of multimedia-based learning systems,

a number of discoveries have been made. They relate to learners, staff, and system issues. Eikenberg (1987) noted that the slow acceptance of multimedia-based learning in the classroom can often be attributed to people's conservative attitudes toward an unknown entity. As might be expected, teachers/trainers who have not had computer experience are hesitant about its use. In-service programs must be used to overcome this problem.

Learner Related Issues

Learners have preconceived ideas about how they relate to computers. If they believe the relationship is negative, effort must be made by the teacher/trainer to change that perception. Some students are very positive about their ability to learn from these systems. Also they like the fact that the multimedia-based learning instruction is more available than a time-specific class and they can spend as much time as necessary learning the material.

In general, learners who are not part of a formal educational program seem to prefer shorter programs. They want to get what they need quickly. Adults prefer a series of short sessions rather than one long session. When possible learners should schedule their own time. Students prefer to sign up for one or two 30-minute blocks in a single setting.

Adult learners like the personalization of multimedia-based learning. The computer always calls on them to respond, often by name. In a typical classroom students may or may not get a chance to respond. The computer always waits for their response, rather than rushing ahead like some classroom instructors do. The computer provides patient, non-threatening feedback. The system doesn't force students to keep up with others as often happens in a classroom setting. The idea that the computer provides a personal (one-on-one) education for students is important.

Low computer anxiety and high motivation are major components for learner success. Contrary to popular belief, learner age by itself should not be assumed to be a factor related to computer anxiety. The most significant concern is the influence of human interaction. Teachers/trainers need to understand that the amount of intervention required is related to the level of academic ability. Higher achieving students need less intervention. Interveners must have outstanding personal skills. Motivating and encouraging students is their most important activity. However, teachers should strive to make students as independent as possible.

Staff-related Issues

Many teachers, trainers, and administrators will need to be taught the fundamentals of multimedia-based learning operations and applications. Everyone will need to explore the possible uses of multimedia-based learning. This is best accomplished through demonstration and hands-on experience. It is important that the initial exposure of teachers, trainers, and administrators be a very positive one, so all precautions should be taken to insure success of the training program. The training program should promote everyone working together and encourage experimentation on the part of the users.

Instructors need training if they are to use multimedia-based learning effectively. The authors suggest that the training should take approximately 4 hours (two, two hour time blocks with a break between), plus ample time to have them explore the software on their own time and become familiar with operating a workstation if they have not used one before. A number of training possibilities exist. Local colleges and universities have courses on multimedia-based learning. Faculty members from universities or consultants from business and industry may be invited to work with instructors. Workshops may also be used. However, the best method is for instructors to get hands-on experience with the multimedia-based learning system. A resource person should be available to provide minimal instruction and to answer questions.

It is difficult to predict how much learner time it will take to complete activities on the computer. Instructors must be willing to be very flexible. Teachers and trainers must change their roles from presenters of information to managers of instruction.

System-related Issues

Students will also need to be instructed in the proper utilization of multimedia-based learning before they can use it for learning. In some cases, the instruction will need to begin with how to turn on the computer. The students will need to learn how to "log-on" to the computer, proper handling of computer diskettes, videodiscs, and CD-ROMs, how to access specific sections of the multimedia-based learning program, and what to do if the system malfunctions.

In addition to demonstrations and hands-on instruction, directions for operation of the multimedia-based learning system should be available. One technique for decreasing the amount of supervision needed and to avoid repetition of simple instructions is to place large, clearly stated sets of instructions on the wall above each system. These posters should cover basic operations such as logging on the system, inserting computer diskettes, videodiscs, and CD-ROM, using the program, and logging off the system. Rules for proper computer diskette, videodisc, and CD-ROM care should also be posted prominently near each system. If there are any idiosyncrasies of particular machines, they should be brought to the attention of the students as well.

A responsible person should be available when the multimedia-based learning systems are being used. A group of student assistants can be used to assist the teacher in charge. In some cases, better students can aid beginning students. Concern about security problems can be reduced by adequate supervision.

Computers are prone to theft. Theft of the computers themselves can be decreased if the computers are securely fastened to desks, carts, or carrels, or if motion dectectors are attached to the machines. If they are to be moved from room to room, fasten them onto a cart. A plan will need to be developed to prevent theft of the computer diskettes and the videodiscs themselves. In most cases a check-in/check-out procedure for diskettes and videodiscs will greatly reduce the losses. Make sure the computer location is well locked when not in use. Don't underestimate the value of good security. At some learning centers, students must leave their student ID card to borrow a disc. They also must log-in and log-out.

Scheduling

One common reason for purchasing a multimedia-based learning system is to provide students with greater learning flexibility (Fahy, 1984). The organization's philosophy should allow as many learners as possible to have access to the multimedia-based learning equipment and materials as long as the use does not interfere with scheduled instructional uses. The systems may be used by students, trainees, staff, faculty, and the community. There may be requests to use the materials during the day, in the evenings, and on weekends. A decision will have to be made as to whether anyone can use the multimedia-based learning systems or whether use should be limited to certain individuals or for specific purposes. The policy should be established by staff and administration. Rules will need to be developed to maintain order and to provide equipment and software security.

The on-site coordinator, working with facilitators and administrators, should determine a policy and guidelines specifying a priority of use. This policy, like the scheduling policy, should be as flexible as possible. Reasonable rules and guidelines should be developed regarding the length of time that one person can use a given multimedia-based learning system when there is demand. Priority of usage will have to be addressed. Many organizations have a first-come, first-served policy.

The on-site coordinator, with the approval of the computer planning task force, will need to develop a scheduling procedure. The procedures should also be approved by administration/management and teachers/trainers. The most common scheduling procedure is to place a printed schedule near the multimedia-based learning system. Clearly mark the times that the center or individual multimedia-based learning system can be used. Provide a calendar of open spaces on the schedule for students to sign-up. Some institutions allow making reservations, and some set time-limits on workstation use.

Maintaining/Replacing

One person should be in charge of problems, repairs, and maintenance. The on-site coordinator should do as much minor maintenance as he/she is competently able to do. However, service facilities and technicians should be lined up for major repairs that the on-site coordinator cannot handle. Most computer suppliers either have repair services or can recommend authorized service centers. Many universities use personnel from the school's computer science, computer technology, data processing, or managment information systems department.

In order to be able to repair or replace worn-out equipment, it is advisable to plan ahead and to budget about 10% of your capital investment per year for that purpose. Of course, the more heavily used equipment will have to be replaced more frequently. Based on experience, most equipment will eventually break down. The key is to acknowledge who will repair the equipment and allot enough time for that individual to complete these repairs, find new equipment to replace the old equipment or get along without it, and allow money to be accessible to pay for repairs.

Future Trends

Research Opportunities

Relatively little formal research has been done on learning with multimedia environments. Most efforts in the field are focused on development because the field is still evolving (Kozma, 1991). The technology trend finds an explosion of CD-ROM and videodisc choices because the use of CD-ROM and videodiscs have skyrocketed in education and business and industry. There is no doubt multimedia has had an impact on instruction. There is a growing understanding of the mechanisms of learning with media but the cognitive effects of multimedia environments need to be explored (Kozma, 1991). The multimedia environment provides a great opportunity to study the interaction of multimedia with the learner.

The authors have implemented multimedia-based learning as a delivery system at a university regional campus for students in a basic mathematics course. An investigation is being conducted to examine multimedia-based learning as a supplement to regular instruction. The emphasis is on achievement effects and learner effectiveness for two types of adult learners in the course: the older adult who is returning to school after a delayed absence, and the adult learner right out of high school who is weak in math skills.

Conclusion

Within the next decade, as technology evolves, direct retrieval of text and image will be standard practice. Schools, homes, businesses, libraries, and other information resource centers will be electronically connected to each other. Vast amounts of data will be accessible electronically.

With rapid changes resulting from knowledge and technology growth, requirements to hold a job will continue to change. Re-education will be required more and more often. Multimedia computing will serve as a major delivery system for this purpose. With the explosion of information in almost every field, the focus is going to be on accessing information rather than committing information to memory. Individuals will learn more on their own. The "places" of learning will become more dispersed. Learning will be done in the home, at least as much as in formal educational settings, on a multimedia computer.

The use of multimedia training by business and industry is increasing rapidly. "Just-in-time training" enables employees to receive instructions when and where they need it. Virtual reality environments will permit users to act as if they were really at a work site. Movements of the fingers, hands, arms, and head, without a mouse or keyboard, will serve as inputs to the computer. Verbal communication to and from the computer system will greatly increase the friendliness of the user's environment.

Through all of the changes, implementation will always be a key to successful application. If an application of multimedia-based learning is to be effective, a very large percentage of effort must be given to the strategies of implementation.

Appendix A:
Checklist for Selecting Multimedia-Based Learning Software

If the item on the checklist correctly describes the software you are reviewing, circle the number in the "weight" column. The criteria weighted 3 are most important, 2 somewhat important, and 1 least important but desirable. After completing the entire checklist, add up the circled weights. Use this total for comparing software packages.

Content	**Weight**
Instructional objectives are clearly stated.	3
The software matches instructional objectives of the curriculum.	3
The information is accurate and answers are correct.	3
The sequences of lessons and instructions are logical and clear.	3

Instruction	
The instruction follows sound educational techniques.	3
The program provides feedback to the student.	3
The amount of learning correlates well with time spent by student.	3
The instruction accomplishes stated objectives.	3
Questions are randomly generated.	3
Students are actively involved.	3
Students are able to get a summary of their performances	1
Students have control over the rate of presentation.	3
The system provides whole class summaries of performance for the instructor.	1

The number of times a student must iterate through
a try-again loop is minimized (not more than 3).　　　　3

Student

Program contains examples relevant to student.　　　　3

Students have control over the selection of lessons.　　　　1

Prerequisite skills for students are clearly identified.　　　　3

Readability of text is appropriate for intended users.　　　　3

Operation

The software allows the user to correct his/her typing errors.　　　3

The management system is easy to use and is
flexible.　　　　3

The keys used to execute commands are consistent
throughout the program.　　　　2

On screen instructions:

　can be skipped if already known.　　　　2

　are simple, clear, and concise.　　　　2

　are presented <u>both</u> in the program and in a manual.　　　2

　tell the student what to do next at critical points in the program.　3

The program is easy to load and instructions for doing so are clear.　3

The program accepts abbreviations for common　　　　3
responses (e.g., Y for yes, N for no).

The system will function without the instructor　　　　3
to assisting users during operation.

The student does not need computer knowledge.　　　　3

References to a manual are kept to an absolute minimum.　　　2

Students can review previous frames of information.　　　　3

A clear and useful summary of program operation is provided.   3

Design

The instructor can change rates of instruction and mastery level.   1

Color is used appropriately.   2

Graphics and/or animation are used appropriately.   2

Sound is used appropriately.   2

The screen displays:

  are clear, not busy or cluttered.   3

  avoid cryptic abbreviations and codes.   3

Flashing text and other forms of highlighting
are used only for important emphasis.   2

When going from one screen to another, scrolling is avoided.   2

Student response is required before proceeding to a new page.   2

Incorrect selection of commands or keys does <u>not</u> cause
program to abort.   3

Menus and features are "user friendly".   3

A minimum of keystrokes is required to execute any command.   2

Messages are provided to inform the student of
noticeable pauses in a program.   2

Students are prompted on the format of the expected response.   2

Package

Suggestions for integration into the curriculum are provided.   2

Supplemental materials are provided.   1

Interesting follow-up activities and/or projects are suggested.   1

Documentation is complete and clearly written.   3

TOTAL (add weights for items checked)   ___

Appendix B: Checklist for Selecting
Multimedia-Based Learning Hardware

Software selected:
    Name
    Vendor:
    Vendor Contact:
    Address:
    Phone:

	Requirements of Software Selected	Specification of Hardware Being Considered
1. Computer Considerations:		
Type		
Manufacturer	_____	_____
Model	_____	_____
Operating System	_____	_____
Memory	_____	_____
Floppy Drive (size)	_____	_____
Hard drive (size)	_____	_____
Color (Y/N)	_____	_____
Video Quality	_____	_____
Compatible with available video overlay board	_____	_____
Mouse	_____	_____
2. Multimedia Add-Ons		
Laserdisc Player	_____	_____
Video Overlay Board	_____	_____
CD-ROM Player	_____	_____
Digital Audio Board/Speakers	_____	_____
3. Other Peripherals		
Printer (check one)		
Dot matrix	_____	_____
Ink jet	_____	_____
Laser	_____	_____

Special Input Device
       Touch Screen   _____   _____
Microphone

4. Other Considerations

Documentation available?   _____   _____
Technical support available? _____   _____
Warranty   _____   _____

Service Contract   _____   _____
System Cost   _____   _____

References

Alderman, D. L., Appel, L., & Murphy, R. (1978). PLATO and TICCIT: An evaluation of CAI in the community college. *Educational Technology*, 18, 40-45.

Askov, E. N., & Turner, T. C. (1989). Using computers for teaching basic skills to adults. *Lifelong Learning*, 12(6), 28-31.

Campbell-Bonar, K., & Grisdale, L. (1991). Applying principles of collaboration to videodisc design: Profile of a successful project. *Canadian Journal of Educational Communications*, 20(3), 189-203.

Carrier, C., Post, T. R., & Heck, W. (1985). Using microcomputers with fourth-grade students to Reinforce arithmetic skills. *Journal for Research in Mathematics Education*, 16(1), 45-51.

Carter, J. H., & Honeywell, R. (1991). Training older adults to use computers. *Performance and Instruction*, 30(2), 9-15.

Cockayne, S. (1991). Effects on small group sizes on learning with interactive videodisc. *Educational Technology*, 31(2), 43-45.

Charp, S., (1981). Effectiveness of computers in instruction. *Viewpoints in Teaching and Learning*, 57(2), 28-32.

Dalton, D.W. (1986). How effective is interactive video in improving performance and attitude? *Educational Technology*, 26(1), 27-29.

Dockterman, D. A. (1990). *Great teaching in the one computer classroom*. Cambridge, MA: Tom Synder Production, Inc.

Eikenger, D. (1987, September 4). Honeymoon's over for interactive: time to grow up. *Backstage*, pp. 1, 8, 38, 40.

Fahy, P. J. (1984). Learning about computerized instruction with adults: One school's trials, errors, and successes. *Educational Technology*, 24(7), 11-16.

Fletcher, J. D. (1991) The effectiveness and cost of interactive videodisc instruction. *Machine-Mediated Learning*, 3, 361-385.

Fuson, K. C. & Brinko, K. T. (1985). The comparative effectiveness of microcomputers and flash cards in the drill and practice of basic mathematics facts. *Journal for Research in Mathematics Education*, 16(3), 225-232.

Gayeski, D. M. (1989). Why information technologies fail. *Educational Technology*, 29(2), 9-17.

Henderson, R. W., Landesman, E. M., & Kachuck, I. (1985). Computer-video instruction in mathematics: Field test of an interactive approach, *Journal for Research in Mathematics Education,* 16(3), 207-224.

Hoffer, T., Radke, J., & Lord, R. (1992). Qualitative/quantitative study of the effectiveness of computer-assisted interactive video instruction: The hyperiodic table of elements. *Journal of Computers in Mathematics and Science Teaching,* 11, 3-12.

Kearsley, G., Hunter, B., & Seidel, R. J. (1983). Two decades of computer based instruction projects: What have we learned? *T.H.E. Journal,* 10(2),90-94.

Kozma, R. B. (1991). Learning with media. *Review of Educational Research,* 61(2), 179-211.

Kulik, J. (1983). Effects of computer-based teaching on secondary school students. *Journal of Educational Psychology,* 75(1), 19-26.

Leonard, W. H. (1992). A comparison of student performance following instruction by interactive videodisc versus conventional laboratory. *Journal of Research in Science Teaching,* 20(1), 93-102.

Lewis, L. H. (1988). Adults and computer anxiety: Fact or fiction? *Lifelong Learning,* 11(8), 5-8, 12.

Maclay, C. M., & Askov, E. N. (1987). Computer-aided instruction for mom and dad. *Issues in Science and Technology,* 4(1), 88-92.

McNeil, B. J., & Nelson, K. R. (1991). Meta-analysis of interactive video instruction: A 10 year review of achievement effects. *Journal of Computer-Based Instruction,* 18(1), 1-6.

Summers, J. A. (1991). Effect of interactivity upon student achievement, completion intervals, and affective perceptions. *Journal of Educational Technology Series,* 19(1), 53-57

Turkle, S. (1984). *The second self.* New York: Simon & Schuster.

Turner, T. C. (1988). An overview of computers in adult literacy programs. *Lifelong Learning,* 11(8), 9-12.

Vickers, M. (1984). Reset your button and drive into computer-assisted math. *Academic Therapy,* 19(4), 465-471.

Chapter 17

Using Multimedia
to Help Students Learn
Knowledge Acquisition

Jay Liebowitz
George Washington University

Karen Bland
IBM Corporation

Multimedia is an emerging technology which is playing a major role in education and training. KARTT (Knowledge Acquisition Research and Teaching Tool) has been developed as a multimedia tool to help students learn knowledge acquisition methods in expert systems development. This tool helps prospective knowledge engineers in better understanding the concepts and methodologies associated with knowledge acquisition.

One of the fastest growing technologies today is interactive multimedia. Multimedia combines text and data with audio and visual information (e.g., speech, music, still images, and full-motion video). Multimedia applications are being developed for education and training, business presentations, marketing, information retrieval, publishing, entertainment, and a host of other areas. Already, in California, citizens can renew their driver's license at multimedia kiosks in shopping malls. There are multimedia applications for exploring the Mayan ruins at Palenque, for training software engineers at the Software Engineering Institute interested in code inspection, for training commuter aircraft pilots, for understanding written and spoken Japanese, for safety instruction for truck drivers, and for a myriad of other tasks.

IBM forecasts that by 1994, more than 40 percent of all IBM personal systems sold will be multimedia machines. Interactive technologies, particularly interactive multimedia, have many benefits. More than 30 studies have found that interactive technologies reduce learning time requirements by an average of 50 percent. Other benefits include reduced cost, instructional consistency, increased retention, increased motivation, increased access, and flexible training periods.

In the School of Business and Public Management at George Washington University, interactive multimedia is being taught as part of our Masters program in information systems. We are also beginning to use interactive multimedia to help our graduate students learn various subjects.

The focus of this chapter is to describe the development and use of a hypertext, multimedia-based tool called KARTT (Knowledge Acquisition Research and Teaching Tool) for our "Knowledge Acquisition" course in the Master of Science-Applied Artificial Intelligence (AI) and Expert Systems program. We will begin by briefly describing the knowledge acquisition process and its importance in developing quality knowledge based systems.

We will go on to describe the knowledge engineering skills required to acquire knowledge. Finally we will describe KARTT and its use in training knowledge engineers.

Knowledge Acquisition and Knowledge Engineering Skills

As expert systems become more commonplace in today's society worldwide, the need for better educating prospective knowledge engineers on knowledge acquisition has become more evident.

Knowledge acquisition is the process via which a knowledge engineer (KE) acquires the expertise, i.e. rules of thumb and sets of facts, that will be used to develop the knowledge base of the expert system. As might be expected, the quality and reliability of the expert system is highly dependent on the system's ability to emulate the expert's expertise. Hence, how knowledge is acquired and analyzed is of paramount importance to the success of the expert system. The knowledge acquisition (KA) process consists of four broad phases (Klahr and Waterman, 1986):

- Discovery of preliminary knowledge and problem range.
- Identifying sources of information.
- Acquiring detailed knowledge from sources.
- Analyzing, coding, and documenting knowledge.

During the first phase of KA the knowledge engineer attempts to gain a general understanding of the problem domain, the major tasks the expert system is to perform, and the sequential order of those tasks. In addition, the knowledge engineer must ascertain the scope of the effort being undertaken. This includes a preliminary decision on the functions to be included and excluded in the expert system. During the second phase of the KA process the KE begins to identify sources of expertise. Sources may include not only human experts, but written sources of expertise like manuals, training guides, policy guidelines etc.. The third phase of the knowledge acquisition process is the most important and time consuming. During this phase the KE will begin to acquire the expert's expertise in earnest. This includes learning the steps the expert performs to complete the task, identifying the task characteristics, understanding how the expert reasons through the task, and how the expert uses information to draw inferences. During the final phase of the acquisition process the knowledge retrieved is analyzed for accuracy and completeness. More importantly, a conceptual model that depicts the sub-tasks of the problem, the inferences made, and the information used to support these inferences is developed. This conceptual model is of great importance since it not only serves as an intermediate representation of the system to be developed, but is used to guide the rest of development process.

From the above description it might be easy to assume that knowledge acquisition is essentially the same process used by software engineers to define the requirements of a conventional system. However, such an assumption belies the differences between the objective of the software engineer and the knowledge engineer. The former acquires information, the latter acquires knowledge. The difference between knowledge and information is best described by Feigenbaum (1983). He asserted that knowledge is information that has been interpreted, categorized, applied and revised. There are generally considered to be five different categories of knowledge: (1) Declarative Knowledge—"what" things are; (2) Procedural Knowledge—considers the manner in which things work under different sets of circumstances; (3) Semantic Knowledge—reflects cognitive structure that involves the use of long term memory (e.g., words and other symbols); (4) Episodic Knowledge—organized as a case or episode; (5) Metaknowledge—knowledge about knowledge. As you might expect, acquiring these different types of knowledge requires different knowledge acquisition techniques. Thus, the knowledge engineer must not only know how to elicit knowledge using various techniques, he must know what technique is appropriate for a specific type of knowledge.

Eliciting and acquiring knowledge is both a difficult and time consuming task. A study by Cullen and Bryman (1988) highlighted some of the major types of problems encountered in this process. As shown in Figure 1, over 47% of the respondents reported "quality of expertise" as a major source of KA problems. More important than the problems encountered during the acquisition process, is the amount of time required to elicit knowledge. Clearly, 34% of the respondents had problems associated with accessibility to experts and project time constraints. This problem has come to be known as the knowledge acquisition bottleneck.

The knowledge acquisition bottleneck has been well documented (Scott et al., 1991; McGraw and Harbison-Briggs, 1989; Medsker et al., 1990). Studies have shown that a single day of

---

Development Problems Experienced
_____

Knowledge Acquisition Problems	% Sample
None reported	22.6
Quality of expertise	47.2
Communication with experts	20.8
Software problems	9.4
Problems with Experts	
None Reported	23.8
Conflicting expertise	7.5
Misunderstanding instructions	22.7
Uncooperative attitudes	11.3
Access and time constraints	34.0
Main Development Constraints	
None reported	33.3
Human resistance	37.0
Limited system capabilities	16.7
Software problems	13.0

Source: Cullen, J., Bryman, A., "The Knowledge Acquisition Bottleneck: Time for Reassessment", Expert System Journal Vol.5, No.3, August 1988

Figure 1: Knowledge Based System Development Problems Experienced

knowledge acquisition can produce 300-500 pages of knowledge elicitation transcripts. If people talk continuously, studies indicate that the rate would be about 10,000 words/hour. Studies also indicate that one day of the expert's time is usually needed for every four days of the knowledge engineer's time. Generally speaking, the sources of these problems can be said to fall into three major categories:

1. Communication difficulties between the KE and the expert.
2. Inability of the expert to describe expertise.
3. Inability of the KE to 'capture' expertise.

Hayes-Roth, Waterman and Lenat (1983) expressed the difficulties of expertise elicitation as a problem with communication between two professionals from diverse backgrounds:

> Knowledge acquisition is a bottleneck in the construction of expert systems. The knowledge engineer's job is to act as a go between to help an expert build a system. Since the knowledge engineer (KE) has far less knowledge of the domain than the expert, however, communication problems impede the process of transferring expertise into a program. The vocabulary initially used by the expert to talk about the domain with a novice is often inadequate for problem-solving; thus the knowledge engineer and expert must work together to extend and refine it.

As the above suggests, for the KE to overcome this problem it becomes necessary for them to become somewhat versed in the problem domain. This task requires a considerable amount of time. Indeed, studies suggest a direct relationship between the complexity of the problem domain and the time/effort required for the KE to obtain sufficient knowledge. The greater the complexity of the area, the longer it takes for the KE to adequately communicate with the expert.

Quite often the expert may be unable to describe expertise. One major reason for this is known as the Paradox of Expertise (Knowledge Engineering Paradox). This paradox states that the more competent domain experts become, the less able they are to describe the knowledge they use to solve problems. According to this paradox: Experts have a tendency to state their conclusions and the reasoning behind them in general terms that are too broad for effective machine analysis (Westphal and McGraw, 1989).

It is advantageous to have the machine work at a more basic

level, dealing with clearly defined pieces of basic information that it can build into more complex judgments. In contrast, the expert seldom operates at a basic level. S/he makes complex judgments rapidly, without laboriously reexamining and restating each step in his reasoning process. The pieces of basic knowledge are assumed and are combined so quickly that it is difficult for her/him to describe the process. When s/he examines a problem, s/he cannot easily articulate each step and may even be unaware of the individual steps taken to reach a solution. S/he may ascribe to intuition or label a hunch which is the result of a very complex reasoning process based upon a large amount of remembered data and experience. In subsequently explaining her/his conclusion or hunch, s/he will repeat only the major steps, often leaving out most of the smaller ones, which may have seemed obvious to him at the time. This is not as surprising as it sounds since knowing what to consider basic and relevant, and not requiring further reevaluation, is what makes a person an "expert."

According to Chan and Benbasat (1991), the inability of the KE to 'capture' expertise is caused by several factors including:

- Experts may lack time or may be unwilling to cooperate.
- Testing and refining knowledge is complicated.
- Methods for knowledge elicitation may be poorly defined.
- System builders have a tendency to collect knowledge from one source, but the relevant knowledge may be scattered across several sources.
- Builders may attempt to collect documented knowledge rather than use experts. The knowledge collected may be incomplete.
- It is difficult to recognize specific knowledge when it is mixed up with irrelevant data.
- Experts may change their behavior when they are being observed and/or interviewed.
- Problematic interpersonal communication factors may exist between the knowledge engineer and the expert.

Other knowledge acquisition studies point to other sources of problems. A KA study in Japan by Motoda et al. (1991) found:

- Task analysis and identification of the problem-solving functions involved in the task are a difficult first step.
- No uniform formal methods have emerged as most appropriate.
- The role of KA changes with the developmental stage, and different requirements must be supported at each stage in the life cycle.

For some organizations, like DuPont, the difficulty of transferring knowledge is rectified by having the expert build his/her own expert system without the need for a knowledge engineer. DuPont uses the "let 1,000 flowers bloom" grass roots approach where they train their experts on how to use PC-based expert system shells. These experts then develop their own expert systems. DuPont's average cost of expert system development is $25,000, but the annual average savings is $100,000 per expert system. The problem with this approach is that the expert may have latent biases, causing extraction of his own expertise to become a difficult, if not flawed, task. However, DuPont feels that it is easier for a domain expert to learn about AI than it is for an AI specialist to learn the domain.

Required Skills of Knowledge Engineers

What are the skills that knowledge engineers should possess?
According to DEC and other sources the knowledge engineer needs to know four major knowledge areas (Liebowitz, 1991b).
These are:

• Understanding of management functions, business in general, and the particular business (domain) in question.
• Understanding of knowledge in general, how human experts think, reason, learn, etc.
• Understanding of, and skills in, applying AI technology, including AI methodologies, programming, foundations, techniques, and tools.
• Understanding of information system implementation skills including software project management, database management systems, human factors, networking, systems analysis, etc.

DeSalvo and Liebowitz (1990), and Cantu-Ortiz (1991) provide a list of professional requirements for the knowledge engineer, which can be summarized as follows:

• *Communication skills:* These are essential tools for knowledge acquisition. The knowledge engineer must possess verbal talents that can be enhanced and developed through an appropriate training program.
• *Abstraction and modeling abilities:* These are critical skills for constructing knowledge representations. The important features of the problem solution must be identified and modeled by the

knowledge engineer.
- *Technical background in computing:* An understanding of hardware and software system design is necessary for developing expert systems.

Oxman (1992) suggests that a knowledge engineer should possess: self-work skills (self-motivation); ability to take a problem and analyze it until a solution is developed or becomes clear; the ability to use case (experiential) information from others and put it to effective use; basic knowledge engineering and acquisition skills; ability to design new solutions when old solutions do not fit; basic tool skills using off-the-shelf tools and techniques; ability to work in small development groups; and ability/desire to read/analyze new literature and put it to use.

Turban (1992) identifies required skills of the knowledge engineer as follows:

- Computer Skills.
- Tolerance and ambivalence.
- Effective communication abilities.
- Broad education.
- Advanced, socially sophisticated verbal skills.
- Fast-learning capabilities (of the domain).
- Understanding of organizations and individuals.
- Wide experience in knowledge engineering.
- Intelligence.
- Empathy and patience.
- Persistence.
- Logical thinking.
- Versatility and inventiveness.
- Self-confidence.

Many of these skills focus at the heart of knowledge acquisition. Because of the difficulty in acquiring and eliciting knowledge, potential knowledge engineers clearly need a stronger foundation in the fundamentals, methodologies, techniques, and tools for acquiring knowledge. Universities, such as the Universidad Politecnica de Madrid, George Washington University, the Center for Knowledge Technology at Utrecht, The Netherlands, and others, are offering curricula in knowledge engineering/applied artificial intelligence and expert systems. A critical component of these knowledge engineering curricula should be a course on knowledge acquisition. The Master of Science program in Applied AI and Expert Systems at

George Washington University requires a course on knowledge acquisition.

While clearly there is a great need for formal training in this area, the need for supplemental instruction is equally as great. The vast number of topic areas in knowledge acquisition simply cannot be covered in a single semester of study. What is needed is a mechanism that would allow students to supplement classroom instruction, thereby providing the student with the ability to focus on specific topics in greater depth. In response to this need we have developed KARTT, a hypermedia teaching tool (Bland and Liebowitz, 1993).

Hypermedia and Computer Based Instruction

A hypermedia system is an interactive multimedia system that is based on the principles of hypertext. In hypertext, text segments, or nodes, are accessed by links which function similarly to keywords. As a result, hypertext systems provide interactive instruction by essentially providing users with subject text navigation control. In hypermedia, nodes may be composed of any kind of media including, video, audio, graphics, and animation.

Hypermedia offers a number of advantages over traditional based instruction. One of the key advantages is learner control. Many studies have shown that learner controlled instruction is associated with increased learning. Research in learner controlled instruction suggests this observation is the result of three factors.

First, learner controlled instruction allows the student to study course material at a pace that suits his/her needs. This in turn helps to increase knowledge retention. Gagne (1985) suggested that learner control of the pace of instruction provides the learner the opportunity to encode information. According to this theory, transfer of information occurs during a phase called encoding, in which the learner organizes the information in a manner which reflects his/her learning style.

It is this consistency between the lesson characteristics and the learning style of the learner which improves retention and retrieval of knowledge. Other researchers go further to suggest that knowledge encoding is the process of the learner's integrating incoming knowledge with previous knowledge (Redding, 1990). In their opinion, learner control provides the student with the ability to incorporate the new knowledge within the framework of previous knowledge. This in turn not only increases retention and retrieval of knowledge, but also provides the learner with the ability to draw inferences and generate new knowledge.

Second, learner controlled instruction provides the learner with the ability to control the order via which the instruction content is presented. Keller (1983), using his model of learning entitled, Motivation Theory, suggested that the ability of the learner to control the sequence of subject presentation increased learning by making learning more relevant to the student. This in turn would improve the learner's motivation, and ultimately learning outcomes. Indeed, some authors have found that intrinsically motivated students, such as those found in college classrooms, performed better when they controlled the learning process (Redding, 1992).

Lastly, learner controlled instruction allows the student to choose the portion of the content materials he or she wishes to study. This frees the student to select material at will, ostensively selecting materials that would be relevant to past, present, or future needs.

Another advantage of hypermedia over traditional instruction is its provisions for non-linear access to information. Such accessibility provides the learner with the opportunity to discover different perspectives on the subject area being learned. Moreover, it allows the learner to explore related topic areas, thereby resulting in knowledge attainment that covers a greater breadth of the subject area. Tazelaar (1988) put it this way:

> Imagine if you will, walking into the New York Public Library and picking up a book on Mozart. You begin to read and learn that Mozart was an Austrian composer in the late 1700's. You wonder what else was happening in Austria then, so you go to the card catalog, find a book on Austrian history, go back to the stacks, locate the volume, (if it's not checked out), and read it before you continue. In this book you find a reference to old Salzburg, and you wonder what it looked like. Back to the card catalog, and the stacks to find the book with images from that time. Finally, you get back to Mozart and read of a piano concerto you've never heard. This process continues until you have either satisfied your desire for knowledge on the subject, or worn yourself out searching for it, whichever come first.

In addition to providing non-linear access to information, hypermedia systems, by their mere function, provide cues that help focus the learner on the specific knowledge to be learned. Links in hypermedia are highlighted. Such highlights help to identify important lesson features by drawing the user's attention. Hannafin & Hooper (1989) suggested that highlighted terms used throughout a lesson act like mnemonics in that they help the user recall lesson features and reinforce the relationship between a term and its definition. Some other authors have suggested that the node structure in hypertext facilitates learning. Research performed by Bork (1984) showed that segmented text, as found in hypertext nodes, was more easily encoded by learners than non-segmented text. He hypothesized that segmented text increased encoding efficiency because it essentially reduced the cognitive demands on the user. In addition to the benefits described so far, previous research has shown that multimedia, especially visual media, can promote learning. Kobayashi (1986) found that humans appear to be particularly adept visual learners. His research, along with others, found evidence to suggest that learning recall was enhanced when information was presented visually. Hannafin (1983) suggested that this was because visual information is coded both verbally and pictorially. This redundancy in encoding, he asserted, increased recall. Thus, combining visual media with accompanying text further increases learning recall. Others have suggested that visual media help increase the appeal of displayed text. This results in an increase in learner attention to the subject matter (Surber & Leeder, 1988). Moreover, visual media can aid the learner grasp concepts that are more easier shown than described. Thus, abstract information, procedural information, or information that requires an understanding of spatial relationships, is communicated most effectively through media that can display the salient features of the concept being presented (Rieber & Kini, 1991).

So far we have described some of the many benefits of hypermedia. In the next section we will describe a hypermedia system that has been developed to help individuals learn about knowledge acquisition approaches for developing expert systems.

KARTT Operating System Overview

KARTT is a hypermedia application that combines hypertext with audio/visual segments of different knowledge acquisition techniques. The system was programmed using a PC hypertext software package by IBM called HYPERWIN. HYPERWIN can be used on any IBM compatible workstation, operating in the DOS or OS/2 environment. An accompanying editor helps developers enter node text quite quickly. This enabled the first release of KARTT to be developed in approximately 12 weeks, with one developer working full time on this project and one other working one-quarter time. KARTT is currently about 80% hypertext, with the other 20% consisting of video segments of knowledge elicitation sessions. KARTT has been operational since the Spring 1992 semester.

The video segments were recorded using a standard camcorder. The segments were then captured using MediaScript. MediaScript is a multimedia authoring language that is based on DVI technology. DVI (Digital Video Interactive) is an integrated video, audio, and graphics technology that integrates software programs, text, graphics, sound, and full-motion video. Ultimedia, IBM's multimedia OS/2 system platform, is used in the current release of KARTT. The advantages of Ultimedia are two-fold. First, Ultimedia is easy to use, requiring the user to use few commands for manipulating information. Second, Ultimedia takes advantage of window technologies. This allows the video segment to be presented in windows that can be moved or scaled at will. As common with most hypertext systems, the hypertext nodes in KARTT are organized in a semantic network. This provides the user with the ability to navigate through the system using multiple, and even recursive paths. To provide the student with instructional and navigational guidance, a hierarchical structure is laid over the semantic network. The result is a system that appears to the user to be organized as a book, complete with chapters, sections, and tables of contents.

This material is represented in KARTT on over 100 nodes, residing on 22 ASCII files.

KARTT Subject Content and Organization

KARTT was proposed as a system to be used by both beginning and advanced students. As a result, KARTT provides information at multiple levels of detail. Background information in subject areas is provided to acquaint new students with basic AI and knowledge engineering concepts. This background knowledge, which concisely represents portions of five student text books used in the courses offered at George Washington University, covers the following topic areas:

• Definition and categories of artificial intelligence.
• Definition of knowledge based systems.
• Components of knowledge based systems.
• Definition and discussion of knowledge representation formalism.
• Comparison of conventional systems and knowledge based systems.
• Discussion of the knowledge based system development process.
• Discussion of knowledge verification and validation techniques.
• Discussion of knowledge engineering and its role in the knowledge

based system development process.
* Definition and discussion of the different types of knowledge.
* Definition and discussion of the major approaches used for acquiring knowledge.
* Comparison of knowledge acquisition approaches.
* Knowledge acquisition selection criteria.
* The problems associated with acquiring knowledge.

Links in background subject text nodes allow the reader to access more advanced information. Advanced students may elect to access more detail information on the various knowledge acquisition methods directly. KARTT currently has approximately 100 recent papers on knowledge acquisition. These are presented to the user in the form of abstracts. These abstracts are organized into 14 topics, representing the breadth of the field of knowledge acquisition approaches and issues surrounding these approaches. The following topics are presented in KARTT:

* Case-based knowledge acquisition.
* Text-analysis, including natural language processing and hypertext.
* Application of machine learning techniques.
* Manual techniques like interviewing and protocol analysis.
* Computer-based elicitation aids.
* Model-based acquisition.
* Theoretical and conceptual issues associated with knowledge, knowledge organization, and acquisition methods.
* Issues in knowledge elicitation.
* Future trends in knowledge acquisition.
* Comparative studies, including empirical research, case studies and surveys.
* Verification, evaluation, and validation techniques.
* Automated and manual knowledge refinement techniques.
* Knowledge acquisition methodologies.
* Utilizing multiple experts in the acquisition process.

Subject Organization. As stated earlier, KARTT is organized as a book, complete with chapters and sections. A main menu presents the user with a high level view of available subjects. Selecting an item from the main menu will cause a subject main menu to be presented. This menu provides considerably more information on the topic area. Selection of a topic from this background subject area menu provides the reader with a high level overview of the topic area.

Located in the overviews are links to nodes that provide detailed information on sub-topic subjects. In addition, links to advanced readings and references are also found.

The advance reading section of KARTT is organized in a somewhat similar fashion. Reading topics are presented in a readings menu. Selection of a topic area results in a display of the readings available in the area. These sub-topic menus present not only the list of available readings, but also a high level introduction to the sub-topic. Thus, the reader can quickly become familiar with the area to be discussed. Moreover, each sub-menu provides access to author notes. These notes, depending on the area, provide the user with a quick overview of the subject areas discussed by the authors. The author notes can also provide:

• Analysis of the information presented.
• References and links to other related topics included within KARTT.
• Links to the glossary.
• Additional references outside the scope of this system.
• Definition of important terms used throughout the abstracts.
• Commentaries on authors' works or techniques discussed.
• Suggested reading lists.

In addition to the above, many abstract modules have notes or other information links attached to them. Thus, a reader is provided with the option of perusing other related topics, readings, or notes.

The use of short, concise, segmented text nodes and graphics in both the beginner and advanced sections has several benefits. Not only does this format enable the reader to become quickly familiar with an area, it also reduces cognitive demands on the reader. According to several authors, the greater the density of a display screen, the greater the demands on the student's cognitive processing (Morrison et al., 1989). Reducing the instructional text into concise segments, as implemented in KARTT, helps focus the reader's attention to the major ideas expressed. This in turn can produce more favorable attitudes towards learning. Moreover, additional research in this area suggests that better readers, as one might expect to find in college and graduate level classes, are more likely to prefer low text density screen displays (Muter, Latremouille, & Treurniet, 1982). Such displays provide skilled readers with adequate contextual support, while at the same time reducing reading time.

KARTT Program Features

Three important criteria can be used to ascertain the quality of a system: usability of the system, instructional quality, and maintainability. The next sections will describe the features in KARTT that correspond to these criteria.

Ease of use is an important aspect of usability that has been carefully considered by the developers. KARTT is fast and easy to learn. Because it is not command driven, the user does not really have to learn how to use the system. Hence, a user can become proficient in using the system with speed. Because KARTT incorporates a hierarchical structure within a semantic network, the user is provided with the best of both worlds. The hierarchical structure provides the user with an interface that is immediately familiar and user friendly, while at the same time providing a certain level of instructional guidance. Moreover, organization of the hypertext nodes into chapters helps alleviate one of the common ailments of large hypertext systems: learner disorientation. Learner disorientation occurs when the reader loses his/her sense of location and direction while navigating in a hypertext system. By overlaying the semantic network with a hierarchical organization structure, the learner can proceed through the system in a more orderly manner. Some authors assert that hierarchical structures, like tables of contents, provide the learner with cognitive cues, which in turn enhance learner recall and retention (Hannafin & Carney, 1991; Schuerman & Peck, 1991; Hannafin & Hooper, 1989). The semantic network structure, on the other hand, provides the user with the freedom to choose a multitude of paths through the instructional material. This also allows the user to move across subject and topic domains.

An additional usability feature in KARTT is the user navigational controls. These controls provide the user with fast path access to menus and previous nodes. Presentation format consistency in KARTT also adds to its usability by helping the learner know where to find different types of information. For example, user navigational controls are always found in the left bottom corner of the screen. Sub-topic menus begin with a brief topic overview, followed by a list of available articles, authors notes, and navigational controls. Consistent frame design, as employed in this manner, not only helps to orient the learner, but also facilitates recall by providing a visual map-like organization which enhances user search for information (Aspillaga, 1991; Hannafin & Hooper, 1989).

While visual media can improve learning, dual presentation of text and visual media, according to some authors, may actually deter learning. Paivio (1979) asserted that multiple modal presentations tend to be distracting, particularly if the presentations do not reinforce each other. The single mode presentation in KARTT works towards avoiding distractions. Video and text are displayed separately. Graphics and tables are displayed with text, only when such graphics support the text.

Finally, the system provides user help for navigating and developing additional panels. An on-line help facility available to the user not only helps the learner use the system, but also provides valuable guidance for novice developers. Each panel of the system also comes complete with user instructions.

Instructional Delivery and Content Quality. Since the system is essentially user driven, the learner is free to learn at his or her own pace. The system also encourages the user to become an active participant in the learning environment by providing the user with the power of choice. Thus, the user/learner chooses what to learn.

KARTT provides the user with multiple learning opportunities. For example, the user can learn about protocol analysis by viewing the glossary, selecting the topic from the sub-menu, or reviewing it in context with interviewing or elicitation techniques. In addition, if the user wanted to see protocol analysis in action, a one-minute video clip of a knowledge engineer using this method can be shown and accessed by the user. In KARTT, thus far, video segments have been incorporated under the general heading "Interviewing Techniques Overview." This visual information allows the student to see how the concepts discussed in the text are applied in an actual acquisition setting.

Cross subject links allow the user to relate subject areas. For example, the topic called "machine learning" is linked to other topics, including explanation-based learning, similarity learning, and empirical inductions. Thus, the user is capable of obtaining a broader understanding of the subject text. This understanding can be further enhanced by the presence of the author's notes. As stated earlier, these notes provide useful insights into the subject domain. The notes also provide useful criticism, where appropriate, and point the learner to readings that serve to support such criticism. Recognizing that the information may not always be as extensive as an individual may desire, KARTT gives the user a list of other references he/she may use to obtain more information outside the system.

KARTT was developed to cover the broad spectrum of knowledge acquisition. Reading sections are composed of recent articles from some of the foremost authors in the various areas. In many cases, where authors of these articles may have used different terminology for the same concept, the KARTT developers have attempted to include all these terms in the subject glossary. Besides covering the major areas in tools and techniques, the abstracts in this system reflect a wide range of journals that touch upon a large number of professions. Included in these abstracts are discussions of knowledge acquisition in medicine, chemistry, civil engineering, computer human engineering, education, management, and manufacturing. This allows the user to understand how expert system development is viewed in other professional communities.

Maintainability. Modular construction of system code has long been seen as one of the most effective means for easing maintenance of software. KARTT was created with this in mind. Though KARTT is based on a semantic network, it is organized in a top-down structured format. This type of structuring ensures that the impact of a single change can be isolated within the software. Adding a new reading to an already existing topic area, for example, is a matter of adding a link to a sub-topic menu, and adding the text to be shown. The main menu file, nor any other topic file need be touched. Moreover, since the sub-topic menu and the abstract text for each reading is included within the same file, this type of change would impact only a single file.

Maintainability is enhanced by use of naming standards and code documentation. For example, each text module in the knowledge acquisition reading area begins with the prefix "KARD". Each text module ends with the file extension "TXT". The table of contents, on the other hand, end with the file extension "TBL". These file extensions enhance the developers', or maintenance team's, ability to easily recognize important members. It also enhances portability by making it easy to copy files from disk to disk.

In addition to the above, the topic areas included within a file are documented in the file banner. This provides for quick identification of text by file. Since the link for a specific article is associated with the title, knowing the title of the article helps the developer identify the link, no matter where the link may appear.

Disadvantages and Limitations of KARTT

While we have discussed the numerous advantages of KARTT, the system is not without its disadvantages. Complete learner control of instruction has been shown in some cases to result in less actual learning (Carrier, Davidson & Williams, 1985; Skinner, 1990).

Learner control allows a student to choose the material s/he wishes to learn. Implicit in this statement is the fact that the student may choose to disregard certain portions of the lesson. Another major factor in the effectiveness of KARTT is its reliance on passive indices. In passive indexed structures, links are defined by the developer. Cross references to related topic areas are also defined by the developer. Hence, the user is completely reliant on the developer to define all possible relationships among all text segments. More important, however, is the lack of a means for directly accessing a specific piece of information. If the user does not know what sub-topic heading an item of information falls within, s/he has no hope of finding the information, short of walking through each link and node. This would suggest that KARTT would be most effective for students who have significant previous knowledge in the area. Hence, as it stands today KARRT is best employed as a classroom supplement, rather than a stand alone CAI.

Perhaps KARTT's greatest limitation is its lack of provisions for self assessment. It has been well established that student self assessment in the form of question and answer formats provides the means by which students can measure their own learning attainment. Such assessments should usually occur after a concept has been presented (approximately every two to three frames). Without this capability the student has no way of determining, (short of actually utilizing the techniques discussed), what s/he knows, and how much s/he knows.

Future Directions for KARTT

The field of knowledge acquisition is currently more an art than a science. One way of remedying this situation is to develop more automated and aided knowledge acquisition tools, create more structured methodologies for knowledge acquisition (like Europe's KADS methodology), and perform more experimental research in comparing knowledge acquisition approaches. KARTT is a step toward improving the student's ability in understanding knowledge acquisition/elicitation techniques. A formal evaluation of KARTT will be conducted during the "Knowledge Acquisition" graduate course in Fall, 1993.

Multimedia is a powerful technology to aid the knowledge acquisition process. Various multimedia, hypertext-based, computer-assisted knowledge engineering (CAKE) tools like KARTT should be further developed to provide ways of improving the knowledge acquisition process. In the near term, KARTT will be expanded to include more video segments of the knowledge engineer using different knowledge acquisition/elicitation approaches with the expert(s). Direct access links will also be created to allow for faster access of topic information. More hypertext descriptions of knowledge acquisition methods and readings will also be incorporated into KARTT. Lastly, an experiment will be conducted to measure KARTT's effectiveness in regard to the student's level of understanding of knowledge acquisition versus other traditional knowledge acquisition methods.

Conclusions

This chapter described the development of a multimedia, hypertext-based tool called KARTT for helping students learn about knowledge acquisition methods and skills. Knowledge acquisition is probably still the biggest bottleneck in expert systems development. Through multimedia and hypertext technologies, KARTT has potentially developed into a useful tool, particularly for those graduate students taking the "Knowledge Acquisition" course. As multimedia platforms become more affordable and accessible over the next few years, increasing interest in multimedia technology will surge, particularly in education and training. Integration of multimedia and expert systems will take place, and the knowledge acquisition bottleneck will likely be reduced.

References

Aspillaga, M. (1991), "Screen Design: Location of Information and Its Effects on Learning", *Journal of Computer-Based Instruction*, Vol.18, No.3, (Bellingham: Association for the Development of Computer Based Instruction Systems, Summer).

Bland, K., and J. Liebowitz (1993), "KARTT: A Multimedia Tool to Help Students Learn Knowledge Acquisition" *Journal of End User Computing* (Harrisburg, Idea Group Publishing, Winter).

Bork, A. (1989), "Courseware Design: Design Considerations", cited in M.J. Hannafin and S.Hooper, "Integrated Framework for CBI Screen Design and Layout", *Computers in Human Behavior*, Vol.5, No.3, (New York: Pergamon Press).

Cantu-Ortiz, F. (1991), "Human Resources Formation in Knowledge Engineering: in Staffing Expert Systems Development Teams" *Heuristics: The Journal of Knowledge Engineering*, Vol.4, No.2, (Gaithersburg: International Association of Knowledge Engineers, Summer).

Carrier, C.A., G. Davidson, and M. Williams (1989), "The Selection of Instructional Options in a Computer-Based Coordinate Concept Lesson" cited in G.R. Morrison et.al., "Implication for the Design of Computer-Based

Instruction Screens". *Computers in Human Behavior*, Vol.5, No.3, (New York: Pergamon Press).

Chan, C., and I. Benbasat (1991), "Case Research on Knowledge Acquisition: Observations and Lessons", *The Knowledge Engineering Review* Vol 6., No.2, (Cambridge, England: Cambridge University Press, June).

Cohen, Y. (1989), "Hypertext- A New Challenge", *Proceedings from the 4th Israel Conference on Computer Systems and Software Engineering* (Piscataway: IEEE Service Center).

Cullen, J., and A. Bryman (1988), "The Knowledge Acquisition Bottleneck: Time for Reassessment?", *Expert System Journal*, Vol.5, No.3, (Oxford, England: Learned Information Ltd., August).

DeSalvo, D., and J. Liebowitz (1990), *Managing Artificial Intelligence and Expert Systems*, (Englewood Cliffs: Prentice Hall).

Feigenbaum, E. (1990), "Knowledge Engineering: the Applied Side of Artificial Intelligence", cited in B. Gaines "Knowledge Acquisition Systems" in H. Adeli (ed.) *Knowledge Engineering: Vol. I Fundamentals*, (New York: McGraw-Hill Publishing).

Gagne, R.M. (1985), *The Conditions of Learning* (4th ed.) (New York: Holt Rinehart and Winston).

Hannafin, M.J. (1991), "The Effects of Instructional Stimulus Loading on Recall of Abstract and Concrete Prose" cited in L.P Rieber and A.S. Kini, "Theoretical Foundations of Instructional Applications of Computer-Generated Animated Visuals", *Journal of Computer Based Instruction*, Vol.18, No.3, (Bellingham: Association for the Development of Computer Based Instruction Systems, Summer).

Hannafin, M.J, and B.W Carney (1991), "Effects of Elaboration Strategies on Learning and Depth of Processing During Computer-Based Instruction", *Journal of Computer-Based Instruction*, Vol.18, No.3, (Bellingham: Association for the Development of Computer Based Instruction Systems, Summer).

Hannafin, M.J, and S. Hooper (1989), "Integrated Framework for CBI Screen Design and Layout", *Computers in Human Behavior*, Vol.5, No.3, (New York: Pergamon Press).

Hayes-Roth, F., D.A. Waterman, and D.B. Lenat (Eds.) (1990), "Building Expert Systems", cited in B. Gaines "Knowledge Acquisition Systems" in H. Adeli (ed.) *Knowledge Engineering: Vol. I Fundamentals*, (New York: McGraw-Hill Publishing).

Keller, J.M. (1983), "Motivational Design of Instruction", In C.M. Reigeluth (Ed.), *Instructional Design Theories and Models: An Overview of Their Current Status* pp.383-434 (Hillsdale: Lawrence Erlbaum Associates).

Klahr, P. and D. Waterman (1986), *Expert Systems: Techniques ,Tools, and Applications* (Reading, MA: Addison Wesley).

Kobayashi, S. (1991), "Theoretical Issues Concerning Superiority of Pictures Over Words and Sentences in Memory", cited in L.P. Rieber, and A.S. Kini, "Theoretical Foundations of Instructional Applications of Computer-Generated Animated Visuals", *Journal of Computer-Based Instruction*, Vol.18, No.3, (Bellingham: Association for the Development of Computer Based Instruction Systems, Summer).

Liebowitz, J. (1991a), *Institutionalizing Expert Systems: A Handbook for Managers*, (Englewood Cliffs: Prentice Hall).

Liebowitz, J. (1991b), "Education of Knowledge Engineers", *Heuristics: The Journal of Knowledge Engineering* Vol.4, No.2, (Gaithersburg: International Association of Knowledge Engineers, Summer).

McGraw, K.L., and K. Harbison-Briggs (1989), *Knowledge Acquisition: Principles and Guidelines* (Englewood Cliffs: Prentice Hall).

Medsker, L., A.J. LaSalle, and D. Hillmer (1990), "Knowledge Acquisition and the Expert System Life Cycle", *Proceedings of the IEEE Conference on Managing Expert System Programs and Projects*, (Los Alamitos: IEEE Computer Society Press, September).

Milheim, W.D., and B.L. Martin (1991), "Theoretical Bases for the Use of Learner Control: Three Different Perspectives", *Journal of Computer-Based Instruction*, Vol.18, No.3, (Bellingham: Association for the Development of Computer Based Instruction Systems, Summer).

Morrison, G.R., S.M. Ross, J.K. O'dell, C.W Schulotz, and N. Higginbotham Wheat (1989), "Implication for the Design of Computer-Based Instruction Screens". *Computers in Human Behavior*, Vol.5, No.3, (New York: Pergamon Press).

Motoda, H., R. Mizoguchi, J. Boose, and B. Gaines (1991), "Knowledge Acquisition for Knowledge Based Systems", *IEEE Expert*, (Los Alamitos: IEEE Computer Society, August).

Muter, P., S.A. Latremouille, and W.C. Treurniet (1989), "Extending Reading of Continuous Text on Television Screens", cited in G.R. Morrision et. al., "Implication for the Design of Computer-Based Instruction Screens". *Computers in Human Behavior*, Vol.5, No.3, (New York: Pergamon Press).

Oxman, S. (1992), Discussions of Working Group on AI in Industry, Academia, and Government, (Annapolis: Oxko Corporation, May).

Paivio, A. (1989), "Imagery and Verbal Processes", cited in M.J. Hannafin and S. Hooper, *Integrated Framework for CBI Screen Design and Layout Computers in Human Behavior*, Vol.5, No.3, (New York: Pergamon Press).

Prerau, D. (1986), *Developing and Managing Expert Systems*, (Reading, MA: Addison Wesley).

Redding, R.E. (1990), "Individual Differences and Training Program Development", *Proceedings of the Human Factors Society* (Santa Monica: Human Factors Society Inc.).

Rieber, L.P., and A.S. Kini (1991), "Theoretical Foundations of Instructional Applications of Computer-Generated Animated Visuals", *Journal of Computer-Based Instruction*, Vol.18, No.3, (Bellingham: Association for the Development of Computer-Based Instruction Systems, Summer).

Schuerman, R.L., K.L. Peck (1991), "Pull-Down Menus, Menu Design, and Usage Patterns in Computer Assisted Instruction", *Journal of Computer-Based Instruction*, Vol.18, No.3, (Bellingham: Association for the Development of Computer-Based Instruction Systems, Summer).

Scott, A.C., J.E. Clayton, and E.L. Gibson (1991), *A Practical Guide to Knowledge Acquisition*, (Reading, MA: Addison Wesley).

Skinner, M. (1990), "Effects of Computer-Based Instruction on the

Achievement of College Students as a Function of Achievement Status and Mode", *Computers in Human Behavior*, Vol.6, (New York: Pergamon Press).

Surber, J., and J. Leeder (1988), "The Effect of Graphic Feedback on Student Motivation", *Journal of Computer-Based Instruction* Vol, 15, No.1, (Bellingham: Association for the Development of Computer-Based Instruction Systems).

Tazelaar, J. (1988), "Hypertext", *Byte*, (Peterborough, NH: McGraw Hill, October).

Turban, E. (1992), *Expert Systems and Applied Artificial Intelligence*, (New York, Macmillan).

Turban, E. and J. Liebowitz (Eds.) (1992), *Managing Expert Systems*, (Harrisburg, PA: Idea Publishing Company).

Westphal, C., and K. McGraw (eds.) (1989), "Special Issue on Knowledge Acquisition", *SIGART Newsletter*, No.108, (New York: ACM Press, April).

Woolf, B.P., E. Soloway, W.J Clancey, K. Van Lehn, and D. Suthers (1991), "Knowledge-Based Environments for Teaching and Learning" *AI Magazine*, Vol.11, No.5, (Menlo Park, CA: American Assocation for Artificial Intelligence, January).

Chapter 18

The Magic of Multimedia in Education:
Promises of the 21st Century

Ronald G. Ragsdale and Alnaaz Kassam
The Ontario Institute for
Studies in Education

This chapter explores the potential for multimedia in education, both with a view to its strengths in the delivery of content and its capabilities for evaluation. The authors, however, advice caution in the wholesale introduction of this technology into the classroom, both in the light of experience with previous technologies such as television and computers and in the light of their overall philosophy of education. The chapter examines the importance of providing education that incorporates the values of all world civilizations and religions, while at the same time being open to the benefits of new technologies.

Go and tell this people: 'Be ever hearing, but never understanding; be ever seeing, but never perceiving' (Isaiah, 6:9).

In recent years computer technology has been embraced with speed and enthusiasm into the classroom environment. While it has delivered a new level of "hearing" and "seeing," its promises of

---

* An earlier version of this material was presented by the first author as an invited address at *Implementatie van interactieve Media in het Hoger Onderwijs* on **November 27, 1992, in Ede, The Netherlands.**

"understanding" and "perceiving" have not always been met.

Multimedia with all its "magical" capabilities is fast taking over the hype that surrounds computing. Will it too prove to be a false prophet? This chapter looks at the role of multimedia in the context of the classroom. We shall start off by exploring the technical capabilities of multimedia as well as its potential influence on other aspects of the classroom including individualized and situated learning, cognition, visualization and the role of values in multimedia. Questions of implementation of multimedia in education will also be considered. The chapter will conclude with a brief analysis on the place of multimedia technology in the role of education in society.

What is Multimedia?

According to Gayeski, multimedia can be defined in the following manner:

> Multimedia is a class of computer-driven interactive communication systems which create, store, transmit, and retrieve textual, graphic, and auditory networks of information (Gayeski, 1992; p. 9).

Embedded in the above definition are three elements: the computer, graphics and networks, which when combined provide a new and powerful technology. Gayeski however, points out that not all components of the technology need be present for multimedia to occur, i.e. text-only applications such as electronic mail also qualify as multimedia (Gayeski, 1992, pp. 9-11).

The term multimedia could therefore include electronic mail or a complex configuration of computers, interactive video, CD-ROM, camcorders or mixers. Because many of these technologies have existed before, this chapter takes the perspective that we can learn from past research in their implementation. This means that previous television or previous computer research could bring valuable insights to the field of multimedia in the classroom.

What Can Multimedia Be Used For?

There are many and varied uses of multimedia: in business, government, industry and education. In all the varied promises of multimedia for educational use made by its enthusiasts, certain themes emerge consistently and clearly. These are its potential for an interactive, individualized and realistic approach to learning and its unique potential for situated learning, cognition and visualization.

We shall explore these themes in more detail by firstly providing a platform to the enthusiasts of multimedia technology. After this we shall question and analyze the enthusiasm by drawing in the views of other technology experts.

The Promise of Multimedia and Interactive, Individualized and Realistic Learning

One of the most important claims of multimedia is that because it combines the technology of video and computers, it offers a unique environment for interactivity, learner control and student interest and motivation.

In a foreword to a book entitled *Interactive Multimedia* (Ambron & Hooper, 1988 cited in Reeves, 1992), John Sculley, Chief Executive Officer of Apple Computer, Inc., describes this new technology:

> Imagine a classroom with a window on all the world's knowledge. Imagine a teacher with the capability to bring to life any image, any sound, any event. Imagine a student with the power to visit any place on earth at any time in history. Imagine a screen that can display in vivid color the inner workings of a cell, the births and deaths of stars, the clashes of armies, and the triumphs of art. And then imagine that you have access to all of this and more by exerting little more effort than simply asking that it appear. It seems like magic even today. Yet the ability to provide this kind of environment is within our grasp (Sculley, 1988, p. vii in Reeves, 1992, p. 48).

Multimedia is also touted as being superior to all other technologies in providing individualized learning and mastery.

> Multimedia provides a higher level of mastery over the subject matter. It gives students "hands-on" learning, better retention, specific feedback and increased levels of understanding. We can't consistently make these statements about videotape, text, text with graphics, traditional classroom learning, or even computer-based training (Roden, 1991 pp. 80-81).

Another oft-cited advantage of multimedia is the speed of response to the individual learner's needs:

> The difference in multimedia excitement is in how it is made to respond to the participant. That instant, personal response is more than a reward to the user...It is the supreme compliment. People live lives full of deferred response. Tulips don't bloom until spring. Even the incredible idea has to wait for a meeting. And your brilliant performance on the job still waits until review time for its response. But in truly interactive media, your response is *now*. And the quality of that instant response defines the quality of multimedia... all else is filler (Hon, 1992, p. 17).

At first glance, it seems obvious that instruction that provides control over learning should prove superior to that which delegates all control to the instructor. However, research with educational technology shows that students do not react uniformly to this type of instruction (Collis, 1991, p. 138). In fact she quotes Salomon who states that:

> There is a growing body of evidence to indicate that no media variable, minute or gross as it may be, affects all groups of learners in one and the same way (Salomon, cited by Schramm, 1977, p. 94).

Furthermore Collis concludes that recent research shows that it is impossible to make general conclusions about the effectiveness of particular design variables in media. Such effectiveness is very much dependent upon the context in which it is used. She defines context as including: "characteristics of the learner, of the learning goals and context, and of the relationship of the media use to other aspects of the instructional setting" (Collis, 1991; p. 139).

To a large extent, Salomon and Gardner (1986) agree with this analysis. They state that there cannot be a one-to-one correspondence between what a feature or activity allows or has potential for, and what actually occurs.

Thus a science simulator may be designed for control over physical phenomena, but it cannot be assumed that the control is "mindfully experienced" by the user (Chanowitz & Langer, cited by Salomon and Gardner, 1986).

While users would naturally be influenced by differences in ability and prior knowledge in the way they process computer or multimedia technology, they are also affected by how they process the information or execute the activity. The individual's motivation, perception of task, and preferred learning strategy also play a crucial role (Anderson & Lorch, 1983; Salomon & Leigh, 1984 cited by Salomon and Gardner, 1986). Thus the effect of a particular medium is only half the story - the other half is played by the user's choice - whether to get involved or not, to process the information more deeply or whether to create meaning from the learning experience. According to Salomon and Gardner, these issues are more important in those activities where more learner control is required:

> As Chanowitz and Langer (1980) argue, there are distinguishable ways in which one can go through (or be put through) the motions of control. One can go through them quite mindlessly, relying on previously made distinctions and seeking perhaps to show good performance (Dweck & Bempechat, 1980); or one can got through them in a more mindful exploratory manner, intending to reach higher levels of mastery and hoping to effect new distinctions and to generate new hypotheses. The behaviors may look alike, but the way control is experienced in both is quite different, and hence may lead to entirely different learning outcomes (Salomon & Gardner, 1986; p. 16).

Salomon and Gardner discuss this in the context of LOGO. While LOGO provides users with the opportunity for more mindful control, there is no assurance that the majority of children will not use the program for producing impressive graphics or "fooling around" as opposed to discovering the underlying math involved. Salomon & Gardner then state that the lesson to be learned is one stated long ago by Schramm, Lyle and Parker (1961), in the context of television:

> Ask not what television (read: the computer) does to the children but rather what the children do with television (computers) (Salomon & Gardner, 1986, p. 16).

Salomon and Gardner go onto explain:

> Computer-afforded activities, promising as they may appear to be, may only suggest how students' minds could beome engaged. But whether they do and in what way they do are issues not easily accounted for by descriptions of the input

or the kinds of activities afforded. A few children may indeed become LOGO aces or thoughtful experimenters with science simulators. How do the others construe the experience? (Salomon & Gardner, 1986, p. 16).

In the same context, we could exchange the words television and computers with multimedia. And in fact, because multimedia is more interactive and individualized than television, student input and involvement is all the more vital.

Clearly, having students take advantage of individualized learning is not just a matter of making multimedia available to them. It also includes preparation of the students' environment, an understanding of the context of the learning situation involved and it includes an appreciation of the students' personal and intellectual needs.

The preparation will also include having students be critically aware of the effects of the technology they use. This will be dealt with in more detail later in this chapter.

The Promise of Multimedia and Situated Learning

In the previous section on interactive, individualized and realistic learning and multimedia, we discussed the potential of multimedia for individualized teaching, instant response, and provision of a realistic and exciting learning environment. Armed with all of these advantages, it seems natural that multimedia should become a tool for apprenticeship training. Whether the training involves a simulation of the corporate environment (Dede, 1992, p. 58) or a policeman on the beat (Reeves, 1992, p. 48), multimedia provides a unique opportunity for "situated learning."

What is "situated learning"? According to Reeves (1992, pp. 47-53), a major concern for education and training is the degree to which transfer of learning takes place from artificial learning environments to the contexts where these skills are actually used. He cites the research of Collins, Brown and Newman (1989) who propose using a "cognitive apprenticeship" model of instruction as opposed to using didactic teaching methods. In this model, students acquire knowledge and skills that are instrumental to the accomplishment of meaningful tasks. As Reeves writes:

> Collins *et al.* (1989) propose a "cognitive apprenticeship" model of instruction as an effective alternative to traditional instruction. The researchers maintain that traditional

knowledge abstracts knowledge and skills from their uses in the world. In apprenticeship learning, on the other hand, knowledge and skills are seen as instrumental to the accomplishment of meaningful tasks. The apprenticeship model is based on modeling, coaching, scaffolding, articulating, reflecting, and exploring as opposed to didactic teaching strategies such as telling and correcting (Reeves, 1992, p. 51).

This model of instruction is termed "situated learning" or "situated cognition."

According to Reeves, well-designed interactive multimedia support simulated apprenticeships, while also providing learning and support activities such as modeling and coaching. He believes that environments that promote situated learning can be constructed through the use of multimedia. A focal event or problem situation serves as the "anchor" or focus for learners to retrieve and construct new knowledge through a meaningful and relevant context. He cites a hypothetical example of a simulation using multimedia technology that would provide sales training for a retail store chain with a high employee turnover. The program would train new employees in the chain's sales strategies by providing a set of typical sales problems that would illustrate to the employee how each strategy influences the company's success. The multimedia system would allow users to switch perspectives from that of the sales person, to the customer, to the manager or even, to a bystander.

There would also be access to a "mentor" who would provide expert advice on various problems and strategies to improve opportunities provided in the program. Multimedia technology allows automated response-capture routines that would track the paths and progress of the trainee through the simulation. Such an environment would presumably provide a learning situation that is interesting, relevant and keyed to the individual needs of a learner. It would also allow for a detailed evaluation of student responses.

It is certainly true that students who have undergone an apprenticeship, are more likely to acquire and retain learning than knowledge that is presented to students in encapsulated format, where it is left up to the student to generate connections among problems and ways to solve these problems. As Reeves explains, knowledge that is learned in a context of use will be used in that and similar contexts (1992, p. 50). Thus it would seem that simulations of scientific and social contexts, should encourage students to acquire a deeper and more realistic understanding of reality, than a simple didactic method of teaching.

However, simulations do alter interpretation of reality. In our research (Ragsdale, Durell, Griffith, Moore & Kassam, 1989 & 1993) with the implementation of computers in schools, we had the opportunity to observe the use of a simulation called *Flame Life*. The program is a simulation of a simple scientific experiment repeated in schools throughout the world - the lighting of a candle, the placing of a glass over it and watching the flame die down. In one case, one of the authors of this chapter, watched a teacher conduct this experiment in reality - without having the students carry it out on the computer. It became clear that the entire experience of the experiment became different - it was richer and had deeper impact on students. It is increasingly becoming clear that technology affects one's interpretation of reality. In fact no technology is neutral (Ellul, 1964).

Ragsdale in discussing discovery learning and the use of technology makes the following comments:

> Discovery learning can be a powerful way of learning, so that the learner has a personal and deep understanding of new concepts. Many people make a false distinction, however, between "guided discovery" and free exploration using computer tools. **When we use technology to explore, we are guided by the technology.** I have traveled between Oslo and Tromsoum by plane, train, bus, and boat, "discovering" very different things with each form of transportation. In particular, crossing the Arctic Circle by train was very different from crossing it by plane or boat (Ragsdale, 1991, p. 164).

In fact, the experience of the Arctic landscape was different with each mode of transportation. In travelling by air, from the window of the plane the author could see only the high mountain peaks. And when travelling by train, his views of the Arctic as barren and harsh, were fulfilled. But in making the journey by boat, he was surprised by the lushness and greenery of the surroundings.

It must also be pointed out that human beings, in experiencing reality, create meaning for themselves. The experience of Paris may be intense and personal for one whose first child was born there, while it may be totally different for one who is there on transit from Africa on their way to Toronto. The fatigue of the former and the latter persons is quite different. Human beings are creatures that create meaning for themselves and their environments.

However, technology—and technology that is as powerful as multimedia, could alter meanings that human beings would normally create from immediate experiences of an environment.

It could be argued that multimedia is "anchored" (see above) in a learning experience. Furthermore, this experience is geared toward different interpretations, so that in the simulation described above, the student could explore the sales simulation through the perspective of various personalities. Nevertheless, it must be pointed out that each of these interpretations has been pre-programmed by the creators of the simulations, and therefore they are not reality but rather representations of reality created by other people. Students therefore experience a world (virtual reality), that is removed from the world around themselves.

In this context, Helsel describes a virtual reality where students, rather than reading about an historical event could partake in it themselves and interact with simulated persons from that historical era. She states that this reality would be a creation of various "experts": historians, psychologists, anthropologists, educators, etc. (Helsel, 1992, p. 41).

In this context one needs to ask: what is history? Is it the experience of events by historical characters, or is it an interpretation of one's past that gives meaning to the present? For the authors, the creation of history is seen as an interpretation of the past made by people, whatever expertise they may possess. It is an exploration of human beings and the meaning they create for themselves and their lives. History is the exploration of ideas that not only tell us about our past, but also shed light on our present.

What then is more important in the study of history: an experience in a simulation that allows one to "become" a character from the past or an analysis of one's past that would allow students to explore changing interpretations of important issues in our lives? Certainly the creation of a simulation where students become characters of history does not preclude an analytical approach to history—but we challenge the implication that in "becoming" a historical character, one acquires true understanding. We shall explore this issue further in the section on multimedia use in the classroom.

In a different light, our research (Ragsdale, Durell, Griffith, Moore & Kassam, 1989 & 1993) has shown that students react differently to simulations and text material. And it is interesting to note that a combination of the two provides for a richer experience. In the following quotation, one of the authors (RGR) is interviewing a student regarding her use of a history simulation:

RGR: Did you also study this using a book?

Yolanda: Yes, she gave us papers and stuff. See, the computer ... It's sort of hard to get to know the rebellion through the computer because it just goes through simulations and you walk down the street and see the houses you might see in that time, so it doesn't tell much about the actual rebellion. So the sheets helped a lot.

RGR: So you needed that for background. Is it like needing the newspaper today to understand what's happening, rather than just seeing it as you walk down the street?

Yolanda: Yes, I think so.

RGR: So your understanding of why the rebellions happened would come from what you read, rather than from the program?

Yolanda: Yes.

RGR: What is the advantage of using the program?

Yolanda: Well, it's fun, it was fun to go through it and basically you do see what life was like back then. Because when you go through the simulation it has different questions about like what kind houses you might have seen, what kind of writing utensils you might have used back then, so you get to compare what you have today with what they had back then. So you do get to see the way their life was back then.

RGR: Is there any sort of "message" - similar to the message or theme in a TV program?

Yolanda: With the computer?

RGR: Yes, or is it just a bunch of questions about life back then?

Yolanda: Yes, I think that's it.

RGR: It just shows you the way life was at that time?

Yolanda: Yes.

Here we see that the student uses the text material to enhance her experience of the simulation, thereby providing more background and analysis than a simple absorption of the experience.

In this context, Helsel believes that with virtual reality, education will move from its reliance on written text to reliance on imagery. She believes that images are easier for human beings to comprehend than is text:

> Very possibly, virtual reality will lead to an emphasis on learning via symbols. People comprehend images much more quickly than they can grasp columns of numbers or lines of text. The brain's visual processing power has been described by Larry Smarr, director of the National Center for Supercomputing Applications at the University of Illinois: "The eye-brain system is incredibly advanced. Looking at the world, we absorb the equivalent of a billion bits of information per second, as much as the text in 1,000 copies of a magazine. But our mental 'text computer' is limited by the fact that we can read only about 100 bites (sic) - or characters - per second." (Helsel, 1992, pp. 41-42).

This seems a rather inflated portrayal of the brain's visual processing power. It is necessary to point out that we may absorb a billion bits of data, but we process and interpret only what "makes sense" to us. This means that from an entire view of a forest, we may only choose to experience the smell and texture of a tiny leaf. Thus the eye may be exposed to all the data available but it is the total human being that chooses to interpret what he/she wishes.

Similarly, our responses to multimedia are governed by our interpretation of what human beings do to process and learn about their environments. We need to ask ourselves whether instruction must only be geared toward making learning easier for the student. Is there not a tradition of knowledge that one wants to make available to students? Are those questions that can only be explored in the abstract, and through text no longer valid? Is only the visual aspect of our cultural heritage to be retained and expanded upon?

In fact, in moving away from the abstract to the visual, we are not only discussing issues of content, but rather also of our perception of ourselves as human beings. As Ellul explains: The reference to a need of images is a falsehood.

People are being plunged into an artificial world which will cause them to lose their sense of reality and to abandon their search for truth (Ellul, 1990, p. 337).

To add another dimension to the discussion, we must refer to Brown, Collins and Duguid's 1989 article: *Situated Cognition and the Culture of Learning.* In their emphasis on an "apprentice" model of instruction, these authors make it clear that learning is a cultural experience:

> Conceptual tools... reflect the cumulative wisdom of the culture in which they are used and the insights and experience of individuals. Their meaning is not invariant but a product of negotiation within the community... Just as carpenters and cabinet makers use chisels differently, so physicists and engineers use mathematical formulae differently. Activity, concept and culture are interdependent. No one can be totally understood without the other two. Learning must involve all three (Brown, Collins & Duguid, 1989, p. 39).

Brown *et al.* continue to state that a collaborative environment where students and teachers partake is an important component of situated cognition:

> Groups are not just a convenient way to accumulate the individual knowledge of their members. They give rise synergistically to insights and solutions that would not come about without them (p. 40).

And in fact, Brown, Collins and Duguid believe that the teacher's role as master to apprentices in an authentic domain is increasingly important (p. 40). Thus we can see that situated learning through "virtual reality" alone will not solve all problems of learning. In fact, simulations are enriched and empowered by human interaction that provides analysis of experiences. This will be demonstrated later in the chapter when we deal with the use of multimedia in the classroom.

Finally, in changing technologies to explore learning, we abandon old ways of teaching. Schools have limited time to deal with the curriculum: once an item is covered in one medium, it is unlikely that it will be covered again in another context. And, in fact, when topics are covered a second time (as in techniques common to math and science) achieving transfer is extremely difficult. In fact students often fail to apply knowledge and skills learned in one context to other situations (Perkins, 1988). Because of this, students may not have occasion to analyze and explore or even be aware of different interpretations of reality.

To summarize, it would seem that multimedia offers possibilities for an experience of situated learning, but it is important that this experience not be isolated from human interaction and analysis.

The Promise of Multimedia and Cognition and Visualization

Dede explains that the "magic" of multimedia is that it can provide situations that mimic reality where one can experience situations that may be dangerous or expensive in real life. However, it also allows learners to manipulate this reality:

> ..adding the ability to magically act in ways impossible in the real world opens up new dimensions for instruction, as well as opportunities for fantasy and curiosity. Through visualization, learners can manipulate typically intangible entities such as molecules and mental models; through virtual communities, students can interact in rich psychosocial environments populated by simulated beings (Dede, 1992, p. 57).

Dede goes on to describing an example of the use of multimedia, where a medical student enters a virtual room labeled "Laboratory." Inside the room would be three categories of objects with which the learner can interact. The first category of object would be the traditional laboratory devices such as microscopes and centrifuges. The second category of object would be the intangible physical one such as a molecule. The learner would be able to manipulate the molecule to view it in three dimensions, or manoeuvre two molecules to observe how one catalyzes a change in another (Dede, 1992, p. 57). The third category of object introduces us to perhaps the most exciting promise of multimedia: here the learner would be able to manipulate typically intangible cognitive objects such as mental models or knowledge structures, looking for patterns that would expose similarities and differences in contrasting theories. The use of the first two categories of objects, Dede terms "sensory traducers." They allow users to access previously imperceptible phenomena such as molecules. However, the manipulation of the third category of object is termed a "cognitive transducer."

According to Dede, this form of visualization makes knowledge structures visible and manipulable. Designers of educational "microworlds" (simulations in which the user can change the rules by which the virtual environment functions) incorporate the use of cognitive transducers:

> As one example of applying cognitive transducers in education, the author has conducted preliminary research on the functional design of an information tool to aid instructional developers (Dede & Jayaram, 1990). By allowing the user to traverse virtual cognitive space, such an application could image the mental models that underlie training. The viewer could navigate through a virtual environment populated by cognitive entities represented as physical objects. In addition, the user could transcend the metaphor of physical space by shifting among alternate contexts (e.g. informational, relational, diagnostic) that provide different perspectives on a particular cognitive entity. Special capabilities to minimize complexity (i.e. guided tours, filters) would also be available (Dede, 1992, p. 57).

Reeves also discusses knowledge-dependent learning and multimedia.

> According to Glaser (1984) and other cognitive psychologists, knowledge begets knowledge. In other words, the ability to construct new knowledge is a function of both the amount and quality of existing knowledge one has as well as one's reasoning and other intellectual abilities. Because learning depends heavily on what students or trainees already know, IMM (Interactive Multimedia) should be designed to provide "cognitive bootstrapping" for the construction of knowledge and the development of intellectual skills (Resnick, 1989 quoted in Reeves, 1992, p. 50).

Reeves identifies methods of "bootstrapping" as allowing students to resolve discrepant events, providing them with multiple perspectives of phenomena, and assisting them with perceptual discrimination of complex processes. One way new knowledge can be developed is to enable students to confront misconceptions they have about different ideas. He says:

Exposing learners to discrepant events permits them to confront their everyday conceptions of the phenomena involved. IMM can be designed to assist learners in resolving discrepancies and ultimately constructing new knowledge on the reconfigured foundations of what they previously "knew" (Reeves, 1992, p. 50).

Reeves goes on to explain that the case-based approach to learning could also aid in students' linking newly acquired knowledge in the form of active responses to simulated problems. This could be done through providing realistic cases rich with problems to be solved, and then presenting conceptual knowledge, skills and even attitudes as required by the individual cases. However, multimedia technology is certainly not the first to offer knowledge construction to its users. LOGO was one of the first and most widely known programs to offer such promise. In describing a microworld, a term that is now often associated with virtual reality, Papert states:

Newton "understood" the universe by reducing whole planets to points that move according to a fixed set of laws in motion. Is this grasping the essence of the real or hiding its complexities? Part of what it means to be able to think like a scientist is to have an intuitive understanding of these epistemological issues and I believe that working with Turtles can give children an opportunity to know them.

It is in fact easy for children to understand how the Turtle defines a self-contained world in which certain questions are relevant and others are not... Children get to know what it is like to explore the properties of a chosen microworld undisturbed by extraneous questions. In doing so they learn to transfer habits of exploration from their personal lives to the formal domain of scientific theory construction (Papert, 1980, p. 117).

Papert describes microworlds as protected areas where children can interact with objects and learn in a natural manner, rather like a baby acquiring the use of language by being surrounded with it.

However, Salomon and Gardner, while acknowledging that research shows that LOGO does affect children's metacognitions

(Clements & Gullo, 1984), believe that it does not show why such results are obtained nor what computer qualities are responsible for them. Were the positive results arrived at by Clements & Gullo obtained by the juxtaposition of two symbol systems in a way that allowed students to translate concepts from one system to another? Or was it that the tutorial guidance provided in the research by Clements and Gullo made the learners more mindful of their own metacognitions? Recent research on computers also provides similar findings. Linn (1985) found in her study of teaching BASIC programming, that under typical instructional settings high-ability students progressed far more than their less able peers. However, under "exemplary" as opposed to "typical" conditions the differences between the two groups of students was far smaller (Salomon & Gardner, 1986, p. 17). Collis (1991) finds similar results. She states that although there is evidence of educational effectiveness from the use of LOGO, computer-assisted instruction and problem solving software, unstructured use is generally ineffective.

Similarly in the case of primary level students, Cohen summarizes previous research that shows that unstructured instruction around LOGO is not as effective as Papert believed:

> Research evidence suggests that while, in general, children enjoy exploring Turtle graphics programming and derive a variety of social-emotional and cognitive benefits from this experience (Clements, 1985, 1986a, 1986b) the standard full-blown version of LOGO is too cognitively demanding for most primary grade students (Cuneo, 1986; Fay & Mayer, 1987; Geva & Cohen, 1987; Lehrer & Smith, 1986; Pea & Kurland, 1983). Thus young children require extensive instructional support to help them learn even the most basic LOGO programming concepts (Clements, 1985; Cohen, 1987; Kull, 1986) quoted in (Cohen, 1991, p. 113).

The finding that different students react to the same technological instruction in different ways is also echoed by Salomon & Leigh in their analysis of predispositions about learning from print and TV.

Salomon and Leigh (1984) show that student expectations and preconceptions of TV affect their response to it. They cite Wright and Huston (1981) who showed that informativeness of formal features is meaningful only to those viewers who actively seek to understand content at the level beyond superficial enjoyment. In fact, to appreciate features for their informativeness, viewers must be able to encode content, form hypotheses and develop a context of expectations (Wright & Huston, 1981, p. 77). Salomon and Leigh state the present research shows that children who fail to seek actively to understand television content at deeper levels can still enjoy a program without being able to gain much knowledge from it.

They believe that what students expect to receive influences their experience with TV. However, they conclude by stating that the development of this "context of expectations" is influenced by factors such as the programs one views, the family context in which viewing takes place, parental control over viewing patterns, etc.

> One learns what to expect from TV and then uses this knowledge to "contextualize" the viewing experience (Salomon & Leigh, p. 135).

Similarly, Ragsdale (1991) in his research with computer use in education has shown that computers can be an effective part of "active learning", but:

> ... not only do our studies indicate that computer use within an active learning environment is not necessarily supportive, but active learning without computers is viable in itself (Ragsdale, 1991, p. 160).

In discussing the *Geometric Supposer*, Gordon says:

> First, we have learned that technology can serve as a catalyst for change, but it can't carry the day. We believe that technology - with appropriate software, with appropriate materials, with an appropriate pedagogy, and with appropriate support for the learning community that is the classroom - can catalyze change....

> Second, we have learned that teachers are central to the constructivist approach and must be supported. If we want to take advantage of the constructivist approach to learning and teaching with technology, we must resolve to support teachers with adequate time and appropriate mechanisms for study and preparation, and with appropriate curricular materials. We must question whether the existing school structures allow for the kind of collegial interaction among

teachers that we have come to believe is necessary for the success of this approach to education (Gordon, 1990, pp. 8-9).

Similarly, in the HOTS (Higher Order Thinking Skills) program (Pogrow, 1988; Gore, 1991), Pogrow maintains that "understanding conversations" between teacher and student are crucial to the development of higher order thinking skills.

Barth (1991) shows that lasting improvements in education must come from within the schools themselves. He writes, "School is not a place for important people who do not need to learn and unimportant people who do. Instead, school is a place where students discover, and adults rediscover the joys, the difficulties, and the satisfactions of learning" (p. 43).

Our own results (Ragsdale, Durell, Griffith, Moore & Kassam, 1989 and 1993), from six elementary schools with student/computer ratios as low as 6/1, indicate that direct teacher involvement in student computer use is crucial. Snyder supports this view, based on his teaching experience and with the software he has developed (Snyder & Palmer, 1986; Snyder, 1988).

In fact, as Collis (1991) points out, it is not the particular medium that makes instructional impact but rather the intersection of capabilities of the medium, the user's characteristics, and the implementation of design strategies to absorb these characteristics. Collis believes that a technology's educational value can be determined by its flexibility to meet the range of user needs and characteristics.

In the previous analysis, we have seen that multimedia is flexible and capable of meeting varying users' needs, but it is the creators of the programs that would have to take into consideration the various factors outlined above. Once a program arrives in the school, the context of the learning environment, both in terms of the individual's personal and intellectual involvement and the surroundings that he or she finds him/herself in, becomes crucial. This discussion illustrates that while multimedia does offer unique possibilities for visualization and cognition, previous experience with varied technologies shows that the learning context, i.e. the teacher, the curriculum, the environment and most important of all, the student, play vital roles in the successful implementation of any technology.

The Promise of Multimedia and Values

In her paper entitled "Virtual Reality and Education", Helsel describes virtual worlds in the following manner:

> Only most recently have humans been able to interact with artificial worlds via simulations or expertly designed multimedia programs. For the future, it will not only be possible for a user to interact within virtual worlds as her very own persona, but also it will be possible for that user to mentally become another person - much as Sherry Turkle predicted almost 10 years ago in *Second Self* when she wrote of new technologies:
>
>> You inhabit someone else's mind...You are Scarlett O'Hara, opening the door to Tara. You are Rhett Butler, deciding to stay rather than leave" (Turkle, 1984, p. 78) cited in (Helsel, 1992, p. 39).

And in the following paragraph Dede explains virtual communities:

> Visualization is one form of magic that empowers learning in multimedia environments; a second type of magic is virtual communities. Learners can interact in psychosocial environments populated both by video-links to other people and by simulated beings. These simulated beings may be avatars (computer graphics representations of people) or knowbots (machine-based agents); each adds an important dimension to education in virtual worlds (Dede, 1992, pp. 57-58).

While the implications of these simulated virtual communities are quite far-reaching, we shall limit ourselves to a description of one such environment in this section. Dede provides a graphic description of Lucasfil 1's *Habitat* (Morningstar and Farmer, 1991 quoted in Dede, 1992):

> *Habitat* was initially designed to be an on-line entertainment m um in which people could meet in a virtual environment to play adventure games. Users, however, extended the system into a full-fledged virtual community with a unique culture; rather than playing pre-scripted fantasy games, they focused on creating new lifestyles and utopian societies (Dede, 1992, p. 59).

Habitat, according to Dede, provided its participants with opportunities to get married or divorced without real-world repercussions, to start businesses without risking real money, establish religions without real-world persecution, and even provided opportunities to murder others' avatars without moral qualms. Users could tailor their own personal avatar to assume a range of personal identities, e.g movie stars, dragons, etc.

According to Dede, what people want from these virtual societies is "magic" which, by definition, the real world cannot provide. Dede gives the example of *Change-o-Matic*, a gender alteration machine which was one of the most popular devices of *Habitat* (Dede, 1992, pp. 58-59). Both the use of *Habitat* and the use of the virtual world outlined by Helsel above, harbor important implications for the impartation of human values.

In the above example, we see how technology can affect the way we interpret and deal with such complex and important human issues as family, marriage, religion, life and death. It is one thing for adults to indulge in such games at their own discretion, but it is quite another to place them in the hands of young people, especially if this is done without prior discussion of the issues at hand. As Roszak states:

> ... the computer brings with it a hidden curriculum that impinges upon the ideals (one) would teach. For this is indeed a powerful teaching tool, a smart machine that brings with it certain deep assumptions about the nature of mentality. Embodied in the machine there is an idea of what the mind is and how it works...
>
> No other teaching tool has ever brought intellectual luggage of so consequential a kind with it. A conception of mind - even if it is no better than a caricature - easily carries over into a prescription for character and value. When we grant anyone the power to teach us *how* to think, we may also be granting them the chance to teach us *what to think, where to begin thinking, where to stop* (Roszak, 1986, p. 217).

What could be the possible effects of multimedia in the form of virtual reality? On the one hand, it could have beneficial effects in that this reality could introduce students to important concepts and could aid in their metacognitive abilities. However, we have discussed these aspects above and have shown how very difficult these are to achieve and how important design, context and individual user characteristics are to their success.

The authors of this chapter, however, are not so much concerned about the effectiveness of imparting skills through multimedia as they are of the view of reality that such endeavors may unconsciously impart. As Postman states:

> ... embedded in every tool is an ideological bias, a predisposition to construct the world as one thing rather than another, to value one thing over another, to amplify one sense or skill or attitude more loudly than another (Postman, 1992, p. 13).

It has been stated above that because multimedia absorbs both the technology of the computer and that of television or live video, we can and should learn from the implementation of these technologies. Extensive work has been conducted on the effects of television on the lives of people, especially on their world view. Here we quote from Ellul:

> Television ... abolishes the relation to space... There is naturally no reason for human relations to be formed. Thus the idea of the global village is a snare and delusion. ... When I meet a beggar or one of the unemployed, I look at this person in the same superficial and disembodied way as I do at the living skeletons in the Third World that television shows me from time to time (Ellul, 1990, p. 335).

In fact, as Dede points out, that while the psychosocial implications of multimedia are complex and depend in part on how the interchange between learners and subject matter takes place, the medium also shapes the message. Dede discusses the impact of technology on human beings:

> The single greatest experiential input for many Americans now is the pervasive sensory, informational, and normative environment created by television, radio, videogames, movies, and videotapes. In this situation, people's knowledge and values can be constrained by the characteristics of these communications channels (Dede, 1992, p. 59).

Dede discusses the cultural consequences of such media as television in our lives. With television, people have a wider range of vicarious experience and more contact with specialized human resources than they would otherwise have had in the context of their own local environments. On the other hand, to the extent that our perceptions of family life come from situation comedies, of crime from police shows and of sexuality from soap operas, this does not bode well for the kind of world-view our children would have (Dede, 1992, p. 59).

Similarly, Postman believes that television approaches reality from a different standpoint than does text.

> On the one hand, there is the world of the printed word with its emphasis on logic, sequence, history, exposition, objectivity, detachment and discipline. On the other, there is the world of television with its emphasis on imagery, narrative, presentness, simultaneity, intimacy, immediate gratification and quick emotional response (Postman, 1992, p. 167).

But if television, and by extension multimedia's emphasis on imagery and moving graphics focuses on learning skills that detract from abstract thinking, they also affect values as Ellul states above. In this context, we would like to quote from Roszak who believes that computer technology is leading us to a view of education that is concentrated on the imparting of information, severed from values. Roszak believes that our obsession with the information society is based on a concept of information that is superficial and misleading - it is also based on how the computer perceives information - as code:

> ..in its new technical sense, *information* has come to denote whatever can be coded for transmission through a channel that connects a source with a receiver, regardless of semantic content (Roszak, 1986, p. 13).

Computers, now regarded as information-processing machines - are considered almost intelligent - even if they do not really understand what they are processing. What is even more dangerous is that some conclude that humans are like that too. Minsky, through his use of frames, shows how even complex human abilities like creativity, common sense and intuition can be explained away by this computational model (Roszak, 1986, p. 39).

Roszak quotes Turkle, who has studied children's use of computers to show how children can be affected by this. In one school, which was highly computerized, some children describe themselves as: "feeling computers, emotional machines" (Roszak, 1986, p. 40).

Roszak shows how, through the use of computers in the

curriculum, even the most creative and mysterious of human activities is assigned to the computer without any analysis of how differently human beings arrive at it. Roszak quotes from Daniel Watt's *Learning with LOGO*, where he is teaching students to get the computer to write poetry using grouping and a randomized list:

> When I see a computer can produce a poem it makes me stop and think just a little ... You and I know that the computer was just following a procedure. The procedure tells it to select cert in types of words according to a fixed pattern. It selects the words from several long lists of different types of words: nouns, verbs, adjectives, etc... But wasn't I doing the same thing when I wrote my poem? I was following a procedure too. The only difference was that I had a much larger choice of patterns and a bigger list of words in my head from which to choose. .. How is that different from what the computer was doing? (Roszak, 1986, pp. 80-81).

What shocks Roszak even further is that no attempt is made after that to help the student analyze how a human being produces a poem. Do poets really only make choices from patterns and lists of words in their heads or rather as, Roszak explains:

> ... they mean to *say* something, and that something preexists the words as a whole thought. They are not simply shuffling parts of speech through arbitrary patterns." (Roszak, 1986, p. 80).

Roszak believes that introducing the computer into the classroom brings with it a hidden agenda that is very dangerous: that of the computational model of the human being.

In this context, we should look at how computerized simulations could also affect values. While computerized simulations are not necessarily multimedia, they share common characteristics with virtual reality.

A simulation is a model of reality - it is not an exact copy but a metaphor of some aspect of reality that is sufficiently large and complex and yet amenable to manipulation. Students entering these metaphorical environments are free to play "what if" games - to explore, experiment and experience the results of their experiments without real-world risk. They can take the role of another person to gain another perspective or can experiment with interwoven variables that form part of the simulation (Snyder, 1988, p. 40).

Simulations on computers can operate at several levels - they can be applications where students see the effects of manipulating a model without knowledge of the underlying rules or structure or they can see the rules and change them. At the highest level, students would be able to create the rules of the simulation themselves (Fugler, 1989, p. 36). Of course, at each of these levels a higher intellectual skill is demanded. Simulations are usually valued for their role in facilitating the acquisition of problem-solving, reasoning, decision-making and interpersonal skills. They are also valued for increasing students' motivation to learn. Finally, cooperative aspects of simulations encourage the development of team-work and communication. As Snyder states:

> the greatest virtue of the simulations is that they get students working together, cooperating, helping, reasoning in groups, and taking responsibility for their own learning (Snyder, 1988).

Simulations are not always cooperative, they can be competitive too. This sometimes depends on the design of the software. However, it often also depends on the teacher's approach:

> If games are introduced in a competitive environment, there will be a different impact on the attitudes of the students than attempts at encouraging a cooperative learning environment (Fugler, 1989).

The design of a piece of simulation may betray values that are absurd but dangerous too. Ragsdale points out that in the early days of computers, a simulation was developed where inadvertently (we hope) extra points were given to a ruler who starved his subjects to maintain optimum population growth (Ragsdale, 1982, p. 5). But simulations more than any other form of computer software demand the presence of the teacher:

> The harder developers work to make simulations rich enough to be worthwhile, with exciting things going on in the program between the players, the harder they are going to be **pedagogically** to use. Why? Because simulations beg for intense teacher involvement, and the better the simulation the greater the requisite involvement. There is no getting around the conflict between increasingly rich simulations and teachers' willingness to tolerate the attendant ambiguity

and interactivity. Teacher training may help, but what we're dealing with here is something which, although it can be learned, cannot readily be taught (Snyder, 1986, pp. 142-143).

It is obvious that with greater teacher involvement one must reappraise teaching strategies and classroom organization. Can we afford to work with a crowded curriculum that covers everything from crafts to physics, a classroom with 35 children of varying abilities, a teacher that stands only in the front of the room, and above all, a curriculum that has no goal, no focus, no overlying philosophy?

We must ask ourselves what view of reality, of nature is being conveyed to our students through the use of multimedia. Is it a conception of reality that mirrors science, or is it one that encourages multiple perspectives, including the moral? Are we to continue to make the decision that human values and traditions hold no place in the school and in our simulations, or will we use the power of multimedia to introduce students to alternative views of mankind?

As Salomon and Gardner (1986, p. 8) point out, science simulators can be used by students for exploratory purposes, by arranging differing times and locations for the use of one simulation. Thus a science simulation could be used in a Physics class, but also in a Social Studies class and even more importantly in a Religious Education class. It could be juxtaposed with alternate views of reality of various world-cultures and world-views. This would allow students to critique the scientific perspective, while at the same time have access to philosophies that embed moral values within themselves.

For example, in viewing Nature through the eyes of the scientist, and then exploring it through the eyes of the North American Native for whom Nature is replete with symbols and meaning, one would provide important insights for students.

In a later section of the chapter we shall discuss the view of education the authors would like to see in the schools. However, before concluding this section it is important to point out that virtual reality should not doom us to views of humanity that are severed from morality. To summarize, while it is true that technology directs us in certain manners, our interpretation of technology rests in our hands. It is the task of educators to help students understand the non-neutrality of technology, and in fact to use the technology to develop critical thinking skills and an independence from it.

The Implementation of Multimedia Technology in Education

Menzies (1989), in discussing the speed at which new innovations are introduced, and the resulting shortening of the relevant decision processes, asserts that the implications of the latter are that we no longer have control of the former. Ely and Plomp (1986) have taken a long and sober look at the history of educational technology and conclude that there is little evidence of a technological revolution in education. They state that the common elements of unsuccessful implementations were confused goals, an emphasis on the medium, resistance to change, lack of support systems, lack of skills, inadequate budgeting, lack of quality software, and lack of a system focus. Those factors most frequently found in successful implementations included meeting critical educational needs, being oriented toward individual learners, cost-effectiveness, simple and available delivery systems, well-designed systems, and having training goals rather than educational ones:

> Projects and programs which succeed are more often involved in training than in education. Since the purposes of training are more often directed toward measurable skill competencies, it is logical that such efforts would yield specific positive results. The wider range and amorphous quality of education makes it difficult to assess whether goals have been attained, for these goals are usually of a more general nature (Ely & Plomp, 1986, pp. 257-258).

Ely and Plomp (1986) suggest seven guidelines for successful implementation: beginning with a problem to be solved, analyzing the context, designing materials to reflect the philosophy and strategies to be used, focusing on individual learners, selecting simple and available media, determining the role of the teacher, and setting up appropriate support systems.

Similarly, Collis states that it is not the technology but the instructional implementation of the technology that determines its effects on learning. She goes on to outline several key points that contribute towards effective implementation. These include the fact that any implementation of media will affect different learners in different ways. Overall effectiveness is affected by the context in which the media are introduced. Students generally like media in a learning context. Nevertheless, media are generally more effective as a supplement to an overall, integrated instructional setting, rather than as the sole or major components of the setting.

Interactivity is important but it can be organized in different ways. The flexibility of a medium reflects its ability to meet user needs and characteristics, and thereby its educational potential (Collis, 1991, p. 146).

As will be noted, many of these factors have been dealt with in the course of this chapter. However, perhaps the most important point, we believe that Collis makes is:

> The basis for media use in education should be first, the identification of an instructional need, and second, an assessment of the characteristics of various media to see which can be best used to address the need (Collis, 1991, p. 146).

What then is the instructional need? It is important that as opposed to defining instruction for each piece of knowledge, we have first of all, an overall perspective on what we believe education to be.

Multimedia Technology and the Role of Education in Society

One of the most important aspects of an individual's education is the understanding of his/her culture's world-view. While skills and specific content in particular disciplines are important, it is the world-view that will equip the individual to deal with the problems and challenges that life offers.

What then is the world-view, the philosophy that one wants to impart to students? While this chapter is too short to do justice to a subject as this, we should quote Postman's views on the redefinition of education to resist the technocrat view of schooling:

> ...the theme of the ascent of humanity gives us a nontechnical, noncommercial definition of education. It is a definition drawn from an honorable humanistic tradition and reflects a concept of the purposes of academic life that goes counter to the biases of the technocrats. I am referring to the idea that to become educated means to become aware of the origins of knowledge and knowledge systems........ In other words, it is an education that stresses history, the scientific mode of thinking, the disciplined use of language, a wide-ranging

knowledge of the arts and religion, and the continuity of human enterprise. It is education as an excellent corrective to the anti-historical information-saturated technology-loving character of technopoly (Postman, 1992, pp. 188-189).

What is the role of education in the 21st century? To celebrate the human being as an emotional, spiritual and intellectual being. To analyze and critique human history, the present and the future. This chapter has shown that analytical and critical skills do not come from within the computer, but rather from the human being. The role of education is to look for answers to humanity's problems with a view to incorporating its traditions, while also improving upon the lives of all.

As Newman has pointed out, the Bible tells us that "Where there is no vision, the people perish" (Proverbs 29:18, KJV). The same can be said about schools and school people without visions. It might also be said that schools with a vision will flourish:

> When we create schools we value for our children and ourselves, we will have created schools of value to others as well (Newman, 1990, p. 176).

What should be the role of technology in the vision we create? To answer this question, it would be important to recall Roszak who said that the computer is just an information-processor. It may provide for us a means to organize ourselves better, but it is human beings that create and possess true knowledge. Thus it is important to point out that while computers are powerful tools, the skills of questioning, analyzing, appreciating and acquiring a sense of awe and a love of learning will not come from a computer system, no matter how exciting. These qualities come from an understanding and appreciation of a culture that imbibes these values. This can only be acquired from the study of traditional subjects such as History, Literature, Art and the Sciences in their purest forms. As Roszak says:

> Those cultures are blessed which can call upon Homer, or Biblical tales, or the Mahabharata to educate the young. Though the children's grasp of such literature may be simple and playful, they are in touch with material of high seriousness. From the heroic examples before them, they learn that growing up means making projects with full responsibility for one's choices. In short, taking charge of one's life in the

presence of a noble standard. Young minds reach out for this guidance; they exercise their powers of imagination in working up fantasies of great quests, great battles, great deeds of cunning, daring, passion, sacrifice. They craft their identities to the patterns of gods and goddesses, kings and queens, warriors, hunters, saints, ...Education begins with giving the mind images - not data points or machines - to think with (Roszak, 1986, p. 215).

Our children are growing up in a complex world. In providing them with a sense of balance between the wonder and beauty of human life, and the need for practical skills and knowledge of the world, we prepare them for this complexity. For this reason it is important to remember that content is as important as method. As Roszak says:

In a time when our schools are filling up with advanced educational technology, it may seem almost perverse to go in search of educational ideals in ancient and primitive societies that had little else to teach with than word of mouth. But it may take that strong a contrast to stimulate a properly critical view of the computer's role in educating the young. At least it reminds us that all societies, modern and traditional, have had to decide *what* to teach their children before they could ask *how* to teach them. Content before means, the message before the medium (Roszak, 1986, p. 217).

What then should be the role of multimedia in the classroom? In the next section, we shall describe the use of a computerized history simulation used widely in schools in Ontario, Canada. Most of the analyses that follows stems from two research projects (Ragsdale, Durell, Griffith, Moore, Kassam, 1989 & 1993) that have studied the impact of computers in classrooms in several boards of education around Ontario for the past 6 years.

Multimedia Use in the Classroom

The Bartletts Saga is a series of historical simulations that was created to give intermediate students of Canadian history a greater understanding of the early settlement and history of Loyalists (those who remained loyal to the British monarchy, and were opposed to American independence.)

The Bartletts are a United Empire Loyalist family that arrive in Upper Canada as a result of the American Revolution taking place in 1776. According to the description of the historical context given at the beginning of the manual that accompanies the program, the Bartletts possess resources and face situations that are typical among Loyalists:

> They face the climate, labour market, colonial administration and rudimentary society encountered by actual Loyalist families. The variable factors in their lives are partly under their own control and partly the product of circumstances (Bemrose & Moore, 1984, p. 3).

In the simulation, students role play the Bartlett family in their struggle for survival in harsh circumstances. Students take part in various decision-making tasks from the amount of food to buy, where to worship, whether to cut off ties with the "rebellious " Americans to what crops to plant.

In participating in this struggle, it was intended that students would not only learn about pioneer life in Canada, but would also learn to reason, evaluate options, solve problems, make decisions, and if they were working in groups, defend each decision (Bemrose & Moore, 1984, p. 3).

The simulation was intially released as a single episode, but eventually more parts were added. Students could explore Loyalist history through the playing of different roles: the Bartlett family members, or a journalist documenting news and social events of the time. The three parts that cover the Saga are: Refugees in the Wilderness, United Empire Loyalists, 1784-1793; The Rebels: Rebellion in Upper Canada, 1830-1844; and United We Stand: Confederation, 1864-1873. In 1987, *The Bartletts: An Interactive History*, a multimedia version of the original program was released in videodisc format. However, its use is not as widespread as the computer program itself, largely because of expense and the absence of needed equipment to run the videodisc simulation in schools. (This is an important consideration for the implementation of multimedia in schools. It is unlikely, given present budgetary and financial constraints, that many schools will be able to implement such multimedia to a large scale.)

While our discussion does not center around the videodisc aspect of the simulation, per se, it will be clear that our research findings are relevant to multimedia. In fact, all *The Bartletts Saga* programs come equipped with media such as an online dictionary, atlas, bibliography, electronic notepad and bulletin board, allowing students to record and share observations.

In the next section we shall examine the justification provided by the authors of the program for the use of computers in History.

The Role of the Computer in the Bartletts Saga Simulation

According to the manual that accompanies the program, participation in *The Bartletts Saga* simulation would help students realize that studying History was an active process. Thus, if, for example, the Bartlett family did not plant corn one year, their livestock might die of starvation the following winter. The student-participant would be both an observer and an actor in the process of history (Bemrose & Moore, 1984, p. 7).

The simulation was also supposed to increase team involvement because students would be sharing scant computer resources and would then indirectly be involved in interacting and discussing "historical issues intelligently because they had immediate access to a "friendly" source of information" (Bemrose & Moore, 1984, p. 8).

It was also believed that the presence of the computer would allow students to have a better grasp of factors affecting decisions.

> Because the simulation would force them to deal with variables such as physical geography, climate, value systems, economics, politics, agriculture and available technology, it would help them that realize that the factors that influenced the Bartlett family two centuries ago continue to influence us today (Bemrose & Moore, 1984, p. 8).

The computer simulation would also show students that decisions have consequences, sometimes in cross-connected ways. Thus, in the simulation, a decision to refuse some Indians permission to fish from their land results in the Indians' refusing to trade with the Bartletts at a later point. The computer demonstrates that the consequences of actions are not always instantaneous (Bemrose & Moore, 1984, p. 8). And furthermore, because of the fact that *The Bartlett Saga* simulation was presented in the form of a game, it was believed that it would provide added challenge to the students as it would demand logic, concentration and alertness at all times from the players (Bemrose & Moore, 1984, p. 8). Finally it was believed that the computer would help towards self-understanding:

The computer simulation can be a catalyst encouraging innovative thinking and improving understanding of our past and the forces that shape the present (Bemrose & Moore, 1984, p. 8).

The Bartlett Saga in the Classroom

In this section it will be shown that a simulation such as *The Bartletts Saga* is not a program that would by its very presence stimulate students to learn about their history. In fact one could state that *The Bartlett Saga* is not a program, but a cultural experience that absolutely requires the presence of the teacher to translate for students as much as he/she would a film, a book, a field-trip, etc.

In his observations of many classrooms, Ragsdale (1990) became aware that students were not using the simulation in ways that were intended by its authors, nor was it being used to improve students' knowledge and learning skills. Several examples from his observations of *The Bartlett Saga* series will illustrate. In various instances, Ragsdale observed that students would concentrate on obtaining the highest possible scores in the simulation, at the expense of acquiring even the most basic understanding of the historical context. The following is an excerpt from fieldnotes:

> Ervin notices that Nate is moving briskly through the items and reminds him that they are supposed to be taking notes on the simulation material. Nate objects strenuously, saying that he took notes on the introduction material, but "on the game, give me a break", assuring Ervin that it is only necessary for him to get a good score (above 100) to show that he knew everything (May 28, 1990).

In another context during a teachers' discussion of the program, a teacher commented that her students had tried to develop a strategy that would kill off the Bartletts as fast as possible.

A common observation of several researchers was that students would seek out small games that formed part of the simulation. Students would then get engrossed in the games, which were supposed to be minor diversions and forget the overall purpose of the program. A stew-making program that allowed users to add alchohol, tobacco and gopher meat to the recipe proved particularly popular.

On questioning the students about their comprehension of the goals of the program, it became clear that they had not understood its most basic framework. Students confused *The Bartletts Saga* with another program created by the same software developers. This program belongs to a totally different historical location and time period. On one occasion, when asked what was meant by Confederation (the title of one of the modules of the program), students had no idea that it had anything to do with the Canadian government or the forming of the country. Other examples of this misuse and misunderstanding of the program abound in the research. From these examples of the implementation of the simulation into the classroom, we can conclude that new technology by itself does not guarantee improvement in pedagogy. Students can easily "hijack" quality materials to suit their own purposes.

In the next section, we shall explore ways in which simulations, computerized or multi-media, can be used in more positive ways.

Preparation of the Context of the Simulation

The materials that accompany *The Bartlett Saga* recommend that the teacher prepare students in various ways. These range from doing creative writing, art, drama, debate to the examination of values, to field trips to various pioneer museums, villages, forts, etc.

In the extremely busy schedule of the classroom teacher, it is unlikely that he/she could implement more than one of these. We suggest that given limited time and resource constraints, teachers should have students approach the simulation as a situation that presents historical and ethical issues to be discussed. It is vital that students come to realize that the simulation is the creation of its authors and that there are other interpretations of similar situations. In the case of the *The Bartlett Saga*, students have been introduced to a sympathetic view of the life of the pioneers, but there also existed other views; the natives, the black people, and the American "rebels."

In this context, it is vital for teachers to work with students through the simulation, pointing out to them biases or sympathies of the authors. It is interesting that teachers in introducing novels, rarely thrust them at students expecting them to work their way through plots, themes and author bias. However, in the case of computer simulations, it is often the case that teachers expect that the computer will "teach" students. As Bowers notes:

> The teacher cannot match the machine when it comes to the tireless reproduction of factual information or the knowledge

base that can be made available through the microcomputer. But only the teacher can amplify those aspects of the cultural transmission process that are reduced by the selective characteristics of the microcomputer. This involves restoring to teachers responsibility for recognizing when to intervene in the educational process by clarifying the conceptual problems that arise from metaphorical thinking, by pointing that the objective knowledge reflects somebody's interpretative framework and that this framework must be understood in terms of underlying cultural assumptions (1988, p. 46).

Teachers must build the simulation as part of a whole learning experience. In the case of the Bartletts, students had to come to understand the historical period with its hardships, its technological progress, and the values of the people involved. This can be done by the teacher providing students with a framework where students could use the simulation as a starting point to research such issues as colonization, the formation of a country, changing technology, the role of the family, etc.

Students should also be given structure where they would be *assigned* work in the form of a project, for which they would receive feedback and evaluation. This would result in students taking the task seriously and being more accountable to the teacher.

Above all, teachers and students need to realize that a simulation is a model of reality based on an interpretation of the real world by an author. Teachers and students must come to critically examine this context. Thus the simulation is an interpretation of reality - what happens in the classroom is an interpretation of the interpretation of this reality. It is important that students appreciate their own role in the experience of historical simulations.

The Bartlett Saga and Multimedia Technology in the Classroom

While the above research data on the simulation did not incorporate motion video, the implementation of the *The Bartlett Saga* does involve different media. Students are expected to maintain a score of their financial and material progress, deal with a variety of political, personal and social scenarios and role play different personalities.

The simulations themselves come equipped with online dictionaries, atlases, bibliographies, notebooks and bulletin boards. Furthermore, as stated above, teachers are encouraged to incorporate such learning experiences as creative writing, art, drama, debate and field trips to enrich the simulation. It is likely that the presence of motion video would have made the program more realistic, but there is no certainty that this would result in students' working to task when left to their own devices.

This brief foray into the classroom has shown that careful design and high quality materials do not necessarily result in corresponding improvement in education. It has also shown that technology, without the presence of the teacher to *explain* the material, can produce unexpected outcomes.

Throughout this chapter the authors have emphasized that research has shown that technology by itself does not solve problems. The successful introduction of technology requires good design, educational content and careful assimilation into student needs and the overall classroom goals. The role of the teacher in this assimilation is vital.

Conclusion

In this chapter we have explored various aspects of multimedia - its unique capabilities for individualized, interactive learning, and its strong potential for visualization and cognition. We have also shown how situated learning can benefit from multimedia technology. We have explored questions of values and the place of multimedia technology in the role of education in society. It is the opinion of the authors that no technology is in itself a solution to the problems of education. It is also our opinion that we cannot reject technology because it threatens our way of thinking. It is important to be open to what technology offers, while at the same time being critical of its influence on our way of life.

Thus, before we pass final judgement on the promise of multimedia in education, it is important to think carefully about the content, philosophy, and the presentation of the technology into the world of the classroom. This must be done each time that we bring any technology into the curriculum.

Postman (1992) and Ellul (1990) analyze our society as being one mesmerized with technology. Are our schools to be reflections of this mesmerization or will they be islands where students can reflect upon, analyze, critique and celebrate society? In such islands, technology is not the centre of knowledge, but rather only one limited tool in humanity's search for wisdom.

References

Barth, Roland S. (1990). *Improving schools from within - teachers, parents and principals can make the difference.* Jossey-Bass Publishers.

Bemrose, John & Komar, A. (1984). *The Bartlett family: A united empire loyalist family in upper Canada.* Toronto: Ministry of Education, Ontario Educational Software Service.

Bowers, C.A. (1988). Teaching a nineteenth-century mode of thinking through a twentieth-century machine. *Educational Theory,* 38(1), 41-45.

Brown, J.S., Collins, A., & Duguid, P. (1989). Situated cognition and the culture of learning. *Educational Researcher,* 18(1), 32-42.

Cohen, R. (1991). Formative evaluation of pre-logo programming environments: A collaborative effort of researchers, teachers and children. *Journal of Computer-Based Instruction,* 15 (4).

Collis, B. (1991). Anticipating the impact of multimedia in education: lessons) from the literature. *Computers in Adult Education and Training,* 2(2), 136-149.

Dede, C. (1992). Making the most of multimedia. *The Electronic School,* pp. A13-A15.

Ellul, J. (1964). *The technological society.* New York: Vintage Books.

Ellul, J. (1990). *The Technological Bluff.* Grand Rapids, MI: Wm. B. Eerdmans Publishing Co.

Ely, D. P., & Plomp, T. (1986). The promises of educational technology: A reassessment. *International Review of Education,* 32, 231-250.

Fugler, D. (1989). The impact of computer-based simulations and games on the teaching/learning process. *ECOO Output,* 9(6), 35-40; 46.

Gayeski, D. M. (1992). Making sense of multimedia: Introduction to special issue. *Educational Technology,* XXXII(5), 9-13.

Gordon, M. (1990). *What is the geometric supposer a case of?* (Tech Rep. No. 90-5). Newton, MA: Education Development Center.

Gore, K. (1991). Computers and thinking skills: the HOTS program. *Language Arts,* 68, 153-158.

Helsel, S. (1992). Virtual reality and education. *Educational Technology,* XXXII (5), 38-42.

Hon, D. (1992). Butcher, baker, candlestick maker: Skills required for effective multimedia development. *Educational Technology,* XXXII(5), 14-18.

Menzies, H. (1989). *Fast forward and out of control: How technology is changing your life.* Toronto: MacMillan.

Newman, J.M. (1990). *Finding our own way: Teachers exploring their assumptions.* Portsmouth, NH: Heinemann.

Papert, S. (1980). *Mindstorms, children, computers and powerful ideas.* New York: Basic Books.

Perkins, David N. (1988). Teaching for transfer. *Educational Leadership,* 46(1), 22-32.

Pogrow, S. (1988). Teaching thinking to at-risk elementary students. *Educational Leadership,* 79-85.

Postman, N. (1992). *Technopoly: The surrender of culture to technology.*

New York: Alfred A. Knopf.

Ragsdale, R.G., Durell, B., Griffith, A. and Kassam, A. (1989). *Toward a taxonomy of possible computer effects in elementary classrooms. (Ontario Ministry of Education Transfer Grant research project).*

Ragsdale, R.G., Durell, B., Griffith, A., Moore, S. and Kassam, A. (1993). *Intentions versus outcomes: Unravelling the organizational web of computers in education.* (Social Science and Humanities Research Council funded research project).

Ragsdale, R.G. (1990). *Computers and teachers as cultural agents.* (Presented at Annual Meeting of Canadian Society for the Study of Education, Victoria, B.C.).

Ragsdale, R.G. (1982). *Computers in the schools: A guide for planning.* Toronto: OISE Press.

Ragsdale, R.G. (1988). Effective tools in education: Teachers, tools and training. *Education and Computers, 7*(3,4), 157-166.

Ragsdale, R.G. (1988). *Permissible computing in education: Values, assumptions and needs.* New York: Praeger.

Reeves, T.C. (1992). Evaluating interactive multimedia: *Educational Technology, XXXII*(5), 47-53.

Roszak, T. (1986). *The cult of information.* New York: Pantheon Books.

Salomon, G. & Gardner, H. (1986). The computer as educator. Lessons from television research. *Educational Researcher, 15*(1), 13-19.

Salomon, G. & Leigh, T. (1984). Predisposition about learning from print and television. *Journal of Communication, 34,* 119-135.

Snyder, T. (1988). Tools for teachers. *The Computing Teacher, 16*(1), 8-11; 13-14; 16.

Snyder, T. and Palmer, J. (1986). *In search of the most amazing thing.* Reading, MA: Addison-Wesley.

Glossary

American National Standards Institute (ANSI) A US government agency whose function is to develop and adopt standards for many areas including business systems functions such as quality assurance and information processing.

Analog: Sound, pictures, or video stored or transmitted in the form of a continuously varying electrical signal. Broadcast video, consumer audio and videotape formats, and videodisc are all examples of analog media

Animation: In a computer system, animation refers to the rapid generation of a sequence of screens, such that one screen may be an alteration of the previous one. Animation may be used to communicate temporal changes, both abstract and physical.

Audiolization: The communication of information via combinations of characteristics of sounds.

Authoring software: Used to create multimedia presentations, these programs specify elements that should be included and combined.

Authoring system: A system used to create hypermedia or multimedia applications.

Browsing: An undirected search for information. In a system featuring hypertext, this is accomplished by navigating using links.

Byte: memory space required to store one character of information.

CD-ROM: Compact Disc-Read Only Memory. a 120 mm-diameter disc which can store text, sound, graphics, still images, animation, and video. One disc can store the equivalent of 250,000 pages of text or the content of a 20 volume encyclopedia

CD-I: Compact Disc-Interactive uses proprietary algorithms for still images, complex graphics, and run-length coding for simple graphics.

Component: A chunk of information in a hypermedia or multimedia system.

Computer-assisted instruction (CAI) The classification of computer systems and software which are used to augment the delivery of educational instruction.

Computer Based Instruction (CBI): A forerunner of today's multimedia, covering a broad range of computer-based training methods utilizing varying degrees of multimedia computing.

Courseware: computer materials designed for classroom use, including software and accompanying printed materials.

Daisy-wheel printer: an impact printer which prints preformed characters that are located on a removable wheel.

Data flow diagram (DFD) An information systems analysis and design tool which is used to shown the flow of information through an enterprise system.

Desktop Video(DTV): Video production using video equipment and desktop computers.

Digital: Information stored or transmitted as a series of binary numbers. Computers and compact discs (both audio and CD-ROM) are digital media.

Documentation: Assistance provided to the user of a compuer system to aid learning and use. It may be printed, as in a manual, or on-line.

Dot-matrix printer: an impact printer which prints characters composed of dots formed by a wire matrix print head.

Drill and practice: computer programs which provide repetitive opportunities for students to pair stimuli with appropriate responses.

Evaluation: data collection and analysis activities focused on improving multimedia programs and/or assessing their effectiveness and worth within a specific context of use.

End user computing The phenomenon wherein the ultimate beneficiaries of computer systems are directly involved with the development and acquisition of those systems and are directly responsible for the operation and management of those systems.

Expert System: a computer program that emulates the behavior of a human expert in a well-defined domain of knowledge.

Hard disk: a high-density, rigid magnetic disk which has a greater storage capacity than a diskette.

Hardware: the tangible, physical components of a computer.

Human-computer interface: In a computer system, the means of communication between humans and the underlying functionality of the computer system.

Hypermedia: A hypertext using components of diverse media (see multimedia).

Hypertext: Information organized into a set of nodes and connected by links such that the information may be accessed nonsequentially.

Icon: A static image used to communicate information visually.

Impact printer: a printer with elements that strike against a ribbon and paper to make impressions.

Information system development life cycle (ISDLC) The popular prescribed set of ordered stages in which information systems professionals engage in the planning and creation of information systems.

Ink jet printer: a non-impact printer which uses a stream of charged ink to form a character.

Input device: a device used to enter information into a computer.

Iterative design: A design process often used in the design of human-computer interfaces where user feedback is a necessary part of the design. This feedback helps to guide the changes made to the system.

International Standards Organization (ISO) A multinational agency whose function is to develop and adopt standards to be applied in the global community.

Knowledge acquisition: the process of gathering information from the domain expert and other sources in building an expert system.

Laser printer: a non-impact printer which uses a laser to make high-quality impressions.

Learner Control : the degree to which an interactive multimedia program allows learners to make decisions about what sections to study and/or what paths to follow through it.

Learning Environment: a multimedia program design to provide a comprehensive range of exploratory pedagogical options for developing new knowledge, skills, and/or attitudes within a given domain, e.g., chemistry.

Mental Model: a model of the structure and internal relationships of a system that evolves in the mind of a user as the user is learning and interacting with an interactive multimedia program or some other type of system; it is the source of the user's expectations about the effects of actions, can guide navigation or planning of actions, and contributes in interpretation of feedback.

Metaphors: A presentation of the functionality of a computer application that provides conceptual cues for its operation. Metaphors are taken from known situations and environments. For example, many of today's graphical user interfaces are based on the desktop metaphor, wth objects found on physical desktops having electronic counterparts in the user interface.

Microworld: a self-contained discovery learning program such as the Logo programming language.

Modular programming: The set of practices related to software design and creation wherein the focus is on subdividing programs in to concise, logical, independent modules with the intention of building quality programs which are easier to maintain after the programs have been implemented.

Monitor: a video display unit that is often used as an output device for a computer.

Mouse: a small hand-held input device with a rotating ball underneath. A computer screen pointer may be controlled by moving the mouse on the desktop.

MPCMC: The Multimedia Personal Computer Marketing Council. An subsidiary of the Software Publishers Association formed to promote industry standards.

Multimedia: In a computer system, the use of multiple media to present information. These media include text, hypertext, still photographs, static graphics, animations, motion video, and sound.

Multimedia-based learning: a computer-based software and hardware system for the presentation of text, sound, graphics, still images, animation, and video.

Navigation : the act of moving from screen to screen or interaction to interaction within an interactive multimedia program.

Output device: a device that allows the user to receive information from a computer. Printers and monitors are common output devices.

Pedagogy: the art and science of teaching.

Peripherals: any device that is connected to and controlled by a computer.

Prototyping The approach to information systems development wherein the system is designed and constructed iteratively, with each iteration becoming closer in nature to the ultimate system.

Readability: An assessment of the effectiveness of textual information in communication with readers.

Simulation: an experience designed to give illusion of reality.

Software: programs used to instruct a computer.

Software engineering: The philosophy and practices pertaining to the proper, orderly and logical design and creation of high quality computer programs, to include such concepts as modular programming and structured programming.

Structured programming The set of practices related to software design and creation wherein the focus is on the exclusive use of the sequence, selection and iteration logical control patterns with the intention of building quality programs that are easier to maintain after the programs have been implemented.

Task analysis: In the design of human-computer interfaces, the process of identifying and analyzing the tasks performed by users.

Total quality management (TQM): The relentless pursuit of quality assurance that focuses on identifying customer needs and on creating and monitoring high quality processes that will produce high quality products to meet those needs.

Usability: An assessment of the effectiveness of a human-computer interface in allowing a user to interact with the system functionality.

Usability attribute: A particular aspect of usability that can me measured, e.g. performance speed and error rate.

User Interface: those aspects of an interactive multimedia program that are perceived by the user as permitting interactions with the program.

Videodisc: an optical disc that contains analog, pre-recorded video material.

Videodisc player: a peripheral that reads prerecorded videodiscs.

Virtual Reality: an interactive multimedia program that incorporates an unusually high degree of experiential fidelity, often accomplished via the incorporation of special interface devices such as "data gloves" and "three dimensional goggles."

Walkthroughs: A team concept often applied in the enlightened approach to information systems and program development wherein the team members regularly meet and scrutinize each other's work in order to assure high quality.

Author Biographies

EDITOR

Sorel Reisman is a professor of Information Systems in the School of Business at California State University, Fullerton. Dr. Reisman has more than 25 years of experience in the research, development, and marketing of multimedia computing systems, hardware, software, and applications. After a career in industry that included a variety of senior management positions with American, Japanese, and British multinational corporations, Dr. Resiman joined Cal State Fullerton in 1986, where he has writtwritten numerous papers on MMC application development; he also serves as academic advisor to the university's Multimedia Learning Center, which he co-founded. Dr. Reisman is the faculty representative on multimedia computing to the Academic Communications Network Committee of the California State University System. He is a member of the IEEE Computer Society, a founding editorial board member of IEE Multimedia magazine and write a regular colum, *End User*, for IEE Software magazine. He is also an editorial board member of the *Journal of End User Computing* and *Journal of Global Information Management.*

AUTHORS

Kuriakose K. Athappilly, Professor of Information Systems, College of Business, Western Michigan University, author of several books and journal articles in the field of information systems.

Barbara A. Baker is Marketing Manager at Starlight Networks, Inc. She has extensive experience marketing applications in emerging markets. Her background includes marketing OEM voice processing products for Voysys Corporation and development of vertical market voice applications through VAR channels for Octel Communications. She has also worked in the electronics practice for McKinsey & Company. Ms. Baker received her M.B.A. from Harvard Business School and a B.A. in Computer Science from the University of California, Berkeley.

Karen Bland is an Advisory Systems Analyst at IBM's Federal Systems Corporation in Rockville, Maryland. She is a doctoral candidate in the Management Science department at George Washington University. She earned a bachelors of science degree from Northwestern University and a Masters of Public Administration from George Washington University.

Donald A. Carpenter is Associate Professor and Department Chair of Computer Science and Information Systems at the University of Nebraska at Kearney, where the classes he teaches include information systems development and multimedia systems. He has published articles in the Journal of Computer Information Systems and in the conference proceedings of several professional societies, including the Association for Computing Machinery, The Decision Sciences Institute and the International Association for Information Management. He has consulted to more than two hundred businesses regarding the development of computerized information systems.

Joyce J. Elam is the James L. Knight Eminent Scholar in Management Information Systems in the Department of Decision Sciences and Information Systems, College of Business Administration, Florida International University, Miami, Florida. Before joining the faculty at Florida International University in 1990, she was an assistant professor at the University of Pennsylvania's Wharton School, an associate professor in the College of Business Administration at the University of Texas at Austin, and a Marvin Bower Fellow at the Harvard Business School. Dr Elam earned both her Ph.D. in operational research (1977) and her BA in mathematics (1970) from the University of Texas. Dr. Elam's research deals with the competitive use of information technology, the management of the information services function, and the use of information technology to support both individual and group decision making. She is the author of numerous articles appearing in such journals as *Information Systems Research, Decision Sciences, Operations Research,* and *Decision Support Systems* on these topics. She id the co-author of the book, *Transforming the IS Organization,* published by ICIT Press, Washington, D.C., in 1988. She has served as associate editor for *MIS Quarterly* and is currently on the editorial board for *Information Systems Research.*

Richard G. Feifer is Associate Professor of Computer and Information Sciences at USIU. Previous to that, he was on the faculty at Northwestern University's Institute for the Learning Sciences (ILS) since its founding in 1989. At ILS he was responsible for the design of multimedia learning environments. From 1983 to 1989 Feifer was at the Center for the Study of Evaluation in the Graduate School of Education at UCLA and at the Artificial Intelligence Laboratory in the Computer Science Department at UCLA. His work at UCLA involved designing, building and evaluating intelligent tutoring systems. Dr. Feifer received his BA from California State University in 1973, his MA from a joint program between Hebrew Union College and the University of Southern California in 1976, and his PhD from the University of California, Los Angeles in 1989.

Edward A. Fox is associate director for research at the Computing Center and associate professor of computer science at Virginia Polytechnic Institute and State University. He directed the Virginia Disc series of CD-ROMs and Virginia Tech work on interac 've digital video. His interests, research projects, and publications are in the area of information storage and retrieval, library automation, hypertext/hyper rmedia/multimedia, computational linguistics, CD-ROM and optical disc technology, electronic publishing, hashing, and expert systems. Fox received a BS in electrical engineering from MIT and an MS and a PhD in computer science from Cornell University. He serves ACM as a member of the Publications Board, chairman of the Special Interest Group on Information Retrieval (SIGIR), and associate editor of ACM Transactions on Information Systems.

Martin D. Fraser received the B.S. and M.S. degrees in mathematics, and the Ph. D. degree in mathematics, major in statistics, from St. Louis University, St. Louis, MO. He is a Professor in the Department of Mathematics and Computer Science at Georgia State University. He has held the positions of Statistical Analysis Manager at American Greetings Corp., of Information Systems Member at Western Electric Co., and of Software Analyst (Captain, USAF) at the Air Force Satellite Test Center, Sunnyvale, CA. His current research interests include software engineering, formal specification methods. modeling and simulation, neural networks, and distributed resource allocation.

Stephen W. Harmon, Ed.D., an assistant professor of Computer Education at the University of Houston at Clear Lake, teaches instructional design and computer-based education courses. He was formerly a teacher in Egypt, and has been active in the Association for the Development of Computer-based Instructional Systems (ADCIS) and other professional associations. His research interests include multimedia user interface issues, instructional technology in developing countries, and the roles of instructional technology in primary and secondary education.

Alnaaz Kassam has been at the Ontario Institute for Studies in Education since 1981. She has worked as the Supervisor of the Microcomputer Room in the library and as a researcher studying the effects of computers in the classroom. She has recently completed her dissertation entitled *Teaching for Creativity in the Era of Computers: An Ethnographic Study.* She is presently working on a program that will use telecommunications to introduce Canadian students to varying interpretations of development from the perspectives of people around the world. She is particularly interested in the preservation of world cultures in the face of new technologies.

Peeter J.Kirs is an assistant professor of Information Systems in the Department of Decision Decision Sciences and Information Systems, College of Business, Florida International University, Miami, Florida. He received his Ph.D. in Information Systems in 1987 from the State University of New York at Buffalo, and has published a number of research articles in such journals as *Management Information Systems Quarterly, Information and Management,* and *The Journal of Database Administration.* His current Research Interests are in Information Systems Analysis and Design, Database Design and Implementation, and Man-Machine Interfaces.

Jay Liebowitz is Professor of Management Science in the School of Business and Public Management at George Washington University. He is the editor-in-chief of the international journal, *Expert Systems With Applications,* and he has published over 14 books and 150 journal articles on expert systems. He is the founder and Chairman of The World Congress on Expert Systems.

J. Morgan Morris has been an Assistant Professor in the Department of Mathematics and Computer Science at Georgia State University in Atlanta, Georgia since 1989. He received his undergraduate degree in Computer Science from the University of Missouri at Rolla, and his M.S. and Ph. D. from the Georgia Institute of Technology in Information and Computer Science. His research interests include user interface design, multimedia, and computer science education.

G. Scott Owen is currently ACM SIGGRAPH Director for Education, Director of the Hypermedia and Visualization LAboratory, and Professor of Mathematics and Computer Science at Georgia State University. He has been doing scientific and graphics programming for over twenty years. He received his undergraduate degree from Harvey Mudd College and his Ph. D. in Physical Chemistry from the University of

Washington. He taught at Atlanta University, in the chemistry department, from 1972-1984 and moved to GSU in 1984. He has published and presented papers in a variety of areas including multimedia, computer graphics, software engineering, computer graphics education, computer science education, and the use of computers in science education.

Joseph W. Pang is responsible for research and development of multimedia services and protocols at Starlight Networks, Inc. Dr. Pang previously was part of the Broadband Network Research group at Pacific Bell, where he worked on a variety of broadband network issues and services, including SMDS, broadband network management, integrated services, and high-bandwidth applications. He received his Ph.D. in Electrical Engineering from Stanford University.

Ronald G. Ragsdale has been at the Ontario Institute for Studies in Education since 1966 and is a Professor in the Departmentof Measurement, Evaluation, and Computer Applications. His primary interests are evaluating the impact of computers on the educational process, with a particular focus on the contrast between expectations and outcomes. He has authored two books published by OISE Press, *Computers in the Schools: A Guide for Planning* and *Evaluation of Microcomputer Courseware*. His most recent book, published by Praeger, is *Permissible Computing in Education: Values, Assumptions, and Needs*.

Thomas C. Reeves, Ph.D., a professor of Instructional Technology at The University of Georgia, teaches program evaluation, instructional design, and research methods courses. He has developed and evaluated interactive technologies since 1974, and has been an invited speaker in Australia, Bulgaria, Finland, Peru, Russia, Switzerland, Taiwan, and elsewhere. His research interests include mental models, electronic performance support systems, adult literacy, multimedia user interface issues, and instructional technology in developing countries.

James D. Russell is Professor of Instructional Research and Development at Purdue University. In addition, he is a faculty consultant for the Center for Instructional Services on campus. he assists in conducting faculty development workshops and works with faculty to improve instruction. His specialty is the design and development of training programs and materials. he teaches courses in snstructional development, media utilization, and adult education. he is co-author of Instructional Media and the New Technologies of Instruction.

Marc J. Schniederjans is Professor of Management at the University of Nebraska - Lincoln. He has published numerous books and journal articles in the disciplines of management science, production and operations management, and information systems.

J. P. Shim is Professor of Information Systems and Management Science at Mississippi State University. His research has focused on hypermedia, decision support systems, and decision analysis. Professor Shim is the coauthor of several books, including *Micro Management Science, Micro Manager, Selected Abstracts in Data Processing* and *Management Information Systems* and others. He has published numerous articles in the leading journals such as *Decision Support Systems, Journal of the Operational Research Society, Computers and Operations Research, OMEGA, Long Range Planning, Socio-Economic Planning Sciences, Human Relations, Journal of Multi-Criteria Decision Analysis, Interface*. He has also served as a referee/editorial review board member for 15 leading journals. Dr. Shim has garnered a number of awards for his accomplishments. His faculty colleagues have awarded him three awards, Outstanding Faculty Member, Outstanding Researcher, and Outstanding Service Member. Professor Shim is a frequent invited lecturer at universities in the U.S., France, Korea, and Taiwan.

Dennis H. Sorge is Director of Academic Services for the School of Scinece, Purdue University. He serves as Outreach Coordinator for the Mathematics Department. This responsibility involves working with K-12 schools for the improvement of instruction and learning. He directed a six-year project to implement interactive video instruction for adult learners. Currently he is presenting workshops for K-12 teachers on implementing computer-based learning in the classroom. he has published more than 20 articles and made over 50 presentations about mathematics, computers, and the implementation of computers in education.

Sun-Gi Chun is Assistant Professor of Computer Information Systems at Alabama State University. Dr. Chun is a member of ACM (special interest group in Hyperlink), DSI, and TIMS/ORSA. He has published in the *Journal of the Operational Research Society*. His research interests include business applications of hypermedia and multimedia, graphical representation of network model, and strategic use of user interface information technologies.

Fouad Tobagi is Chief Technical Officer at Starlight Networks, Inc. A Professor of Electrical Engineering at Stanford University, Dr. Tobagi's expertise and international reputation covers LANs and high-speed packet networks. He is a Fellow of the Institute of Electronics and Electrical Engineers (IEEE) and has served as editor for a number of IEEE publications. Dr. Tobagi coauthored the first papers on Carrier Sense Multiple Access (CSMA). His contributions also include work on high-speed fiber optics networks, broadband integrated services digital networks (Binds), and ATM fast packet-switching. Dr. Tobagi received his Ph.D. from the University of California, Los Angeles, where he was Research Staff Project Manager with the ARPA project.

Gary A. Walter is a doctoral student in the Decision Sciences and Information Systems Department at Florida International University. He received his B.S. from the University of Illinois and his M.B.A. from Florida International University. In 1990 and 1991 he was coordinator of the Coral Reef Project at New Era Video Inc. His research interests are hypermedia and expert systemsand man-machine interfaces.

Ginger L. Weibaker is an Evaluation Specialist and a doctoral candidate at Purdue University. her doctoral dissertation involved a study to examine the effects on achievement when interactive video is used as a supplement to instruction in a college-level basic mathematics course. She is the computer laboratory coordinator in the division of Educational Computing and Instructional Development.

J. Christopher Westland is currently an assistant professor in information systems at the University of Southern California. Previously he worked in industry for eight years, first as a certified public accountant for Touche Ross in Chicago and later as a database administrator and computer security analyst for Rockwell International. He has been awarded an Andersen Foundation Fellowship, a FLAS Fellowship by the U.S. Department of Education, several Paton Fellowships, a Dykstra Fellowship for Teaching Excellence, and a FRIF Grant to study politics and conflict resolution in information systems resource sharing. His current research focuses on the economics of information systems management and information technologies, on new technologies for software engineering, and on organizational and strategic applications of information technology.

Index